ELEMENTS OF
ARGUMENT

FOURTH EDITION

ELEMENTS OF ARGUMENT

A Text and Reader

Annette T. Rottenberg

BEDFORD BOOKS OF ST. MARTIN'S PRESS
BOSTON

For Alex

For Bedford Books
Publisher: Charles H. Christensen
Associate Publisher/General Manager: Joan E. Feinberg
Managing Editor: Elizabeth M. Schaaf
Developmental Editor: Stephen A. Scipione
Production Editor: Michelle McSweeney
Copyeditor: Cynthia Insolio Benn
Text Design: Claire Seng-Niemoeller
Cover Design: Richard Emery
Cover Art: Detail of *Un Candidate* by Honoré Daumier. Lithograph, 11¾ × 9⁹⁄₁₆″. The Armand Hammer Collection, The Armand Hammer Museum of Art and Cultural Center, Los Angeles. Photographed by Paula Goldman.

For information, write: St. Martin's Press, Inc.
175 Fifth Avenue, New York, N.Y. 10010
Editorial Offices: Bedford Books *of* St. Martin's Press,
29 Winchester Street, Boston, MA 02116

ISBN 0-312-08640-7

ACKNOWLEDGMENTS

Adelphi advertisement, "There's a place in this world for unusual people." Reprinted by permission of Adelphi University.

Charlotte Allen, "Boys Only." Reprinted by permission of *The New Republic*, © 1992, The New Republic, Inc.

Gordon Allport, "The Nature of Prejudice." From the 17th Claremont Reading Conference Yearbook, 1952. Reprinted by permission of the Claremont Reading Conference.

American Forest and Paper Association advertisement, "The great American forest is closer than you think." Reprinted by permission of the American Forest and Paper Association.

Molefi Kete Asante, "Response to Diane Ravitch." Reprinted from *The American Scholar*, Volume 60, No. 2, Spring 1991. Copyright © 1991 by the author.

Acknowledgments and copyrights are continued at the back of the book on pages 683–687, which constitute an extension of the copyright page.

Preface
for Instructors

PURPOSE

Argumentation as the basis of a composition course should need no defense, especially at a time of renewed pedagogical interest in critical thinking. A course in argumentation encourages practice in close analysis, use of supporting materials, and logical organization. It encompasses all the modes of development around which composition courses are often built. It teaches students to read and to listen with more than ordinary care. Not least, argument can engage the interest of students who have been indifferent or even hostile to required writing courses. Because the subject matter of argument can be found in every human activity, from the most trivial to the most elevated, both students and teachers can choose the materials that appeal to them. And those materials need not be masterpieces of the genre, as in courses based on literature; students can exercise their critical skills on flawed arguments that allow them to enjoy a well-earned superiority.

Composition courses using the materials of argument are, of course, not new. But the traditional methods of teaching argument through mastery of the formal processes of reasoning cannot account for the complexity of arguments in practice. Even more relevant to our purposes as teachers of composition is the tenuous relationship between learning about induction and deduction, however helpful in analysis, and the actual process of student composition. E. D. Hirsch, Jr., in *The Philosophy of Composition*, wrote, "I believe, as a practical matter, that instruction in logic is a very inefficient way to give instruction in writing."[1] The challenge has been to find a method of teaching argument

---

[1] *The Philosophy of Composition* (Chicago: University of Chicago Press, 1977), p. 142.

that assists students in defending their claims as directly and efficiently as possible, a method that reflects the way people actually go about organizing and developing claims outside the classroom.

One such method, first adapted to classroom instruction by teachers of rhetoric and speech, uses a model of argument advanced by Stephen Toulmin in *The Uses of Argument*. Toulmin was interested in producing a description of the real *process* of argument. His model was the law. "Arguments," he said, "can be compared with law-suits, and the claims we make and argue for in extra-legal contexts with claims made in the courts."[2] Toulmin's model of argument was based on three principal elements: claim, evidence, and warrant. These elements answered the questions, "What are you trying to prove?" "What have you got to go on?" "How did you get from evidence to claim?" Needless to say, Toulmin's model of argument does not guarantee a classroom of skilled arguers, but his questions about the parts of an argument and their relationship are precisely the ones that students must ask and answer in writing their own essays and analyzing those of others. They lead students naturally into the formulation and development of their claims.

My experience in supervising hundreds of teaching assistants over a number of years has shown that they also respond to the Toulmin model with enthusiasm. They appreciate its clarity and directness and the mechanism it offers for organizing a syllabus.

In this text I have adapted — and greatly simplified — some of Toulmin's concepts and terminology for freshman students. I have also introduced two elements of argument with which Toulmin is not directly concerned. Most rhetoricians consider them indispensable, however, to discussion of what actually happens in the defense or rejection of a claim. One is motivational appeals — warrants based on appeals to the needs and values of an audience, designed to evoke emotional responses. A distinction between logic and emotion may be useful as an analytical tool, but in producing or attacking arguments human beings find it difficult, if not impossible, to make such a separation. In this text, therefore, persuasion through appeals to needs and values is treated as a legitimate element in the argumentative process.

I have also stressed the significance of audience as a practical matter. In the rhetorical or audience-centered approach to argument, to which I subscribe in this text, success is defined as acceptance of the claim by an audience. Arguers in the real world recognize intuitively that their primary goal is not to demonstrate the purity of their logic, but to win the adherence of their audiences. To gain this adherence, students need to be reminded of the necessity for establishing themselves as credible sources for their readers.

---

[2] *The Uses of Argument* (Cambridge: Cambridge University Press, 1958), p. 7

ORGANIZATION

In Part One, after an introductory overview, a chapter each is devoted to the chief elements of argument — the claims that students make in their arguments (Chapter 2), the definitions and support they must supply for their claims (Chapters 3 and 4), the warrants that underlie their arguments (Chapter 5), the language that they use (Chapter 6). Popular fallacies, as well as induction and deduction, are treated in Chapter 7; because fallacies represent errors of the reasoning process, a knowledge of induction and deduction can make clear how and why fallacies occur. Each chapter ends with an advertisement illustrating the element of argument treated in that chapter. In all, Part One contains twenty-eight readings and eight advertisements, accompanied by critical thinking exercises and writing suggestions.

I have tried to provide examples, readings, discussion questions, and writing suggestions that are both practical and stimulating. With the exception of several student dialogues, the examples are real, not invented; they have been taken from speeches, editorial opinions, letters to the editor, advertisements, interviews, and news reports. They reflect the liveliness and complexity that invented examples often suppress.

The readings in Part One support the discussions in several important ways. First, they illustrate the elements of argument; in each chapter, one or more essays have been analyzed to emphasize the chapter's principles of argument. Second, they are drawn from current publications and cover as many different subjects as possible to convince students that argument is a pervasive force in the world they read about and live in. Third, some of the essays are obviously flawed and thus enable students to identify the kinds of weaknesses they should avoid in their own essays.

Part Two takes up the process of writing and researching. Chapter 8 explains how to find a topic, define the issues that it embraces, organize the information, and draft and revise an argument. Chapter 9 introduces students to the business of finding sources, in the field and in the library, including information from computer catalogs, and using these sources effectively in research papers. The chapter concludes with two annotated student research papers, one of which represents research in the social and natural sciences and uses a modified American Psychological Association (APA) documentation style, the other of which employs the materials of literature and the Modern Language Association (MLA) documentation system.

Part Three, "Opposing Viewpoints," exhibits arguers in action, using informal and formal language, debating head-on. The subjects — abortion, animal rights, children's rights, endangered species, euthanasia, freedom of speech, gay and lesbian rights, multicultural studies, and sex education — capture headlines every day. Despite their immediacy, these subjects are likely to arouse passions and remain controversial for a long time. Whether as matters of national policy or personal choice, they call for decisions based on familiarity with their competing views.

Finally, Part Four, "Classic Arguments," reprints nine selections that have stood the tests of both time and the classroom. Drawn from the works of Plato, Andrew Marvell, Jonathan Swift, Mary Wollstonecraft, Henry David Thoreau, Virginia Woolf, George Orwell, and Martin Luther King, Jr., they are among the arguments that teachers find invaluable in any composition course.

The editor's notes provide additional suggestions for using the book, as well as for finding and using the enormous variety of materials available in a course on argument.

I hope this text will lead students to discover not only the practical and intellectual rewards of learning how to argue but the real excitement of engaging in civilized debate.

NEW TO THIS EDITION

Revising a successful textbook — the publisher says that *Elements of Argument* is the bestselling book of its kind — presents both a challenge and an opportunity. The challenge is to avoid undoing features that have been well received in the earlier editon. The opportunity is to tap into the experiences of instructors and students who have used the earlier editions and to make use of their insights to improve what needs improvement. This is how we have approached this revision, and it accounts for all that we have done, and not done, in preparing the new edition.

The principles and concerns of the book have not changed. Rather, I have included a greater breadth of material to increase the book's usefulness as a teaching tool. Instructors who requested more explanations in Part One of warrants, induction, and deduction will find an expanded discussion, including new analyses of the different ways in which warrants operate. A reference chart with additional examples of the three main kinds of warrants appears on the endpapers of the book. In Part Two, library and field research is now covered in more detail in Chapter 9, with a brief introduction to computer catalogs and a list of some of the principal databases. This chapter also includes *two* annotated student research papers. In addition to the one that appeared in the earlier editions using the APA documentation style, I have added "When a Fairy Tale Is Not Just a Fairy Tale," an example of research in the humanities and the use of the MLA documentation system. In Part Three, the number of "Opposing Viewpoints" remains the same, but five of the topics are new, reflecting the most recent public controversies. Four popular topics from the third edition have been retained — Abortion, Animal Rights, Euthanasia, Freedom of Speech — and brought up to date with fresh material from many sources. The five new topics, which should appeal strongly to students, are: Children's Rights, Endangered Species, Gay and Lesbian Rights, Multicultural Studies, and Sex Education. As further proof of the wide range of arguments in the print media, each chapter of "Opposing Viewpoints" ends with a cartoon that treats the topic with humor and irony. In Part Four, the anthology of classic arguments, students can encounter still another genre as a vehicle of argument in Andrew Marvell's poem, "To His Coy Mistress."

The number of selections in the fourth edition has grown to 122, the majority of them new, with a corresponding increase in the number of debatable issues and teaching options. Taken as a whole, the changes in the fourth edition should further enhance the versatility of the book, deepen students' awareness of how pervasive argument is, and increase their ability to think critically and communicate persuasively.

This book has profited from the critiques and suggestions of Patricia Bizzell, College of the Holy Cross; Richard Fulkerson, East Texas State University; William Hayes, California State College — Stanislaus; Marcia MacLennan, Kansas Wesleyan University; Lester Faigley, University of Texas at Austin; Cheryl W. Ruggiero, Virginia Polytechnic Institute; Michael Havens, University of California at Davis; Judith Kirscht, University of Michigan; Richard Katula, University of Rhode Island; Carolyn R. Miller, North Carolina State University at Raleigh; A. Leslie Harris, Georgia State University; Richard S. Hootman, University of Iowa; Donald McQuade, University of California at Berkeley; David L. Wagner; Ron Severson, Salt Lake Community College; Paul Knoke, East Carolina University; and Robert H. Bentley, Lansing Community College. The editor's notes are the better for the contributions of Gail Stygall of the University of Washington.

Many instructors helped improve the book by responding to a questionnaire. I appreciate the thoughtful consideration given by: Timothy C. Alderman, Yvonne Alexander, John V. Andersen, William Arfin, Karen Arnold, David B. Axelrod, Peter Banland, Carol A. Barnes, Marci Bartolotta, Dr. Bonnie C. Bedford, Frank Beesley, Don Beggs, Martine Bellen, Scott Bentley, Don Black, Kathleen Black, Stanley S. Blair, Laurel Boyd, Dianne Brehmer, Alan Brown, Paul L. Brown, Bill Buck, W. K. Buckley, Alison A. Bulsterbaum, Clarence Bussinger, Gary T. Cage, Ruth A. Cameron, Barbara R. Carlson, Gail Chapman, Roland Christian, Dr. Thomas S. Costello, David J. Cranmer, Edward Crothers, Mimi Dane, Judy Davidson, Philip E. Davis, Stephanie Demma, Julia Dietrich, Marcia B. Dinnech, Jane T. Dodge, L. Leon Duke, P. Dunsmore, Bernard Earley, Carolyn L. Engdahl, David Estes, Kristina Faber, B. R. Fein, Delia Fisher, Evelyn Flores, David D. Fong, Donald Forand, Mary A. Fortner, Leslye Friedberg, Sondra Frisch, Maureen Furniss, Diane Gabbard, Frieda Gardner, Gail Garloch, Darcey Garretson, Victoria Gaydosik, E. R. Gelber-Beechler, Scott Giantralley, Michael Patrick Gillespie, Paula Gillespie, Wallace Gober, Sara Gogol, Stuart Goodman, Mildred Gronek, Marilyn Hagans, Linda L. Hagge, Lee T. Hamilton, Phillip J. Hanse, Susan Harland, Carolyn G. Hartz, Fredrik Hausmann, Ursula K. Heise, Anne Helms, Diane Price Herndl, Heidi Hobbs, William S. Hochman, Sharon E. Hockensmith, Joyce Hooker, Clarence Hundley, Richard Ice, Mary Griffith Jackson, Ann S. Jagoe, Katherine James, Ruth Jeffries, Owen Jenkins, Ruth Y. Jenkins, Iris Jennings, Linda Johnson, Janet Jubnke, E. C. Juckett, George T. Karnezis, Mary Jane Kearny, Joanne Keel, Patricia Kellogg-Dennis, N. Kesinger, Joanne Kirkland, Nancy Klug, John H. Knight, Paul D. Knoke, Frances Kritzer, Barbara Ladd, Marlene J. Lang, Sara R. Lee, William Levine, Mary Levitt, Diana M. Liddle, Cynthia Lowenthal, Marjorie Lynn, Patrick McGuire, Ray McKerrow, Pamela J. McLagen, Suzanne McLaughlin, Dennis McMillan, Christina M. McVay, D'Ann Madewell, Beth Madison, Susan Maloney, Barbara A. Manrigue, Joyce Marks, Michael Matzinger, Charles May, Jean-Pierre Meterean, Lisa K. Miller, Logan D. Moon, Dennis D. Moore, Dan Morgan, Karen L. Morris, Curt Mortenson, Philip A. Mottola, Thomas Mullen, Michael B. Naas, Joseph Nassar, Byron Nelson, Elizabeth A. Nist, Jody Noerdlinger, Dr. Mary Jean Northcutt, Thomas O'Brien, James F. O'Neil, Mary O'Riordan, Amy Olsen, Richard D. Olson, Lori Jo Oswald, Sushil K. Oswald, Jo. Patterson, Leland S. Person, Betty Peters, Susan T. Peterson, Steve Phelan, Mildred Postar, Ralph David Powell, Jr., Teresa Marie Purvis, Barbara E. Rees, Karen L. Regal, Pat Regel, Charles Reinhart, Janice M. Reynolds, Douglas F. Rice, G. A. Richardson, Katherine M. Rogers, Judith Klinger Rose, Cathy Rosenfeld, Robert A. Rubin, Lori Ruediger, Norma L. Rudinsky, Richard Ruppel, Joseph L. Sanders, Suzette Schlapkohl, Sybil Schlesinger, Richard Schneider, Eileen Schwartz, Esther L. Schwartz, Eugene Senff, Lucy Sheehey, Sallye J. Sheppeard, Sally Bishop Shigley, John Shout, Thomas Simmons, Michael Simms, Richard Single-tary, Thomas S. Sloane, Beth Slusser, Denzell Smith, Rebecca Smith, Katherine Sotol, Richard Spilman, Martha L. Stephens, Arlo Stoltenberg, Elissa L. Stuchlik, Judy Szaho, Andrew Tadie, Fernanda G. Tate-Owens, R. Terhorst, Marguerite B. Thompson, Arline R. Thorn, Mary Ann Tre-vathan, Sandia Tuttle, Whitney G. Vanderwerff, Jennie VerSteeg, Linda D. Warwick, Carol Adams Watson, Roger D. Watson, Karen Webb, Ray-mond E. Whelan, Betty E. White, Toby Widdicombe, Mary Louise Willey, Heywood Williams, Alfred Wong, and Laura Zlogar.

I thank the people at Bedford Books whose efforts have made the progress of the fourth edition a pleasure as well as a business: Elizabeth Chapman, Laura McCready, and Elizabeth Schaaf. Most of all I thank Charles H. Christensen, Joan E. Feinberg, Michelle McSweeney, Lori Chong, and especially the editor with whom I have worked most closely for three editions, Steve Scipione.

Brief Contents

PART THREE

PART FOUR

Contents

Two physicians examine the frightening and potentially lethal
effects of cocaine abuse.

A journalist evaluates the lessons teens learn in "universities of
suburban materialism."

A teacher argues that forcing unmotivated students to stay in
school is a fruitless waste of energy and resources and a drag
on those who truly want to learn.

Two researchers for "The Garbage Project" at the University of
Arizona make some surprising assertions about the physical
reality inside a landfill.

A film critic declares that "Hollywood no longer reflects — or
even respects — the values that most Americans cherish."

Gambling is destructive to society, charges an editorial in the
Wall Street Journal, and when government "substitutes
gambling for taxation it relinquishes its moral authority."

A spokesman for a conservative African-American think tank
musters evidence to show that opposition to capital
punishment runs counter to our religious and legal tradition.

A former chief justice of the United States examines the
historical roots of the Second Amendment in order to
construct an appeal for gun control.

The author of *Growing Up Absurd* argues that if the goal of higher education is education, we should use tests that foster learning, not competition.

A physician and a professor of biology propose that fetal brain development ought to be the guideline for determining when life begins.

"It's made from an endangered species for that one person in a thousand who couldn't care less." [cartoon] **444**

THINKING AND WRITING ABOUT ENDANGERED SPECIES **445**

14. Euthanasia 446

Death by Choice
DANIEL C. MAGUIRE **447**

According to a professor of ethics, though few of us would grant a doctor, a family, or a panel of experts the moral right to end someone else's existence, we can't decide the question *whether* without considering *who.*

In Defense of Voluntary Euthanasia
SIDNEY HOOK **452**

Having survived a life-threatening illness during which he asked to be allowed to die, a philosopher explains why he still believes that his request should have been honored.

Active and Passive Euthanasia
JAMES RACHELS **454**

The American Medical Association has condemned "mercy killing" but has condoned allowing a terminally ill patient to die. A philosopher of ethics asks whether it is truly kinder to watch someone yield to a slow and painful death than to hasten the patient's inevitable end.

That Right Belongs Only to the State
MORTIMER OSTOW **460**

A doctor argues that, just as no member of our society is entitled to take a life by murder or suicide, so the burden of making life-or-death decisions in medical cases should not fall on individuals.

Cozy Little Homicides
JOHN LEO **461**

A contributing editor for *U.S. News and World Report* warns that a proposed euthanasia bill in Washington is modeled too closely after the Dutch system, an alleged model program "shot through with dishonesty."

Consequences of Imposing the Quality-of-Life Ethic
EILEEN DOYLE **463**

In the attempts of euthanasia proponents to substitute a "quality-of-life" ethic for a "right-to-life" ethic, a nurse perceives a covert attack on cherished American principles.

In the Face of Death: Rights, Choices, Beliefs
JAMES M. WALL **466**

A lesbian writer urges heterosexuals to become involved in the fight for gay rights because "Homophobia hurts you almost as much as it hurts us."

Although sympathetic to "domestic partnership possibilities," this political science professor opposes the legality of gay marriage because marriage is about the possibility of creating and raising children.

The editor of *The New Republic* explains why allowing gays and lesbians to marry is not a "radical step" but a fair and practical advance of existing laws.

A U.S. Army colonel believes that gays should not be allowed into the military because they will destroy morale and fighting spirit.

A retired army officer claims that the integration of gays, even if disruptive, will openly acknowledge the presence of gays in the military and represent a victory for equality.

A former assistant U.S. secretary of education argues that while a pluralistic approach encourages students and teachers to understand the many ethnic and racial strains that contribute to an American community, particularists threaten to undermine public education in their attempts to implement an ethnocentric curriculum.

The chair of the African-American Studies Department at
Temple University refutes Ravitch's assertations and challenges
her version of multiculturalism as one riddled with her own
Eurocentric assumptions.

Value Free?

While it is important that a multicultural curriculum teach
children about other people's values, writes the president of
the American Federation of Teachers, "this does not mean
teaching students that they need not hold other people's
practices — and our own — up to moral scrutiny."

Whose Culture Is It Anyway?

"A curriculum that reflects the achievement of the world's
great cultures, not merely the West's is not 'politicized'; rather
it situates the West as one of a community of civilizations,"
claims the head of the Afro-American Studies Department at
Harvard.

Report on Minority Cultures in the Classroom

A report on education to the New York Board of Regents, in
affirming the right of students to study the contributions of
minority cultures, reminds us that "the schoolroom is one of
the places where this cultural interdependence must be
reflected."

Toward a Divisive Diversity

A Pulitzer Prize–winning historian in a dissent from the "Report
on Minority Cultures in the Classroom" deplores the emphasis
on separatism as well as the failure to recognize the European
sources of American democracy. Public education, he argues,
"should aim to strengthen, not weaken . . . the bonds of
national cohesion."

In Defense of Multiculturalism

A Harvard professor of education and sociology suggests that
the present-day multicultural movement is a result of the
failure of the African-American community to fully assimilate
into American society and represents a worthy attempt to
overcome this failure.

Ugh! Oops.

A humanities professor lists "multicultural no-nos" from the
Dictionary of Cautionary Words and Phrases, a serious

guideline for political correctness written by a group of journalists.

18. Sex Education   585

A former U.S. secretary of education argues that birth control clinics in schools represent an abdication of responsibility by school officials and a legitimization of sexual activity.

"The sex battle is lost. The front-line issue is pregnancy." A doctor turned political commentator asks us to face that reality and confront the problem in our schools.

A letter to the *New York Times* suggests that condom advocates, in avoiding the question "Should children have sex?" are overlooking the fact that "in child sex someone always gets hurt."

A nurse practitioner responds to O'Leary's letter by asserting that children "understand that teaching about AIDS prevention does not mean we condone their sexual activity, but that we care about them."

A social worker presses for school reforms that will allow parents to be informed of the content in sex education courses and to exercise a veto over student attendance because the "primary right to determine what a child is exposed to in school rests with the parents."

A researcher who has studied several sex education courses in U.S. schools asks whether Sweden's liberal mandatory sex education program, which has been effective in reducing pregnancy and abortion, would be successful in the United States.

In this 1946 essay, the author of *Nineteen Eighty-Four* suggests why the hand that pens a stale metaphor should not be trusted with the reins of government.

Letter from Birmingham Jail
MARTIN LUTHER KING, JR. **663**

In 1963, the imprisoned civil-rights leader argues that nonviolent victims of unjust laws have the right to break those laws so long as they use nonviolent actions.

I Have a Dream
MARTIN LUTHER KING, JR. **678**

This stirring exhortation to marchers at a 1963 civil-rights rally rings out like a church bell with rhythm, imagery, joy, hope, and deep conviction. Don't just read the words — listen to the music!

ELEMENTS OF
ARGUMENT

PART ONE

The Structure of Argument

CHAPTER ONE

Introduction to Argument

THE NATURE OF ARGUMENT

A conversation overheard in the school cafeteria:

"Hey, how come you didn't order the meat loaf special? It's pretty good today."

"Well, I read this book about vegetarianism, and I've decided to give up meat. The book says meat's unhealthy and vegetarians live longer."

"Don't be silly. Americans eat lots of meat, and we're living longer and longer."

"Listen, this book tells how much healthier the Danes were during World War II because they couldn't get meat."

"I don't believe it. A lot of these health books are written by quacks. It's pretty dumb to change your diet after reading one book."

These people are having what most of us would call an argument, one that sounds dangerously close to a quarrel. There are, however, significant differences between the colloquial meaning of argument as a quarrel and its definition as a process of reasoning and advancing proof, although even the exchange reported above exhibits some of the characteristics of formal argument. The kinds of arguments we deal with in this text are not quarrels. They often resemble ordinary discourse about controversial issues. You may, for example, overhear a conversation like this one:

"This morning while I was trying to eat breakfast I heard an announcer describing the execution of that guy in Texas who raped

3

> and murdered a teenaged couple. They gave him an injection, and
> it took him ten minutes to die. I almost lost my breakfast listening
> to it."
>
> "Well, he deserved it. He didn't show much pity for his victims,
> did he?"
>
> "Okay, but no matter what he did, capital punishment is really
> awful, barbaric. It's murder, even if the state does it."
>
> "No, I'd call it justice. I don't know what else we can do to show
> how we feel about a cruel, pointless murder of innocent people.
> The punishment ought to be as terrible as we can make it."

Each speaker is defending a value judgment about an issue that tests
ideas of good and evil, right and wrong, and that cannot be decided by
facts.

In another kind of argument the speaker or writer proposes a
solution for a specific problem. Two men, both under twenty, are engaged in a conversation.

> "I'm going to be broke this week after I pay my car insurance.
> I don't think it's fair for males under twenty to pay such high rates.
> I'm a good driver, much better that my older sister. Why not consider
> driving experience instead of age or sex?"
>
> "But I always thought that guys our age had the most accidents.
> How do you know that driving experience is the right standard to
> apply?"
>
> "Well, I read a report by the Highway Commission that said it's
> really driving experience that counts. So I think it's unfair for us to
> be discriminated against. The law's behind the times. They ought to
> change the insurance laws."

In this case someone advocates a policy that appears to fulfill a desirable goal — making it impossible to discriminate against drivers just
because they are young and male. Objections arise that the arguer must
attempt to answer.

In these three dialogues, as well as in all the other arguments you
will read in this book, human beings are engaged in explaining and
defending their own actions and beliefs and opposing those of others.
They do this for at least two reasons: to justify what they do and think
both to themselves and to their opponents and, in the process, to solve
problems and make decisions, especially those dependent on a consensus between conflicting views.

Unlike the examples cited so far, the arguments you will read and
write will not usually take the form of dialogues, but arguments are
implicit dialogues. Even when our audience is unknown, we write to
persuade the unconvinced, to acquaint them with good reasons for
changing their minds. As one definition has it, "Argumentation is the

art of influencing others, through the medium of reasoned discourse, to believe or act as we wish them to believe or act."[1] This process is inherently dramatic; a good argument can create the kinds of tensions generated at sporting events. Who will win? What are the factors that enable a winner to emerge? One of the most popular and enduring situations on television is the courtroom debate, in which two lawyers (one, the defense attorney, the hero, unusually knowledgeable and persuasive; the other, the prosecuting attorney, bumbling and corrupt) confront each other before an audience of judge and jury that must render a heart-stopping verdict. Tensions are high because a life is in the balance. In the classroom the stakes are neither so intimidating nor so melodramatic, but even here a well-conducted argument can throw off sparks.

Most of the arguments in this book will deal with matters of public controversy, an area traditionally associated with the study of argument. As the word *public* suggests, these matters concern us as members of a community. "They are," according to one rhetorician, "the problems of war and peace, race and creed, poverty, wealth, and population, of democracy and communism. . . . Specific issues arise on which we must take decision from time to time. One day it is Suez, another Cuba. One week it is the Congo, another it is the plight of the American farmer or the railroads. . . . On these subjects the experts as well as the many take sides."[2] Today the issues are different from the issues that writers confronted more than twenty years ago. Today we are concerned about the nuclear freeze, unemployment, illegal immigration, bilingual education, gun control, homosexual rights, drug abuse, prayer in school, to name only a few,

Clearly, if all of us agreed about everything, if harmony prevailed everywhere, the need for argument would disappear. But given what we know about the restless, seeking, contentious nature of human beings and their conflicting interests, we should not be surprised that many controversial questions, some of them as old as human civilization itself, will not be settled nor will they vanish despite the energy we devote to settling them. Unresolved, they are submerged for a while and then reappear, sometimes in another form, sometimes virtually unchanged. Capital punishment is one such stubborn problem; abortion is another. Nevertheless, we value the argumentative process because it is indispensable to the preservation of a free society. In *Areopagitica,* his great defense of free speech, John Milton, the seventeenth-century poet, wrote, "I cannot praise a fugitive and cloistered virtue, unexercised and unbreathed, that never sallies out and sees her adversary." How

---

[1] J. M. O'Neill, C. Laycock, and R. L. Scale, *Argumentation and Debate* (New York: Macmillan, 1925), p. 1.

[2] Karl R. Wallace, "Toward a Rationale for Teachers of Writing and Speaking," *English Journal,* September 1961, p. 386.

can we know the truth, he asked, unless there is a "free and open encounter" between all ideas? "Give me liberty to know, to utter, and to argue freely according to conscience, above all liberties."

WHY STUDY ARGUMENT?

Perhaps the question has already occurred to you: Why *study* argument? Since you've engaged in some form of the argumentative process all your life, is there anything to be learned that experience hasn't taught you? We think there is. If you've ever felt frustration in trying to decide what is wrong with an argument, either your own or someone else's, you might have wondered if there were rules to help in the analysis. If you've ever been dissatisfied with your attempt to prove a case, you might have wondered how good arguers, the ones who succeed in persuading people, construct their cases. Good arguers do, in fact, know and follow rules. Studying and practicing these rules can provide you with some of the same skills.

You will find yourself using these skills in a variety of situations, not only in arguing important public issues. You will use them, for example, in your academic career. Whatever your major field of study — the humanities, the social sciences, the physical sciences, business — you will be required to defend views about materials you have read and studied.

Humanities. Why have some of the greatest novels resisted translation into great films?

Social Science. What is the evidence that upward social mobility continues to be a positive force in American life?

Physical Science. What will happen to the world climate as the amount of carbon dioxide in the atmosphere increases?

Business. Are the new tax laws beneficial or disadvantageous to the real estate investor?

For all these assignments, different as they may be, you would use the same kinds of analysis, research techniques, and evaluation. The conventions or rules for reporting results might differ from one field of study to another, but for the most part the rules for defining terms, evaluating evidence, and arriving at conclusions cross disciplinary lines. Many employers, not surprisingly, are aware of this. One sheriff in Arizona advertised for an assistant with a degree in philosophy. He had discovered, he said, that the methods used by philosophers to solve problems were remarkably similar to the methods used in law enforcement.

Whether or not you are interested in serving as sheriff's assistant, you will encounter situations in the workplace that call for the same analytical and argumentative skills employed by philosophers and law enforcement personnel. Almost everywhere — in the smallest businesses as well as the largest corporations — a worker who can articulate his or her views clearly and forcefully has an important advantage in gaining access to positions of greater interest and challenge. Even when they are primarily informative, the memorandums, reports, instructions, questions, and explanations that issue from offices and factories obey the rules of argumentative discourse.

You may not anticipate doing the kind of writing or speaking at your job that you will practice in your academic work. It is probably true that in some careers, writing constitutes a negligible part of a person's duties. But outside the office, the studio, and the salesroom, you will be called on to exhibit argumentative skills as a citizen, as a member of a community, and as a consumer of leisure. In these capacities you can contribute to decision making if you are knowledgeable and prepared. By writing or speaking to the appropriate authorities, you can argue for a change in the meal ticket plan at your school or the release of pornographic films at the neighborhood theater or against a change in automobile insurance rates. Most of us are painfully aware of opportunities we lost because we were uncertain of how to proceed, even in matters that affected us deeply.

A course in argumentation offers another invaluable dividend: It can help you to cope with the bewildering confusion of voices in the world around you. It can give you tools for distinguishing between what is true and what is false, what is valid and what is invalid, in the claims of politicians, promoters of causes, newscasters, advertisers, salespeople, teachers, parents and siblings, employers and employees, neighbors, friends, and lovers, any of whom may be engaged at some time in attempting to persuade you to accept a belief or adopt a course of action. It can even offer strategies for arguing with yourself about a personal dilemma.

So far we have treated argument as an essentially pragmatic activity that benefits the individual. But choosing argument over force or evasion has clear moral benefits for society as well. We can, in fact, defend the study of argumentation for the same reasons that we defend universal education despite its high cost and sometimes controversial results. In a democracy, widespread literacy ultimately benefits all members of society, not only those who are the immediate beneficiaries of education, because only an informed citizenry can make responsible choices. One distinguished writer explains that "democracy depends on a citizenry that can reason for themselves, on men who know whether a case has been proved, or at least made probable."[3]

---

[3] Wayne C. Booth, "Boring from Within: The Art of the Freshman Essay," adapted

It is not too much to say that argument is a civilizing influence, the very basis of democratic order. In totalitarian countries, coercion, which may express itself in a number of reprehensible forms — censorship, imprisonment, exile, torture, or execution — is a favored means of removing opposition to establishment "truth." In free societies, argument and debate remain the preeminent means of arriving at consensus.

Of course, rational discourse in a democracy can and does break down. Confrontations with police at nuclear power plants, shouting and heckling at a meeting to prevent a speaker from being heard, student sit-ins in college administrators' offices — such actions have become common in recent years. The demands of the demonstrators are often passionately and sincerely held, and the protesters sometimes succeed through force or intimidation in influencing policy changes. When this happens, however, we cannot be sure that the changes are justified. History and experience teach us that reason, to a far greater degree than other methods of persuasion, ultimately determines the rightness or wrongness of our actions.

A piece of folk wisdom sums up the superiority of reasoned argument as a vehicle of persuasion: "A man convinced against his will is of the same opinion still." Those who accept a position after engaging in a dialogue offering good reasons on both sides will think and act with greater willingness and conviction than those who have been coerced or denied the privilege of participating in the decision.

Why Write?

If we agree that studying argumentation provides important critical tools, one last question remains: Why *write?* Isn't it possible to learn the rules by reading and talking about the qualities of good and bad arguments? Not quite. All writers, both experienced and inexperienced, will probably confess that looking at what they have written, even after long thought, can produce a startled disclaimer: But that isn't what I meant to say! They know that more analysis and more hard thinking are in order. Writers are also aware that words on paper have an authority and a permanency that invite more than casual deliberation. It is one thing to make an assertion, to express an idea or a strong feeling in conversation, and perhaps even to deny it later; it is quite another to write out an extended defense of your own position or an attack on someone else's that will be read and perhaps criticized by people unsympathetic to your views.

from a speech delivered to the Illinois Council of College Teachers of English in May 1963.

Students are often told that they must become better thinkers if they are to become better writers. It works the other way, too. In the effort to produce a clear and convincing argument, a writer matures as a thinker and a critic. The very process of writing calls for skills that make us better thinkers. An authority on language, the British etymologist Eric Partridge, put it this way.

> Good — that is, clear, effective, entirely adequate — speaking and writing will ease and smooth the passage of general thought and the conveyance of a particular thought or impression in statement or question or command. Bad speaking and writing do just the opposite and, worse, set up doubt and ambiguity.[4]

In sum, writing argumentative essays tests and enlarges important mental abilities — developing and organizing ideas, evaluating evidence, observing logical consistency, expressing ourselves clearly and economically — that we need to exercise all our lives in our various social roles, whether or not we continue to write after college.

THE TERMS OF ARGUMENT

One definition of argument, emphasizing audience, has been given earlier: "Argumentation is the art of influencing others, through the medium of reasoned discourse, to believe or act as we wish them to believe or act." A distinction is sometimes made between argument and persuasion. Argument, according to most authorities, gives primary importance to logical appeals. Persuasion introduces the element of ethical and emotional appeals. The difference is one of emphasis. In real-life arguments about social policy, the distinction is hard to measure. In this book we use the term *argument* to represent forms of discourse that attempt to persuade readers or listeners to accept a claim, whether acceptance is based on logical or emotional appeals or, as is usually the case, on both. The following brief definition includes other elements: *An argument is a statement or statements offering support for a claim.*

An argument is composed of at least three parts: the claim, the support, and the warrant.[5]

---

[4] "Speaking of Books: Degraded Language," *New York Times Book Review,* September 18, 1966, p. 2.

[5] Some of the terms and analyses used in this text are adapted from Stephen Toulmin's *The Uses of Argument* (Cambridge: Cambridge University Press, 1958).

The Claim

The claim (also called a *proposition*) answers the question "What are you trying to prove?" It may appear as the thesis statement of your essay, although in some arguments it may not be stated directly. There are three principal kinds of claim (discussed more fully in Chapter 2): claims of fact, of value, and of policy. (The three dialogues at the beginning of this chapter represent these three kinds of claim respectively.) *Claims of fact* assert that a condition has existed, exists, or will exist and are based on facts or data that the audience will accept as being objectively verifiable:

> The present cocaine epidemic is not unique. From 1885 to the 1920s, cocaine was as widely used as it is today.
>
> Horse racing is the most dangerous sport.
>
> California will experience colder, stormier weather for the next ten years.

All these claims must be supported by data. Although the last example is an inference or an educated guess about the future, a reader will probably find the prediction credible if the data seem authoritative.

Claims of value attempt to prove that some things are more or less desirable than others. They express approval or disapproval of standards of taste and morality. Advertisements and reviews of cultural events are one common source of value claims, but such claims emerge whenever people argue about what is good or bad, beautiful or ugly.

> One look and Crane [writing paper] says you have a tasteful writing style.
>
> *Tannhäuser* provides a splendid viewing as well as listening experience.
>
> Football is one of the most dehumanizing experiences a person can face. — Dave Meggyesy
>
> Ending a patient's life intentionally is absolutely forbidden on moral grounds. — Presidential Commission on Medical Ethics, 1983

Claims of policy assert that specific policies should be instituted as solutions to problems. The expression *should, must,* or *ought to* usually appears in the statement.

> Prisons should be abolished because they are crime-manufacturing concerns.
>
> Our first step must be to immediately establish and advertise drastic policies designed to bring our own population under control. — Paul Ehrlich, biologist
>
> The New York City Board of Education should make sure that qualified women appear on any new list [of candidates for Chancellor of Education].

Policy claims call for analysis of both fact and value. (A full discussion of claims follows in Chapter 2.)

The Support

Support consists of the materials used by the arguer to convince an audience that his or her claim is sound. These materials include *evidence* and *motivational appeals*. The evidence or data consist of facts, statistics, and testimony from experts. The motivational appeals are the ones that the arguer makes to the values and attitudes of the audience to win support for the claim. The word *motivational* points out that these appeals are the reasons that move an audience to accept a belief or adopt a course of action. For example, in his argument advocating population control, Ehrlich first offered statistical evidence to prove the magnitude of the population explosion. But he also made a strong appeal to the generosity of his audience to persuade them to sacrifice their own immediate interests to those of future generations. (See Chapter 4 for detailed coverage of support.)

The Warrant

The warrant is an inference or an assumption, a belief or principle that is taken for granted. A warrant is a guarantee of reliability; in argument it guarantees the soundness of the relationship between the support and the claim. It allows the reader to make the connection between the support and the claim.

Warrants or assumptions underlie all the claims we make. They may be stated or unstated. If the arguer believes that the audience shares his assumption, he may feel it unnecessary to express it. But if he thinks that the audience is doubtful or hostile, he may decide to state the assumption in order to emphasize its importance or argue for its validity.

This is how the warrant works. In the dialogue beginning this chapter, one speaker made the claim that vegetarianism was more healthful than a diet containing meat. As support he offered the evidence that the authors of a book he had read recommended vegetarianism for greater health and longer life. He did not state his warrant — that the authors of the book were trustworthy guides to theories of healthful diet. In outline form the argument looks like this:

CLAIM: Adoption of a vegetarian diet leads to healthier and longer life.

SUPPORT: The authors of *Becoming a Vegetarian Family* say so.

WARRANT: The authors of *Becoming a Vegetarian Family* are reliable sources of information on diet.

A writer or speaker may also need to offer <u>support for the warrant</u>. In the case cited above, the second speaker is reluctant to accept the unstated warrant, suggesting that the authors may be quacks. The first speaker will need to provide support for the assumption that the authors are trustworthy, perhaps by introducing proof of their credentials in science and medicine. Notice that although the second speaker accepts the evidence, he cannot agree that the claim has been proved unless he also accepts the warrant. If he fails to accept the warrant — that is, if he refuses to believe that the authors are credible sources of information about diet — then the evidence cannot support the claim.

The following example demonstrates how a different kind of warrant, based on values, can also lead an audience to accept a claim.

> CLAIM: Laws making marijuana illegal should be repealed.
>
> SUPPORT: People should have the right to use any substance they wish.
>
> WARRANT: No laws should prevent citizens from exercising their rights.

Support for repeal of the marijuana laws often consists of medical evidence that marijuana is harmless. Here, however, the arguer contends that an important ethical principle is at work: Nothing should prevent people from exercising their rights, including the right to use any substance, no matter how harmful. Let us suppose that the reader agrees with the supporting statement, that individuals should have the right to use any substance. But in order to accept the claim, the reader must also agree with the principle expressed in the warrant, that government should not interfere with the individual's right. He or she can then agree that laws making marijuana illegal should be repealed. Notice that this warrant, like all warrants, certifies that the relationship between the support and the claim is sound.

One more element of argument remains to be considered — *definition.* Definition, of course, is important in all forms of exposition, but it can be crucial in argument. For this reason we've devoted a whole chapter to it in this text. Many of the controversial questions you will encounter in your reading about public affairs are primarily arguments about the definition of terms. Such terms as *abortion, pornography, equality, poverty,* and *insanity* must be defined before useful public policies about them can be formulated. (For more on warrants, see Chapter 5.)

THE AUDIENCE

All arguments are composed with an audience in mind. We have already pointed out that an argument is an implicit dialogue or exchange. Often the writer of an argument about a public issue is responding to another writer or speaker who has made a claim that needs to be supported or opposed. In writing your own arguments, you should assume that there is a reader who may not agree with you. Throughout this book, we will continue to refer to ways of reaching such a reader.

Speechmakers are usually better informed than writers about their audience. Some writers, however, are familiar with the specific persons or groups who will read their arguments; advertising copywriters are a conspicuous example. They discover their audiences through sophisticated polling and marketing techniques and direct their messages to a well-targeted group of prospective buyers. Other professionals may be required to submit reports to persuade a specific and clearly defined audience of certain beliefs or courses of action: An engineer may be asked by an environmental interest group to defend his plans for the building of a sewage treatment plant; or a town planner may be called on to tell the town council why she believes that rent control may not work; or a sales manager may find it necessary to explain to his superior why a new product should be launched in the Midwest rather than the South.

In such cases the writer asks some or all of the following questions about the audience:

Why has this audience requested this report? What do they want to get out of it?

How much do they already know about the subject?

Are they divided or agreed on the subject?

What is their emotional involvement with the issues?

Assessing Credibility

Providing abundant evidence and making logical connections between the parts of an argument may not be enough to win agreement from an audience. In fact, success in convincing an audience is almost always inseparable from the writer's credibility, or the audience's belief in the writer's trustworthiness. Aristotle, the Greek philosopher who wrote a treatise on argument that has influenced its study and practice for more than two thousand years, considered credibility — what he called *ethos* — the most important element in the arguer's ability to persuade the audience to accept his or her claim.

Aristotle named "intelligence, character, and goodwill" as the attributes that produce credibility. Today we might describe these qualities somewhat differently, but the criteria for judging a writer's credibility remain essentially the same. First, the writer must convince the audience that he is knowledgeable, that he is as well informed as possible about the subject. Second, he must persuade his audience that he is not only truthful in the presentation of his evidence but also morally upright and dependable. Third, he must show that, as an arguer with good intentions, he has considered the interests and needs of others as well as his own.

As an example in which the credibility of the arguer is at stake, consider a wealthy Sierra Club member who lives on ten acres of a magnificent oceanside estate and who appears before a community planning board to argue against future development of the area. His claim is that more building will destroy the delicate ecological balance of the area. The board, acting in the interests of all the citizens of the community, will ask themselves: Has the arguer proved that his information about environmental impact is complete and accurate? Has he demonstrated that he sincerely desires to preserve the wilderness, not merely his own privacy and space? And has he also made clear that he has considered the needs and desires of those who might want to live in a housing development by the ocean? If the answers to all these questions are yes, then the board will hear the arguer with respect, and the arguer will have begun to establish his credibility.

A reputation for intelligence, character, and goodwill is not often won overnight. And it can be lost more quickly than it is won. Once a writer or speaker has betrayed an audience's belief in her character or judgment, she may find it difficult to persuade an audience to accept subsequent claims, no matter how sound her data and reasoning are. "We give no credit to a liar," said Cicero, "even when he speaks the truth."

Political life is full of examples of lost and squandered credibility. After it was discovered that President Lyndon Johnson had deceived the American public about U.S. conduct in the Vietnam War, he could not regain his popularity. After senator Edward Kennedy failed to persuade the public that he had behaved honorably at Chappaquiddick, his influence and power in the Democratic party declined. After President Gerald Ford pardoned former President Richard Nixon for his complicity in the Watergate scandal, Ford was no longer a serious candidate for reelection.

We can see the practical consequences when an audience realizes that an arguer has been guilty of a deception — misusing facts and authority, suppressing evidence, distorting statistics, violating the rules of logic. But suppose the arguer is successful in concealing his or her manipulation of the data and can persuade an uninformed audience to take the action or adopt the idea that he or she recommends. Even supposing that the argument promotes a "good" cause, is the arguer justified in using evasive or misleading tactics?

The answer is no. To encourage another person to make a decision on the basis of incomplete or dishonestly used data is profoundly unethical. It indicates lack of respect for the rights of others — their right to know at least as much as you do about the subject, to be allowed to judge and compare, to disagree with you if they challenge your own interests. If the moral implications are still not clear, try to imagine yourself not as the perpetrator of the lie but as the victim.

There is also a danger in measuring success wholly by the degree to which audiences accept our arguments. Both as writers and readers, we must be able to respect the claim, or proposition, and what it tries to demonstrate. Toulmin has said: "To conclude that a proposition is true, it is not enough to know that this man or that finds it 'credible': the proposition itself must be *worthy* of credence."[6]

Acquiring Credibility

You may wonder how you can acquire credibility. You are not yet an expert in many of the subjects you will deal with in assignments, although you are knowledgeable about many other things, including your cultural and social activities. But there are several ways in which you can create confidence by your treatment of topics derived from academic disciplines, such as politics, psychology, economics, sociology, and art, on which most assignments will be based.

First, you can submit evidence of careful research, demonstrating that you have been conscientious in finding the best authorities, giving credit, and attempting to arrive at the truth. Second, you can adopt a thoughtful and judicious tone that reflects a desire to be fair in your conclusion. Tone expresses the attitude of the writer toward his or her subject. When the writer feels strongly about the subject and adopts a belligerent or complaining tone, for example, he or she forgets that readers who feel differently may find the tone disagreeable and unconvincing. In the following excerpt a student expresses his feelings about standard grading, that is, grading by letter or number on a scale that applies to a whole group.

> You go to school to learn, not to earn grades. To be educated, that's what they tell you. "He's educated, he graduated Magna Cum Laude." What makes a Magna Cum Laude man so much better than a man that graduates with a C? They are both still educated, aren't they? No one has a right to call someone less educated because they got a C instead of an A. Let's take both men and put them in front of a car. Each car has something wrong with it. Each man must fix his broken car. Our C man goes right to work while our Magna Cum Laude man hasn't got the slightest idea where to begin. Who's more educated now?

Probably a reader who disagreed with the claim — that standard grading should not be used — would find the tone, if not the evidence itself, unpersuasive. The writer sounds as if he is defending his own ability to do something that an honors graduate can't do, while ignoring the acknowledged purposes of standard grading in academic subjects. He sounds, moreover, as if he's angry because someone has done him

---

[6]*An Examination of the Place of Reason in Ethics* (Cambridge: Cambridge University Press, 1964), p. 71.

an injury. Compare the preceding passage to the following one, written by a student on the same subject.

> Grades are the play money in a university Monopoly game. As long as the tokens are offered, the temptation will be largely irresistible to play for them. Students are so busy taking notes, doing tests, and getting tokens that they have forgotten to ask: Of what worth is all this? Or perhaps they ask and the grade is their answer.
>
> One certainly learns something in the passive lecture-note-read-note-test process: how to do it all more efficiently next time (in the hope of eventually owning Boardwalk and Park Place). As Marshall McLuhan has said, we learn what we do. In this process most students come to view learning as studying and remembering what other people have learned. They assume that knowledge is logically and for practical reasons divided up into discrete pieces called "disciplines" and that the highest knowledge is achieved by specializing in a discipline. By getting good grades in a lot of disciplines they conclude they have learned a lot. They have indeed, and it is too bad.[7]

Most readers would consider this writer more credible, in part because he has adopted a tone that seems moderate and impersonal. That is, he does not convey the impression that he is interested only in defending his own grades. Notice also that the language of this passage suggests a higher level of learning and research.

Sometimes, of course, an expression of anger or even outrage is appropriate and morally justified. But if readers do not share your sense of outrage, you must try to reach them through a more moderate approach. In his autobiography, Benjamin Franklin recounted his attempts to acquire the habit of temperate language in argument:

> Retaining . . . the habit of expressing myself in terms of modest diffidence; . . . never using, when I advanced anything that may possibly be disputed, the words *"certainly, undoubtedly,"* or any others that give the air of positiveness to an opinion; but rather say, I conceive or apprehend a thing to be so and so; it appears to me, *I should think it is so or so,* for such and such reasons; or *I imagine it to be so;* or *it is so, if I am not mistaken.* This habit, I believe, has been of great advantage to me when I have had occasion to inculcate my opinions, and persuade men into measures that I have been from time to time engaged in promoting.[8]

This is not to say that the writer must hedge his or her opinions or confess uncertainty at every point. Franklin suggests that the writer must recognize that other opinions may also have validity and that, although the writer may disagree, he or she respects the other opinions.

---

[7] Roy E. Terry in "Does Standard Grading Encourage Excessive Competitiveness?" *Change,* September 1974, p. 45.

[8] *The Autobiography of Benjamin Franklin* (New York: Pocket Library, 1954), pp. 22–23.

Such an attitude will also dispose the reader to be more generous in evaluating the writer's argument.

A final method of establishing credibility is to produce a clean, literate, well-organized paper, with evidence of care in writing and proofreading. Such a paper will help persuade the reader to take your efforts seriously.

SAMPLE ANALYSIS

The Declaration of Independence
THOMAS JEFFERSON

credibility

When in the course of human events, it becomes necessary for one people to dissolve the political bands which have connected them with another, and to assume among the Powers of the earth, the separate and equal station to which the Laws of Nature and Nature's God entitle them, a decent respect to the opinions of mankind requires that they should declare the causes which impel them to the separation. warrants

We hold these truths to be self-evident, that all men are created equal, that they are endowed by their Creator with certain unalienable Rights, that among these are Life, Liberty and the pursuit of Happiness.

That to secure these rights, Governments are instituted among Men, deriving their just powers from the consent of the governed.

That whenever any Form of Government becomes destructive of these ends, it is the Right of the People to alter or to abolish it, and to institute a new Government laying its foundation on such principles and organizing its powers in such form, as to them shall seem most likely to effect their Safety and Happiness. Prudence, indeed, will dictate that Governments long established should not be changed for light and transient causes; and accordingly all experience hath shown that mankind are more disposed to suffer, while evils are sufferable, than to right themselves by abolishing the forms to which they are accustomed. But when a long train of abuses and usurpations pursuing invariably the same Object evinces a design to reduce them under absolute Despotism, it is their right, it is their duty, to throw off such government, and to provide new Guards for their future security.

change for credibility

Such has been the patient sufferance of these Colonies; and such is now the necessity which constrains them to alter their former Systems of Government. The history of the present King of Great Britain is a history of repeated injuries and usurpations, all having in direct object the establishment of an absolute Tyranny over these States. To prove this, let Facts be submitted to a candid world. 5

He has refused his Assent to laws, the most wholesome and necessary for the public good.

He has forbidden his Governors to pass Laws of immediate and pressing importance, unless suspended in their operation till his Assent should be obtained; and when so suspended, he has utterly neglected to attend to them.

He has refused to pass other Laws for the accommodation of large districts of people, unless those people would relinquish the right of Representation in the Legislature, a right inestimable to them and formidable to tyrants only.

He has called together legislative bodies at places unusual, uncomfortable, and distant from the depository of their Public Records, for the sole purpose of fatiguing them into compliance with his measures.

He has dissolved Representative Houses repeatedly, for opposing with manly firmness his invasions on the rights of the people.   10

He has refused for a long time, after such dissolutions, to cause others to be elected; whereby the Legislative Powers, incapable of Annihilation, have returned to the People at large for their exercise; the State remaining in the mean time exposed to all the danger of invasion from without, and convulsions within.

He has endeavored to prevent the population of these States; for that purpose obstructing the Laws of Naturalization of Foreigners; refusing to pass others to encourage their migration hither, and raising the conditions of new Appropriations of Lands.

He has obstructed the Administration of Justice, by refusing his Assent to Laws for establishing Judiciary Powers.

He has made Judges dependent on his Will alone, for the tenure of their offices, and the amount and payment of their salaries.

He has erected a multitude of New Offices, and sent hither swarms   15
of Officers to harass our People, and eat out their substance.

He has kept among us, in time of peace, Standing Armies without the consent of our Legislature.

He has affected to render the Military independent of and superior to the Civil Power.

He has combined with others to subject us to jurisdictions foreign to our constitution, and unacknowledged by our laws; giving his Assent to their acts of pretended Legislation:

For quartering large bodies of armed troops among us:

For protecting them, by a mock Trial, from Punishment for any   20
Murders which they should commit on the Inhabitants of these States:

For cutting off our Trade with all parts of the world:

For imposing Taxes on us without our Consent:

For depriving us in many cases, of the benefits of Trial by Jury:

For transporting us beyond Seas to be tried for pretended offenses:

For abolishing the free System of English Laws in a Neighbouring   25
Province, establishing therein an Arbitrary government, and enlarging

its boundaries so as to render it at once an example and fit instrument *Support*
for introducing the same absolute rule into these Colonies:

For taking away our Charters, abolishing our most valuable Laws,
and altering fundamentally the Forms of our Governments:

For suspending our own legislatures, and declaring themselves invested with Power to legislate for us in all cases whatsoever.

He has abdicated Government here, by declaring us out of his
Protection and waging War against us.

He has plundered our seas, ravaged our Coasts, burnt our towns
and destroyed the Lives of our people.

He is at this time transporting large Armies of foreign Mercenaries   30
to compleat the works of death, desolation and tyranny, already begun
with circumstances of Cruelty & perfidy scarcely paralleled in the most
barbarous ages, and totally unworthy the Head of a civilized nation.

He has constrained our fellow Citizens taken Captive on the high
Seas to bear Arms against their Country, to become the executioners
of their friends and Brethren, or to fall themselves by their Hands.

He has excited domestic insurrections amongst us, and has endeavored to bring on the inhabitants of our frontiers, the merciless Indian
Savages, whose known rule of warfare is an undistinguished destruction
of all ages, sexes, and conditions.

In every stage of these Oppressions We Have Petitioned for Redress
in the most humble terms. Our repeated petitions have been answered
only by repeated injury. A Prince, whose character is thus marked by
every act which may define a Tyrant, is unfit to be the ruler of a free
People.

Not have We been wanting in attention to our British brethren. We
have warned them from time to time of attempts by their legislature to
extend an unwarrantable jurisdiction over us. We have reminded them
of the circumstances of our emigration and settlement here. We have
appealed to their native justice and magnanimity and we have conjured
them by the ties of our common kindred to disavow these usurpations,
which would inevitably interrupt our connections and correspondence.
They too have been deaf to the voice of justice and of consanguinity.
We must, therefore, acquiesce in the necessity, which denounces our
Separation, and hold them, as we hold the rest of mankind, Enemies in
War, in Peace Friends.

We, therefore, the Representatives of the United States of America,   35
in General Congress, Assembled, appealing to the Supreme Judge of the
world for the rectitude of our intentions, do, in the Name, and by
Authority of the good People of these Colonies, solemnly publish and
declare, That these United Colonies are, and of Right ought to be, Free
and Independent States; that they are Absolved from all Allegiance to
the British Crown, and that all political connection between them and
the State of Great Britain, is and ought to be totally dissolved; and that
as Free and Independent States, they have full power to levy War,

conclude Peace, contract Alliances, establish Commerce, and to do all other Acts and Things which Independent States may of right do. And for the support of this Declaration, with a firm reliance on the protection of Divine Providence, we mutually pledge to each other our lives, our Fortunes and our sacred Honor.

Analysis

Claim: What is Jefferson trying to prove? *The American colonies are justified in declaring their independence from British rule.* Jefferson and his fellow signers might have issued a simple statement such as appears in the last paragraph, announcing the freedom and independence of these United Colonies. Instead, however, they chose to justify their right to do so.

Support: What does Jefferson have to go on? The Declaration of Independence bases its claim on two kinds of support: *factual evidence* and *motivational appeals* or appeals to the values of the audience.

Factual Evidence: Jefferson presents a long list of specific acts of tyranny by George III, beginning with "He has refused his Assent to Laws, the most wholesome and necessary for the public good." This list constitutes more than half the text. Notice how Jefferson introduces these grievances: "The history of the present King of Great Britain is a history of repeated injuries and usurpations, all having in direct object the establishment of an absolute Tyranny over these States. *To prove this, let Facts be submitted to a candid world*" (italics for emphasis added). Jefferson hopes that a recital of these specific acts will convince an honest audience that the United Colonies have indeed been the victims of an intolerable tyranny.

Appeal to Values: Jefferson also invokes the moral values underlying the formation of a democratic state. These values are referred to throughout. In the second and third paragraphs he speaks of equality, "Life, Liberty and the pursuit of Happiness," "Just powers," "Consent of the governed," and safety. In the last paragraph he refers to freedom and independence. Jefferson believes that the people who read his appeal will, or should, share these fundamental values. Audience acceptance of these values constitutes the most important part of the support. Some historians have called the specific acts of oppression cited by Jefferson trivial, inconsequential, or distorted. Clearly, however, Jefferson felt that the list of specific grievances was vital to definition of the abstract terms in which values are always expressed.

Warrant: How does Jefferson get from support to claim? *People have a right to revolution in order to free themselves from oppression.* This warrant is explicit: "But when a long train of abuses and usurpations pursuing invariably the same Object evinces a design to reduce them under absolute Despotism, it is their right, it is their duty, to throw off such government, and to provide new Guards for their future security." Some members of Jefferson's audience, especially those whom he accuses of oppressive acts, will reject the principle that any subject people have earned the right to revolt. But Jefferson believes that the decent opinion of mankind will accept this assumption. Many of his readers will also be aware that the warrant is supported by seventeenth-century political philosophy, which defines government as a social compact between the government and the governed.

If Jefferson's readers do, in fact, accept the warrant and if they also believe in the accuracy of the factual evidence and share his moral values, then they will conclude that his claim has been proved, that Jefferson has justified the right of the colonies to separate themselves from Great Britain.

Audience: The Declaration of Independence is addressed to several audiences: to the American colonists; to the British people; to the British Parliament; to the British king, George III; and to mankind or a universal audience.

Not all the American colonists were convinced by Jefferson's argument. Large numbers remained loyal to the King and for various reasons opposed an independent nation. In the next-to-the-last paragraph, Jefferson refers to previous addresses to the British people. Not surprisingly, most of the British citizenry as well as the King also rejected the claims of the Declaration. But the universal audience, the decent opinion of mankind, found Jefferson's argument overwhelmingly persuasive. Many of the liberal reform movements of the eighteenth and nineteenth centuries were inspired by the Declaration. In basing his claim on universal principles of justice and equality, Jefferson was certainly aware that he was addressing future generations.

EXERCISES FOR CRITICAL THINKING

1. From the following list of claims, select the ones you consider most controversial. Tell why they are difficult to resolve. Are the underlying assumptions controversial? Is support hard to find or disputed? Can you think of circumstances under which some of these claims might be resolved?
   a. Congress should endorse the right-to-life amendment.
   b. Solar power can supply 20 percent of the energy needs now satisfied by fossil and nuclear power.
   c. Homosexuals should have the same job rights as heterosexuals.
   d. Rapists should be treated as mentally ill rather than depraved.
   e. Whale hunting should be banned by international law.
   f. Violence on television produces violent behavior in children who watch more than four hours a day.

g. Both creationism and evolutionary theory should be taught in the public schools.

h. Mentally defective men and women should be sterilized or otherwise prevented from producing children.

i. History will pronounce Reggie Jackson a greater all-round baseball player than Joe DiMaggio.

j. Bilingual instruction should not be permitted in the public schools.

k. Some forms of cancer are caused by a virus.

l. Dogs are smarter than horses.

m. Curfews for teenagers will reduce the abuse of alcohol and drugs.

n. The federal government should impose a drinking age of twenty-one.

o. The United States should proceed with unilateral disarmament.

p. Security precautions at airports are out of proportion to the dangers of terrorism.

q. Bodybuilding cannot be defined as a sport; it is a form of exhibitionism.

2. Report on an argument you have heard recently. Identify the parts of that argument — claim, support, warrant — as they are defined in this chapter. What were the strengths and weaknesses in the argument you heard?

3. Choose one of the more controversial claims in the previous list and explain the reasons it is controversial. Is support lacking or in doubt? Are the warrants unacceptable to many people? Try to go as deeply as you can, exploring, if possible, systems of belief, traditions, societal customs. You may confine your discussion to personal experience with the problem in your community or group. If there has been a change over the years in the public attitude toward the claim, offer what you think may be an explanation for the change.

4. Write your own argument for or against the value of standard grading in college.

5. Discuss an occasion when a controversy arose that the opponents could not settle. Describe the problem and tell why you think the disagreement was not settled.

Chapter Two

Claims

Claims, or propositions, represent answers to the question: "What are you trying to prove?" Although they are the conclusions of your arguments, they often appear as thesis statements. Claims can be classified as *claims of fact, claims of value,* and *claims of policy.*

CLAIMS OF FACT

Claims of fact assert that a condition has existed, exists, or will exist and their support consists of factual information — that is, information such as statistics, examples, and testimony that most responsible observers assume can be verified.

Many facts are not matters for argument: Our own senses can confirm them, and other observers will agree about them. We can agree that a certain number of students were in the classroom at a particular time, that lions make a louder sound than kittens, and that apples are sweeter than potatoes.

We can also agree about information that most of us can rarely confirm for ourselves — information in reference books, such as atlases, almanacs, and telephone directories; data from scientific resources about the physical world; and happenings reported in the media. We can agree on the reliability of such information because we trust the observers who report it.

However, the factual map is constantly being redrawn by new data in such fields as history and science that cause us to reevaluate our conclusions. For example, the discovery of the Dead Sea Scrolls in 1947 revealed that some books of the Bible — *Isaiah,* for one — were far older than we had thought. Researchers at New York Hospital–Cornell

Medical Center say that many symptoms previously thought inevitable in the aging process are now believed to be treatable and reversible symptoms of depression.[1]

In your conversations with other students you probably generate claims of fact every day, some of which can be verified without much effort, others of which are more difficult to substantiate.

> CLAIM: Most of the students in this class come from towns within fifty miles of Boston.

To prove this the arguer would need only to ask the students in the class where they come from.

> CLAIM: Students who take their courses Pass/Fail make lower grades than those who take them for specific grades.

In this case the arguer would need to have access to student records showing the specific grades given by instructors. (In most schools the instructor awards a letter grade, which is then recorded as a Pass or a Fail if the student has elected this option.)

> CLAIM: The Red Sox will win the pennant this year.

This claim is different from the others because it is an opinion about what will happen in the future. But it can be verified (in the future) and is therefore classified as a claim of fact.

More complex factual claims about political and scientific matters remain controversial because proof on which all or most observers will agree is difficult or impossible to obtain.

> CLAIM: Bilingual programs are less effective than English only programs in preparing students for higher education.
>
> CLAIM: The only life in the universe exists on this planet.

Not all claims are so neatly stated or make such unambiguous assertions. Because we recognize that there are exceptions to most generalizations, we often qualify our claims with words such as *generally, usually, probably, as a rule*. It would not be true to state flatly, for example, "College graduates earn more than high school graduates." This statement is generally true, but we know that some high school graduates who are electricians or city bus drivers or sanitation workers earn more than college graduates who are schoolteachers or nurses or social workers. In making such a claim, therefore, the writer should qualify it with a word that limits the claim.

To support a claim of fact, the writer needs to produce sufficient and appropriate data, that is, examples, statistics, and testimony from reliable sources. Provided this requirement is met, the task of estab-

---

[1]*New York Times*, February 20, 1983, Sec. 22, p. 4.

lishing a factual claim would seem to be relatively straightforward. But as you have probably already discovered in ordinary conversation, finding convincing support for factual claims can pose a number of problems. Whenever you try to establish a claim of fact, you will need to ask at least three questions about the material you plan to use: What are sufficient and appropriate data? Who are the reliable authorities? and Have I made clear whether my statements are facts or inferences?

Sufficient and Appropriate Data

The amount and kind of data for a particular argument depend on the importance and complexity of the subject. The more controversial the subject, the more facts and testimony you will need to supply. Consider the claim "The nuclear arsenal of Russia is greater than that of the United States." If you want to prove the truth of this claim, obviously you will have to provide a larger quantity of data than for a claim that says, "By following three steps, you can train your dog to sit and heel in fifteen minutes." In examining your facts and opinions, an alert reader will want to know if they are accurate, current, and typical of other facts and opinions that you have not mentioned.

The reader will also look for testimony from more than one authority, although there may be cases where only one or two experts, because they have achieved a unique breakthrough in their field, will be sufficient. These cases would probably occur most frequently in the physical sciences. The Nobel Prize winners James Watson and Francis Crick, who first discovered the structure of the DNA molecule, are an example of such experts. However, in the case of the so-called Hitler diaries that surfaced in 1983, at least a dozen experts — journalists, historians, bibliographers who could verify the age of the paper and the ink — were needed to establish that they were forgeries.

Reliable Authorities

Not all those who pronounce themselves experts are trustworthy. Your own experience has probably taught you that you cannot always believe the reports of an event by a single witness. The witness may be poorly trained to make accurate observations — about the size of a crowd, the speed of a vehicle, his distance from an object. Or his own physical conditions — illness, intoxication, disability — may prevent him from seeing or hearing or smelling accurately. The circumstances under which he observes the event — darkness, confusion, noise — may also impair his observation. In addition, the witness may be biased for or against the outcome of the event, as in a hotly contested baseball game, where the observer sees the play that he wants to see. You will find the problems associated with the biases of witnesses to be relevant to your work as a reader and writer of argumentative essays.

You will undoubtedly want to quote authors in some of your arguments. In most cases you will not be familiar with the authors. But there are guidelines for determining their reliability: the rank or title of the experts, the acceptance of their publications by other experts, their association with reputable universities, research centers, or think tanks. For example, for a paper on euthanasia, you might decide to quote from an article by Paul Ramsey, identified as the Harrington Spear Paine Professor of Religion at Princeton University. For a paper on prison reform you might want to use material supplied by Tom Murton, a professional penologist, formerly superintendent in the Arkansas prison system, now professor of criminology at the University of Minnesota. Most readers of your arguments would agree that these authors have impressive credentials in their fields.

What if several respectable sources are in conflict? What if the experts disagree? After a preliminary investigation of a controversial subject, you may decide that you have sufficient material to support your claim. But if you read further, you may discover that other material presented by equally qualified experts contradicts your original claim. In such circumstances you will find it impossible to make a definitive claim. (On pp. 121–123, in the treatment of support of a claim by evidence, you will find a more elaborate discussion of this vexing problem.)

Facts or Inferences

We have defined a fact as a statement that can be verified. An inference is "a statement about the unknown on the basis of the known."[2] The difference between facts and inferences is important to you as the writer of an argument because an inference is an *interpretation,* or an opinion reached after informed evaluation of evidence. As you and your classmates wait in your classroom on the first day of the semester, a middle-aged woman wearing a tweed jacket and a corduroy skirt appears and stands in the front of the room. You don't know who this woman is. However, based on what you do know about the appearance of many college teachers and the fact that teachers usually stand in front of the classroom, you may *infer* that this woman is your teacher. You will probably be right. But you cannot be certain until you have more information. Perhaps you will find out that this woman has come from the department office to tell you that your teacher is sick and cannot meet the class today.

You have probably come across a statement such as the following in a newspaper or magazine: "Excessive television viewing has caused

---

[2]S. I. Hayakawa, *Language in Thought and Action* (New York: Harcourt, Brace, Jovanovich, 1978), p. 35.

the steady decline in the reading ability of children and teenagers." Presented this way, the statement is clearly intended to be read as a factual claim that has been or can be proved. But it is an inference. The facts, which can be, and have been, verified, are (1) the reading ability of children and teenagers has declined and (2) the average child views television for six or more hours a day. (Whether this amount of time is "excessive" is also an opinion.) The cause-effect relation between the two facts is an interpretation of the investigator who has examined both the reading scores and the amount of time spent in front of the television set and *inferred* that one is the cause of the other. The causes of the decline in reading scores are probably more complex than the original statement indicates. Since we can seldom or never create laboratory conditions for testing the influence of television separate from other influences in the family and the community, any statement about the connection between reading scores and television viewing can only be a guess.

By definition, no inference can ever do more than suggest probabilities. Of course, some inferences are much more reliable than others and afford a high degree of probability. Almost all claims in science are based on inferences, interpretations of data on which most scientists agree. Paleontologists find a few ancient bones from which they make inferences about an animal that might have been alive millions of years ago. We can never be absolutely certain that the reconstruction of the dinosaur in the museum is an exact copy of the animal it is supposed to represent, but the probability is fairly high because no other interpretation works so well to explain all the observable data — the existence of the bones in a particular place, their age, their relation to other fossils, and their resemblance to the bones of existing animals with which the paleontologist is familiar.

Inferences are profoundly important, and most arguments could not proceed very far without them. But an inference is not a fact. The writer of an argument must make it clear when he or she offers an inference, an interpretation, or an opinion that it is not a fact.

Defending a Claim of Fact

Here is a summary of the guidelines that should help you to defend a factual claim. (We'll say more about support of factual claims in Chapter 4.)

1. Be sure that the claim — what you are trying to prove — is clearly stated, preferably at the beginning of your paper.
2. Define terms that may be controversial or ambiguous. For example, in trying to prove that "radicals" had captured the student government, you would have to define "radicals," distinguishing them from

"liberals" or members of other ideological groups, so that your readers would understand exactly what you meant.

3. As far as possible, make sure that your evidence — facts and opinions, or interpretations of the facts — fulfills the appropriate criteria. The data should be sufficient, accurate, recent, typical; the authorities should be reliable.

4. Make clear when conclusions about the data are inferences or interpretations, not facts. For example, you might write, "The series of lectures, 'Modern Architecture,' sponsored by our fraternity, was poorly attended because the students at this college aren't interested in discussions of art." What proof could you offer that this *was* the reason, that your statement was a *fact?* Perhaps there were other reasons that you hadn't considered.

5. Arrange your evidence in order to emphasize what is most important. Place it at the beginning or the end, the most emphatic positions in an essay, and devote more space to it.

SAMPLE ANALYSIS: CLAIM OF FACT

Cocaine Is Even Deadlier Than We Thought

LOUIS L. CREGLER and HERBERT MARK

To the Editor:

In his July 3 letter about recreational cocaine use, Dr. Carl C. Pfeiffer notes that some of the toxic effects of cocaine on the heart have long been known to those versed in pharmacology. We wish to point out that cardiologists and neurologists are seeing additional complications not previously known. Indeed, little information on the cardiovascular effects of cocaine appeared until recently.

As Dr. Pfeiffer says, cocaine sensitizes the heart to the normal stimulant effects of the body's adrenaline. This ordinarily makes the heart beat much faster and increases blood pressure significantly. Cocaine abuse has also been associated with strokes, heart attacks (acute myocardial infarctions), and sudden deaths. Individuals with weak blood vessels (aneurysms or arteriovenous malformations) in the head are at greatest risk of having a stroke. With the sudden surge in blood

Louis L. Cregler, M.D., is assistant chief of medicine, and Herbert Mark, M.D., is chief of medicine at the Bronx Veterans Administration Medical Center. This article appeared in the *New York Times* on July 30, 1986.

pressure, a blood vessel can burst. Cocaine can also cause blood vessels supplying the heart muscle itself to undergo vasoconstriction (coronary spasm), and this can produce a heart attack.

Deaths have been reported after administration of cocaine by all routes. Most such deaths are attributed to cocaine intoxication, leading to generalized convulsions, respiratory failure, and cardiac arrhythmias, minutes to hours after administration. Much of this information is so new that it has not found its way into the medical literature or standard textbooks.

Cocaine abuse continues to escalate in American society. It is estimated that 30 million Americans have used it, and some 5 million use it regularly. As cocaine has become less expensive, its availability and purity are increasing. It has evolved from a minor problem into a major threat to public health. And as use has increased, greater numbers of emergency-room visits, cocaine-related heart problems, and sudden deaths have been reported. With so many people using cocaine, it is not unexpected that more strokes, heart attacks, and sudden cardiac deaths will be taking place.

Louis L. Cregler, M.D.
Herbert Mark, M.D.

Analysis

The authors of this letter supply data to prove that the deadly effects of cocaine exceed those that are already well known in medicine and pharmacology. Four aspects of this factual claim are noteworthy. First, it is a response to a letter that, according to the authors, ignored significant new evidence. Many factual claims originate in just this way — as answers to previous claims. Second, the authors, both physicians at a large medical center, apparently have expert knowledge of the scientific data they report. Third, the effects of cocaine use are precisely and vividly described. It is, in fact, these specific references to the damage done to heart and blood vessels that make the claim particularly convincing. Finally, the authors make this claim in order to promote a change in our attitudes toward the use of cocaine; they do not call on their readers to abstain from cocaine. This use of a factual claim as a first step in calling for changes in attitude and behavior is a familiar and often effective argumentative strategy.

CLAIMS OF VALUE

Unlike claims of fact, which attempt to prove that something is true and which can be validated by reference to the data, claims of value make a judgment. They express approval or disapproval. They attempt to prove that some action, belief, or condition is right or wrong, good or bad, beautiful or ugly, worthwhile or undesirable.

> CLAIM: Democracy is superior to any other form of government.

> CLAIM: Killing animals for sport is wrong.

> CLAIM: The Sam Rayburn Building in Washington is an aesthetic failure.

Some claims of value are simply expressions of tastes, likes and dislikes, or preferences and prejudices. The Latin proverb "De gustibus non est disputandum" states that we cannot dispute about tastes. Suppose you express a preference for chocolate over vanilla. If your listener should ask why you prefer this flavor, you cannot refer to an outside authority or produce data or appeal to her moral sense to convince her that your preference is justified.

Many claims of value, however, can be defended or attacked on the basis of standards that measure the worth of an action, a belief, or an object. As far as possible, our personal likes and dislikes should be supported by reference to these standards. Value judgments occur in any area of human experience, but whatever the area, the analysis will be the same. We ask the arguer who is defending a claim of value: *What are the standards or criteria for deciding that this action, this belief, or this object is good or bad, beautiful or ugly, desirable or undesirable? Does the thing you are defending fulfill these criteria?*

There are two general areas in which people often disagree about matters of value: aesthetics and morality. They are also the areas that offer the greatest challenge to the writer. What follows is a discussion of some of the elements of analysis that you should consider in defending a claim of value in these areas.

Aesthetics is the study of beauty and the fine arts. Controversies over works of art — the aesthetic value of books, paintings, sculpture, architecture, dance, drama, and movies — rage fiercely among experts and laypeople alike. They may disagree on the standards for judging or, even if they agree, may disagree about how successfully the art object under discussion has met these standards.

Consider a discussion about popular music. Hearing someone praise the singing of a well-known vocalist, Sheila Jordan, you might ask why she is so highly regarded. You expect Jordan's fan to say more than "I like her" or "Man, she's great." You expect the fan to give reasons to support his claim. "She's unique," he says. He shows you a short review from a widely read newspaper that says, "Her singing is filled with fascinating phrasings, twists, and turns, and she's been compared with Billie Holiday for her emotional intensity. . . . She can be so heart-wrenching that conversations stop cold." Her fan agrees with the criteria for judging a singer given by the author of the review: uniqueness, fascinating phrasings, emotional intensity.

You may not agree that these are the only standards or even the significant ones for judging a singer. But the establishment of standards itself offers material for a discussion or an argument. You may argue about the relevance of the criteria, or, agreeing on the criteria, you may argue about the success of the singer in meeting them. Perhaps you prefer cool singers to intense ones. Or, even if you choose intensity over coolness, you may not think Sheila Jordan can be described as "expressive." Moreover, in any arguments about criteria, differences in experience and preparation acquire importance. You would probably take for granted that a writer with formal musical training who has listened carefully to dozens of singers over a period of years, who has read a good deal of musical criticism and discussed musical matters with other knowledgeable people would be a more reliable critic than someone who lacked these qualifications.

It is probably not surprising then, that, despite wide differences in taste, professional critics more often than not agree on criteria and whether an art object has met the criteria. For example, almost all movie critics agreed that *Citizen Kane* and *Gone with the Wind* were superior films. They also agreed that *A Tomato Ate My Sister,* a horror film, was terrible.

Value claims about morality express judgments about the rightness or wrongness of conduct or belief. Here disagreements are as wide and deep as in the arts. The first two examples on page 30 reveal how controversial such claims can be. Although you and your reader may share many values, among them a belief in democracy, a respect for learning, and a desire for peace, you may also disagree, even profoundly, about other values. The subject of divorce, for example, despite its prevalence in our society, can produce a conflict between differing moral standards. Some people may insist on adherence to absolute standards, arguing that the values they hold are based on immutable religious precepts derived from God and Scripture. Since marriage is sacred, divorce is always wrong, they say, whether or not the conditions of society change. Other people may argue that values are relative, based on the changing needs of societies in different places and at different times. Since marriage is an institution created by human beings at a particular time in history to serve particular social needs, they may say, it can also be dissolved when other social needs arise. The same conflicts between moral values might occur in discussions of abortion or suicide.

As a writer you cannot always know what system of values is held by your reader. Yet it might be possible to find a rule on which almost all readers agree. One such rule was expressed by the eighteenth-century German philosopher Immanuel Kant: "Man and, in general, every rational being exists as an end in itself and not merely as a means to be arbitrarily used by this or that will." Kant's prescription urges us not to subject any creature to a condition that it has not freely chosen. In other words, we cannot use other creatures, as in slavery, for our own purposes. (Some philosophers would extend this rule to the treatment of animals by human beings.) This standard of judgment has, in fact, been invoked in recent years against medical experimentation on human beings in prisons and hospitals without their consent and against the sterilization of poor or mentally defective women without their knowledge of the decision.

Nevertheless, even where there is agreement about standards for measuring behavior, you should be aware that a majority preference is not enough to confer moral value. If in a certain neighborhood a majority of heterosexual men decide to harass a few gay men and lesbians, that consensus does not make their action right. In formulating value claims, you should be prepared to ask and answer questions about the way in which your value claims and those of others have been arrived at. Lionel Ruby, an American philosopher, sums it up in these words: "The law of rationality tells us that we ought to justify our beliefs by evidence and reasons, instead of asserting them dogmatically."[3]

Of course, you will not always be able to persuade those with whom you argue that your values are superior to theirs and that they should therefore change their attitudes. Nor, on the other hand, would you want to compromise your values or pretend that they were different in order to win an argument. What you can and should do, however, as Lionel Ruby advises, is give *good reasons* why you think one thing is better than another. If as a child you asked why it was wrong to take your brother's toys, you might have been told by an exasperated parent, "Because I say so." Some adults still give such answers in defending their judgments, but such answers are not arguments and do nothing to win the agreement of others.

Defending a Claim of Value

The following suggestions are a preliminary guide to the defense of a value claim. (We discuss value claims further in Chapter 4.)

1. Try to make clear that the values or principles you are defending should have priority on any scale of values. Keep in mind that you and your readers may differ about their relative importance. For example, although your readers may agree with you that brilliant photography is important in a film, they may think that a well-written script is even more crucial to its success. And although they may agree that freedom of the press is a mainstay of democ-

---

[3] *The Art of Making Sense* (New York: Lippincott, 1968), p. 271.

racy, they may regard the right to privacy as even more fundamental.

2. Suggest that adherence to the values you are defending will bring about good results in some specific situation or bad results if respect for the values is ignored. You might argue, for example, that a belief in freedom of the press will make citizens better informed and the country stronger while a failure to protect this freedom will strengthen the forces of authoritarianism.

3. Since value terms are abstract, use examples and illustrations to clarify meanings and make distinctions. Comparisons and contrasts are especially helpful. If you are using the term *heroism,* can you provide examples to differentiate between *heroism* and *foolhardiness* or *exhibitionism?*

4. Use testimony of others to prove that knowledgeable or highly regarded people share your values.

SAMPLE ANALYSIS: CLAIM OF VALUE

Kids in the Mall:
Growing Up Controlled
WILLIAM SEVERINI KOWINSKI

Butch heaved himself up and loomed over the group. "Like it was different for me," he piped. "My folks used to drop me off at the shopping mall every morning and leave me all day. It was like a big free baby-sitter, you know? One night they never came back for me. Maybe they moved away. Maybe there's some kind of a Bureau of Missing Parents I could check with."

Richard Peck
Secrets of the Shopping Mall,
a novel for teenagers

From his sister at Swarthmore, I'd heard about a kid in Florida whose mother picked him up after school every day, drove him straight to the mall, and left him there until it closed — all at his insistence. I'd heard about a boy in Washington who, when his family moved from one suburb to another, pedaled his bicycle five miles every day to get back to his old mall, where he once belonged.

William Severini Kowinski is a free-lance writer who has been the book review editor and managing arts editor of the *Boston Phoenix.* This excerpt is from his book *The Malling of America: An Inside Look at the Great Consumer Paradise* (1985).

These stories aren't unusual. The mall is a common experience for the majority of American youth; they have probably been going there all their lives. Some ran within their first large open space, saw their first fountain, bought their first toy, and read their first book in a mall. They may have smoked their first cigarette or first joint, or turned them down, had their first kiss or lost their virginity in the mall parking lot. Teenagers in America now spend more time in the mall than anywhere else but home and school. Mostly it is their choice, but some of that mall time is put in as the result of two-paycheck and single-parent households, and the lack of other viable alternatives. But are these kids being harmed by the mall?

I wondered first of all what difference it makes for adolescents to experience so many important moments in the mall. They are, after all, at play in the fields of its little world and they learn its ways; they adapt to it and make it adapt to them. It's here that these kids get their street sense, only it's mall sense. They are learning the ways of a large-scale, artificial environment; its subtleties and flexibilities, its particular pleasures and resonances, and the attitudes it fosters.

The presence of so many teenagers for so much time was not something mall developers planned on. In fact, it came as a big surprise. But kids became a fact of mall life very easily, and the International Council of Shopping Centers found it necessary to commission a study, which they published along with a guide to mall managers on how to handle the teenage incursion.

The study found that "teenagers in suburban centers are bored and 5 come to the shopping centers mainly as a place to go. Teenagers in suburban centers spent more time fighting, drinking, littering and walking than did their urban counterparts, but presented fewer overall problems." The report observed that "adolescents congregated in groups of two to four and predominantly at locations selected by them rather than management." This probably had something to do with the decision to install game arcades, which allow management to channel these restless adolescents into naturally contained areas away from major traffic points of adult shoppers.

The guide concluded that mall management should tolerate and even encourage the teenage presence because, in the words of the report, "The vast majority support the same set of values as does shopping center management." *The same set of values* means simply that mall kids are already preprogrammed to be consumers and that the mall can put the finishing touches to them as hard-core, lifelong shoppers just like everybody else. That, after all, is what the mall is about. So it shouldn't be surprising that in spending a lot of time there, adolescents find little that challenges the assumption that the goal of life is to make money and buy products, or that just about everything else in life is to be used to serve those ends.

Growing up in a high-consumption society already adds inestimable pressure to kids' lives. Clothes consciousness has invaded the grade schools, and popularity is linked with having the best, newest clothes in the currently acceptable styles. Even what they read has been affected. "Miss [Nancy] Drew wasn't obsessed with her wardrobe," noted the *Wall Street Journal.* "But today the mystery in teen fiction for girls is what outfit the heroine will wear next." Shopping has become a survival skill and there is certainly no better place to learn it than the mall, where its importance is powerfully reinforced and certainly never questioned.

The mall as a university of suburban materialism, where Valley Girls and Boys from coast to coast are educated in consumption, has its other lessons in this era of change in family life and sexual mores and their economic and social ramifications. The plethora of products in the mall, plus the pressure on teens to buy them, may contribute to the phenomenon that psychologist David Elkind calls "the hurried child": kids who are exposed to too much of the adult world too quickly and must respond with a sophistication that belies their still-tender emotional development. Certainly the adult products marketed for children — form-fitting designer jeans, sexy tops for preteen girls — add to the social pressure to look like an adult, along with the home-grown need to understand adult finances (why mothers must work) and adult emotions (when parents divorce).

Kids spend so much time at the mall partly because their parents allow it and even encourage it. The mall is safe, doesn't seem to harbor any unsavory activities, and there is adult supervision; it is, after all, a controlled environment. So the temptation, especially for working parents, is to let the mall be their baby-sitter. At least the kids aren't watching TV. But the mall's role as a surrogate mother may be more extensive and more profound.

Karen Lansky, a writer living in Los Angeles, has looked into the 10 subject, and she told me some of her conclusions about the effects on its teenaged denizens of the mall's controlled and controlling environment. "Structure is the dominant idea, since true 'mall rats' lack just that in their home lives," she said, "and adolescents about to make the big leap into growing up crave more structure than our modern society cares to acknowledge." Karen pointed out some of the elements malls supply that kids used to get from their families, like warmth (Strawberry Shortcake dolls and similar cute and cuddly merchandise), old-fashioned mothering ("We do it all for you," the fast-food slogan), and even home cooking (the "homemade" treats at the food court).

The problem in all this, as Karen Lansky sees it, is that while families nurture children by encouraging growth through the assumption of responsibility and then by letting them rest in the bosom of the family from the rigors of growing up, the mall as a structural mother encourages passivity and consumption, as long as the kid doesn't make trouble. Therefore all they learn about becoming adults is how to act and how to consume.

Kids are in the mall not only in the passive role of shoppers — they also work there, especially as fast-food outlets infiltrate the mall's enclosure. There they learn how to hold a job and take responsibility, but still within the same value context. When "CBS Reports" went to Oak Park Mall in suburban Kansas City, Kansas, to tape part of their hour-long consideration of malls, "After the Dream Comes True," they interviewed a teenaged girl who worked in a fast-food outlet there. In a sequence that didn't make the final program, she described the major goal of her present life, which was to perfect the curl on top of the ice-cream cones that were her store's specialty. If she could do that, she would be moved from the lowly soft-drink dispenser to the more prestigious ice-cream division, the curl on top of the status ladder at her restaurant. These are the achievements that are important at the mall.

Other benefits of such jobs may also be overrated, according to Laurence D. Steinberg of the University of California at Irvine's social ecology department, who did a study on teenage employment. Their jobs, he found, are generally simple, mindlessly repetitive and boring. They don't really learn anything, and the jobs don't lead anywhere. Teenagers also work primarily with other teenagers; even their supervisors are often just a little older than they are. "Kids need to spend time with adults," Steinberg told me. "Although they get benefits from peer relationships, without parents and other adults it's one-side socialization. They hang out with each other, have age-segregated jobs, and watch TV."

Perhaps much of this is not so terrible or even so terribly different. Now that they have so much more to contend with in their lives, adolescents probably need more time to spend with other adolescents without adult impositions, just to sort things out. Though it is more concentrated in the mall (and therefore perhaps a clearer target), the value system there is really the dominant one of the whole society. Attitudes about curiosity, initiative, self-expression, empathy, and disinterested learning aren't necessarily made in the mall; they are mirrored there, perhaps a bit more intensely — as through a glass brightly.

Besides, the mall is not without its educational opportunities. There [15] are bookstores, where there is at least a short shelf of classics at great prices, and other books from which it is possible to learn more than how to do sit-ups. There are tools, from hammers to VCRs, and products, from clothes to records, that can help the young find and express themselves. There are older people with stories, and places to be alone or to talk one-on-one with a kindred spirit. And there is always the passing show.

The mall itself may very well be an education about the future. I was struck with the realization, as early as my first forays into Greengate, that the mall is only one of a number of enclosed and controlled environments that are part of the lives of today's young. The mall is just an extension, say, of those large suburban schools — only there's Karmelkorn instead of chem lab, the ice rink instead of the gym: It's high school without the impertinence of classes.

Growing up, moving from home to school to the mall — from enclosure to enclosure, transported in cars — is a curiously continuous process, without much in the way of contrast or contact with unenclosed reality. Places must tend to blur into one another. But whatever differences and dangers there are in this, the skills these adolescents are learning may turn out to be useful in their later lives. For we seem to be moving inexorably into an age of preplanned and regulated environments, and this is the world they will inherit.

Still, it might be better if they had more of a choice. One teenaged girl confessed to "CBS Reports" that she sometimes felt she was missing something by hanging out at the mall so much. "But I'm here," she said, "and this is what I have."

Analysis

Kowinski has chosen to evaluate one aspect of an extraordinarily successful economic and cultural phenomenon — the commercial mall. He asks whether the influence of the mall on adolescents is good or bad. The answer seems to be a little of both. The good values may be described as exposure to a variety of experiences, a protective structure for adolescents who often live in unstable environments, and immersion in a world that may well serve as an introduction to adulthood. But the bad values, which Kowinski thinks are more influential (as the title suggests) are those of the shoppers' paradise, a society that believes in acquisition and consumption of goods as ultimate goals, and too much control over the choices available to adolescents. The tone of the judgment, however, is moderate and reflects a balanced, even scholarly, attitude. More than other arguments, the treatment of values requires such a voice, one which respects differences of opinion among readers. But serious doesn't mean heavy. His style is formal but highly readable, brightened by interesting examples and precise details. The opening paragraph is a strikingly effective lead.

Some of his observations are personal, but others are derived from studies by professional researchers, from "CBS Reports" to a well-known writer on childhood. These studies give weight and authority to his conclusions. Here and there we detect an appealing sympathy for the adolescents in their controlled environment.

Like any thoughtful social commentator, Kowinski casts a wide net. He sees the mall not only as a hangout for teens but as a good deal more, an institution that offers insights into family life and work, the changing urban culture, the nature of contemporary entertainment, even glimpses of a somewhat forbidding future.

CLAIMS OF POLICY

Claims of policy argue that certain conditions should exist. As the name suggests, they advocate adoption of policies or courses of action because problems have arisen that call for solution. Almost always *should* or *ought to* or *must* is expressed or implied in the claim.

> CLAIM: Voluntary prayer should be permitted in public schools.
>
> CLAIM: A dress code should be introduced for all public high schools.
>
> CLAIM: A law should permit sixteen-year-olds and parents to "divorce" each other in cases of extreme incompatibility.
>
> CLAIM: Mandatory jail terms should be imposed for drunk driving violations.

In defending such claims of policy you may find that you must first convince your audience that a problem exists. This will require that, as part of your longer argument, you make a factual claim, offering data to prove that present conditions are unsatisfactory. You may also find it necessary to refer to the values that support your claim. Then you will be ready to introduce your policy, to persuade your audience that the solution you propose will solve the problem.

We will examine a policy claim in which all these parts are at work. The claim can be stated as follows: "The time required for an undergraduate degree should be extended to five years." Immediate agreement with this policy among student readers would certainly not be universal. Some students would not recognize a problem. They would say, "The college curriculum we have now is fine. There's no need for a change. Besides, we don't want to spend more time in school." First, then, the arguer would have to persuade a skeptical audience that there is a problem, that four years of college are no longer enough because the stock of knowledge in almost all fields of study continues to increase. The arguer would provide data to show how many more choices in history, literature, and science students have now compared to the choices in the those fields a generation ago. She would also find it necessary to emphasize the value of greater knowledge and more schooling compared to the value of other goods the audience cherishes, such as earlier independence. Finally, the arguer would offer a plan for putting her policy into effect. Her plan would have to take into consideration initial psychological resistance, revision of the curriculum, the costs of more instruction, and the costs of lost production in the work force. Most important, she would point out the benefits for both individuals and society if this policy were adopted.

In this example, we assumed that the reader would disagree that a problem existed. In many cases, however, the reader may agree that there is a problem but disagree with the arguer about the way of solving it. Most of us, no doubt, will agree that we want to reduce or eliminate the following problems: misbehavior and vandalism in schools, drunk driving, crime on the streets, child abuse, pornography, pollution. But how shall we go about solving those problems? What public policy will give us well-behaved, diligent students who never destroy school property? Safe streets where no one is ever robbed or assaulted? Loving homes where no child is ever mistreated? Some members of society would choose to introduce rules or laws that punish infractions so severely that wrongdoers would be unwilling or unable to repeat their offenses. Other members of society would prefer policies that attempt to rehabilitate or reeducate offenders through training, therapy, counseling, and new opportunities.

Defending a Claim of Policy

The following steps will help you organize arguments for a claim of policy.

1. Make your proposal clear. The terms in the proposal should be precisely defined.
2. If necessary, establish that there is a need for a change. If changes have been ignored or resisted, there may be good or at least understandable reasons why this is so. (It is often wrongly assumed that people cling to cultural practices long after their significance and necessity have eroded. But rational human beings do not continue to observe practices unless those practices serve a purpose. The fact that you and I may see no value or purpose in the activities of another is irrelevant.)
3. Consider the opposing arguments. You may want to state the opposing arguments in a brief paragraph in order to answer them in the body of your argument.
4. Devote the major part of your essay to proving that your proposal is an answer to the opposing arguments and that there are distinct benefits for your readers in adopting your proposal.
5. Support your proposal with solid data, but don't neglect the moral considerations and the common-sense reasons, which may be even more persuasive.

So That Nobody Has to Go to School If They Don't Want To

ROGER SIPHER

A decline in standardized test scores is but the most recent indicator that American education is in trouble.

One reason for the crisis is that present mandatory-attendance laws force many to attend school who have no wish to be there. Such children have little desire to learn and are so antagonistic to school that neither they nor more highly motivated students receive the quality education that is the birthright of every American.

The solution to this problem is simple: Abolish compulsory-attendance laws and allow only those who are committed to getting an education to attend.

This will not end public education. Contrary to conventional belief, legislators enacted compulsory-attendance laws to legalize what already existed. William Landes and Lewis Solomon, economists, found little evidence that mandatory-attendance laws increased the number of children in school. They found, too, that school systems have never effectively enforced such laws, usually because of the expense involved.

There is no contradiction between the assertion that compulsory 5 attendance has had little effect on the number of children attending school and the argument that repeal would be a positive step toward improving education. Most parents want a high school education for their children. Unfortunately, compulsory attendance hampers the ability of public school officials to enforce legitimate educational and disciplinary policies and thereby make the education a good one.

Private schools have no such problem. They can fail or dismiss students, knowing such students can attend public school. Without compulsory attendance, public schools would be freer to oust students whose academic or personal behavior undermines the educational mission of the institution.

Has not the noble experiment of a formal education for everyone failed? While we pay homage to the homily, "You can lead a horse to

---

Roger Sipher is associate professor of history at the State University of New York at Cortland. This article appeared in the *New York Times* on December 22, 1977.

water but you can't make him drink," we have pretended it is not true in education.

Ask high school teachers if recalcitrant students learn anything of value. Ask teachers if these students do any homework. Ask if the threat of low grades motivates them. Quite the contrary, these students know they will be passed from grade to grade until they are old enough to quit or until, as is more likely, they receive a high school diploma. At the point when students could legally quit, most choose to remain since they know they are likely to be allowed to graduate whether they do acceptable work or not.

Abolition of archaic attendance laws would produce enormous dividends.

First, it would alert everyone that school is a serious place where 10 one goes to learn. Schools are neither day-care centers nor indoor street corners. Young people who resist learning should stay away; indeed, an end to compulsory schooling would require them to stay away.

Second, students opposed to learning would not be able to pollute the educational atmosphere for those who want to learn. Teachers could stop policing recalcitrant students and start educating.

Third, grades would show what they are supposed to: how well a student is learning. Parents could again read report cards and know if their children were making progress.

Fourth, public esteem for schools would increase. People would stop regarding them as way stations for adolescents and start thinking of them as institutions for educating America's youth.

Fifth, elementary schools would change because students would find out early that they had better learn something or risk flunking out later. Elementary teachers would no longer have to pass their failures on to junior high and high school.

Sixth, the cost of enforcing compulsory education would be elimi- 15 nated. Despite enforcement efforts, nearly 15 percent of the school-age children in our largest cities are almost permanently absent from school.

Communities could use these savings to support institutions to deal with young people not in school. If, in the long run, these institutions prove more costly, at least we would not confuse their mission with that of schools.

Schools should be for education. At present, they are only tangentially so. They have attempted to serve an all-encompassing social function, trying to be all things to all people. In the process they have failed miserably at what they were originally formed to accomplish.

Analysis

Roger Sipher's article offers a straightforward solution to a distressing educational problem. Following a clear and familiar pattern of organization, the author begins by referring to the problem and the need for change that has induced him to present this solution. He seems sure that his readers will recognize the disciplinary problems arising from compulsory attendance, and he therefore alludes to them but omits any specific mention of them. Instead he concentrates on the unfortunate educational consequences of compulsory attendance. In the third paragraph he states his thesis directly: "Abolish compulsory-attendance laws and allow only those who are committed to getting an education to attend."

Sipher is no doubt aware that his proposal will strike many readers as a radical departure from conventional solutions, perhaps more damaging than the problem itself. He moves at once to dispel the fear that public education will suffer if mandatory attendance laws are repealed. He offers as proof a study by two economists who conclude that compulsory attendance has little effect on the actual number of students who attend school. But in this part of the discussion Sipher is guilty of a seeming contradiction. The reader may ask, "If compulsory-attendance laws make little difference — that is, if students attend in the same numbers regardless of the laws — why abolish them?" Later in the essay Sipher points out that in some large cities almost 15 percent of school-age children are permanently absent. If they are absent, they cannot be the ones who are "polluting the educational atmosphere." Apparently, then, the author is referring to a small number of students uninterested in learning who continue to come to school because they are compelled to do so.

In the middle section Sipher elaborates on the difficulties of teaching those who are uninterested in learning. The use of the imperative mode, of speaking directly to the reader — "Ask high school teachers if recalcitrant students learn anything of value" — is effective. Here, too, however, some readers may want to know if Sipher is aware of the alternative programs introduced into many city schools for reaching unwilling students or whether he knows about them but regards them as unsuccessful.

The strongest part of the argument appears in the last third of the essay, where the author lists six advantages that will follow the repeal of compulsory attendance laws. He also seems to recognize that some readers will have another question: "What will become of the young people who are required to leave school?" His answer — "institutions" — is vague. But since the burden of his proposal is to offer ways of improving the quality of education, Sipher may consider that he is justified in declining to answer this question more fully.

The strengths of Sipher's argument are clear, direct organization, readable language, and listing of the specific dividends that would follow implementation of his proposal. Equally important is the novelty of the proposal, which will outrage some readers and delight others. In either case the proposal will arouse attention and initiate discussion.

However, the originality of the solution may also constitute a weakness. The more original the solution to a problem, the more likely it is to encounter initial resistance. Sipher's argument is too short to answer the many questions his readers might have about possible disadvantages. This argument, in other words, should be considered an introduction to any attempt to solve the problem, a limitation of which Sipher was probably aware.

READINGS FOR ANALYSIS

The Landfill Excavations
WILLIAM L. RATHJE and CULLEN MURPHY

The Garbage Project began excavating landfills primarily for two reasons, both of them essentially archaeological in nature. One was to see if the data being gleaned from garbage fresh off the truck could be cross-validated by data from garbage in municipal landfills. The second, which derived from the Garbage Project's origins as an exercise in the study of formation processes, was to look into what happens to garbage after it has been interred. As it happens, the first landfill excavation got under way, in 1987, just as it was becoming clear — from persistent reports about garbage in the press that were at variance with some of the things the Garbage Project had been learning — that an adequate knowledge base about landfills and their contents did not exist. It was during this period that news of a mounting garbage crisis broke into the national consciousness. And it was during this period that two assertions were given wide currency and achieved a status as accepted fact from which they have yet to be dislodged. One is that accelerating rates of garbage generation are responsible for the rapid depletion and present shortage of landfills. The other is that, nationwide, there are few good places left to put new landfills. Whether these propositions are true or false — they happen, for the most part, to be exaggerations — it was certainly the case that however quickly landfills were being filled, the public, the press, and even most specialists had only

William L. Rathje is a professor of anthropology at the University of Arizona, where he heads the Garbage Project. Cullen Murphy is managing editor of the *Atlantic Monthly*. This excerpt is from their book *Rubbish! The Archeology of Garbage* (1992).

the vaguest idea (at best) of what they were being filled up *with*. Yes, think tanks and consulting firms have done some calculations and come up with estimates of garbage quantities by commodity, based on national production figures and assumptions about rates of discard. But until 1987, when the Garbage Project's archaeologists began systematically sorting through the evidence from bucket-auger wells, no one had ever deliberately dug into landfills with a view to recording the inner reality in minute detail. . . .

One key aim of the landfill excavations was to get some idea of the volume occupied by various kinds of garbage in landfills. Although many Garbage Project studies have relied on garbage weight for comparative purposes, volume is the critical variable when it comes to landfill management: Landfills close not because they are too heavy but because they are too full. And yet reliable data on the volume taken up by plastics, paper, organic material, and other kinds of garbage once it has been deposited in a landfill did not exist in 1987. The Garbage Project set out to fill the gap, applying its usual sorting and weighing procedures to excavated garbage, and then adding a final step: a volume measurement. Measuring volume was not a completely straightforward process. Because most garbage tends to puff up with air once it has been extracted from deep inside a landfill, all of the garbage exhumed was subjected to compaction, so that the data on garbage volume would reflect the volume that garbage occupies when it is squashed and under pressure inside a landfill. The compactor used by the Garbage Project is a thirty-gallon cannister with a hydraulic piston that squeezes out air from plastic bags, newspapers, cereal boxes, mowed grass, hot dogs, and everything else at a relatively gentle pressure of 0.9 pounds per square inch. The data on garbage volume that emerged from the Garbage Project's landfill excavations were the first such data in existence.

What do the numbers reveal? Briefly, that the kinds of garbage that loom largest in the popular imagination as the chief villains in the filling up and closing down of landfills — fast-food packaging, expanded polystyrene foam (the material that coffee cups are made from), and disposable diapers, to name three on many people's most-unwanted list — do not deserve the blame they have received. They may be highly visible as litter, but they are not responsible for an inordinate contribution to landfill garbage. The same goes for plastics. But one kind of garbage whose reputation has thus far been largely unbesmirched — plain old paper — merits increased attention.

Over the years, Garbage Project representatives have asked a variety of people who have never seen the inside of a landfill to estimate what percentage of a landfill's contents is made up of fast-food packaging, expanded polystyrene foam, and disposable diapers. In September of 1989, for example, this very question was asked of a group attending the biennial meeting of the National Audubon Society, and the results were generally consistent with those obtained from surveys conducted at universities, at business meetings, and at conferences of state and local government officials: Estimates at the Audubon meeting of the volume of fast-food packaging fell mainly between 20 and 30 percent of a typical landfill's contents; of expanded polystyrene foam, between 25 and 40 percent; and of disposable diapers, between 25 and 45 percent. The overall estimate, then, of the proportion of a landfill's volume that is taken up by fast-food packaging, foam in general, and disposable diapers ranged from a suspiciously high 70 percent to an obviously impossible 125 percent.

Needless to say, fast-food packaging has few friends. It is designed 5 to be bright, those bold reds and yellows being among the most attention-getting colors on a marketer's palette; this, coupled with the propensity of human beings to litter, means that fast-food packaging gets noticed. It is also greasy and smelly, and on some level it seems to symbolize, as do fast-food restaurants themselves, certain attributes of modern America to which modern Americans remain imperfectly reconciled. But is there really all that much fast-food packaging? Is it "straining" the capacity of America's landfills, as a 1988 editorial in the *New York Times* contended?

The physical reality inside a landfill is, in fact, quite different from the picture painted by many commentators. Of the more than fourteen tons of garbage from landfills that the Garbage Project has sorted, fewer than a hundred pounds was found to consist of fast-food packaging of any kind — that is, containers or wrappers for hamburgers, pizzas, chicken, fish, and convenience-store sandwiches, plus all the accessories, such as cups, lids, straws, sauce containers, and so on, plus all the boxes and bags used to deliver food and other raw materials to the fast-food restaurant. In other words, less than one-half of 1 percent of the weight of the materials excavated from nine municipal landfills over a period of five years (1985–89) consisted of fast-food packaging. As for the amount of space that fast-food packaging takes up in landfills — a more important indicator than weight — the Garbage Project estimate after sorting is that it accounts for no more than one-third of 1 percent of the total volume of a landfill's contents.

What about expanded polystyrene foam — the substance that most people are referring to when they say Styrofoam (which is a registered trademark of the Dow Chemical Corporation, and is baby blue in color and used chiefly to insulate buildings)? Expanding polystyrene foam is, of course, used for many things. Only about 10 percent of all foam plastics that were manufactured in the period 1980–83 were used for fast-food packaging. Most foam was (and is) blown into egg cartons, meat trays, coffee cups (the fast-food kind, yes, but mainly the plain kind that sit stacked upside down beside the office coffee pot), "peanuts" for packing, and the molded forms that protect electronic appliances in their shipping cases. All the expanded polystyrene foam that is thrown away in America every year, from the lowliest packing peanut to the most sophisticated molded carton, accounts for no more than 1 percent of the volume of garbage landfilled between 1980 and 1989.

Expanded polystyrene foam has been the focus of many vocal campaigns around the country to ban it outright. It is worth remembering that if foam were banned, the relatively small amount of space that it takes up in landfills would not be saved. Eggs, hamburgers, coffee, and stereos must still be put in *something.* The most likely replacement for foam is some form of coated cardboard, which can be difficult to recycle and takes up almost as much room as foam in a landfill. Indeed, in cases where cardboard replaced foam, it could often happen that a larger volume of cardboard would be needed to fulfill the same function fulfilled by a smaller volume of foam. No one burns fingers holding a foam cup filled with coffee, because the foam's insulating qualities are so effective. But people burn their fingers so frequently with plastic- or wax-coated cardboard coffee cups (and all cardboard hot-drink cups are coated) that they often put one such cup inside another for the added protection.

As for disposable diapers, the debate over their potential impact on the environment is sufficiently vociferous and complex to warrant its own chapter. . . . Suffice it to say for present purposes, though, that the pattern displayed by fast-food packaging and expanded polystyrene foam is apparent with respect to diapers, too. People *think* that disposable diapers are a big part of the garbage problem; they are not a very significant factor at all.

The three garbage categories that, as we saw, the Audubon respondents believed accounted for 70 to 125 percent of all garbage actually account, together, for only about 3 percent. The survey responses would probably have been even more skewed if respondents had also been asked to guess the proportion of a typical landfill's contents that is made up of plastic. Plastic is surrounded by a maelstrom of mythology; into the very word Americans seem to have distilled all of their guilt over the environmental degradation they have wrought and the culture of consumption they invented and inhabit. Plastic has become an object of scorn — who can forget the famous scene in *The Graduate* (or quote it properly)? — no doubt in large measure because its development corresponded chronologically with, and then powerfully reinforced, the emergence of the very consumerist ethic that is now despised. (What Mr. McGuire, a neighbor, says to Benjamin Braddock is: "I just want to say one word to you. Just one word. Are you listening? . . . Plastics. There is a great future in plastics. Think about it.") Plastic is the Great Satan of garbage. It is the apotheosis of the cheap, the inauthentic; even the attempts to replace or transform plastic — such as the recent ill-fated experiments with "biodegradable" plastic . . . — seem somehow inauthentic. . . .

[But] in landfill after landfill the volume of all plastics — foam, film, and rigid; toys, utensils, and packages — from the 1980s amounted to between 20 and 24 percent of all garbage, as sorted; when compacted along with everything else, in order to replicate actual conditions inside a landfill, the volume of plastics was reduced to under 16 percent.

Even if its share of total garbage is, at the moment, relatively low, is it not the case that plastics take up a larger proportion of landfill space with every passing year? Unquestionably a larger number of physical objects are made of plastic today than were in 1970 or 1950. But a curious phenomenon becomes apparent when garbage deposits from our own time are compared with those from strata characteristic of, say, the 1970s. While the number of individual plastic objects to be found in a deposit of garbage of a constant size has increased considerably in the course of a decade and a half — more than doubling — the proportion of landfill space taken up by these plastics has not changed; at some landfills, the proportion of space taken up by plastics was actually a little less in the 1980s than it was in the 1970s.

The explanation appears to be a strategy that is known in the plastics industry as "light-weighting" — making objects in such a way that the objects retain all the necessary functional characteristics but require the use of less resin. The concept of light-weighting is not limited to the making of plastics; the makers of glass bottles have been light-weighting their wares for decades, with the result that bottles today are 25 percent lighter than they were in 1984. (That is why bottles in landfills are likely to show up broken in the upper, more-recent, strata, whereas lower strata, holding garbage from many years ago, contain many more whole bottles.) Environmentalists might hail light-weighting as an example of source reduction. Businessmen embrace it for a different reason: sheer profit. Using fewer raw materials for a product that is lighter and therefore cheaper to transport usually translates into a competitive edge, and companies that rely heavily on plastics have been light-weighting ever since plastics were introduced. PET soda bottles had a weight of 67 grams in 1974; the weight today is 48 grams, for a reduction of 30 percent. High-density polyethylene (HDPE) milk jugs in the mid-1960s had a weight of 120 grams; the weight today is about 65 grams, for reduction of more than 45 percent. Plastic grocery bags had a thickness of 30 microns in 1976; the thickness today is at most 18 microns, for a reduction of 40 percent. Even the plastic in disposable diapers has been light-weighted, although the super-absorbent material that was added at the same time (1986) ensures that even if diapers enter the house lighter they will leave it heavier than ever. When plastic gets lighter, in most cases it also gets thinner and more crushable. The result, of course, is that many more plastic items can be squeezed into a given volume of landfill space today than could have been squeezed into it ten or twenty years ago.

This fact has frequently been met with skepticism. In 1989, Robert Krulwich, of the CBS network's "Saturday Night with Connie Chung" program, conducted a tour of the Garbage Project's operations in Tucson, and he expressed surprise when told about the light-weighting of plastics. He asked for a crushed PET soda bottle from 1989 and tried to blow it up. The light plastic container inflated easily. He was then given a crushed PET soda bottle found in a stratum dating back to 1981 — a bottle whose plastic would be considerably thicker and stiffer. Try as he might, Krulwich could not make the flattened container inflate.

Discussion Questions

1. What reasons do the authors give for the importance of the Garbage Project? Do their findings seem to justify their "archeological" research?
2. Some factual claims imply a need for changes in behavior. (See the analysis of "Cocaine Is Even Deadlier Than We Thought," p. 28.) Is there any evidence that Rathje and Murphy are interested in influencing behavior?
3. How do they account for the erroneous information held by the public? Does this information reflect certain values or prejudices? Were some of your own views overturned by the authors' conclusions?

Writing Suggestions

1. Describe any changes you or your family might make in your purchases and methods of disposal as a result of reading "The Landfill Excavations." Explain how these changes would affect your life. Would they impose a hardship? If you are not persuaded to make any changes, explain why.
2. Choose another garbage or litter "problem" — one from your own experience or one you have read about — and provide the data to prove that it is or is not a problem. Newspapers and news magazines are one source of information, but remember that expert minority views may be overlooked and unreported. Like the authors of "The Landfill Excavations," select relevant statistics and examples with human interest, wherever possible.

Hollywood's Poison Factory
MICHAEL MEDVED

America's long-running romance with Hollywood is over. For millions of people, the entertainment industry no longer represents a source of enchantment, of magical fantasy, of uplift, or even of harmless diversion. Popular culture is viewed now as an implacable enemy, a

Michael Medved is a cohost of the popular weekly PBS television program, "Sneak Previews." This article first appeared in *Imprimis,* a publication of Hillsdale College, in November 1992. It is based on his latest book, *Hollywood vs. America* (HarperCollins, 1992).

threat to their basic values and a menace to the raising of their children. The Hollywood dream factory has become the poison factory.

This disenchantment is reflected in poll after poll. An Associated Press Media General poll released in 1990 showed that 80 percent of Americans objected to the amount of foul language in motion pictures; 82 percent objected to the amount of violence, 72 percent objected to the amount of explicit sexuality, and by a ratio of 3 to 1 they felt that movies today are worse than ever.

Hollywood no longer reflects — or even respects — the values that most Americans cherish.

Take a look, for example, at the most recent Oscars. Five very fine actors were nominated for best actor of the year. Three of them portrayed murderous psychos: Robert DeNiro in *Cape Fear,* Warren Beatty in *Bugsy,* and Anthony Hopkins in *The Silence of the Lambs* (this last a delightful family film about two serial killers — one eats and the other skins his victims). A fourth actor, Robin Williams, was nominated for playing a delusional homeless psycho in *The Fisher King.* The most wholesome character was Nick Nolte's, a good old-fashioned manic-depressive-suicidal neurotic in *The Prince of Tides.*

These are all good actors, delivering splendid performances, com- 5 pelling and technically accomplished. But isn't it sad when all this artistry is lavished on films that are so empty, so barren, so unfulfilling? Isn't it sad when at the Academy Awards — the annual event that celebrates the highest achievement of which the film industry is capable — the best we can come up with is movies that are so floridly, strangely whacked out?

I repeat: The fundamental problem with Hollywood has nothing at all to do with the brilliance of the performers, or the camera work, or the editing. In many ways, these things are better than ever before. Modern films are technically brilliant, but they are morally and spiritually empty.

The Messages

What are the messages in today's films? For a number of years I have been writing about Hollywood's antireligious bias, but I must point out that this hostility has never been quite as intense as in the last few years. The 1991 season boasted one religion-bashing movie after another in which Hollywood was able to demonstrate that it was an equal-opportunity offender.

For Protestants there was *At Play in the Fields of the Lord,* a lavish $35 million rainforest spectacle about natives and their wholesome primitive ways and the sick, disgusting missionaries who try to ruin their lives. And then for Catholics there was *The Pope Must Die,* which was re-released as *The Pope Must Diet.* It didn't work either way. It features scenes of the Holy Father flirting with harlot nuns and hiding in a closet pigging out on communion wafers. For Jews there was *Naked Tango,* written and directed by the brother of the screenwriter for *The Last Temptation of Christ.* This particular epic featured religious Jews operating a brutal bordello right next door to a synagogue and forcing women into white slavery.

And then most amazingly there was *Cape Fear,* which was nominated for a number of the most prestigious Academy Awards. It wasn't an original concept. *Cape Fear* was a remake of a 1962 movie in which Robert Mitchum plays a released convict intent on revenge who tracks down his old defense attorney. Gregory Peck portrays the defense attorney, a strong, stalwart, and upright man who defends his family against this crazed killer. In the remake, by *Last Temptation* director Martin Scorsese, there is a new twist: The released convict is not just an ordinary maniac, but a "Killer Christian from Hell." To prevent anyone from missing the point, his muscular back has a gigantic cross tattooed on it, and he has Biblical verses tattooed on both arms.

When he is about to rape the attorney's wife, played by Jessica   10
Lange, he says, "Are you ready to be born again? After just one hour with me, you'll be talking in tongues." He carries a Bible with him in scenes in which he is persecuting his family, and he tells people that he is a member of a Pentecostal church.

The most surprising aspect of this utterly insulting characterization is that it drew so little protest. Imagine that DeNiro's character had been portrayed as a gay rights activist. Homosexual groups would have howled in protest, condemning this caricature as an example of bigotry. But we are so accustomed to Hollywood's insulting stereotypes of religious believers that no one even seems to notice the hatred behind them.

The entertainment industry further demonstrates its hostility to organized religion by eliminating faith and ritual as a factor in the lives of nearly all the characters it creates. Forty to fifty percent of all Americans go to church or synagogue every week. When was the last time you saw anybody in a motion picture going to church, unless that person was some kind of crook, or a mental case, or a flagrant hypocrite?

Hollywood even removes religious elements from situations in which they clearly belong. The summer of 1991 offered a spate of medical melodramas like *Regarding Henry, Dying Young,* and *The Doctor.* Did you notice that all these characters go into the operating room without once invoking the name of God, or whispering one little prayer, or asking for clergy? I wrote a nonfiction book about hospital life once, and I guarantee that just as there are no atheists in foxholes, there are no atheists in operating rooms — only in Hollywood.

Religion isn't Hollywood's only target; the traditional family has also received surprisingly harsh treatment from today's movie moguls. Look again at *Cape Fear.* The remake didn't only change the killer; it also changed the hero, and this brings me to the second message that Hollywood regularly broadcasts. As I mentioned, the original character Gregory Peck plays is a decent and honorable man. In the remake, Nick Nolte's character is, not to put too fine a point on it, a sleazeball. He is repeatedly unfaithful to his wife; when his wife dares to question that practice, he hits her. He tries to beat up his daughter on one occasion because she is smoking marijuana. He is not a likable person. That a happily married, family-defending hero — the kind of person that people can identify with — is transformed into a sadistic, cheating, bitter man, says volumes about the direction of American movies.

Did you ever notice how few movies there are about happily mar- 15 ried people? There are very few movies about married people at all, but those that are made tend to portray marriage as a disaster, as a dangerous situation, as a battleground — with a long series of murderous marriage movies.

There was *Sleeping with the Enemy,* in which Patrick Bergin beats up Julia Roberts so mercilessly that she has to run away. When he comes after her, she eventually kills him. There was also *Mortal Thoughts,* in which Bruce Willis beats up *his* wife and he is killed by his wife's best friend. In *Thelma and Louise,* there is another horrible, brutal, and insensitive husband to run away from. In *A Kiss Before Dying,* Matt Dillon persuades twin sisters to marry him. He kills the first one and then tries to kill the second, but she gets to him first.

In *She-Devil,* Roseanne Barr torments her cheating husband Ed Begley, Jr., and in *Total Recall,* Sharon Stone pretends to be married to Arnold Schwarzenegger and tries to kill him. When he gets the upper hand, she objects, "But you can't hurt me! I'm your wife." Arnold shoots her through the forehead and says, "Consider that a divorce." And then there was a more recent film, *Deceived,* starring Goldie Hawn. The advertisement for the movie says, "She thought her life was perfect," and, of course, her model husband turns out to be a murderous monster. *Deceived* is an appropriate title, because we all have been deceived by Hollywood's portrayal of marriage. It even applies to television. The *New York Times* reports that in the past TV season there were seven different pregnancies. What did six of the seven pregnancies have in common? They were out of wedlock. The message is that marriage is outmoded, it is dangerous, oppressive, unhealthy.

But is it true? Recently, I made an interesting discovery. The conventional wisdom is that the divorce rate in America stands at 50 percent. This figure is used repeatedly in the media. But the 1990 U.S. Census Bureau has a category listing the number of people who have ever been married and who have ever been divorced. Less than 20 percent have been divorced! The evidence is overwhelming that the idea of a 50 percent divorce rate is more than a slight overstatement; it is a destructive and misleading myth.

Yet for years Hollywood has been selling divorce. Remember *The*

Last Married Couple in America, starring the late Natalie Wood? That may be a Hollywood prophecy, but it is not the reality of the American heartland. In this matter, as in so many others, by overstating the negative, the film industry leads viewers to feel terrified and/or insecure, and their behavior is adversely affected. I know many people who say, "I'm reluctant to get married because I know there's a 50 percent chance I'm going to get divorced." Wouldn't it make a difference if they knew there was an 80 percent chance of staying together?

Rekindling Our Love Affair with Hollywood

There are many indications that the entertainment industry may [20] be eager to reconnect with the grass roots — and to entertain an expanded notion of its own obligations to the public. The industry has, in some areas, behaved responsibly. In the past five years it changed its message about drugs. No longer is it making movies in which marijuana, cocaine, and other drugs are glamorized. Hollywood made a decision. Was it self-censorship? You bet. Was it responsible? Yes.

We can challenge the industry to adopt a more wholesome outlook, to send more constructive messages. We can clamor for movies that don't portray marriage as a living hell, that recognize the spiritual side of man's nature, that glorify the blessings in life we enjoy as Americans and the people who make sacrifices to ensure that others will be able to enjoy them.

The box-office crisis put Hollywood in a receptive mood. Already two film corporations have committed to a schedule of family movies for a very simple reason: They are wildly successful. Only 2 percent of movies released in 1991 were G-rated — just fourteen titles — but at least eight of these fourteen proved to be unequivocally profitable. (By comparison, of more than six hundred other titles, *at most* 20 percent earned back their investment.) Look at *Beauty and the Beast,* my choice for Best Movie of 1991. It was a stunning financial success. We need many more pictures like this, and not just animated features geared for younger audiences. Shouldn't it be possible to create movies with adult themes but without foul language, graphic sex, or cinematic brutality? During Hollywood's golden age, industry leaders understood that there was nothing inherently *mature* about these unsettling elements.

People tell me sometimes, "Boy, the way you talk, it sounds as though you really hate movies." The fact is that I don't. I'm a film critic because I *love* movies. And I want to tell you something: All of the people who are trying to make a difference in this business love movies and they love the industry, despite all its faults. They love what it has done in the past, and they love its potential for the future. They believe that Hollywood can be the dream factory again.

When I go to a screening, sit in a theater seat, and the lights go down, there's a little something inside me that hopes against all rational expectation that what I'm going to see on the screen is going to delight me, enchant me, and entice me, like the best movies do. I began by declaring that America's long-running romance with Hollywood is over. It is a romance, however, that can be rekindled, if this appalling, amazing industry can once again create movies that are worthy of love and that merit the ardent affection of its audience.

Discussion Questions

1. The title suggests the author's attitude toward Hollywood movies today. Explain the terms *poison* and *dream* as indicative of the values that Medved wants to promote.
2. Medved takes it for granted that most Americans share his values. Does he provide evidence to support this assumption?
3. Do you agree that all the movies he cites as "poisonous" are antagonistic to mainstream American values? If you disagree with some of his interpretations, point out the differences.

Writing Suggestions

1. Choose some examples of recent movies that might represent Hollywood as "dream" factory. Try to decide if there are enough of them to refute Medved's claim.
2. Medved thinks that movies should "delight," "enchant," and "entice." Why do *you* go to the movies? Pick out several reasons and tell why they satisfy some basic needs. Use examples of specific movies to make the reasons clear.
3. Do prime-time TV shows reflect "dreams" or "poison" or both? Examine several popular shows to prove that TV is like or unlike Hollywood in its presentation of values.

Green Eggs & Ham
THE WALL STREET JOURNAL

To paraphrase Dr. Seuss, "I do like gambling, Sam-I-Am, I really like it, and I can. For I can do it in a plane, on a boat, at the track, and in the rain. I can do it in a casino, with the lottery, or with Keno." In a plane? Not quite yet, but the latest proposal is to equip airline seats with a video terminal that can eat credit cards and bankrupt you while you're still belted in, which is in many ways the opposite of what happens to a Strasbourg goose.

Some estimates suggest that gambling revenues are higher than the

This editorial is from the April 27, 1992 edition of the *Wall Street Journal.*

defense budget, and they are now poised to take a leap to the next energy level as technology threatens to bring casinos to every home and conveyance. Mayor Daley of Chicago is backing "gaming executives" who want to build a 100-acre $2 billion palace of sin in what the AP [Associated Press] calls "downtown" Chicago: Finding a 100-acre site in downtown Chicago will be only the first problem. Riverboat gambling is back on the Mississippi, and Indians are opening casinos all over the West. Thirty-three states have fallen to the lottery and more are on the way. And then there are pull-tabs; blackjack; OTB [off-track betting]; bingo; numbers; video poker; horse, dog, and insect racing (in bars); Reno; Las Vegas; Atlantic City; and Ed McMahon, the classic figure of trust, who periodically announces to every household in America that if it has won $10 million it has won $10 million. (Thank you, Ed.)

Other than littering the desert with immense, metastasized replicas of Port Said bordellos, gambling creates nothing. It reallocates resources from the desperate and the needful to the unspeakable and the inane. It, like the British royal family, is the worst possible model for the poor, being the polar opposite of thrift, discipline, hard work, and ingenuity. It violates every standard, all common sense, and every sensible equation, from ancient religious edicts to the laws of thermodynamics (at least figuratively), and it runs with almost every other form of crime and corruption.

Are we for it because we favor free markets? No, in the same way that we do not favor a free market for recreational drugs, legalized prostitution, or, for that matter, the unrestricted sale of nuclear weapons. The West long ago identified gambling as a sin not because it violates some mystical equilibrium, although it does, but because it, like drunkenness or (as one might now say) spouse-beating, is destructive to society. Among other things, it is the Arnold Schwarzenegger of regressive taxation. And lotteries don't actually pay much to education, which has little to do with money anyway.

In America we once dealt wisely with gambling by isolating it in 5 the middle of a desert surrounded by unexploded practice munitions. This allowed the hardest cases to get to the roulette wheels and served as a safety valve for the ill-effects of absolutism. Now, however, the thing is spreading, and government is the sponsor. But when government substitutes gambling for taxation it relinquishes its moral authority. To the argument that if government does not play, others will, we say, in that case why not have [New York state governor] Mario Cuomo rob jewelry stores?

Although you'd hardly know it from observing our elected officials, government's job is to resist and suppress that which is immoral and destructive, not to form a partnership with it. We would like to hear from the presidential candidates on this subject, for gambling is now almost everywhere, and has achieved a terrible hold on a people raised to think that lunch can be free.

Discussion Questions

1. Why is gambling authorized or sponsored by the government more pernicious than gambling by private enterprise?
2. In the last paragraph the author summarizes his or her objections to gambling as "immoral and destructive." What is immoral about gambling? Why is it destructive?
3. The author at one point seems to advocate a solution to the gambling problem. Would that solution be workable today? Why or why not?

Writing Suggestions

1. Because gambling is widespread among all classes in the United States — and in many other societies — its appeal must be strong and universal. Some observers think it is an addiction. What is the appeal? Use your own experience as a gambler or your acquaintance with gamblers as well as the opinions of psychologists and other experts to explain it.
2. Find evidence from advocates of gambling to justify government sponsorship, especially in state lotteries.
3. Gambling is said to be common on college campuses. What kinds of gambling do college students engage in? Does gambling serve a useful purpose? Is it harmful in any way?

Capital Punishment — An Idea Whose Time Has Come Again

J. A. PARKER

Capital punishment has been the subject of increasing debate in the American society in recent days.

In recent years, few murderers have been executed. In 1957, when 65 executions took place, the nation witnessed 8,060 murders. In 1981, when 1 execution occurred, there were 22,520 murders.

Our murder rate is the highest in the industrial world. It is even higher than the rate of death by violence in certain war zones.

In Northern Ireland, for example, there were 8.8 deaths per 100,000 population in the years 1968–1974. In 1980, in the United States, there were 10.2 deaths per 100,000 by murder.

Similarly, during the German bombardment of London in the years 5

J. A. Parker is the editor of *The Lincoln Review,* the journal of an African-American think tank, where this essay appeared in the summer of 1986.

1940–1945, there were 21.7 deaths per 100,000 as a result. In Detroit, from the years 1972–1978, there were 42.4 deaths per 100,000 from murder.

While there may be disagreement about the element of cause and effect, it is clear that as we have departed from capital punishment our society has seen an epidemic of murder.

Between 1966 and 1972, no death penalties were carried out. In 1972, in the case of *Furman v. Georgia,* the Supreme Court invalidated the death sentence in both state and federal courts. The grounds of the decision were sweeping — that without specific legislative guidelines, the death penalty was automatically an arbitrary punishment. The vote, however, was narrow, 5–4.

Following this decision, states legislatures passed laws clearly setting forth procedures for judging when death was the appropriate punishment. Thirty-eight states adopted this approach. As crimes were committed and sentences passed, the issue once again was litigated in the courts. As a result, from 1972 to 1976, no cases reached the Supreme Court and no executions occurred.

From 1976 to 1981, the Supreme Court used various procedural arguments to invalidate specific death sentences. A judgment in an Ohio case, for example, was thrown out on the grounds that the lower courts had not given sufficient consideration to mitigating factors before invoking the death penalty. An Alabama ruling was invalidated on grounds that the jury was not given an opportunity to find that the crime was not premeditated.

Finally, in 1981, with Justice Potter Stewart having retired and been replaced by Sandra Day O'Connor, the court began to decline to interpose procedural objections to capital punishment, and once again the death penalty has been applied. 10

At the present time, there is only one major challenge to capital punishment laws (the subject of an article in this issue by George C. Smith and Daniel J. Popeo). That challenge is based on statistical studies showing racial disparities in imposition of the death sentence. The Georgia death penalty is being challenged on behalf of a black man sentenced to death for killing a white police officer. The evidence includes a study showing that those who killed whites in Georgia were eleven times more likely to receive the death penalty than those who killed blacks. A Federal appellate court rejected the appeal, but the Supreme Court has decided to hear the case in its next session.

In this case, Warren McCleskey, a black male recidivist, was tried and convicted in 1979 of murdering a police officer, plus two counts of armed robbery. The jury found two statutory aggravating factors — murder in the course of a robbery, plus killing a police officer performing his official duties — and therefore sentenced McCleskey to death. The Eleventh Circuit firmly rejected McCleskey's discrimination arguments by a 9–3 vote.

The theory in the McCleskey case — that the race of the victim rather than the perpetrator of the crime is a key element in determining which murderers are executed and which are not — is viewed by authors Smith and Popeo as revealing that the advocates of such a theory "simply lack the facts to press the more direct case they would much prefer — i.e., a straightforward claim that the death penalty is disproportionately imposed on black defendants." As a result of the Justice Department's 1985 survey of sentencing outcomes, it is now documented that, "Whereas 12 blacks were sent to death row for every 1,000 blacks arrested for murder and non-negligent homicide, a significantly higher ratio of 16 out of 1,000 whites arrested for those same crimes were sent to death row. That means a 33 percent greater probability of receiving the death sentence for the white murderer. . . . Whereas only 1.1 percent of black death-row inmates were actually executed, 1.7 percent of white death-row inmates were executed. The white inmate thus has a 55 percent greater likelihood of actual execution than his black counterpart."

Since the facts contradict the notion that race is a primary factor in their convictions or executions, the notion that the victim's race is a key element appears particularly strained. Placing racial considerations aside, however, the debate over the morality and deterrent effect of capital punishment is likely to continue for some time.

Is it, somehow, "immoral" to execute murderers? At the present 15 time, there are some in the religious community and elsewhere in the American society who argue that it is. In the Judeo-Christian tradition, however, the weight of evidence may be found on the opposite side.

The distinguished Christian writer C. S. Lewis argued that, "We can rest contentedly in our sins and in our stupidities . . . but pain insists on being attended to. God whispers to us in our pleasures, speaks in our conscience, but shouts in our pains: It is His megaphone to rouse a deaf world. A bad man, happy, is a man without the least inkling that his actions do not 'answer,' that they are not in accord with the laws of the universe. A perception of this truth lies at the back of the universal human feeling that bad men ought to suffer. It is no use turning up our noses at this feeling, as if it were wholly base. . . . Some enlightened people would like to banish all conceptions of retribution or desert from their theory of punishment and place its value wholly in the deterrence of others or the reform of the criminal himself. They do not see that by doing so they render all punishment unjust. What can be more immoral than to inflict suffering on me for the sake of deterring others if I do not *deserve* it? And if I do deserve it, you are admitting the claims of 'retribution.' And what can be more outrageous than to catch me and submit me to a disagreeable process of moral improvement without my consent, unless (once more) I *deserve* it?"

The Sixth Commandment, it is widely recognized, is correctly translated from the Hebrew as "Thou shalt not murder." The Mosaic Code, in fact, provided the death penalty for murder and for many other crimes, most of which would not be considered capital offenses today. Christian forgiveness, while a mandate for individuals, is not such for duly constituted governmental authority. St. Paul wrote that government "does not bear the sword in vain" but is appointed by God "to execute His wrath on the wrongdoer." The dictum of Jesus that, "All who take the sword will perish by the sword" may be seen as a declaration that the death penalty for murder is indeed just.

Some critics of capital punishment argue that it violates the Eighth Amendment, which forbids cruel and unusual punishments. Yet, they forget that the Eighth Amendment was made part of the Constitution in 1791 at a time when governments throughout the world had established methods of execution which were intended to inflict maximum suffering such as burning, drawing and quartering, impalement, and pressing. It is such actions which were viewed as "cruel and unusual," not the act of executing a murderer. Indeed, capital punishment existed in the United States before the adoption of the Bill of Rights — and has continued to exist for more than two hundred years.

Yet another argument presented by critics of capital punishment is that, placing the moral and constitutional questions aside, it simply does not deter crime. In this instance, while some data seems to support the critics' assessment, the burden of the evidence would lead to an opposite conclusion.

Professor Isaac Ehrlich of the University of Chicago has concluded [20] that over the period 1933–1969, "an additional execution per year . . . may have resulted on the average in seven or eight fewer murders." Dr. Ehrlich has shown that previous investigations, which did not find deterrent effects of the death penalty, suffer from fatal defects. He believes that it is possible to demonstrate the marginal deterrent effect of the death penalty statistically.

What we know with certainty is that as executions for murder have declined, murder itself has dramatically increased. Those who argue that life imprisonment is a sufficient deterrent to protect society overlook the fact that most of the killers sentenced to life in prison are back on the streets in approximately fourteen years. "Today, there is no true life sentence," declared Robert Johnson, assistant professor of justice at American University's School of Justice. "It all depends on individual parole boards, but on a first-degree murder conviction a realistic minimum term served would be between seven and fourteen years." In New York, prisoners serving life sentences become eligible for parole in just nineteen months.

To the argument that capital punishment degrades the condemned and the executioner equally, New York City's Mayor Edward Koch responds: "Let me ask you to consider which one of the following cases disgraces and outrages human dignity more. One Lemuel Smith was convicted last year in Dutchess County for murder. He had already been convicted in Schenectady for a kidnapping and rape, for which he received two twenty-five-years-to-life sentences. He had also already been convicted of murder in Albany, for which he received another twenty-five-years-to-life sentence. While serving these three life sentences in Green Haven Prison, Smith lured a woman corrections officer . . . into the Catholic chaplain's office and there strangled her to death and mutilated her body. . . . A fourth life sentence is meaningless. The status of the law in New York has effectively given him a license to kill. . . ."

Mayor Koch argues that, "Only moral ciphers could equate the infliction of a supremely just legal penalty with the horrifying ordeals that . . . innocent human beings . . . endured. And this says nothing of the endless grief visited upon those who loved them. . . . Murder is sui generis in the realm of social and moral evil. The sanctity of human life cannot credibly be proclaimed without capital punishment. . . . Capital punishment must be endorsed and, in the appropriate cases, applied, if we are to have a truly civilized society."

The distinguished English legal philosopher Sir James Stephen declared that, "The fact that men are hanged for murder is one great reason why murder is considered so dreadful a crime."

It is the simple justice of capital punishment which has been clear 25
throughout history to most observers. In a debate on the subject more than a decade ago, the late Senator John McClellan (D-Ark.) asked: "What other punishment is 'just' for a man, found to be sane, who would stab, strangle, and mutilate eight student nurses? What other punishment is 'just' for men who would invade the home of members of a rival religious sect and shoot to death men, women, and children, after forcing a mother to watch as her three young children were drowned before her eyes? What other punishment is 'just' for a band of social misfits who would invade the homes of people they had never even met and stab and hack to death a woman eight and a half months pregnant and her guests?"

The overwhelming majority of the American people support capital punishment. Recent polls indicate that 72 percent of Americans favored executing murderers, the highest percentage since 1936. Support for the death penalty has risen sharply since 1966, when 42 percent of those interviewed favored the death penalty. A majority of all groups — men and women, whites and blacks — supported capital punishment.

Justice Oliver Wendell Holmes wrote, in "The Common Law," that, "The first requirement of a sound body of law is that it should correspond with the actual feelings and demands of the community. . . ."

It is high time that we rejected the notion that sadistic murderers can be "rehabilitated." The job of society and those who act in its name is to remove murderers from our midst, not provide them with an opportunity to kill again. Beyond this, retribution is a legitimate function of society. Professor Walter Berns notes that, "We in the United States have always recognized the legitimacy of retribution. We have schedules of punishment in every criminal code according to which punishments are designed to fit the crime and not simply to fit what social science tells us about deterrence and rehabilitation; the worse the crime, the more severe the punishment. Justice requires criminals (as well as the rest of us) to get what they (and we) deserve, and what criminals deserve depends on what they have done."

It is a misreading of our religious tradition to believe that men are not responsible for the consequences of their actions and that it is in violation of our moral teachings to execute murderers. "Whoso sheddeth man's blood, by man shall his blood be shed," states Genesis (9:6). In the Bible (Exodus 21:12), exactly twenty-five verses after the Sixth Commandment, "Thou shalt not kill," the Law says, "He that smiteth a man so that he die, shall be surely put to death." This sentiment is repeated in Leviticus (24:17) which states, "He who kills a man shall be put to death." Again, in Numbers (35:30–31) it is said: "If anyone kills a person, the murderer shall be put to death on the evidence of witnesses. . . . Moreover, you shall accept no ransom for the life of a murderer who is guilty of death; but he shall be put to death."

The philosophical position of opponents of capital punishment con tradicts not only our religious and legal tradition, but common sense as well. Florida's Governor Graham, who has signed nearly fifty death warrants, cites the case of a restaurant robbery seen by a customer. "Afterward," recounts Graham, "he was the only witness. So the two guys took him out to the Everglades and shot him in the back of the head. If they had felt that being convicted of robbery and first-degree murder was sufficiently different, they might have had second thoughts." 30

Indeed, those critics of capital punishment who argue that it is not, in fact, a deterrent, are, in most cases, opposed to executing murderers regardless of the deterrent fact.

In this connection, Professor Ernest van den Haag writes: "Common sense, lately bolstered by statistics, tells us that the death penalty will deter murder, if anything can. People fear nothing more than death. Therefore, nothing will deter a criminal more than the fear of death. Death is final. But where there is life there is hope. Wherefore, life in prison is less feared. Murderers clearly prefer it to execution — otherwise, they would not try to be sentenced to life in prison instead of death (only an infinitesimal percentage of murderers are suicidal). Therefore, a life sentence must be less deterrent than a death sentence. And we must execute murderers as long as it is merely possible that their execution protects citizens from future murder. . . . I have occasionally asked abolitionists if they would favor the death penalty were it shown that every execution deters, say, five hundred murders. The answer to this admittedly hypothetical question, after some dodging, has always been no. . . . Abolitionists want to abolish the death penalty regardless of whether it deters. The nondeterrence argument they use is a sham. . . . It is fair to conclude that they would rather save the life of a convicted murderer than that of any number of innocent victims. In their eyes, the sanctity of the life of the murderer exceeds that of any future murder victims."

Given our escalating murder rate, and the intellectual and moral bankruptcy of the arguments of those who have opposed the execution of murderers, it seems clear that capital punishment is an idea whose time has come — again.

Discussion Questions

1. List the objections to capital punishment that Parker attempts to refute (there are at least eight). Which of his rebuttals is the most convincing? Which is the least convincing? Explain.
2. Does the fact that Parker is black affect our acceptance of his argument?
3. Explain the comment by Sir James Stephen: "The fact that men are hanged for murder is one great reason why murder is considered so dreadful a crime."
4. Explain Walter Berns's opinion of *rehabilitation*.
5. Would Anna Quindlen (see "Death Penalty's False Promise: An Eye for an Eye," p. 166) take a favorable view of Parker's arguments?

Writing Suggestions

1. Choose one or two of Parker's issues and develop an opposing view. You may need to support your claim with statistics, expert opinion, and examples of noteworthy cases. (Notice how Quindlen uses the case of Ted Bundy.)
2. Try to explain the views of abolitionists who "want to abolish the death penalty regardless of whether it deters."

The Right to Bear Arms
WARREN E. BURGER

Our metropolitan centers, and some suburban communities of America, are setting new records for homicides by handguns. Many of our large centers have up to ten times the murder rate of all of Western Europe. In 1988, there were 9,000 handgun murders in America. Last year, Washington, D.C., alone had more than 400 homicides — setting a new record for our capital.

The Constitution of the United States, in its Second Amendment,

Warren E. Burger was Chief Justice of the United States from 1969 to 1986. This article is from the January 14, 1990 issue of *Parade* magazine.

guarantees a "right of the people to keep and bear arms." However, the meaning of this clause cannot be understood except by looking to the purpose, the setting, and the objectives of the draftsmen. The first ten amendments — the Bill of Rights — were not drafted at Philadelphia in 1787; that document came two years later than the Constitution. Most of the states already had bills of rights, but the Constitution might not have been ratified in 1788 if the states had not had assurances that a national Bill of Rights would soon be added.

People of that day were apprehensive about the new "monster" national government presented to them, and this helps explain the language and purpose of the Second Amendment. A few lines after the First Amendment's guarantees — against "establishment of religion," "free exercise" of religion, free speech and free press — came a guarantee that grew out of the deep-seated fear of a "national" or "standing" army. The same First Congress that approved the right to keep and bear arms also limited the national army to 840 men; Congress in the Second Amendment then provided:

> A well regulated Militia, being necessary to the security of a free State, the right of the people to keep and bear Arms, shall not be infringed.

In the 1789 debate in Congress on James Madison's proposed Bill of Rights, Elbridge Gerry argued that a state militia was necessary:

> to prevent the establishment of a standing army, the bane of liberty. . . . Whenever governments mean to invade the rights and liberties of the people, they always attempt to destroy the militia in order to raise an army upon their ruins.

We see that the need for a state militia was the predicate of the 5 "right" guaranteed; in short, it was declared "necessary" in order to have a state military force to protect the security of the state. That Second Amendment clause must be read as though the word "because" was the opening word of the guarantee. Today, of course, the "state militia" serves a very different purpose. A huge national defense establishment has taken over the role of the militia of 200 years ago.

Some have exploited these ancient concerns, blurring sporting guns — rifles, shotguns, and even machine pistols — with all firearms, including what are now called "Saturday night specials." There is, of course, a great difference between sporting guns and handguns. Some regulation of handguns has long been accepted as imperative; laws relating to "concealed weapons" are common. That we may be "over-regulated" in some areas of life has never held us back from more regulation of automobiles, airplanes, motorboats, and "concealed weapons."

Let's look at the history.

First, many of the 3.5 million people living in the thirteen original Colonies depended on wild game for food, and a good many of them required firearms for their defense from marauding Indians — and later from the French and English. Underlying all these needs was an important concept that each able-bodied man in each of the thirteen independent states had to help or defend his state.

The early opposition to the idea of national or standing armies was maintained under the Articles of Confederation; that confederation had no standing army and wanted none. The state militia — essentially a part-time citizen army, as in Switzerland today — was the only kind of "army" they wanted. From the time of the Declaration of Independence through the victory at Yorktown in 1781, George Washington, as the commander in chief of these volunteer-militia armies, had to depend upon the states to send those volunteers.

When a company of New Jersey militia volunteers reported for duty   10
to Washington at Valley Forge, the men initially declined to take an oath to "the United States," maintaining, "Our country is New Jersey." Massachusetts Bay men, Virginians, and others felt the same way. To the American of the eighteenth century, his state was his country, and his freedom was defended by his militia.

The victory at Yorktown — and the ratification of the Bill of Rights a decade later — did not change people's attitudes about a national army. They had lived for years under the notion that each state would maintain its own military establishment, and the seaboard states had their own navies as well. These people, and their fathers and grandfathers before them, remembered how monarchs had used standing armies to oppress their ancestors in Europe. Americans wanted no part of this. A state militia, like a rifle and powder horn, was as much a part of life as the automobile is today; pistols were largely for officers, aristocrats — and dueling.

Against this background, it was not surprising that the provision concerning firearms emerged in very simple terms with the significant predicate — basing the right on the *necessity* for a "well regulated militia," a state army.

In the two centuries since then — with two world wars and some lesser ones — it has become clear, sadly, that we have no choice but to maintain a standing national army while still maintaining a "militia" by way of the National Guard, which can be swiftly integrated into the national defense forces.

Americans also have a right to defend their homes, and we need not challenge that. Nor does anyone seriously question that the Constitution protects the right of hunters to own and keep sporting guns for hunting game any more than anyone would challenge the right to own and keep fishing rods and other equipment for fishing — or to own automobiles. To "keep and bear arms" for hunting today is essentially a recreational activity and not an imperative of survival, as it was 200 years ago; "Saturday night specials" and machine guns are not recreational weapons and surely are as much in need of regulation as motor vehicles.

Americans should ask themselves a few questions. The Constitution 15
does not mention automobiles or motorboats, but the right to keep and
own an automobile is beyond question; equally beyond question is the
power of the state to regulate the purchase or the transfer of such
vehicle and the right to license the vehicle and the driver with reasonable standards. In some places, even a bicycle must be registered, as
must some household dogs.

If we are to stop this mindless homicidal carnage, is it unreasonable:

1. to provide that, to acquire a firearm, an application be made reciting
   age, residence, employment, and any prior criminal convictions?
2. to require that this application lie on the table for ten days (absent
   a showing for urgent need) before the license would be issued?
3. that the transfer of a firearm be made essentially as that of a motor
   vehicle?
4. to have a "ballistic fingerprint" of the firearm made by the manufacturer and filed with the license record so that, if a bullet is found
   in a victim's body, law enforcement might be helped in finding the
   culprit?

These are the kinds of questions the American people must answer
if we are to preserve the "domestic tranquility" promised in the Constitution.

Discussion Questions

1. Why does Burger recount the history of the Second Amendment so fully?
   Explain his reason for arguing that the Second Amendment does not guarantee the right of individuals to "bear arms."
2. Burger also uses history to argue that there is a difference between legislation against sporting guns and legislation against handguns. Summarize
   his argument.
3. How effective is his analogy between licensing vehicles and licensing handguns?

Writing Suggestions

1. Other people interpret "the right to bear arms" differently. Look at some
   of their arguments and write an essay summarizing their interpretations
   and defending them.
2. Burger outlines a policy for registration of handguns that would prevent
   criminal use. But at least one sociologist has pointed out that most guns
   used by criminals are obtained illegally. Examine and evaluate some of the
   arguments claiming that registration is generally ineffective.
3. Analyze arguments of the National Rifle Association, the nation's largest
   gun lobby. Do they answer Burger's claims?

The great American forest is closer than you think.

Wherever you are.

Because after giving up land to build our cities and highways, after meeting our constantly growing demands for wood and paper products, we still have three-fourths as much forestland as we had when Columbus landed.

Even more surprising, this 761 *million* acres is still widely distributed all across the country—it's not all just "out West" or "down South." 51% of New York State is forest. 65% of Rhode Island. And 51% of New Jersey—the most densely populated state. As a matter of fact, more than half of the forest in the continental United States is located in the east-ern part of the country.

Because America's forest is truly an *American* forest, growing in many different elevations and rainfalls and temperatures and soils, its six distinct natural regions provide us with a constant variety, too, from the Douglas firs of the Northwest to the hardwoods of the Northeast.

Much of the forest has been harvested and regrown three or four times. And, public or private, government or individually owned, much of it is available for hunting and fishing, picnicking and camping—as millions of outdoorsmen from Maine to California can tell you. So if you haven't seen it lately, why wait?

It's right there in your back-yard, keeping America green—and growing.

For the whole story on America's forest today, get "Forests USA." For your copy of this full-color, 16-page booklet, send 25¢ to AFI, 1619 Massachusetts Avenue, N.W., Washington, D.C. 20036

Name

Address

City

State   Zip

American Forest Institute

Discussion Questions

1. What fears does this ad respond to? Does it succeed in reassuring the reader? If so, how?
2. How does the advertiser go beyond the facts to reach the audience?

The advertisement reads:

The initials of a friend

You will find these letters on many tools by which electricity works. They are on great generators used by electric light and power companies; and on lamps that light millions of homes.

They are on big motors that pull railway trains; and on tiny motors that make hard housework easy.

By such tools electricity dispels the dark and lifts heavy burdens from human shoulders. Hence the letters G-E are more than a trademark. They are an emblem of service—the initials of a friend.

GENERAL ELECTRIC

This advertisement first appeared in 1923. Today, you'll find our initials on many more things — from appliances, plastics, motors and lighting to financial services and medical equipment. Wherever you see our initials, we want them to mean the same thing to you — the initials of a friend.

We bring good things to life.

Discussion Questions

1. To what need does the ad make an appeal?
2. What devices in the ad — both objects and the choice of objects to discuss — contribute to the effectiveness of the message?
3. How does the company's present-day slogan compare?

Nuclear energy can help America find a way out of our dangerous dependence on foreign oil

Oil imports are increasing to dangerous levels. As the uncertainty in the Persian Gulf continues, the ability to rely on America's nuclear energy becomes more important than ever.

During the 1973 embargo, when we were importing 35% of our oil, prices skyrocketed as supply nose-dived. In the last 18 months, America's dependence on OPEC oil has increased dramatically. We're even more dependent now than we were in 1973. Oil imports have risen by over 25% while domestic oil production has fallen nearly 10%. Looking to the future, the situation is even worse.

In fact, if projections from the Department of Energy are correct, America may be importing as much as 50% of our oil by 1990. That would seriously jeopardize our national energy security.

Nuclear Energy Saves Oil

Electricity generated from America's 108 commercial nuclear electric plants saves us over 750,000 barrels of oil a day. Every day. Without nuclear energy's contribution, we would need to import even more foreign oil than we already do.

Nuclear Energy for the Future

America's use of electricity has been growing steadily to fuel our growing economy. At current growth rates, electricity demand will overtake supply in the early 1990s.

New nuclear electric plants should be in planning *now*. But they are not, despite the fact that most Americans believe that nuclear energy is important and that we will need more.

Too many financial, political, licensing, and regulatory uncertainties stand in the way of America's being able to fully utilize its nuclear energy resources. For example, it has taken some plants as long as 12 years to be completed. If nothing changes, that means that a plant begun now might not be operating before the year 2000.

As America's economy continues to grow, America must find ways to keep pace with its growing electricity needs. Nuclear energy can play a major role in meeting those needs as well as keeping us less dependent on foreign oil.

For a free booklet on energy independence, write to the U.S. Council for Energy Awareness, P.O. Box 66103, Dept. NS02, Washington, D.C. 20035. Please allow 2-3 weeks for delivery.

Information about energy America can count on
U.S. COUNCIL FOR ENERGY AWARENESS

©1988 USCEA

As seen in March 1988 issues of Reader's Digest, National Geographic, Newsweek, U.S. News & World Report, The Economist, and State Legislatures and in April 1988 issues of National Geographic, TIME, Newsweek, Sports Illustrated, U.S. News & World Report, Smithsonian, Forbes, Scientific American, Natural History, National Journal, and State Legislatures.

Discussion Questions

1. How does the format of the ad affect the message?
2. What words in the headline are meant to rouse an emotional response in the reader?
3. How are the objections to nuclear energy handled?
4. Is this a successful policy claim?

EXERCISES FOR CRITICAL THINKING

1. Look for personal advertisements (in which men and women advertise for various kinds of companionship) in a local or national paper or magazine. (The *Village Voice,* a New York paper, is an outstanding source.) What inferences can you draw about the people who place these particular ads? About the "facts" they choose to provide? How did you come to these conclusions? You might also try to infer the reasons that more men than women place ads and why this might be changing.

2. "I like Colonel Sanders" is the title of an article that praises ugly architecture, shopping malls, laundromats, and other symbols of "plastic" America. The author claims that these aspects of the American scene have unique and positive values. Defend or refute his claim by pointing out what the values of these things might be, giving reasons for your own assessments.

3. A psychiatrist says that in pro football personality traits determine the positions of the players. Write an essay developing this idea and providing adequate evidence for your claim. Or make inferences about the relationship between the personalities of the players and another sport that you know well.

4. At least one city in the world — Reykjavik, the capital of Iceland — bans dogs from the city. Defend or attack this policy by using both facts and values to support your claim.

5. Write a review of a movie, play, television program, concert, restaurant, or book. Make clear your criteria for judgment and their order of importance.

6. The controversy concerning seat belts and air bags in automobiles has generated a variety of proposals, one of which is mandatory use of seat belts in all the states. Make your own policy claim regarding laws about safety devices (the wearing of motorcycle helmets is another thorny subject), and defend it by using both facts and values — facts about safety, values concerning individual freedom and responsibility.

7. Select a ritual with which you are familiar and argue for or against the value it represents. *Examples:* the high school prom, Christmas gift-giving, a fraternity initiation, a wedding, a confirmation or bar mitzvah, a funeral ceremony, a Fourth of July celebration.

8. Choose a recommended policy — from the school newspaper or elsewhere — and argue that it will or will not work to produce beneficial changes. *Examples:* expansion of core requirements, comprehensive tests as a graduation requirement, reinstitution of a physical education requirement, removal of junk food from vending machines.

CHAPTER THREE

Definition

THE PURPOSES OF DEFINITION

Before we examine the other elements of argument, we need to consider definition, a component you may have to deal with early in writing an essay. Definition may be used in two ways: to clarify the meanings of vague or ambiguous terms or as a method of development for the whole essay. In some arguments your claims will contain words that need explanation before you can proceed with any discussion. But you may also want to devote an entire essay to the elaboration of a broad concept or experience that cannot be adequately defined in a shorter space.

The Roman statesman Cicero said, "Every rational discussion of anything whatsoever should begin with a definition in order to make clear what is the subject of dispute." You have probably already discovered the importance of definition in argument. If you have ever had a disagreement with your parents about using the car or drinking or dyeing your hair or going away for a weekend or staying out till three in the morning, you know that you were really arguing about the meaning of the term "adolescent freedom."

Arguments often revolve around definitions of crucial terms. For example, how does one define *democracy*? Does a democracy guarantee freedom of the press, freedom of worship, freedom of assembly, freedom of movement? In the United States, we would argue that such freedoms are essential to any definition of *democracy*. But countries in which these freedoms are nonexistent also represent themselves as democracies or governments of the people. In the words of Senator Daniel J. Moynihan, "For years now the most brutal totalitarian regimes have called themselves 'people's' or 'democratic' republics." Rulers in such governments are aware that defining their regimes as democratic may win the approval of people who would otherwise condemn them. In his formidable attack on totalitarianism, *Nineteen Eighty-Four,* George Orwell coined the slogans "War Is Peace" and "Slavery Is Freedom," phrases that represent the corrupt use of definition to distort reality.

But even where there is no intention to deceive, the snares of definition are difficult to avoid. How do you define *abortion?* Is it "termination of pregnancy"? Or is it "murder of an unborn child"? During a celebrated trial in 1975 of a physician who performed an abortion and was accused of manslaughter, the prosecution often used the word *baby* to refer to the fetus, but the defense referred to "the products of conception." These definitions of *fetus* reflected the differing judgments of those on opposite sides. Not only do judgments create definitions; definitions influence judgments. In the abortion trial, the definitions of *fetus* used by both sides were meant to promote either approval or disapproval of the doctor's action.

Definitions can indeed change the nature of an event or a "fact." How many farms are there in the state of New York? The answer to the question depends on the definition of *farm.* In 1979 the *New York Times* reported:

> Because of a change in the official definition of the word "farm," New York lost 20 percent of its farms on January 1, with numbers dropping from 56,000 to 45,000. . . .
>
> Before the change, a farm was defined as "any place from which $250 or more of agricultural products is sold" yearly or "any place of 10 acres or more from which $50 or more of agricultural products is sold" yearly. Now a farm is "any place from which $1,000 or more of agricultural products is sold" in a year.[1]

A change in the definition of poverty can have similar results. An article in the *New York Times,* whose headline reads, "Who's in Poverty? Depends on Definition," makes this clear.

> The official poverty definition includes money income only. According to this definition 13.5 percent of Americans . . . were below the poverty threshold in 1987. [But] including the value of noncash benefits, such as food stamps, subsidized housing, and Medicare . . . reduces the general poverty level to 8.5 percent.[2]

The differences in the numbers are wholly a matter of definition, as the editorial writer recognizes by inserting the phrase, "According to this definition." Such differences can, of course, have serious personal consequences for those who are being defined.

In fact, local and federal courts almost every day redefine traditional

---

[1] *New York Times,* March 4, 1979, Sec. 1, p. 40.
[2] *New York Times,* November 2, 1988, Sec. B, p. 1.

concepts that can have a direct impact on our everyday lives. The definition of the family, for example, has undergone significant changes that acknowledge the existence of new relationships. In January 1990 the New Jersey Supreme Court ruled that a family may be defined as "one or more persons occupying a dwelling unit as a single nonprofit housekeeping unit, who are living together as a stable and permanent living unit, being a traditional family unit or the *functional equivalent* thereof" (italics for emphasis added). This meant that ten Glassboro State College students, unrelated by blood, could continue to occupy a single-family house despite the objection of the borough of Glassboro.[3] Even the legal definition of maternity has shifted. Who is the mother — the woman who contributes the egg or the woman (the surrogate) who bears the child? Several states, acknowledging the changes brought by medical technology, now recognize a difference between the "birth mother" and the "legal mother."

DEFINING THE TERMS IN YOUR ARGUMENT

In some of your arguments you will introduce terms that require definition. We've pointed out that a definition of poverty is crucial to any debate on the existence of poverty in the United States. The same may be true in a debate about the legality of euthanasia, or mercy killing. Are the arguers referring to passive euthanasia, that is, the withdrawal of life-support systems, or to active euthanasia, in which death is hastened through the direct administration of drugs?

It is not uncommon, in fact, for arguments about controversial questions to turn into arguments about the definition of terms. If, for example, you wanted to argue in favor of the regulation of religious cults, you would first have to define *cult.* In so doing, you might discover that it is not easy to distinguish clearly between conventional religions and cults. Then you would have to define *regulation,* spelling out the legal restrictions you favored so as to make them apply only to cults, not to established religions. An argument on the subject might end almost before it began if writer and reader could not agree on definitions of these terms. While clear definitions do not guarantee agreement, they do ensure that all parties understand the nature of the argument.

Defining Vague and Ambiguous Terms

You will need to define other terms in addition to those in your claim. If you use words and phrases that have two or more meanings, they may appear vague and ambiguous to your reader. In arguments of value and policy abstract terms such as *freedom, justice, patriotism,*

---

[3]*New York Times,* February 1, 1990, Sec. B, p. 5.

and *equality* require clarification. Despite their vagueness, however, they are among the most important in the language because they represent the ideals that shape our laws. When conflicts arise, the courts must define these terms to establish the legality of certain practices. Is the Ku Klux Klan permitted to make disparaging public statements about ethnic and racial groups? That depends on the court's definition of "free speech." Can execution for some crimes be considered "cruel and unusual punishment"? That, too, depends on the court's definition of "cruel and unusual punishment." In addition, such terms as *happiness, mental health, success,* and *creativity* often defy precise definition because they reflect the differing values within a society or a culture.

The definition of *success,* for example, varies not only among social groups but also among individuals within the group. One scientist has postulated five signs by which to judge the measure of success: wealth (including health), security (confidence in retaining the wealth), reputation, performance, and contentment.[4] Consider whether all of these are necessary to your own definition of *success.* If not, which may be omitted? Do you think others should be added? Notice that one of the signs — reputation — depends on definition by the community; another — contentment — can be measured only by the individual. The assessment of performance probably owes something to both the group and the individual.

Christopher Atkins, a young actor, gave an interviewer an example of an externalized definition of success, that is, a definition based on the standards imposed by other people:

> Success to me is judged through the eyes of others. I mean, if you're walking around saying, "I own a green Porsche," you might meet somebody who says, "Hey, that's no big deal, I own a green Porsche and a house." So all of a sudden, you don't feel so successful. Really, it's in the eyes of others.[5]

So difficult is the formulation of a universally accepted measure for success that some scholars regard the concept as meaningless. Nevertheless, we continue to use the word as if it represented a definable concept because the idea of success, however defined, is important for the identity and development of the individual and the group. It is clear, however, that when crossing subcultural boundaries, even within a small group, we need to be aware of differences in the use of the word. If "contentment" — that is, the satisfaction of achieving a small personal goal — is enough, then a person lying under a palm tree subsisting on handouts from picnickers may be a success. But you should not expect all your readers to agree that these criteria are enough to define *success.*

In arguing about aesthetic matters, whose vocabulary is almost always abstract, the criteria for judgment must be revealed, either

---

[4] Gwynn Nettler, *Social Concerns* (New York: McGraw-Hill, 1976), pp. 196–197.
[5] *New York Times,* August 6, 1982, Sec. III, p. 8.

directly or indirectly, and then the abstract terms that represent the criteria must be defined. If you want to say that a film is distinguished by great acting, have you made clear what you mean by *great*? That we do not always understand or agree on the definition of *great* is apparent, say, on the morning after the Oscar winners have been announced.

Even subjects that you feel sure you can identify may offer surprising insights when you rethink them for an extended definition. One critic, defining rock music, argued that the distinguishing characteristic of rock music was *noise* — not the beat, not the harmonies, not the lyrics, not the vocal style, but noise, "nasty, discordant irritating noise — or, to its practitioners, unfettered, liberating, expressive noise."[6] In producing this definition, the author had to give a number of examples to prove that he was justified in rejecting the most familiar criteria.

Robert Sommer, an architect who is critical of the "hard" architecture of prison cells, dormitory rooms, and public facilities such as picnic tables and restrooms, explains the meaning of *hard* by setting down its characteristics: strength, resistance to human imprint, lack of permeability between inside and out. He defines the last term by giving details.

> Often this [lack of permeability] means an absence of windows, a style referred to in Berkeley as post-revolutionary architecture. At first glance the Bank of America on Berkeley's Telegraph Avenue seems to have windows but these are really reflecting metal surfaces. The new postal center in Oakland, with its tiny slit windows, looks as if it were intended for urban guerrilla warfare. Older buildings that still have plate glass use steel shutters and gates that can be drawn across the exterior in a matter of minutes. Some corporations are moving their data-processing machinery underground where they are less vulnerable to attack.[7]

References to other matters of taste outside the arts — food, fashion, cars — also require definition of criteria if arguer and reader are to understand each other. How does the reviewer define "very good" for the restaurant to which she awards two stars? How does the wearer define Jordache jeans as "better" than Wrangler jeans? How does the maker of a Mercedes-Benz define its car as "superior" to a BMW?

METHODS FOR DEFINING TERMS

The following strategies for defining terms in an argument are by no means mutually exclusive. You may use all of them in a single argumentative essay.

---

[6] Jon Pareles, "Noise Evokes Modern Chaos for a Band," *New York Times,* March 9, 1986, Sec. H., p. 26.

[7] Robert Sommer, *Tight Spaces: Hard Architecture and How to Humanize It* (Englewood Cliffs, N.J.: Prentice-Hall, 1974), p. 7.

Dictionary Definition

Giving a dictionary definition is the simplest and most obvious way to define a term. An unabridged dictionary is the best source because it usually gives examples of the way a word can be used in a sentence; that is, it furnishes the proper context.

In many cases, the dictionary definition alone is not sufficient. It may be too broad or too narrow for your purpose. Suppose, in an argument about pornography, you wanted to define the word *obscene*. *Webster's New International Dictionary* (third edition, unabridged) gives the definition of *obscene* as "offensive to taste; foul; loathsome; disgusting." But these synonyms do not tell you what qualities make an object or an event or an action "foul," "loathsome," and "disgusting." In 1973 the Supreme Court, attempting to narrow the definition of *obscenity,* ruled that obscenity was to be determined by the community in accordance with local standards. One person's obscenity, as numerous cases have demonstrated, may be another person's art. The celebrated trials in the early twentieth century about the distribution of novels regarded as pornographic — D. H. Lawrence's *Lady Chatterley's Lover* and James Joyce's *Ulysses* — emphasized the problems of defining obscenity.

Another dictionary definition may strike you as too narrow. *Patriotism,* for example, is defined in one dictionary as "love and loyal or zealous support of one's country, especially in all matters involving other countries." Some readers may want to include an unwillingness to support government policies they consider wrong.

Stipulation

In stipulating the meaning of a term, the writer asks the reader to accept a definition that may be different from the conventional one. He or she does this in order to limit or control the argument. Someone has said, "Part of the task of keeping definitions in our civilization clear and pure is to keep a firm democratic rein on those with the power, or craving the power, to stipulate meaning." Perhaps this writer was thinking of a term like *national security,* which can be defined by a nation's leaders in such a way as to sanction persecution of citizens and reckless military adventures. Likewise, a term such as *liberation* can be appropriated by terrorist groups whose activities often lead to oppression rather than liberation.

Religion is usually defined as a belief in a supernatural power to be obeyed and worshiped. But in an article entitled "Civil Religion in America," a sociologist offers a different meaning.

> While some have argued that Christianity is the national faith, and others that church and synagogue celebrate only the generalized religion

of "the American way of life," few have realized that there actually exists alongside of and rather clearly differentiated from the churches an elaborate and well-institutionalized civil religion in America. This article argues not only that there is such a thing, but also that this religion . . . has its own seriousness and integrity and requires the same care in understanding that any other religion does.[8]

When the author adds, "This religion — there seems no other word for it — was neither sectarian nor in any specific sense Christian," he emphasizes that he is distinguishing his definition of religion from definitions that associate religion and church.

Even the word *violence,* which the dictionary defines as "physical force used so as to injure or damage" and whose meaning seems so clear and uncompromising, can be manipulated to produce a definition different from the one normally understood by most people. Some pacifists refer to conditions in which "people are deprived of choices in a systematic way" as "institutionalized quiet violence." Even where no physical force is employed, this lack of choice in schools, in the workplace, in the black ghettos is defined as violence.[9]

In *Through the Looking-Glass* Alice asked Humpty Dumpty "whether you can make words mean so many different things."

"When I use a word," Humpty Dumpty said scornfully, "it means just what I choose it to mean, neither more nor less."[10]

A writer, however, is not free to invent definitions that no one will recognize or that create rather than solve problems between writer and reader.

Negation

To avoid confusion it is sometimes helpful to tell the reader what a term is *not.* In discussing euthanasia, a writer might say, "By euthanasia I do not mean active intervention to hasten the death of the patient."

A negative definition may be more extensive, depending on the complexity of the term and the writer's ingenuity. The critic of rock music quoted earlier in this chapter arrived at his definition by rejecting attributes that seemed misleading. The ex-Communist Whittaker Chambers, in a foreword to a book on the spy trial of Alger Hiss, defined communism this way:

> First, let me try to say what Communism is not. It is not simply a vicious plot hatched by wicked men in a subcellar. It is not just the writings

---

[8] Robert N. Bellah, "Civil Religion in America," *Daedalus,* Winter 1967, p. 1.

[9] Newton Garver, "What Violence Is," in *Moral Choices,* edited by James Rachels (New York: Harper and Row, 1971), pp. 248–249.

[10] Lewis Carroll, *Alice in Wonderland and Through the Looking-Glass* (New York: Grosset and Dunlap, 1948), p. 238.

of Marx and Lenin, dialectical materialism, the Politburo, the labor theory of value, the theory of the general strike, the Red Army secret police, labor camps, underground conspiracy, the dictatorship of the proletariat, the technique of the coup d'état. It is not even those chanting, bannered millions that stream periodically, like disorganized armies, through the heart of the world's capitals: Moscow, New York, Tokyo, Paris, Rome. These are expressions, but they are not what Communism is about.[11]

This, of course, is only part of the definition. Any writer beginning a definition in the negative must go on to define what the term *is*.

Examples

One of the most effective ways of defining terms in an argument is the use of examples. Both real and hypothetical examples can bring life to abstract and ambiguous terms. The writer in the following passage defines *preferred categories* (classes of people who are meant to benefit from affirmative action policies) by invoking specific cases:

> The absence of definitions points up one of the problems with preferred categories. . . . These preferred categories take no account of family wealth or educational advantages. A black whose father is a judge or physician deserves preferential treatment over any nonminority applicant. The latter might have fought this way out of the grinding poverty of Appalachia, or might be the first member of an Italian-American or a Polish-American family to complete high school. But no matter.[12]

Insanity is a word that has been used and misused to describe a variety of conditions. Even psychiatrists are in dispute about its meaning. In the following anecdote, examples narrow and refine the definition.

> Dr. Zilboorg says that present-day psychiatry does not possess any satisfactory definition of mental illness or neurosis. To illustrate, he told a story: A psychiatrist was recently asked for a definition of a "well-adjusted person" (not even slightly peculiar). The definition: "A person who feels in harmony with himself and who is not in conflict with his environment." It sounded fine, but up popped a heckler. "Would you then consider an anti-Nazi working in the underground against Hitler a maladjusted person?" "Well," the psychiatrist hemmed, "I withdraw the latter part of my definition." Dr. Zilboorg withdrew the first half for him. Many persons in perfect harmony with themselves, he pointed out, are in "distinctly pathological states."[13]

[11] *Witness* (New York: Random House, 1952), p. 8.
[12] Anthony Lombardo, "Quotas Work Both Ways," *U.S. Catholic,* February 1974, p. 39.
[13] Quoted in *The Art of Making Sense,* p. 48.

Extended Definition

When we speak of an extended definition, we usually refer not only to length but also to the variety of methods for developing the definition. Let's take the word *materialism*. A dictionary entry offers the following sentence fragments as definitions: "1. the doctrine that comfort, pleasure, and wealth are the only or highest goals or values. 2. the tendency to be more concerned with material than the spiritual goals or values." But the term *materialism* has acquired so many additional meanings, especially emotional ones, that an extended definition serves a useful purpose in clarifying the many different ideas surrounding our understanding of the term.

Below is a much longer definition of *materialism,* which appears at the beginning of an essay entitled, "People and Things: Reflections on Materialism."[14]

> There are two contemporary usages of the term, materialism, and it is important to distinguish between them. On the one hand we can talk about *instrumental materialism,* or the use of material objects to make life longer, safer, more enjoyable. By instrumental, we mean that objects act as essential means for discovering and furthering personal values and goals of life, so that the objects are instruments used to realize and further those goals. There is little negative connotation attached to this meaning of the word, since one would think that it is perfectly sensible to use things for such purposes. While it is true that the United States is the epitome of materialism in this sense, it is also true that most people in every society aspire to reach our level of instrumental materialism.
>
> On the other hand the term has a more negative connotation, which might be conveyed by the phrase *terminal materialism.* This is the sense critics use when they apply the term to Americans. What they mean is that we not only use our material resources as instruments to make life more manageable, but that we reduce our ultimate goals to the possession of things. They believe that we don't just use our cars to get from place to place, but that we consider the ownership of expensive cars one of the central values in life. Terminal materialism means that the object is valued only because it indicates an end in itself, a possession. In instrumental materialism there is a sense of directionality, in which a person's goals may be furthered through the interactions with the object. A book, for example, can reveal new possibilities or widen a person's view of the world, or an old photograph can be cherished because it embodies a relationship. But in terminal materialism, there is no sense of reciprocal interaction in the relation between the object and the end. The end is valued as final, not as itself a means to further ends. And quite often it is only the status label or image associated with the object that is valued, rather than the actual object.

---

[14]Mihaly Csikszentmihalyi and Eugene Rochberg-Halton, "People and Things: Reflections on Materialism," *University of Chicago Magazine,* Spring 1978, pp. 7–8.

In the essay from which this passage is taken, the authors distinguish between two kinds of materialism and provide an extended explanation, using contrast and examples as methods of development. They are aware that the common perception of materialism, the love of things for their own sake, is a negative one. But this view, according to the authors, doesn't fully account for the attitudes of many Americans toward the things they own. There is, in fact, another more positive meaning that the authors call *instrumental materialism.* You will recognize that the authors are *stipulating* a meaning with which their readers might not be familiar. In their essay they distinguish between *terminal materialism,* in which "the object is valued only because it indicates an end in itself" and *instrumental materialism,* "the use of material objects to make life longer, safer, more enjoyable." Since *instrumental materialism* is the less familiar definition, the essay provides a great number of examples that show how people of three different generations value photographs, furniture, musical instruments, plants, and other objects for their memories and personal associations rather than as proof of the owners' ability to acquire the objects or win the approval of others.

THE DEFINITION ESSAY

The argumentative essay can take the form of an extended definition. An example of such an essay is the one from which we've just quoted, as well as the three essays at the end of this chapter. The definition essay is appropriate when the idea under consideration is so controversial or so heavy with historical connotations that even a paragraph or two cannot make clear exactly what the arguer wants his or her readers to understand. For example, if you were preparing a definition of patriotism, you would want to answer some or all of the following questions. You would probably use a number of methods to develop your definition: personal narrative, examples, stipulation, comparison and contrast, and cause and effect analysis.

1. *Dictionary Definition.* Is the dictionary definition the one I will elaborate on? Do I need to stipulate other meanings?

2. *Personal History.* Where did I first acquire my notions of patriotism? What was taught? How and by whom was it taught?

3. *Cultural Context.* Has my patriotic feeling changed in the last few years? Why or why not? Does my own patriotism reflect the mood of the country or the group to which I belong?

4. *Values.* What is the value of patriotism? Does it make me more humane, more civilized? Is patriotism consistent with tolerance of other systems and cultures? Is patriotism the highest duty of a

citizen? Do any other values take precedence? What was the meaning of President Kennedy's injunction: "Ask not what your country can do for you; ask rather what you can do for your country"?

5. *Behavior.* How do I express my patriotism (or lack of it)? Can it be expressed through dissent? What sacrifice, if any, would I make for my country?

WRITING AN ESSAY OF DEFINITION

The following list suggests several important steps to be taken in writing an essay of definition.

1. Choose a term that needs definition because it is controversial or ambiguous, or because you want to offer a personal definition that differs from the accepted interpretation. Explain why an extended definition is necessary. Or choose an experience that lends itself to treatment in an extended definition. One student defined "culture shock" as she had experienced it while studying abroad in Hawaii among students of a different ethnic background.
2. Decide on the thesis — the point of view you wish to develop about the term you are defining. If you want to define "heroism," for example, you may choose to develop the idea that this quality depends on motivation and awareness of danger rather than on the specific act performed by the hero.
3. Begin by consulting the dictionary for the conventional definition, the one with which most readers will be familiar. Make clear whether you want to elaborate on the dictionary definition or take issue with it because you think it is misleading or inadequate.
4. Distinguish wherever possible between the term you are defining and other terms with which it might be confused. If you are defining "love," can you make a clear distinction between the different kinds of emotional attachments contained in the word?
5. Try to think of several methods of developing the definition — using examples, comparison and contrast, analogy, cause and effect analysis. However, you may discover that one method alone — say, use of examples — will suffice to narrow and refine your definition. See the sample essay "The Nature of Prejudice" on page 90 for an example of such a development.
6. Arrange your supporting material in an order that gives emphasis to the most important ideas.

Addiction Is Not a Disease

STANTON PEELE

Why Addiction Is Not a Disease

Medical schools are finally teaching about alcoholism; Johns Hopkins will require basic training for all students and clinicians. . . . Alcoholism, as a chronic disease, offers "a fantastic vehicle to teach other concepts," says Jean Kinney [of Dartmouth's Cork Institute]. . . . William Osler, Kinney remarks, coined the aphorism that "to know syphilis is to know medicine," . . . Now, she says, the same can be said of alcoholism.

"The Neglected Disease in Medical Education," *Science*[1]

OCD (obsessive-compulsive disorder) is apparently rare in the general population.

American Psychiatric Association, 1980[2]

The evidence is strong OCD is a common mental disorder that, like other stigmatized and hidden disorders in the past, may be ready for discovery and demands for treatment on a large scale.

National Institute of Mental Health, 1988[3]

In America today, we are bombarded with news about drug and alcohol problems. We may ask ourselves, "How did we get here?" Alternatively, we may wonder if these problems are really worse now than they were five or ten years ago, or fifty or one hundred. Actually, in many cases the answer is no. Estimates of the number of alcoholics requiring treatment are wildly overblown, and reputable epidemiological researchers find that as little as 1 percent of the population fits the clinical definition of alcoholism — as opposed to the 10 percent figure regularly used by the alcoholism industry. Meanwhile, cocaine use is

---

Stanton Peele, who received his Ph.D. in social psychology from the University of Michigan, has taught at Harvard and Columbia Universities, the University of California, and is coauthor of the bestselling *Love and Addiction* (1975). This excerpt is from *Diseasing of America* (Boston: Houghton Mifflin, 1989).

[1] C. Holden, "The Neglected Disease in Medical Education," *Science* 229 (1985) pp. 741–742.

[2] *Diagnostic and Statistical Manual of Mental Disorders,* 3rd ed. (Washington, D.C.: American Psychiatric Association, 1980).

[3] M. Karno et al., "The Epidemiology of Obsessive-Compulsive Disorder in Five US Communities," *Archives of General Psychiatry* 45 (1988) pp. 1094–1099.

down. All indicators are that very few young people who try drugs ever become regular users, and fewer still get "hooked."

Of course, we have real problems. The nightly news carries story after story of inner-city violence between crack gangs and of totally desolate urban environments where drugs reign supreme. The cocaine problem has resolved itself — not exclusively, but very largely — into a ghetto problem, like many that face America. A *New York Times* front-page story based on an eight-year study of young drug users showed that those who abuse drugs have a number of serious background problems, and *that these problems don't disappear from their lives when they stop using drugs.*[4] In other words, the sources — and solutions — for what is going on in our ghettos are only very secondarily a matter of drug availability and use.

America is a society broken into two worlds. The reality of the crack epidemic and of inner cities and poor environments sometimes explodes and impinges unpleasantly on our consciousness. For the most part, however, our reality is that of the middle class, which fills our magazines with health stories and warnings about family problems and the strivings of young professionals to find satisfaction. And for some time now, this other world has also focused on addiction. But this new addiction marketplace is only sometimes linked to alcohol and drugs. Even when it is, we have to redefine alcoholism as the new Betty Ford kind, which is marked by a general dull malaise, a sense that one is drinking too much, and — for many, like Betty Ford and Kitty Dukakis — relying on prescribed drugs to make life bearable.

However we define loss-of-control drinking, Betty Ford didn't experience it. But treating problems like hers and those of so many media stars is far more rewarding and profitable than trying to deal with street derelicts or ghetto addicts. At the same time, *everything can be an addiction.* This remarkable truth — which I first described in *Love and Addiction* in 1975 — has so overwhelmed us as a society that we have gone haywire. We want to pass laws to excuse compulsive gamblers when they embezzle money to gamble and to force insurance companies to pay to treat them. We want to treat people who can't find love and who instead (when they are women) go after dopey, superficial men or (when they are men) pursue endless sexual liaisons without finding true happiness. And we want to call all these things — and many, many more — addictions.

Since I was part of the movement to label non-drug-related behav- 5 iors as addictions, what am I complaining about? My entire purpose in writing *Love and Addiction* was to explain addictions as part of a larger description of people's lives. Addiction is an experience that people

---

[4]S. Blakeslee, "8-Year Study Finds 2 Sides to Teen-Age Drug Use," *New York Times,* July 21, 1988, p. 1, Sec. A, p. 23.

can get caught up in but that still expresses their values, skills at living, and personal resolve — or lack of it. The label *addiction* does not obviate either the meaning of the addictive involvement within people's lives, or their responsibility for their misbehavior or for their choices in continuing the addiction. Forty million Americans have quit smoking. What, then, are we to think about the people who do not quit but who sue a tobacco company for addicting them to cigarettes after they learn they are going to die from a smoking-related ailment?

This discrepancy between understanding addiction within the larger context of a person's life and regarding it as an *explanation* of that life underlies my opposition to the "disease theory" of addiction, which I contest throughout this book. My view of addiction explicitly refutes this theory's contentions that (1) the addiction exists *independently* of the rest of a person's life and *drives* all of his or her choices; (2) it is progressive and irreversible, so that the addiction *inevitably worsens* unless the person seeks medical treatment or joins an AA-type support group; (3) addiction means the person is incapable of controlling his or her behavior, either in relation to the addictive object itself or — when the person is intoxicated or in pursuit of the addiction — in relation to the person's dealings with the rest of the world. Everything I oppose in the disease view is represented in the passive, *1984*-ish phrase, *alcohol abuse victim,* to replace *alcohol abuser.* On the contrary, this book maintains that people are *active agents* in — not passive victims of — their addictions.

While I do believe that a host of human habits and compulsions can be understood as addictions, I think the disease version of addiction does *at least* as much harm as good. An addiction does not mean that God in heaven decided which people are alcoholics and addicts. There is no biological urge to form addictions, one that we will someday find under a microscope and that will finally make sense of all these different cravings and idiocies (such as exercising to the point of injury or having sex with people who are bad for you). No medical treatment will ever be created to excise addictions from people's lives, and support groups that convince people that they are helpless and will forever be incapable of controlling an activity are better examples of self-fulfilling prophecies than of therapy.

What is this new addiction industry meant to accomplish? More and more addictions are being discovered, and new addicts are being identified, until all of us will be locked into our own little addictive worlds with other addicts like ourselves, defined by the special interests of our neuroses. What a repugnant world to imagine, as well as a hopeless one. Meanwhile, *all of the addictions we define are increasing.* In the first place, we tell people they can never get better from their "diseases." In the second, we constantly find new addicts, looking for them in all sorts of new areas of behavior and labeling them at earlier ages on the basis of more casual or typical behaviors, such as getting drunk at holiday celebrations ("chemical-dependency disease") or checking to see whether they locked their car door ("obsessive-compulsive disorder").

We must oppose this nonsense by understanding its sources and contradicting disease ideology. . . . Our society is going wrong in excusing crime, compelling people to undergo treatment, and wildly mixing up moral responsibility with disease diagnoses. Indeed, understanding the confusion and self-defeating behavior we display in this regard is perhaps the best way to analyze the failure of many of our contemporary social policies. . . . [We must] confront the actual social, psychological, and moral issues that we face as individuals and as a society — the ones we are constantly repressing and mislabeling through widening our disease nets. It is as though we were creating distorted microscopes that actually muddy our vision and that make our problems harder to resolve into components we can reasonably hope to deal with.

What are real diseases?   If we are to distinguish between addiction 10 and other diseases, then we first need to understand what have been called diseases historically and how these differ from what are being called diseases today. To do so, let us review three generations of diseases — physical ailments, mental disorders, and addictions.

The *first* generation of diseases consists of disorders known through their physical manifestations, like malaria, tuberculosis, cancer, and AIDS. The era of medical understanding that these diseases ushered in began with the discovery of specific microbes that cause particular diseases and for which preventive inoculations — and eventually antibodies — were developed. These maladies are the ones we can unreservedly call diseases without clouding the issue. This first generation of diseases differs fundamentally from what were later called diseases in that the former are *defined by their measurable physical effects.* They are clearly connected to the functioning of the body, and our concern is with the damage the disease does to the body.

The *second* generation of diseases are the so-called mental illnesses (now referred to as emotional disorders). They are not defined in the same way as the first generation. Emotional disorders are apparent to us not because of what we measure in people's bodies but because of the feelings, thoughts, and behaviors that they produce in people, which we can only know from what the sufferers say and do. We do not diagnose emotional disorders from a brain scan; if a person cannot tell reality from fantasy, we call the person mentally ill, no matter what the person's EEG says.

The *third* generation of diseases — addictions — strays still farther from the model of physical disorder to which the name *disease* was first applied by modern medicine. That is, unlike a mental illness such as schizophrenia, which is indicated by disordered thinking, addictive disorders *are known by the goal-directed behaviors they describe.* We call a person a drug addict who consumes drugs compulsively or excessively and whose life is devoted to seeking out these substances. If an addicted smoker gives up smoking or if a habituated coffee drinker decides to drink coffee only after Sunday dinner, then each ceases to be addicted. We cannot tell whether a person is addicted or will be addicted in the absence of the ongoing behavior — the person with a hypothetical alcoholic predisposition (say, one who has an alcoholic parent or whose face flushes when drinking) but who drinks occasionally and moderately is not an alcoholic.

In order to clarify the differences between third-generation and first-generation diseases, we often have to overcome shifting definitions that have been changed solely for the purpose of obscuring crucial differences between problems like cancer and addiction. After a time, we seem not to recognize how our views have been manipulated by such gerrymandered disease criteria. For example, by claiming that alcoholics are alcoholics even if they haven't drunk for fifteen years, alcoholism is made to seem less tied to drinking behavior and more like cancer. Sometimes it seems necessary to remind ourselves of the obvious: that a person does not get over cancer by stopping a single behavior or even by changing a whole life-style, but the sole and essential indicator for successful remission of alcoholism is that the person ceases to drink.

Addictions involve appetites and behaviors. While a connection can   15
be traced between individual and cultural beliefs and first- and second-generation diseases, this connection is most pronounced for addictions. Behaviors and appetites are addictions only in particular cultural contexts — obviously, obesity matters only where people have enough to eat and think it is important to be thin. Symptoms like loss-of-control drinking depend *completely* on cultural and personal meanings, and cultural groups that don't understand how people can lose control of their drinking are almost immune to alcoholism. What is most important, however, is not how cultural beliefs affect addictions but how our defining of addictions as diseases affects our views of ourselves as individuals and as a society. . . .

What Is Addiction, and How Do People Get It?

While individual practitioners and recovering addicts — and the whole addiction movement — may believe they are helping people, they succeed principally at expanding their industry by finding more addicts and new types of addictions to treat. I too have argued — in books from *Love and Addiction* to *The Meaning of Addiction* — that addiction *can* take place with any human activity. Addiction is *not,* however, something people are born with. Nor is it a biological imperative, one that means the addicted individual is not able to consider or choose alternatives. The disease view of addiction is equally untrue when applied to gambling, compulsive sex, and everything else that it has been used to explain. Indeed, the fact that people become addicted to all these things *proves* that addiction is not *caused* by chemical or biological forces and that it is not a special disease state.

The nature of addiction. People seek specific, essential human experiences from their addictive involvement, no matter whether it is drinking, eating, smoking, loving, shopping, or gambling. People can come to depend on such an involvement for these experiences until — in the extreme — the involvement is totally consuming and potentially destructive. Addiction can occasionally veer into total abandonment, as well as periodic excesses and loss of control. Nonetheless, even in cases where addicts die from their excesses, an addiction must be understood as a human response that is motivated by the addict's desires and principles. All addictions *accomplish something for the addict.* They are ways of coping with feelings and situations with which addicts cannot otherwise cope. What is wrong with disease theories as science is that they are *tautologies;* they avoid the work of understanding *why* people drink or smoke in favor of simply declaring these activities to be addictions, as in the statement "He drinks so much because he's an alcoholic."

Addicts seek experiences that satisfy needs they cannot otherwise fulfill. Any addiction involves three components — the person, the situation or environment, and the addictive involvement or experience (see Table 1). In addition to the individual, the situation, and the ex-

TABLE 1

The Person	The Situation	The Addictive Experience
Unable to fulfill essential needs	Barren and deprived: disadvantaged social groups, war zones	Creates powerful and immediate sensations; focuses and absorbs attention
Values that support or do not counteract addiction: e.g., lack of achievement motivation	Antisocial peer groups Absence of supportive social groups; disturbed family structure	Provides artificial or temporary sense of self-worth, power, control, security, intimacy, accomplishment
Lack of restraint and inhibition	Life situations: adolescence, temporary isolation, deprivation, or stress	
Lack of self-efficacy; sense of powerlessness vis-à-vis the addiction		Eliminates pain, uncertainty, and other negative sensations

perience, we also need to consider the overall cultural and social factors that affect addiction in our society.

The social and cultural milieu. We must also consider the enormous social-class differences in addiction rates. That is, the farther down the social and economic scale a person is, the more likely the person is to become addicted to alcohol, drugs, or cigarettes, to be obese, or to be a victim or perpetrator of family or sexual abuse. How does it come to be that addiction is a "disease" rooted in certain social experiences, and why in particular are drug addiction and alcoholism associated primarily with certain groups? A smaller range of addiction and behavioral problems are associated with the middle and upper social classes. These associations must also be explained. Some addictions, like shopping, are obviously connected with the middle class. Bulimia and exercise addiction are also primarily middle-class addictions.

Finally, we must explore why addictions of one kind or another 20 appear on our social landscape all of sudden, almost as though floodgates were released. For example, alcoholism was unknown to most colonial Americans and to most Americans earlier in this century; now it dominates public attention. This is not due to greater consumption, since we are actually drinking *less* alcohol than the colonists did. Bulimia, PMS, shopping addiction, and exercise addiction are wholly new inventions. Not that it isn't possible to go back in time to find examples of things that appear to conform to these new diseases. Yet their widespread — almost commonplace — presence in today's society must be explained, especially when the disease — like alcoholism — is supposedly biologically inbred. . . .

Are addicts disease victims? The development of an addictive lifestyle is an accumulation of patterns in people's lives of which drug use is neither a result nor a cause but another example. Sid Vicious was the consummate drug addict, an exception even among heroin users. Nonetheless, we need to understand the extremes to gain a sense of the shape of the entire phenomenon of addiction. Vicious, rather than being a passive victim of drugs, seemed intent on being and remaining addicted. He avoided opportunities to escape and turned every aspect of his life toward his addictions — booze, Nancy, drugs — while sacrificing anything that might have rescued him — music, business interests, family, friendships, survival instincts. Vicious was pathetic; in a sense, he was a victim of his own life. But his addiction, like his life, was more an active expression of his pathos than a passive victimization.

Addiction theories have been created because it stuns us that people would hurt — perhaps destroy — themselves through drugs, drinking, sex, gambling, and so on. While people get caught up in an addictive dynamic over which they do not have full control, it is at least as accurate to say that people consciously select an addiction as it is to say an addiction has a person under its control. And this is why addiction is so hard to ferret out of the person's life — because it fits the person. The bulimic woman who has found that self-induced vomiting helps her to control her weight and who feels more attractive after throwing up is a hard person to persuade to give up her habit voluntarily. Consider the homeless man who refused to go to one of Mayor Koch's New York City shelters because he couldn't easily drink there and who said, "I don't want to give up drinking; it's the only thing I've got."

The researcher who has done the most to explore the personalities of alcoholics and drug addicts is psychologist Craig MacAndrew. MacAndrew developed the MAC scale, selected from items on the MMPI (a personality scale) that distinguish clinical alcoholics and drug abusers from normal subjects and from other psychiatric patients. This scale identifies antisocial impulsiveness and acting out: "an assertive, aggressive, pleasure-seeking character," in terms of which alcoholics and drug abusers closely "resemble criminals and delinquents."[5] These characteristics are not the *results* of substance abuse. Several studies have measured these traits in young men *prior* to becoming alcoholics and in young drug and alcohol abusers.[6] This same kind of antisocial thrill-seeking characterizes most women who become alcoholic. Such women more often have disciplinary problems at school, react to boredom by "stirring up some kind of excitement," engage in more disapproved sexual practices, and have more trouble with the law.[7]

The typical alcoholic, then, fulfills antisocial drives and pursues immediate, sensual, and aggressive rewards while having underdeveloped inhibitions. MacAndrew also found that another, smaller group comprising both men and women alcoholics — but more often women — drank to alleviate internal conflicts and feelings like depression. This group of alcoholics viewed the world, in MacAndrew's words, "primarily in terms of its potentially punishing character." For them, "alcohol functions as a palliation for a chronically fearful, distressful internal state of affairs." While these drinkers also sought specific rewards in drinking, these rewards were defined more by internal states

---

[5] C. MacAndrew, "What the MAC Scale Tells Us about Men Alcoholics," *Journal of Studies on Alcohol* 42 (1981) p. 617.

[6] H. Hoffman, R. G. Loper, and M. L. Kammeier, "Identifying Future Alcoholics with MMPI Alcoholism Scores," *Quarterly Journal of Studies on Alcohol* 35 (1974) pp. 490–498; M. C. Jones, "Personality correlates and Antecedents of Drinking Patterns in Adult Males," *Journal of Consulting and Clinical Psychology* 32 (1968) pp. 2–12; R. G. Loper, M. L. Kammeier, and H. Hoffman, "MMPI Characteristics of College Freshman Males Who Later Become Alcoholics," *Journal of Abnormal Psychology* 82 (1973) pp. 159–162; C. MacAndrew, "Toward the Psychometric Detection of Substance Misuse in Young Men," *Journal of Studies on Alcohol* 47 (1986) pp. 161–166.

[7] C. MacAndrew, "Similarities in the Self-Depictions of Female Alcoholics and Psychiatric Outpatients," *Journal of Studies on Alcohol* 47 (1986) pp. 478–484.

than by external behaviors. Nonetheless, we can see that this group too did not consider normal social strictures in pursuing feelings they desperately desired.

MacAndrew's approach in this research was to identify particular   25
personality types identified by the experiences they looked to alcohol to provide. But even for alcoholics or addicts without such distinct personalities, the purposeful dynamic is at play. For example, in *The Lives of John Lennon,* Albert Goldman describes how Lennon — who was addicted over his career to a host of drugs — would get drunk when he went out to dinner with Yoko Ono so that he could spill out his resentments of her. In many families, drinking allows alcoholics to express emotions that they are otherwise unable to express. The entire panoply of feelings and behaviors that alcohol may bring about for individual drinkers thus can be motivations for chronic intoxication. While some desire power from drinking, others seek to escape in alcohol; for some drinking is the route to excitement, while others welcome its calming effects.

Alcoholics or addicts may have more emotional problems or more deprived backgrounds than others, but probably they are best characterized as feeling powerless to bring about the feelings they want or to accomplish their goals without drugs, alcohol, or some other involvement. Their sense of powerlessness then translates into the belief that the drug or alcohol is extremely powerful. They see in the substance the ability to accomplish what they need or want but can't do on their own. The double edge to this sword is that the person is easily convinced that he or she cannot function without the substance or addiction, that he or she requires it to survive. This sense of personal powerlessness, on the one hand, and of the extreme power of an involvement or substance, on the other, readily translates into addiction.[8]

People don't manage to become alcoholics over years of drinking simply because their bodies are playing tricks on them — say, by allowing them to imbibe more than is good for them without realizing it until they become dependent on booze. Alcoholics' long drinking careers are motivated by their search for essential experiences they cannot gain in other ways. The odd thing is that — despite a constant parade of newspaper and magazine articles and TV programs trying to convince us otherwise — most people recognize that alcoholics drink for specific purposes. Even alcoholics, however much they spout the party line, know this about themselves. Consider, for example, . . . Monica Wright, the head of a New York City treatment center, [who] describes how she drank over the twenty years of her alcoholic marriage to cope with her insecurity and with her inability to deal with her husband and children.

---

[8] G. A. Marlatt, "Alcohol, the Magic Elixir," in *Stress and Addiction,* eds. E. Gottheil et al. (New York: Brunner/Mazel, 1987); D. J. Rohsenow, "Alcoholics' Perceptions of Control," in *Identifying and Measuring Alcoholic Personality Characteristics,* ed. W. M. Cox (San Francisco: Jossey-Bass, 1983).

It is impossible to find an alcoholic who does not express similar reasons for his or her drinking, once the disease dogma is peeled away. . . .

Analysis

Peele is not the only writer to take issue with the popular practice of defining all kinds of mental and social problems as addictions. (A recent satirical newspaper article is entitled, "It's Not Me That's Guilty. My Addiction Just Took Over.") Peele's definition will be disputed by many doctors, psychologists, and a powerful industry of self-appointed healers. But definitions that attack popular opinions are often the liveliest and most interesting both to read and to write. In addition, they may serve a useful purpose, even if they are misguided, in encouraging new thinking about apparently intractable problems.

In defense of a controversial definition, an author must do at least two things: (1) make clear why a new definition is needed, that is, why the old definition does not work to explain certain conditions, and (2) argue that the new definition offers a better explanation and may even lead to more effective solutions of a problem.

The first part of Peele's argument is definition by negation. (Notice the title of this section.) Peele insists that the number of drug and alcohol addicts among both the poor and the well-to-do is not nearly so large as practitioners would have it. Next, he points out that addiction is not an explanation of a person's life, as some have insisted, nor does it mean that the addict is a victim to be absolved of responsibility for the consequences of his actions. Last, he provides the reasons that addiction is not a disease, basing his argument on the historic definition of disease as a bodily ailment whose physical effects are measurable. Defining mental illness and addiction as diseases is, Peele thinks, an evasion of the truth.

Some readers will question the narrowness of Peele's stipulation. Since the term *disease* has come to signify almost everywhere (including the dictionary) a disorder that need not be biological in origin, these readers may feel that Peele is attacking a nonexistent problem. But in the next section — "What Is Addiction?" — he elaborates on his major point: Addicts are not passive victims. Addiction is a choice, derived from the addict's desires and principles. Because this is the heart of the controversy, Peele devotes the rest of his essay to its development. In "The Nature of Addiction" he gives an overview of the motives that lead addicts to alcohol or drugs. Later, in "Are Addicts Disease Victims?" he enlarges on the descriptions of their behavior and identifies specific reasons for their actions. One of the strengths of his argument is the breadth of the analysis. In a few pages he touches on all the relevant causes of the addict's choices: the individual, the situation, the addictive experience, the social and cultural milieu.

The support for his claim is not exhaustive, but it offers a variety of evidence: examples of familiar individuals and types (Sid Vicious, John Lennon, the bulimic, the homeless man, the head of a treatment center) clear explanations of different kinds of addictive behavior, and a detailed summary of expert opinion.

All this evidence, if it is to work, must make an appeal to the common sense and experience of the reader. As Peele says, "The odd thing is that — despite a constant parade of newspaper and magazine articles and TV programs trying to convince us otherwise — most people recognize that alcoholics drink for specific purposes." Most readers, of course, will not be experts, but if they find the evidence consistent with their knowledge of and experience with addiction, they will find Peele's definition deserving of additional study.

READINGS FOR ANALYSIS

The Nature of Prejudice
GORDON ALLPORT

Before I attempt to define prejudice, let us have in mind four instances that I think we all would agree are prejudice.

The first is the case of the Cambridge University student who said, "I despise all Americans. But," he added, a bit puzzled, "I've never met one that I didn't like."

The second is the case of another Englishman, who said to an American, "I think you're awfully unfair in your treatment to Negroes. How *do* Americans feel about Negroes?" The American replied, "Well, I suppose some Americans feel about Negroes just the way you feel about the Irish." The Englishman said, "Oh, come now. The Negroes are human beings."

Then there's the incident that occasionally takes place in various parts of the world (in the West Indies, for example, I'm told). When an American walks down the street the natives conspicuously hold their noses till the American goes by. The case of odor is always interesting. Odor gets mixed up with prejudice because odor has great associative power. We know that some Chinese deplore the odor of Americans. Some white people think Negroes have a distinctive smell and vice versa. An intrepid psychologist recently did an experiment; it went as follows. He brought to a gymnasium an equal number of white and

Gordon Allport (1897–1967) was a psychologist who taught at Harvard University from 1924 until his death. He was author of numerous books, among them *Personality: A Psychological Interpretation* (1937). Allport delivered "The Nature of Prejudice" at the Seventeenth Claremont Reading Conference in 1952. The speech was published as a paper in 1952 in the Seventeenth Claremont Reading Conference Yearbook.

colored students and had them take shower baths. When they were nice and clean he had them exercise vigorously for fifteen minutes. Then he brought his judges in, and each went to the sheeted figures and sniffed. They were to say "white" or "black," guessing at the identity of the subject. The experiment seemed to prove that when we are sweaty we all smell the same way. It's good to have experimental demonstration of the fact.

The fourth example I'd like to bring before you is a piece of writing that I quote. Please ask yourselves who, in your judgment, wrote it. It's a passage about the Jews.

> The synagogue is worse than a brothel. It's a den of scoundrels. It's a criminal assembly of Jews, a place of meeting for the assassins of Christ, a den of thieves, a house of ill fame, a dwelling of iniquity. Whatever name more horrible to be found, it could never be worse than the synagogue deserves.
>
> I would say the same things about their souls. Debauchery and drunkenness have brought them to the level of lusty goat and pig. They know only one thing: to satisfy their stomachs and get drunk, kill, and beat each other up. Why should we salute them? We should not even have the slightest converse with them. They are lustful, rapacious, greedy, perfidious robbers.

Now who wrote that? Perhaps you say Hitler, or Goebbels, or one of our local anti-Semites? No, it was written by Saint John Chrysostom, in the fourth century A.D. Saint John Chrysostom, as you know, gave us the first liturgy in the Christian church still used in the Orthodox churches today. From it all services of the Holy Communion derive. Episcopalians will recognize him also as the author of that exalted prayer that closes the offices of both matins and evensong in the *Book of Common Prayer.* I include this incident to show how complex the problem is. Religious people are by no means necessarily free from prejudice. In this regard be patient even with our saints.

What do these four instances have in common? You notice that all of them indicate that somebody is "down" on somebody else — a feeling of rejection, or hostility. But also, in all these four instances, there is indication that the person is not "up" on his subject — not really informed about Americans, Irish, Jews, or bodily odors.

So I would offer, first a slang definition of prejudice: *Prejudice is being down on somebody you're not up on.* If you dislike slang, let me offer the same thought in the style of St. Thomas Aquinas. Thomists have defined prejudice as *thinking ill of others without sufficient warrant.*

You notice that both definitions, as well as the examples I gave, specify two ingredients of prejudice. First there is some sort of faulty generalization in thinking about a group. I'll call this the process of *categorization.* Then there is the negative, rejective, or hostile ingredient, a *feeling* tone. "Being down on something" is the hostile ingredient; "that you're not up on" is the categorization ingredient; "thinking ill of others" is the hostile ingredient; "without sufficient warrant" is the faulty categorization.

Parenthetically I should say that of course there is such a thing as positive prejudice. We can be just as prejudiced *in favor of* as we are *against.* We can be biased in favor of our children, our neighborhood or our college. Spinoza makes the distinction neatly. He says that *love prejudice* is "thinking well of others, through love, more than is right." *Hate prejudice,* he says, is "thinking ill of others, through hate, more than is right." 10

Discussion Questions

1. This was a speech, obviously not delivered extemporaneously but read to the audience. What characteristics suggest an oral presentation?
2. Allport has arranged his anecdotes carefully. What principle of organization has he used?
3. This essay was written in 1952. Are there any references or examples that seem dated? Why or why not?

Writing Suggestions

1. Some media critics claim that negative prejudice exists in the treatment of certain groups in movies and television. If you agree, select a group that seems to you to be the object of prejudice in these media, and offer evidence of the prejudice and the probable reasons for it. Or disagree with the media critics and provide evidence that certain groups are *not* the object of prejudice
2. Can you think of examples of what Allport calls *positive prejudice?* Perhaps you can find instances that are less obvious than the ones Allport mentions. Explain in what way these prejudices represent a love that is "more than is right."

What Sexual Harassment Is — and Is Not

ELLEN BRAVO and ELLEN CASSEDY

Louette Colombano was one of the first female police officers in her San Francisco district. While listening to the watch commander, she and the other officers stood at attention with their hands behind their backs. The officer behind her unzipped his fly and rubbed his penis against her hands.

Ellen Bravo is the national director of 9to5, an organization for working women. Ellen Cassedy, a founder of 9to5, writes a column for the *Philadelphia Daily News.* This

Diane, a buyer, was preparing to meet an out-of-town client for dinner when she received a message: her boss had informed the client that she would spend the night with him. Diane sent word that she couldn't make it to dinner. The next day she was fired.

Few people would disagree that these are clear-cut examples of sexual harassment. Touching someone in a deliberately sexual way, demanding that an employee engage in sex or lose her job — such behavior is clearly out of bounds. (It's also *illegal*. . . .) But in less obvious cases, many people are confused about where to draw the line.

Is It Harassment?

Is all sexual conversation inappropriate at work? Is every kind of touching off limits? Consider the following examples. In your opinion, which, if any, constitute sexual harassment?

- A male manager asks a female subordinate to lunch to discuss a new project.
- A man puts his arm around a woman at work.
- A woman tells an off-color joke.
- These comments are made at the workplace:

  "Your hair looks terrific."
  "That outfit's a knockout."
  "Did you get any last night?"

The answer in each of these cases is, "It depends." Each one *could* 5 be an example of sexual harassment — or it could be acceptable behavior.

Take the case of the manager asking a female subordinate to lunch to discuss a new project. Suppose this manager often has such lunchtime meetings with his employees, male and female. Everyone is aware that he likes to get out of the office environment in order to get to know the associates a little better and to learn how they function — for example, whether they prefer frequent meetings or written reports, detailed instructions or more delegation of responsibility. The female subordinate in this case may feel she's being treated just like other colleagues and be glad to receive the individual attention.

On the other hand, suppose this subordinate has been trying for some time, unsuccessfully, to be assigned to an interesting project. The only woman who does get plum assignments spends a lot of time out of the office with the boss; the two of them are rumored to be sleeping

article is excerpted from their book, *The 9 to 5 Guide to Combating Sexual Harassment* (New York: John Wiley & Sons, 1992).

together. The lunch may represent an opportunity to move ahead, but it could mean that the manager expects a physical relationship in return. In this case, an invitation to lunch with the boss is laden with unwelcome sexual overtones.

An arm around the shoulder, an off-color joke, comments about someone's appearance, or even sexual remarks may or may not be offensive. What matters is the relationship between the two parties and how each of them feels.

"Your hair looks terrific," for instance, could be an innocuous compliment if it were tossed off by one co-worker to another as they passed in the hall. But imagine this same phrase coming from a male boss bending down next to his secretary's ear and speaking in a suggestive whisper. Suddenly, these innocent-sounding words take on a different meaning. The body language and tone of voice signify something sexual. While the comment itself may not amount to much, the secretary is left to wonder *what else the boss has in mind.*

On the other hand, even words that may seem grossly inappropriate — "Did you get any last night?" — can be harmless in certain work situations. One group of male and female assembly-line workers talked like this all the time. What made it okay? They were friends and equals — no one in the group had power over any of the others. They were all comfortable with the banter. They hadn't drawn up a list specifying which words were acceptable to the group and which were not. But they had worked together for some time and knew one another well. Their remarks were made with affection and accepted as good-natured. No one intended to offend — and no one was offended. The assembly-line area was relatively isolated, so the workers weren't in danger of bothering anyone outside their group. Had a new person joined the group who wasn't comfortable with this kind of talk, the others would have stopped it. They might have thought the new person uptight, they might not have liked the new atmosphere, but they would have respected and honored any request to eliminate the remarks.

This is the essence of combating sexual harassment — creating a workplace that is built on mutual respect.

Looking at Harassment

Try assessing whether each of the following scenarios constitutes sexual harassment. Then consider the analysis that follows.

Scenario 1: Justine works in a predominantly male department. She has tried to fit in, even laughing on occasion at the frequent sexual jokes. The truth is, though, that she gets more irritated by the jokes each day. It is well known in the department that Justine has an out-of-town boyfriend whom she sees most weekends. Nonetheless, Franklin, one of Justine's co-workers, has said he has the "hots" for her and that —

*boyfriend or not — he's willing to do almost anything to get a date with
her. One day, Sarah, another of Justine's co-workers, overheard their
boss talking to Franklin in the hallway. "If you can get her to go to bed
with you," the boss said, "I'll take you out to dinner. Good luck." They
chuckled and went their separate ways.* (From the consulting firm of
Jane C. Edmonds & Associates, Inc., *Boston Globe,* 10/24/91.)

The boss is out of line. True, he probably didn't intend anyone to
overhear him. But why was he having this conversation in the hallway?
What was he doing having the conversation at all? The boss is responsible for keeping the workplace free of harassment. Instead, he's giving
Franklin an incentive to make sexual advances to a co-worker and then
to brag about it.

The conversation may constitute harassment not only of Justine   15
but also of Sarah, who overheard the conversation. A reasonable woman
might easily wonder, "Who's he going to encourage to go after *me*?"
Ideally, Sarah should tell the two men she was offended by their remarks. But given that one of them is her boss, it would be understandable if she were reluctant to criticize his behavior.

Franklin isn't just romantically interested in Justine; he "has the
hots" for her and is willing to "do almost anything" to get a date with
her. Justine could well be interested in a "fling" with Franklin. But she's
irritated by the sexual remarks and innuendoes in the workplace. It's
unlikely that she would be flattered by attention from one of the men
responsible for this atmosphere.

Justine can just say no to Franklin. But she may well object to
having to say no over and over. And most women are not pleased to
be the brunt of jokes and boasts. Some may argue that whether Franklin
and Justine get together is a personal matter between the two of them.
The moment it becomes the subject of public boasting, however, Franklin's interest in Justine ceases to be just a private interaction.

The law doesn't say Justine should be tough enough to speak up
on her own — it says the company is responsible for providing an
environment free of offensive or hostile behavior. As the person in
charge, the boss ought to know what kind of remarks are being made
in the workplace and whether employees are offended by them. Instead
of making Franklin think the way to win favor with him is to pressure
a co-worker into bed, the manager might want to arrange for some
training on sexual harassment.

*Scenario 2:   Freda has been working for Bruce for three years. He
believes they have a good working relationship. Freda has never complained to Bruce about anything and appears to be happy in her job.
Bruce regularly compliments Freda on her clothing; in his opinion, she
has excellent taste and a good figure. Typically, he'll make a remark
like "You sure look good today." Last week, Freda was having a bad
day and told Bruce that she was "sick and tired of being treated like a*

sex object." Bruce was stunned. (From the consulting firm of Jane C. Edmonds & Associates, Inc., *Boston Globe,* 10/24/91.)

There's really not enough information to come to any conclusion 20 in this case. The scenario explains how Bruce feels, but not Freda. In the past, when he said, "Hey, you look good today," did Freda usually answer, "So do you"? Or did he murmur, "Mmm, you look go-o-o-o-d," and stare at her chest while she crossed her arms and said, "Thank you, sir"? In addition to complimenting Freda's appearance, did Bruce ever praise her work? Did he compliment other women? Men?

It is plausible that Freda might have been upset earlier. She probably wouldn't say she was tired of being treated like a sex object unless she'd felt that way before. Why didn't she speak up sooner? It's not uncommon for someone in Freda's situation to be reluctant to say anything for fear of looking foolish or appearing to be a "bad sport." Remember, Bruce is her boss.

Bruce states that he was stunned when Freda blew up at him. He needs to consider whether Freda might have given him any signals he ignored. He should ask himself how his compliments fit in with the way he treats other employees. Has he really given Freda an opening to object to his remarks?

The most comfortable solution might be for Bruce and Freda to sit down and talk. Perhaps Freda doesn't really mind the compliments themselves but wants more attention paid to her work. If Freda has been upset about the compliments all along, Bruce is probably guilty only of not paying close attention to her feelings. He should let her know that he values her work *and* her feelings, listen carefully to what she has to say, and encourage her to speak up promptly about issues that may arise in the future.

Scenario 3: Barbara is a receptionist for a printing company. Surrounding her desk are five versions of ads printed by the company for a beer distributor. The posters feature women provocatively posed with a can of beer and the slogan, "What'll you have?" On numerous occasions, male customers have walked in, looked at the posters, and commented, "I'll have you, baby." When Barbara tells her boss she wants the posters removed, he responds by saying they represent the company's work and he's proud to display them. He claims no one but Barbara is bothered by the posters.

The legal standard in this case is not how the boss feels, but 25 whether a "reasonable woman" might object to being surrounded by such posters. The company has other products it could display. Barbara has not insisted that the company refuse this account or exclude these posters from the company portfolio. She has merely said she doesn't want the posters displayed around *her* desk. Barbara's view is substantiated by how she's been treated; the posters seem to give customers license to make suggestive remarks to her.

Scenario 4: Therese tells Andrew, her subordinate, that she needs him to escort her to a party. She says she's selecting him because he's the most handsome guy on her staff. Andrew says he's busy. Therese responds that she expects people on her staff to be team players.

Therese may have wanted Andrew merely to accompany her to the party, not to have a sexual relationship with her. And Andrew might have been willing to go along if he hadn't been busy. Nevertheless, a reasonable employee may worry about what the boss means by such a request, particularly when it's coupled with remarks about personal appearance.

Andrew might not mind that Therese finds him handsome. But most people would object to having their job tied to their willingness to make a social appearance with the boss outside of work. The implicit threat also makes Therese's request unacceptable. The company should prohibit managers from requiring subordinates to escort them to social engagements.

Scenario 5: Darlene invites her co-worker Dan for a date. They begin a relationship that lasts several months. Then Darlene decides she is no longer interested and breaks up with Dan. He wants the relationship to continue. During the workday, he frequently calls her on the interoffice phone and stops by her desk to talk. Darlene tries to brush him off, but with no success. She asks her manager to intervene. The manager says he doesn't get involved in personal matters.

Most managers are rightly reluctant to involve themselves in em- 30 ployees' personal relationships. Had Darlene asked for help dealing with Dan outside of work, the manager would have been justified in staying out of it. He could have referred her to the employee assistance program, if the company had one.

Once Dan starts interfering with Darlene's work, however, it's a different story. The company has an obligation to make sure the work environment is free from harassment. If Darlene finds herself less able to do her job or uncomfortable at work because of Dan and if her own efforts have failed, the manager has both the right and the responsibility to step in and tell Dan to back off.

Scenario 6: Susan likes to tell bawdy jokes. Bob objects. Although he doesn't mind when men use such language in the office, he doesn't think it's appropriate for women to do so.

An employee who objects to off-color jokes shouldn't have to listen to them at work, and management should back him up. Bob's problem, however, is restricted to jokes told by women. If he doesn't have the same problem when men tell such jokes, it's his problem — not the company's. Management can't enforce Bob's double standard.

Scenario 7: Janet is wearing a low-cut blouse and short shorts. John, her co-worker, says, "Now that I can see it, you gotta let me have some." Janet tells him to buzz off. All day, despite Janet's objections, John continues to make similar remarks. When Janet calls her supervisor over to complain, John says, "Hey, can you blame me?"

The company has a right to expect clothing appropriate to the job. 35 If Janet's clothes are inappropriate, management should tell her so. But Janet's outfit doesn't give John license to say or do whatever he likes. Once she tells him she doesn't like his comments, he should stop — or be made to do so.

Scenario 8: Someone posts a Hustler *magazine centerfold in the employee men's room. No women use this room.*

Some would say that if the women aren't aware of the pinups in the men's room, they can't be offensive. But when men walk out of the restroom with such images in their mind's eye, how do they view their female co-workers? And when the women find out about the pinups — as they will — how will they feel? As the judge ruled in a 1991 Florida case involving nude posters at a shipyard, the presence of such pictures, even if they aren't intended to offend women, "sexualizes the work environment to the detriment of all female employees."

A Common-Sense Definition

Sexual harassment is not complicated to define. To harass someone is to bother him or her. Sexual harassment is bothering someone in a sexual way. The harasser offers sexual attention to someone who didn't ask for it and doesn't welcome it. The unwelcome behavior might or might not involve touching. It could just as well be spoken words, graphics, gestures, or even looks (not any look — but the kind of leer or stare that says, "I want to undress you").

Who decides what behavior is offensive at the workplace? The recipient does. As long as the recipient is "reasonable" and not unduly sensitive, sexual conduct that offends him or her should be changed.

That doesn't mean there's a blueprint for defining sexual harass- 40 ment. "Reasonable" people don't always agree. Society celebrates pluralism. Not everyone is expected to have the same standards of morality or the same sense of humor. Still, reasonable people will agree *much of the time* about what constitutes offensive behavior or will recognize that certain behavior or language can be expected to offend some others. Most people make distinctions between how they talk to their best friends, to their children, and to their elderly relatives. Out of respect, they avoid certain behavior in the presence of certain people. The same distinctions must be applied at work.

Sexual harassment is different from the innocent mistake — that is, when someone tells an off-color joke, not realizing the listener will be offended, or gives what is meant as a friendly squeeze of the arm to a co-worker who doesn't like to be touched. Such behavior may represent insensitivity, and that may be a serious problem, but it's usually not sexual harassment. In many cases, the person who tells the joke that misfires or who pats an unreceptive arm *knows right away* that he or she has made a mistake. Once aware or made aware, this individual will usually apologize and try not to do it again.

Do They Mean It?

Some offensive behavior stems from what University of Illinois psychologist Louise Fitzgerald calls "cultural lag." "Many men entered the workplace at a time when sexual teasing and innuendo were commonplace," Fitzgerald told the *New York Times.* "They have no idea there's anything wrong with it." Education will help such men change their behavior.

True harassers, on the other hand, *mean* to offend. Even when they know their talk or action is offensive, they continue. Sexual harassment is defined as behavior that is not only unwelcome but *repeated.* (Some kinds of behavior are *always* inappropriate, however, even if they occur only once. Grabbing someone's breast or crotch, for example, or threatening to fire a subordinate who won't engage in sexual activity does not need repetition to be deemed illegal.)

The true harasser acts not out of insensitivity but precisely because of the knowledge that the behavior will make the recipient uncomfortable. The harasser derives pleasure from the momentary or continuing powerlessness of the other individual. In some cases, the harasser presses the victim to have sex, but sexual pleasure itself is not the goal. Instead, the harasser's point is to dominate, to gain power over another. As University of Washington psychologist John Gottman puts it, "Harassment is a way for a man to make a woman vulnerable."

Some harassers target the people they consider the most likely to   45
be embarrassed and the least likely to file a charge. Male harassers are sometimes attempting to put "uppity women" in their place. In certain previously all-male workplaces, a woman who's simply attempting to do her job may be considered uppity. In this instance, the harassment is designed to make the woman feel out of place, if not to pressure her out of the job. Such harassment often takes place in front of an audience or is recounted to others afterwards ("pinch and tell").

Dr. Frances Conley, the renowned neurosurgeon who quit her job at Stanford Medical School after nearly twenty-five years of harassment, told legislators at a sexual harassment hearing in San Diego, California, that the "unsolicited touching, caressing, comments about my physical attributes" she experienced "were always for effect in front of an audience. . . ."

Part of the Job

Some harassers who don't consciously set out to offend are nevertheless unwilling to curb their behavior even after they're told it's offensive. If a woman doesn't like it, they figure that's her problem. And some harassers consider sexual favors from subordinates to be a "perk," as much a part of the job as a big mahogany desk and a private executive bathroom. A young woman on President Lyndon Johnson's staff, according to *A Sexual Profile of Men in Power* (Prentice-Hall, 1977), by Sam Janus and others, "was awakened in her bedroom on his Texas ranch in the middle of the night by a searching flashlight. Before she could scream, she heard a familiar voice: 'Move over. This is your president.'"

Men can be harassed by women, or both harasser and victim can be of the same sex. Overwhelmingly, however, sexual harassment is an injury inflicted on women by men. While the number of hard-core harassers is small, their presence is widely felt. Sexual harassment is ugly. And it's damaging — to the victims, to business, and to society as a whole.

DEFINING SEXUAL HARASSMENT

Sexual harassment means bothering someone in a sexual way.

Sexual harassment is behavior that is not only unwelcome but in most cases *repeated.*

The goal of sexual harassment is not sexual pleasure but gaining power over another.

Some male harassers want to put "uppity women" in their place.

The essence of combating sexual harassment is fostering mutual respect in the workplace.

Discussion Questions

1. This definition is developed almost entirely through examples of specific actions. Why is that a particularly effective strategy for defining sexual harassment?
2. The authors say, " 'Reasonable' people will agree *much of the time* about what constitutes offensive behavior. . . ." Are there any examples of sexual harassment in this article with which you disagree? If so, explain your objection.
3. How would you characterize the tone of the article? Does it contribute to the effectiveness of the definition? Tell why or why not.

Writing Suggestions

1. Consider the reasons that sexual harassment has become a national issue. What social, political, and economic factors might account for the rise in complaints and public attention? Are some reasons more important than others?

2. The Clarence Thomas–Anita Hill case in October 1991 was a nationally televised hearing on sexual harassment which continues to reverberate. Look up the facts in several national newsmagazines. Then summarize them and come to a conclusion of your own about the justice of the accusations, emphasizing those areas of the debate that support your claim.

Deconstructing Date Rape

SUZANNE FIELDS

Every young girl, at least until recently, has thrilled to that famous stairway scene in *Gone with the Wind* when Scarlett beguilingly says, "No, no, no," and Rhett sweeps her into his arms to carry her upstairs anyway.

Today, certain "sex awareneess counselors" and feminist radicals insist that Rhett was not a dreamboat after all, but a rapist, and what Scarlett might have thought about the experience that romantic night at Tara is as irrelevant as her contented smile the morning after. In fact, even if Scarlett had said, "Yes, yes, yes," the man-haters would call it rape anyhow.

Rape has suddenly become the four-letter word with more meanings than snow has in Eskimo. It is, according to feminist writer Robin Warshaw, our constant companion, a crime "more common than left-handedness or heart attacks or alcoholism." Indeed, it seems that rape has become a metaphor. In the rush to find rape everywhere, radical feminists have trivialized, if not ignored, the central issue: whether a woman has consented to, or even welcomed, sexual intercourse. To read much of the feminist literature on the subject, consent is no defense at all against the charge of rape.

Susan Estrich, onetime Dukakis campaign manager who now teaches law at the University of Southern California, writes: "Many feminists would argue that so long as women are powerless relative to men, viewing 'yes' as a sign of true consent is misguided." Given this sort of logic, even a false charge of rape can be seen as having redeeming political merit because it registers a protest against oppression.

Suzanne Fields is a syndicated columnist. This essay is taken from the April 1992 issue of *Heterodoxy,* published by the Center for the Study of Popular Culture in Studio City, California.

"To use the word [yes] carefully would be to be careful for the sake 5
of the violator, and the survivors don't care a hoot about him," says
Catherine Comins, assistant dean of Student Life at Vassar. Comins
believes that even the falsely accused can have a valuable experience
of a different kind: "I think it ideally initiates a process of self-explora-
tion. 'How do I see women?' 'Do I have the potential to do to her what
they say I did?' Those are good questions."

Ms. Comins would be at home at Dartmouth University, a place
where feeling speaks louder than fact. Philip Weiss in *Harper's* describes
how Dartmouth women have formed sex-offense brigades. Like the
witch hunters of Salem, they prosecute vendettas against men they
merely *imagine* violated them, even when the alleged victims did not
necessarily express outrage at the time of the putative crime. One
woman succeeded in getting a man suspended for a semester for "sexual
assault," although she waited three years to complain. She conceded,
moreover, that she did not object when he penetrated her with his
fingers in the men's room of his dorm one evening when they both had
had too much to drink.

At Brown, women write the names of accused rapists on bathroom
walls. Women at the University of Wisconsin are concerned about the
thought as well as the deed, warning in a brochure that men should
"stop fantasizing about rape." A Swarthmore College pamphlet describes
"acquaintance rape" as incidents "ranging from crimes legally defined
as rape to verbal harassment and inappropriate innuendo." *Innuendo?*

There has been more writing on rape and less real study of it, it is
safe to say, than of any other major crime. Feminists often cite Mary
Koss, who is frequently identified as the "leading scholar" in the field,
to substantiate their claims that date rape is a clear and unambiguous
offense. The data Koss collected about rape comes from interviews she
conducted with 6,159 college students for a "study" funded by the
Center for Antisocial and Violent Behavior of the National Institute of
Mental Health. Koss found that 15 percent of the women had been raped
and another 11 percent experienced attempted rape. Yet although this
study is regarded as "authoritative," these are in fact not real statistics
and the answers reported are not necessarily the answers given by
respondents in the study but merely Koss's *interpretations* of the answers. Fully 73 percent of the women Koss identified as having been
raped said they did not themselves think they were raped, and "raped"
or not, 42 percent had sexual intercourse again with their "rapist." Koss
actually identifies 2,024 experiences of unwanted sexual contact against
a woman's will including fondling, kissing, or petting. Who's counting
here?

Rape is the bandwagon on which most of our leading feminists
have climbed to establish their moral bona fides. Susan Brownmiller,
who could be described as the mother of date rape scholarship, grounds
her argument in the fundamental differences between the sexes: "[Rape]

is nothing more or less than a conscious process of intimidation by which *all men* keep *all women* in a state of fear." Andrea Dworkin goes even farther, describing all women as making up an occupied country of inferiors and stops just short of calling every episode of intercourse, including loving intercourse, rape. Naomi Wolf, author of *The Beauty Myth,* sees little distinction between rape and sex: "Sexual violence is seen as normal by young women as well as young men."

It is little wonder that when Betty Friedan complained that feminists 10 spend too much time protesting rape when women have many other concerns, she was viciously set upon by her sisters for "ignoring the victims."

Nancy Ziegenmeyer, who was raped by a stranger who threatened to kill her and who went public in a famous series in the Des Moines *Register,* lectures young college women that date rape is "just as serious" as what happened to her and says that rape "will touch one of every three women in this country, although only one in ten will report it. *Mademoiselle* picks up the same theme, asking its readers: "How can it be that three of the twelve women in your aerobics class, or two of the eight women in your office, will be or have been raped?"

Where do these figures come from? What can they really mean? We're never told. The avalanche of statistics keeps overwhelming us. *Mademoiselle* went to Dr. Diana Russell, a sociologist and author of *Sexual Exploitation,* who, after interviewing a cross section of women in San Francisco, said that half the rape victims she spoke to had been raped more than once. Many had been raped or abused as children. "The perpetrators in most of those cases were an acquaintance or intimate of the victim," Russell writes. "It's a pattern of revictimization."

The definition of "rape victim" is crucial to these discussions. In the Middle Ages, rape was punished by castration and blinding, and not so long ago it was a hanging offense nearly everywhere in America with the suspect being lucky to get a trial in many places. The sexual revolution, which scrambled so many of the signals between men and women, transformed certainty into conjecture. "Date rape" is in this sense the offspring of a one night stand between the sexual revolution and the feminist movement which society as a whole is being forced to adopt and support.

Nearly all newspapers continue to withhold identification of the rape victim, although Alan Dershowitz, Harvard professor and trial lawyer, has argued that the notion is outdated, based on the idea that a woman not a virgin at marriage was "damaged goods." Even so, Dershowitz nevertheless concedes that naming a woman who charges "date rape" is different from naming a woman who is jumped by a man from behind the bushes. When a *New York Post* editorial called for making clear legal distinctions between stranger rape and a sexual encounter which has been preceded by a series of "consensual activi-ties" — drinking, a visit to a man's home, a walk on a deserted beach at three o'clock in the morning, feminists were enraged. Their project to make rape, whatever the adjective placed in front of it, symbolic of relations between the sexes had been challenged.

The ultimate tragedy of all this political jousting is that it trivializes 15 what is one of the most capital offenses. If yes means no just as much as no means no, and if a victim does not need to know she has been victimized, then how can we distinguish the crime from the rhetoric? If rape is merely in the eye of the social scientist or feminist activist, one of the most heinous crimes known to mankind becomes merely a "misunderstanding." Guilt and innocence melt into each other and we are all victims.

Discussion Questions

1. The author criticizes several studies that are meant to prove the prevalence of date rape. What is the basis of her criticism? Do you find any weaknesses in her objections?
2. What is the significance of the author's reference to punishment for rape in earlier times?
3. Why does the author deplore the attempt by some people to define rape so broadly? How do you think the author would define rape? Would she distinguish date rape from other kinds of rape?

Writing Suggestions

1. If there has been public concern on your campus about date rape, describe what measures, both official and unofficial, have been taken to deal with it. Evaluate the effectiveness of the measures. Suggest any other steps that in your view would reduce the problem.
2. Try to explain the reasons that date rape has become so common, "more common than left-handedness or heart attacks or alcoholism," according to one writer. Is it merely a matter of definition? Or is it a reality born of changing social conditions?

I acquired the painting of my dreams.
Only to discover it was a brilliant forgery.

I bought stocks like they were going out of style.
And they were.

I married for love.
Then found I was being married for money.

I bought myself a Waterman.

There are some decisions one never lives to regret.

Pens write. A Waterman pen expresses. For more than a century, this distinction has remained constant. The creation shown here, for example, has been crafted from sterling silver, painstakingly tooled and balanced to absolute precision. Those who desire such an instrument of expression will find Waterman pens in a breadth of styles, prices and lacquers.

WATERMAN
— PARIS —

© 1993 Waterman Pen Company

Discussion Questions

1. This ad is divided into two parts. The part in small print extols the distinctive attributes of the Waterman pen. Why does the advertiser relegate the description of his pen to the small print?
2. How does the advertiser define a superior "instrument of expression"? Does calling a pen an "instrument of expression" add something to the definition?
3. What contrast is the reader invited to examine in the humorous first part of the ad?

EXERCISES FOR CRITICAL THINKING

1. Choose one of the following statements and define the italicized term. Make the context as specific as possible (for example, by referring to the Declaration of Independence or your own experience).
    a. All men are created *equal.*
    b. I believe in *God.*
    c. This school doesn't offer a *liberal education.*
    d. The marine corps needs *good men.*
    e. "Roseanne" is a *better* television show than "Seinfeld."
2. Many recent controversial movements and causes are identified by terms that have come to mean different things to different people. Choose one of the following and define it, explaining both the favorable and unfavorable connotations of the term. Use examples to clarify the meaning.
    a. comparative worth
    b. Palestinian homeland
    c. affirmative action
    d. co-dependency
    e. nationalism
3. Choose two words that are sometimes confused and define them to make their differences clear. *Examples:* authoritarianism and totalitarianism; envy and jealousy; sympathy and pity; cult and established church; justice and equality; liberal and radical; agnostic and atheist.
4. Define a good parent, a good teacher, a good husband or wife. Try to uncover the assumptions on which your definition is based. (For example, in defining a good teacher, students sometimes mention the ability of the teacher to maintain order. Does this mean that the teacher alone is responsible for classroom order?)
5. Define any popular form of entertainment, such as the soap opera, western, detective story, or science fiction story or film. Support your definition with references to specific shows or books. *Or* define an idealized type from fiction, film, the stage, advertising, or television, describing the chief attributes of that type and the principal reasons for its popularity.
6. From your own experience write an essay describing a serious misunderstanding that arose because two people had different meanings for a term they were using.
7. Write about an important or widely used term whose meaning has changed since you first learned it. Such terms often come from the slang of particular groups: teenagers, drug users, rock music fans, musicians, athletes.
8. Define the differences between *necessities, comforts,* and *luxuries.* Consider how they have changed over time.

CHAPTER FOUR

Support

TYPES OF SUPPORT: EVIDENCE AND APPEALS TO NEEDS AND VALUES

All the claims you make — whether of fact, of value, or of policy — must be supported. Support for a claim represents the answer to the question, "What have you got to go on?"[1] There are two basic kinds of support in an argument: evidence and appeals to needs and values.

Evidence, as one dictionary defines it, is "something that tends to prove; ground for belief." When you provide evidence, you use facts, including statistics, and opinions, or interpretations of facts, both your own and those of experts. In the following conversation, the first speaker offers facts and the opinion of an expert to convince the second speaker that robots are exceptional machines.

> *"You know, robots do a lot more than work on assembly lines in factories."*
>
> *"Like what?"*
>
> *"They shear sheep, pick citrus fruit, and even assist in neuro-surgery. And by the end of the century, every house will have a robot slave."*
>
> *"No kidding. Who says so?"*
>
> *"An engineer who's the head of the world's largest manufacturer of industrial robots."*

---

[1] Stephen Toulmin, *The Uses of Argument* (Cambridge: Cambridge University Press, 1958), p. 98.

A writer often appeals to readers' needs, that is, requirements for physical and psychological survival and well-being, and values, or standards for right and wrong, good and bad. In the following conversation, the first speaker makes an appeal to the universal need for self-esteem and to the principle of helping others, a value the second speaker probably shares.

> *"I think you ought to come help us at the nursing home. We need an extra hand."*

> *"I'd like to, but I really don't have the time."*

> *"You could give us an hour a week, couldn't you? Think how good you'd feel about helping out, and the old people would be so grateful. Some of them are very lonely."*

Although they use the same kinds of support, conversations are less rigorous than arguments addressed to larger audiences in academic or public situations. In the debates on public policy that appear in the media and in the courts, the quality of support can be crucial in settling urgent matters. The following summary of a well-known court case demonstrates the critical use of both evidence and value appeals in the support of opposing claims.

On March 30, 1981, President Ronald Reagan and three other men were shot by John W. Hinckley, Jr., a young drifter from a wealthy Colorado family. Hinckley was arrested at the scene of the shooting. In his trial the factual evidence was presented first: There were dozens of reliable witnesses who had seen the shooting at close range. Hinckley's diaries, letters, and poems revealed that he had planned the shooting to impress actress Jodie Foster. Opinions, consisting of testimony by experts, were introduced by both the defense and the prosecution. This evidence was contradictory. Defense attorneys produced several psychiatrists who defined Hinckley as insane. If this interpretation of his conduct convinced the jury, then Hinckley would be confined to a mental hospital rather than a prison. The prosecution introduced psychiatrists who interpreted Hinckley's motives and actions as those of a man who knew what he was doing and knew it was wrong. They claimed he was *not* insane by legal definition. The fact that experts can make differing conclusions about the meaning of the same information indicates that interpretations are less reliable than other kinds of support.

Finally, the defense made an appeal to the moral values of the jury. Under the law, criminals judged to be insane are not to be punished as harshly as criminals judged to be sane. The laws assume that criminals who cannot be held responsible for their actions are entitled to more compassionate treatment, confinement to a mental hospital rather than prison. The jury accepted the interpretive evidence supporting the claim of the defense, and Hinckley was pronounced not guilty by reason of insanity. Clearly the moral concern for the rights of the insane proved to be decisive.

In your arguments you will advance your claims, not unlike a lawyer, with these same kinds of support. But before you begin, you should ask two questions: Which kind of support should I use in convincing an audience to accept my claim? and How do I decide that each item of support is valid and worthy of acceptance? This chapter presents the different types of evidence and appeals you can use to support your claim and examines the criteria by which you can evaluate the soundness of that support.

EVIDENCE

Factual Evidence

In Chapter 2, we defined facts as statements possessing a high degree of public acceptance. In theory, facts can be verified by experience alone. Eating too much will make us sick; we can get from Hopkinton to Boston in a half hour by car; in the Northern Hemisphere it is colder in December than in July. The experience of any individual is limited in both time and space, so we must accept as fact thousands of assertions about the world that we ourselves can never verify. Thus we accept the report that human beings landed on the moon in 1969 because we trust those who can verify it. (Country people in Morocco, however, received the news with disbelief because they had no reason to trust the reporters of the event. They insisted on trusting their senses instead. One man said, "I can see the moon very clearly. If a man were walking around up there, wouldn't I be able to see him?")

Factual evidence appears most frequently as examples and statistics, which are a numerical form of examples.

Examples

Examples are the most familiar kind of factual evidence. In addition to providing support for the truth of a generalization, examples can enliven otherwise dense or monotonous prose.

In the following paragraph the writer supports the claim in the topic sentence by offering a series of specific examples. (The article claims that most airport security is useless.)

> Meanwhile, seven hijacking incidents occurred last year (twenty-one in 1980 and eleven the year before), despite the security system. Two involved the use of flammable liquids. . . . In four other cases, hijackers claimed to have flammables or explosives but turned out to be bluffing. In the only incident involving a gun, a man brushed past the security system and brandished the weapon on the plane before being wrestled to the

ground. One other hijacking was aborted on the ground, and the remaining five were concluded after some expense, fright, and delay — but no injuries or deaths.[2]

Hypothetical examples, which create imaginary situations for the audience and encourage them to visualize what might happen under certain circumstances, can also be effective. The following paragraph, taken from the same article as the preceding paragraph, illustrates the use of hypothetical examples.

> But weapons can get through nonetheless. Some are simply over-looked; imagine being one of those 10,000 "screeners" staring at X-rayed baggage, day in and day out. Besides, a gun can be broken down into unrecognizable parts and reassembled past the checkpoint. A hand grenade can be hidden in an aerosol shaving-cream can or a photographer's lens case. The ingredients of a Molotov cocktail can be carried on quite openly; any bottle of, say, duty-free liquor or perfume can be emptied and refilled with gasoline. And the possibilities for bluffing should not be forgotten; once on board, anyone could claim that a bottle of water was really a Molotov cocktail, or that a paper bag contained a bomb.[3]

All claims about vague or abstract terms would be boring or unintelligible without examples to illuminate them. For example, if you claim that a movie contains "unusual sound effects," you will certainly have to describe some of the effects to convince the reader that your generalization can be trusted.

Statistics

Statistics express information in numbers. In the following example statistics have been used to express raw data in numerical form.

> Surveys have shown that almost half of all male high school seniors — and nearly 20 percent of all ninth grade boys — can be called "problem drinkers." . . . Over 5,000 teenagers are killed yearly in auto accidents due to drunken driving.[4]

These grim numbers probably have meaning for you, partly because you already know that alcoholism exists even among young teenagers and partly because your own experience enables you to evaluate the numbers. But if you are unfamiliar with the subject, such numbers may be difficult or impossible to understand. Statistics, therefore, are more effective in comparisons that indicate whether a quantity is relatively large or small and sometimes even whether a reader should interpret

---

[2] Patrick Brogan, "The $310 Million Paranoia Subsidy," *Harper's,* September 1982, p. 18.

[3] Ibid.

[4] "The Kinds of Drugs Kids Are Getting Into" (Spring House, Penn.: McNeil Pharmaceutical, n.d.).

the result as gratifying or disappointing. For example, if a novice gambler were told that for every dollar wagered in a state lottery, 50 percent goes back to the players as prizes, would the gambler be able to conclude that the percentage is high or low? Would he be able to choose between playing the state lottery and playing a casino game? Unless he had more information, probably not. But if he were informed that in casino games, the return to the players is over 90 percent and in slot machines and racetracks the return is around 80 percent, the comparison would enable him to evaluate the meaning of the 50 percent return in the state lottery and even to make a decision about where to gamble his money.[5]

Comparative statistics are also useful for measurements over time. A national survey by The Institute for Social Research of the University of Michigan, in which 17,000 of the nation's 2.7 million high school seniors were questioned about their use of drugs, revealed a continuing downward trend.

> 50.9 percent of those questioned in 1989 reported that they had at least tried an illicit drug like marijuana or cocaine, as against 53.9 percent in 1988 and 56.6 percent in 1987.[6]

Diagrams, tables, charts, and graphs can make clear the relations among many sets of numbers. Such charts and diagrams allow readers to grasp the information more easily than if it were presented in paragraph form. The bar graph[7] that is shown on page 112 summarizes the information produced by a poll on gambling habits. A pie chart[8] such as the one on page 113 can also clarify lists of data.

Opinions: Interpretations of the Facts

We have seen how opinions of experts influenced the verdict in the trial of John Hinckley. Facts alone were not enough to substantiate the claim that Hinckley was guilty of attempted assassination. Both the defense and the prosecution relied on experts — psychiatrists — to interpret the facts. Opinions or interpretations about the facts are the inferences discussed in Chapter 2. They are an indispensable source of support for your claims.

Suppose a nightclub for teenagers — Studio 44: A Young Adult Dance Club — has opened in your town. That is a fact. What is the significance of it? Is the club's existence good or bad? What consequences will it have for the community? Some parents oppose the idea of a nightclub, fearing that it may allow teenagers to escape from

---

[5] Curt Suphee, "Lotto Baloney," *Harper's,* July 1983, p. 201.

[6] *New York Times,* February 14, 1990, Sec. A, p. 16.

[7] *New York Times,* May 28, 1989, p. 24.

[8] *Wall Street Journal,* February 2, 1990, Sec. B, p. 1.

Want to Bet?

Please tell me whether or not you have done any of the following in the past 12 months:

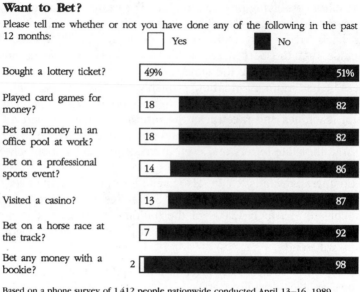

	Yes	No
Bought a lottery ticket?	49%	51%
Played card games for money?	18	82
Bet any money in an office pool at work?	18	82
Bet on a professional sports event?	14	86
Visited a casino?	13	87
Bet on a horse race at the track?	7	92
Bet any money with a bookie?	2	98

Based on a phone survey of 1,412 people nationwide conducted April 13–16, 1989.

Bar graph

parental control and engage in dangerous activities. Other parents approve of a club, hoping that it will serve as a substitute for unsupervised congregation in the streets. The importance of these interpretations is that they, not the fact itself, help people decide what actions they should take. If the community accepts the interpretation that Studio 44 is a source of delinquency, they may decide to revoke the owner's license and close the club. As one writer puts it, "The interpretation of data becomes a struggle over power."

Opinions or interpretations of facts generally take three forms: (1) They may suggest the cause for a condition or a causal connection between two sets of data; (2) they may offer predictions about the future; (3) they may suggest solutions to a problem.

1. Causal Connection

Anorexia is a serious, sometimes fatal, disease, characterized by self-starvation. It is found largely among young women. Physicians, psychologists, and social scientists have speculated about the causes, which remain unclear. A leading researcher in the field, Hilde Bruch, believes that food refusal expresses a desire to postpone sexual development. Another authority, Joan Blumberg, believes that one cause may be biological, a nervous dysfunction of the hypothalamus. Still others

Plastic That Goes to Waste

Components of municipal solid waste, by volume

Types of plastic in municipal solid waste, by weight

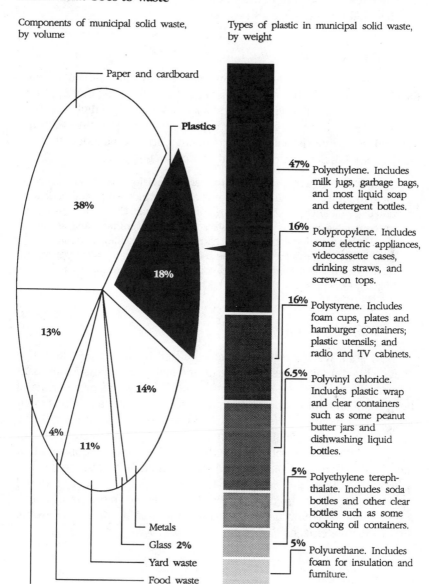

Paper and cardboard

Plastics

38%

18%

13%

14%

4%

11%

Metals

Glass 2%

Yard waste

Food waste

Other

47% Polyethylene. Includes milk jugs, garbage bags, and most liquid soap and detergent bottles.

16% Polypropylene. Includes some electric appliances, videocassette cases, drinking straws, and screw-on tops.

16% Polystyrene. Includes foam cups, plates and hamburger containers; plastic utensils; and radio and TV cabinets.

6.5% Polyvinyl chloride. Includes plastic wrap and clear containers such as some peanut butter jars and dishwashing liquid bottles.

5% Polyethylene terephthalate. Includes soda bottles and other clear bottles such as some cooking oil containers.

5% Polyurethane. Includes foam for insulation and furniture.

4.5% Other plastics.

Source: Franklin Associates Ltd.

Pie chart

infer that the causes are cultural, a response to the admiration of the thin female body.[9]

2. Predictions about the Future.

In the fall and winter of 1989–1990 extraordinary events shook Eastern Europe, toppling Communist regimes and raising more popular forms of government. Politicians and scholars offered predictions about future changes in the region. One expert, Zbigniew Brzezinski, former national security adviser under President Carter, concluded that the changes for the Soviet Union might be destructive.

> It would be a mistake to see the recent decisions as marking a break-through for democracy. Much more likely is a prolonged period of democ-ratizing chaos. One will see the rise in the Soviet Union of increasingly irreconcilable conflicts between varying national political and social as-pirations, all united by a shared hatred for the existing Communist no-menklatura. One is also likely to see a flashback of a nationalist type among the Great Russians, fearful of the prospective breakup of the existing Great Russian Empire.[10]

3. Solutions to Problems

How shall we solve the problems caused by young people in our cities "who commit crimes and create the staggering statistics in teen-age pregnancies and the high abortion rate"? The minister emeritus of the Abyssinian Baptist Church in New York City proposes establishment of a national youth academy with fifty campuses on inactive military bases. "It is a 'parenting' institution. . . . It is not a penal institution, not a prep school, not a Job Corps Center, not a Civilian Conservation Camp, but it borrows from them." Although such an institution has not been tried before, the author of the proposal thinks that it would represent an effort "to provide for the academic, moral, and social development of young people, to cause them to become responsible and productive citizens."[11]

Expert Opinion

For many of the subjects you discuss and write about, you will find it necessary to accept and use the opinions of experts. Based on their reading of the facts, experts express opinions on a variety of contro-versial subjects: whether capital punishment is a deterrent to crime;

---

[9] Phyllis Rose, "Hunger Artists," *Harper's,* July 1988, p. 82.

[10] *New York Times,* February 9, 1990, Sec. A, p. 13.

[11] Samuel D. Proctor, "To the Rescue: A National Youth Academy," *New York Times,* September 16, 1989, Sec. A, p. 27.

whether legalization of marijuana will lead to an increase in its use; whether children, if left untaught, will grow up honest and cooperative; whether sex education courses will result in less sexual activity and fewer illegitimate births. The interpretations of the data are often profoundly important because they influence social policy and affect our lives directly and indirectly.

For the problems mentioned above, the opinions of people recognized as authorities are more reliable than those of people who have neither thought about nor done research on the subject. But opinions may also be offered by student writers in areas in which they are knowledgeable. If you were asked, for example, to defend or refute the statement that work has advantages for teenagers, you could call on your own experience and that of your friends to support your claim. You can also draw on your experience to write convincingly about your special interests.

One opinion, however, is not as good as another. The value of any opinion depends on the quality of the evidence and the trustworthiness of the person offering it.

EVALUATION OF EVIDENCE

Before you begin to write, you must determine whether the facts and opinions you have chosen to support your claim are sound. Can they convince your readers? A distinction between the evaluation of facts and the evaluation of opinions is somewhat artificial because many facts are verified by expert opinion, but for our analysis we discuss them separately.

Evaluation of Factual Evidence

As you evaluate factual evidence, you should keep in mind the following questions:

1. Is the evidence up to date? The importance of up-to-date information depends on the subject. If you are defending the claim that suicide is immoral, you will not need to examine new data. For many of the subjects you write about, recent research and scholarship will be important, even decisive, in proving the soundness of your data. "New" does not always mean "best," but in fields where research is ongoing — education, psychology, technology, medicine, and all the natural and physical sciences — you should be sensitive to the dates of the research.

In writing a paper a few years ago warning about the health hazards of air pollution, you would have used data referring only to outdoor pollution produced by automobile and factory emissions. But writing about air pollution today, you would have to take into account new data about indoor pollution, which has become a serious problem as a result of attempts to conserve energy. Because research studies in indoor pollution are continually being updated, recent evidence will probably be more accurate than past research.

2. Is the evidence sufficient?   The amount of evidence you need depends on the complexity of the subject and the length of your paper. Given the relative brevity of most of your assignments, you will need to be selective. For the claim that indoor pollution is a serious problem, one example would obviously not be enough. For a 750-to-1,000-word paper, three or four examples would probably be sufficient. The choice of examples should reflect different aspects of the problem: in this case, different sources of indoor pollution — gas stoves, fireplaces, kerosene heaters, insulation — and the consequences for health.

Indoor pollution is a fairly limited subject for which the evidence is clear. But more complex problems require more evidence. A common fault in argument is generalization based on insufficient evidence. In a 1,000-word paper you could not adequately treat the causes of unrest in the Middle East; you could not develop workable solutions for the health-care crisis; you could not predict the development of education in the next century. In choosing a subject for a brief paper, determine whether you can produce sufficient evidence to convince a reader who may not agree with you. If not, the subject may be too large for a brief paper.

3. Is the evidence relevant?   All the evidence should, of course, contribute to the development of your argument. Sometimes the arguer loses sight of the subject and introduces examples that are wide of the claim. In defending a national health care plan, one student offered examples of the success of health maintenance organizations, but such organizations, although subsidized by the federal government, were not the structure favored by sponsors of a national health-care plan. The examples were interesting but irrelevant.

Also keep in mind that not all readers will agree on what is relevant. Is the unsavory private life of a politician relevant to his or her performance in office? If you want to prove that a politician is unfit to serve because of his or her private activities, you may first have to convince some members of the audience that private activities are relevant to public service.

4. Are the examples representative?   This question emphasizes your responsibility to choose examples that are typical of all the examples you do not use. Suppose you offered Vermont's experience to support your claim that passage of a bottle bill would reduce litter. Is the experience of Vermont typical of what is happening or may happen in other states? Or is Vermont, a small, mostly rural New England state, different enough from other states to make the example unrepresentative?

5. Are the examples consistent with the experience of the audience? The members of your audience use their own experiences to judge the soundness of your evidence. If your examples are unfamiliar or extreme, they will probably reject your conclusion. Consider the following excerpt from a flyer distributed on a university campus by the Revolutionary Communist Party.

> What is growing up female in a capitalist society? Growing up to Laverne and Shirley and the idea that female means scatterbrained broad? Being chained to the kitchen and let out on a leash to do cheap labor? Over-burdened by the hardships of trying to raise children in this putrid, degenerate society — with or without husbands?

If most members of the audience find such a characterization of female experience inconsistent with their own, they will probably question the validity of the claim.

Evaluation of Statistics

The questions you must ask about examples also apply to statistics. Are they recent? Are they sufficient? Are the relevant? Are they typical? Are they consistent with the experience of the audience? But there are additional questions directed specifically to evaluation of statistics.

1. Do the statistics come from trustworthy sources? Perhaps you have read newspaper accounts of very old people, some reported to be as old as 135, living in the Caucasus or the Andes, nourished by yogurt and hard work. But these statistics are hearsay; no birth records or other official documents exist to verify them. Now two anthropologists have concluded that the numbers were part of a rural mythology and that the ages of the people were actually within the normal range for human populations elsewhere.[12]

Hearsay statistics should be treated with the same skepticism accorded to gossip or rumor. Sampling a population to gather statistical information is a sophisticated science; you should ask whether the reporter of the statistics is qualified and likely to be free of bias. Among the generally reliable sources are polling organizations such as Gallup, Roper, and Louis Harris and agencies of the U.S. government such as the Census Bureau and the Bureau of Labor Statistics. Other qualified sources are well-known research foundations, university centers, and

---

[12] Richard B. Mazess and Sylvia H. Forman, "Longevity and Age Exaggeration in Vilcabamba, Ecuador," *Journal of Gerontology,* 1979, pp. 94–98.

insurance companies that prepare actuarial tables. Statistics from underdeveloped countries are less reliable for obvious reasons: lack of funds, lack of trained statisticians, lack of communication and transportation facilities to carry out accurate censuses.

2. Are the terms clearly defined?   In an example in Chapter 3, the reference to "poverty" (p. 70) made clear that any statistics would be meaningless unless we knew exactly how "poverty" was defined by the user. "Unemployment" is another term for which statistics will be difficult to read if the definition varies from one user to another. For example, are seasonal workers "employed" or "unemployed" during the off-season? Are part-time workers "Employed"? (In Russia they are "unemployed.") Are workers on government projects "employed"? (During the 1930s they were considered "employed" by the Germans and "unemployed" by the Americans.) The more abstract or controversial the term, the greater the necessity for clear definition.

3. Are the comparisons between comparable things?   Folk wisdom warns us that we cannot compare apples and oranges. Population statistics for the world's largest city, for example, should indicate the units being compared. Greater London is defined in one way; greater New York in another; and greater Tokyo in still another. The population numbers will mean little unless you can be sure that the same geographical units are being compared.

4. Has any significant information been omitted?   *The Plain Truth,* a magazine published by the World-Wide Church of God, advertises itself as follows:

> *The Plain Truth* has now topped 5,000,000 copies per issue. It is now the fastest-growing magazine in the world and one of the widest circulated mass-circulation magazines on earth. Our circulation is now greater than *Newsweek.* New subscribers are coming in at the rate of around 40,000 per week.

What the magazine neglects to mention is that it is *free.* There is no subscription fee, and the magazine is widely distributed in drugstores, supermarkets, and airports. *Newsweek* is sold on newsstands and by subscription. The comparison therefore omits significant information.

Evaluation of Opinions

When you evaluate the reliability of opinions in subjects with which you are not familiar, you will be dealing almost exclusively with opinions of experts. Most of the following questions are directed to an evaluation of authoritative sources. But you can also ask these questions of students or of others with opinions based on their own experience and research.

1. Is the source of the opinion qualified to give an opinion on the subject? The discussion on credibility in Chapter 1 (pp. 15–17) pointed out that certain achievements by the interpreter of the data — publications, acceptance by colleagues — can tell us something about his or her competence. Although these standards are by no means foolproof — people of outstanding reputations have been known to falsify their data — nevertheless they offer assurance that the source is generally trustworthy. The answers to questions you must ask are not hard to find: Is the source qualified by education? Is the source associated with a reputable institution — a university or a research organization? Is the source credited with having made contributions to the field — books, articles, research studies? Suppose in writing a paper recommending relaxation of rules on prescription drugs you came across an article by Michael J. Halberstam. He is identified as follows:

> Michael J. Halberstam, M.D., is a practicing cardiologist, associate clinical professor of medicine at George Washington University School of Medicine, and editor-in-chief of *Modern Medicine.* He is also a member of the advisory committee of the Center for Health Policy Research at the American Enterprise Institute.[13]

These credentials would suggest to almost any reader that Halberstam is a reliable source of information about prescription drugs.

If the source is not so clearly identified, you should treat the data with caution. Such advice is especially relevant when you are dealing with popular works about such subjects as miracle diets, formulas for instant wealth, and sightings of monsters and UFOs. Do not use such data until you can verify them from other, more authoritative sources.

In addition, you should question the identity of any source listed as "spokesperson" or "reliable source" or "an unidentified authority." The mass media are especially fond of this type of attribution. Sometimes the sources are people in public life who plant stories anonymously or off the record for purposes they prefer to keep hidden.

Even when the identification is clear and genuine, you should ask if the credentials are relevant to the field in which the authority claims expertise. So specialized are areas of scientific study today that scientists in one field may not be competent to make judgments in another. William Shockley is a distinguished engineer, a Nobel Prize winner for his contribution to the invention of the electronic transistor. But when he made the claim, based on his own research, that blacks are genetically inferior to whites, geneticists accused Shockley of venturing into

---

[13] Michael Halberstam, "Too Many Drugs?" (Washington, DC: Center for Policy Health Research, 1979), inside cover.

a field where he was unqualified to make judgments. Similarly, advertisers invite stars from the entertainment world to express opinions about products with which they are probably less familiar than members of their audience. All citizens have the right to express their views, but this does not mean that all views are equally credible or worthy of attention.

2. Is the source biased for or against his or her interpretation? Even authorities who satisfy the criteria for expertise may be guilty of bias. Bias arises as a result of economic reward, religious affiliation, political loyalty, and other interests. The expert may not be aware of the bias; even an expert can fall into the trap of ignoring evidence that contradicts his or her own intellectual preferences. A British psychologist has said:

> The search for meaning in data is bound to involve all of us in distortion to greater or lesser degree. . . . Transgression consists not so much in a clear break with professional ethics, as in an unusually high-handed, extreme or self-deceptive attempt to promote one particular view of reality at the expense of all others.[14]

Before accepting the interpretation of an expert, you should ask: Is there some reason why I should suspect the motives of this particular source?

Consider, for example, an advertisement claiming that sweetened breakfast cereals are nutritious. The advertisement, placed by the manufacturer of the cereal, provides impeccable references from scientific sources to support its claims. But since you are aware of the economic interest of the company in promoting sales, you may wonder if they have reproduced only facts that favor their claims. Are there other facts that might prove the opposite? As a careful researcher you would certainly want to look further for data about the advantages and disadvantages of sugar in our diets.

It is harder to determine bias in the research done by scientists and university members even when the research is funded by companies interested in a favorable review of their products. If you discover that a respected biologist who advocates the use of sugar in baby food receives a consultant's fee from a sugar company, should you conclude that the research is slanted and that the scientist has ignored contrary evidence? Not necessarily. The truth may be that the scientist arrived at conclusions about the use of sugar legitimately through experiments that no other scientist would question. But it would probably occur to you that a critical reader might ask about the connection between the results of the research and the payment by a company that profits from

---

[14] Liam Hudson, *The Cult of the Fact* (New York: Harper and Row, 1972), p. 125.

the research. In this case you would be wise to read further to find confirmation or rejection of the claim by other scientists.

The most difficult evaluations concern ideological bias. Early in our lives we learn to discount the special interest that makes a small child brag, "My mother (or father) is the greatest!" Later we become aware that the claims of people who are avowed Democrats or Republicans or Marxists or Yankee fans or zealous San Franciscans or joggers must be examined somewhat more carefully than those of people who have no special commitment to a cause or a place or an activity. This is not to say that all partisan claims lack support. They may, in fact, be based on the best available support. But whenever special interest is apparent, there is always the danger that an argument will reflect this bias.

3. Has the source bolstered the claim with sufficient and appropriate evidence? In an article attacking pornography, one author wrote, "Statistics prove that the recent proliferation of porno is directly related to the increasing number of rapes and assaults on women."[15] But the author gave no further information — neither statistics nor proof that a cause-effect relation exists between pornography and violence against women. The critical reader will ask, "What are the numbers? Who compiled them?"

Even those who are reputed to be experts in the subjects they discuss must do more than simply allege that a claim is valid or that the data exist. They must provide facts to support their interpretations.

When Experts Disagree

Authoritative sources can disagree. Such disagreement is probably most common in the social sciences. They are called the "soft" sciences precisely because a consensus about conclusions in these areas is more difficult to arrive at than in the natural and physical sciences. Consider the influence of television viewing on children, an issue that has divided the experts for more than a generation. Dr. William Dietz, chairman of an American Academy of Pediatrics subcommittee on children's television, deplores the effect of TV watching on children. He has said, "I have to wonder whether our children wouldn't be better off spending that time bored rather than watching television. . . . Boredom generates creativity and self-reliance." However, a recent study for the Department of Education by Daniel R. Anderson, a professor of psychology at the University of Massachusetts, and Patricia A. Collins — "The Impact of Children's Education: Television's Influence on Cognitive Development" — finds little or no evidence that television "stifles a child's

---

[15] Charlotte Allen, "Exploitation for Profit," *Daily Collegian* [University of Massachusetts], October 5, 1976, p. 2.

imagination or has a negative effect on school performance."[16] The resolution of this issue is complicated by the difficulty of controlling all the factors that affect human behavior.

But even in the natural and physical sciences, where the results of observation and experiment are more conclusive, we encounter heated differences of opinion. A popular argument concerns the extinction of the dinosaurs. Was it the effect of a comet striking the earth? Or widespread volcanic activity? Or a cooling of the planet? All these theories have their champions among the experts.

Environmental concerns also produce lively disagreements. Scientists have lined up on both sides of a debate about the importance of protecting the tropical rain forest as a source of biological, especially mammalian, diversity. Dr. Edward O. Wilson, a Harvard biologist, whose books have made us familiar with the term *biodiversity,* says, "The great majority of organisms appears to reach maximum diversity in the rain forest. There is no question that the rain forests are the world's headquarters of diversity." But in the journal *Science* another biologist, Dr. Michael Mares, a professor of zoology at the University of Oklahoma, argues that "if one could choose only a single South American habitat in which to preserve the greatest mammalian diversity, it would be the dry lands. . . . The dry lands are very likely far more highly threatened than the largely inaccessible rain forests."[17] A debate of more immediate relevance concerns the possible dangers in experiments with the AIDS virus. Dr. Robert Gallo and his colleagues at the National Cancer Institute have published a warning that "laboratory experiments involving the growing of AIDS viruses in cells that are infected with mouse viruses could generate more pathogenic AIDS viruses," which might find new routes of transmission through the air. But two experts, Dr. Stephen Goff, a molecular biologist at the College of Physicians and Surgeons at Columbia University, and Dr. Mark Feinberg, a molecular biologist at the Whitehead Institute for Biomedical Research in Cambridge, Massachusetts, are not alarmed. Dr. Feinberg says that there is no proof that "new and more deadly AIDS virus strains are being produced."[18]

How can you choose between authorities who disagree? If you have applied the tests discussed so far and discovered that one source is less qualified by training and experience or makes claims with little support or appears to be biased in favor of one interpretation, you will have no difficulty in rejecting that person's opinion. If conflicting sources prove to be equally reliable in all respects, then continue reading other authorities to determine whether a greater number of experts support one opinion rather than another. Although numbers alone, even of experts, don't guarantee the truth, nonexperts have little

[16] *Wall Street Journal,* June 13, 1989, Sec. A, p. 13.

[17] *New York Times,* April 7, 1992, Sec. C, p. 4.

[18] *New York Times,* February 16, 1990, Sec. A, p. 19.

choice but to accept the authority of the greater number until evidence to the contrary is forthcoming. Finally, if you are unable to decide between competing sources of evidence, you may conclude that the argument must remain unsettled. Such an admission is not a failure; after all, such questions are considered controversial because even the experts cannot agree, and such questions are often the most interesting to consider and argue about.

APPEALS TO NEEDS AND VALUES

Good factual evidence is usually enough to convince an audience that your factual claim is sound. Using examples, statistics, and expert opinion, you can prove, for example, that women do not earn as much as men for the same work. But even good evidence may not be enough to convince your audience that unequal pay is wrong or that something should be done about it. In making value and policy claims, an appeal to the needs and values of your audience is absolutely essential to the success of your argument. If you want to persuade the audience to change their minds or adopt a course of action — in this case, to demand legalization of equal pay for equal work — you will have to show that assent to your claim will bring about what they want and care deeply about.

As a writer, you cannot always know who your audience is; it's impossible, for example, to predict exactly who will read a letter you write to a newspaper. Even in the classroom, you have only partial knowledge of your readers. You may not always know or be able to infer what the goals and principles of your audience are. You may not know how they feel about big government, the draft, private school education, feminism, environmental protection, homosexuality, religion, or any of the other subjects you might write about. If the audience concludes that the things you care about are very different from what they care about, if they cannot identify with your goals and principles, they may treat your argument with indifference, even hostility, and finally reject it. But you can hope that decent and reasonable people will share many of the needs and values that underlie your claims.

Appeals to Needs

Suppose that you are trying to persuade Joan Doakes, a friend who is still undecided, to attend college. In your reading you have come across a report about the benefits of a college education written by Howard Bowen, a former professor of economics at Claremont (California) Graduate School, former president of Grinnell College, and a specialist in the economics of higher education. Armed with his testimony, you write to Joan. As support for your claim that she should attend college, you offer evidence that (1) college graduates earn more throughout their lifetime than high school graduates; (2) college graduates are more active and exert greater influence in their communities than high school graduates; and (3) college graduates achieve greater success as partners in marriage and as thoughtful and caring parents.[19]

Joan writes back that she is impressed with the evidence you've provided — the statistics, the testimony of economists and psychologists — and announced that she will probably enroll in college instead of accepting a job offer.

How did you succeed with Joan Doakes? If you know your friend pretty well, the answer is not difficult. Joan has needs that can be satisfied by material success; more money will enable her to enjoy the comforts and luxuries that are important to her. She also needs the esteem of her peers and the sense of achievement that political activity and service to others will give her. Finally, she needs the rootedness to be found in close and lasting family connections.

Encouraged by your success with Joan Doakes, you write the same letter to another friend, Fred Fox, who has also declined to apply for admission to college. This time, however, your argument fails. Fred, too, is impressed with your research and evidence. But college is not for him, and he repeats that he has decided not to become a student.

Why such a different response? The reason, it turns out, is that you don't know what Fred really wants. Fred Fox dreams of going to Alaska to live alone in the wilderness. Money means little to him, influence in the community is irrelevant to his goals, and at present he feels no desire to become a member of a loving family.

Perhaps if you had known Fred better, you would have offered different evidence to show that you recognized what he needed and wanted. You could have told him that Bowen's study also points out that "college-educated persons are healthier than are others," that "they also have better ability to adjust to changing times and vocations," that "going to college enhances self-discovery" and enlarges mental resources, which encourage college graduates to go on learning for the rest of their lives. This information might have persuaded Fred that college would also satisfy some of his needs.

As this example demonstrates, you have a better chance of persuading your reader to accept your claim if you know what he or she wants and what importance he or she assigns to the needs that we all share. Your reader must, in other words, see some connection between your evidence and his or her needs.

The needs to which you appealed in your letters to Joan and Fred are the requirements for physiological or psychological well-being. The

---

[19] "The Residue of Academic Learning," *Chronicle of Higher Education,* November 14, 1977, p. 13.

most familiar classification of needs was developed by the psychologist Abraham H. Maslow in 1954.[20] These needs, said Maslow, motivate human thought and action. In satisfying our needs, we attain both long- and short-term goals. Because Maslow believed that some needs are more important than others, he arranged them in hierarchical order from the most urgent biological needs to the psychological needs that are related to our roles as members of a society.

Physiological Needs. Basic bodily requirements: food and drink; health; sex

Safety Needs. Security; freedom from harm; order and stability

Belongingness and Love Needs. Love within a family and among friends; roots within a group or a community

Esteem Needs. Material success; achievement; power, status, and recognition by others

Self-actualization needs. Fulfillment in realizing one's potential

For most of your arguments you won't have to address the audience's basic physiological needs for nourishment or shelter. The desire for health, however, now receives extraordinary attention. Appeals to buy health foods, vitamin supplements, drugs, exercise and diet courses, and health books are all around us. Many of the claims are supported by little or no evidence, but readers are so eager to satisfy the need for good health that they often overlook the lack of facts or authoritative opinion. The desire for physical well-being, however, is not so simple as it seems; it is strongly related to our need for self-esteem and love.

Appeals to our needs to feel safe from harm, to be assured of order and stability in our lives are also common. Insurance companies, politicians who promise to rid our streets of crime, and companies that offer security services all appeal to this profound and nearly universal need. (We say "nearly" because some people are apparently attracted to risk and danger.) At this writing those who monitor global warming are attempting both to arouse fear for our safety and to suggest ways of reducing the dangers that make us fearful.

The last three needs in Maslow's hierarchy are the ones you will find most challenging to appeal to in your arguments. It is clear that these needs arise out of human relationships and participation in society. Advertisers make much use of appeals to these needs.

Belongingness and Love Needs.
"Whether you are young or old, the need for companionship is universal." (ad for dating service)

---

[20]*Motivation and Personality* (New York: Harper and Row, 1954), pp. 80–92.

"Share the Fun of High School with Your Little Girl!" (ad for a Barbie Doll)

Esteem Needs.
"Enrich your home with the distinction of an Oxford library."
"Apply your expertise to more challenges and more opportunities. Here are outstanding opportunities for challenge, achievement, and growth." (Perkin-Elmer Co.)

Self-actualization Needs.
"Be all that you can be." (U.S. Army)
"Are you demanding enough? Somewhere beyond the cortex is a small voice whose mere whisper can silence an army of arguments. It goes by many names: integrity, excellence, standards. And it stands alone in final judgment as to whether we have demanded enough of ourselves and, by that example, have inspired the best in those around us." *(New York Times)*

Of course, it is not only advertisers who use these appeals. We hear them from family and friends, from teachers, from employers, from editorials and letters to the editor, from people in public life.

Appeals to Values

Needs give rise to values. If we feel the need to belong to a group, we learn to value commitment, sacrifice, and sharing. And we then respond to arguments that promise to protect our values. It is hardly surprising that values, the principles by which we judge what is good or bad, beautiful or ugly, worthwhile or undesirable, should exercise a profound influence on our behavior. Virtually all claims, even those that seem to be purely factual, contain expressed or unexpressed judgments. The two scientists quoted in Chapter 2 (pp. 28–29) who presented evidence that cocaine was "deadlier than we thought," did so not for academic reasons but because they hoped to persuade people that using the drug was bad.

For our study of argument, we will speak of groups or systems of values because any single value is usually related to others. People and institutions are often defined by such systems of values. We can distinguish, for example, between those who think of themselves as traditional and those who think of themselves as modern by listing their differing values. One writer contrasts such values in this way:

> Among the values of traditionalism are: merit, accomplishment, competition, and success; self-restraint, self-discipline, and the postponement of gratification; the stability of the family; and a belief in certain moral universals. The modernist ethos scorns the pursuit of success; is egalitarian and redistributionist in emphasis; tolerates or encourages sensual gratifi-

cation; values self-expression as against self-restraint; accepts alternative or deviant forms of the family; and emphasizes ethical relativism.[21]

Systems of values are neither so rigid nor so distinct from one another as this list suggests. Some people who are traditional in their advocacy of competition and success may also accept the modernist values of self-expression and alternative family structures. One editorial writer explained the popularity of the governor of New York, Mario Cuomo:

> He embodies that rare combination of an old-fashioned liberal who has traditional, conservative family values — calling for compassion for the needy and afflicted while inveighing against a lack of discipline in American life.[22]

Values, like needs, are arranged in a hierarchy; that is, some are clearly more important than others to the people who hold them. Moreover, the arrangement may shift over time or as a result of new experiences. In 1962, for example, two speech teachers prepared a list of what they called "Relatively Unchanging Values Shared by Most Americans."[23] Included were "puritan and pioneer standards of morality" and "perennial optimism about the future." More than thirty years later, an appeal to these values might fall on a number of deaf ears.

You should also be aware of not only changes over time but also different or competing value systems that reflect a multitude of subcultures in our country. Differences in age, sex, race, ethnic background, social environment, religion, even in the personalities and characters of its members define the groups we belong to. Such terms as "honor," "loyalty," "justice," "patriotism," "duty," "responsibility," "equality," "freedom," and "courage" will be interpreted very differently by different groups.

All of us belong to more than one group, and the values of the several groups may be in conflict. If one group to which you belong, say, peers of your own age and class, is generally uninterested in and even scornful of religion, you may nevertheless hold to the values of your family and continue to place a high value on religious belief.

How can a knowledge of your readers' values enable you to make a more effective appeal? Suppose you want to argue in favor of a sex education program in the junior high school you attended. The program you support would not only give students information about contraception and venereal disease but also teach them about the pleasures of sex, the importance of small families, and alternatives to heterosexuality. If the readers of your argument are your classmates or your

---

[21] Joseph Adelson, "What Happened to the Schools," *Commentary,* March 1981, p. 37.

[22] *New York Times,* June 21, 1983, Sec. I, p. 29.

[23] Edward Steele and W. Charles Redding, "The American Value System: Premises for Persuasion," *Western Speech,* Vol. 26, Spring 1962, pp. 83–91.

peers, you can be fairly sure that their agreement will be easier to obtain than that of their parents, especially if their parents think of themselves as conservative. Your peers are more likely to value experimentation, tolerance of alternative sexual practices, freedom, and novelty. Their parents are more likely to value restraint, conformity to conventional sexual practices, obedience to family rules, and foresight in planning for the future.

Knowing that your peers share your values and your goals will mean that you need not spell out the values supporting your claim; they are understood by your readers. Convincing their parents, however, who think that freedom, tolerance, and experimentation have been abused by their children, will be a far more challenging task. In one written piece you have little chance of changing their values, a result that might be achieved only over a longer period of time. So you might first attempt to reduce their hostility by suggesting that, even if a community-wide program were adopted, students would need parental permission to enroll. This might convince some parents that you share their values regarding parental authority and primacy of the family. Second, you might look for other values to which the parents subscribe and to which you can make an appeal. Do they prize maturity, self-reliance, responsibility in their children? If so, you could attempt to prove, with authoritative evidence, that the sex education program would promote these qualities in students who took the course.

But familiarity with the value systems of prospective readers may also lead you to conclude that winning assent to your argument will be impossible. It would probably be fruitless to attempt to persuade a group of lifelong pacifists to endorse the use of nuclear weapons. The beliefs, attitudes, and habits that support their value systems are too fundamental to yield to one or two attempts at persuasion.

EVALUATION OF APPEALS TO NEEDS AND VALUES

If your argument is based on an appeal to the needs and values of your audience, the following questions will help you evaluate the soundness of your appeal.

1. Have the values been clearly defined? If you are appealing to the patriotism of your readers, can you be sure that they agree with your definition? Does patriotism mean "Our country, right or wrong!" or does it mean dissent, even violent dissent, if you think your country is wrong? Because value terms are abstractions, you must make their meaning explicit by placing them in context and providing examples.

2. Are the needs and values to which you appeal prominent in the reader's hierarchy at the time you are writing? An affluent community, fearful of further erosion of quiet and open countryside, might resist an appeal to allow establishment of a high-technology firm, even though the firm would bring increased prosperity to the area.

3. Is the evidence in your argument clearly related to the needs and values to which you appeal? Remember that the reader must see some connection between your evidence and his or her goals. Suppose you were writing an argument to persuade a group of people to vote in an upcoming election. You could provide evidence to prove that only 20 percent of the town voted in the last election. But this evidence would not motivate your audience to vote unless you could provide other evidence to show that their needs were not being served by such a low turnout.

SAMPLE ANALYSIS

Bar the Door
DANIEL JAMES

By September 30, well over 1 million people will have crossed the Mexican border into the United States illegally in the past twelve months. Illegal aliens, mainly from Mexico and Central America, have arrived at the same rate annually since 1989, the Immigration and Naturalization Service says — and the trend is upward.

Up to 5 million people are living in the United States without legal immigration papers. About 700,000 immigrants enter each year legally.

A Tulane University demographer, Leon Bouvier, projects that at least 15 million immigrants, including illegals, will arrive during the 1990s. The influx, he projects, will continue unabated until at least the year 2020. Thus we can expect perhaps 30 million or more newcomers in the first two decades of the twenty-first century. That will make the immigration wave which began in 1965 the longest and biggest ever, adding 61 million people to the population.

This influx provided the tinder for rioting in Los Angeles and the Washington Heights section of New York City. About 45 percent of South-Central Los Angeles is Hispanic, the Census Bureau says, and many of the newcomers participated in the riots.

Daniel James is the author of *Illegal Immigration — An Unfolding Crisis.* This article appeared in the *New York Times* on July 25, 1992.

Incredibly, the immigration question has received no attention from 5
Governor Bill Clinton, President Bush, and their parties, although the
statistics expose a formidable problem that increasingly impinges on
every aspect of our lives.

California, November's biggest prize, is a basket case, largely because of a flood of immigrants in the 1980s that increased its population
by 30.5 percent, to 31 million. The demands on social, health, and
educational services are soaring and threaten to cause them to break
down. No wonder California is broke. Its budget deficit is a record $14.5
billion. Even before the Los Angeles riots, it sought $1.1 billion in U.S.
aid to cover not only welfare and education needs but also health care
for 1.3 million newly legalized immigrants.

And no wonder seven out of ten Californians think the state should
limit immigration. That seems to be the national consensus, too. A
Roper poll taken between March 27 and April 14 found that 69 percent
of respondents would like to "reduce" immigration. Eight out of ten
think our immigration policies "need revision."

What revisions would prove effective and reasonable?

First, a freeze on immigration for up to five years (except for
spouses and minor children of U.S. citizens and legal residents) could
prove beneficial. This moratorium would reduce unfair competition for
scarce jobs; give our economy a chance to recover; cut social, health,
and educational costs; and relieve pressure on the environment. Above
all, it would give the millions of immigrants here an opportunity to
assimilate.

Second, we must launch an all-out drive to halt illegal entries. This 10
would involve erecting unsurmountable barriers along the fifty miles of
southern border where 90 percent of illegal aliens cross. The cost,
about $300 million, hardly compares with the $5 billion spent yearly on
benefits for illegal families. The Border Patrol should be increased to
6,000 agents (4,324 are now assigned to 2,000 miles of border), and the
National Guard and Army should be used when necessary.

Third, we should offer Mexico, the biggest source of immigrants,
an incentive: The United States would underwrite a joint effort to
"green" its northern border, enabling Mexico to increase food production and farm employment in order to deter Mexicans from heading
north for food and work.

Fourth, President Bush should air the issue with President Carlos
Salinas of Mexico and try to persuade him to discard its policy of
considering the United States a safety valve for its vast army of unemployed. He should obtain Mr. Salinas's approval to deport illegals
into the Mexican interior, where they usually originate — a key point,
since it would drastically cut the number of illegals who easily reenter
the United States because Mexican law permits them to be deported
only to the Mexican side of the border.

Our immigration policy is conducive to the proliferation of a foreign underclass that may become permanently unassimilable, thus fostering inner-city ghettoes and ethnic tensions. What's more, the economic effects of the growth of such an underclass will weaken our power to compete in the global marketplace.

Immigration Still Makes America What It Is

HARRY A. DEMELL

To the Editor:

In "Bar the Door" (Op-Ed, July 25) Daniel James tries to make a case for the closing of our borders to legal as well as undocumented immigration. The article represents a naive and uninformed approach to this complex situation. I am an immigration lawyer, and my insights and experience contradict Mr. James's conclusions.

Legal immigration is not the problem he suggests. In every generation there was a minority who felt the current wave of immigration would somehow ruin our country. In postrevolutionary America there was a wave of German immigration. The ethnic English Americans thought the Germans would destroy their society. Later the ethnic English and Germans thought the Irish immigrants would ruin the country. The nativists have always been wrong.

Between the Revolutionary War and the Civil War the population of the United States grew ten times, primarily through immigration, and still we maintained our national character while growing economically, geographically, and culturally.

Subsequent generations had their own minority opinion that the immigration of Italians, Jews, Chinese, and many others would somehow hurt the United States. We took in these immigrants, and America prospered and grew in ways unimagined at the time. The grandchildren of these immigrants continue to make the United States the most vital society the world has known. These same people are bringing ideas of democracy, freedom, individual equality, and fair play to their ethnic cousins all over the world, further increasing our country's security.

Mr. James's call to prevent legal immigration is ill advised and 5 unworkable. Restrictions on legal immigration would only bar those most likely to comply with our laws. Now we are burdened with a complex body of immigration laws and regulations that accomplish

Harry A. DeMell is an immigration attorney whose response to Daniel James appeared in the *New York Times* on August 8, 1992.

little and discourage compliance. Economic realities create a magnet for poor undocumented workers. Mexicans and others who are lucky to earn $5 a day at home will come to a country where they can earn more than that per hour.

An enlightened U.S. government policy would understand the realities of the situation and work to harness, legalize, and tax these workers. This requires workable procedures. When it becomes more profitable to comply with the law than to flout it, employers and alien workers will comply.

— Harry A. DeMell

Analysis

The subject of immigration has always generated strong reactions, both for and against, and the two authors select different evidence and appeals to different values to support their opposing claims.

The longer article by Daniel James is a policy claim, which, as the title tells us, urges tight restrictions on immigration, especially from Mexico and Central America. James's evidence for restrictions rests on a formidable array of statistics, some of which are documented, others of which must be accepted without attribution. He mentions the Immigration and Naturalization Service, a Tulane University demographer, the Census Bureau, and a Roper opinion poll, sources that confer some credibility on his numbers. But some statistics — the number of illegal immigrants, the projections into the future — are more difficult to confirm.

The numbers are very large — tens of millions of people, billions of dollars — and are clearly intended to frighten the reader. The emotional appeal throughout is primarily to fear, fear of crime and violence, which James attributes in part to Hispanic immigrants in Los Angeles and New York, higher taxes for welfare and health care, "unfair competition" for jobs, pressure on the environment, the growth of ghettoes. The language, with its selection of loaded words, is likewise inflammatory: "proliferation of a foreign underclass," "permanently unassimilable," "ethnic tensions," "unfair competition," "weaken our power to compete."

The careful organization of the argument is worth noting. It follows the classic debate form of presenting stock issues: need, plan, and advantage. (See p. 259 for discussion of this type of organization.)

DeMell's argument is a value claim, as the title makes clear. It avoids the statistical approach. Its vehicle is history and an appeal to the positive values that have made America "the most vital society the world has known." Where James frightens, DeMell reassures. Within the limits of a brief letter, his history is reasonably detailed. He cites specific waves of emigrating aliens beginning in the early nineteenth century and the hostile reception they received from those already here. By analogy, he assures his readers that, just as previous generations misjudged the impact of immigration, so the present generation has nothing to fear from present and future immigrants. On the contrary. Immigrants bring not only economic prosperity but the moral values that are the basis of a democratic society: "ideas of democracy, freedom, individual equality, and fair play." Notice that James's "illegal aliens" becomes DeMell's "undocumented workers," a far less provocative term.

DeMell's credibility is based on his own experience as an immigration lawyer. This leads him to treat only what he is most familiar with, legal immigration. The fact that he ignores James's arguments about illegal immigration may be a weakness. Some readers may also look for specific recommendations for changes in the law to oppose James's long, detailed list of proposals for controlling immigration. DeMell's aim, however, is more modest. He wants merely to counter James's pessimistic prophecies with a broad view of immigration as a continuing beneficial force in American life. But an argument by analogy is always vulnerable to the charge that differences between the things being compared — in this case, past and future immigration — may be greater than the author acknowledges.

READINGS FOR ANALYSIS

Playing Favorites
PATRICIA KEEGAN

There is strong evidence today that nurture — in the role of parents, teachers, and a society still influenced by sex stereotypes — plays an important part in determining how and what boys and girls learn. There is even stronger evidence that, particularly since the advent of the computer, the American education system is geared more closely to boys' learning styles than to those of girls. It is a bias that a growing number of projects are aiming to correct.

Studies of school and college classrooms have helped broadly define gender differences in learning. Boys, for example, are competitive, girls cooperative. Boys often prefer individual work, girls do better in groups. Boys seek leadership roles, girls are more willing to be led. Boys believe that they earn high grades, while girls more often attribute their success to luck. "How we treat boys and girls obviously affects

Patricia Keegan is a free-lance writer based in New York State who specializes in writing about education. This selection is from the Education Life supplement in the *New York Times,* August 16, 1989.

the way they learn and what they learn," said Dr. Myra Sadker, acting dean of the school of education at American University in Washington, D.C.

Dr. Sadker and her husband, Dr. David Sadker, also a professor of education at American University, have studied classroom interactions in all levels for more than a decade. In one study financed by the National Institute of Education, field researchers who observed more than one hundred fourth-, sixth-, and eight-grade classrooms in four states and the District of Columbia found that male students received more attention from teachers and were given more time to talk in class.

While boys are more assertive than girls — they are eight times more likely to call out answers — the Sadkers found that teachers also called on boys more often and gave them more positive feedback than girls. Boys also received more precise feedback from teachers — praise, criticism, or help with the answers they gave in class; girls, the Sadkers said, more often received bland and diffuse responses, such as "O.K." and "uh-huh." Most of the researchers in this and other studies found that boys got more attention whether the teachers were male or female.

Parents also affect how and what their children learn. According   5 to Dr. Jacquelynne Eccles, who is both a professor of psychology at the University of Colorado and senior research scientist at the University of Michigan, parents — particularly mothers — believe in sex-stereotyped ability more strongly today than they did in the mid-1970s when she began her research.

"Parents, teachers, and kids think boys have more ability in mathematics and sports and girls slightly more in English and music," said Dr. Eccles, who surveyed 1,000 Michigan families with school-age children. She reinterviewed one hundred families after news stories appeared on research showing that boys were genetically better in math. About half the families had read the stories. Among those who had, the parents, particularly the mothers, had lowered their opinions of their daughters' math ability.

"Their attitudes have more of an impact on kids' confidence than grades, but certainly affect the likelihood that kids will spend more time on those subjects," Dr. Eccles said.

In response to the continuing low number of girls entering the technical fields, some schools have begun programs to encourage them to take math and science courses. For example, in seventh- and eighth-grade science classes at the Montgomery Middle School, just outside Princeton, N.J., female students act as group leaders and teach lessons to their male and female classmates. Their teachers find that assigning girls leadership roles that most would not take on their own, and setting up small groups, builds the girls' self-confidence and interests in these fields.

Proponents of women's colleges take these findings a step further, arguing that their environment — in which, in the absence of men, women must assume leadership positions — encourages women to enter male-dominated fields such as science and math. A 1985 study by the Women's College Coalition, which represents most of the nation's ninety-four women's colleges, found that 5.4 percent of its graduates earned degrees in biology compared with 3.6 percent of women at coeducational colleges. In physics, the figures were 1.7 percent compared with 1.2 percent and in math, 2.3 percent compared with 1.5 percent.

The different treatment of students based on their gender has been   10
observed at all levels. In a 1975 study of classroom interaction in Suffolk County, New York, involving more than 200 children in nursery schools, two psychologists then affiliated with the State University of New York at Stony Brook, Lisa Serbin and K. Daniel O'Leary, found that teachers showed boys how to staple pieces of construction paper together for a crafts project, then let the boys do their own stapling. But the teachers did the stapling for the girls.

"Girls Taught to Be Dependent"

Although no studies of the same children have been done over the long term, Dr. O'Leary said, "The findings would suggest that girls are taught to be more dependent and boys more independent." Dr. Serbin said that in this study and in later studies of nursery-school children, she found that girls "tend to remain close to the teacher while boys are more comfortable exploring on their own, working independently without teacher structure."

Similarly, in colleges and graduate schools, professors show male students how to use equipment and perform lab experiments, while they did the work for female students.

After looking at many of the studies on college-classroom interactions, the Association of American Colleges concluded that male students also receive more eye contact and far more of the professor's attention than do female students.

The classroom climate obviously affects women's learning and intellectual self-esteem. "Women students are much less likely than their male classmates to feel confident about their preparation for and their ability to do graduate work," according to the association's 1982 report.

Yet at least one recent study shows that things can change over   15
time. Research among 4,500 adult learners at Empire State College of the State University of New York found that the women's perception of learning ability jumps ahead of the men's in their late twenties and continues higher through the early retirement years. In the midlife transition phase, between ages thirty-seven and forty-three, men think their academic acumen is significantly below that of midlife women.

Follow-up interviews, explained Dr. Timothy Lehmann, associate vice president for research and evaluation, indicate that: "By reentering college, women students more than men clearly recognize they are at a transition point. They go on to have a greater graduation rate than men."

One instrument that has provided researchers with a rich opportunity to study gender-related learning differences is the computer. In a 1987 survey of and interviews with forty-four fifth-graders, Dr. Lise Motherwell of the Massachusetts Institute of Technology found that 75 percent of the boys thought the computer was more like a machine and 60 percent of the girls said it was more like a person. "Computers have become the erector sets and doll houses of the eighties," Dr. Motherwell writes in a paper soon to be published by the National Organization for Women.

What Computers Are to Girls and Boys

A federally funded study to encourage girls' use of computers, conducted by the Women's Action Alliance, a national nonprofit organization furthering equality for women, based in New York City, yielded similar findings in its final report in 1986, titled, "The Neuter Computer: Computers for Boys and Girls." It read, "While many boys seem to enjoy the computer for its own sake — playing around with it just to see what it can do — many girls seem to value the computer for how it can help them do what they want or have to do. In other words, computers are often means for girls but ends for boys."

A 1984 survey by the Alliance as part of the same study, which examined 700 seventh- and eighth-grade students in California, Nebraska, and Vermont, found boys far more likely than girls to use the computer in school during free time and more likely to have a home computer and use it.

Hoping to reduce the disparity, the Women's Action Alliance, with money from the National Science Foundation, is sponsoring what it calls a computer-equity project involving six school districts in New York State. One of these, Orchard Park Middle School, in a suburb of Buffalo, started a computer club just for girls. The female students liked choosing their own computer activities, instead of the militaristic, competitive games usually chosen by the boys, according to Barbara Chmura, district computer coordinator. Once the girls developed more confidence about using computers, they were more likely to take part in joint projects with boys, she said. 20

Recent evidence indicates that gender-related differences in attitudes toward computers and technology continue through adulthood, even among those who use computers in their careers.

The Center for Children and Technology of the Bank Street College of Education in New York City interviewed more than seventy men and women in technological fields including architecture, engineering, computer programming, and video production. "Women in technological fields want their work to be useful, helpful, and empower others," said

Dr. Margaret Honey, senior research scientist at the center. "Men don't talk that way."

When the subjects were asked to create a perfect technological instrument, women proposed ways to humanize the computer, Dr. Honey said, while men "believed the computer has the goods and they want to be connected to it."

The ongoing Bank Street project, financed by the Spencer Foundation, now is interviewing adolescent boys and girls to find out how they view technology. The goal, as with the other programs, is to develop alternate learning programs so that girls will feel more comfortable choosing careers in technological fields still dominated by men.

Discussion Questions

1. What is the principal kind of support Keegan uses to establish her claim that parents and teachers treat boys more favorably than they treat girls? Is it convincing? Why or why not?
2. List some of the differences in the treatment of male and female students. How can they be explained? Mention some of the consequences for learners.
3. Keegan points out that things can change over time." Discuss some of the changes and their causes.

Writing Suggestions

1. Does your own experience with parents and teachers confirm or deny Keegan's conclusion? Are girls favored in some ways not treated in the article? Whether you agree or disagree with Keegan, make clear in your essay that your argument is based on limited experience.
2. Some feminists have argued that men and women perceive and react to the world differently. Keegan refers to a few of these differences in the use of computers. Are there advantages to the individual and society in reducing the differences? Are there also disadvantages?

Not Just Read and Write, but Right and Wrong

KATHLEEN KENNEDY TOWNSEND

In a suburban high school's crowded classroom, a group of juniors explained to me why drugs are difficult to control. "You see, Mrs. Townsend, what if you want a new pair of Reeboks? You could sell drugs and make $250 in an afternoon. It's a lot easier and quicker than working at McDonald's. You'd have to work there a whole week."

Kathleen Kennedy Townsend is the director of the Maryland Student Service Alliance,

In my work helping teachers, I've walked into countless high schools where I could have filled a garbage bag with the trash in the halls. Yet I rarely hear teachers asking students to pick up the garbage — or telling them not to litter in the first place.

Of course, many students obey the law, stay away from drugs, and perform selfless acts: They tutor, work with the elderly, or run antidrug campaigns. But too many lack a sense of duty to a larger community.

A survey conducted for People for the American Way asked just over 1,000 Americans between fifteen and twenty-four what goals they considered important. Three times as many selected career success as chose community service — which finished dead last. Only one-third said they could countenance joining the military or working on a political campaign. During one focus group interview for the study, some young people were asked to name qualities that make this country special. There was a long silence until one young man came up with an answer: "Cable TV."

The study concluded, "Young people have learned only half of America's story. . . . [They] reveal notions of America's unique character that emphasize freedom and license almost to the complete exclusion of service or participation . . . they fail to perceive a need to reciprocate by exercising the duties and responsibilities of good citizenship."

Failure of Schools

While it is easy enough to blame this problem on the "me-ism" of the Reagan years, it's time to recognize that *it's also the result of deliberate educational policy.* One principal I know speaks for too many others. "Schools," she says, "cannot impose duties on the students. Students come from different backgrounds. They have different standards."

Twice since 1982 the Maryland Department of Education has sent our questionnaires to local education departments soliciting opinions about values education. The answers are typical of those found across the United States. Many respondents were indifferent, simply stating that values education is "inherent" in teaching. Other answers were more hostile: "Specific training in values is a new development which we do not consider essential," and "A special effort would cause trouble."

The consensus of the high school teachers and administrators participating in a curriculum workshop I ran last summer said it all: "Values — we can't get into that."

Schools across America have simply refused to take responsibility for the character of their students. They wash their hands of the teach-

a state-sponsored program designed to get students involved with community service. This article first appeared in *The Washington Monthly,* January 1990.

ing of virtue, doing little to create an environment that teaches children the importance of self-discipline, obligation, and civic participation. As one teacher training text says, "There is no right or wrong answer to any question of value."

Is it any surprise that students tend to agree? These days it seems 10 they're all relativists. A collection of high school interviews quotes one eleventh-grader as saying, "What one person thinks is bad or wrong, another person might think that it is good or right. I don't think morals should be taught because it would cause more conflicts and mess up the student's mind." One of her classmates adds, "Moral values cannot be taught and people must learn what works for them. In other words, 'Whatever gets you through the night, it's alright.'"

Sensitivity Needed

Now it's obvious that the public schools are a ticklish arena for instilling values. Our pluralistic society is justly worried about party lines of any kind. That means that teaching values in the schools — whether as an integral part of the traditional classes or as a separate course — requires subtle skills and real sensitivity to student and community needs. Of course, families and churches should play a part, but neither are as strong or effective as they were a generation ago. Only the schools are guaranteed to get a shot at kids. That's why their current fumbling of anything smacking of right and wrong is so disastrous.

The importance of teaching values in the schools was barely mentioned at the education summit presided over by George Bush at the University of Virginia. The meeting was dominated by talk of federal funding and drug education. The underlying valuelessness of American education — an obstacle to the intelligent use of scarce resources and a root cause of drug problems — really didn't come up.

Such a curious oversight at Thomas Jefferson's school! Jefferson fought for public education because he believed that the citizen's virtue is the foundation of democracy. Only virtuous citizens, he knew, would resist private gain for the public good. And to know the public good, you have to study literature, philosophy, history, and religion.

For many years, Jefferson's wisdom about education prevailed. James Q. Wilson attributes America's low level of crime during the nineteenth century to the efforts of educators to instill self-discipline. "In the 1830s," he explains, "crime began to rise rapidly. New York had more murders than London, even though New York was only a tiny fraction of the size of London. However, rather than relying on police forces or other government programs, the citizens concentrated on education.

"Sunday schools were started. It was an all-day effort to provide 15 education in morality, education in punctuality, in decency, in following rules, and accepting responsibility, in being generous, in being kind.

"The process was so successful that in the second half of the nineteenth century, despite urbanization, despite the enormous influx into this country of immigrants from foreign countries all over Europe, despite the widening class cleavages, despite the beginning of an industrial proletariat, despite all those things which textbooks today teach us cause crime to go up, crime went down. And it went down insofar as I, or any historian, can tell because this effort to substitute the ethic of self-control for what appeared to be the emerging ethic of self-expression succeeded." In 1830 the average American drank ten gallons of distilled liquor a year. By 1850, it was down to two.

Basic Values

The flavor of this nineteenth-century approach to education is preserved today in many state constitutions. North Dakota's is typical in declaring that public schools should "emphasize all branches of knowledge that tend to impress upon the mind the importance of truthfulness, temperance, purity, public spirit, and respect for honest labor of every kind." In current educational jargon, this approach is called "values inculcation." . . .

In 1981 the California State Assembly considered a bill that spelled out values that should be included in public school instructional materials. Among those values were: honesty, acceptance of responsibility, respect for the individuality of others, respect for the responsibility inherent in being a parent or in a position of authority, the role of the work ethic in achieving personal goals, universal values of right and wrong, respect for property, the importance of the family unit, and the importance of respect for the law.

The bill was defeated.

How have we reached the point where a list of basic values like   20 that is considered unsuitable for schools? . . .

The major criticism of not teaching values is very simple: There are some values that teachers should affirm. Not all values are the same. My daughter is the only girl on her soccer team, and recently some of the boys on the team spit at her. The coach shouldn't have the boys *justify* their actions. He should have them *stop.* He should make sure they know they were wrong. That's what he should do. What he actually did tells you a lot about the schools today. He did nothing.

Discussion Questions

1. What different kinds of support does Townsend provide to establish her claim? Is the evidence sufficient to prove that instruction in values is necessary?
2. What values above all others would the author seek to promote? Why do you think she has chosen these particular values?

3. Would the nineteenth-century Sunday school effort described by James Q. Wilson work today to reduce crime? Why or why not?
4. Do you think any of the values listed in the 1981 California bill are controversial? Explain.

Writing Suggestions

1. If you have been a student in a public, private, or Sunday school where specific values were taught, directly or through literature and history, describe and evaluate the experience. Was it successful — that is, did the values taught have a meaningful influence on your life?
2. Are there some actions that are always right or wrong, regardless of the circumstances? If you think there are, choose one or two and defend your choice. (You would probably agree with Ted Koppel, who reminds us that they are the Ten Commandments, not the Ten Suggestions.) If, on the other hand, you believe that all values are relative or situational — dependent, that is, on particular circumstances — argue the proposition that any view on the rightness or wrongness of a specific action is contingent on the situation.
3. Look up President Clinton's pronouncements on a plan for national service for young people. Summarize the values that such service is intended to promote. Is national service an effective vehicle for achieving these goals?

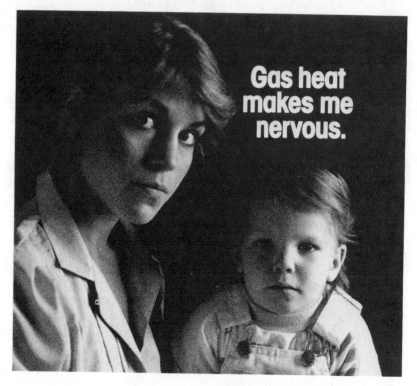

Discussion Questions

1. What strong emotional appeal does the ad make? Is it justified?
2. How would you verify the validity of the appeal?

EXERCISES FOR CRITICAL THINKING

1. What kind of evidence would you offer to prove to a skeptic that the moon landings — or any other space ventures — have actually occurred? What objections would you anticipate?

2. A group of heterosexual people in a middle-class community who define themselves as devout Christians have organized to keep a group of homosexuals from joining their church. What kind of support would you offer for your claim that the homosexuals should be welcomed into the church? Address your argument to the heterosexuals unwilling to admit the group of homosexuals.

3. In the summer of 1983, after an alarming rise in the juvenile crime rate, the mayor of Detroit instituted a curfew for young people under the age of eighteen. What kind of support can you provide for or against such a curfew?

4. "Racism [or sexism] is [not] a major problem on this campus [or home town or neighborhood]." Produce evidence to support your claim.

5. Write a full-page advertisement to solicit support for a project or cause that you believe in.

6. How do you account for the large and growing interest in science fiction films and literature? In addition to their entertainment value, are there other less obvious reasons for their popularity?

7. According to some researchers soap operas are influential in transmitting values, life-styles, and sexual information to youthful viewers. Do you agree? If so, what values and information are being transmitted? Be specific.

8. Choose one of the following stereotypical ideas and argue that it is true or false or partly both. Discuss the reasons for the existence of the stereotype.
   a. Jocks are stupid.
   b. The country is better than the city for bringing up children.
   c. TV is justly called "the boob tube."
   d. A dog is man's best friend.
   e. Beauty contests are degrading to women.

9. Defend or refute the view that organized sports build character.

10. The philosopher Bertrand Russell said, "Most of the work that most people have to do is not in itself interesting, but even such work has certain advantages." Defend or refute this assertion. Use your own experience as support.

CHAPTER FIVE

Warrants

We now come to the third element in the structure of the argument — the warrant. In the first chapter we defined the warrant as an assumption, a belief we take for granted, or a general principle. Claim and support, the other major elements we have discussed, are more familiar in ordinary discourse, but there is nothing mysterious or unusual about the warrant. All our claims, both formal and informal, are grounded in warrants or assumptions that the audience must share with us if our claims are to prove acceptable.

These warrants reflect our observations, our personal experience, and our participation in a culture. But because these observations, experiences, and cultural associations will vary, the audience may not always agree with the warrants or assumptions of the writer. The British philosopher Stephen Toulmin refers to warrants as "general, hypothetical statements, which can act as bridges" and "entitle one to draw conclusions or make claims."[1] The word *bridges* to denote the action of the warrant is crucial. One dictionary defines warrant as a "guarantee or justification." We use the word *warrant* to emphasize that in an argument it guarantees a connecting link — a bridge — between the claim and the support. This means that even if a reader agrees that the support is sound, the support cannot prove the validity of the claim unless the reader also agrees with the underlying warrant. Recall the sample argument outlined in Chapter 1 (p. 11):

> **CLAIM:** Adoption of a vegetarian diet leads to healthier and longer life.

---

[1] Stephen Toulmin, *The Uses of Argument* (Cambridge: Cambridge University Press, 1958), p. 98.

SUPPORT: The authors of *Becoming a Vegetarian Family* say so.

WARRANT: The authors of *Becoming a Vegetarian Family* are reliable sources of information on diet.

Notice that the reader must agree with the assumption that the testimony of experts is trustworthy before he or she arrives at the conclusion that a vegetarian diet is healthy. Simply providing evidence that the authors say so is not enough to prove the claim.

The following dialogue offers another example of the relationship between the warrant and the other elements of the argument.

"I don't think that Larry can do the job. He's pretty dumb."

"Really? I thought he was smart. What makes you say he's dumb?"

"Did you know that he's illiterate — can't read above third-grade level? In my book that makes him dumb."

If we put this into outline form, the warrant or assumption in the argument becomes clear.

CLAIM: Larry is pretty dumb.

EVIDENCE: He can't read above third-grade level.

WARRANT Anybody who can't read above third-grade level must be dumb.

We can also represent the argument in diagram form, which shows the warrant as a bridge between the claim and the support.

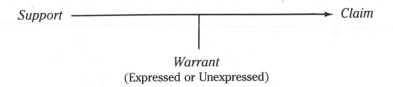

Support ⟶ *Claim*

Warrant
(Expressed or Unexpressed)

The argument above can then be written like this:

Support ⟶ *Claim*
Larry can't read above He's pretty dumb.
third-grade level.

Warrant
Anybody who can't read above third-grade
level must be pretty dumb.

Is this warrant valid? We cannot answer this question until we consider the *backing*. Every warrant or assumption rests on something else that gives it authority; this is what we call backing. Backing or authority for the warrant in this example would consist of research data that prove a relationship between stupidity and illiteracy. This particular warrant, we would discover, lacks backing because we know that the failure to learn to read may be due to a number of things unrelated to intelligence. So, if the warrant is unprovable, the claim — that Larry is dumb — is also unprovable, even if the evidence is true. In this case, then, the evidence does not guarantee the soundness of the claim.

Now consider this example of a somewhat more complicated warrant: The beautiful and unspoiled Eastern Shore of Maryland is being discovered by thousands of tourists, vacationers, and developers who will, according to the residents, change the landscape and the way of life, which is now based largely on fishing and farming. In a few years the Eastern Shore may become a noisy, crowded string of resorts. Mrs. Walkup, the Kent County commissioner, says,

> Catering to the wealthy puts property back on the tax rolls, but it's going to make the Eastern Shore look like the rest of the country. Everything that made our way of life so special is being eroded. We are a fragile area. The Eastern Shore is still special, but it is feeling pressure from all directions. Lots of people don't seem to appreciate the fact that God made us to need a little peace and quiet now and then.[2]

In simplified form the argument of those opposed to development would be outlined this way:

CLAIM: Development will bring undesirable changes to the present way of life on the Eastern Shore, a life of farming and fishing, peace and quiet.

SUPPORT: Developers will build express highways, condominiums, casinos, and nightclubs.

WARRANT: A pastoral life of fishing and farming is superior to the way of life brought by expensive, fast-paced modern development.

Notice that the warrant is a broad generalization that can apply to a number of different situations, while the claim is about a specific place and time. It should be added that in other arguments the warrant may not be stated in such general terms. However, even in arguments in which the warrant makes a more specific reference to the claim, the reader can infer an extension of the warrant to other similar arguments. In both the vegetarian diet example (p. 3, outlined on p. 11) and the example of the authority warrant below (p. 152), the warrants mention specific authors. But it is clear that such warrants can be generalized to apply to other arguments in which we accept a claim based on the credibility of the sources.

---

[2]Michael Wright, "The Changing Chesapeake," *New York Times Magazine,* July 10, 1983, p. 27.

To be convinced of the validity of Mrs. Walkup's claim, you must first find that the support is true, that the developers plan to introduce drastic changes that will destroy the pastoral life of the Eastern Shore. You may, however, believe that the support is not entirely sound, that the development will be much more modest than residents fear, and that the Eastern Shore will not be seriously altered. Next, you may want to see more justification for the warrant. Is pastoral life superior to the life that will result from large-scale development? Perhaps you have always thought that a life of fishing and farming means poverty and limited opportunities for the majority of the residents. Although the superiority of a way of life is largely a matter of taste and therefore difficult to prove, Mrs. Walkup may need to produce backing for her belief that the present way of life is more desirable than one based on developing the area for new residents and summer visitors. If you find either the support or the warrant unconvincing, you cannot accept the claim.

Remember that a claim is often modified by one or more qualifiers, which limit the claim. Mrs. Walkup might have said, "Development will *probably* destroy *some aspects of* the present way of life on the Eastern Shore." Warrants can also be modified or limited by *reservations,* which remind the reader that there are conditions under which the warrants will not be relevant. Mrs. Walkup might have added, ". . . unless increased prosperity and exposure to the outside world brought by development improve some aspects of our lives."

A diagram of Mrs. Walkup's argument shows the additional elements:

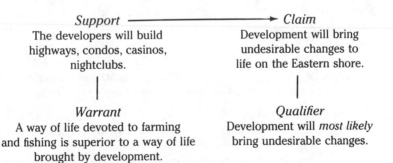

Support ──────────────▶ *Claim*
The developers will build
highways, condos, casinos,
nightclubs.

Development will bring
undesirable changes to
life on the Eastern shore.

| |

Warrant
A way of life devoted to farming
and fishing is superior to a way of life
brought by development.

Qualifier
Development will *most likely*
bring undesirable changes.

Backing
We have experienced crowds, traffic,
noise, rich strangers, high-rises, and
they destroy peace and quiet.

|

Reservation
But increased development might
improve some aspects of our lives.

Claim and support (or lack of support) are relatively easy to uncover in most arguments. One thing that makes the warrant different
is that it is often unexpressed and therefore unexamined by both writer
and reader because they take it for granted. In the argument about
Larry's intelligence, the warrant was stated. But in the argument about
development on the Eastern Shore, Mrs. Walkup did not state her warrant directly, although her meaning is perfectly clear. She probably felt
that it was not necessary to be more explicit because her readers would
understand and supply the warrant.

We can make the discovery of warrants even clearer by examining
another argument, in this case a policy claim. We've looked at a factual
claim — that Larry is dumb — and a value claim — that Eastern Shore
development is undesirable. Now we examine a policy claim that rests
on one expressed and one unexpressed warrant. Policy claims are
usually more complicated than other claims because the statement of
policy is preceded by an array of facts and values. In addition, such
claims may represent chains of reasoning in which one argument is
dependent on another. These complicated arguments may be difficult
or impossible to summarize in a simple diagram, but careful reading,
asking the same kinds of questions that the author may have asked
about his claim, can help you to find the warrant or chain of warrants
that must be accepted before evidence and claim can be linked.

In the article we examine,[3] the author argues for a radical reform
in college sports — the elimination of subprofessional intermural team
sports, as practiced above all in football and basketball. The claim is
clear, and evidence for the professional character of college sports not
hard to find: the large salaries paid to coaches, the generous perquisites
offered to players, the recruitment policies which ignore academic
standing, the virtually full-time commitment of the players, the lucrative
contracts with TV. But can this evidence support the author's claim
that such sports do not belong on college campuses? Advocates of
these sports may ask, Why not? In the conclusion of the article the
author states one warrant or assumption underlying his claim.

> Even if the money to pay college athletes could be found, though, a
> larger question must be answered — namely, why should a system of
> professional athletics be affiliated with universities at all? For the truth is
> that the requirements of athletics and academics operate at cross purposes,
> and the attempt to play both games at once serves only to reduce the level
> of performance of each.

In other words, the author assumes that the goals of an academic
education on the one hand and the goals of big-time college sports on
the other hand are incompatible. In the article he develops the ways in
which each enterprise harms the other.

But the argument clearly rests on another warrant that is not

---

[3] D. G. Myers, "Why College Sports?" *Commentary,* December 1990, pp. 49–51.

expressed because the author takes for granted that his readers will supply it: The academic goals of the university are primary and should take precedence over all other collegiate activities. This is an argument based on an authority warrant, the authority of those who define the goals of the university — scholars, public officials, university administrators, and others. (Types of warrants are discussed in the following section.)

This warrant makes clear that the evidence of the professional nature of college sports cited above supports the claim that they should be eliminated. If quasiprofessional college sports are harmful to the primary educational function of the college or university, then they must go. In the author's words, "The two are separate enterprises, to be judged by separate criteria. . . . For college sports, the university is not an educational institution at all; it is merely a locus, a means of coordinating the different aspects of the sporting enterprise."

Arguers will often neglect to state their warrants for one of two reasons: First, like Mrs. Walkup, they may believe that the warrant is obvious and need not be expressed; second, they may want to conceal the warrant in the hope that the reader will overlook its weakness.

What kinds of warrants are so obvious that they need not be expressed? Here are a few that will probably sound familiar.

Mothers love their children.

The more expensive the product, the more satisfactory it will be.

A good harvest will result in lower prices for produce.

First come, first served.

These statements seem to embody beliefs that most of us would share and that might be unnecessary to make explicit in an argument. The last statement, for example, is taken as axiomatic, an article of faith that we seldom question in ordinary circumstances. Suppose you hear someone make the claim, "I deserve to get the last ticket to the concert." If you ask why he is entitled to a ticket that you also would like to have, he may answer in support of his claim, "Because I was here first." No doubt you accept his claim without further argument because you understand and agree with the warrant that is not expressed: "If you arrive first, you deserve to be served before those who come later." Your acceptance of the warrant probably also takes into account the unexpressed backing that is based on a belief in justice: "It is only fair that those who sacrifice time and comfort to be first in line should be rewarded for their trouble."

In this case it may not be necessary to expose the warrant and examine it. Indeed, as Stephen Toulmin tells us, "If we demanded the credentials of all warrants at sight and never let one pass unchallenged, argument could scarcely begin."[4]

---

[4]*The Uses of Argument* (Cambridge: Cambridge University Press, 1958), p. 106.

But even those warrants that seem to express universal truths invite analysis if we can think of claims for which these warrants might not, after all, be relevant. "First in line," for example, may justify the claim of a person who wants a concert ticket, but it cannot in itself justify the claim of someone who wants a vital medication that is in short supply. Moreover, offering a rebuttal to a long-held but unexamined warrant can often produce an interesting and original argument. If someone exclaims, "All this buying of gifts! I think people have forgotten that Christmas celebrates the birth of Christ," she need not express the assumption — that the buying of gifts violates what ought to be a religious celebration. It goes unstated by the speaker because it has been uttered so often that she knows the hearer will supply it. But one writer, in an essay titled "Let's Keep Christmas Commercial," argued that, contrary to popular belief, the purchase of gifts, which means the expenditure of time, money, and thought on others rather than oneself, is not a violation but an affirmation of the Christmas spirit.[5]

The second reason for refusal to state the warrant lies in the arguer's intention to disarm or deceive the reader, although the arguer may not be aware of this. For instance, failure to state the warrant is common in advertising and politics, where the desire to sell a product or an idea may outweigh the responsibility to argue explicitly. The following advertisement is famous not only for what it says but for what it does not say:

> In 1918 Leona Currie scandalized a New Jersey beach with a bathing suit cut above her knees. And to irk the establishment even more, she smoked a cigarette. Leona Currie was promptly arrested.
>
> Oh, how Leona would smile if she could see you today.
>
> You've come a long way, baby. *Virginia Slims.* The taste for today's woman.

What is the unstated warrant? The manufacturer of Virginia Slims hopes we will agree that being permitted to smoke cigarettes is a significant sign of female liberation. But many readers would insist that proving "You've come a long way, baby" requires more evidence than women's freedom to smoke (or wear short bathing suits). The shaky warrant weakens the claim.

Politicians, too, conceal warrants that may not survive close scrutiny. In the 1983 mayoral election in Chicago, one candidate revealed that his opponent had undergone psychiatric treatment. He did not have to state the warrant supporting his claim. He knew that many in his audience would assume that anyone who had undergone psychiatric treatment was unfit to hold public office. This same assumption contributed to the withdrawal of a vice-presidential candidate from the 1972 campaign.

---

[5] April Oursler Armstrong, *Saturday Evening Post,* December 18, 1965, p. 8.

TYPES OF WARRANTS

In this section we show how arguments may be classified according to the types of warrants offered as proof. Because warrants represent the reasoning process by which we establish the relationship between support and claim, analysis of warrants enables us to see the whole argument as a sum of its parts.

Warrants may be organized into three categories: "*authoritative, substantive,* and *motivational.*"[6] We have already given examples of these types of warrants in this chapter and in Chapter 1. The *authoritative warrant* (see p. 12) is based on the credibility or trustworthiness of the source. If we assume that the source of the data is authoritative, then we find that the support justifies the claim. A *substantive warrant* is based on beliefs about reliability of factual evidence. In the example on page 145 the speaker assumes, although mistakenly, that the relationship between illiteracy and stupidity is a verifiable datum, one that can be proved by objective research. A *motivational warrant,* on the other hand, is based on the needs and values of the audience. For example, the warrant on page 12 reflects a preference for individual freedom, a value that would cause a reader who held it to agree that laws against marijuana should be repealed.

Seven types of warrants in these categories are examined below. Authority, of course, represents the authoritative warrant. Generalization, sign, cause and effect, comparison, and analogy are substantive warrants, based on relationships between facts in the external world. Under values you will find examples of motivational warrants, which are subjective, or a reflection of feelings and attitudes.

There are at least two good reasons for summarizing the types of warrants. First, reading these summaries will give you a number of additional examples of warrants as they work (or don't work) to justify claims. Second, it will become clear as you examine them that each type of warrant requires a different set of questions for testing its soundness. At the end of this discussion on page 159 a list of questions will help you to decide whether a particular kind of warrant is valid and can justify a particular claim. The list is not exhaustive, and you may be able to think of other criteria for evaluating warrants.

Authority

Arguments from authority depend on the credibility of their sources, as in this example.

---

[6] D. Ehninger and W. Brockriede, *Decision by Debate* (New York: Dodd, Mead, 1953).

[Benjamin] Bloom maintains that most children can learn everything that is taught them with complete competence.[7]

Because Benjamin Bloom is a professor of education at the University of Chicago and a widely respected authority on educational psychology, his statement about the educability of children carries considerable weight. Notice that Professor Bloom has qualified his claim by asserting that "most" children, but not all, can learn everything. The reader might also recognize the limits of the warrant — the authority could be mistaken, or there could be disagreement among authorities.

> CLAIM: Most children can learn everything that is taught them with complete competence.
>
> SUPPORT: Professor Bloom attests that this is so.
>
> WARRANT: Professor Bloom's testimony is sufficient because he is an accepted authority on educational achievement.
>
> RESERVATIONS: Unless the data for his studies were inaccurate, unless his criteria for evaluation were flawed, and so on.

Generalization

Arguments from generalization are based on the belief that we can derive a general principle from a series of examples. But these warrants are credible only if the examples are representative of the whole group being described and not too many contradictory examples have been ignored. In the following excerpt the author documents the tragic effects for children born "unnaturally" (outside the mother's womb) or without knowledge of their fathers.

> For years I've collected bits of data about certain unfortunate people in the news: Son of Sam, the Hillside strangler, the Pennsylvania shoemaker who raped and brutalized several women, a Florida man who killed at least thirty-four women, the man sought in connection with the Tylenol scare. All of them grew up not knowing at least one of their natural parents; most knew neither.[8]

In outline the argument takes this form:

> CLAIM: People brought up without a sense of identity with their natural parents will respond to the world with rage and violence.
>
> SUPPORT: Son of Sam, the Hillside strangler, the Pennsylvania shoemaker, the Florida murderer, the man in the Ty-

---

[7] Michael Alper, "All Our Children Can Learn," *University of Chicago Magazine,* Summer 1982, p. 3.

[8] Lorraine Dusky, "Brave New Babies?" *Newsweek,* December 6, 1982, p. 30.

lenol scare responded to the world with rage and violence.

WARRANT: What is true of this sample is true for others in this class.

RESERVATIONS: Unless this sample is too small or exceptions have been ignored.

Sign

As the name suggests, in arguments based on sign the arguer offers an observable datum as an indicator of a condition. The warrant that a sign is convincing can be accepted only if the sign is appropriate, if it is sufficient, and if other indicators do not dispute it. We have already examined one such argument, in which the enjoyment of Virginia Slims is presented as a sign of female liberation. In the following example the warrant is stated:

> There are other signs of a gradual demoting of the professions to the level of ordinary trades and businesses. The right of lawyers and physicians to advertise, so as to reintroduce money competition and break down the "standard practices," is being granted. Architects are being allowed to act as contractors. Teachers have been unionized.[9]

Here, too, a reservation is in order.

CLAIM: Professions are being demoted to the level of ordinary trades and businesses.

SUPPORT: Lawyers and physicians advertise, architects act as contractors, teachers have been unionized.

WARRANT: These business practices are signs of the demotion of the professions.

RESERVATION: Unless these practices are not widespread.

Cause and Effect

Causal reasoning assumes that one event or condition can bring about another. We can reason from the cause to the effect or from the effect to the cause. The following is an example of reasoning from effect (the claim) to cause (the warrant). The quotation is taken from the famous Supreme Court decision of 1954, *Brown v. Board of Education,* which mandated the desegregation of public schools throughout the United States.

> Segregation of white and colored children in public schools has a detrimental effect upon the colored children. The impact is greater when

---

[9] Jacques Barzun, "The Professions Under Siege," *Harper's,* October 1978, p. 66.

it has the sanction of the law; for the policy of separating the races is usually interpreted as denoting the inferiority of the Negro group. A sense of inferiority affects the motivation of a child to learn. Segregation with the sanction of law, therefore, has a tendency to [retard] the educational and mental development of Negro children and to deprive them of some of the benefits they would receive in a racial[ly] integrated school system.[10]

The outline of the argument would take this form:

CLAIM

(EFFECT): Colored children have suffered mental and emotional damage in legally segregated schools.

SUPPORT: They suffer from feelings of inferiority, which retard their ability to learn. They are being deprived of important social and educational benefits.

WARRANT

(CAUSE): Legal segregation has a tendency to retard the emotional and mental development of Negro children.

In cause-effect arguments the reasoning may be more complicated than an outline suggests. For one thing, events and conditions in the world are not always the result of single causes, nor does a cause necessarily produce a single result. It is probably more realistic to speak of chains of causes as well as chains of effects. A recent headline emphasizes this form of reasoning: "Experts Fear That Unpredictable Chain of Events Could Bring Nuclear War." The article points to the shooting of the Archduke Francis Ferdinand of Austria-Hungary in the Bosnian city of Sarajevo in 1914, which "set in motion a series of events that the world's most powerful leaders could not stop" — that is, World War I.

Or, as another example, opinion polls a few years ago indicated Americans' unwillingness to "approve any bellicose activity, unless U.S. interests are seen as truly vital and are clearly defined."[11] The immediate cause of this isolationism is usually attributed to the "Vietnam syndrome," the relic of a bitter experience in an unpopular war. But this single cause, according to some students of the problem, is insufficient to explain the current mood. History, they say, reveals "decades of similar American resistance to foreign involvements."

Causes can also be either *necessary* or *sufficient*. That is, to contract tuberculosis, it is necessary to be exposed to the bacillus, but this exposure in itself may not be sufficient to bring on the disease. However, if the victim's immune system is depressed for some reason, exposure to the bacillus will be sufficient to cause the illness. Or, to take an example from law and politics: To reduce the incidence of drunk driving,

---

[10] *Brown v. Board of Education of Topeka,* 347 U.S. 487–496 (May 17, 1954).
[11] *Public Opinion,* April–May 1982, p. 16.

it would be necessary to enact legislation that penalized the drunk driver. But that would not be sufficient unless the police and the courts were diligent in making arrests and imposing sentences.

If you are aware of the intricate relations between causes and effects, you will be cautious about proposing simple explanations or inferring simple results from some of the complex subjects you examine.

Comparison

In some arguments we compare characteristics and circumstances in two or more cases to prove that what is true in one case ought to be true in another. Unlike the elements in analogies, which we will discuss next, the things being matched in comparisons belong to the same class. The following is a familiar argument based on a comparison of similar activities in different countries at different times. On the basis of these apparent similarities the author makes a judgment about America's future.

> Perhaps I'm wrong, but the auguries seem to me threatening. Like the bourgeoisie of pre–World War I in Europe, we are retreating into our well-furnished houses, hoping the storm, when it comes, will strike someone else, preferably the poor. Our narcissistic passion for sports and fitness reminds me of Germany in the twenties and early thirties, when the entire nation turned to hiking, sun-bathing, and the worship of the body beautiful, in part so as not to see what was happening to German politics — not to speak of the family next door. The belief that gold in the garden is more important than government helped to bring France to defeat in 1940 and near civil war in the 1950s. When the middle class stops believing in government or in the future, it's all over, time truly to sew the diamonds in the lining of your coat and make a run for it.[12]

This is the argument in outline form:

CLAIM: The behavior of many middle-class Americans today threatens our future.

SUPPORT: The same kind of behavior by the Germans in the twenties and thirties and by the French in the thirties and forties led to disaster.

WARRANT: Because such behavior brought disaster to Germany and France, it will bring disaster to America.

But is this warrant believable? Are the dissimilarities between our country now and these European countries in earlier decades greater than the similarities? For example, if our present passion for sports and fitness is caused by very different social forces than those that operated

---

[12] Michael Korda, "The New Pessimism," *Newsweek,* June 14, 1982, p. 20.

in Germany in the twenties and thirties, then the comparison warrant is too weak to support the author's claim.

Analogy

An analogy warrant assumes a resemblance in some characteristics between dissimilar things. Analogies differ in their power to persuade. Some are explanatory; others are merely descriptive. Those that describe are less likely to be useful in a serious argument. In conversation we often liken human beings to other animals — cows, pigs, rats, chickens. Or we compare life and happiness to a variety of objects: "Life is a cabaret," "Life is just a bowl of cherries," "Happiness is a warm puppy." But such metaphorical uses are more colorful than precise. In those examples one quality is abstracted from all the others, leaving us with two objects that remain essentially dissimilar. Descriptive analogies promise immediate access to the reader, as do paintings or photographs. For this reason you may find the idea of such short cuts tempting, but descriptive analogies are seldom enough to support a claim. Consider the following example, which appears in a speech by Malcolm X, the black civil-rights leader, criticizing the participation by whites in the march on Washington in 1962 for black rights and employment:

> It's just like when you've got some coffee that's too black, which means it's too strong. What do you do? You integrate it with cream, you make it weak. But if you pour too much cream in it, you won't even know you ever had coffee.[13]

This is the outline of the argument:

CLAIM: Integration of black and white people in the march on Washington weakened the black movement for rights and jobs.

SUPPORT: Putting white cream into black coffee weakens the coffee.

WARRANT: Weakening coffee with cream is analogous to weakening the black rights movement by allowing white people to participate.

The imagery is vivid, but the analogy does not represent convincing proof. The dissimilarities between whitening coffee with cream and integrating a political movement are too great to convince the reader of the damaging effects of integration. Moreover, words like *strong* and *weak* as they apply to a civil-rights movement need careful definition. To make a convincing case, the author would have to offer not imagery but facts and authoritative opinion.

---

[13] "Message to the Grass Roots," *Roots of Rebellion,* edited by Richard P. Young (New York: Harper and Row, 1970), p. 357.

The following analogy is more successful because it is explanatory rather than descriptive. The elements on both sides of the analogy are failing or sick human beings and less than productive tests. This excerpt appears in an article by Albert Shanker, president of the American Federation of Teachers, deploring the low scores of American students in national mathematics tests.

> It's not the first time we've heard about the dismal performance of U.S. students in math: NAEP [National Assessment of Educational Progress] has been giving us the same bad news for twenty years. So it should come as no surprise that our kids are nowhere near "first in the world." What can we expect now? Only, I'm afraid, that another test will be administered two years from now to see if we're doing any better.
>
> Suppose you were feeling terrible and went to a doctor who tested you, said you had a fever, and asked you to come back in two weeks. And suppose you returned every couple of weeks for a year or so to be tested, and every time, you got the same bad news but still no diagnosis and no advice. Few of us would think much of a doctor who did nothing but test us and give us bad news. But that's what's been going on in education for twenty years.[14]

Mr. Shanker's argument may be outlined like this:

CLAIM: Testing students in math year after year without proposing remedies is fruitless.

SUPPORT: Testing a sick person again and again without offering a diagnosis or treatment would be considered unacceptable medical practice.

WARRANT: Math tests which fail to diagnose the problem and propose remedies are analogous to medical tests which offer no diagnosis or treatment for the patient.

This analogy, however, suffers from the weakness of all analogies — dissimilarities between the objects being compared. Many physical illnesses may be easier to diagnose and cure than deficiencies in math. The latter are certainly due to a variety of social, economic, and personal problems that are difficult or impossible for the educational system to treat.

Values

Warrants may also reflect needs and values, and readers accept or reject the claim to the extent that they find the warrants relevant to their own goals and standards. Mrs. Walkup and others based their opposition to development of the Eastern Shore on a value warrant: Rural life is superior to the way of life being introduced by developers.

---

[14] "Testing Is Not Enough," *New York Times,* October 20, 1991, Sec. E, p. 7.

Clearly, numbers of outsiders who valued a more sophisticated way of life did not agree.

The persuasive appeal of advertisements, as we know, leans heavily on value warrants, which are often unstated. Sometimes they include almost no printed message, except the name of the product accompanied by a picture. The advertisers expect us to assume that if we use their product, we can acquire the desirable characteristics of the attractive people shown using it.

Value warrants are indispensable in arguments on public policy. In the following excerpt from a radio debate, a professor of statistics at Berkeley argues in favor of affirmative action policies to promote the hiring of women faculty. Her claim has been made earlier, but her warrant and any reservations remain unstated. This is her supporting material.

> 6.9 percent is [a] very tiny proportion of the faculty. You still have to go a long ways to see a woman teaching in this university. Most all of the students go to this university and never, ever have a woman professor, a woman associate professor, even a woman assistant professor teaching them. There's a lack of role models, there's a lack of teaching, and it brings a lack of breadth into the teaching.[15]

The Berkeley professor's argument may be outlined like this:

CLAIM: The proportion of women on the Berkeley faculty should be increased.

SUPPORT: Because women are only 6.9 percent of the faculty, most students never have a woman teacher.

WARRANT: Exposure of students to women faculty is a desirable educational goal.

RESERVATION: Unless individual women faculty members are significantly less competent than men.

EVALUATION OF WARRANTS

We've pointed out that the warrant underlying your claim will define the kind of argument you are making. Answering the following questions about warrants, whether expressed or unexpressed, will help you to judge the soundness of your arguments.

---

[15] Elizabeth Scott, quoted in "Affirmative Action: Not a Black and White Issue," National Public Radio, week of April 25, 1977, p. 7.

1. *Authority*

   Is the authority sufficiently respected to make a credible claim?

   Do other equally reputable authorities agree with the authority cited?

   Are there equally reputable authorities who disagree?

2. *Generalization*

   Are sufficient examples given to convince us that a general statement is justified? That is, are the examples given representative of the whole community?

   Are there sufficient negative instances to weaken the generalization?

3. *Sign*

   Is the sign used appropriate as an indicator?

   Is the sign sufficient to account for the claim?

   Are negative signs — that is, other indicators — available that might contradict the claim?

4. *Cause and Effect*

   Does the cause given seem to account entirely for the effect?

   Are other possible causes equally important as explanations for the effect?

   Is it possible to prove that the stated cause produced the effect?

5. *Comparison*

   Are the similarities between the two situations greater than the differences?

   Have all or only a few of the important characteristics been compared? Have some important dissimilarities been overlooked?

6. *Analogy*

   Is the analogy explanatory or simply descriptive?

   Are there sufficient similarities between the two elements to make the analogy appropriate?

7. *Values*

   Is the value one that the audience will regard as important?

   Is the value relevant to the claim?

The Case for Torture

MICHAEL LEVIN

It is generally assumed that torture is impermissible, a throwback to a more brutal age. Enlightened societies reject it outright, and regimes suspected of using it risk the wrath of the United States.

I believe this attitude is unwise. There are situations in which torture is not merely permissible but morally mandatory. Moreover, these situations are moving from the realm of imagination to fact.

Suppose a terrorist has hidden an atomic bomb on Manhattan Island which will detonate at noon on July 4 unless . . . (here follow the usual demands for money and release of his friends from jail). Suppose, further, that he is caught at 10 A.M. of the fateful day, but — preferring death to failure — won't disclose where the bomb is. What do we do? If we follow due process — wait for his lawyer, arraign him — millions of people will die. If the only way to save those lives is to subject the terrorist to the most excruciating possible pain, what grounds can there be for not doing so? I suggest there are none. In any case, I ask you to face the question with an open mind.

Torturing the terrorist is unconstitutional? Probably. But millions of lives surely outweigh constitutionality. Torture is barbaric? Mass murder is far more barbaric. Indeed, letting millions of innocents die in deference to one who flaunts his guilt is moral cowardice, an unwillingness to dirty one's hands. If *you* caught the terrorist, could you sleep nights knowing that millions died because you couldn't bring yourself to apply the electrodes?

Once you concede that torture is justified in extreme cases, you 5 have admitted that the decision to use torture is a matter of balancing innocent lives against the means needed to save them. You must now face more realistic cases involving more modest numbers. Someone plants a bomb on a jumbo jet. He alone can disarm it, and his demands cannot be met (or if they can, we refuse to set a precedent by yielding to his threats). Surely we can, we must, do anything to the extortionist to save the passengers. How can we tell 300, or 100, or 10 people who never asked to be put in danger, "I'm sorry, you'll have to die in agony, we just couldn't bring ourselves to. . . ."

Here are the results of an informal poll about a third, hypothetical,

---

Michael Levin is a professor of philosophy at the City College of New York. This essay is reprinted from the June 7, 1982 issue of *Newsweek.*

case. Suppose a terrorist group kidnapped a newborn baby from a hospital. I asked four mothers if they would approve of torturing kidnappers if that were necessary to get their own newborns back. All said yes, the most "liberal" adding that she would administer it herself.

I am not advocating torture as punishment. Punishment is addressed to deeds irrevocably past. Rather, I am advocating torture as an acceptable measure for preventing future evils. So understood, it is far less objectionable than many extant punishments. Opponents of the death penalty, for example, are forever insisting that executing a murderer will not bring back his victim (as if the purpose of capital punishment were supposed to be resurrection, not deterrence or retribution). But torture, in the cases described, is intended not to bring anyone back but to keep innocents from being dispatched. The most powerful argument against using torture as a punishment or to secure confessions is that such practices disregard the rights of the individual. Well, if the individual is all that important — and he is — it is correspondingly important to protect the rights of individuals threatened by terrorists. If life is so valuable that it must never be taken, the lives of the innocents must be saved even at the price of hurting the one who endangers them.

Better precedents for torture are assassination and preemptive attack. No Allied leader would have flinched at assassinating Hitler, had that been possible. (The Allies did assassinate Heydrich.) Americans would be angered to learn that Roosevelt could have had Hitler killed in 1943 — thereby shortening the war and saving millions of lives — but refused on moral grounds. Similarly, if nation A learns that nation B is about to launch an unprovoked attack, A has a right to save itself by destroying B's military capability first. In the same way, if the police can by torture save those who would otherwise die at the hands of kidnappers or terrorists, they must.

There is an important difference between terrorists and their victims that should mute talk of the terrorists' "rights." The terrorist's victims are at risk unintentionally, not having asked to be endangered. But the terrorist knowingly initiated his actions. Unlike his victims, he volunteered for the risks of his deed. By threatening to kill for profit or idealism, he renounces civilized standards, and he can have no complaint if civilization tries to thwart him by whatever means necessary.

Just as torture is justified only to save lives (not extort confessions 10 or recantations), it is justifiably administered only to those *known* to hold innocent lives in their hands. Ah, but how can the authorities ever be sure they have the right malefactor? Isn't there a danger of error and abuse? Won't We turn into Them?

Questions like these are disingenuous in a world in which terrorists proclaim themselves and perform for television. The name of their game is public recognition. After all, you can't very well intimidate a government into releasing your freedom fighters unless you announce that it is your group that has seized its embassy. "Clear guilt" is difficult to define, but when 40 million people see a group of masked gunmen seize an airplane on the evening news, there is not much question about who the perpetrators are. There will be hard cases where the situation is murkier. Nonetheless, a line demarcating the legitimate use of torture can be drawn. Torture only the obviously guilty, and only for the sake of saving innocents, and the line between Us and Them will remain clear.

There is little danger that the Western democracies will lose their way if they choose to inflict pain as one way of preserving order. Paralysis in the face of evil is the greater danger. Some day soon a terrorist will threaten tens of thousands of lives, and torture will be the only way to save them. We had better start thinking about this.

Analysis

Levin's controversial essay attacks a popular assumption which most people have never thought to question — that torture is impermissible under any circumstances. Levin argues that in extreme cases torture is morally justified in order to bring about a greater good than the rights of the individual who is tortured.

Against the initial resistance that most readers may feel, Levin makes a strong case. Its strength lies in the backing he provides for the warrant that torture is sometimes necessary. This backing consists in the use of two effective argumentative strategies. One is the anticipation of objections. Unprecedented? No. Unconstitutional? No. Barbaric? No. Second, and more important, are the hypothetical examples that compel readers to rethink their positions and possibly arrive at agreement with the author. Levin chooses extreme examples — kidnapping of a newborn child, planting a bomb on a jumbo jet, detonating an atomic bomb in Manhattan — that draw a line between clear and murky cases and make agreement easier. And he bolsters his moral position by insisting that torture is not to be used as punishment or revenge but only in order to save innocent lives.

To support such an unpopular assumption the writer must convey the impression that he is a reasonable man, and this Levin attempts to do by a searching definition of terms, the careful organization and development of his argument, including references to the opinions of other people, and the expression of compassion for innocent lives.

Another strength of the article is its readability — the use of contractions, informal questions, conversational locutions. This easy, familiar style is disarming; the reader doesn't feel threatened by heavy admonitions from a writer who affects a superior, moral attitude.

A Proposal to Abolish Grading

PAUL GOODMAN

Let half a dozen of the prestigious Universities — Chicago, Stanford, the Ivy League — abolish grading, and use testing only and entirely for pedagogic purposes as teachers see fit.

Anyone who knows the frantic temper of the present schools will understand the transvaluation of values that would be effected by this modest innovation. For most of the students, the competitive grade has come to be the essence. The naive teacher points to the beauty of the subject and the ingenuity of the research; the shrewd student asks if he is responsible for that on the final exam.

Let me at once dispose of an objection whose unanimity is quite fascinating. I think that the great majority of professors agree that grading hinders teaching and creates a bad spirit, going as far as cheating and plagiarizing. I have before me the collection of essays, *Examining in Harvard College,* and this is the consensus. It is uniformly asserted, however, that the grading is inevitable; for how else will the graduate schools, the foundations, the corporations *know* whom to accept, reward, hire? How will the talent scouts know whom to tap?

By testing the applicants, of course, according to the specific task-requirements of the inducting institution, just as applicants for the Civil Service or for licenses in medicine, law, and architecture are tested. Why should Harvard professors do the testing *for* corporations and graduate schools?

The objection is ludicrous. Dean Whitla, of the Harvard Office of 5 Tests, points out that the scholastic-aptitude and achievement tests used for *admission* to Harvard are a super-excellent index for all-around Harvard performance, better than high-school grades or particular Harvard course-grades. Presumably, these college-entrance tests are tailored for what Harvard and similar institutions want. By the same logic, would not an employer do far better to apply his own job-aptitude test rather than to rely on the vagaries of Harvard section-men? Indeed, I doubt that many employers bother to look at such grades; they are more likely to be interested merely in the fact of a Harvard diploma,

---

Paul Goodman (1911–1972) was a college professor and writer whose outspoken views were popular with students during the 1960s. This essay is from *Compulsory Miseducation* (1964).

whatever that connotes to them. The grades have most of their weight with the graduate schools — here, as elsewhere, the system runs mainly for its own sake.

It is really necessary to remind our academics of the ancient history of Examination. In the medieval university, the whole point of the grueling trial of the candidate was whether or not to accept him as a peer. His disputation and lecture for the Master's was just that, a masterpiece to enter the guild. It was not to make comparative evaluations. It was not to weed out and select for an extramural licensor or employer. It was certainly not to pit one young fellow against another in an ugly competition. My philosophic impression is that the medievals thought they knew what a good job of work was and that we are competitive because we do not know. But the more status is achieved by largely irrelevant competitive evaluation, the less will we ever know.

(Of course, our American examinations never did have this purely guild orientation, just as our faculties have rarely had absolute autonomy; the examining was to satisfy Overseers, Elders, distant Regents — and they as paternal superiors have always doted on giving grades, rather than accepting peers. But I submit that this set-up itself makes it impossible for the student to *become* a master, to *have* grown up, and to commence on his own. He will always be making A or B for some overseer. And in the present atmosphere, he will always be climbing on his friend's neck.)

Perhaps the chief objectors to abolishing grading would be the students and their parents. The parents should be simply disregarded; their anxiety has done enough damage already. For the students, it seems to me that a primary duty of the university is to deprive them of their props, their dependence on extrinsic valuation and motivation, and to force them to confront the difficult enterprise itself and finally lose themselves in it.

A miserable effect of grading is to nullify the various uses of testing. Testing, for both student and teacher, is a means of structuring, and also of finding out what is blank or wrong and what has been assimilated and can be taken for granted. Review — including high-pressure review — is a means of bringing together the fragments, so that there are flashes of synoptic insight.

There are several good reasons for testing, and kinds of test. But if the aim is to discover weakness, what is the point of down-grading and punishing it, and thereby inviting the student to conceal his weakness, by faking and bulling, if not cheating? The natural conclusion of synthesis is the insight itself, not a grade for having had it. For the important purpose of placement, if one can establish in the student the belief that one is testing *not* to grade and make invidious comparisons but for his own advantage, the student should normally seek his own level, where he is challenged and yet capable, rather than trying to get by. If the 10 student dares to accept himself as he is, a teacher's grade is a crude instrument compared with a student's self-awareness. But it is rare in our universities that students are encouraged to notice objectively their vast confusion. Unlike Socrates, our teachers rely on power-drives rather than shame and ingenuous idealism.

Many students are lazy, so teachers try to goad or threaten them by grading. In the long run this must do more harm than good. Laziness is a character-defense. It may be a way of avoiding learning, in order to protect the conceit that one is already perfect (deeper, the despair that one *never* can be). It may be a way of avoiding just the risk of failing and being down-graded. Sometimes it is a way of politely saying, "I won't." But since it is the authoritarian grown-up demands that have created such attitudes in the first place, why repeat the trauma? There comes a time when we must treat people as adult, laziness and all. It is one thing courageously to fire a do-nothing out of your class; it is quite another thing to evaluate him with a lordly F.

Most important of all, it is often obvious that balking in doing the work, especially among bright young people who get to great universities, means exactly what it says: The work does not suit me, not this subject, or not at this time, or not in this school, or not in school altogether. The student might not be bookish; he might be school-tired; perhaps his development ought now to take another direction. Yet unfortunately, if such a student is intelligent and is not sure of himself, he *can* be bullied into passing, and this obscures everything. My hunch is that I am describing a common situation. What a grim waste of young life and teacherly effort! Such a student will retain nothing of what he has "passed" in. Sometimes he must get mononucleosis to tell his story and be believed.

And ironically, the converse is also probably commonly true. A student flunks and is mechanically weeded out, who is really ready and eager to learn in a scholastic setting, but he has not quite caught on. A good teacher can recognize the situation, but the computer wreaks its will.

Discussion Questions

1. Why do you think Goodman calls on "half a dozen of the prestigious Universities" instead of all universities to abolish grading?
2. Where does the author reveal the purposes of his proposal?
3. Most professors, Goodman argues, think that grading hinders teaching. Why, then, do they continue to give grades? How does Goodman reply to their objections?
4. What does Goodman think the real purpose of testing should be? How does grading "nullify the various uses of testing"?

Writing Suggestions

1. Do you agree that grading prevents you from learning? If so, write an essay in which you support Goodman's thesis by reporting what your own experience has been.
2. If you disagree with Goodman, write an essay that outlines the benefits of grading.
3. Is there a better way than grading to evaluate the work of students — a way that would achieve the goals of education Goodman values? Suggest a method and explain why it would be superior to grading.

Death Penalty's False Promise:
An Eye for an Eye

ANNA QUINDLEN

Ted Bundy and I go back a long way, to a time when there was a series of unsolved murders in Washington State known only as the Ted murders. Like a lot of reporters, I'm something of a crime buff. But the Washington Ted murders — and the ones that followed in Utah, Colorado, and finally in Florida, where Ted Bundy was convicted and sentenced to die — fascinated me because I could see myself as one of the victims. I looked at the studio photographs of young women with long hair, pierced ears, easy smiles, and I read the descriptions: polite, friendly, quick to help, eager to please. I thought about being approached by a handsome young man asking for help, and I knew if I had been in the wrong place at the wrong time I would have been a goner.

By the time Ted finished up in Florida, law enforcement authorities suspected he had murdered dozens of young women. He and the death penalty seemed made for each other.

The death penalty and I, on the other hand, seem to have nothing in common. But Ted Bundy has made me think about it all over again, now that the outlines of my sixties liberalism have been filled in with a decade as a reporter covering some of the worst back alleys in New York City and three years as a mother who, like most, would lay down her life for her kids.

Anna Quindlen is a regular columnist for the *New York Times.* For several years she authored "Life in the 30s," a weekly column in the same newspaper where this article appeared on September 17, 1986.

Simply put, I am opposed to the death penalty. I would tell that to any judge or lawyer undertaking the voir dire of jury candidates in a state in which the death penalty can be imposed. That is why I would be excused from such a jury. In a rational, completely cerebral way, I think the killing of one human being as punishment for the killing of another makes no sense and is inherently immoral.

But whenever my response to an important subject is rational and completely cerebral, I know there is something wrong with it — and so it is here. I have always been governed by my gut, and my gut says I am hypocritical about the death penalty. That is, I do not in theory think that Ted Bundy, or others like him, should be put to death. But if my daughter had been the one clubbed to death as she slept in a Tallahassee sorority house, and if the bite mark left in her buttocks had been one of the prime pieces of evidence against the young man charged with her murder, I would with the greatest pleasure kill him myself.

The State of Florida will not permit the parents of Bundy's victims to do that, and, in a way, that is the problem with an emotional response to capital punishment. The only reason for a death penalty is to exact retribution. Is there anyone who really thinks that it is a deterrent, that there are considerable numbers of criminals out there who think twice about committing crimes because of the sentence involved? The ones I have met in the course of my professional duties have either sneered at the justice system, where they can exchange one charge for another with more ease than they could return a shirt to a clothing store, or they have simply believed that it is the other guy who will get caught, get convicted, get the stiffest sentence. Of course, the death penalty would act as a deterrent by eliminating recidivism, but then so would life without parole, albeit at greater taxpayer expense.

I don't believe deterrence is what most proponents seek from the death penalty anyhow. Our most profound emotional response is to want criminals to suffer as their victims did. When a man is accused of throwing a child from a high-rise terrace, my emotional — some might say hysterical — response is that he should be given an opportunity to see how endless the seconds are from the thirty-first story to the ground. In a civilized society that will never happen. And so what many people want from the death penalty, they will never get.

Death is death, you may say, and you would be right. But anyone who has seen someone die suddenly of a heart attack and someone else slip slowly into the clutches of cancer knows that there are gradations of dying.

I watched a television reenactment one night of an execution by lethal injection. It was well done; it was horrible. The methodical approach, people standing around the gurney waiting, made it more awful. One moment there was a man in a prone position; the next moment that man was gone. On another night I watched a television movie about a little boy named Adam Walsh, who disappeared from a shopping center in Florida. There was a reenactment of Adam's parents coming to New York, where they appeared on morning talk shows begging for their son's return, and in their hotel room, where they received a call from the police saying that Adam had been found: not all of Adam, actually, just his severed head, discovered in the waters of a Florida canal. There is nothing anyone could do that is bad enough for an adult who took a six-year-old boy away from his parents, perhaps tortured, then murdered, him and cut off his head. Nothing at all. Lethal injection? The electric chair? Bah.

And so I come back to the position that the death penalty is wrong, 10 not only because it consists of stooping to the level of the killers, but also because it is not what it seems. Just before Ted Bundy's most recent execution date was postponed, pending further appeals, the father of his last known victim, a twelve-year-old girl, said what almost every father in his situation must feel. "I wish they'd bring him back to Lake City," said Tom Leach of the town where Kimberly Leach lived and died, "and let us all have at him." But the death penalty does not let us all have at him in the way Mr. Leach seems to mean. What he wants is for something as horrifying as what happened to his child to happen to Ted Bundy. And that is impossible.

Discussion Questions

1. "An eye for an eye" is a biblical injunction that is often misunderstood. What kind of vengeance does it prescribe?
2. What claim does Quindlen defend in this essay? (The title of the essay is a clue.) Is it explicitly stated anywhere?
3. What conflict in herself is Quindlen trying to resolve? How does she respond to the conventional arguments against capital punishment?
4. Why does she use Ted Bundy throughout as an example of the criminal condemned to death? Is his example an effective one? Explain your answer.
5. What personal references contribute most strongly to her argument?

Writing Suggestions

1. If you disagree with Quindlen's claim about capital punishment, offer a rebuttal to her argument.
2. Although it isn't always easy to make a clear distinction, we all make decisions based on both reason and emotion. Think of an important decision — choosing a lover or a marriage partner, deciding to have children, selecting a career, choosing to commit (or not commit) an illegal act — and explain how you came or would come to a conclusion based on a compromise between reason and emotion or a rejection of one in favor of the other.

Mainstreaming My Son

BARBARA GERBASI

When my son, who is afflicted with cerebral palsy and epilepsy, was nine years old, he had the opportunity to leave the school for handicapped children he had always attended and enroll in a special class in our neighborhood public school to be what is known as "mainstreamed."

Mainstreaming is the concept of placing handicapped children in the "least restrictive environment," in the words of Public Law 94-142 of 1975, the federal measure that directed the states to provide all handicapped children with a free and appropriate education. That environment was envisioned by the law's writers as one that most closely approximated the "real world," with which all children, handicapped or not, must eventually learn to deal. In practice it meant, where feasible, classrooms in public schools with "normal," or nonhandicapped children.

We parents of youngsters with disabilities uniformly applauded that idea, though we were divided into two camps. The first group said thanks, but no thanks; their children were doing just fine where they were. They had no desire to send them to a regular public school and risk exposure to possible ridicule, prejudice, and misunderstanding. They also cited the myriad of special services such as occupational, speech, and physical therapy that their children needed. Such services, they felt, could best be coordinated and provided by a special facility.

Then there were parents like myself, who embraced the concept of mainstreaming wholeheartedly. My reasons were the usual ones. Special facilities, no matter how expert, were not the real world and children attending them were too sheltered. Surrounded for the most part by others like themselves, they had few role models. Secluded, how would they learn to relate to normal people?

Professionals knowledgeable about the disabled have long agreed 5 that in the larger scheme of things social adjustment is the most important factor contributing to a satisfying existence for a handicapped individual. If a disabled person is able to function successfully in social situations, other impediments become secondary. I had serious concerns whether such social skills could be learned in a special school. Mainstreaming appeared to be the answer. Despite these beliefs, the decision to send my son to a regular school was not made easily. I

Barbara Gerbasi was a parent living in New Hyde Park, Long Island, when her article appeared in the *New York Times* Education Survey Supplement on April 4, 1985.

didn't know of any child as disabled as he who had been mainstreamed. Did he have the inner resources necessary to cope with such a change? How would the other children and the staff react to him? It was risky, but after careful thought my husband and I agreed that the possible benefits outweighed the risks.

It was 1979, and for many educators mainstreaming was an idea whose time had come. The principal of the school my son was to attend was a forward-thinking administrator who welcomed him with enthusiasm. The classroom teacher welcomed the challenge. Together they overcame all obstacles and developed a program for my son. My concern about the reaction of the other students proved unfounded. Their response was positive. Not only did they accept him, but they also vied with one another to push his wheelchair and help him in the lunchroom. He became an instant celebrity, and in the three years he spent there he thrived.

So enthralled was I about the success of this placement that I wrote about it in a newspaper article. As a result I was asked to speak about mainstreaming to various groups of parents and educators. I became a champion for the cause. My message was optimistic and convincing. See, I proclaimed, mainstreaming can indeed work. Even a very disabled child can find acceptance in a regular school. In retrospect, my vision was more than a bit shortsighted.

Elementary-school children, especially those in upper-middle-class neighborhoods, are for the most part aware, sensitive, and accepting. The problem begins in adolescence. The same qualities continue to exist, but as this stage evolves the adolescent develops a heightened awareness of himself along with accompanying doubts and insecurities. More self-absorbed now and struggling with their own perceived inadequacies, adolescents become perfunctory and superficial in their involvement with a disabled peer.

As my son has entered adolescence, the social advantages of mainstreaming have dimmed. I know it's part of puberty, but in a disabled youth, whose emotional outlets are few, the difficulties of this stage are magnified. The boy who once looked forward eagerly to Monday morning and school now can't wait for Friday. It is difficult to get him out of bed in the morning and he often says that he doesn't want to go to school.

The list of complaints is long. Everyone, he says, stares at him in 10 his wheelchair, especially the girls, and he's embarrassed. While they might converse with him in the classroom or cafeteria, they don't invite him to parties and he's unable to join their teams. Most painful of all, he can only fantasize about being part of the life of the pretty cheerleader who waves gaily to him in the hall. The attention he does receive from girls is not kind he craves. He says they pat his head and treat him like a baby. They tell him he's cute. He tells me he doesn't want to be cute. It's "cool" he aspires to be. Maybe, he says hopefully, a leather jacket and slicked-back hair would help.

Then there's also the problem of communication. Other students often have difficulty understanding him and quickly lose interest in what he has to say. Not long ago I found him removing pictures taken on vacation from the family photo album and putting them into his knapsack. They might help, he said, when he tried to tell the kids about our trip. I marvel at his ingenuity while acknowledging that it's not enough to bridge the gap.

He arrived home from school recently excited and charged with anticipation. Two of the boys had said they would be coming over on their bikes that afternoon to see him. He checked out our cookie supply and asked my opinion as to whether cocoa or juice would be the better thing to serve, and did I think they might like to play Atari. Then he positioned himself by the living room window to wait. And wait. Nervously, I busied myself in the next room, wondering what could be done to cushion the blow I was afraid was coming. Finally he asked me to call their homes and I did, already knowing the answer. Dejected, he took refuge in front of the TV.

I have begun to think that maybe he would be happier in a school with children like himself. No, it's still not the real world, but at this time in his life it might be a more comforting environment. My feelings about mainstreaming are more reserved. I don't know how realistic it is to expect that a disabled child will be accepted totally when he reaches adolescence. Change is always complex. What is right and appropriate at one stage of life may be terribly out of sync with the next.

This summer, I have arranged for my son to attend a day program for handicapped children. Maybe he'll be happier. Maybe he'll meet a cheerleader who will do more than just wave. He'll be one of the crowd again, no special treatment, and maybe that will be an adjustment. But that too is what an adolescent, handicapped or not, wants — to be one of a group; not to stand out, to be just like the others.

Discussion Questions

1. What is the warrant underlying the author's claim that mainstreaming a handicapped child may not be in his or her best interest? Has she provided backing for the warrant?
2. Summarize the issues on both sides of the debate about mainstreaming.
3. Why did the onset of adolescence create problems for the author's son? How does the author develop the answer? What is the appeal of her evidence?

4. How would you characterize the tone and language of this article? Would the message have been stronger if the language were more passionate? Explain your answer.

Writing Suggestions

1. The author suggests that her son was rejected by other adolescents in part because he was disabled. Yet some adolescents who are not disabled but who do not conform to certain standards may also be rejected by their schoolmates. What standards control adolescent attitudes and behavior? Who determines the standards? Why are most adolescents fearful of violating them? Choose a limited area for discussion — your own high school or neighborhood, an identifiable social group, a specific experience — and examine the social criteria that determine who belongs and who doesn't. Try to evaluate the significance of the consequences.
2. If your college or university offers examples of successful or unsuccessful social integration of the disabled, discuss the reasons for their success or failure.
3. Do some research into expert opinion on the advantages of mainstreaming. Elaborate on some of the advantages mentioned by the author. Try to find examples of successful mainstreaming of disabled adolescents and decide what circumstances were responsible.

THERE'S A PLACE IN THIS WORLD FOR UNUSUAL PEOPLE.

ADELPHI.

Approximately 12.6 million high school seniors will be applying to college this year.

Approximately six or seven hundred of them look at this magazine every now and then.

Approximately fifty or sixty check out the ads.

And maybe four or five, at best, bother reading them.

Congratulations. You're part of that last group. This is an ad for you.

Being significantly different from the average American high school student, perhaps you'll be interested in a significantly different university:

A school that questions the value of a typical 20th century college education as much as you probably do, and a school that attempts to provide answers to your questions with questions of its own.

And a school whose ads, instead of blathering on and on, simply invite you to learn more by calling the number below.

We sincerely hope all four or five of you flood us with replies.

ADELPHI UNIVERSITY For more information call 1-800-ADELPHI.

The Bettmann Archive

Discussion Questions

1. Which of the warrants is represented by this ad? What is its major appeal? Did you feel that the ad was really addressed to *you?* Why or why not?
2. How does the format of the ad — almost all text with a tiny picture of Theodore Roosevelt — contribute to the message of the advertiser? Why a picture of Theodore Roosevelt?
3. Through careful use of language, the writer attempts to personalize the ad. What language strategies did you notice?

Exercises for Critical Thinking

1. What are some of the assumptions underlying the preference for *natural* foods and medicines? Can *natural* be clearly defined? Is this preference part of a broader philosophy? Try to evaluate the validity of the assumption.
2. Is plagiarism wrong? What assumptions about education are relevant to the issue of plagiarism? (Some students defend it. What kinds of arguments do they provide?)
3. Choose an advertisement and examine the warrants on which the advertiser's claim is based.
4. "Religious beliefs are (or are not) necessary to a satisfactory life." Explain the warrants underlying your claim. Define any ambiguous terms.
5. Should students be given a direct voice in the hiring of faculty members? On what warrants about education do you base your answer?
6. Discuss the validity of the warrant in this statement from *The Watch Tower* (a publication of the Jehovah's Witnesses) about genital herpes: "The sexually loose are indeed 'receiving in themselves the full recompense, which was due for their error' (Romans 1:27)."
7. Read the following passage about suicide by the Greek philosopher Aristotle (adapted from his *Ethics*). Then defend or attack his argument, being careful to make clear both Aristotle's and your own warrants.

   > Just as a murderer does not have the right to take a mother from her family or a child from her parents and simultaneously to deny society the use of a productive citizen, so the suicide, even though he or she freely chooses to be his or her own victim, does not possess the right to thus diminish the welfare of so many others.

8. In view of the increasing attention to health in general, and nutrition and exercise in particular, do you think that universities and colleges should impose physical education requirements? If so, what form should they take? If not, why not? Defend your reasons.
9. In recent years both state and federal governments have been embroiled in controversies concerning the rights of citizens to engage in harmful practices. In Massachusetts, for example, a mandatory seat belt law was repealed by rebellious voters who considered the law an infringement of their freedom. What principles do you think ought to guide government regulation of dangerous practices?
10. The author of the following passage, Katherine Butler Hathaway, became a hunchback as a result of a childhood illness. Here she writes about the relationship between love and beauty from the point of view of someone who is deformed. Discuss the warrants on which the author bases her conclusion.

    > I could secretly pretend that I had a lover . . . but I could never risk showing that I thought such a thing was possible for me . . . with any man. Because of my repeated encounters with the mirror and my irrepressible tendency to forget what I had seen, I had begun to force myself to believe and to remember, and especially to remember, that I would never be chosen for what I imagined to be the supreme and most intimate of all experience. I thought of sexual love as an honor that was too great and too beautiful for the body in which I was doomed to live.

CHAPTER SIX

Language
and Thought

THE POWER OF WORDS

Words play such a critical role in argument that they deserve special treatment. Elsewhere we have referred directly and indirectly to language: Chapter 3 discusses definitions and Part Two discusses style — the choice and arrangement of words and sentences — and shows how successful writers express arguments in language that is clear, vivid, and thoughtful. An important part of these writers' equipment is a large and active vocabulary, but no single chapter in a book can give this to you; only reading and study can widen your range of word choices. Even in a brief chapter, however, we can point out how words influence the feelings and attitudes of an audience, both favorably and unfavorably.

One kind of language responsible for shaping attitudes and feelings is *emotive language,* language that expresses and arouses emotions. Understanding it and using it effectively is indispensable to the arguer who wants to move an audience to accept a point of view or undertake an action.

Long before you thought about writing your first argument, you learned that words had the power to affect you. Endearments and affectionate and flattering nicknames evoked good feelings about the speaker and yourself. Insulting nicknames and slurs produced dislike for the speaker and bad feelings about yourself. Perhaps you were told, "Sticks and stones may break your bones, but words will never hurt you." But even to a small child it is clear that ugly words are as painful as sticks and stones and that the injuries are sometimes more lasting.

Nowhere is the power of words more obvious and more familiar than in advertising, where the success of a product may depend on the feelings that certain words produce in the prospective buyer. Even the names of products may have emotive significance. In recent years a new industry, composed of consultants who supply names for products, has emerged. Although most manufacturers agree that a good name won't save a poor product, they also recognize that the right name can catch the attention of the public and persuade people to buy a product at least once. According to an article in the *Wall Street Journal*, a product name not only should be memorable but also should "remind people of emotional or physical experiences." One consultant created the name Magnum for a malt liquor from Miller Brewing Company: "The product is aimed at students, minorities, and lower-income customers." The president of the consulting firm says that Magnum "implies strength, masculinity, and more bang for your buck."[1]

Even scientists recognize the power of words to attract the attention of other scientists and the public to discoveries and theories that might otherwise remain obscure. A good name can even enable the scientist to visualize a new concept. One scientist says that "a good name," such as "quark," "black hole," "big bang," "chaos," or "great attractor," "helps in communicating a theory and can have substantial impact on financing."

It is not hard to see the connection between the use of words in conversation and advertising and the use of emotive language in the more formal arguments you will be writing. Emotive language reveals your approval or disapproval, assigns praise or blame — in other words, makes a judgment about the subject. Keep in mind that unless you are writing purely factual statements, such as scientists write, you will find it hard to avoid expressing judgments. Neutrality does not come easily, even where it may be desirable, as in news stories or reports of historical events. For this reason you need to attend carefully to the statements in your argument, making sure that you have not disguised judgments as statements of fact. Of course, in attempting to prove a claim, you will not be neutral. You will be revealing your judgment about the subject, first in the selection of facts and opinions and the emphasis you give to them and second in the selection of words.

Like the choice of facts and opinions, the choice of words can be effective or ineffective in advancing your argument, moral or immoral in the honesty with which you exercise it. The following discussions offer some insights into recognizing and evaluating the use of emotive language in the arguments you read, as well as into using such language in your own arguments where it is appropriate and avoiding it where it is not.

---

[1] *Wall Street Journal*, August 5, 1982, p. 19.

CONNOTATION

The connotations of a word are the meanings we attach to it apart from its explicit definition. Because these added meanings derive from our feelings, connotations are one form of emotive language. For example, the word *rat* denotes or points to a kind of rodent, but the attached meanings of "selfish person," "evil-doer," "betrayer," and "traitor" reflect the feelings that have accumulated around the word.

In Chapter 3 we observed that definitions of controversial terms, such as *poverty* and *unemployment,* may vary so widely that writer and reader cannot always be sure that they are thinking of the same thing. A similar problem arises when a writer assumes that the reader shares his or her emotional response to a word. Emotive meanings originate partly in personal experience. The word *home,* defined merely as "a family's place of residence," may suggest love, warmth, and security to one person; it may suggest friction, violence, and alienation to another. The values of the groups to which we belong also influence meaning. Writers and speakers count on cultural associations when they refer to our country, our flag, and heroes and enemies we have never seen. The arguer must also be aware that some apparently neutral words trigger different responses from different groups — words such as *cult, revolution, police, beauty contest,* and *corporation.*

Various reform movements have recognized that words with unfavorable connotations have the power not only to reflect but also to shape our perceptions of things. The words *Negro* and *colored* were rejected by the civil-rights movement in the 1960s because they bore painful associations with slavery and discrimination. Instead, the word *black,* which was free from such associations, became the accepted designation; more recently, the Reverend Jesse Jackson suggested another change, African American, to reflect ethnic origins. People of "Spanish-Hispanic" origin (as they are designated on the 1990 census) are now engaged in a debate about the appropriate term for a diverse population of more than 22 million American residents from Mexico, Puerto Rico, Cuba, and more than a dozen Central and South American countries. To some, the word *Hispanic* is unacceptable because it is an Anglicization and recalls the colonization of America by Spain and Portugal.

The women's liberation movement also insisted on changes that would bring about improved attitudes toward women. The movement condemned the use of *girl* for a female over the age of eighteen and the use in news stories of descriptive adjectives that emphasized the physical appearance of women. And the homosexual community succeeded in reintroducing the word *gay,* a word current centuries ago, as a substitute for words they considered offensive. Now *queer,* a word long regarded as offensive, has been adopted as a substitute for *gay* by a new generation of militant gays and lesbians, although it is still considered unacceptable by many, if not most members of the homosexual community.

Members of certain occupations have invented terms to confer greater respectability on their work. The work does not change, but the workers hope that public perceptions will change if janitors are called custodians, garbage collectors are called sanitation engineers, if undertakers are called morticians, if people who sell makeup are called cosmetologists. Events considered unpleasant or unmentionable are sometimes disguised by polite terms, called *euphemisms.* During the 1992–1993 recession new terms emerged which disguised, or tried to, the grim fact that thousands of people were being dismissed from their jobs: "skill mix adjustment," "work force imbalance correction," "redundancy elimination," "downsizing," "indefinite idling," even a daring "career-change opportunity." Many people refuse to use the word *died* and choose *passed away* instead. Some psychologists and physicians use the phrase "negative patient care outcome" for what most of us would call "death." Even when referring to their pets, some people cannot bring themselves to say "put to death" but substitute "put to sleep" or "put down." In place of a term to describe an act of sexual intercourse, some people use "slept together" or "went to bed together" or "had an affair."

Polite words are not always so harmless. If a euphemism disguises a shameful event or condition, it is morally irresponsible to use it to mislead the reader into believing that the shameful condition does not exist. In his powerful essay "Politics and the English Language" (reprinted in Part Four), George Orwell pointed out that politicians and reporters have sometimes used terms like "pacification" or "rectification of frontiers" to conceal acts that result in torture and death for millions of people. An example of such usage was cited by a member of Amnesty International, a group monitoring human rights violations throughout the world. He objected to a news report describing camps in which the Chinese were promoting "reeducation through labor." This term, he wrote, "makes these institutions seem like a cross between Police Athletic League and Civilian Conservation Corps camps." On the contrary, he went on, the reality of "reeducation through labor" was that the victims were confined to "rather unpleasant prison camps." The details he offered about the conditions under which people lived and worked gave substance to his claim.[2] More recently, when news organizations referred to the expulsion of Romanian gypsies from Germany as part of a "deportation treaty," an official of Germany's press agency objected to the use of the word "deportation." "You must know that by using

---

[2] Letter to the *New York Times,* August 30, 1982, p. 25.

words such as 'deportation' you are causing great sadness. . . . We prefer that you use the term readmission or retransfer."[3]

Perhaps the most striking examples of the way that connotations influence our perceptions of reality occur when people are asked to respond to questions of poll-takers. Sociologists and students of poll-taking know that the phrasing of a question, or the choice of words, can affect the answers and even undermine the validity of the poll. In one case poll-takers first asked a selected group of people if they favored continuing the welfare system. The majority answered no. But when the poll-takers asked if they favored government aid to the poor, the majority answered yes. Although the terms "welfare" and "government aid to the poor" refer to essentially the same forms of government assistance, "welfare" has acquired for many people negative connotations of corruption and shiftless recipients.

A *New York Times*/CBS News poll conducted in January 1989 asked, "If a woman wants to have an abortion and her doctor agrees to it, should she be allowed to have an abortion or not?" Sixty-one percent said yes, 25 percent said no, and 25 percent said it depended on the circumstances. But when the pollsters asked, "Should abortion be legal as it is now, or legal only in such cases as rape, incest, or to save the life of the mother, or should it not be permitted at all?" a much higher percentage said that abortion depended on the circumstances. Only 46 percent said it should be legal as it is now, and 41 percent said it should be legal only in such cases as rape, incest, or to save the life of the mother. According to polling experts, people are far more likely to say that they support abortion when the question is asked in terms of the "woman's right to choose" than when the question asks about "protecting the unborn child." "How the question is framed," say the experts, "can affect the answers."[4]

This is also true in polls concerning rape, another highly charged subject. Dr. Neil Malamuth, a psychologist at the University of California at Los Angeles, says, "When men are asked if there is any likelihood they would force a woman to have sex against her will if they could get away with it, about half say they would. But if you ask them if they would rape a woman if they knew they could get away with it, only about 15 percent say they would." The men who change their answers aren't aware that "the only difference is in the words used to describe the same act."[5]

The wording of an argument is crucial. Because readers may interpret the words you use on the basis of feelings different from your own, you must support your word choices with definitions and with evidence that allows readers to determine how and why you made them.

---

[3] *International Herald Tribune,* November 5, 1992.
[4] *New York Times,* January 1, 1989, p. 21.
[5] *New York Times,* August 29, 1989, Sec. C, p. 1.

SLANTING

Slanting, says one dictionary, is "interpreting or presenting in line with a special interest." The term is almost always used in a negative sense. It means that the arguer has selected facts and words with favorable or unfavorable connotations to create the impression that no alternative view exists or can be defended. For some questions it is true that no alternative view is worthy of presentation, and emotionally charged language to defend or attack a position that is clearly right or wrong would be entirely appropriate. We aren't neutral, nor should we be, about the tragic abuse of human rights anywhere in the world or even about less serious infractions of the law, such as drunk driving or vandalism, and we should use strong language to express our disapproval of these practices.

Most of your arguments, however, will concern controversial questions about which people of goodwill can argue on both sides. In such cases, your own judgments should be restrained. Slanting will suggest a prejudice — that is, a judgment made without regard to all the facts. Unfortunately, you may not always be aware of your bias or special interest; you may believe that your position is the only correct one. You may also feel the need to communicate a passionate belief about a serious problem. But if you are interested in persuading a reader to accept your belief and to act on it, you must also ask: If the reader is not sympathetic, how will he or she respond? Will he or she perceive my words as "loaded" — one-sided and prejudicial — and my view as slanted?

R. D. Laing, a Scottish psychiatrist, defined prayer in this way: "Someone is gibbering away on his knees, talking to someone who is not there."[6] This description probably reflects a sincerely held belief. Laing also clearly intended it for an audience that already agreed with him. But the phrases "gibbering away" and "someone who is not there" would be offensive to people for whom prayer is sacred.

The following remark by an editor of *Penthouse* appeared in a debate on women's liberation.

> I haven't noticed that there is such a thing as a rise in the women's liberation movement. It seems to me that it's a lot of minor sound and a tiny fury. There are some bitty bitty groups of some disappointed ladies who have some objective or other.[7]

An unfriendly audience would resent the use of language intended to diminish the importance of the movement: "minor sound," "tiny fury,"

---

[6] "The Obvious," in *The Dialectics of Liberation,* edited by David Cooper (Penguin Books, 1968), p. 17.

[7] "Women's Liberation: A Debate" (Penthouse International Ltd., 1970).

"bitty bitty group of some disappointed ladies," "some objective or other." But even audiences sympathetic to the claim may be repelled or embarrassed by intense, colorful, obviously loaded words. In 1970, Senators George McGovern and Mark Hatfield introduced an amendment to enforce America's withdrawal from the Vietnam War. A New York newspaper, violently opposed to the amendment, named it the "White Flag Amendment." An editorial called it a "bug-out scheme" designed to "sucker fence-sitting senators," "a simple and simple-minded solution" supported by "defeatists and Reds," a "cheap way out" that would reveal "the jelly content of America's spine," a "skedaddle scheme." Most readers, including those who agreed with the claim, might feel that the name-calling, slang, and exaggeration revealed a lack of dignity inappropriate to the cause they were defending. Such language is better suited to informal conversation than to serious argument.

We find slanting everywhere, not only in advertising and propaganda, where we expect to find it, but in news stories, which should be strictly neutral in their recounting of events, and in textbooks. In the field of history, for example, it is often difficult for scholars to remain impartial about significant events. Like the rest of us, they may approve or disapprove, and their choice of words will reflect their judgments.

The following passage by a distinguished Catholic historian describes the events surrounding the momentous decision by Henry VIII, king of England, to break with the Roman Catholic Church in 1534, in part because of the Pope's refusal to grant him a divorce from the Catholic princess Catherine of Aragon so that he could marry Anne Boleyn.

> The *protracted* delay in receiving an annulment was very *irritating* to the *impulsive* English king. . . . Gradually Henry's former *effusive* loyalty to Rome gave way to a settled conviction of the tyranny of the papal power, and there *rushed* to his mind the recollections of efforts of earlier English rulers to restrict that power. A few *salutary* enactments against the Church might *compel* a favorable decision from the Pope.
>
> Henry seriously opened his campaign against the Roman Church in 1531, when he *frightened* the clergy into paying a fine of over half a million dollars for violating an *obsolete* statute . . . and in the same year he *forced* the clergy to recognize himself as supreme head of the Church. . . .
>
> His *subservient* Parliament then empowered him to stop the payments of annates to the Pope and to appoint bishops in England without recourse to the papacy. *Without waiting longer* for the decision from Rome, he had Cranmer, *one of his own creatures,* whom he had just named Archbishop of Canterbury, declare his marriage null and void. . . .
>
> Yet Henry VIII encountered considerable *opposition* from the *higher clergy,* from the monks, and from many *intellectual leaders.* . . . A *popular uprising* — the Pilgrimage of Grace — was *sternly* suppressed, and such men as the *brilliant* Sir Thomas More and John Fisher, the *aged* and *saintly*

bishop of Rochester, were beheaded because they retained their former belief in papal supremacy.[8] [Italics added]

In the first paragraph the italicized words help make the following points: that Henry was rash, impulsive, and insincere and that he was intent on punishing the church (the word *salutary* means healthful or beneficial and is used sarcastically). In the second paragraph the choice of words stresses Henry's use of force and the cowardly submission of his followers. In the third paragraph the adjectives describing the opposition to Henry's campaign and those who were executed emphasize Henry's cruelty and despotism. Within the limits of this brief passage the author has offered support for his strong indictment of Henry VIII's actions, both in defining the statute as obsolete and in describing the popular opposition. In a longer exposition you would expect to find a more elaborate justification with facts and authoritative opinion from other sources.

The advocate of a position in an argument, unlike the reporter or the historian, must express a judgment, but the preceding examples demonstrate how the arguer should use language to avoid or minimize slanting and to persuade readers that he or she has come to a conclusion after careful analysis. The careful arguer must not conceal his or her judgments by presenting them as if they were statements of fact, but must offer convincing support for his or her choice of words and respect the audience's feelings and attitudes by using temperate language.

Depending on the circumstances, *exaggeration* can be defined, in the words of one writer, as "a form of lying." An essay in *Time* magazine, "Watching Out for Loaded Words," points to the danger for the arguer in relying on exaggerated language as an essential part of the argument.

> The trouble with loaded words is they tend to short-circuit thought. While they may describe something, they simultaneously try to seduce the mind into accepting a prefabricated opinion about the something described.[9]

PICTURESQUE LANGUAGE

Picturesque language consists of words that produce images in the mind of the reader. Students sometimes assume that vivid picture-making language is the exclusive instrument of novelists and poets, but writers of arguments can also avail themselves of such devices to heighten the impact of their messages.

---

[8] Carlton J. H. Hayes, *A Political and Cultural History of Modern Europe,* Vol. 1 (New York: Macmillan Company, 1933), pp. 172–173.
[9] *Time,* May 24, 1982, p. 86.

Picturesque language can do more than render a scene. It shares with other kinds of emotive language the power to express and arouse deep feelings. Like a fine painting or photograph, it can draw readers into the picture where they partake of the writer's experience as if they were also present. Such power may be used to delight, to instruct, or to horrify. In 1741 the Puritan preacher Jonathan Edwards delivered his sermon "Sinners in the Hands of an Angry God," in which people were likened to repulsive spiders hanging over the flames of Hell to be dropped into the fire whenever a wrathful God was pleased to release them. The congregation's reaction to Edwards's picture of the everlasting horrors to be suffered in the netherworld included panic, fainting, hysteria, and convulsions. Subsequently Edwards lost his pulpit in Massachusetts, in part as a consequence of his success at provoking such uncontrollable terror among his congregation.

Language as intense and vivid as Edwards's emerges from very strong emotion about a deeply felt cause. In an argument against abortion, a surgeon recounts a horrifying experience as if it were a scene in a movie.

> You walk toward the bus stop. . . . It is all so familiar. All at once you step on something soft. You feel it with your foot. Even through your shoe you may have the sense of something unusual, something marked by a special "give." It is a foreignness upon the pavement. Instinct pulls your foot away in an awkward little movement. You look down, and you see . . . a tiny naked body, its arms and legs flung apart, its head thrown back, its mouth agape, its face serious. A bird, you think, fallen from the nest. But there is no nest here on 73rd Street, no bird so big. It is rubber, then. A model, a . . . a joke. And you bend to see. Because you must. And it is no joke. Such a gray softness can be but one thing. It is a baby, and dead. You cover your mouth, your eyes. You are fixed. Horror has found its chink and crawled in, and you will never be the same as you were. Years later you will step from a sidewalk to a lawn, and you will start at its softness and think of that upon which you have just trod.[10]

Here the use of the pronoun *you* serves to draw readers into the scene and intensify their experience.

The rules governing the use of picturesque language are the same as those governing other kinds of emotive language. Is the language appropriate? Is it too strong, too colorful for the purpose of the message? Does it result in slanting or distortion? What will its impact be on a hostile or indifferent audience? Will they be angered, repelled? Will they cease to read or listen if the imagery is too disturbing?

We expect strong language in arguments about life and death. For subjects about which your feelings are not so passionate, your choice

---

[10] Richard Selzer, *Mortal Lessons: Notes on the Art of Surgery* (New York: Simon and Schuster, 1974), pp. 153–154.

of words will be more moderate. The excerpt below, from an article arguing against repeal of Sunday closing laws, creates a sympathetic picture of a market-free Sunday. Most readers, even those who oppose Sunday closing laws, would enjoy the picture and perhaps react more favorably to the argument.

> Think of waking in the city on Sunday. Although most people no longer worship in the morning, the city itself has a reverential air. It comes to life slowly, even reluctantly, as traffic lights blink their orders to empty streets. Next, joggers venture forth, people out to get the paper, families going to church or grandma's. Soon the city is its Sunday self: People cavort with their children, discuss, make repairs, go to museums, gambol. Few people go to work, and any shopping is incidental. The city on Sunday is a place outside the market. Play dominates, not the economy.[11]

CONCRETE AND ABSTRACT LANGUAGE

Writers of argument need to be aware of another use of language — the distinction between concrete and abstract. Concrete words point to real objects and real experiences. Abstract words express qualities apart from particular things and events. *Beautiful roses* is concrete; we can see, touch, and smell them. *Beauty* in the eye of the beholder is abstract; we can speak of the quality of beauty without reference to a particular object or event. *Returning money found in the street to the owner, although no one has seen the discovery* is concrete. *Honesty* is abstract. In abstracting we separate a quality shared by a number of objects or events, however different from each other the individual objects or events may be.

Writing that describes or tells a story leans heavily on concrete language. Although arguments also rely on the vividness of concrete language, they use abstract terms far more extensively than other kinds of writing. Using abstractions effectively, especially in arguments of value and policy, is important for two reasons: (1) Abstractions represent the qualities, characteristics, and values that the writer is explaining, defending, or attacking; and (2) they enable the writer to make generalizations about his or her data. Equally important is knowing when to avoid abstractions that obscure the message.

In some textbook discussions of language, abstractions are treated as inferior to concrete and specific words, but such a distinction is misleading. Abstractions allow us to make sense of our experience, to come to conclusions about the meaning of the bewildering variety of emotions and events we confront throughout a lifetime. One writer

---

[11] Robert K. Manoff, "New York City, It is Argued, Faces 'Sunday Imperialism,'" *New York Times,* January 2, 1977, Sec. IV, p. 13.

summarized his early history as follows: "My elementary school had the effect of *destroying* any *intellectual motivation,* of *stifling* all *creativity,* of *inhibiting personal relationships* with either my teachers or my peers" (emphasis added). Writing in the humanities and in some social and physical sciences would be impossible without recourse to abstractions that express qualities, values, and conditions.

You should not, however, expect abstract terms alone to carry the emotional content of your message. The effect of even the most suggestive words can be enhanced by details, examples, and anecdotes. One mode of expression is not superior to the other; both abstractions and concrete detail work together to produce clear, persuasive argument. This is especially true when the meanings assigned to abstract terms vary from reader to reader.

In establishing claims based on the support of values, for example, you may use such abstract terms as *religion, duty, freedom, peace, progress, justice, equality, democracy,* and *pursuit of happiness.* You can assume that some of these words are associated with the same ideas and emotions for almost all readers; others require further explanation. Suppose you write, "We have made great progress in the last fifty years." One dictionary defines *progress* as "a gradual betterment," another abstraction. How will you define "gradual betterment" for your readers? Can you be sure that they have in mind the same references for progress that you do? If not, misunderstandings are inevitable. You may offer examples: supersonic planes, computers, shopping malls, nuclear energy. Many of your readers will react favorably to the mention of these innovations, which to them represent progress; others, for whom these inventions represent change but not progress, will react unfavorably. You may not be able to convince all of your readers that "we have made great progress," but all of them will now understand what you mean by "progress." And intelligent disagreement is preferable to misunderstanding.

Abstractions tell us what conclusions we have arrived at; details tell us how we got there. But there are dangers in either too many details or too many abstractions. For example, a writer may present only concrete data without telling readers what conclusions are to be drawn from them. Suppose you read the following:

> To Chinese road-users, traffic police are part of the grass . . . and neither they nor the rules they're supposed to enforce are paid the least attention. . . . Ignoring traffic-lights is only one peculiarity of Chinese traffic. It's normal for a pedestrian to walk straight out into a stream of cars without so much as lifting his head; and goodness knows how many Chinese cyclists I've almost killed as they have shot blindly in front of me across busy main roads.[12]

---

[12] Philip Short, "The Chinese and the Russians," *The Listener,* April 8, 1982, p. 6.

These details would constitute no more than interesting gossip until we read, "It's not so much a sign of ignorance or recklessness . . . but of fatalism." The details of specific behavior have now acquired a significance expressed in the abstraction *fatalism.*

A more common problem, however, in using abstractions is omission of details. Either the writer is not a skilled observer and cannot provide the details, or he or she feels that such details are too small and quiet compared to the grand sounds made by abstract terms. These grand sounds, unfortunately, cannot compensate for the lack of clarity and liveliness. Lacking detailed support, abstract words may be misinterpreted. They may also represent ideas that are so vague as to be meaningless. Sometimes they function illegitimately as short cuts (discussed on pp. 188–195), arousing emotions but unaccompanied by good reasons for their use. The following paragraph exhibits some of these common faults. How would you translate it into clear English?

> We respectively petition, request, and entreat that due and adequate provision be made, this day and the date hereinafter subscribed, for the satisfying of these petitioners' nutritional requirements and for the organizing of such methods of allocation and distribution as may be deemed necessary and proper to assure the reception by and for said petitioners of such quantities of baked cereal products as shall, in the judgment of the aforesaid petitioners, constitute a sufficient supply thereof.[13]

If you had trouble decoding this, it was because there were almost no concrete references — the homely words *baked* and *cereal* leap out of the paragraph like English signposts in a foreign country — and too many long words or words of Latin origin when simple words would do: *requirements* instead of *needs, petition* instead of *ask.* An absence of concrete references and an excess of long Latinate words can have a depressing effect on both writer and reader. The writer may be in danger of losing the thread of the argument, the reader at a loss to discover the message.

The paragraph above, according to James B. Minor, a lawyer who teaches courses in legal drafting, is "how a federal regulation writer would probably write, 'Give us this day our daily bread.'" This brief sentence with its short, familiar words and its origin in the Lord's Prayer has a deep emotional effect. The paragraph composed by Minor deadens any emotional impact because of its preponderance of abstract terms and its lack of connection with the world of our senses.

That passage was invented to educate writers in the government bureaucracy to avoid inflated prose. But writing of this kind is not uncommon among professional writers, including academics. If the subject matter is unfamiliar and the writer an acknowledged expert, you may have to expend a special effort in penetrating the language.

---

[13] *New York Times,* May 10, 1977, p. 35.

But you may also rightly wonder if the writer is making unreasonable demands on you.

> The human race is now entering upon a new phase of evolutionary consciousness and progress, a phase in which, impelled by the forces of evolution itself, it must converge upon itself and convert itself into one single human organism infused by a reconciliation of knowing and being in their inner unity and destined to make a qualitative leap into a higher form of consciousness as we know it, or otherwise destroy itself. For the entire universe is one vast field, potential for incarnation, and achieving incandescence here and there of reason and spirit. And in the whole world of *quality* with which by the nature of our minds we necessarily make contact, we here and there apprehend preeminent value. This can be achieved only if we recognize that we are unable to focus our attention on the particulars of the whole, without diminishing our comprehension of the whole, and of course, conversely, we can focus on the whole only by diminishing our comprehension of the particulars which constitute the whole.[14]

You probably found this paragraph even more baffling than the previous example. Although there is some glimmer of meaning here — that mankind must attain a higher level of consciousness, or perish — you should ask whether the extraordinary overload of abstract terms is justified. In fact, most readers would be disinclined to sit still for an argument with so little reference to the real world. One critic of social science prose maintains that if preeminent thinkers like Bertrand Russell can make themselves clear but social scientists continue to be obscure, "then you can justifiably suspect that it might all be nonsense."[15]

Finally, there are the moral implications of using abstractions that conceal a disagreeable reality. George Orwell pointed them out more than forty years ago in "Politics and the English Language." Another essayist, Joseph Wood Krutch, in criticizing the attitude that cheating "doesn't really hurt anybody," observed, "'It really doesn't hurt anybody' means it doesn't do that abstraction called society any harm." The following news story reports a proposal with which Orwell and Krutch might have agreed. His intention, says the author, is to "slow the hand of any President who might be tempted to unleash a nuclear attack."

> It has long been feared that a President could be making his fateful decision while at a "psychological distance" from the victims of a nuclear barrage; that he would be in a clean, air-conditioned room, surrounded by well-scrubbed aides, all talking in abstract terms about appropriate military responses in an international crisis, and that he might well push to the

---

[14] Ruth Nanda Anshen, "Credo Perspectives," introduction to *Two Modes of Thought* by James Bryant Conant (New York: Simon and Schuster, 1964), p. x.

[15] Stanisslav Andreski, *Social Sciences as Sorcery* (New York: St. Martin's Press, 1972), p. 86.

back of his mind the realization that hundreds of millions of people would be exterminated.

So Roger Fisher, professor of law at Harvard University, offers a simple suggestion to make the stakes more real. He would put the codes needed to fire nuclear weapons in a little capsule, and implant the capsule next to the heart of a volunteer, who would carry a big butcher knife as he accompanied the President everywhere. If the President ever wanted to fire nuclear weapons, he would first have to kill, with his own hands, that human being.

He has to look at someone and realize what death is — what an innocent death is. "It's reality brought home," says Professor Fisher.[16]

The moral lesson is clear: It is much easier to do harm if we convince ourselves that the object of the injury is only an abstraction.

SHORT CUTS

Short cuts are arguments that depend on readers' responses to words. Short cuts, like other devices we have discussed so far, are a common use of emotive language but are often mistaken for valid argument.

Although they have power to move us, these abbreviated substitutes for argument avoid the hard work necessary to provide facts, expert opinion, and analysis of warrants. Even experts, however, can be guilty of using short cuts, and the writer who consults an authority should be alert to that authority's use of language. Two of the most common uses of short cuts are clichés and slogans.

Clichés

"I'm against sloppy, emotional thinking. I'm against fashionable thinking. I'm against the whole cliché of the moment."[17] This statement by the late Herman Kahn, the founder of the Hudson Institute, a famous think tank, serves as the text for this section. A cliché is an expression or idea grown stale through overuse. Clichés in language are tired expressions that have faded like old photographs; readers no longer see anything when clichés are placed before them. Clichés include phrases like "cradle of civilization," "few and far between," "rude awakening," "follow in the footsteps of," "fly in the ointment."

But more important to recognize and avoid are clichés of thought. A cliché of thought may be likened to a formula, which one dictionary defines as "any conventional rule or method for doing something, especially when used, applied, or repeated without thought." Clichés of

---

[16]*New York Times,* September 7, 1982, Sec. C, p. 1.
[17]*New York Times,* July 8, 1983, Sec. B, p. 1.

thought represent ready-made answers to questions, stereotyped so-lutions to problems, "knee-jerk" reactions. Two writers who call these forms of expression "mass language" describe it this way: "Mass language is language which presents the reader with a response he is expected to make without giving him adequate reason for having this response."[18] These "clichés of the moment" are often expressed in single words or phrases. For example, the phrase "the Me generation" has been repeated so often that it has come to represent an indisputable truth for many people, one they no longer question. The acceptance of this cliché, however, conceals the fact that millions of very different kinds of people from ages eighteen to thirty-five are being thoughtlessly lumped together as selfish and materialistic.

Certain cultural attitudes encourage the use of clichés. The liberal American tradition has been governed by hopeful assumptions about our ability to solve problems. A professor of communications says that "we tell our students that for every problem there must be a solution."[19] But real solutions are hard to come by. In our haste to provide them, to prove that we can be decisive, we may be tempted to produce familiar responses that resemble solutions.

History teaches us that a solution to an old and serious problem is almost always accompanied by unexpected drawbacks. As the writer quoted in the previous paragraph warns us, "Life is not that simple. There is no one answer to a given problem. There are multiple solutions, all with advantages and disadvantages." By solving one problem, we often create another. Automobiles, advanced medical techniques, in-dustrialization, and liberal divorce laws have all contributed to the solution of age-old problems: lack of mobility, disease, poverty, domes-tic unhappiness. We now see that these solutions bring with them new problems that we nevertheless elect to live with because the advantages seem greater than the disadvantages. A well-known economist puts it this way: "I don't look for solutions; I look for trade-offs. I think the person who asks, 'What is the solution to this problem?' has a funda-mental misconception of the way the world works. We have trade-offs, and that's all we have."[20]

This means that we should be skeptical of solutions promising everything and ignoring limitations and criticism. Such solutions have probably gone around many times. Having heard them so often, we are inclined to believe that they have been tried and proven. Thus they escape serious analysis.

---

[18] Richard E. Hughes and P. Albert Duhamel, *Rhetoric: Principles and Usage* (Engle-wood Cliffs, NJ: Prentice-Hall, 1962), p. 161.

[19] Malcolm O. Sillars, "The New Conservatism and the Teacher of Speech," *Southern Speech Journal* 21 (1956), p. 240.

[20] Thomas Sowell, "Manhattan Report" (edited transcript of *Meet the Press*) (New York: International Center for Economic Policy Studies, 1981), p. 10.

Some of these problems and their solutions represent the fashionable thinking to which Kahn objected. They confront us everywhere, like the public personalities who gaze at us week after week from the covers of magazines and tabloid newspapers at the checkout counter in the supermarket. Alarms about the failures of public education, about drug addiction or danger to the environment or teenage pregnancy are sounded throughout the media continuously. The same solutions are advocated again and again: "Back to basics"; "Impose harsher sentences"; "Offer sex education." Their popularity, however, should not prevent us from asking: Are the problems as urgent as their prominence in the media suggests? Are the solutions workable? Does sufficient evidence exist to justify their adoption?

Your arguments will not always propose solutions. They will sometimes provide interpretations of or reasons for social phenomena, especially for recurrent problems. Some explanations have acquired the status of folk wisdom, like proverbs, and careless arguers will offer them as if they needed no further support. One object of stereotyped responses is the problem of juvenile delinquency, which liberals attribute to poverty, lack of community services, meaningless education, and violence on TV. Conservatives blame parental permissiveness, decline in religious influence, lack of individual responsibility, lenient courts. Notice that the interpretations of the cause of juvenile delinquency are related to an ideology, to a particular view of the world that may prevent the arguer from recognizing any other way of examining the problem. Other stereotyped explanations for a range of social problems include inequality, competition, self-indulgence, alienation, discrimination, technology, lack of patriotism, excessive governmental regulation, and lack of sufficient governmental regulation. All of these explanations are worthy of consideration, but they must be defined and supported if they are to be used in a thoughtful, well-constructed argument.

Although formulas change with the times, some are unexpectedly hardy and survive long after critics have revealed their weaknesses. Overpopulation is an often-cited cause of poverty, disease, and war. It can be found in the writing of the ancient Greeks 2,500 years ago. "That perspective," says the editor of *Food Monitor,* a journal published by World Hunger Year, Inc., "is so pervasive that most Americans have simply stopped thinking about population and resort to inane clucking of tongues."[21] If the writer offering overpopulation as an explanation for poverty were to look further, he or she would discover that the explanation rested on shaky data. The Netherlands, the most densely populated country in the world (931 persons per square mile) is also one of the richest ($13,065 per capita income per year). Chad, one of the most sparsely populated (11 persons per square mile) is also one

---

[21] Letter to the *New York Times,* October 4, 1982, Sec. A, p. 18.

of the poorest ($158 per capita income per year).[22] Strictly defined, overpopulation may serve to explain some instances of poverty; obviously it cannot serve as a blanket to cover all or even most instances. "By repeating stock phrases," one columnist reminds us, "we lose the ability, finally, to hear what we are saying."

Clichés sometimes appear in less familiar guise. In summer 1983 Nigeria elected a new government, an important, peaceful event that received less media attention than violent events of much more trivial significance. An editorial in the *Wall Street Journal* attributed this lack of interest to our inability to look beyond cherished clichés:

> Let's be frank about this: An awful lot of people in the industrialized West just can't take seriously the idea of these underdeveloped countries conducting their own affairs in any sensible or civilized way. The cliché on the right is that you're lucky if someone imposes stability on the country long enough to let a proper mix of economic policies take hold. And the left thinks that elections aren't as important as a government that will force a presumably more equal restructuring of the nation's wealth.[23]

Slogans

> I have always been rather impressed by those people who wear badges stating where they stand on certain issues. The badges have to be small, and therefore the message has to be small, concise, and without elaboration. So it comes out as "I hate something" or "I love something," or ban this or ban that. There isn't space for argument, and I therefore envy the badge-wearer who is so clear-cut about his or her opinions.[24]

The word *slogan* has a picturesque origin. A slogan was the war cry or rallying cry of a Scottish or Irish clan. From that early use it has come to mean a "catchword or rallying motto distinctly associated with a political party or other group" as well as a "catch phrase used to advertise a product."

Slogans, like clichés, are short, undeveloped arguments. They represent abbreviated responses to often complex questions. As a reader you need to be aware that slogans merely call attention to a problem; they cannot offer persuasive proof for a claim in a dozen words or less. As a writer you should avoid the use of slogans that evoke an emotional response "without giving [the reader] adequate reason for having this response."

Advertising slogans are the most familiar. Some of them are probably better known than nursery rhymes: "Reach out and touch someone," "It costs more, but I'm worth it," "Don't leave home without it." Advertisements may, of course, rely for their effectiveness on more than

---

[22] *World Almanac and Book of Facts 1990* (New York: World Almanac, 1990), pp. 737, 698.

[23] *Wall Street Journal,* August 15, 1983, p. 16.

[24] Anthony Smith, "Nuclear Power — Why Not?" *The Listener,* October 22, 1981, p. 463.

slogans. They may also give us interesting and valuable information about products, but most advertisements give us slogans that ignore proof — short cuts substituting for argument.

The persuasive appeal of advertising slogans is heavily dependent on the connotations associated with products. In Chapter 4 (see "Appeals to Needs and Values"), we discussed the way in which advertisements promise to satisfy our needs and protect our values. Wherever evidence is scarce or nonexistent, the advertiser must persuade us through skillful choice of words and phrases (as well as pictures), especially those that produce pleasurable feelings. "Coke — it's the real thing." "Real" — as opposed to artificial or unnatural — sounds like a desirable quality. But what is "real" about Coke? Probably even the advertiser would find it hard to define the "realness" of Coke. Another familiar slogan — "Noxzema, clean makeup" — also emphasizes a quality that we approve of, but what is "clean" makeup? Since the advertisers are silent, we are left with warm feelings about the word and not much more.

Advertising slogans are persuasive because their witty phrasing and punchy rhythms produce an automatic "yes" response. We react to them as we might react to the lyrics of popular songs, and we treat them far less critically than we treat more straightforward and elaborate arguments. Still, the consequences of failing to analyze the slogans of advertisers are usually not serious. You may be tempted to buy a product because you were fascinated by a brilliant slogan, but if the product doesn't satisfy, you can abandon it without much loss. However, ignoring ideological slogans, coined by political parties or special interest groups, may carry an enormous price, and the results are not so easily undone.

Ideological slogans, like advertising slogans, depend on the power of connotation, the emotional associations aroused by a word or phrase. In the 1960s and 1970s, a period of well-advertised social change, slogans flourished; they appeared by the hundreds of thousands on buttons, T-shirts, and bumper stickers. One of them read, "Student Power!" To some readers of the slogan, distrustful of young people and worried about student unrest on campuses and in the streets, the suggestion was frightening. To others, mostly students, the idea of power, however undefined, was intoxicating. Notice that "Student Power!" is not an argument; it is only a claim. (It might also represent a warrant.) As a claim, for example, it might take this form: Students at this school should have the power to select the faculty. Of course, the arguer would need to provide the kinds of proof that support his or her claim, something the slogan by itself cannot do. Many people, whether they accepted or rejected the claim, supplied the rest of the argument without knowing exactly what the issues were and how a developed argument would proceed. They were accepting or rejecting the slogan largely on the basis of emotional reaction to words.

American political history is, in fact, a repository of slogans. Leaf through a history of the United States and you will come across "Tippecanoe and Tyler, too," "manifest destiny," "fifty-four forty or fight," "make the world safe for democracy," "the silent majority," "the domino theory," "the missile gap," "the window of vulnerability." Each administration tries to capture the attention and allegiance of the public by coining catchy phrases. Roosevelt's New Deal in 1932 was followed by the Square Deal and the New Frontier. Today, slogans must be carefully selected to avoid offending groups that are sensitive to the ways in which words affect their interests. In 1983 Senator John Glenn, announcing his candidacy for president, talked about bringing "old values and new horizons" to the White House. "New horizons" apparently carried positive connotations. His staff, however, worried that "old values" might suggest racism and sexism to minorities and women.

A professor of politics and international affairs at Princeton University explains why public officials use slogans, despite their obvious shortcomings:

> Officials long have tried to capture complicated events and to dominate public discussion of foreign policy by using simple phrases and slogans. They engage in phrase-making in order to reach wide audiences. . . .
>
> Slogans and metaphors often express the tendencies of officials and academics who have a common wish to be at once sweeping, unequivocal, easily understood, and persuasive. The desire to capture complicated phenomena through slogans stems also from impatience with the particular and unwillingness or inability to master interrelationships.[25]

Over a period of time slogans, like clichés, can acquire a life of their own and, if they are repeated often enough, come to represent an unchanging truth we no longer need to examine. "Dangerously," says the writer quoted above, "policy makers become prisoners of the slogans they popularize."

The arguments you write will not, of course, be one-sentence slogans. Unfortunately, many longer arguments amount to little more than sloganeering or series of suggestive phrases strung together to imitate the process of argumentation. Following are two examples. The first is taken from a full-page magazine advertisement in 1983, urging the formation of a new political party. The second is part of the second inaugural address of George C. Wallace, governor of Alabama, in 1971. These extracts are typical of the full advertisement and the full speech.

> We can't dislodge big money from its domination over the two old parties, but we can offer the country something better: a new party that represents the people and responds to their needs. . . . How can we solve any problem without correcting the cause — the structure of the Dem/Rep machine and the power of the military-industrial establishment? . . . The power of the people could be a commanding force if only we could get

---

[25] Henry Bienen, "Slogans Aren't the World," *New York Times,* January 16, 1983, Sec. IV, p. 19.

together — Labor, public-interest organizations, blacks, women, antinu-clear groups, and all the others.[26]

The people of the South and those who think like the South, represent the majority viewpoint within our constitutional democracy, but they are not organized and do not speak with a loud voice. Until the day arrives when the voice of the people of the South and those who think like us is, within the law, thrust into the face of the bureaucrats, only then can the "people's power" express itself legally and ethically and get results. . . . Too long, oh, too long, has the voice of the people been silenced by their own disruptive government — by governmental bribery in quasi-govern-mental handouts such as H.E.W. and others that exist in America today! An aroused people can save this nation from those evil forces who seek our destruction. The choice is yours. The hour is growing late![27]

Whatever power these recommendations might have if their pro-posals were more clearly formulated, as they stand they are collections of slogans and loaded words. (Even the language falters; can the voice of the people be thrust into the face of the bureaucrats?) We can visualize some of the slogans as brightly colored banners: "Dislodge Big Money!" "Power to the People!" "Save This Nation from Evil Forces!" "The Choice Is Yours!" Do all the groups mentioned share identical interests? If so, what are they? Given the vagueness of the terms, it is not surprising that arguers on opposite sides of the political spec-trum — loosely characterized as liberal and conservative — sometimes resort to the same clichés and slogans: the language of populism, or a belief in the virtues of the "common people" in these examples.

Slogans have numerous shortcomings as substitutes for the devel-opment of an argument. First, their brevity presents serious disadvan-tages. Slogans necessarily ignore exceptions or negative instances that might qualify a claim. They usually speak in absolute terms without describing the circumstances in which a principle or idea might not work. Their claims therefore seem shrill and exaggerated. In addition, brevity prevents the sloganeer from revealing how he or she arrived at conclusions.

Second, slogans may conceal unexamined warrants. When Japanese cars were beginning to compete with American cars, the slogan "Made in America by Americans" appeared on the bumpers of thousands of American-made cars. A thoughtful reader would have discovered in this slogan several implied warrants: American cars are better than Japanese cars; the American economy will improve if we buy American; patriot-ism can be expressed by buying American goods. If the reader were to ask a few probing questions, he or she might find these warrants un-convincing.

Silent warrants that express values hide in other popular and influ-ential slogans. "Pro-life," the slogan of those who oppose abortion,

---

[26] *The Progressive,* September 1983, p. 38.
[27] Second Inaugural Address as Governor of Alabama, January 18, 1971.

assumes that the fetus is a living being entitled to the same rights as individuals already born. "Pro-choice," the slogan of those who favor abortion, suggests that the freedom of the pregnant woman to choose is the foremost or only consideration. The words *life* and *choice* have been carefully selected to reflect desirable qualities, but the words are only the beginning of the argument.

Third, although slogans may express admirable sentiments, they often fail to tell us how to achieve their objectives. They address us in the imperative mode, ordering us to take an action or refrain from it. But the means of achieving the objectives may be nonexistent or very costly. If the sloganeer cannot offer workable means for implementing his or her goals, he or she risks alienating the audience.

Sloganeering is one of the recognizable attributes of propaganda. Propaganda for both good and bad purposes is a form of slanting, of selecting language and facts to persuade an audience to take a certain action. Even a good cause may be weakened by an unsatisfactory slogan. The slogans of some organizations devoted to fundraising for the physically handicapped have come under attack for depicting the handicapped as helpless. According to one critic, the popular slogan "Jerry's kids" promotes the idea that Jerry Lewis is the sole support of children afflicted with muscular dystrophy. Perhaps increased sensitivity to the needs of the handicapped will produce new words and new slogans. If you assume that your audience is sophisticated and alert, you will probably write your strongest arguments, devoid of clichés and slogans.

SAMPLE ANALYSIS

On the Need for Asylums

LEWIS THOMAS

From time to time, medical science has achieved an indisputable triumph that is pure benefit for all levels of society and deserving of such terms as "breakthrough" and "medical miracle." It is not a long list, but the items are solid bits of encouragement for the future. The conquests of tuberculosis, smallpox, and syphilis of the central nervous system should be at the top of anyone's list. Rheumatic fever, the most

Lewis Thomas, Professor Emeritus at the Cornell School of Medicine, has been president of the Memorial Sloan-Kettering Cancer Center in New York City. Trained as a doctor, he is also a renowned essayist. This piece is from his third collection of essays, *Late Night Thoughts on Listening to Mahler's Ninth Symphony* (New York: Viking Press, 1983).

common cause of heart disease forty years ago, has become a rare, almost exotic disorder, thanks to the introduction of antibiotics for treating streptococcal sore throat. Some forms of cancer — notably childhood leukemias, Hodgkin's disease, and certain sarcomas affecting young people — have become curable in a high proportion of patients. Poliomyelitis is no longer with us.

But there is still a formidable agenda of diseases for which there are no cures, needing much more research before their underlying mechanisms can be brought to light. Among these diseases are some for which we have only halfway technologies to offer, measures that turn out to be much more costly than we had guessed and only partly, sometimes marginally, effective. The transplantation of major organs has become successful, but only for a relatively small number of patients with damaged kidneys and hearts, and at a financial cost much too high for applying the technologies on a wide scale. Very large numbers of patients with these fatal illnesses have no access to such treatments. Renal dialysis makes it possible to live for many months, even a few years, with failed kidneys, but it is a hard life.

The overestimation of the value of an advance in medicine can lead to more trouble than anyone can foresee, and a lot of careful thought and analysis ought to be invested before any technology is turned loose on the marketplace. It begins to look as if coronary bypass surgery, for example, is an indispensable operation for a limited number of people, but it was probably not necessary for the large number in whom the expensive procedure has already been employed.

There are other examples of this sort of premature, sweeping adoption of new measures in medicine. Probably none has resulted in more untoward social damage than the unpredicted, indirect but calamitous effects of the widespread introduction twenty or so years ago of Thorazine and its chemical relatives for the treatment of schizophrenia. For a while, when it was first used in state hospitals for the insane, the new line of drugs seemed miraculous indeed. Patients whose hallucinations and delusions impelled them to wild, uncontrollable behavior were discovered to be so calmed by the treatment as to make possible the closing down of many of the locked wards in asylums. Patients with milder forms of schizophrenia could return, at least temporarily, to life outside the institutions. It was the first real advance in the treatment of severe mental disease, and the whole world of psychiatry seemed to have been transformed. Psychopharmacology became, overnight, a bright new discipline in medicine.

Then came the side effect. Not a medical side effect (although there were some of these) but a political one, and a disaster. On the assumption that the new drugs made hospitalization unnecessary, two social policies were launched with the enthusiastic agreement of both the professional psychiatric community and the governmental agencies responsible for the care of the mentally ill. Brand-new institutions, 5 ambitiously designated "community mental health centers," were deployed across the country. These centers were to be the source of the new technology for treating schizophrenia, along with all other sorts of mental illness: in theory, patients would come to the clinics and be given the needed drugs, and, when necessary, psychotherapy. And at the same time orders came down that most of the patients living in the state hospitals be discharged forthwith to their homes or, lacking homes, to other quarters in the community.

For a while it looked like the best of worlds, on paper, anyway. Brochures with handsome charts were issued by state and federal agencies displaying the plummeting curves of state hospital occupancy, with the lines coinciding marvelously with the introduction of the new drugs. No one noted that the occupancy of private mental hospitals rose at the same time — though it could not rise very high, with the annual cost of such hospitalization running around $40,000 per bed. The term "breakthrough" was used over and over again, but after a little while it came to be something more like a breakout. The mentally ill were out of the hospital, but in many cases they were simply out on the streets, less agitated but lost, still disabled but now uncared for. The community mental health centers were not designed to take on the task of custodial care. They could serve as shelters only during the hours of appointment, not at night.

All this is still going on, and it is not working. To be sure, the drugs do work — but only to the extent of allaying some of the most distressing manifestations of schizophrenia. They do not turn the disease off. The evidences of the mind's unhinging are still there, coming and going in cycles of remission and exacerbation just as they have always done since schizophrenia was first described. Some patients recover spontaneously and for good, as some have always done. The chronically and permanently disabled are better off because they are in lesser degrees of mental torment when they have their medication; but they are at the same time much worse off because they can no longer find refuge when they are in need of it. They are, instead, out on the streets, or down in the subways, or wandering in the parks, or confined in shabby rooms in the shabbiest hotels, alone. Or perhaps they are living at home, but not many of them living happily; nor are many of their families happy to have them at home. One of the high risks of severe mental disease is suicide, and many of these abandoned patients choose this way out, with no one to stop them. It is an appalling situation.

It is claimed that the old state hospitals were even more appalling. They were called warehouses for the insane, incapable of curing anything, more likely to make it worse by the process known in psychiatric circles as "institutionalization," a steady downhill course toward total dependency on the very bleakness of the institution itself. The places were badly managed, always understaffed, repellent to doctors, nurses, and all the other people needed for the care of those with sick minds.

Better off without them, it was said. Cheaper too, although this wasn't said so openly.

What never seems to have been thought of, or at least never discussed publicly, was changing the state hospitals from bad to good institutions, given the opportunity for vastly improved care that came along with the drugs. It was partly the history of such places that got in the way. For centuries the madhouses, as they were called, served no purpose beyond keeping deranged people out of the public view. Despite efforts at reform in the late nineteenth and early twentieth centuries, they remained essentially lockups.

But now it is becoming plain that life in the state hospitals, bad as it was, was better than life in the subways or in the doorways of downtown streets, late on cold nights with nothing in the shopping bag to keep a body warm, and no protection at all against molestation by predators or the sudden urge for self-destruction. What now? 10

We should restore the state hospital system, improve it, expand it if necessary, and spend enough money to ensure that the patients who must live in these institutions will be able to come in off the streets and live in decency and warmth, under the care of adequately paid, competent professionals and compassionate surrogate friends.

If there is not enough money, there are ways to save. There was a time when many doctors were glad to volunteer their services on a part-time basis, indeed competed to do so, unpaid by state or federal funds and unreimbursed by insurance companies, in order to look after people unable to care for themselves. We should be looking around again for such doctors, not necessarily specialists in psychiatric medicine, but well-trained physicians possessing affection for people in trouble — a quality on which recruitment to the profession of medicine has always, we hope, been based. We cannot leave the situation of insane human beings where it is today.

A society can be judged by the way it treats its most disadvantaged, its least beloved, its mad. As things now stand, we must be judged a poor lot, and it is time to mend our ways.

Analysis

The essay by Lewis Thomas makes a constructive contrast with one of the other essays in this chapter. The essay by Neusner is a sample of a very different kind of language, an expression of anger, contempt, and resentment about what the author regards as a distressing academic problem. Thomas, in writing about a destructive policy which *he* deplores, might also have resorted to intemperate language to express impatience with the architects of that policy. But the language of "On the Need for Asylums" is moderate in tone and nonaccusatory. It emphasizes compassion for the victims rather than anger at those responsible for the policy. Paragraph 7 gives a moving description of the lives of abandoned schizophrenics. The emotional appeal is an essential ingredient of his argument, but Thomas's voice is one of restrained sadness. The only censorious word is "appalling" at the end of the paragraph.

Thomas uses several language devices to deflect specific blame. Sometimes it is the passive voice of the verb. For example, where he says, "two social policies were launched" and "Brand-new institutions . . . were deployed," the people who launched the social policies and deployed the new institutions are not identified. Other writers on the subject have been quick to name and indict the authors of these unsuccessful programs. When an indictment seems relevant, Thomas resorts to general rather than specific terms: "orders came down," "state and federal agencies," "a lot of careful thought and analysis ought to be invested. . . ." Elsewhere when he refers to the "calamitous effects" of the adoption of Thorazine, he includes the words "unpredicted, indirect" as if to avoid charging the medical profession with carelessness. In the last paragraph he lays blame for the ruinous policy of discharging the mentally ill from state hospitals, but he does not separate himself from the policymakers: "[W]e must be judged a poor lot, and it is time to mend our ways."

Thomas is a deservedly popular essayist, not only for the variety of subjects and the breadth of information in his award-winning collections of essays, but for the person he seems to be as the author of those reflections: thoughtful, modest, humorous, friendly. Part of his appeal is his use of language, that of an intelligent layman — although he is a respected scientist — neither technical nor literary and often close to conversation in the use of contractions, short words and phrases, and sentence fragments. "It was partly the history of such places that got in the way." "All this is still going on, and it is not working." "For a while it looked like the best of worlds, on paper anyway." "Better off without them, it was said. Cheaper, too, although this wasn't said so openly."

Of course, there are conditions which call for anger, when the arguer is right to speak in a loud voice. But sometimes a quiet voice, reflecting a thoughtful and conciliatory arguer, is a more effective strategy for persuading a general audience.

The Speech the Graduates Didn't Hear

JACOB NEUSNER

We the faculty take no pride in our educational achievements with you. We have prepared you for a world that does not exist, indeed, that cannot exist. You have spent four years supposing that failure leaves no record. You have learned at Brown that when your work goes poorly, the painless solution is to drop out. But starting now, in the world to which you go, failure marks you. Confronting difficulty by quitting leaves you changed. Outside Brown, quitters are no heroes.

With us you could argue about why your errors were not errors, why mediocre work really was excellent, why you could take pride in routine and slipshod presentation. Most of you, after all, can look back on honor grades for most of what you have done. So, here grades can have meant little in distinguishing the excellent from the ordinary. But tomorrow, in the world to which you go, you had best not defend errors but learn from them. You will be ill-advised to demand praise for what does not deserve it, and abuse those who do not give it.

For four years we created an altogether forgiving world, in which whatever slight effort you gave was all that was demanded. When you did not keep appointments, we made new ones. When your work came in beyond the deadline, we pretended not to care.

Worse still, when you were boring, we acted as if you were saying something important. When you were garrulous and talked to hear yourself talk, we listened as if it mattered. When you tossed on our desks writing upon which you had not labored, we read it and even responded, as though you earned a response. When you were dull, we pretended you were smart. When you were predictable, unimaginative, and routine, we listened as if to new and wonderful things. When you demanded free lunch, we served it. And all this why?

Despite your fantasies, it was not even that we wanted to be liked 5 by you. It was that we did not want to be bothered, and the easy way out was pretense: smiles and easy Bs.

It is conventional to quote in addresses such as these. Let me quote

---

Jacob Neusner, formerly university professor at Brown University, is Distinguished Professor of Religious Studies at the University of South Florida in Tampa. His speech appeared in Brown's *The Daily Herald* on June 12, 1983.

someone you've never heard of: Professor Carter A. Daniel, Rutgers University (*Chronicle of Higher Education,* May 7, 1979):

> College has spoiled you by reading papers that don't deserve to be read, listening to comments that don't deserve a hearing, paying attention even to the lazy, ill-informed, and rude. We had to do it, for the sake of education. But nobody will ever do it again. College has deprived you of adequate preparation for the last fifty years. It has failed you by being easy, free, forgiving, attentive, comfortable, interesting, unchallenging fun. Good luck tomorrow.

That is why, on this commencement day, we have nothing in which to take much pride.

Oh, yes, there is one more thing. Try not to act toward your co-workers and bosses as you have acted toward us. I mean, when they give you what you want but have not earned, don't abuse them, insult them, act out with them your parlous relationships with your parents. This too we have tolerated. It was, as I said, not to be liked. Few professors actually care whether or not they are liked by peer-paralyzed adolescents, fools so shallow as to imagine professors care not about education but about popularity. It was, again, to be rid of you. So go, unlearn the lies we taught you. To Life!

Discussion Questions

1. Pick out some of the words and phrases — especially adjectives and verbs — used by Neusner to characterize both students and teachers. Do you think these terms are loaded? Explain.
2. Has Neusner chosen "facts" to slant his article? If so, point out where slanting occurs. If not, point out where the article seems to be truthful.
3. As a student you will probably object to Neusner's accusations. How would you defend your behavior as a student in answer to his specific charges?

Writing Suggestions

1. Rewrite Neusner's article with the same "facts" — or others from your experience — using temperate language and a tone of sadness rather than anger.
2. Write a letter to Neusner responding to his attack. Support or attack his argument by providing evidence from your own experience.
3. Write your own short commencement address. Do some things need to be said that commencement speakers seldom or never express?
4. Write an essay using the same kind of strong language as Neusner uses about some aspect of your education of which you disapprove. Or write a letter to a teacher using the same form as "The Speech the Graduates Didn't Hear."

Bring Back Carl's Plaque

DAVE BARRY

I say we put Carl Sagan into a rocket and send him out to retrieve Pioneer 10 before we all get killed.

For those of you beer-swilling semiliterates who don't know what I'm talking about, let me explain that Pioneer 10 is a space probe that recently left the solar system, and Carl Sagan is a famous science personality who goes on public television and earns big buckeroos explaining the universe. Carl's technique is to use the word "billion" a lot. It's written into his contract that he gets to say "billion" an average of twice per sentence, so the viewers won't forget what a deep thinker he is.

Carl will pick up a golf ball, and he'll say, "To most of you, this golf ball is a mere golf ball, but it actually contains a billion billion billion billion tiny particles. If each of these particles were the size of a grapefruit, my hand would have to be a billion billion billion billion billion times the size of the Houston Astrodome to hold them all. This should give you a rough idea of the kind of heavy thinking I'm doing all day while you're trying to decide whether to have spaghetti or tuna surprise. Billion billion billion. Good night."

People listen to Carl prattling on this way, and they naturally conclude he's some kind of major genius. That's what got us into this space-probe trouble that's going to get us all killed.

See, when they decided to send Pioneer 10 up, Carl sold the gov-   5
ernment on the idea that we should attach a plaque to it, so that if alien beings found it they'd be able to locate the Earth. This is easily the stupidest idea a scientific genius ever sold to the government, surpassing even the time a bunch of scientists convinced Gerald Ford we were going to have the legendary swine flu epidemic, which eventually had to be canceled due to a lack of actual germs.

What I'm saying is that the last thing we need is alien beings. I don't know about you, but in the vast majority of the movies I've seen, the alien beings have turned out to be disgusting. A whole lot of them have tentacles, and those are the good-looking ones. Some of them are just blobs of slime. Almost all of them are toxic.

So it's all well and good for Carl Sagan to *talk* about how neat it would be to get in touch with the aliens, but I bet he'd change his mind pronto if they actually started oozing under his front door. I bet he'd be whapping at them with his golf clubs just like the rest of us.

Heralded as "the funniest man in America" by the *New York Times,* Dave Barry is a syndicated columnist based in Miami. This essay appeared in his book, *Bad Habits* (New York: Henry Holt, 1985).

But the really bad part is what they put on the plaque. I mean, if we're going to have a plaque, it ought to at least show the aliens what we're really like, right? Maybe a picture of people eating cheeseburgers and watching "The Dukes of Hazzard." Then if aliens found it, they'd say, "Ah. Just plain folks."

But no. Carl came up with this incredible science-fair-wimp plaque that features drawings of — you are not going to believe this — *a hydrogen atom and naked people.* To represent the entire Earth! This is crazy! Walk the streets of any town on this planet, and the two things you will almost never see are hydrogen atoms and naked people. On top of that, the man on the plaque is clearly deranged. He's cheerfully waving his arm, as if to say, "Hi! Look at me! I'm naked as a jaybird!" The woman is not waving, because she's obviously embarrassed. She wishes she'd never let the man talk her into posing naked for this plaque.

So that's it, gang. That's the plaque that's supposed to tell the aliens 10 what you're like. Now if Pioneer 10 is picked up, I figure it will be picked up by some kind of Intergalactic Police, the alien equivalent of rural police officers. They'll look at it, and they'll say, "Looks to me like what we got here is we got a race of hydrogen-obsessed pervert science wimps who force the women to go around naked and probably say 'billion' a lot. I say we vaporize their planet and then ooze over to the diner for something to eat."

And that will be that, unless we send Carl out to retract the plaque, or at least explain that it represents only him and a few close friends. We can do it. A nation that can land a man on the moon can remove Carl Sagan from the solar system. I've given this a lot of thought. Billion billion billion.

Discussion Questions

1. A comic writer often assumes a *persona.* This persona is not the author but a character that the author has created in whose voice he speaks. How would you describe the person that Barry pretends to be in this article?
2. Who and what are the real objects of Barry's attacks? (Some may not be directly named in the article.) Which seem serious? Which trivial?
3. What examples and language elements — vocabulary, grammar, metaphors — does Barry use to comic advantage? Are they consistent with the character of the persona?

Writing Suggestions

1. Try rewriting Barry's argument as a serious claim of policy, without insulting Carl Sagan and treating seriously, even if unfavorably, the design of the plaque on Pioneer 10.

2. If you are brave, write a funny piece about some subject whose absurdities have either amused or angered you. The subjects are everywhere. Some may even be found in the serious arguments you have been reading in this book: malls, mandatory school attendance, sexual harassment, prejudice, gun control. (Not surprisingly, all of these subjects have, in fact, been treated satirically by humor columnists like Russell Baker, Art Buchwald, and Mike Royko.) And, of course, there are always advertisements as objects of humorous attack.

AMERICANS. HELPING FRIENDS. RELATIVES — ESPECIALLY STRANGERS — WITHOUT QUESTION OR PAUSE. IT'S A TRADITION OF TEACHERS. CAREGIVERS. FIREMEN AND POLICE. A TRADITION OF VOLUNTEERISM. FROM MANHATTAN BEACH. CALIFORNIA. TO MANHATTAN ISLAND. NEW YORK. NONE CARE AS THEY CARE. OR GIVE AS THEY GIVE. SO, AT MUTUAL OF AMERICA WE HAVE A SINGULAR MISSION: TO PROTECT THEIR FUTURES WITH PENSION AND RETIREMENT PROGRAMS BACKED BY NO-NONSENSE GENERAL ACCOUNT ASSETS. MANAGED FOR GROWTH. NOT RISK. AND.THROUGH OUR NETWORK OF REGIONAL OFFICES. A SPECIAL KIND OF PERSONAL ATTENTION YOU THOUGHT HAD . DISAPPEARED. ALL SO THAT YOU CAN REST EASILY. TODAY, ORGANIZATIONS LIKE YOURS, AND THE MEN AND WOMEN WHO WORK FOR THEM. TRUST IN THE STRENGTH. THE STABILITY. THE SPIRIT OF AMERICA - MUTUAL OF AMERICA.

THE STRENGTH. THE STABILITY.

THE SPIRIT OF AMERICA...

MUTUAL OF AMERICA
666 Fifth Ave. New York, NY 10103

Discussion Questions

1. What psychological need does the advertiser appeal to?
2. What language is used to make the readers of the ad feel both flattered and included? How successful are these strategies?
3. What language does the advertiser use to establish the virtues of the company?
4. What function does the picture serve?

EXERCISES FOR CRITICAL THINKING

1. Select one or two related bumper stickers visible in your neighborhood. Examine the hidden warrants on which they are based and assess their validity.
2. For a slogan found on a bumper sticker or elsewhere, supply the evidence to support the claim in the slogan. Or find evidence that disproves the claim.
3. Examine a few periodicals from fifty or more years ago. Select either an advertising or a political slogan in one of them and relate it to beliefs or events of the period. Or tell why the slogan is no longer relevant.
4. Discuss the origin of a cliché or slogan. Describe, as far as possible, the backgrounds and motives of its users.
5. Make up your own slogan for a cause that you support. Explain and defend your slogan.
6. Discuss the appeal to needs and values of some popular advertising or political slogan.
7. Choose a cliché and find evidence to support or refute it. *Examples:* People were much happier in the past. Mother knows best. Life was much simpler in the past. Money can't buy happiness.
8. Choose one of the statements in exercise 7 or another statement and write a paper telling why you think such a statement has persisted as an explanation.
9. Select a passage, perhaps from a textbook, written largely in abstractions, and rewrite it using simpler and more concrete language.

CHAPTER SEVEN

Induction, Deduction, and Logical Fallacies

Throughout the book we have pointed out the weaknesses that cause arguments to break down. In the vast majority of cases these weaknesses represent breakdowns in logic or the reasoning process. We call such weaknesses *fallacies,* a term derived from the Latin. Sometimes these false or erroneous arguments are deliberate; in fact, the Latin word *fallere* means to deceive. But more often these arguments are either carelessly or unintentionally constructed. Thoughtful readers learn to recognize them; thoughtful writers learn to avoid them.

The reasoning process was first given formal expression by Aristotle, the Greek philosopher, almost 2,500 years ago. In his famous treatises, he described the way we try to discover the truth — observing the world, selecting impressions, making inferences, generalizing. In this process Aristotle identified two forms of reasoning: *induction* and *deduction.* Both forms, he realized, are subject to error. Our observations may be incorrect or insufficient, and our conclusions may be faulty because they have violated the rules governing the relationship between statements. The terms we've introduced may be unfamiliar, but the processes of reasoning, as well as the fallacies that violate these processes are not. Induction and deduction are not reserved only for formal arguments about important problems; they also represent our everyday thinking about the most ordinary matters. As for the fallacies, they, too, unfortunately, may crop up anywhere, whenever we are careless in our use of the reasoning process.

In this chapter we will examine some of the most common fallacies. First, however, a closer look at induction and deduction will make clear what happens when fallacies occur.

INDUCTION

Induction is the form of reasoning in which we come to conclusions about the whole on the basis of observations of particular instances. If you notice that prices on the four items you bought in the campus bookstore are higher than similar items in the bookstore in town, you may come to the conclusion that the campus store is a more expensive place to shop. If you also noticed that all three of the instructors you saw on the first day of school were wearing faded jeans and sandals, you might say that your teachers are generally informal in their dress. In both cases you have made an *inductive leap,* reasoning from what you have learned about a few examples to what you think is true of a whole class of things.

How safe are you in coming to these conclusions? As we've noticed in discussing data and generalization warrants, the reliability of your conclusion depends on the quantity and quality of your observations. Were four items out of the thousands available in the campus store a sufficiently large sample? Would you come to the same conclusion if you chose fifty items? Might another selection have produced a different conclusion? As for the casually dressed instructors, perhaps further investigation would disclose that the teachers wearing jeans were all teaching assistants and that associate and full professors usually wore business clothes. Or the difference might lie in the academic discipline; anthropology teachers might turn out to dress less formally than business school teachers.

In these two situations, you could come closer to verifying your conclusions by further observation and experience, that is, by buying more items at both stores over a longer period of time and by coming into contact with a greater number of professors during a whole semester. Even without pricing every item in both stores or encountering every instructor on campus, you would be more confident of your generalization as the quality and quantity of your samples increased.

In some cases you can observe all the instances in a particular situation. For example, by acquiring information about the religious beliefs of all the residents of the dormitory, you can arrive at an accurate assessment of the number of Buddhists. But since our ability to make definitive observations about everything is limited, we must also make an inductive leap about categories of things that we ourselves can never encounter in their entirety. For some generalizations, as we have learned about evidence, we rely on the testimony of reliable witnesses who report that they have experienced or observed many more instances of the phenomenon. A television documentary may give us information about unwed teenage mothers in a city neighborhood; four girls are interviewed and followed for several days by the reporter. Are these girls typical of thousands of others? A sociologist on the program assures us that, in fact, they are. She herself has consulted with hundreds of other young mothers and can vouch for the fact that a conclusion about them, based on our observation of the four, will be sound. Obviously, though, our conclusion can only be probable, not certain. The sociologist's sample is large, but she can account only for hundreds, not thousands, and there may be unexamined cases that will seriously weaken our conclusions.

In other cases, we may rely on a principle known in science as "the uniformity of nature." We assume that certain conclusions about oak trees in the temperate zone of North America, for example, will also be true for oak trees growing elsewhere under similar climatic conditions. We also use this principle in attempting to explain the causes of behavior in human beings. If we discover that institutionalization of some children from infancy results in severe emotional retardation, we think it safe to conclude that under the same circumstances all children would suffer the same consequences. As in the previous example, we are aware that certainty about every case of institutionalization is impossible. With rare exceptions, the process of induction can offer only probability, not certain truth.

SAMPLE ANALYSIS: AN INDUCTIVE ARGUMENT

Not All Men Are Sly Foxes

ARMIN A. BROTT

If you thought your child's bookshelves were finally free of openly (and not so openly) discriminatory materials, you'd better check again. In recent years groups of concerned parents have persuaded textbook publishers to portray more accurately the roles that women and minorities play in shaping our country's history and culture. *Little Black Sambo* has all but disappeared from library and bookstore shelves; feminist fairy tales by such authors as Jack Zipes have, in many homes, replaced the more traditional (and obviously sexist) fairy tales. Richard Scarry, one of the most popular children's writers, has reissued new versions of some of his classics; now female animals are pictured doing the same jobs as male animals. Even the terminology has changed: males and females are referred to as mail "carriers" or "firefighters."

Armin A. Brott is a freelance writer. This article appeared in *Newsweek* on July 6, 1992.

There is, however, one very large group whose portrayal continues to follow the same stereotypical lines as always: fathers. The evolution of children's literature didn't end with *Goodnight Moon* and *Charlotte's Web*. My local public library, for example, previews 203 new children's picture books (for the under-five set) each *month*. Many of these books make a very conscious effort to take women characters out of the kitchen and the nursery and give them professional jobs and responsibilities.

Despite this shift, mothers are by and large still shown as the primary caregivers and, more important, as the primary nurturers of their children. Men in these books — if they're shown at all — still come home late after work and participate in the child rearing by bouncing baby around for five minutes before putting the child to bed.

In one of my two-year-old daughter's favorite books, *Mother Goose and the Sly Fox*, "retold" by Chris Conover, a single mother (Mother Goose) of seven tiny goslings is pitted against (and naturally outwits) the sly Fox. Fox, a neglectful and presumably unemployed single father, lives with his filthy, hungry pups in a grimy hovel littered with the bones of their previous meals. Mother Goose, a successful entrepreneur with a thriving lace business, still finds time to serve her goslings homemade soup in pretty porcelain cups. The story is funny and the illustrations marvelous, but the unwritten message is that women take better care of their kids and men have nothing else to do but hunt down and kill innocent, law-abiding geese.

The majority of other children's classics perpetuate the same neg- 5 ative stereotypes of fathers. Once in a great while, people complain about *Babar*'s colonialist slant (little jungle-dweller finds happiness in the big city and brings civilization — and fine clothes — to his backward village). But I've never heard anyone ask why, after his mother is killed by the evil hunter, Babar is automatically an "orphan." Why can he find comfort only in the arms of another female? Why do Arthur's and Celeste's mothers come alone to the city to fetch their children? Don't the fathers care? Do they even have fathers? I need my answers ready for when my daughter asks.

I recently spent an entire day on the children's floor of the local library trying to find out whether these same negative stereotypes are found in the more recent classics-to-be. The librarian gave me a list of the twenty most popular contemporary picture books and I read every one of them. Of the twenty, seven don't mention a parent at all. Of the remaining thirteen, four portray fathers as much less loving and caring than mothers. In *Little Gorilla*, we are told that the little gorilla's "mother loves him" and we see Mama gorilla giving her little one a warm hug. On the next page we're also told that his "father loves him," but in the illustration, father and son aren't even touching. Six of the remaining nine books mention or portray mothers as the only parent, and only three of the twenty have what could be considered "equal" treatment of mothers and fathers.

The same negative stereotypes also show up in literature aimed at the *parents* of small children. In "What to Expect the First Year," the authors answer almost every question the parents of a newborn or toddler could have in the first year of their child's life. They are meticulous in alternating between references to boys and girls. At the same time, they refer almost exclusively to "mother" or "mommy." Men, and their feelings about parenting, are relegated to a nine-page chapter just before the recipe section.

Unfortunately, it's still true that, in our society, women do the bulk of the child care, and that thanks to men abandoning their families, there are too many single mothers out there. Nevertheless, to say that portraying fathers as unnurturing or completely absent is simply "a reflection of reality" is unacceptable. If children's literature only reflected reality, it would be like prime-time TV and we'd have books filled with child abusers, wife beaters, and criminals.

Young children believe what they hear — especially from a parent figure. And since, for the first few years of a child's life, adults select the reading material, children's literature should be held to a high standard. Ignoring men who share equally in raising their children, and continuing to show nothing but part-time or no-time fathers is only going to create yet another generation of men who have been told since boyhood — albeit subtly — that mothers are the truer parents and that fathers play, at best, a secondary role in the home. We've taken major steps to root out discrimination in what our children read. Let's finish the job.

Analysis

An inductive argument proceeds by examining particulars and arriving at a generalization that represents a probable truth. After reading a number of children's books in which the fathers, if they appear at all, are mostly portrayed as irresponsible and uncaring, Brott concludes that fathers are discriminated against in children's literature. Brott reports that he has examined twenty books. Only three of them give equal treatment to fathers and mothers. Even a book of advice for parents treats fathers with comparative indifference.

Because the subject is likely to be familiar to most readers, they will be able to participate in finding their own examples in children's literature to support — or refute — his claim. The success of Brott's argument will depend on finding that the examples in the article are sufficient, representative, and up-to-date. We know that the books he refers to are up-to-date (Brott mentions this in paragraph 6), but they may not be representative (the librarian gave him a list of the twenty "most popular contemporary picture books"), and whether twenty of 203 new books received by the library *each month* is sufficient is somewhat doubtful. Like all inductive arguments, this one too must be judged for probability, not certainty, but high probability would require a much bigger sample.

The examples in the article are not simply a list, however. Brott presents his conclusion within a broad context. In the first and second paragraphs he points out that while many negative racial and sexual stereotypes are disappearing from children's literature, one damaging stereotype remains, that of fathers. In the final paragraph he summarizes the dangers to society of allowing children — and the potential fathers among them — to believe that fathers are unimportant or indifferent to their children. One may find the latter conclusion valid, of course, even if one finds Brott's sample insufficient.

DEDUCTION

While induction attempts to arrive at the truth, deduction guarantees sound relationships between statements. If each of a series of statements, called *premises,* is true, deductive logic tells us that the conclusion must also be true. Unlike the conclusions from induction, which are only probable, the conclusions from deduction are certain. The simplest deductive argument consists of two premises and a conclusion. In outline such an argument looks like this:

MAJOR PREMISE: All students with 3.5 averages and above for three years are invited to become members of Kappa Gamma Pi, the honor society.

MINOR PREMISE: George has had a 3.8 average for over three years.

CONCLUSION: Therefore, he will be invited to join Kappa Gamma Pi.

This deductive conclusion is *valid* or logically consistent because it follows necessarily from the premises. No other conclusion is possible. Validity, however, refers only to the form of the argument. The argument itself may not be satisfactory if the premises are not true — if Kappa Gamma Pi has imposed other conditions or if George has only a 3.4 average. The difference between truth and validity is important because it alerts us to the necessity for examining the truth of the premises before we decide that the conclusion is sound.

One way of discovering how the deductive process works is to look at the methods used by Sherlock Holmes, that most famous of literary detectives, in solving his mysteries. His reasoning process follows a familiar pattern. Through the inductive process, that is, observing the particulars of the world, he came to certain conclusions about those particulars. Then he applied deductive reasoning to come to a conclusion about a particular person or event.

On one occasion Holmes observed that a man sitting opposite him on a train had chalk dust on his fingers. From this observation Holmes deduced that the man was a schoolteacher. If his thinking were outlined, it would take the form of the syllogism, the classic form of deductive reasoning:

MAJOR PREMISE: All men with chalk dust on their fingers are school-teachers.

MINOR PREMISE: This man has chalk dust on his fingers.

CONCLUSION: Therefore, this man is a schoolteacher.

One dictionary defines the syllogism as "a formula of argument consisting of three propositions." The first proposition is called the major premise and offers a generalization about a large group or class. This generalization has been arrived at through inductive reasoning or observation of particulars. The second proposition is called the minor premise, and it makes a statement about a member of that group or class. The third proposition is the conclusion, which links the other two propositions, in much the same way that the warrant links the support and the claim.

If we look back at the syllogism that summarizes Holmes's thinking, we see how it represents the deductive process. The major premise, the first statement, is an inductive generalization, a statement arrived at after observation of a number of men with chalk on their fingers. The minor premise, the second statement, assigns a particular member, the man on the train, to the general class of those who have dust on their fingers.

But although the argument may be logical, it is faulty. The deductive argument is only as strong as its premises. As Lionel Ruby pointed out, Sherlock Holmes was often wrong.[1] Holmes once deduced from the size of a large hat found in the street that the owner was intelligent. He obviously believed that a large head meant a large brain and that a large brain indicated intelligence. Had he lived one hundred years later, new information about the relationship of brain size to intelligence would have enabled him to come to a different and better conclusion.

In this case, we might first object to the major premise, the generalization that all men with chalk dust on their fingers are schoolteachers. Is it true? Perhaps all the men with dusty fingers whom Holmes had so far observed had turned out to be schoolteachers, but was his sample sufficiently large to allow him to conclude that all dust-fingered men, even those with whom he might never have contact, were teachers? Were there no other vocations or situations that might require the use of chalk? Draftsmen or carpenters or tailors or artists might have fingers just as white as those of schoolteachers. In other words, Holmes may have ascertained that all schoolteachers have chalk dust on their fingers, but he had not determined that *only* schoolteachers can be

---

[1] *The Art of Making Sense* (Philadelphia: Lippincott, 1954), ch. 17.

thus identified. Sometimes it is helpful to draw circles representing the various groups in their relation to the whole.

If a large circle (see the figure below) represents all those who have chalk dust on their fingers, we see that several different groups may be contained in this universe. To be safe, Holmes should have deduced that the man on the train *might* have been a schoolteacher; he was not safe in deducing more than that. Obviously, if the inductive generalization or major premise is false, the conclusion of the particular argument is also false or invalid.

The deductive argument may also go wrong elsewhere. What if the minor premise is untrue? Could Holmes have mistaken the source of the white powder on the man's fingers? Suppose it was not chalk dust but flour or confectioner's sugar or talcum or heroin? Any of these possibilities would weaken or invalidate his conclusion.

Another example, closer to the kinds of arguments you will examine, reveals the flaw in the deductive process.

MAJOR PREMISE: All Communists oppose organized religion.

MINOR PREMISE: Robert Roe opposes organized religion.

CONCLUSION: Therefore, Robert Roe is a Communist.

The common name for this fallacy is "guilt by association." The fact that two things share an attribute does not mean that they are the same thing. As in the first example, the diagram on page 215 makes clear that Robert Roe and Communists do not necessarily share all attributes. Remembering that Holmes may have misinterpreted the signs of chalk on the traveler's fingers, we may also want to question whether Robert Roe's opposition to organized religion has been misinterpreted.

An example from history shows us how such an argument may be used. In a campaign speech during the summer of 1952, Senator Joseph McCarthy, who had made a reputation as a tireless enemy of communism, said, "I do not tell you that Schlesinger, Stevenson's number one man, number one braintrust, I don't tell you he's a Communist. I have

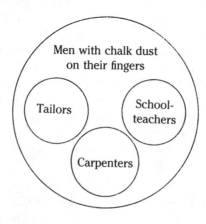

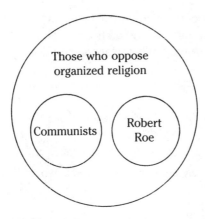

no information on that point. But I do know that if he were a Communist he would also ridicule religion as Schlesinger has done."[2] This is an argument based on a sign warrant. Clearly the sign referred to by Senator McCarthy, ridicule of religion, would not be sufficient to characterize someone as a Communist.

Some deductive arguments give trouble because one of the premises, usually the major premise, is omitted. As in the warrants we examined in Chapter 5, a failure to evaluate the truth of the unexpressed premise may lead to an invalid conclusion. When only two parts of the syllogism appear, we call the resulting form an *enthymeme*. Suppose we overhear the following snatch of conversation:

> *"Did you hear about Jean's father? He had a heart attack last week."*
>
> *"That's too bad. But I'm not surprised. I know he always refused to go for his annual physical checkups."*

The second speaker has used an unexpressed major premise, the cause-effect warrant "If you have annual physical checkups, you can avoid heart attacks." He does not express it because he assumes that it is unnecessary to do so. The first speaker recognizes the unspoken warrant and may agree with it. Or the first speaker may produce evidence from reputable sources that such a generalization is by no means universally true, in which case the conclusion of the second speaker is suspect.

A knowledge of the deductive process can help guide you toward an evaluation of the soundness of your reasoning in an argument you are constructing. The syllogism is often clearer than an outline in establishing the relations between the different parts of an argument.

Suppose you wanted to argue that your former high school should

[2] Joseph R. McCarthy, "The Red-Tinted Washington Crowd," speech delivered to a Republican campaign meeting at Appleton, Wisconsin, November 3, 1952.

introduce a dress code. You might begin by asking these questions: What would be the purpose of such a regulation? How would a dress code fulfill that purpose? What reasons could you provide to support your claim?

Then you might set down part of your argument like this:

> Dressing in different styles makes students more aware of social differences among themselves.
>
> The students in this school dress in many different styles.
>
> Therefore, they are more aware of differences in social status among the student body.

As you diagram this first part of the argument, you should ask two sets of questions:

1. Is the major premise true? Do differences in dress cause awareness of differences in social status? Has my experience confirmed this?
2. Is the minor premise true? Has my observation confirmed this?

The conclusion, of course, represents something that you don't have to observe. You can deduce with certainty that it is true if both the major and minor premises are true.

So far the testing of your argument has been relatively easy because you have been concerned with the testing of observation and experience. Now you must examine something that does not appear in the syllogism. You have determined certain facts about perceptions of social status, but you have not arrived at the policy you want to recommend: that a dress code should be mandated. Notice that the dress code argument is based on acceptance of a moral value.

> Reducing awareness of social differences is a desirable goal for the school.
>
> A uniform dress code would help to achieve that goal.
>
> Therefore, students should be required to dress uniformly.

The major premise in this syllogism is clearly different from the previous one. While the premise in the previous syllogism can be tested by examining sufficient examples to determine probability, this statement, about the desirability of the goal, is a value judgment and cannot be proved by counting examples. Whether equality of social status is a desirable goal depends on an appeal to other, more basic values.

Setting down your own or someone else's argument in this form will not necessarily give you the answers to questions about how to support your claim, but it should clearly indicate what your claims are and, above all, what logical connections exist between your statements.

When Rights Run Wild

SUSAN JACOBY

I'm starting to cover my ears whenever I hear another dissatisfied American belligerently demanding some new "right."

A friend of mine is being relentlessly pursued — and threatened with a lawsuit — by the woman who gave her up for adoption thirty-five years ago and now insists she has a grandmother's right to know her grandchildren.

When my neighborhood librarian tries to get a homeless man, who reeks of alcohol and snores loudly, to leave, he snarls, "I have as much right to be here as anyone else."

The evening news features an endless procession of the rights-obsessed — convicted child abusers who want more babies; drunk drivers outraged by Breathalyzer tests at roadblocks; lawyers fighting for the "freedom" of the mentally ill to refuse treatment and live in the street. And let's not forget the right to live and the right to die — with everyone trying to enforce his or her definition of exactly when those rights begin and end.

Enough! This isn't what our forefathers had in mind when they 5 enshrined the concept of individual rights in the Constitution and Declaration of Independence. In the latter document, the Founding Fathers asserted that all Americans are endowed with the rights to "Life, Liberty, and the pursuit of Happiness."

But too many Americans have twisted the sensible right to *pursue* happiness into the delusion that we are entitled to a *guarantee* of happiness. If we don't get exactly what we want, we assume that someone else must be violating our rights.

Many people blame this "rights inflation" on lawyers because they stand to collect fat fees whenever anyone takes a new injustice to court. But I suspect the lawyers are only responding to our unrealistic expectations. As a people, we're no longer willing to write off some of life's disappointments to simple bad luck.

While researching an article on new treatments for infertility, I interviewed a woman who was planning to sue her insurance company because it refused to pay for any more attempts at test-tube fertilization (at $20,000 a try). She'd already been reimbursed for more than $100,000

Susan Jacoby is a journalist and essayist who frequently writes on issues from a feminist standpoint. This article appeared in the March 10, 1992 issue of *Woman's Day.*

of treatments, and her doctor said she was a poor candidate for further attempts to conceive.

I asked this woman why she didn't consider adopting a child — she was already forty years old — instead of filing a lawsuit. "It's my fundamental human right to have a baby," she declared. "The insurance company, by refusing to pay, is taking that away from me."

This is a perfect example of rights inflation. It is, of course, a 10
fundamental human right to *try* to have a baby without interference from the state. That's why we're so horrified at the Chinese government's policy of forcing women to have abortions in order to limit population growth.

But the right to try to conceive — to pursue the happiness of parenthood — doesn't mean society owes every woman a baby. I understand the pain of being physically unable to have a child, but I don't think the rest of us are obliged to provide unlimited financial support for what may prove to be an impossible dream.

Where do this woman's rights end? When her insurance company has spent $200,000? When other policyholders have watched their premiums skyrocket to cover the cost of her high-tech attempts to conceive?

Regardless of the issue, there is no room for compromise, common sense, and courtesy when people pursue what they consider their rights at any cost.

I am thrilled, for instance, that young girls now have a chance to play on Little League baseball teams. There's no reason why ten-year-old girls and boys can't hit, run, throw, and have fun on the same team. But then there's the girl who's fighting for the right to play on a junior-high football team. To me, it seems obvious that contact sports for adolescents are entirely different from noncontact sports for kids. It's senseless to talk about this girl's rights when the real issue should be safety and fun.

The worst thing about rights inflation is that it encourages people 15
to make competing claims instead of seeking solutions for problems. The continuing battle between smokers and nonsmokers offers a perfect example.

I recently watched a couple threaten to sue a restaurant owner because he had mistakenly filed their reservation in his smoking section. The no-smoking section was already full, so he offered the couple a choice: a table in the small smoking area or an hour's wait (with dinner on the house in either case). The enraged couple wasn't about to accept what I considered a sensible solution; the husband insisted that all smoking should be banned for the night. "But what about the rights of the people in the smoking section?" the owner asked plaintively.

Forget about anyone else's rights. These people had booked a no-smoking table, and they had a right to one. There was no room in their world for an honest mistake — just as there is no place in the mental world of many Americans for any kind of bad luck.

It's time for us to grow up and stop taking a conspiracy view of every disappointment. We all have the right to dream, but none of us is entitled to a guarantee that all of our dreams will come true.

Analysis

A deductive argument proceeds from a general statement that the writer assumes to be true to a conclusion that is more specific. Deductive reasoning is commonplace, but it is seldom so pure as the definition suggests. In Jacoby's article the generalization, or major premise, on which the conclusion is based is expressed in paragraphs 5 and 6: The right to happiness is not guaranteed either in law or in principle. She points out that the Constitution guarantees some individual rights; the Declaration of Independence guarantees only the right to *pursue* happiness. The minor premise reflects Jacoby's observation that more and more dissatisfied Americans are claiming "inalienable rights" to happiness, which are not guaranteed. She concludes that the demand for these rights is unjustified; moreover, it imposes unfair costs on the rest of us.

As in any deductive argument, the validity of the claim depends, first of all, on the soundness of the major premise. Is it true? Jacoby is on firm ground with the Declaration of Independence, which affirms "that [all men] are endowed by their Creator with certain inalienable Rights, that among them are Life, Liberty, and the pursuit of Happiness." In this document "certain inalienable rights" are not further defined, but they will be spelled out in the Bill of Rights, the first ten amendments to the Constitution. The Bill of Rights does not, of course, guarantee the right to happiness. It does, however, define specific individual rights to which all citizens are entitled. Jacoby does not mention these, and here questions about the nature of those rights will be relevant. After reading Jacoby's examples, the reader must decide whether the rights that Jacoby condemns are rights to which people are *not* entitled.

In fact, decisions about the justifications for these rights must be left to the legislatures and the courts that interpret the Bill of Rights. Jacoby has made a strong case by choosing extreme examples, a strategy which is appropriate for the purposes of her argument. The title of her essay, "When Rights Run Wild," makes clear what kinds of rights she will condemn. And her examples are likely to spark a sympathetic response in her readers — the demands for the right of a woman to have a baby, of a young girl to play junior high school football, of the mentally ill to live in the street, of a homeless man to disturb readers in the library. On the other hand, it is worth remembering that courts have sometimes supported the rights that Jacoby finds outrageous — for example, that of the homeless man who was not only allowed to continue visiting the library but was also awarded a large sum of money when he sued the town for violating his civil rights.

The fact that the courts will occasionally disagree with Jacoby does not necessarily invalidate her argument. Court judgments that interpret our constitutional rights are often disputed and frequently overturned. And we remember that the premise must satisfy standards of probability, not certainty. Jacoby depends on the strength of her examples and what one writer has called "the lay common sense of the juryman" to persuade most readers that a guarantee of some individual rights was never meant to guarantee the fulfillment of *all* our dreams.

A Note on the Syllogism and the Toulmin Model

In examining the classical deductive syllogism, you may have noticed the resemblance of its three-part outline to the three-part structure of claim, support, and warrant that we have used throughout the text to illustrate the elements of argument. We mentioned that the syllogism was articulated over two thousand years ago by the Greek philosopher Aristotle. By contrast, the claim-support-warrant structure is based on the model of argument proposed by the modern British philosopher Stephen Toulmin.

Now, there is every reason to think that all models of argument will share some similarities. Nevertheless, the differences between the formal syllogism and the informal Toulmin model suggest that the latter is a more effective instrument for writers who want to know which questions to ask, both before they begin and during the process of developing their arguments.

The syllogism is useful for laying out the basic elements of an argument, as we have seen in several examples. It lends itself more readily to simple arguments. The following syllogism summarizes a familiar argument.

MAJOR PREMISE: Advertising of things harmful to our health should be legally banned.

MINOR PREMISE: Cigarettes are harmful to our health.

CONCLUSION: Therefore, advertising of cigarettes should be legally banned.

Cast in the form of a Toulmin outline, the argument looks like this:

CLAIM: Advertising of cigarettes should be legally banned.

SUPPORT (EVIDENCE):   Cigarettes are harmful to our health.

WARRANT: Advertising of things harmful to our health should be legally banned.

or in diagram form:

Support — — — — — — ⊤ — — — — → *Claim*
Cigarettes are harmful   Advertising of cigarettes
to our health.   should be legally banned.

Warrant
Advertising of things harmful to our
health should be legally banned.

In both the syllogism and the Toulmin model the principal elements of the argument are expressed in three statements. You can see that the claim in the Toulmin model is the conclusion in the syllogism — that is, the proposition that you are trying to prove. The evidence (support) in the Toulmin model corresponds to the minor premise in the syllogism. And the warrant in the Toulmin model resembles the major premise of the syllogism.

But the differences are significant. One difference is the use of language. The syllogism represents an argument "in which the validity of the assumption underlying the inference 'leap' is uncontested."[3] That is, the words "major premise" seem to suggest that the assumption has been proved. They do not emphasize that an analysis of the premise — "Advertising of things harmful to our health should be legally banned" — is necessary before we can decide that the conclusion is acceptable. Of course, a careful arguer will try to establish the truth and validity of all parts of the syllogism, but the terms in which the syllogism is framed do not encourage him or her to examine the real relationship among the three elements. Sometimes the enthymeme (see p. 215), which uses only two elements in the argument and suppresses the third, makes analyzing the relationship even more difficult.

In the Toulmin model, the use of the term *warrant* indicates that the validity of the proposition must be established in order to *guarantee* the claim, or make the crossing from support to claim. It makes clear that the arguer must ask *why* such advertising must be banned.

Nor is the term *minor premise* as useful to the arguer as "support." The word *support* instructs the arguer that he or she must take steps to provide the claim with factual evidence or an appeal to values.

A second difference is that while the syllogism is essentially static, with all three parts logically locked into place, the Toulmin model suggests that an argument is a *movement* from support to claim by way of the warrant, which acts as a bridge. Remember that Toulmin introduced the concept of warrant by asking "How do you get there?" (His

---

[3] Wayne E. Brockenreide and Douglas Ehninger, "Toulmin on Argument: An Interpretation and Application," *Contemporary Theories of Rhetoric: Selected Readings*, Richard L. Johannesen, ed. (New York: Harper and Row, 1971), p. 245. This comparative analysis is indebted to Brockenreide and Ehninger's influential article.

first two questions, introducing the claim and support, were, "What are you trying to prove?" and "What have you got to go on?")

Lastly, recall that in addition to the three basic elements, the Toulmin model offers supplementary elements of argument. The *qualifier,* in the form of words like "probably" or "more likely," shows that the claim is not absolute. The *backing* offers support for the validity of the warrant. The *reservation* suggests that the validity of the warrant may be limited. These additional elements, which refine and expand the argument itself, reflect the real flexibility and complexity of the argumentative process.

COMMON FALLACIES

In this necessarily brief review it would be impossible to discuss all the fallacies listed by logicians, but we can examine the ones most likely to be found in the arguments you will read and write. Fallacies are difficult to classify, first, because there are literally dozens of systems for classifying, and second, because under any system there is always a good deal of overlap. Our discussion of the reasoning process, however, tells us where faulty reasoning occurs.

Inductive fallacies, as we know, result from the wrong use of evidence: That is, the arguer leaps to a conclusion on the basis of an insufficient sample, ignoring evidence that might have altered his or her conclusion. Deductive fallacies, on the other hand, result from a failure to follow the logic of a series of statements. Here the arguer neglects to make a clear connection between the parts of his or her argument. One of the commonest strategies is the introduction of an irrelevant issue, one that has little or no direct bearing on the development of the claim and serves only to distract the reader.

It's helpful to remember that, even if you cannot name the particular fallacy, you can learn to recognize it and not only refute it in the arguments of others but avoid it in your own as well.

1. Hasty Generalization

In Chapter 4 (see pp. 115–117) we discussed the dangers in drawing conclusions on the basis of insufficient evidence. Many of our prejudices are a result of hasty generalization. A prejudice is literally a judgment made before the facts are in. On the basis of experience with two or three members of an ethnic group, for example, we may form the prejudice that all members of the group share the characteristics that we have attributed to the two or three in our experience. (See Gordon Allport, "The Nature of Prejudice," on p. 90.)

Superstitions are also based in part on hasty generalization. As a result of a very small number of experiences with black cats, broken mirrors, Friday the thirteenth, or spilled salt, some people will assume a cause-effect relation between these signs and misfortunes. Superstition has been defined as "a notion maintained despite evidence to the contrary." The evidence would certainly show that, contrary to the superstitious belief, in a lifetime hundreds of such "unlucky" signs are not followed by unfortunate events. To generalize about a connection is therefore unjustified.

2. Faulty Use of Authority

The attempt to bolster claims by citing the opinions of experts was discussed in Chapter 4. Both writers and readers need to be especially aware of the testimony of authorities who may disagree with those cited. In circumstances where experts disagree, you are encouraged to undertake a careful evaluation and comparison of credentials.

3. *Post Hoc* or Doubtful Cause

The entire Latin term for this fallacy is *post hoc, ergo propter hoc,* meaning, "After this, therefore because of this." The arguer infers that because one event follows another event, the first event must be the cause of the second. But proximity of events or conditions does not guarantee a causal relation. The rooster crows every morning at 5:00 and, seeing the sun rise immediately after, decides that his crowing has caused the sun to rise. A month after A-bomb tests are concluded, tornadoes damage the area where the tests were held, and residents decide that the tests caused the tornadoes. After the school principal suspends daily prayers in the classroom, acts of vandalism increase, and some parents are convinced that failure to conduct prayer is responsible for the rise in vandalism. In each of these cases, the fact that one event follows another does not prove a causal connection. The two events may be coincidental, or the first event may be only one, and an insignificant one, of many causes that have produced the second event. The reader or writer of causal arguments must determine whether another more plausible explanation exists and whether several causes have combined to produce the effect. Perhaps the suspension of prayer was only one of a number of related causes: a decline in disciplinary action, a relaxation of academic standards, a change in school administration, and changes in family structure in the school community.

In the previous section we pointed out that superstitions are the result not only of hasty generalization but also of the willingness to find a cause-effect connection in the juxtaposition of two events. A belief in astrological signs also derives from erroneous inferences about cause and effect. Only a very few of the millions of people who consult the astrology charts every day in newspapers and magazines have submitted the predictions to statistical analysis. A curious reader might try this strategy: Save the columns, usually at the beginning or end of the year, in which astrologers and clairvoyants make predictions for events in the coming year, allegedly based on their reading of the stars and other signs. At the end of the year evaluate the percentage of predictions that were fulfilled. The number will be very small. But even if some of the predictions prove true, there may be other less fanciful explanations for their accuracy.

In defending simple explanations against complex ones, philosophers and scientists often refer to a maxim called *Occam's razor,* a principle of the medieval philosopher and theologian William of Occam. A modern science writer says this principle "urges a preference for the simplest hypothesis that does all we want it to do."[4] Bertrand Russell, the twentieth-century British philosopher, explained it this way:

> It is vain to do with more what can be done with fewer. That is to say, if everything in some science can be interpreted without assuming this or that hypothetical entity, there is no ground for assuming it. I have myself found this a most fruitful principle in logical analysis.[5]

In other words, choose the simpler, more credible explanation wherever possible.

We all share the belief that scientific experimentation and research can answer questions about a wide range of natural and social phenomena: evolutionary development, hurricanes, disease, crime, poverty. It is true that repeated experiments in controlled situations can establish what seem to be solid relations suggesting cause and effect. But even scientists prefer to talk not about cause but about an extremely high probability that under controlled conditions one event will follow another.

In the social sciences cause-effect relations are especially susceptible to challenge. Human experiences can seldom be subjected to laboratory conditions. In addition, the complexity of the social environment makes it difficult, even impossible, to extract one cause from among the many that influence human behavior.

4. False Analogy

Problems in the use of analogy have been treated in Chapter 5. Many analogies are merely descriptive — like the analogy used by Malcolm X — and offer no proof of the connection between the two things being compared.

Historians are fond of using analogical arguments to demonstrate

---

[4]Martin Gardner, *The Whys of a Philosophical Scrivener* (New York: Quill, 1983), p. 174.

[5]*Dictionary of Mind, Matter and Morals* (New York: Philosophical Library, 1952), p. 166.

that particular circumstances prevailing in the past are being reproduced in the present. They therefore feel safe in predicting that the present course of history will follow that of the past. British historian Arnold Toynbee argues by analogy that humans' tenure on earth may be limited.

> On the evidence of the past history of life on this planet, even the extinction of the human race is not entirely unlikely. After all, the reign of man on the Earth, if we are right in thinking that man established his present ascendancy in the middle paleolithic age, is so far only about 100,000 years old, and what is that compared to the 500 million or 900 million years during which life has been in existence on the surface of this planet? In the past, other forms of life have enjoyed reigns which have lasted for almost inconceivably longer periods — and which yet at last have come to an end.[6]

Toynbee finds similarities between the limited reigns of other animal species and the possible disappearance of the human race. For this analogy, however, we need to ask whether the conditions of the past, so far as we know them, at all resemble the conditions under which human existence on earth might be terminated. Is the fact that human beings are also members of the animal kingdom sufficient support for this comparison?

5. *Ad Hominem*

The Latin term *ad hominem* means "against the man" and refers to an attack on the person rather than on the argument or the issue. The assumption in such a fallacy is that if the speaker proves to be unacceptable in some way, his or her statements must also be judged unacceptable. Attacking the author of the statement is a strategy of diversion that prevents the reader from giving attention where it is due — to the issue under discussion.

You might hear someone complain, "What can the priest tell us about marriage? He's never been married himself." This accusation ignores the validity of the advice the priest might offer. In the same way an overweight patient might reject the advice on diet by an overweight physician. In politics it is not uncommon for antagonists to attack each other for personal characteristics that may not be relevant to the tasks they will be elected to perform. They may be accused of infidelity to their partners, homosexuality, atheism, or a flamboyant social life. Even if certain accusations should be proved true, voters should not ignore the substance of what politicians do and say in their public offices.

This confusion of private life with professional record also exists

---

[6]*Civilization on Trial* (New York: Oxford University Press, 1948), pp. 162–163.

in literature and the other arts. According to their biographers, the American writers Thomas Wolfe, Robert Frost, and William Saroyan — to name only a few — and numbers of film stars, including Charlie Chaplin, Joan Crawford, and Bing Crosby, made life miserable for those closest to them. Having read about their unpleasant personal characteristics, some people find it hard to separate the artist from his or her creation, although the personality and character of the artist are often irrelevant to the content of the work.

Accusations against the person do *not* constitute a fallacy if the characteristics under attack are relevant to the argument. If the politician is irresponsible and dishonest in the conduct of his or her personal life, we may be justified in thinking that the person will also behave irresponsibly and dishonestly in public office.

6. False Dilemma

As the name tells us, the false dilemma, sometimes called the black-white fallacy, poses an either/or situation. The arguer suggests that only two alternatives exist, although there may be other explanations of or solutions to the problem under discussion. The false dilemma reflects the simplification of a complex problem. Sometimes it is offered out of ignorance or laziness, sometimes to divert attention from the real explanation or solution that the arguer rejects for doubtful reasons.

You may encounter the either/or situation in dilemmas about personal choices. "At the University of Georgia," says one writer, "the measure of a man was football. You either played it or worshiped those who did, and there was no middle ground."[7] Clearly this dilemma — "Love football or you're not a man" — ignores other measures of manhood.

Politics and government offer a wealth of examples. In an interview with the *New York Times* in 1975, the Shah of Iran was asked why he could not introduce into his authoritarian regime greater freedom for his subjects. His reply was, "What's wrong with authority? Is anarchy better?" Apparently he considered that only two paths were open to him — authoritarianism or anarchy. Of course, democracy was also an option, which, perhaps fatally, he declined to consider.

7. Slippery Slope

If an arguer predicts that taking a first step will lead inevitably to a second usually undesirable step, he or she must provide evidence that this will happen. Otherwise, the arguer is guilty of a slippery slope fallacy.

---

[7] Phil Gailey, "A Nonsports Fan," *New York Times Magazine,* December 18, 1983, Sec. VI, p. 96.

Asked by an inquiring photographer on the street how he felt about censorship of a pornographic magazine, a man replied, "I don't think any publication should be banned. It's a slippery slope when you start making decisions on what people should be permitted to read. . . . It's a dangerous precedent." Perhaps. But if questioned further, the man should have offered evidence that a ban on some things leads inevitably to a ban on everything.

Predictions based on the danger inherent in taking the first step are commonplace:

> Legalization of abortion will lead to murder of the old and the physically and mentally handicapped.

> The Connecticut law allowing sixteen-year-olds and their parents to divorce each other will mean the death of the family.

> If we ban handguns, we will end up banning rifles and other hunting weapons.

Distinguishing between probable and improbable predictions — that is, recognizing the slippery slope fallacy — poses special problems because only future developments can verify or refute predictions. For example, in 1941 the imposition of military conscription aroused some opponents to predict that the draft was a precursor of fascism in this country. Only after the war, when ten million draftees were demobilized, did it become clear that the draft had been an insufficient sign for a prediction of fascism. In this case the slippery slope prediction of fascism might have been avoided if closer attention had been paid to other influences pointing to the strength of democracy.

Slippery slope predictions are simplistic. They ignore not only the dissimilarities between first and last steps but also the complexity of the developments in any long chain of events.

8. Begging the Question

If the writer makes a statement that assumes that the very question being argued has already been proved, the writer is guilty of begging the question. In a letter to the editor of a college newspaper protesting the failure of the majority of students to meet the writing requirement because they had failed an exemption test, the writer said, "Not exempting all students who honestly qualify for exemption is an insult." But whether the students are honestly qualified is precisely the question that the exemption test was supposed to resolve. The writer has not proved that the students who failed the writing test were qualified for exemption. She has only made an assertion *as if* she had already proved it.

In an effort to raise standards of teaching, some politicians and educators have urged that "master teachers" be awarded higher salaries. Opponents have argued that such a proposal begs the question because it assumes that the term "master teachers" can be or has already been defined.

Circular reasoning is an extreme example of begging the question: "Women should not be permitted to join men's clubs because the clubs are for men only." The question to be resolved first, of course, is whether clubs for men only should continue to exist.

9. Straw Man

This fallacy consists of an attack on a view similar to but not the same as the one your opponent holds. It is a familiar diversionary tactic. The name probably derives from an old game in which a straw man was set up to divert attention from the real target that a contestant was supposed to knock down.

One of the outstanding examples of the straw man fallacy occurred in the famous Checkers speech of Senator Richard Nixon. In 1952 during his vice-presidential campaign, Nixon was accused of having appropriated $18,000 in campaign funds for his personal use. At one point in the radio and television speech in which he defended his reputation, he said:

> One other thing I probably should tell you, because if I don't they will probably be saying this about me, too. We did get something, a gift, after the election.
>
> A man down in Texas heard Pat on the radio mention the fact that our two youngsters would like to have a dog, and, believe it or not, the day before we left on this campaign trip we got a message from Union Station in Baltimore saying they had a package for us. We went down to get it. You know what it was?
>
> It was a little cocker spaniel dog, in a crate that he had sent all the way from Texas, black and white, spotted, and our little girl, Tricia, the six-year-old, named it Checkers.
>
> And, you know, the kids, like all kids, loved the dog, and I just want to say this, right now, that regardless of what they say about it, we are going to keep it.[8]

Of course, Nixon knew that the issue was the alleged misappropriation of funds, not the ownership of the dog, which no one had asked him to return.

---

[8] Radio and television address of Senator Nixon from Los Angeles on September 23, 1952.

10. Two Wrongs Make a Right

This is another example of the way in which attention may be diverted from the question at issue.

After a speech by President Jimmy Carter in March 1977 attacking the human rights record of the Soviet Union, Russian officials responded:

> As for the present state of human rights in the United States, it is characterized by the following facts: millions of unemployed, racial discrimination, social inequality of women, infringement of citizens' personal freedom, the growth of crime, and so on.[9]

The Russians made no attempt to deny the failure of *their* human rights record; instead they attacked by pointing out that the Americans are not blameless either.

11. *Non Sequitur*

The Latin term *non sequitur,* which means "it does not follow," is another fallacy of irrelevance. An advertisement for a book, *Worlds in Collision,* whose theories about the origin of the earth and evolutionary development have been challenged by almost all reputable scientists, states:

> Once rejected as "preposterous!" Critics called it an outrage! It aroused incredible antagonism in scientific and literary circles. Yet half a million copies were sold and for twenty-seven years it remained an outstanding bestseller.

We know, of course, that the popularity of a book does not bestow scientific respectability. The number of sales, therefore, is irrelevant to proof of the book's theoretical soundness.

12. *Ad Populum*

Arguers guilty of this fallacy make an appeal to the prejudices of the people (*populum* in Latin). They assume that their claim can be adequately defended without further support if they emphasize a belief or attitude that the audience shares with them. One common form of *ad populum* is an appeal to patriotism, which may allow arguers to omit evidence that the audience needs for proper evaluation of the claim. In the following advertisement the makers of Zippo lighters made such an appeal in urging readers to buy their product.

---

[9]*New York Times,* March 3, 1977, p. 1.

It's a grand old lighter. Zippo — the grand old lighter that's made right here in the good old U. S. A.

We truly make an all-American product. The raw materials used in making a Zippo lighter are all right from this great land of ours.

Zippo windproof lighters are proud to be Americans.

13. Appeal to Tradition

In making an appeal to tradition, the arguer assumes that what has existed for a long time and has therefore become a tradition should continue to exist *because* it is a tradition. If the arguer avoids telling his or her reader *why* the tradition should be preserved, he or she may be accused of failing to meet the real issue.

The following statement appeared in a letter defending the membership policy of the Century Club, an all-male club established in New York City in 1847 that was under pressure to admit women. The writer was a Presbyterian minister who opposed the admission of women.

> I am totally opposed to a proposal which would radically change the nature of the Century. . . . A club creates an ethos of its own over the years, and I would deeply deplore a step that would inevitably create an entirely different kind of place.
>
> A club like the Century should surely be unaffected by fashionable whims. . . .[10]

14. Faulty Emotional Appeals

In some discussions of fallacies, appeals to the emotions of the audience are treated as illegitimate or "counterfeit proofs." All such appeals, however, are *not* illegitimate. As we saw in Chapter 4 on support, appeals to the values and emotions of an audience are an appropriate form of persuasion. You can recognize fallacious appeals if (1) they are irrelevant to the argument or draw attention from the issues being argued or (2) they appear to conceal another purpose. Here we treat two of the most popular appeals — to pity and to fear.

Appeals to pity, compassion, and natural willingness to help the unfortunate are particularly hard to resist. The requests for aid by most charitable organizations — for hungry children, victims of disaster, stray animals — offer examples of legitimate appeals. But these appeals to our sympathetic feelings should not divert us from considering other issues in a particular case. It would be wrong, for example, to allow a multiple murderer to escape punishment because he or she had experienced a wretched childhood. Likewise, if you are asked to contribute to a charitable cause, you should try to learn how many unfortunate people or animals are being helped and what percentage of the contri-

---

[10] David H. C. Read, letter to the *New York Times,* January 13, 1983, p. 14.

bution will be allocated to maintaining the organization and its officers. In some cases the financial records are closed to public review, and only a small share of the contribution will reach the alleged beneficiaries.

Appeals to fear are likely to be even more effective. But they must be based on evidence that fear is an appropriate response to the issues and that it can move an audience toward a solution to the problem. (Fear can also have the adverse effect of preventing people from taking a necessary action.) Insurance companies, for example, make appeals to our fears of destitution for ourselves and our families as a result of injury, unemployment, sickness, and death. These appeals are justified if the possibilities of such destitution are real and if the insurance will provide relief. It would also be legitimate to arouse fear of the consequences of drunk driving, provided, again, that the descriptions were accurate. On the other hand, it would be wrong to induce fear that fluoridation of public water supplies causes cancer without presenting sound evidence of the probability. It would also be wrong to instill a fear of school integration unless convincing proof were offered of undesirable social consequences.

An emotional response by itself is not always the soundest basis for making decisions. Your own experience has probably taught you that in the grip of a strong emotion like love or hate or anger you often overlook good reasons for making different and better choices. Like you, your readers want to be given the opportunity to consider all the available kinds of support for an argument.

READINGS FOR ANALYSIS

On Nation and Race
ADOLF HITLER

There are some truths which are so obvious that for this very reason they are not seen or at least not recognized by ordinary people. They sometimes pass by such truisms as though blind and are most astonished when someone suddenly discovers what everyone really ought to know. Columbus's eggs lie around by the hundreds of thousands, but Columbuses are met with less frequency.

Thus men without exception wander about in the garden of Nature;

Adolf Hitler (1889–1945) became the Nazi dictator of Germany in the mid-1930s. "On Nation and Race" (editor's title) begins the eleventh chapter of *Mein Kampf (My Struggle)*, vol. 1, published in 1925.

they imagine that they know practically everything and yet with few exceptions pass blindly by one of the most patent principles of Nature's rule: the inner segregation of the species of all living beings on this earth.

Even the most superficial observation shows that Nature's restricted form of propagation and increase is an almost rigid basic law of all the innumerable forms of expression of her vital urge. Every animal mates only with a member of the same species. The titmouse seeks the titmouse, the finch the finch, the stork the stork, the field mouse the field mouse, the dormouse the dormouse, the wolf the she-wolf, etc.

Only unusual circumstances can change this, primarily the compulsion of captivity or any other cause that makes it impossible to mate within the same species. But then Nature begins to resist this with all possible means, and her most visible protest consists either in refusing further capacity for propagation to bastards or in limiting the fertility of later offspring; in most cases, however, she takes away the power of resistance to disease or hostile attacks.

This is only too natural.   5

Any crossing of two beings not at exactly the same level produces a medium between the level of the two parents. This means: The offspring will probably stand higher than the racially lower parent, but not as high as the higher one. Consequently, it will later succumb in the struggle against the higher level. Such mating is contrary to the will of Nature for a higher breeding of all life. The precondition for this does not lie in associating superior and inferior, but in the total victory of the former. The stronger must dominate and not blend with the weaker, thus sacrificing his own greatness. Only the born weakling can view this as cruel, but he after all is only a weak and limited man; for if this law did not prevail, any conceivable higher development of organic living beings would be unthinkable.

The consequence of this racial purity, universally valid in Nature, is not only the sharp outward delimitation of the various races, but their uniform character in themselves. The fox is always a fox, the goose a goose, the tiger a tiger, etc., and the difference can lie at most in the varying measure of force, strength, intelligence, dexterity, endurance, etc., of the individual specimens. But you will never find a fox who in his inner attitude might, for example, show humanitarian tendencies toward geese, as similarly there is no cat with a friendly inclination toward mice.

Therefore, here, too, the struggle among themselves arises less from inner aversion than from hunger and love. In both cases, Nature looks on calmly, with satisfaction, in fact. In the struggle for daily bread all those who are weak and sickly or less determined succumb, while the struggle of the males for the female grants the right or opportunity to propagate only to the healthiest. And struggle is always a means for improving a species' health and power of resistance and, therefore, a cause of its higher development.

If the process were different, all further and higher development would cease and the opposite would occur. For, since the inferior always predominates numerically over the best, if both had the same possibility of preserving life and propagating, the inferior would multiply so much more rapidly that in the end the best would inevitably be driven into the background, unless a correction of this state of affairs were undertaken. Nature does just this by subjecting the weaker part to such severe living conditions that by them alone the number is limited, and by not permitting the remainder to increase promiscuously, but making a new and ruthless choice according to strength and health.

No more than Nature desires the mating of weaker with stronger   10 individuals, even less does she desire the blending of a higher with a lower race, since, if she did, her whole work of higher breeding, over perhaps hundreds of thousands of years, might be ruined with one blow.

Historical experience offers countless proofs of this. It shows with terrifying clarity that in every mingling of Aryan blood with that of lower peoples the result was the end of the cultured people. North America, whose population consists in by far the largest part of Germanic elements who mixed but little with the lower colored peoples, shows a different humanity and culture from Central and South America, where the predominantly Latin immigrants often mixed with the aborigines on a large scale. By this one example, we can clearly and distinctly recognize the effect of racial mixture. The Germanic inhabitant of the American continent, who has remained racially pure and unmixed, rose to be master of the continent; he will remain the master as long as he does not fall a victim to defilement of the blood.

The result of all racial crossing is therefore in brief always the following:

(a) Lowering of the level of the higher race;

(b) Physical and intellectual regression and hence the beginning of a slowly but surely progressing sickness.

To bring about such a development is, then, nothing else but to sin   15 against the will of the eternal creator.

And as a sin this act is rewarded.

When man attempts to rebel against the iron logic of Nature, he comes into struggle with the principles to which he himself owes his existence as a man. And this attack must lead to his own doom.

Here, of course, we encounter the objection of the modern pacifist, as truly Jewish in its effrontery as it is stupid! "Man's role is to overcome Nature!"

Millions thoughtlessly parrot this Jewish nonsense and end up by really imagining that they themselves represent a kind of conqueror of Nature; though in this they dispose of no other weapon than an idea, and at that such a miserable one, that if it were true no world at all would be conceivable.

But quite aside from the fact that man has never yet conquered   20 Nature in anything, but at most has caught hold of and tried to lift one or another corner of her immense gigantic veil of eternal riddles and secrets, that in reality he invents nothing but only discovers everything, that he does not dominate Nature, but has only risen on the basis of his knowledge of various laws and secrets of Nature to be lord over those other living creatures who lack this knowledge — quite aside from all this, an idea cannot overcome the preconditions for the development and being of humanity, since the idea itself depends only on man. Without human beings there is no human idea in this world; therefore, the idea as such is always conditioned by the presence of human beings and hence of all the laws which created the precondition for their existence.

And not only that! Certain ideas are even tied up with certain men. This applies most of all to those ideas whose content originates, not in an exact scientific truth, but in the world of emotion, or, as it is so beautifully and clearly expressed today, reflects an "inner experience." All these ideas, which have nothing to do with cold logic as such, but represent only pure expressions of feeling, ethical conceptions, etc., are chained to the existence of men, to whose intellectual imagination and creative power they owe their existence. Precisely in this case the preservation of these definite races and men is the precondition for the existence of these ideas. Anyone, for example, who really desired the victory of the pacifistic idea in this world with all his heart would have to fight with all the means at his disposal for the conquest of the world by the Germans; for, if the opposite should occur, the last pacifist would die out with the last German, since the rest of the world has never fallen so deeply as our own people, unfortunately, has for this nonsense so contrary to Nature and reason. Then, if we were serious, whether we liked it or not, we would have to wage wars in order to arrive at pacifism. This and nothing else was what Wilson, the American world savior, intended, or so at least our German visionaries believed — and thereby his purpose was fulfilled.

In actual fact the pacifistic-humane idea is perfectly all right perhaps when the highest type of man has previously conquered and subjected the world to an extent that makes him the sole ruler of this earth. Then this idea lacks the power of producing evil effects in exact proportion as its practical application becomes rare and finally impossible. Therefore, first struggle and then we shall see what can be done. Otherwise mankind has passed the high point of its development and the end is not the domination of any ethical idea but barbarism and consequently chaos. At this point someone or other may laugh, but this planet once moved through the ether for millions of years without human beings and it can do so again some day if men forget that they owe their higher existence, not to the ideas of a few crazy ideologists, but to the knowledge and ruthless application of Nature's stern and rigid laws.

Everything we admire on this earth today — science and art, technology and inventions — is only the creative product of a few peoples and originally perhaps of *one* race. On them depends the existence of this whole culture. If they perish, the beauty of this earth will sink into the grave with them.

However much the soil, for example, can influence men, the result of the influence will always be different depending on the races in question. The low fertility of a living space may spur the one race to the highest achievements; in others it will only be the cause of bitterest poverty and final undernourishment with all its consequences. The inner nature of peoples is always determining for the manner in which outward influences will be effective. What leads the one to starvation trains the other to hard work.

All great cultures of the past perished only because the originally 25 creative race died out from blood poisoning.

The ultimate cause of such a decline was their forgetting that all culture depends on men and conversely; hence that to preserve a certain culture the man who creates it must be preserved. This preservation is bound up with the rigid law of necessity and the right to victory of the best and stronger in this world.

Those who want to live, let them fight, and those who do not want to fight in this world of eternal struggle do not deserve to life.

Even if this were hard — that is how it is! Assuredly, however, by far the harder fate is that which strikes the man who thinks he can overcome Nature, but in the last analysis only mocks her. Distress, misfortune, and diseases are her answer.

The man who misjudges and disregards the racial laws actually forfeits the happiness that seems destined to be his. He thwarts the triumphal march of the best race and hence also the precondition for all human progress, and remains, in consequence, burdened with all the sensibility of man, in the animal realm of helpless misery.

It is idle to argue which race or races were the original represen- 30 tative of human culture and hence the real founders of all that we sum up under the word "humanity." It is simpler to raise the question with regard to the present, and here an easy, clear answer results. All the human culture, all the results of art, science, and technology that we see before us today, are almost exclusively the creative product of the Aryan. This very fact admits of the not unfounded inference that he alone was the founder of all higher humanity, therefore representing the prototype of all that we understand by the word "man." He is the Prometheus of mankind from whose bright forehead the divine spark of genius has sprung at all times, forever kindling anew that fire of knowledge which illumined the night of silent mysteries and thus caused man to climb the path to mastery over the other beings of this earth. Exclude him — and perhaps after a few thousand years darkness will again descend on the earth, human culture will pass, and the world turn to a desert.

Discussion Questions

1. In explaining his ideology, how does Hitler misinterpret the statement that "Every animal mates only with a member of the same species"? How would you characterize this fallacy?
2. Hitler uses the theory of evolution and his interpretation of the "survival of the fittest" to justify his racial philosophy. Find the places in the text where Hitler reveals that he misunderstands the theory in its application to human beings.
3. What false evidence about race does Hitler use in his assessment of the racial experience in North America? Examine carefully the last sentence of paragraph 11: "The Germanic inhabitant of the American continent, who has remained racially pure and unmixed, rose to be master of the continent; he will remain the master as long as he does not fall a victim to defilement of the blood."
4. What criticism of Jews does Hitler offer? How does this criticism help to explain Hitler's pathological hatred of Jews?
5. Hitler believes that pacifism is a violation of "Nature and reason." Would modern scientists agree that the laws of Nature require unremitting struggle and conflict between human beings — until the master race conquers?

Writing Suggestion

Do some research in early human history to discover the degree of truth in this statement: "All human culture, all the results of art, science, and technology that we see before us today, are almost exclusively the creative product of the Aryan." You may want to limit your discussion to one area of human culture.

A Criminal Justifies Himself
TONY PARKER and ROBERT ALLERTON

My first question is this: If you were to describe yourself in one word, would the description invariably be "a criminal"?

Yes, definitely. That's what I am, I never think of myself in any other way.

And have you any intention of changing, of going straight or reforming?

Tony Parker is a British sociologist who has written several books on crime and prisons, including *The Courage of His Convictions* (1962), from which this interview with career criminal Robert Allerton is excerpted.

None whatsoever. There's one thing, though, I'd like to make clear right at the start — and that is, I don't want to try and pass myself off as a "master criminal" or anything like that. I'm not. I've had successes and failures in life like everyone else, and I'm nothing out of the ordinary as far as criminals go. I don't consider myself cleverer than most, or even cleverer than the police, for example: sometimes I have been, and quite obviously sometimes not. On the whole I'd say I was just the ordinary run of professional criminal, similar to — well, let's say to a bank clerk from Surbiton in the straight world. But having said that, still definitely "a criminal," yes . . .

Is there any particular form of crime, or criminal activity, which 5 *you wouldn't commit?*

A year or two ago I used to think I'd never go in for drug-trafficking, but now I'm not so sure about that. I've never actually done it yet, but as I get older I seem to be losing my inhibitions, I don't feel as strongly about it as I used to. There's only one thing I still feel I could never do, and that's poncing.[1] To me it's the worst thing of the lot, I'd never stoop to it — or at least I hope I wouldn't. Maybe I'm old-fashioned, or sentimental about women or something — I just can't stomach the idea of poncing at all. I've nothing but contempt, real, deep contempt, for ponces.

There's no other limit you'd set yourself?

No, I'll go as far as necessary, whatever it is.

What does that mean, exactly?

What it says. If it was ever necessary to kill somebody, well, I'd go 10 up to and including that. I'd kill somebody in a fit of temper, I'm quite capable of that — or if they were trying to stop me getting something I'd really made up my mind to have. Or if they were holding me down, and there was so much at stake that I'd just got to get away. But I think most people have it in them to do murder at some time in their lives, under certain circumstances.

The thing that I find most difficult to understand about you is that you're apparently quite undeterred by your repeated prison sentences. You've now reached the stage, with your record, that when you're caught next time it's more than likely you'll get about eight years' preventive detention. I don't understand how you can be prepared to face that.

I'm not prepared. This is the thing which people like you can never grasp. I'm no more "prepared" to do eight years' P.D. than you're prepared to knock somebody down in your car tomorrow. I don't think too much about the one more than you do about the other. It's an ever-present risk but one doesn't dwell on it — do you see what I mean? . . .

I don't want to do eight years, no — but if I have to I have to, and that's all there is to it. If you're a criminal, what's the alternative to the

---

[1] Pimping. — ED.

risk of going to prison? Coal-miners don't spend their time worrying about the risk they might get killed by a fall at the coal-face either. Prison's an occupational risk, that's all — and one I'm quite prepared to take. I'll willingly gamble away a third of my life in prison, so long as I can live the way I want for the other two-thirds. After all, it's my life, and that's how I feel about it. The alternative — the prospect of vegetating the rest of my life away in a steady job, catching the 8:13 to work in the morning, and the 5:50 back again at night, all for ten or fifteen quid[2] a week — now that really does terrify me, far more than the thought of a few years in the nick.

You don't think, then, that there's anything wrong in not working for your living?

But I do work for my living. Most crime — unless it's the senseless, petty-thieving sort — is quite hard work, you know. Planning a job, working out all the details of the best way to do it — and then carrying it out, under a lot of nervous strain and tension — and having to run round afterwards, if it's goods, fencing the stuff, getting a good price for it, delivering it to the fence, and so on — all this needs a lot of thinking and effort and concentration. It certainly is "work," don't kid yourself about that.

But anyway this whole point's not all that simple. A lot of other people don't "work" for their living, in the way you mean — but nobody goes on at them like they do at criminals. Quite a large proportion of the "upper classes," for instance. You can see them any day round Piccadilly, Vigo Street, Savile Row — nattily dressed half-wits who've never done a stroke of work in their lives, popping in and out of Fortnum's or Scott's, spending all their time trying to get rid of the money their fathers and grandfathers and great-grandfathers left them. And usually it's that sort who get fiercest about people like me, saying we ought to be caned and whipped and flogged because we never do an honest day's work.

I can steal from people like that without the faintest compunction at all, in fact I'm delighted to do it. I remember once screwing the town house of the Duke of . . . well, I'd better not say who, because I didn't get caught for it. The inside of the house was the most beautiful place I've ever been in in my life — gorgeous curtains and furnishings, antique furniture, silver bowls and vases all over the place, exquisite miniatures on the walls — it was a fabulous place. My only regret was I hadn't got a furniture van so I could strip it from top to bottom. His Lordship I suppose was up in Scotland shooting wild birds, or some other civilized hobby, and his house was just standing unused until he chose to come back and live in it again.

I remember after I'd come out I passed an old man in rags, standing

---

[2] Ten or fifteen pounds sterling. — ED.

on the street-corner scraping at a violin to try and earn himself a few coppers, and I thought: "You mug, why don't you go in there and at least get yourself a good sleep in one of his Lordship's unused beds for a night."

All the things that were in that house, all those beautiful possessions, the duke had got for himself without the faintest effort of any kind. Most of them had been handed down to him, and all he'd ever had to do to get the others was write out a check — and he probably didn't even do that for himself but had a flunkey to do it. Never in his whole life had he known what it was like to be short of anything. Well, I had, and I don't think it was wrong to steal enough from him to subsidize me for a bit.

And those people, when they have something nicked, they've got it   20 all insured anyway, so they don't suffer. Sometimes they advertise for its return — you know, "Sentimental value" and all that. I'm sure I'd feel sentimental, too, about losing something worth a few hundred quid, only I'd be a bit more honest about it.

And the stuff I pinched from that particular house I appreciated, I did really. In fact, if it hadn't been too dangerous, I'd gladly have kept a lot of it to have around my own place, because it was so beautiful. But I never felt bad about taking it — why should I? I feel terrific. He'd got no cause for complaint, because it was taken, after all, by someone who could really appreciate its artistic merit, not one of those insensitive thugs who couldn't differentiate between Royal Worcester and a Woolworth's chamber-pot. . . .

What about wages-snatches?

. . . All right, wages-snatches. I'll try and take it from the beginning.

If I can see a chance of earning myself — or making myself, if you prefer it — a few thousand quid all at one go, naturally I'll do it. It's only what people, millions of them, are trying to do on the football pools every week. You could say: "Yes, but they're trying to do it honestly" — to which I'd reply: "It depends on your definition of honest, because while they're trying to get themselves several thousand of someone else's money for the outlay of a few shillings and no work. I'm trying to get it by some careful thinking and plotting, some bloody hard effort, and the risk of my own liberty into the bargain."

So who's doing more to earn the money — me or the pools "inves-   25 tors," as they're called? (By the promoters, of course. It's the old con-man's trick of persuading a mug you're going to give him something for nothing, playing on people's natural avarice and greed.) The "investors" trust to luck to bring them a lot of money — well, I bank on my own efforts.

But there's a difference. Pools winnings come out of what the "investors" hand over voluntarily, so those who lose have no complaint. Workers don't hand over their wages voluntarily for you to steal.

I'll say they don't. But look, don't try to break my heart. Who loses on a wages-snatch — the workers? Of course not. It's the company — and they can usually stand it. It's the same with banks — if I have a few thousand from a bank, theoretically it's their customers' money I've taken. But you never hear of a bank apportioning the losses round their customers, do you? "We're so sorry, Major Bloodworthy, somebody blew our safe last night and took ten thousand quid — and it was your ten thousand that was in there!" Mind you, I'm not saying they shouldn't; to me it's quite an attractive idea.

No, let's face it, most of these people are insured against robberies, so it's only the insurance companies who pay up.

But this doesn't in any way defend the use of violence to get it, does it, by coshing[3] the man carrying the wages-bag for instance? . . .

Bob . . .   30

Yes, all right. So violence is wrong, on a fundamental level, I admit that. But on a day-to-day level it just happens that it's a tool of my trade and I use it — like an engineer uses a slide-rule, or a bus-driver the handbrake, or a dentist the drill. Only when necessary, and only when it can't be avoided. If I've got to whack a bloke with an iron bar to make him let go of the wages-bag he's carrying, O.K., so I'll whack him. If he lets go without any trouble, I don't. That's all.

I don't indulge in it, you know, for the sheer pleasure of the thing. I'm no sadist. This has always been my theory, that I'll take whatever job comes along. If there's a vanload of stuff to be pulled, I'll pull it; a screwing job, I'll screw it; a safe-blowing, I'll blow it — and so on. And if it's a coshing job, well then, I'll use a cosh. . . .

I can remember the first time quite clearly, I was only a kid, sixteen or seventeen, and thought myself a real tearaway of course. There was an old woman, a pawnbroker I think she was, lived in a little house just off Cable Street somewhere. Me and a couple of my mates heard that on Saturday nights she always had a bomb in there. Money was short and we decided to have it.

We went along about nine o'clock one Saturday night with shooters, banging on the door and shouting out: "Mrs. Rosenbloom, Mrs. Rosenbloom!" or whatever her name was. "Let us in, it's urgent, we've got to talk to you." She opened the door, and seeing we were only kids she let us in. When we were inside we shoved her back into her kitchen and knocked her into a chair, telling her to keep quiet while we turned the place inside out looking for the money.

So of course she starts screaming and raving like a mad woman.   35
Before we went in it'd been decided it was going to be my job to keep her quiet. I rammed my shooter up against her ear and said: "Belt up, you old faggot, or I'll pull the trigger."

It made not a blind bit of difference, she just yelled all the louder

---

[3] Hitting with a blackjack. — ED.

for help. The other two were tearing everything to bits trying to find where she'd hidden her money, and this racket she was making was really getting on their nerves, so one of them said: "Oh, for Christ's sake, hit the old bag, can't you? If you don't lay her out she'll have the whole neighborhood on us."

And I just couldn't do it. All I could do was stand there bleating: "Shut up, will you! I'm warning you, I'll pull the trigger." Naturally it didn't stop her. Finally one of the other two walked over, took the gun out of my hand, and belted her unconscious. He put the gun back in my hand, really angry, and he said: "It's her or us, you silly bastard, can't you see that?"

It taught me the lesson, and after that I was all right. . . .

Not long after that there was another job, in a warehouse in Islington: And this one got rid of the last of my scruples about violence. While we were in the place the night watchman heard us moving about and he came up the stairs to the floor we were on, to see what was going on. On the landing were a couple of five-gallon oil drums. When I saw him coming towards us, I lifted one of them right over my head and let him have it. It knocked him back all the way downstairs, but he lay at the bottom yelling blue murder, so I took a fire extinguisher off the wall and went down and laid him out with it. I didn't try to batter him to death or anything, just put him out and stop his noise. I didn't feel angry, savage, anything like that — I don't think I felt anything, just dispassionate about it, knowing it'd got to be done, because he was threatening us and our safety with his noise.

You felt no compunction at all about hitting him like that? 40

No, none. I feel if someone takes a job as night watchman he's got to be prepared to be hit if he tries to make a hero of himself. I wouldn't have touched him if he'd left us alone, but since he tried to stop us he got what he earned. Personally I think he was stupid, he should have kept quiet and kept his nose out of it. What was he trying to do, win himself a medal? And what was he hoping to get from it, anyway — a pat on the shoulder from the guv'nor, "Good fella, Jim," a gold watch when he retired? Anyone who takes a job like that wants his brains testing, to me he does. Perhaps I'm missing something, but I can't see anything admirable in it at all, these heroes trying to win themselves medals for about nine-pounds-ten a week. You read in the papers sometimes — "Last night Mr. Jim Smith tried to tackle some bandits and he's now in hospital recovering from concussion." It always gives me a laugh, if it was a job I was on that it's referring to. O.K., so the bloke's a hero and got his name in the paper. So what's he got for it? Concussion. And what have I got? What I went for, which is what I would have got anyway, and he needn't have got his concussion trying to stop me.

But it's fortunate not everybody uses your methods, isn't it, or else we'd all be living in the jungle?

But we *are* living in a jungle. You've put your finger on it with that word, though, because that's all it is, a question of method. Lots of people take money off others, but they use other ways of doing it. Some of them are considered respectable. Personally I don't think they are — but it's a matter of opinion, that's all.

A landlord gets money out of people when he puts their rents up, by extortion, by playing on the fact they've got nowhere else to live. And the Law upholds him in doing it. Yet really all he's doing is stealing money from people. But if I go along and steal that money from him he screams to the Law, and they come after me to try and get his money back for him. If his tenant screams to the police that his landlord's robbing him, they do nothing of course. No: He perpetrates his crime upheld by all the respectability of society, without any risk on his part of going to prison. Well, personally, I think my method's a lot more straightforward and honest than his is. And I don't pretend to be doing anything other than what I am — stealing. But the landlord does. And what's more, I don't go in for robbing poor people, either, like he does. Thieving off your own kind, that's terrible.

Or take the case of a jeweller. He's a business man, and he's in the   45
game to make money. O.K., so I'm a business man too, and I'm also out to make money. We just use different methods. The jeweller makes a profit — and often a very big profit — out of what he sells. On top of that he fiddles the income tax and the purchase tax, and even the customs duty as well if he can get away with it. That's considered all right by him and others like him, and if he makes enough to buy himself a big house and a posh car everyone looks up to him as a clever fellow, a shrewd business man. But how's he got his money? By rooking people, taking advantage of soft young couples getting engaged to sell them a more expensive ring than they can afford, and fiddling the authorities whenever he can. But at least he didn't steal it. Well, what's in a name? Tell me exactly where the line is between thieving and "shrewd business" and I might believe it. What's more, the jeweller can insure himself against people like me going and pinching his stock. But I can't insure against the police nicking me, can I? The Law's on one side only, the side of the pretenders, that's all.

It's funny, there's a few criminals, you do meet them from time to time, who won't do any violence. A firm I was with once, there was three of them besides me, we were discussing some job we had in view — a wages-snatch I think it was — where it was obvious we'd have to whack someone to get what we wanted. One of the three was one of these humanitarian types, you know, had what you might call a conscientious objection to using violence altogether. He went on about it so long the other two started to dither as well. We had a long argument about it, and my line was the one I've already explained: If violence needs doing, then you've got to do it. Some people won't hand over to you what you want just like that, so you've got to whack them. Well, this whole job fell through because they didn't look at it my way at all, they were scared about the thing. Once you start drawing lines here, there, and everywhere about what you will do, and what you won't, you might as well give up villainy altogether. It's amateurism — and the amateur's the curse of thieving like he is of any other game. The only approach I can go along with is to be a professional, and get on with whatever comes.

Discussion Questions

1. Do you detect fallacious reasoning in the following statements? Examine the statements that precede or follow them in the interview in order to understand the context.
   a. ". . . I think most people have it in them to do murder at some time in their lives, under certain circumstances."
   b. "A lot of other people don't 'work' for their living, in the way you mean — but nobody goes on at them like they do at criminals."
   c. "Never in his whole life had he known what it was like to be short of anything. Well, I had, and I don't think it was wrong to steal enough from him to subsidize me for a bit."
   d. "He [the Duke]'d got no cause for complaint, because it was taken, after all, by someone who could really appreciate its artistic merit, not one of those insensitive thugs who couldn't differentiate between Royal Worcester and a Woolworth's chamber-pot."
   e. "So violence is wrong, on a fundamental level, I admit that. But on a day-to-day level it just happens that it's a tool of my trade and I use it — like an engineer uses a slide-rule, or a bus-driver the handbrake, or a dentist the drill."
2. How does Robert Allerton justify his use of violence against the old woman pawnbroker and the night watchman at the warehouse? Is there any weakness in his defense?
3. Are his analogies between burglar and landlord and burglar and jeweller sound?

Writing Suggestions

1. The introduction to this interview says: "An English career criminal discusses the philosophy of his occupation." Write a letter to the criminal, summarizing your principal criticisms of the reasoning he uses to justify his occupation. Name specific fallacies, if possible. If some of his arguments seem valid, point these out as well.
2. Invent an occupation for yourself (such as mercenary soldier, phony doctor or lawyer, smuggler of contraband goods, drug dealer) that might be regarded dubiously by most people, and write an essay in which you defend your work. Invite your classmates to discover any fallacies.

CHERYL SILAS had a highway collision, was hit twice from behind, and then sold three cars for us.

When Cheryl unbuckled her shoulder harness and lap belt, it took her a moment to realize her Saturn coupe was really a mess. And that, remarkably, she wasn't. That's when she decided to get another SC.

Several other people arrived at similar conclusions. A policeman at the accident scene came in soon after and ordered himself a sedan. As did a buddy of his, also on the force. Then Cheryl's brother, glad he still had a sister, bought yet another Saturn in Illinois.

Now, good referrals are important to any product. And we're always glad to have them. But we'd be more than happy if our customers found less dramatic ways to help spread the word.

A DIFFERENT KIND OF COMPANY. A DIFFERENT KIND OF CAR.

© 1991 Saturn Corporation. M.S.R.P. of 1992 Saturn SC shown is $12,415, including retailer prep and optional sunroof. Tax, license, transportation and other options additional. If you'd like to know more about Saturn, and our new sedans and coupe, please call us at 1-800-522-5000.

Discussion Questions

1. What example of inductive reasoning does the advertiser use? How would you evaluate the probability of the conclusion?
2. To what extent does the use of an alleged real person in a narrative contribute to the effectiveness of the advertiser's pitch? Should the ad have contained more factual information?

EXERCISES FOR CRITICAL THINKING

Decide whether the reasoning in the following examples is faulty. Explain your answers.

1. The presiding judge of a revolutionary tribunal, on being asked why people were being executed without trial: "Why should we put them on trial when we know that they're guilty?"
2. Since good nutrition is essential to the health of its citizens, the government should punish people who eat junk food.
3. A research study demonstrated that children who watched "Seinfeld" rather than "Roseanne" received higher grades in school. So it must be true that "Seinfeld" is more educational than "Roseanne."
4. The meteorologist was wrong in predicting the amount of rain for May. Obviously the meteorologist is unreliable.
5. Women ought to be permitted to serve in combat. Why should men be the only ones to face death and danger?
6. If Cher uses Equal, it must taste better than Sweet 'N Low.
7. People will gamble anyway, so why not legalize gambling in this state?
8. Because so much money was spent on public education in the last decade while educational achievement declined, more money to improve education can't be the answer to reversing the decline.
9. He's a columnist for the campus newspaper, so he must be a pretty good writer.
10. We tend to exaggerate the need for standard English. You don't need much standard English for most jobs in this country.
11. It's discriminatory to mandate that police officers must conform to certain height and weight.
12. A doctor can consult books to make a diagnosis, so a medical student should be able to consult books when being tested.
13. Because this soft drink contains so many chemicals, it must be unsafe.
14. Core requirements should be eliminated. After all, students are paying for their education, so they should be able to earn a diploma by choosing the courses they want.
15. We should encourage a return to arranged marriages in this country since marriages based on romantic love haven't been very successful.
16. I know three redheads who have terrible tempers, and since Annabel has red hair, I'll bet she has a terrible temper, too.
17. Supreme Court Justice Byron White was an All-American football player while at college, so how can you say that athletes are dumb?
18. Benjamin H. Sasway, a student at Humboldt State University in California, was indicted for failure to register for possible conscription. Barry Lynn, president of Draft Action, an antidraft group, said, "It is disgraceful that this Administration is embarking on an effort to fill the prisons with men of conscience and moral commitment."
19. You know Jane Fonda's exercise books must be worth the money. Look at the great shape she's in now that she's in her fifties.
20. James A. Harris, former president of the National Education Association: "Twenty-three percent of schoolchildren are failing to graduate, and an-

other large segment graduate as functional illiterates. If 23 percent of anything else failed — 23 percent of automobiles didn't run, 23 percent of the buildings fell down, 23 percent of stuffed ham spoiled — we'd look at the producer."

21. A professor at Rutgers University: "The arrest rate for women is rising three times as fast as that of men. Women, inflamed by the doctrines of feminism, are pursuing criminal careers with the same zeal as business and the professions."

22. Physical education should be required because physical activity is healthful.

23. George Meany, former president of the AFL-CIO, in 1968: "To these people who constantly say you have got to listen to these younger people, they have got something to say, I just don't buy that at all. They smoke more pot than we do and if the younger generation are the hundred thousand kids that lay around a field up in Woodstock, New York, I am not going to trust the destiny of the country to that group."

24. That candidate was poor as a child, so he will certainly be sympathetic to the poor if he's elected.

25. When the federal government sent troops into Little Rock, Arkansas, to enforce integration of the public school system, the governor of Arkansas attacked the action, saying that it was as brutal an act of intervention as Russia's sending troops into Hungary to squelch the Hungarians' rebellion. In both cases, the governor said, the rights of a freedom-loving, independent people were being violated.

26. Governor Jones was elected two years ago. Since that time constant examples of corruption and subversion have been unearthed. It is time to get rid of the man responsible for this kind of corrupt government.

27. Are we going to vote a pay increase for our teachers or are we going to allow our schools to deteriorate into substandard custodial institutions?

28. You see, the priests were right. After we threw those virgins into the volcano, it quit erupting.

29. The people of Rome lost their vitality and desire for freedom when their emperors decided that the way to keep them happy was to provide them with bread and circuses. What can we expect of our own country now that the government gives people free food and there is a constant round of entertainment provided by television?

30. From Mark Clifton, "The Dread Tomato Affliction" (proving that eating tomatoes is dangerous and even deadly): "Ninety-two point four percent of juvenile delinquents have eaten tomatoes. Fifty-seven point one percent of the adult criminals in penitentiaries throughout the United States have eaten tomatoes. Eighty-four percent of all people killed in automobile accidents during the year have eaten tomatoes."

31. "But can you doubt that air has weight when you have the clear testimony of Aristotle affirming that all elements have weight, including air, and excepting only fire?" (From Galileo, *Dialogues Concerning Two New Sciences*)

32. Robert Brustein, artistic director of the American Repertory Theatre, commenting on a threat by Congress in 1989 to withhold funding from an offensive art show: "Once we allow lawmakers to become art critics, we

take the first step into the world of Ayatollah Khomeini, whose murderous review of *The Satanic Verses* still chills the heart of everyone committed to free expression." (The Ayatollah Khomeini called for the death of the author, Salman Rushdie, because he had allegedly committed blasphemy against Islam in his novel.)

PART TWO

Writing and Researching Arguments

CHAPTER EIGHT

Writing an Argumentative Paper

The person who understands how arguments are constructed has an important advantage in today's world. Television commercials, political speeches, newspaper editorials, and magazine advertisements, as well as many communications between individuals, all draw on the principles we have examined in the preceding chapters. By now you should be fairly adept at picking out claims, support, and warrants (explicit or unstated) in these presentations. The next step is to apply your skills to writing an argument of your own. The process of using what you have learned will enhance your ability to analyze critically the marketing efforts with which we are all bombarded every day. Mastering the writing of arguments also gives you a valuable tool for communicating with other people in school, on the job, and even at home.

In this chapter we will move through the various stages involved in creating an argumentative paper: choosing a topic, defining the issues, organizing the material, writing the essay, and revising. We will also consider the more general question of how to use the principles already discussed in order to convince a real audience. The more carefully you follow the guidelines set out here and the more thought you give to your work at each point, the better you will be able to utilize the art of argument when this course is over.

FINDING AN APPROPRIATE TOPIC

An old British recipe for jugged hare is said to begin, "First, catch your hare." To write an argumentative paper, you first must choose your topic. This is a relatively easy task for someone writing an argument as part of his or her job — a lawyer defending a client, for example, or an advertising executive presenting a campaign. For a student, however, it can be daunting. Which of the many ideas in the world worth debating would make a good subject?

Several guidelines can help you evaluate the possibilities. Perhaps your assignment limits your choices. If you have been asked to write a research paper, you obviously must find a topic on which research is available. If your assignment is more open-ended, you need a topic that is worth the time and effort you expect to invest in it. In either case, your subject should be one that interests you. Don't feel you have to write about what you know — very often finding out what you don't know will turn out to be more satisfying. You should, however, choose a subject that is familiar enough for you to argue about without fearing you're in over your head.

Invention Strategies

As a starting point, think of conversations you've had in the past few days or weeks that have involved defending a position. Is there some current political issue you're concerned about? Some dispute with friends that would make a valid paper topic? One of the best sources is controversies in the media. Keep your project in mind as you watch TV, read, or listen to the radio. You may even run into a potential subject in your course reading assignments or classroom discussions. Fortunately for the would-be writer, nearly every human activity includes its share of disagreement.

As you consider possible topics, write them down. One that looks unlikely at first glance may suggest others or may have more appeal when you come back to it later. Further, simply putting words on paper has a way of stimulating the thought processes involved in writing. Even if your ideas are tentative, the act of converting them into phrases or sentences can often help in developing them.

Evaluating Possible Topics

Besides interesting you, your topic must interest your audience. Who is the audience? For a lawyer it is usually a judge or jury; for a columnist, anyone who reads the newspaper in which his or her column appears. For the student writer, the audience is to some extent hypothetical. You should assume that your paper is directed at readers who are reasonably intelligent and well informed, but who have no specific knowledge of the subject. It may be useful to imagine you are writing for a local or school publication — this may be the case if your paper turns out well.

Be sure, too, that you choose a topic with two sides. The purpose of an argument is to defend or refute a thesis, which means the thesis must be debatable. In evaluating a subject that looks promising, ask yourself: Can a case be made for the opposing view? If not, you have no workable ground for building your own case.

Finally, check the scope of your thesis. Consider how long your paper will be, and whether you can do justice to your topic in that amount of space. For example, suppose you want to argue in favor of worldwide nuclear disarmament. Is this a thesis you can support persuasively in a short paper? One way to find out is by listing the potential issues or points about which arguers might disagree. Consider the thesis: "The future of the world is in danger as long as nuclear weapons exist." Obviously this statement is too general. You would have to specify what you mean by the future of the world (the continuation of human life? of all life? of the earth itself?) and exactly how nuclear weapons endanger it before the claim would hold up. You could narrow it down: "Human beings are error-prone; therefore as long as nuclear weapons exist there is the chance that a large number of people will be killed accidentally." Though this statement is more specific and includes an important warrant, it still depends on other unstated warrants: that one human being (or a small group) is in the position to discharge a nuclear weapon capable of killing a large number of people; that such a weapon could, in fact, be discharged by mistake, given current safety systems. Can you expect to show sufficient evidence for these assumptions in the space available to you?

By now it should be apparent that arguing in favor of nuclear disarmament is too broad an undertaking. A more workable approach might be to defend or refute one of the disarmament proposals under consideration by the U.S. Congress, or to show that nuclear weapons pose some specific danger (such as long-term water pollution) that is sufficient reason to strive for disarmament.

Can a thesis be too narrow? Certainly. If this is true of the one you have chosen, you probably realized it when you asked yourself whether the topic was debatable. If you can prove your point convincingly in a paragraph, or even a page, you need a broader thesis.

At this preliminary stage, don't worry if you don't know exactly how to word your thesis. It's useful to write down a few possible phrasings to be sure your topic is one you can work with, but you need not be precise. The information you unearth as you do research will help you to formulate your ideas. Also, stating a thesis in final terms is premature until you know the organization and tone of your paper.

To This Point

Let's assume you have surveyed a range of possible topics and chosen one that provides you with a suitable thesis for your paper. Before you go on, check your thesis against the following questions:

1. Is this topic one that will interest both me and my audience?
2. Is the topic debatable?
3. Is my thesis appropriate in scope for a paper of this length?
4. Do I know enough about my thesis to have a rough idea of what ideas to use in supporting it and how to go about finding evidence to back up these ideas?

DEFINING THE ISSUES

Preparing an Initial Outline

An outline, like an accounting system or a computer program, is a practical device for organizing information. Nearly every elementary and high school student learns how to make an outline. What will you gain if you outline your argument? Time and an overview of your subject. The minutes you spend organizing your subject at the outset generally save at least double the time later, when you have few minutes to spare. An outline also enables you to see the whole argument at a glance.

Your preliminary outline establishes an order of priority for your argument. Which supporting points are issues to be defended, which are warrants, and which are evidence? Which supporting points are most persuasive? By constructing a map of your territory, you can identify the research routes that are likely to be most productive. You can also pinpoint any gaps in your reasoning.

List each issue as a main heading in your outline. Next, write below it any relevant support (or sources of support) that you are aware of. Then reexamine the list and consider which issues appear likely to offer the strongest support for your argument. You should number these in order of importance.

Case Study: Coed Bathrooms

To see how we raise and evaluate issues in a specific context, let's look at a controversy that surfaced recently at a large university. Students living in coed dorms elected to retain their coed bathrooms. The university administration, however, withdrew its approval, in part because of growing protests from parents and alumni.

The students raised these issues:

1. The rights of students to choose their living arrangements
2. The absence of coercion on those who did not wish to participate
3. The increase in civility between the sexes as a result of sharing accommodations

4. The practicality of coed bathrooms, which preclude the necessity for members of one sex to travel to a one-sex bathroom on another floor
5. The success of the experiment so far

On the other side, the administration introduced the following issues:

1. The role of the university *in loco parentis*
2. The necessity for the administration to retain the goodwill of parents and alumni
3. The dissatisfaction of some students with the arrangement
4. The inability of immature students to respect the right of others and resist the temptation of sexual activity

Now let's analyze these issues, comparing their strengths and weaknesses.

1. It is clear that not all the issues in this dispute were equally important. The arguers decided, therefore, to give greater emphasis to the issues that were most likely to be ultimately persuasive to their audiences and less attention to those that were difficult to prove or narrower in their appeal. The issue of convenience, for example, seemed a minor point. How much cost is imposed in being required to walk up or down a flight of stairs?

2. It was also clear that, as in several of the other cases we have examined, the support consisted of both factual data and appeals to values. In regard to the factual data, each side reported evidence to prove that

a. The experiment was or was not a success.
b. Civility had or had not increased.
c. The majority of students did or did not favor the plan.
d. Coercion had or had not been applied.

The factual data were important. If the administration could prove that the interests of some students had been injured, then the student case for coed bathrooms would be weakened.

But let us assume that the factual claims either were settled or remained in abeyance. We now turn our attention to a second set of issues, a contest over the values to be served.

3. Both sides claimed adherence to the highest principles of university life. Here the issues, while no easier to resolve, offered greater opportunity for serious and fruitful discussion.

The first question to be resolved was that of democratic control. The students asserted, "We should be permitted to have coed bathrooms because we can prove that the majority of us want them." The students hoped that the university community would agree with the implied analogy: that the university community should resemble a political democracy and that students should have full rights as citizens of that community. (This is an argument also made in regard to other areas of university life.)

The university denied that it was a democracy in which students had equal rights and insisted that it should not be. The administration offered its own analogical proof: Students are not permitted to hire their own teachers or to choose their manner of instruction, their courses of study, their grades, or the rules of admission. The university, they insisted, represented a different kind of community, like a home, in which the experienced are required to lead and instruct the inexperienced.

Students responded by pointing out that coed bathrooms or any other aspect of their living arrangements were areas in which *they* were experts and that freedom to choose living arrangements was not to be confused with a demand for equal participation in academic matters. Moreover, it was also true that in recent years the verdict had increasingly been rendered in favor of rights of special groups as against those of institutions. Students' rights have been among those that have benefited from the movement toward freedom of choice.

4. The second issue was related to the first but introduced a practical consideration, namely, the well-being of the university. The administration argued that more important than the wishes of the students in this essentially minor dispute was the necessity for retaining the support and goodwill of parents and alumni, who are ultimately responsible for the very existence of the university.

The students agreed that this support was necessary but felt that parents and alumni could be persuaded to consider the good reasons in the students' argument. Some students were inclined to carry the argument over goals even further. They insisted that if the university could maintain its existence only at the cost of sacrificing principles of democracy and freedom, then perhaps the university had forfeited its right to exist.

In making our way through this debate, we have summarized a procedure for tackling the issues in any controversial problem.

1. Raise the relevant issues and arrange them in order of importance. Plan to devote more time and space to issues you regard as crucial.
2. Produce the strongest evidence you can to support your factual claims, knowing that the opposing side or critical readers may try to produce conflicting evidence.
3. Defend your value claims by finding support in the fundamental principles with which most people in your audience would agree.
4. Argue with yourself. Try to foresee what kinds of refutation are possible. Try to anticipate and meet the opposing arguments.

ORGANIZING THE MATERIAL

Once you are satisfied that you have identified all the issues that will appear in your paper, you should begin to determine what kind of organization will be most effective for your argument. Now is the time to organize the results of your thinking into a logical and persuasive form. If you have read about your topic, answered questions, and acquired some evidence, you may already have decided on ways to approach your subject. If not, you should look closely at your outline now, recalling your purposes when you began your investigation, and develop a strategy for using the information you have gathered to achieve those purposes.

The first point to establish is what type of thesis you plan to present. Is your intention to make readers aware of some problem? To offer a solution to the problem? To defend a position? To refute a position held by others? The way you organize your material will depend to a great extent on your goal. With that goal in mind, look over your outline and reevaluate the relative importance of your issues. Which ones are most convincing? Which are backed up by the strongest support? Which ones relate to facts, and which concern values?

With these points in mind, let us look at various ways of organizing an argumentative paper. It would be foolish to decide in advance how many paragraphs a paper ought to have; however, you can and should choose a general strategy before you begin writing. If your thesis presents an opinion or recommends some course of action, you may choose simply to state your main idea and then defend it. If your thesis argues against an opposing view, you probably will want to mention that view and then refute it. Both these organizations introduce the thesis in the first or second paragraph (called the *thesis paragraph*). A third possibility is to start establishing that a problem exists and then introduce your thesis as the solution; this method is called *presenting the stock issues.* Although these three approaches sometimes overlap in practice, examining each one individually can help you structure your paper. Let's take a look at each arrangement.

Defending the Main Idea

All forms of organization will require you to defend your main idea, but one way of doing this is simple and direct. Early in the paper state the main idea that you will defend throughout your argument. You can also indicate here the two or three points you intend to develop in support of your claim; or you can raise these later as they come up. Suppose your thesis is that widespread vegetarianism would solve a number of problems. You could phrase it this way: "If the majority of people in this country adopted a vegetarian diet, we would see improvements in the economy, in the health of our people, and in moral sensitivity." You would then develop each of the claims in your list with appropriate data and warrants. Notice that the thesis statement in the first (thesis) paragraph has already outlined your organizational pattern.

Defending the main idea is effective for factual claims as well as policy claims, in which you urge the adoption of a certain policy and give the reasons for its adoption. It is most appropriate when your thesis is straightforward and can be readily supported by direct statements.

Refuting the Opposing View

Refuting an opposing view means to attack it in order to weaken, invalidate, or make it less credible to a reader. Since all arguments are dialogues or debates — even when the opponent is only imaginary — refutation of the other point of view is always implicit in your arguments. As you write, keep in mind the issues that an opponent may raise. You will be looking at your own argument as an unsympathetic reader may look at it, asking yourself the same kinds of critical questions and trying to find its weaknesses in order to correct them. In this way every argument you write becomes a form of refutation.

You do you plan a refutation? Here are some general guidelines.

1. If you want to refute the argument in a specific essay or article, read the argument carefully, noting all the points with which you disagree. This advice may seem obvious, but it cannot be too strongly emphasized. If your refutation does not indicate scrupulous familiarity with your opponent's argument, he or she has the right to say, and often does, "You haven't really read what I wrote. You haven't really answered my argument."

2. If you think that your readers are sympathetic to the opposing view or are not familiar with it, summarize it at the beginning of your paper, providing enough information to give readers an understanding of exactly what you plan to refute. When you summarize, it's important to be respectful of the opposition's views. You don't want to alienate readers who might not agree with you at first.

3. If your argument is long and complex, choose only the most important points to refute. Otherwise the reader who does not have the original argument on hand may find a detailed refutation hard to follow. If the argument is short and relatively simple — a claim supported by only two or three points — you may decide to refute all of them, devoting more space to the most important ones.

4. Attack the principal elements in the argument of your opponent.

a. Question the evidence. (See pp. 115–121 in the text.) Question whether your opponent has proved that a problem exists.

b. Attack the warrants or assumptions that underlie the claim. (See pp. 158–159 in the text.)

c. Attack the logic or reasoning of the opposing view. (Refer to the discussion of fallacious reasoning on pp. 222–231 in the text.)

d. Attack the proposed solution to a problem, pointing out that it will not work.

5. Be prepared to do more than attack the opposing view. Supply evidence and good reasons in support of your own claim.

Presenting the Stock Issues

Presenting the stock issues, or stating the problem before the solution, is a type of organization borrowed from traditional debate format. It works for policy claims when an audience must be convinced that a need exists for changing the status quo (present conditions) and for introducing plans to solve the problem. You begin by establishing that a problem exists (need). You then propose a solution (plan), which is your thesis. Finally, you show reasons for adopting the plan (advantages). These three elements — need, plan, and advantages — are called the stock issues.

For example, suppose you wanted to argue that measures for reducing acid rain should be introduced at once. You would first have to establish a need for such measures by defining the problem and providing evidence of damage. Then you would produce your thesis, a means for improving conditions. Finally you would suggest the benefits that would follow from implementation of your plan. Notice that in this organization your thesis paragraph usually appears toward the middle of your paper, although it may also appear at the beginning.

Ordering Material for Emphasis

Whichever way you choose to work, you should revise your outline to reflect the order in which you intend to present your thesis and supporting ideas. Not only the placement of your thesis paragraph but also the wording and arrangement of your ideas will determine what points in your paper receive the most emphasis.

Suppose your purpose is to convince the reader that cigarette smoking is a bad habit. You might decide to concentrate on three unpleasant attributes of cigarette smoking: (1) it is unhealthy; (2) it is dirty; (3) it is expensive. Obviously, these are not equally important as possible deterrents. You would no doubt consider the first reason the most compelling, accompanied by evidence to prove the relationship between cigarette smoking and cancer, heart disease, emphysema, and other diseases. This issue, therefore, should be given greater emphasis than the others.

There are several ways to achieve emphasis. One is to make the explicit statement that you consider a certain issue the most important.

> Finally, and *most importantly,* human culture is often able to neutralize or reverse what might otherwise be genetically advantageous consequences of selfish behavior.[1]

This quotation also reveals a second way — placing the material to be emphasized in an emphatic position, either first or last in the paper. The end position, however, is generally more emphatic.

A third way to achieve emphasis is to elaborate on the material to be emphasized, treating it at greater length, offering more data and reasons for it than you give for the other issues.

Considering Scope and Audience

With a working outline in hand that indicates the order of your thesis and claims, you are almost ready to begin turning your notes into prose. First, however, it is useful to review the limits on your paper to be sure your writing time will be used to the best possible advantage.

The first limit involves scope. As mentioned earlier, your thesis should introduce a claim that can be adequately supported in the space available to you. If your research has opened up more aspects than you anticipated, you may want to narrow your thesis to one major subtopic. Or you could emphasize only the most persuasive arguments for your position (assuming these are sufficient to make your case) and omit the others. In a brief paper (three or four pages), three issues are probably all you have room to develop. On the other hand, if you suspect your thesis can be proved in one or two pages, look for ways to expand it. What additional issues might be brought in to bolster your argument? Alternatively, is there a larger issue for which your thesis could become a supporting idea?

Other limits on your paper are imposed by the need to make your points in a way that will be persuasive to an audience. The style and tone you choose depend not only on the nature of the subject, but also on how you can best convince readers that you are a credible source. *Style* in this context refers to the elements of your prose — simple versus complex sentences, active versus passive verbs, metaphors, analogies, and other literary devices. *Tone* is the approach you take to your topic — solemn or humorous, detached or sympathetic. Style and tone together compose your voice as a writer.

Many students assume that every writer has only one voice. In fact, a writer typically adapts his or her voice to the material and the audience. Perhaps the easiest way to appreciate this is to think of two

---

[1] Peter Singer, *The Expanding Circle* (New York: New American Library, 1982), p. 171.

or three works by the same author that are written in different voices. Or compare the speeches of two different characters in the same story, novel, or film. Every writer has individual talents and inclinations that appear in most or all of his or her work. A good writer, however, is able to amplify some stylistic elements and diminish others, as well as to change tone, by choice.

It is usually appropriate in a short paper to choose an *expository* style, which emphasizes the elements of your argument rather than your personality. You many want to appeal to your readers' emotions as well as their intellects, but keep in mind that sympathy is most effectively gained when it is supported by believable evidence. If you press your point stridently, your audience is likely to be suspicious rather than receptive. If you sprinkle your prose with jokes or metaphors, you may diminish your credibility by detracting from the substance of your case. Both humor and analogy can be useful tools, but they should be used with discretion.

You can discover some helpful pointers on essay style by reading the editorials in newspapers such as the *New York Times,* the *Washington Post,* or the *Wall Street Journal.* The authors are typically addressing a mixed audience comparable to the hypothetical readers of your own paper. Though their approaches vary, each writer is attempting to portray himself or herself as an objective analyst whose argument deserves careful attention.

Again, remember your goals. You are trying to convince your audience of something; an argument is, by its nature, directed at people who may not initially agree with its thesis. Therefore, your voice as well as the claims you make must be convincing.

To This Point

The organizing steps that come between preparation and writing are often neglected. Careful planning at this stage, however, can save much time and effort later. As you prepare to start writing, you should be able to answer the following questions:

1. Is the purpose of my paper to persuade readers to accept a potentially controversial idea, to refute someone else's position, or to propose a solution to a problem?
2. Have I decided on an organization that is likely to accomplish this purpose?
3. Does my outline arrange my thesis and issues in an appropriate order to emphasize the most important issues?
4. Does my outline show an argument whose scope suits the needs of this paper?
5. What questions of style and tone do I need to keep in mind as I write to ensure that my argument will be persuasive?

WRITING

Beginning the Paper

Having found a claim you can defend and the voice you will adopt toward your audience, you must now think about how to begin. An introduction to your subject should consist of more than just the first paragraph of your paper. It should invite the reader to give attention to what you have to say. It should also point you in the direction you will take in developing your argument. You may want to begin the actual writing of your paper with the thesis paragraph. It is useful to consider the whole paragraph rather than simply the thesis statement for two reasons. First, not all theses are effectively expressed in a single sentence. Second, the rest of the paragraph will be closely related to your statement of the main idea. You may show why you have chosen this topic or why your audience will benefit from reading your paper. You may introduce your warrant, qualify your claim, and in other ways prepare for the body of your argument. Because readers will perceive the whole paragraph as a unit, it makes sense to approach it that way.

Consider first the kind of argument you intend to present. Does your paper make a factual claim? Does it address values? Does it recommend a policy or action? Is it a rebuttal of some current policy or belief? The answers to those questions will influence the way you introduce the subject.

If your thesis makes a factual claim, you may be able to summarize it in one or two opening sentences. "Whether we like it or not, money is obsolete. The currency of today is not paper or coin, but plastic." Refutations are easy to introduce in a brief statement: "Contrary to popular views on the subject, the institution of marriage is as sound today as it was a generation ago."

A thesis that defends a value is usually best preceded by an explanatory introduction. "Some wars are morally defensible" is a thesis that can be stated as a simple declarative opening sentence. However, readers who disagree may not read any further than the first line. Someone defending this claim is likely to be more persuasive if he or she first gives an example of a situation in which war is or was preferable to peace or presents the thesis less directly.

One way to keep such a thesis from alienating the audience is to phrase it as a question. "Are all wars morally indefensible?" Still better would be to prepare for the question:

> Few if any of us favor war as a solution to international problems. We are too vividly aware of the human suffering imposed by armed conflict, as well as the political and financial turmoil that inevitably result. Yet can we honestly agree that no war is ever morally defensible?

Notice that this paragraph gains appeal from use of the first person *we.* The author implies that he or she shares the readers' feelings but has good reasons for believing those feelings are not sufficient grounds for condemning all wars. Even if readers are skeptical, the conciliatory phrasing of the thesis should encourage them to continue reading.

For any subject that is highly controversial or emotionally charged, especially one that strongly condemns an existing situation or belief, you may sometimes want to express your indignation directly. Of course, you must be sure that your indignation can be justified. The author of the following introduction, a physician and writer, openly admits that he is about to make a case that may offend readers.

> Is there any polite way to introduce today's subject? I'm afraid not. It must be said plainly that the media have done about as sorry and dishonest a job of covering health news as is humanly possible, and that when the media do not fail from bias and mendacity, they fail from ignorance and laziness.[2]

If your thesis advocates a policy or makes a recommendation, it may be a good idea, as in a value claim, to provide a short background. The following paragraph introduces an argument favoring relaxation of controls in high schools.

> "Free the New York City 275,000" read a button worn by many young New Yorkers some years ago. The number was roughly the total of students enrolled in the City's high schools.
> The condition of un-freedom which is described was not, however, unique to the schools of one city. According to the Carnegie Commission's comprehensive study of American public education, *Crisis in the Classroom*, public schools across the country share a common characteristic, namely, "preoccupation with order and control." The result is that students find themselves the victims of "oppressive and petty rules which give their schools a repressive, almost prison-like atmosphere."[3]

There are also other ways to introduce your subject. One is to begin with an appropriate quotation.

> "Reading makes a full man, conversation makes a ready man, and writing makes an exact man." So Francis Bacon told us around 1600. Recently I have been wondering how Bacon's formula might apply to present-day college students.[4]

Or you may begin with an anecdote. In the following introduction to an article about the relation between cancer and mental attitude, the author recounts a personal experience.

---

[2] Michael Halberstam, "TV's Unhealthy Approach to Health News," *TV Guide*, September 20–26, 1980, p. 24

[3] Alan Levine and Eve Carey, *The Rights of Students* (New York: Avon Books, 1977), p. 11.

[4] William Aiken, "The Conversation on Campus Today Is, Uh . . . ," *Wall Street Journal*, May 4, 1982, p. 18.

Shortly after I moved to California, a new acquaintance sat in my San Francisco living room drinking rose-hip tea and chainsmoking. Like so many residents of the Golden West, Cecil was "into" all things healthy, from jogging to *shiatsu* massage to kelp. Tobacco didn't seem to fit, but he told me confidently that there was no contradiction. "It all has to do with energy," he said. "Unless you have a lot of negative energy about smoking cigarettes, there's no way they can hurt you; you won't get cancer."[5]

Finally, you may introduce yourself as the author of the claim.

I wish to argue an unpopular cause: the cause of the old, free elective system in the academic world, or the untrammeled right of the undergraduate to make his own mistakes.[6]

My subject is the world of Hamlet. I do not of course mean Denmark, except as Denmark is given a body by the play; and I do not mean Elizabethan England, though this is necessarily close behind the scenes. I mean simply the imaginative environment that the play asks us to enter when we read it or go to see it.[7]

You should, however, use such introductions with care. They suggest an authority about the subject that you shouldn't attempt to assume unless you can demonstrate that you are entitled to it.

Guidelines for Good Writing

In general, the writer of an argument follows the same rules that govern any form of expository writing. Your style should be clear and readable, your organization logical, your ideas connected by transitional phrases and sentences, your paragraphs coherent. The main difference between an argument and other kinds of expository writing, as noted earlier, is the need to persuade an audience to adopt a belief or take an action. You should assume your readers will be critical rather than neutral or sympathetic. Therefore, you must be equally critical of your own work. Any apparent gap in reasoning or ambiguity in presentation is likely to weaken the argument.

As you read the essays in this book and elsewhere, you will discover that good style in argumentative writing shares several characteristics:

- Variety in sentence structure: a mixture of both long and short sentences, different sentence beginnings
- Rich but standard vocabulary: avoidance of specialized terms unless they are fully explained, word choice appropriate to a thoughtful argument

[5] Joel Guerin, "Cancer and the Mind," *Harvard Magazine,* November–December 1978, p. 11.
[6] Howard Mumford Jones, "Undergraduates on Apron Strings," *Atlantic Monthly,* October 1955, p. 45.
[7] Maynard Mack, "The World of Hamlet," *Yale Review,* June 1952, p. 502.

- Use of details and examples to illustrate and clarify abstract terms, principles, and generalizations.

You should take care to avoid the following:

- Unnecessary repetition: making the same point without new data or interpretation
- Exaggeration or stridency, which can create suspicion of your fairness and powers of observation
- Short paragraphs of one or two sentences, which are common in advertising and newspaper writing to get the reader's attention but are inappropriate in a thoughtful essay

In addition to these stylistic principles, seven general points are worth keeping in mind:

1. Although *you,* like *I,* should be used judiciously, it can be found even in the treatment of weighty subjects. Here is an example from an essay by the distinguished British mathematician and philosopher, Bertrand Russell.

> Suppose you are a scientific pioneer and you make some discovery of great scientific importance and suppose you say to yourself, "I am afraid this discovery will do harm": you know that other people are likely to make the same discovery if they are allowed suitable opportunities for research; you must therefore, if you do not wish the discovery to become public, either discourage your sort of research or control publication by a board of censors.[8]

Don't be afraid to use *you* or *I* when it is useful to emphasize the presence of the person making the argument.

2. Don't pad. This point should be obvious; the word *pad* suggests the addition of unnecessary material. Many writers find it tempting, however, to enlarge a discussion even when they have little more to say. It is never wise to introduce more words into a paper that has already made its point. If the paper turns out to be shorter than you had hoped, it may mean that you have not sufficiently developed the subject or that the subject was less substantial than you thought when you selected it. Padding, which is easy to detect in its repetition and sentences empty of content, weakens the writer's credibility.

3. For any absolute generalization — a statement containing words such as *all* or *every* — consider the possibility that there may be at least one example that will weaken the generalization. Such a precaution means that you won't have to backtrack and admit that your generalization is not, after all, universal. A student who was arguing against capital punishment for the reason that all killing was wrong

---

[8] "Science and Human Life," in *What Is Science?* edited by James R. Newman (New York: Simon and Schuster, 1955), p. 12.

suddenly paused in her presentation and added, "On the other hand, if given the chance, I'd probably have been willing to kill Hitler." This admission meant that she recognized important exceptions to her rule and that she would have to qualify her generalization in some significant way.

When offering an explanation, especially one that is complicated or extraordinary, look first for a cause that is easier to accept, one that doesn't strain credibility. (In Chapter 7, we called attention to this principle. See p. 224.) For example, a few years ago a great many people were bemused by reports about the mysterious Bermuda Triangle, which had apparently swallowed up ships and planes since the mid-nineteenth century. The forces at work were variously described as space-time warps, UFOs that transported earthlings to other planets, and sea monsters seeking revenge. But a careful investigation revealed familiar, natural causes. A reasonable person interested in the truth would have searched for more conventional explanations before accepting the bizarre stories of extraterrestrial creatures. He or she would also exercise caution when confronted by conspiracy theories that try to account for controversial political events, such as the assassination of John Kennedy.

5. Check carefully for questionable warrants. Your outline should specify your warrants. When necessary, these should be included in your paper to link claims with support. Many an argument has failed because it depended on an unstated warrant with which the reader did not agree. If you were arguing for a physical education requirement at your school, you might make a good case for all the physical and psychological benefits of such a requirement. But you would certainly need to introduce and develop the warrant on which your claim was based — that it is the proper function of a college or university to provide the benefits of a physical education. Many readers would agree that physical education is valuable, but they might question the assumption that an academic institution should introduce a nonintellectual enterprise into the curriculum. At any point where you draw a controversial or tenuous conclusion, be sure your reasoning is clear and logical.

6. Avoid conclusions that are merely summaries. Summaries may be needed in long technical papers, but in brief arguments they create endings that are without force or interest. In the closing paragraph you should find a new idea that emerges naturally from the development of the whole argument.

7. Strive for a paper that is unified, coherent, and emphatic where appropriate. A *unified* paper stays focused on its goal and directs each claim, warrant, and piece of evidence toward that goal. Extraneous information or unsupported claims impair unity. *Coherence* means that all ideas are fully explained and adequately connected by transitions. To ensure coherence, give especially close attention to the beginnings and ends of your paragraphs: Is each new concept introduced in a way

that shows it following naturally from the one that preceded it? *Emphasis,* as we have mentioned, is a function partly of structure and partly of language. Your most important claims should be placed where they are certain of receiving the reader's attention: key sentences at the beginning or end of a paragraph, key paragraphs at the beginning or end of your paper. Sentence structure can also be used for emphasis. If you have used several long, complex sentences, you can emphasize a significant point by stating it briefly and simply. You can also create emphasis with verbal flags, such as "The primary issue to consider . . ." or "Finally, we cannot ignore. . . ."

All clear expository prose will exhibit the qualities of unity, coherence, and emphasis. But the success of an argumentative paper is especially dependent on these qualities because the reader may have to follow a line of reasoning that is both complicated and unfamiliar. Moreover, a paper that is unified, coherent, and properly emphatic will be more readable, the first requisite of an effective argument.

REVISING

The final stage in writing an argumentative paper is revising. The first step is to read through what you have written for mistakes. Next, check your work against the guidelines listed under "Organizing the Material" and "Writing." Have you omitted any of the issues, warrants, or supporting evidence on your outline? Is each paragraph coherent in itself? Do your paragraphs work together to create a coherent paper? All the elements of the argument — the issues raised, the underlying assumptions, and the supporting material — should contribute to the development of the claim in your thesis statement. Any material that is interesting but irrelevant to that claim should be cut. Finally, does your paper reach a clear conclusion that reinforces your thesis?

Be sure, too, that the style and tone of your paper are appropriate for the topic and the audience. Remember that people choose to read an argument because they want the answer to a troubling question or the solution to a recurrent problem. Besides stating your thesis in a way that invites the reader to join you in your investigation, you must retain your audience's interest through a discussion that may be unfamiliar or contrary to their convictions. The outstanding qualities of argumentative prose style, therefore, are clarity and readability.

Style is obviously harder to evaluate in your own writing than organization. Your outline provides a map against which to check the structure of your paper. Clarity and readability, by comparison, are somewhat abstract qualities. Two procedures may be helpful. The first is to read two or three (or more) essays by authors whose style you admire and then turn back to your own writing. Awkward spots in your prose are sometimes easier to see if you get away from it and respond to someone else's perspective than if you simply keep rereading your own writing.

The second method is to read aloud. If you have never tried it, you are likely to be surprised at how valuable this can be. Again, start with someone else's work that you feel is clearly written, and practice until you achieve a smooth rhythmic delivery that satisfies you. And listen to what you are reading. Your objective is to absorb the patterns of English structure that characterize the clearest, most readable prose. Then read your paper aloud and listen to the construction of your sentences. Are they also clear and readable? Do they say what you want them to say? How would they sound to a reader? According to one theory, you can learn the rhythm and phrasing of a language as you learn the rhythm and phrasing of a melody. And you will often *hear* a mistake or a clumsy construction in your writing that has escaped your eye in proofreading.

PREPARING THE MANUSCRIPT

Type on one side of 8½-by-11-inch 20-pound white typing paper, double-spacing throughout. Leave margins of 1 to 1½ inches on all sides and indent each paragraph five spaces. Unless a formal outline is part of the paper, a separate title page is unnecessary. Instead, beginning about one inch from the top of the first page and flush with the left margin, type your name, the instructor's name, the course title, and the date, each on a separate line; then double-space and type the title, capitalizing the first letter of the first and last words of the title and all other words except articles, prepositions, and conjunctions. Quadruple-space and type the body of the paper.

Number all but the first page at the top right corner, typing your last name before each page number in case pages are mislaid. If an outline is included, number its pages with lowercase roman numerals.

Proofread the paper carefully for mistakes in grammar, spelling, and punctuation. Make corrections with liquid correction fluid or, if there are only a few mistakes, cross them out and neatly write the correction above the line.

REVIEW CHECKLIST FOR ARGUMENTATIVE PAPERS

A successful argumentative paper meets the following criteria:

1. It presents a thesis that is of interest to both the writer and the audience, is debatable, and can be defended in the amount of space available.

2. Each statement offered in support of the thesis is backed up with enough evidence to give it credibility. Data cited in the paper come from a variety of sources. All quotations and direct references to primary or secondary sources are fully documented.
3. The warrants linking claims to support are either specified or implicit in the author's data and line of reasoning. No claim should depend on an unstated warrant with which skeptical readers might disagree.
4. The thesis is clearly presented and adequately introduced in a thesis paragraph, which indicates the purpose of the paper.
5. Supporting statements and data are organized in a way that builds the argument, emphasizes the author's main ideas, and justifies the paper's conclusions.
6. All possible opposing arguments are anticipated and refuted.
7. The paper is written in a style and tone appropriate to the topic and the intended audience. The author's prose is clear and readable.
8. The manuscript is clean, carefully proofed, and typed in an acceptable format.

CHAPTER NINE

Researching an Argumentative Paper

The success of any argument, short or long, depends in large part on the quantity and quality of the support behind it. Research, therefore, can be crucial for any argument outside your own experience. Some papers will benefit from research in the library and elsewhere because development of the claim requires facts, example, statistics, and informed opinions that are available only from experts. This chapter offers information and advice to help you work through the steps of writing a research paper, from getting started to preparing the finished product.

GETTING STARTED

The following guidelines will help you keep your research on track:

1. Focus your investigation on building your argument, not merely on collecting information about the topic. Do follow any promising leads that turn up from the sources you consult, but don't be diverted into general reading that has no direct bearing on your thesis.

2. Look for at least two pieces of evidence to support each point you make. If you cannot find sufficient evidence, you may need to revise or abandon the point.

3. Use a variety of sources. Check not only different publications but information drawn from different fields as well.

4. Be sure your sources are authoritative. We have already pointed out elsewhere the necessity for examining the credentials of sources. Although it may be difficult or impossible for those outside the field to conclude that one authority is more trustworthy than another, some guidelines are available. Articles and essays in scholarly journals are probably more authoritative than articles in college newspapers. Au-

thors whose credentials include many publications and years of study at reputable institutions are probably more reliable than newspaper columnists and the so-called man in the street. However, we can judge reliability much more easily if we are dealing with facts and inferences than with values and emotions.

5. Don't let your sources' opinions outweigh your own. Your paper should demonstrate that the thesis and ideas you present are yours, arrived at after careful reflection and supported by research. The thesis need not be original, but your paper should be more than a collection of quotations or a report of the facts and opinions you have been reading. It should be clear to the reader that the quotations and other materials support *your* claim and that *you* have been responsible for finding and emphasizing the important issues, examining the data, and choosing between strong and weak opinions.

MAPPING RESEARCH: A SAMPLE OUTLINE

To explore a range of research activities, let's suppose that you are preparing a research paper, six to ten pages long. You have chosen to defend the following thesis: *Conventional zoos should be abolished because they are cruel to animals and cannot provide the benefits to the public that they promise.* To keep your material under control and give directions to your reading, you would sketch a preliminary outline, which might look like this:

Why We Don't Need Zoos

I. Moral Objection: Animals have fundamental right to liberty
   A. Must prove animals are negatively affected by captivity
      1. research?
      2. research?
   B. Must refute claims that captivity is not detrimental to animals
      1. Brownlee's description of dolphin: "seeming stupor"; eating "half-heartedly"; not behaving like wild dolphins
      2. Personal experience: watching leopards running in circles in cages for hours
II. Practical Objection: Zoos can't accomplish what they claim to be their goals
   A. "Educational benefits" zoo provides are inaccurate at best: Public is not learning about wild animals at all but about domesticated descendants of same (support with research from [I.A] above)
   B. Conservation programs at zoos are ineffective
      1. It's difficult to breed animals in zoos

2. Resultant offspring, when there is any, is victim of inbreeding.
Leads to inferior stock that will eventually die out (research?)

Now you need to begin the search for the materials that will support
your argument. There are two principal ways of gathering the materials — field research and library research. Most writers will not want to
limit themselves to one kind of research, but one method may work
better than another for a particular project.

USING SOURCES: FIELD RESEARCH

The term *field research* describes the search for firsthand information in the field — that is, outside the library. By firsthand we mean
information taken directly from the original source. It can include interviews and conversations, surveys, questionnaires, personal observations, and experiments. If your topic relates to a local issue, one
involving your school or your town, or is based on the experience of
someone whose story has been unreported, firsthand information may
be more useful than library research. The library, however, is also a
source of original materials. For example, documents containing raw
data that have not yet been interpreted — such as statistics compiled
by the Census Bureau of the United States — will be most readily available in the library.

One of the rewards of field research is that it often generates new
information which in turn produces new interpretations of familiar
conditions. It is a favored method for anthropologists and sociologists,
and most physical and natural scientists use observation and experiment at some point as essential tools in their research. Notice that both
of the student research papers at the end of this chapter used firsthand information gained from personal observation and interviews in
addition to their library research.

How does field research work? Suppose you decide to investigate
the food services on campus, about which you have heard numerous
complaints. You may have one or two purposes in mind: First, you may
want to establish the fact that a problem exists, because you think that
not all members of the community are sufficiently aware of it. In this
case, then, having determined that the problem is real, you may want
to propose a solution. You can go directly to primary sources without
consulting books or journals.

After talking informally with students about their reactions to the
food in the dining commons, the coffee shops, the snack bars, and
elsewhere, you might distribute a questionnaire to a selected group to
get information about the specific grounds for complaint — nutritional
value, cost, variety, quantity of food, quality of service. Eliciting useful
information from a questionnaire is not, however, as simple as it seems,

and you should probably consult a sociologist or psychologist on campus to find the most reliable sample of students and the most appropriate questions for your particular study.

You will also, of course, want to ask questions of those in charge of the food service to discover their view of the problem. If they agree with the students that the service is unsatisfactory, perhaps they can offer reasons that they consider beyond their control. Or they may disagree and point out the injustice of the students' complaints.

The answers to these questions might then lead you to interview university officials and to consult records about food purchases and budgets, if they are accessible. And even an investigation into a local problem can benefit from library research and a look at journal articles about the ways other schools have solved, or failed to solve, the same problems.

USING SOURCES: THE LIBRARY

For freshman research papers the most common resource is still the library. If you were going to write a research paper on why we don't need zoos, you would probably want to rely on materials available in the library for most of your evidence. Although you could collect some firsthand information by visiting a zoo yourself (as did the author of the paper at the end of this chapter) and by interviewing zoo directors and other animal scientists, the published opinions of a wide range of scholars will be far more easily obtained in the library and will probably carry more weight in your argument. Having drawn up a preliminary outline to help map out your reading, how can you most effectively use the library to research the fate of wild animals in captivity?

It's a good idea to consult the librarian before starting your research; he or she will be able to direct you to specific reference works relevant to your subject, which could save you a lot of time. Your library also contains useful systems for recovering material of all kinds, including the card catalog or catalog access system; dictionaries and encyclopedias; magazine, newspaper, and specialized indexes; and abstracting services.

The Card Catalog and Catalog Access System

The card catalog is an alphabetical listing of books arranged by title, author, and subject. Usually the title and author cards are found in one file, and the subject cards are found in another. The information on all three types of cards is the same. Every card in the file will tell you a book's title, author, and publisher, the city and date of publication, the book's size and length, and whether the book contains illustrations,

Subject Card

```
                        ANIMALS, TREATMENT OF -- MORAL AND ETHICAL
                        ASPECTS
     HV
     4711               Singer, Peter.
     .A56                   Animal rights and human obligations / edited
     1976               by Tom Regan and Peter Singer. -- Englewood
                        Cliffs, N. J. : Prentice Hall. 1976.
                            250 p. ; 23 cm.
                            Includes bibliography.
                            ISBN 0-13-037523-3

                            1. Animals, Treatment of.  2. Animals,
                        Treatment of -- Moral and ethical aspects.
                        I.  Regan, Tom.  II. Singer, Peter.
```

Author Card

```
     HV
     4711               Singer, Peter.
     .A56                   Animal rights and human obligations / edited
     1976               by Tom Regan and Peter Singer. -- Englewood
                        Cliffs, N. J. : Prentice Hall, 1976.
                            250 p. ; 23 cm.
                            Includes bibliography.
                            ISBN 0-13-037523-3

                            1. Animals, Treatment of.  2. Animals,
                        Treatment of -- Moral and ethical aspects.
                        I. Regan, Tom.  II. Singer, Peter.
```

Title Card

```
     HV                     Animal rights and human obligations
     4711               Singer, Peter.
     .A56                   Animal rights and human obligations / edited
     1976               by Tom Regan and Peter Singer. -- Englewood
                        Cliffs, N. J. : Prentice Hall, 1976.
                            250 p. ; 23 cm.
                            Includes bibliography.
                            ISBN 0-13-037523-3

                            1. Animals, Treatment of.   2. Animals,
                        Treatment of -- Moral and ethical aspects.
                        I. Regan, Tom.  II. Singer, Peter.
```

an introduction, a bibliography, or an index. The call number appears in the upper left corner of the card or at the bottom of the card.

Unless you already know of specific authors and titles you wish to look up, you will probably begin with the subject file. No matter what your subject, keep an open mind: You may have to use your imagination to find the listings you need. For example, the entry for "Zoo" reads "See Zoological gardens," but the books under that topic are mainly descriptive and therefore not very useful. You might look next under "Animals," and then "Animals, treatment of." Preliminary reading may also have suggested the key words and phrases "Endangered species," "Conservation," and "Preservation." If you're having trouble finding the specific heading for the subject you want to research, the *Library of Congress Subject Headings* can help you determine the heading you need. These large red books are usually kept near the catalog.

When you find a citation for a book that interests you, copy down the complete call number. Most libraries have a great many books with almost identical call numbers, so if you don't write the number down, or if you write down a shortened form of the call number, you could search the stacks for hours without finding the book you want.

Many libraries have replaced their card catalogs with microfilm or on-line computer catalogs. Both of these systems allow a large amount of material to be stored in a much smaller space than the standard card catalog allows.

Databases

Some libraries also subscribe to database services that list sources available at libraries throughout the United States and Canada. If your library subscribes to a database, you might be able to use it yourself, or you might have to ask the librarian to print out a listing of materials for you (usually for a price). Specialized databases exist for almost any discipline you would want to search, but you should find out which databases your library subscribes to before you decide to consult any one of them. Some of the most popular databases are:

ERIC (Educational Research Information Center)

DIALOG (includes over 250 databases)

BRS (Bibliographical Retrieval Services)

RLIN (Research Libraries Information Network)

OCLC (Online Computer Library Center)

FirstSearch Catalog

WorldCat (a cornerstone database containing 26 million records from 15,000 libraries worldwide)

It should be pointed out that some databases contain references not only to books but to items such as sound recordings, videocassettes, musical scores, manuscripts, audiovisuals, and other sources.

Encyclopedias

When beginning your research, you will find that general encyclopedias can provide a useful overview of your subject and also suggest related terms under which you might look. Two general encyclopedias that are probably on the shelves of your library are the *Encyclopedia Americana* and the *Encyclopedia Britannica.* You will also find many specialized encyclopedias in the research section of your library. Some encyclopedias you might fine useful include:

Britannica Encyclopedia of American Art

Cassell's Encyclopedia of World Literature

Encyclopedia of Biological Sciences

Encyclopedia of Education

Encyclopedia of Environmental Science

Encyclopedia of Philosophy

Encyclopedia of Physics

International Encyclopedia of the Social Sciences

McGraw-Hill Encyclopedia of Science and Technology

New Illustrated Encyclopedia of World History

For a list of specialized encyclopedias in your library, consult the subject file of the card catalog under "Encyclopedias."

Indexes

Magazine indexes. The *Readers' Guide to Periodical Literature* is likely to be useful if your subject is particularly timely. While there may not be any books published yet on your topic, you will probably find some articles. The *Readers' Guide* lists articles published in over one hundred of the best-known magazines in the country in volumes arranged by year. As in the card catalog, entries are organized by the author's name, title of the article, or subject of the article. For a controversial or timely subject, it makes sense to start with the most recent volumes and work backward. (If you are researching a specific event, you should start with the year in which it took place.) If your library does not carry the periodicals you need, the librarian will be able to direct you to a library that does.

Newspaper indexes.   Newspaper indexes are an excellent source for articles on current events. While books can contain detailed analyses of events that occurred years ago and magazines can give you a thorough discussion of the events of last week or last month, newspapers cover the stories that are in the news right now. Like the *Readers' Guide,* newspaper indexes are arranged by year, with entries organized according to author, title, and subject.

The most popular newspaper index is the *New York Times Index.* Indexes also exist for the *Wall Street Journal* and the *Christian Science Monitor,* and the *National Newspaper Index* includes indexes for the *Chicago Tribune,* the *Los Angeles Times,* the *New Orleans Times-Picayune,* and the *Washington Post.*

Specialized indexes.   Most college libraries carry specialized indexes citing more sophisticated articles from scholarly and professional journals and magazines. The articles listed in these indexes will be more difficult to read than the articles listed in the *Readers' Guide,* but they will also be more substantial and authoritative. Your paper might give you reason to consult one of these specialized indexes:

Applied Science and Technology Index

Art Index

Biological and Agricultural Index

Business Periodicals Index

Education Index

Humanities Index

Index to Legal Periodicals

Music Index

Philosopher's Index

Social Sciences Index

Abstracts

If you want to know the main points of a book or article before you take the time to read it, then you might want to consult an abstract. Collections of abstracts index books and articles on a particular subject and summarize them briefly. Abstracting services include:

Abstracts in Anthropology

Biological Abstracts

Book Review Digest

Chemical Abstracts

Congressional Abstracts

Historical Abstracts

Physics Abstracts

Psychological Abstracts

Sociological Abstracts

Women's Studies Abstracts

READING WITH A PURPOSE

When you begin studying your sources, read first to acquire general familiarity with your subject. Make sure that you are covering both sides of the question — in this case arguments both for and against the existence of zoos — as well as facts and opinions from a variety of sources. In investigating this subject, you will encounter data from biologists, ecologists, zoo directors, anthropologists, animal-rights activists, and ethical philosophers; their varied points of view will contribute to the strength of your claim.

As you read, look for what seem to be the major issues. They will probably be represented in all or most of your sources. For the claim about zoos the major issues may be summarized as follows: (1) the fundamental right wild animals have to liberty; (2) the harm done to animals who are denied this right and kept in captivity. On the other side, these issues will emerge: (1) the lack of concrete evidence that animals suffer or are harmed by being in zoos; (2) the benefits, in terms of entertainment, education, and conservation efforts that the public derives from zoos. The latter two, of course, are the issues you will have to refute. Your note taking should emphasize these important issues.

Write down questions as they occur to you in your reading. Why do zoos exist? What are their major goals, and how well do they meet them? What happens to animals who are removed from the wild and placed in zoos? What happens to animals born and reared in captivity? How do these groups compare with their wild counterparts, who are free to live in their natural habitats? Do animals really have a right to liberty? What are the consequences of denying them this right? Are there consequences to humanity?

Taking Notes

While everyone has his or her own method for taking notes, here are a few suggestions that should be useful to any writer.

Summarize instead of quoting long passages, unless you feel the quotation is more effective than anything you can write and can provide crucial support for your argument. Summarizing as you read can save you a great deal of time.

When you do quote, make sure to quote exactly. Copy the material word for word, leaving all punctuation exactly as it appears and inserting ellipsis points if you delete material. Make sure to enclose all quotations in quotation marks and to copy complete information about your source, including page numbers and publishing information as well as the author's name and the title of the book or article. If you quote an article that appears in an anthology or collection, make sure you record complete information about the book itself.

Keep index cards for each source you use, and write down complete bibliographical information for each source *as you use it.* That way you will have all the information necessary to document your paper when you need it. Some people find it useful to keep two sets of note cards: one set for the bibliographical information and one set for the notes themselves. Each source appears on one card by itself, ready to be arranged in alphabetical order for the Works Cited or References page of the paper.

Note Card with Quotation

Hediger   25

"The wild animal, with its marked tendency to escape, is notorious for the fact that it is never completely released from that all-important activity, avoiding enemies, even during sleep, but is constantly on the alert."

Note Card with Summary

Hediger   25

Animals who live in the wild have to be on the watch for predators constantly.

Note Card with Statistics

Reiger   32

By end of decade, worldwide extinction
rate will be one species per hour.

Other statistics, too, in Reiger,
"The Wages of Growth," Field and
Stream, July 1981: 32.

Bibliography Note Card

Hediger, Heini. The Psychology and Behavior of
Animals in Zoos and Circuses. Trans.
Geoffrey Sircom. New York: Dover, 1968..

As you take notes, refer to your outline frequently to ensure that you are acquiring sufficient data to support all the points you intend to use. You will also be revising your outline during the course of your research, as issues are clarified and new ones emerge. Keeping close track of your outline will prevent you from recording material that is interesting but not relevant. If you aren't sure whether you will want to use a certain piece of information later, don't copy the whole passage. Instead, make a note for future reference so that you can find it again if you need it. Taking too many notes is, however, preferable to taking too few, a problem that will force you to go back to the library for missing information. For the ideas and quotations in your notes, you should always take down enough information to enable you to find the references again as quickly as possible.

When researching your topic, you will find words and ideas put together by other people that you will want to use in your paper. Relying on the knowledge of others is an important part of doing research; expert opinions and eloquent arguments will help support your claims when your own expertise is limited. But remember, this is *your* paper. Your ideas and your insights into other people's ideas are just as important as the ʾformation you uncover at the library. Try to achieve a balance between solid information and original interpretation.

Quoting

You may want to quote passages or phrases from your sources if they express an idea in words more effective than your own. In this particular project, you might come across a statement that provides succinct, irrefutable evidence for an issue you wish to support. If the author of this statement is a professional in his or her field, someone with a great deal of authority on the subject, it would be appropriate to quote that author. Suppose, during the course of your research for the zoo paper, you find that many sources agree that zoos don't have the money or space necessary to maintain large enough animal populations to ensure successful captive breeding programs. But so far you only have opinions to that effect. You have been unable to find any concrete documentation of this fact until you come across Ulysses S. Seal's address to the National Zoological Park Symposia for the Public, September 1982. Here is how you could use Seal's words in your paper:

> Bear in mind that "none of these [zoo] budgets is allocated specifically for species preservation. Zoos have been established primarily as recreational institutions and are only secondarily developing programs in conservation, education and research" (Seal 74).

Notice the use of brackets (not parentheses) in the first sentence, which enclose material that did not appear in the original source but is necessary for clarification. Brackets must be used to indicate any such changes in quoted material.

Quotations should be introduced logically and gracefully in your text. Make sure that the quoted material either supports or illustrates the point you have just made or the point you are about to make and that your writing remains grammatically correct once the quotation is introduced.

Quotations are an important tool for establishing your claims, but it is important not to overuse them. If you cannot say most of what you want to say in your own words, you probably haven't thought hard enough about what it is you want to say.

Paraphrasing

Paraphrasing involves restating the content of an original source in your own words. It is most useful when the material from your source is too long for your paper, can be made clearer to the reader by rephrasing, or is written in a style markedly different from your own.

A paraphrase should be as true to the original source as you can make it: Do not change the tone or the ideas, or even the order in which the ideas are presented. Take care not to allow your own opinions to creep into your paraphrase of someone else's argument. Your readers should always be aware of which arguments belong to you and which belong to outside sources.

Like a quotation, a paraphrase must *always* include documentation, or you will be guilty of plagiarism. Even though you are using your own words, the ideas in a paraphrase belong to someone else, and that person deserves credit for them. One final caveat: When putting a long passage into your own words, beware of picking up certain expressions and turns of phrase from your source. If you do end up using your source's exact words, make sure to enclose them in quotation marks.

Below is a passage from Shannon Brownlee's "First It Was 'Save the Whales,' Now It's 'Free the Dolphins'" (*Discover* Dec. 1986: 70–72), along with a good paraphrase of the passage and two unacceptable paraphrases.

ORIGINAL PASSAGE:

But are we being good caretakers by holding a dolphin or a sea lion in a tank? Yes, if two conditions are met: that they're given the best treatment possible and, no less important, that they're displayed in a way that educates and informs us. Captive animals must be allowed to serve as ambassadors for their species (72).

A PARAPHRASE THAT PLAGIARIZES:

In "First It Was 'Save the Whales,' Now It's 'Free the Dolphins,'" Shannon Brownlee argues that it's all right for people to hold animals in captivity as long as (1) the animals are treated as well as possible, and (2) the animals are displayed in a way that educates the public. Brownlee insists that animals be allowed to serve as "ambassadors for their species" (p. 72).

A PARAPHRASE THAT ALTERS THE MEANING OF THE ORIGINAL PASSAGE:

According to Shannon Brownlee, a captive animal is being treated fairly as long as it's kept alive and its captivity gives people pleasure. In her essay, "First It Was 'Save the Whales,' Now It's 'Free the Dolphins,'" she argues that people who keep animals in cages are responsible to the animals in only two ways: (1) they should treat their captives as well as possible (even if a small tank is all that can be provided), and (2) they should make sure that the spectators enjoy watching them (p. 72).

A GOOD PARAPHRASE:

Shannon Brownlee holds that two criteria are necessary in order for the captivity of wild animals to be considered worthwhile. First, the animals should be treated as well as possible. Second, their captivity should have educational value for the people who come to look at them. "Captive animals," Brownlee claims, "must be allowed to serve as ambassadors for their species" (p. 72).

Summarizing

A summary is like a paraphrase, but it involves shortening the original passage as well as putting it in your own words. It gives the gist of the passage. Summarizing is useful when the material from your source is too long for the purposes of your paper. As with a paraphrase, a summary should not alter the meaning of the original passage.

In the paper at the end of this chapter, for instance, the statement, "It is generally acknowledged that there is a great deal of difficulty involved in breeding zoo animals" is not a direct quotation, but the idea comes from Jon Luoma's article in *Audubon.* The statement in the paper is both a summary and a paraphrase. Returning to the source makes it clear that neither quoting nor paraphrasing would have been suitable choices in this instance, since for the writer's purposes it was possible to reduce the following passage from Luoma's article to one sentence.

> But the successful propagation of entire captive species poses awesome management problems. . . . Sanford Friedman, the Minnesota Zoo's director of biological programs, had explained to me that long-term maintenance of a species in captivity demands solutions to these fundamental problems. "First, we have to learn *how* to breed them. Second, we have to decide *who* to breed. And third, we have to figure out *what* to do with them and their offspring once we've bred them."

This passage is far too long to include in a brief research paper, but it is easily summarized without losing any of its effectiveness.

Avoiding Plagiarism

Plagiarism is the use of someone else's words or ideas without adequate acknowledgment — that is, presenting such words or ideas as your own. Putting something in your own words is not in itself a defense against plagiarism; the source of the ideas must be identified as well. Giving credit to the sources you use serves three important purposes: (1) It reflects your own honesty and seriousness as a researcher; (2) it enables the reader to find the source of the reference and read further, sometimes to verify that the source has been correctly used; and (3) it adds the authority of experts to your argument. Deliberate plagiarism is nothing less than cheating and theft, and it is an offense that deserves serious punishment. Accidental plagiarism can be avoided if you take a little care when researching and writing your papers.

The writer of the zoo paper, for instance, uses and correctly introduces the following direct quotation by James Rachels:

As James Rachels (1976) writes:

> Humans have a right to liberty because they have var-
> ious other interests that will suffer if their freedom is
> unduly restricted. The right to liberty--the right to be
> free of external constraints on one's actions--may
> then be seen as derived from a more basic right not to
> have one's interests needlessly harmed. (p. 210)

If the writer of the zoo paper had chosen to state this idea more briefly, in her own words, the result might have been something like this: "Human beings believe in their fundamental right to liberty because they all agree that they would suffer without it. The right to liberty, then, stems from the right not to suffer unnecessarily." Although the wording has been significantly altered, if this statement appeared as is, undocumented, the author of the paper would be guilty of plagiarism because the ideas are not original. To avoid plagiarism, the author needs to include a reference to James Rachels at the beginning of the summary and a citation of the page number at the end. Taking care to document sources is an obvious way to avoid plagiarism. You should also be careful in taking notes and, when writing your paper, indicating where your ideas end and someone else's ideas begin.

When taking notes, make sure either to quote word-for-word *or* to paraphrase: one or the other, not a little bit of both. If you quote, enclose any language that you borrow from other sources in quotation marks. That way, when you look back at your note cards weeks later, you won't mistakenly assume that the language is your own. If you know that you aren't going to use a particular writer's exact words in your paper, then take the time to summarize that person's ideas right away. That will save you time and trouble later.

When using someone else's ideas in your paper, always let the reader know where that person's ideas begin and end. Here is an example from the zoo paper:

> When zoo animals do mate successfully, the offspring is often weakened by
> inbreeding. According to geneticists, this is because a population of 150
> breeder animals is necessary in order to "assure the more or less perma-
> nent survival of a species in captivity" (Ehrlich & Ehrlich, 1981, p. 211).

The phrase "according to geneticists" indicates that the material to follow comes from another source, cited parenthetically at the end of the borrowed material. If the student had not included the phrase "according to geneticists," it might look as if she only borrowed the passage in quotation marks, and not the information that precedes that passage.

Material that is considered common knowledge — that is, familiar or at least accessible to the general public — does not have to be

documented. The author of *Hamlet,* the date the Declaration of Independence was signed, or the definition of *misfeasance,* while open to
dispute (some scholars, for example, claim that William Shakespeare
did not write *Hamlet*) are indisputably considered to be common knowledge in our culture. Unfortunately, it is not always clear whether a
particular fact *is* common knowledge. Although too much documentation can clutter a paper and distract the reader, it's still better to cite
too many sources than to cite too few and risk being accused of
dishonesty. In general, if you are unsure whether or not to give your
source credit, you should document the material.

Keeping Research under Control

Your preliminary outline provides guideposts for your research.
You will need to revise it as you go along to make room for new ideas
and evidence and for the questions that come up as you read. Rather
than try to fit each new piece of information into your outline, you can
use the numbering or lettering system in your outline to cross-reference
your notebooks or file cards.

As much as possible, keep all materials related to the same point
in the same place. You might do this by making a separate pile of file
cards for each point and its support and questions or by reserving
several pages in your notebook for information bearing on each point.

How do you know when you have done enough research? If you
have kept your outline updated, you have a visual record of your
progress. Check this against the guidelines on pages 270–271: Is each
point backed by at least two pieces of support? Do your sources represent a range of authors and of types of data? If a large proportion of
your support comes from one book, or if most of your references are
to newspaper articles, you probably need to keep working. On the other
hand, if your notes cite five different authorities making essentially the
same point, you may have collected more data than you need. It can
be useful to point out that more than one authority holds a given view
and to make notes of examples that are notably different from one
another. But it is not necessary to take down all the passages or
examples expressing the same idea.

To This Point

Before you leave the library or your primary sources for your
typewriter, check to make sure your research is complete.

1. Does your working outline show any gaps in your argument?
2. Have you found adequate data to support your claim?
3. Have you identified the warrants linking your claim with data and
   ensured that these warrants too are adequately documented?

4. If you intend to quote or paraphrase sources in your paper, do your notes include exact copies of all statements you may want to use and complete references?
5. Have you answered all the relevant questions that have come up during your research?
6. Do you have enough information about your sources to document your paper?

MLA System for Citing Publications

One of the simplest methods of crediting sources is the MLA in-text system, which is used in the research paper on fairy tales in this chapter. In the text of your paper, immediately after any quotation, paraphrase, or anything else you wish to document, simply insert a parenthetical mention of the author's last name and the page number on which the material appeared. You don't need a comma after the author's name or an abbreviation of the word "page." For example, the following sentence appears in the fairy tale paper:

> Famines in the seventeenth century often reduced the peasantry to a diet of "bad black bread, acorns, and roots" (Weber 96).

The parenthetical reference tells the reader that the information in this sentence came from page 96 of the book or article by Eugen Weber that appears in the Works Cited, at the end of the paper. The complete reference on the Works Cited page provides all the information readers need to locate the original source in the library:

> Weber, Eugen. "Fairies and Hard Facts: The Reality of Folktales." Journal of the History of Ideas 42 (1981): 93-113.

If the author's name is mentioned in the same sentence, it is also acceptable to place only the page numbers in parentheses; it is not necessary to repeat the author's name. For example:

> Bettelheim sees symbolic meaning in every motif and element in the story, and assumes that children interpret these symbolically as well (159-66).

The list of works cited includes all material you have used to write your research paper. This list appears at the end of your paper and always starts on a new page. Center the title Works Cited, double-space between the title and the first entry, and begin your list, which should be arranged alphabetically by author. Each entry should start at the left margin; indent all subsequent lines of the entry five spaces. Number each page, and double-space throughout.

Another method of documenting sources is to use notes, either footnotes (at the foot of the page) or endnotes (on a separate page at the end of the paper). The note method is not as commonly used today as the in-text system for two reasons: (1) Reference notes repeat almost all the information already given on the Works Cited page. (2) If footnotes are used, it requires careful calculation during typing to fit them on the page so that there is a consistent bottom margin throughout the paper.

Nevertheless, it is a valid method, so we illustrate it here. Superscript numbers go at the end of the sentence or phrase being referenced:

> Roman authors admit to borrowing frequently from earlier Greek writers for their jokes, although no joke books in the original Greek survive today.[1]

The reference note for this citation would be:

> [1]Alexander Humez and Nicholas Humez, Alpha to Omega. (Boston: Godine, 1981) 79.

On the Works Cited page this reference would be:

> Humez, Alexander, and Nicholas Humez. Alpha to Omega. Boston: Godine, 1981.

Notice that the page number for a book citation is given in the note but not the reference, and that the punctuation differs. Otherwise the information is the same. Number the notes consecutively throughout your paper.

One more point: *Content notes,* which provide additional information not readily worked into a research paper, are also indicated by superscript numbers. Susan Bennett's paper on fairy tales features four such notes, included on a Notes page before the list of Works Cited.

Following are examples of the citation forms you are most likely to need as you document your research. In general, for both books and magazines, information should appear in the following order: author, title, and publication information. Each item should be followed by a period. When using as a source an essay that appears in this book, follow the citation model for "Material reprinted from another source," unless your instructor indicates otherwise. Consult the third edition of the *MLA Handbook for Writers of Research Papers* by Joseph Gibaldi and Walter S. Achert (New York: Modern Language Association of America, 1988) for other documentation models and a list of acceptable shortened forms of publishers.

A BOOK BY A SINGLE AUTHOR

Kinder, Chuck. The Silver Ghost. New York: Harcourt, 1979.

AN ANTHOLOGY OR COMPILATION

Abrahams, William, ed. Prize Stories 1980: The O. Henry Awards. Garden City: Doubleday, 1980.

A BOOK BY TWO AUTHORS

Danzig, Richard, and Peter Szanton. National Service: What Would It Mean? Lexington: Lexington, 1986.

Note: This form is followed even for two authors with the same last name.

Ehrlich, Paul, and Anne Ehrlich. Extinction: The Causes and Consequences of the Disappearance of Species. New York: Random, 1981.

A BOOK BY TWO OR MORE AUTHORS

Heffernan, William A., Mark Johnston, and Frank Hodgins. Literature: Art and Artifact. San Diego: Harcourt, 1987.

If there are more than three authors, name only the first and add: "et al." (and others).

A BOOK BY A CORPORATE AUTHOR

Poets & Writers, Inc. The Writing Business: A Poets & Writers Handbook. New York: Poets & Writers, 1985.

A WORK IN AN ANTHOLOGY

Morton, Eugene S. "The Realities of Reintroducing Species to the Wild." Animal Extinctions: What Everyone Should Know. Ed. J. R. Hoage. National Zoological Park Symposia for the Public Series. Washington: Smithsonian Institution, 1985. 71-95.

AN INTRODUCTION, PREFACE, FOREWORD, OR AFTERWORD

Borges, Jorge Luis. Preface. New Islands. By Maria Luisa Bombal. Trans. Richard and Lucia Cunningham. New York: Farrar, 1982.

MATERIAL REPRINTED FROM ANOTHER SOURCE

Barry, Dave. "Bring Back Carl's Plaque." Bad Habits. New York: Henry
    Holt. 1985. Rpt. in Elements of Argument: A Text and Reader.
    Annette T. Rottenberg. 4th ed. New York: Bedford-St. Martin's, 1994.
    202.

A MULTIVOLUME WORK

Skotheim, Robert Allen, and Michael McGiffert, eds. Since the Civil War.
    Vol. 2 of American Social Thought: Sources and Interpretations. 2
    vols. Reading: Addison, 1972.

AN EDITION OTHER THAN THE FIRST

Cassill, R.V., ed. The Norton Anthology of Short Fiction, 2nd ed. New York:
    Norton, 1985.

A TRANSLATION

Allende, Isabel. The House of the Spirits. Trans. Magda Bogin. New York:
    Knopf, 1985.

A REPUBLISHED BOOK

Weesner, Theodore. The Car Thief. 1972. New York: Vintage-Random,
    1987

Note: The only information about original publication you need to
provide is the publication date, which appears immediately after the
title.

A BOOK IN A SERIES

Eady, Cornelius. Victims of the Latest Dance Craze. Omnation Press Dia-
    logues on Dance Series 5. Chicago: Omnation, 1985.

ARTICLE FROM A DAILY NEWSPAPER

Dudar, Helen. "James Earl Jones at Bat." New York Times 22 Mar. 1987,
    sec. 2: 1+.

ARTICLE FROM A PERIODICAL

O'Brien, Conor Cruise. "God and Man in Nicaragua." Atlantic Monthly
    Aug. 1986: 50-72.

UNSIGNED EDITORIAL

"Medium, Message." Editorial. Nation 28 Mar. 1987: 383-84.

ANONYMOUS WORKS

"The March Almanac." Atlantic Mar. 1993: 18.

Citation World Atlas. Maplewood: Hammond, 1987.

**ARTICLE FROM JOURNAL WITH SEPARATE
PAGINATION FOR EACH ISSUE**

Brewer, Derek. "The Battleground of Home: Versions of Fairy Tales."
    Encounter 54.4 (1980): 52-61.

**ARTICLE IN A JOURNAL WITH CONTINUOUS
PAGINATION THROUGHOUT VOLUME**

McCafferty, Janey. "The Shadders Go Away." New England Review and
    Bread Loaf Quarterly 9 (1987): 332-42.

Note that the issue number is not mentioned here; because the volume
has continuous pagination throughout the year, only the volume number (9) is needed.

A REVIEW

Walker, David. Rev. of A Wave, by John Ashbery. Field 32 (1985): 63-71.

AN INTERVIEW

Hines, Gregory. Interview. With D. C. Denison. The Boston Globe Maga-
    zine 29 Mar. 1987: 2.

Note: An interview conducted by the author of the paper would be
documented as follows:

Hines, Gregory. Personal interview. 29 Mar. 1987.

AN ARTICLE IN A REFERENCE WORK

"Bylina." The Princeton Encyclopedia of Poetry and Poetics. Ed. Alex
    Preminger. Enlarged ed. Princeton: Princeton UP, 1974.

GOVERNMENT DOCUMENT

United States. National Endowment for the Arts. 1989 Annual Report.
    Washington: Office of Public Affairs, 1990.

Frequently the Government Printing Office (GPO) is the publisher of
federal government documents.

COMPUTER SOFTWARE

XyQuest. XyWrite. Vers. III Plus. Computer Software. XyQuest, 1988. PC-
　　DOS 2.0, 384KB, disk.

Note here that the version is given in roman numerals, since it appears
that way in the title; usually software versions are given in decimals
(e.g., Vers. 2.1).

DATABASE SOURCE (INFORMATION SERVICE)

Gura, Mark. The Gorgeous Mosaic Project: A Work of Art by the School-
　　children of the World. Teacher's packet. East Brunswick: Children's
　　Atelier, 1990. ERIC ED 347 257.

Kassebaum, Peter. Cultural Awareness Training Manual and Study Guide.
　　ERIC, 1992. ED 347 289.

The ERIC documentation number at the end of the entry indicates that
the reader can obtain this source solely or primarily through ERIC
(Educational Resources Information Center). When no other publishing
information is given, treat ERIC (without a city of publication) as the
publisher, as shown in the second entry. ERIC also catalogs many
previously published articles with documentation numbers beginning
with EJ rather than ED. Treat these simply as articles in periodicals,
not as material from an information service; that is, omit the EJ number.
　　NTIS (National Technical Information Service) is another information service.

UNPUBLISHED MANUSCRIPT

Leahy, Ellen. "An Investigation of the Computerization of Information Sys-
　　tems in a Family Planning Program." Unpublished master's degree
　　project. Div. of Public Health, U of Massachusetts, Amherst, 1990.

LETTER TO THE EDITOR

Flannery, James W. Letter. New York Times Book Review 28 Feb. 1993: 34.

PERSONAL CORRESPONDENCE

Bennett, David. Letter to the author. 3 Mar. 1993.

LECTURE

Calvino, Italo. "Right and Wrong Political Uses of Literature." Symposium
　　on European Politics. Amherst College. Amherst, 25 Feb. 1976.

FILM

The Voice of the Khalam. Prod. Loretta Pauker. With Leopold Senghor, Okara, Birago Diop, Rubadiri, and Francis Parkes. Contemporary Films/McGraw-Hill, 1971. 16 mm, 29 min.

Other pertinent information to give in film references, if available, is the writer and director (see model for radio/TV program for style).

TV OR RADIO PROGRAM

The Shakers: Hands to Work, Hearts to God. Narr. David McCullough. Dir. Ken Burns and Amy Stechler Burns. Writ. Amy Stechler Burns, Wendy Tilghman, and Tom Lewis. PBS. WGBY, Springfield. 28 Dec. 1992.

VIDEOTAPE

Style Wars! Videotape. Prod. Tony Silver and Henry Chalfont. New Day Films, 1985. 69 min.

PERFORMANCE

Quilters: A Musical Celebration. By Molly Newman and Barbara Damashek. Dir. Joyce Devlin. Musical dir. Faith Fung. Mt. Holyoke Laboratory Theatre, South Hadley, MA. 26 Apr. 1991. Based on The Quilters: Women and Domestic Art by Patricia Cooper and Norma Bradley Allen.

CARTOON

Henley, Marian. "Maxine." Cartoon. Valley Advocate 25 Feb. 1993: 39.

SAMPLE RESEARCH PAPER (MLA STYLE)

The following paper, prepared in the MLA style, was written for an advanced composition course. Told to compose a research paper on a literary topic, Susan A. Bennett chose to write on fairy tales — a subject literary enough to satisfy her instructor, yet general enough to encompass her own interest in developmental psychology. But as she explored the subject, she found herself reading in a surprising array of disciplines, including folklore, anthropology, and history. Although she initially expected to report on the psychological importance of fairy tales, Bennett at last wrote an argument about the importance of their historical and cultural roots. Her paper, as is typical for literary papers, anchors its argument in the events and details of its chosen text, "Hansel and Gretel." But it also makes effective use of sources to help readers understand that there is more to the tale than a story that sends children happily off to sleep.

Include a title page if an outline is part of the paper. If no outline is required, include name, instructor's name, course name, and and date at the upper left corner of page 1.

When a Fairy Tale Is Not Just a Fairy Tale

By

Susan A. Bennett

Professor Middleton

English 2A

May 1993

Topic outline. Some instructors require a thesis statement under "Outline" heading and before the outline itself.

Outline

I. Introduction:

   A. Dictionary definition of "fairy tale"

   B. Thesis: "Hansel and Gretel" has historical roots

II. Origin and distribution of tale

III. Historical basis of motifs

   A. Physical and economic hardship

      1. Fear of the forest

      2. Poverty and starvation

      3. Child abandonment

      4. Fantasies of finding treasure

   B. Cruel stepmother

   C. Wicked witch

      1. Eating meat associated with cannibalism and upper classes

      2. Elderly caretaker for unwanted children

      3. Witches in community

      4. Witchcraft as remnant of ancient fertility religion

IV. Rebuttals to historical approach

   A. Motivation for telling realistic tales

   B. Psychological interpretations

      1. Fairy tales dreamlike, not literal

      2. Freudian interpretation

V. Conclusion

When a Fairy Tale Is Not Just a Fairy Tale

"Hansel and Gretel" is a well-known fairy tale, beloved of many children in both Europe and North America.[1] Athough it has no fairies in it, it conforms to the definition of "fairy tale" given in Webster's Ninth New Collegiate Dictionary: "a narrative of adventures involving fantastic forces and beings (as fairies, wizards, and goblins)." As anyone familiar with this tale will remember, Hansel and Gretel are two children on an adventure in the woods, where they encounter a wicked witch in a gingerbread house, who plans to fatten and eat them. Through their ingenuity they outsmart her, burn her up in her own oven, and return home triumphantly with a hoard of riches found in her house.

We think of fairy tales as being lighthearted fantasies that entertain but don't have much relevance to daily life. We often borrow the word to describe a movie with an unlikely plot, or a person not quite grounded in reality: "Oh, he's living in a fairy tale world; he hasn't got his head on his shoulders." In fact, the second definition of "fairy tale" in Webster's is "a made-up story usually designed to mislead."

So what is the meaning of "Hansel and Gretel"? Is it simply a story of make-believe, or something more? Fairy tales are told, read, and heard in the context of a time and place. Today we are exposed to them through illustrated storybooks, cartoons, and film. But in Europe, before technologies in printing made mass publishing possible, folktales were passed on orally. They were told by adults mostly for adult audiences, although people often first heard them as children. They served to entertain and to relieve the boredom of repetitive work in the fields during the day and in the home in the evening (Weber 93, 113). In peasant and aboriginal communities, that is often still the case (Taggart 437).

I believe that "Hansel and Gretel" has historical meaning. Embedded in this simple narrative is a record of the experiences and events once common in the lives of the people who first told and listened to it.

Where did "Hansel and Gretel" come from? We do not know for certain. In oral form this tale shows wide distribution. Different versions have been recorded all over Europe, India, Japan, Africa, the Caribbean, Pacific Islands, and among

---

Margin notes:

Title centered

Raised, superscript number refers to notes giving information at the end to the paper.

Writer briefly summarizes tales to orient readers.

In-text citation of author and pages; citation appears at the end of the sentence before the period.

Thesis with claim of fact that the writer must support

Writers's name;
page number

Bennett   2

native North and South Americans ("Hansel and Gretel"). As
with all folktales, there is no agreement among folklorists[2]
about whether all these versions migrated from one place to
another, sprang up independently, or derive from some combi-

Reference to en-
cyclopedia arti-
cle — page num-
ber not necessary

nation of the two ("Hansel and Gretel"). Most oral versions of
it have been recorded in Europe (Aarne 117). This does not
prove that the tale originated there--it may simply reflect the
eagerness of people in Europe during the nineteenth and
twentieth centuries to record their own folk history--but it is
the best guideline for now.

The tale may be very ancient, since folktales can be
passed on faithfully from one generation to another without
change. (The origins of "Cinderella," for example, can be

Square brackets
used to represent
parentheses
within parenthe-
ses

traced back to China in the ninth century [Thompson, Folktale
126].) But we can't know that for sure. So, even though "Hansel and Gretel" may have originated hundreds or even thousands of years ago, it probably is only safe to compare a tale
with the historical period when the tale was first recorded.
For "Hansel and Gretel" this means Europe in the seventeenth
to nineteenth centuries.[3]

Eugen Weber is one historian who sees direct parallels
between the characters and motifs in "Hansel and Gretel" (and
other Grimms' fairy tales), and the social and economic conditions in Europe during this period. One of the central themes
in the tale is poverty and abandonment. Recall how the tale

Specific support
from the tale
cited

begins: Hansel and Gretel live with their parents near a huge
forest; their father is a woodcutter. The family is facing starvation because there is a famine. Twice their parents abandon
them in the woods to save themselves. The first time the children are able to find their way home, but the second time they
get lost.

As Weber points out, until the middle of the nineteenth

Consecutive refer-
ences immedi-
ately following an
identified source
("Weber") cite
only the pages
within the source
without repeating
the source.

century, the forest, especially for northern Europeans, carried
the real potential for encountering danger in the form of rob-
bers, wild animals, and getting lost (96-97). Moreover, conditions of poverty, starvation, early death, and danger from unknown adults were common throughout Europe for peasants
and the working class (96). The majority of Europeans at the
beginning of the eighteenth century were farmers, and the av-

erage life expectancy was about twenty-five years (Treasure
660, 667). Famines in the seventeenth century often reduced
the peasantry to a diet of "bad black bread, acorns, and roots"
(Weber 96). Hansel and Gretel are treated by the witch to a
dinner of pancakes and sugar, milk, nuts, and apples (101).
This may not sound particularly nourishing to our ears because we assume a healthy dinner must have vegetables and/
or meat. But when you're starving, anything is likely to taste
good; this would have been a sumptuous meal for Hansel and
Gretel.

> Narrative details linked to histori-cal facts

Childhood was thought of differently then than today.
"Valued as an extra pair of hands or deplored as an extra
mouth to feed, the child belonged to no privileged realm of
play and protection from life's responsibilities" (Treasure
664). Social historian John Boswell estimates that anywhere
from 10 to 40 percent of children in towns and cities were
abandoned during the eighteenth century. Parental motivation
included removing the stigma of illegitimate or physically deformed children, being unable to support their children and
hoping to give them a better life with strangers, desiring to
promote one child's inheritance over another's, or simply lacking interest in raising the child (48, 428).

> Source cited after direct quotation

Weber points out that peasants had very little cash and
didn't use banks. Hiding and finding treasure--gold, silver, and
jewelry--was a much more common occurrence two centuries
ago than it is today (101), a kind of lottery for the poor. In
this light, the riches the children find in the witch's house
could reflect the common person's fantasy of striking it rich.

> Writer's interpre-tation of one as-pect of the story

A central motif in the story is the stepmother who wants
to abandon the children to keep herself and her husband from
starving. (The father, at first reluctant, eventually gives in to
his wife's plan.) As Weber and others have noted, stepmothers
were not unusual in history. The death rate among childbearing women was much higher in past centuries than it is today.
When women died in childbirth, there was strong economic
motivation for fathers to remarry. In the seventeenth and
eighteenth centuries, 20 to 80 percent of widowers remarried
within the year of their wife's death. By the mid-nineteenth

Bennett   4

century, after life expectancy rose, only 15 percent of widowers did so (94, 112).

What accounts for the stereotype of the heartless stepmother? Weber suggests that stepmothers were assigned the
role of doing evil to children for economic reasons: The family
would risk losing its good name and perhaps its land if a biological parent killed a child (107). There is also the issue of
inheritance from the stepmother's point of view: If her husband dies, her husband's children, not she, would inherit the-
land and property. Literary and legal evidence of stepmothers
plotting to eliminate stepchildren, especially stepsons, shows
up in European literature as far back as two millennia ago
(Boswell 128).

Transition to new
topic: witches

Another major theme in "Hansel and Gretel" is the
wicked witch, which also shows up in lots of other fairy tales.
Were there witches in European history, and if so, where did
the reputation for eating children come from?

Weber notes that in fairy tales only evil figures eat meat
of any kind, whether animal or human flesh. Before the middle of the nineteenth century the peasantry rarely ate meat,
but the aristocracy and bourgeoisie did. This discrepancy may
be the origin of the motif in some fairy tales of evil figures of
upper-class background wanting to eat children (112, 101).
Weber seems to imply that child-eating witches symbolized to
the peasantry either resentment of or paranoia about the aristocracy.

Although the witch's cottage in "Hansel and Gretel" is
not described as grand or large, there are other allusions to
wealth and comfort. The witch puts the two children to bed
between clean sheets, a luxury for much of the peasantry, who
slept on straw and for whom bed lice were a common reality
(Treasure 661-62). And of course there is the hoard of coin
money and jewelry the children later discover there. Perhaps
more significantly, the witch herself has a lot of power, just as
the aristocracy was perceived to have, including the power to
deceive and take away life.

David Bakan suggests that the historical basis for the
witch is the unmarried elderly woman in the community who

took in unwanted, illegitimate children and was often paid to
do this (66-67). There is also evidence that witchcraft, ranging from white magic to sorcery (black magic), was practiced
by both individual women and men among the peasantry during this time. For example, "the 'cunning folk' were at least as
numerous in sixteenth-century England as the parish clergy.
Moreover, in their divinatory, medical, and religious functions
they were far more important in peasant society than were
the official clergy" (Horsley 697). Witches were called on to
influence the weather, provide love potions, find lost objects,
midwife, identify thieves, and heal illnesses (698). Some services performed by witches were ambiguous: "Apparently some
peasants would conjure the storms or weather spirits to avoid
striking their own fields--but to strike someone else's instead,"
but for the most part the wisewomen and sorcerers were different people (698).

The idea that an organized witch cult, as portrayed by
the Catholic Church during the Middle Ages, actually existed is
dismissed today by most social historians. Jesse Nash thinks
we should reconsider the possibility that some of the behavior
witches were accused of, including ritual cannibalism and sexual orgies in the woods, actually occurred in some form (12).
He sees witchcraft as "a surviving remnant of a religion which
was concerned with the fertility of crops, animals, humans,
and with the alteration of seasons and with the identification
of humans with animals" (13). These practices date back to a
matriarchal goddess religion which flourished in Europe 5,000
to 7,000 years ago, before invasion of the patriarchal cultures
from India (Marija Gimbutas in Nash 12). This religion included human sacrifice and was based on the concept of maintaining balance in the universe: The goddess of life was at the
same time the goddess of death. Wood-wives and fairies, who
lived in the forest, "were mediators of sacred knowledge to
their communities" (16).

Nash suggests that in Europe, although Christianity became the official way of thinking about the world, it did not
replace the old beliefs entirely, despite strong attempts by the
Church to eliminate them. Religious beliefs and practices can
persist hidden for generations if need be.[4] The peasants were

Source within a
source cited

able to live with and practice both Christianity and paganism in combination for centuries (25).

So we have seen there is validity to the claim that many of the motifs of "Hansel and Gretel" have historical roots.

Having supported her major claim, the writer continues by anticipating and addressing possible rebuttals.

However, one might well ask why people would want to hear stories so close to their own experiences. If oral tales during this time were meant as entertainment mostly for adults, wouldn't they want something to take their minds off their troubles? Weber suggests a couple of motivations for telling fairy tales. One was to experience "the delights of fear" (97). Fairy tales were told along with ghost stories, gossip, jokes, and fables. I suspect it was similar to the thrill some people get today watching scary movies with happy endings.

Second, fairy tales helped to explain how the world worked. To most people not able to read, the world of cause and effect was mysterious and could only be explained through symbolism and analogy. Folktales had been used in church

Two sources cited at once

sermons since the fourteenth century (Weber 110, Zipes 22).

But the industrial age ushered in the scientific revolution, and with it came the concept of explaining the unknown by breaking it down into working parts (Weber 113). Reading became available to large numbers of people. By this time fairy tales were no longer meaningful ways to explain the world for ordinary adults, so they became the province of children's entertainment (113).

Competing theories presented

Folklorist Alan Dundes thinks it is naive to assume fairy tales have literal meaning. In recent years he and a number of other people have looked to psychology to explain the origin of fairy tales. "Fairy tales are like dreams--can you find the

Telephone interview — no page numbers

historic origin of dreams?" (Dundes). In their structure and characters fairy tales do have a number of dreamlike aspects: They rarely state the feelings of the hero directly, and all inner experiences of the hero are projected outward into objects in nature and other people (Tatar 91). The other characters seem not to have separate lives of their own; all their actions and intentions relate to the hero (Brewer 55). Also, magical things happen: Elements of nature speak, granting favors to the hero or threatening success or even life. In one version of

"Hansel and Gretel," for example, a white duck talks to the children and carries them across a lake on their way home.

The symbolic nature of fairy tales, however, doesn't deny the validity of examining them for historical origins. As anyone who has recorded their own dreams knows, people and objects from mundane, daily life show up regularly in them. Sometimes these elements are disguised as symbols, but other times they are transparently realistic. Similarly, the talking duck and the gingerbread house in "Hansel and Gretel" may be unreal, but other themes have more literal counterparts in history.

One of the most quoted interpreters of fairy tales is psychologist Bruno Bettelheim, whose The Uses of Enchantment analyzes fairy tales in Freudian terms. In his view, "Hansel and Gretel" represents the task each of us as children must face in coming to terms with anxiety--not the anxiety of facing starvation and being literally abandoned in the woods, but the ordinary fear of separating from our parents (especially mother) in the process of growing up to become independent adults. Bettelheim sees symbolic meaning in every motif and element in the story, and assumes that children interpret these symbolically as well (159-66).

Undeniably, there are themes in "Hansel and Gretel"--as in many of our most common fairy tales--that strike deep psychological chords with both children and adults. The wicked stepmother is a good example: Children often fantasize they are really stepchildren or adopted as a way to account for feeling victimized and abused by their parents. "In real life this fantasy occurs among children with a very high frequency" (Bakan 76).

Partial validity of competing theories acknowledged

These themes help to explain the enduring popularity of fairy tales among middle-class children over the last two centuries. But we cannot treat fairy tales as if they spring full-blown from the unconscious and tell us nothing about the past. For the people who told and heard "Hansel and Gretel" in the seventeenth to nineteenth centuries in Europe, the tale was describing events and phenomena that happened, if not to them, then to someone they knew. Everyone in rural commu-

Having qualified her major claim in light of other theories, student goes on to reiterate the support for her major claim in her conclusion.

nities was likely to have been exposed, whether in person or
by hearsay, to some elderly woman claiming powers to alter
weather patterns, heal the sick, cast spells, midwife, or take in
illegitimate babies. Stepmothers were common, poverty and
famine ongoing, and abandonment and child abuse very real.
In addition to providing entertainment, tales like "Hansel and
Gretel" reassured teller and listener alike that the ordinary
physical hardships, which for most of us today are fictions,
were possible to overcome.

Bennett 9

Notes

^{1} We in the United States know it primarily in printed form, as it has come to us from Germany. Between 1812 and 1857, the Grimm brothers, Jacob and Wilhelm, published several editions of Kinder und Hausmarchen (Children's and Household Tales) (Zipes 6, 41, 79). In addition to "Hansel and Gretel," this book included over 200 other folktales (though not all of them were fairy tales). The anthology increased in popularity until by the turn of the twentieth century it outsold all other books in Germany except the Bible (Zipes 15). To date it has been translated into some seventy languages (Denecke).

^{2} Folklorists collect folktales from around the world and analyze them. Tales are categorized according to type (basic plot line) and motifs (elements within the tale). Two widely used references for folklorists are Antti Aarne's Types of the Folklore and Stith Thompson's Motif-index. "Hansel and Gretel" is type 327A in the Aarne classification.

^{3} The Grimms were the first to record tale type 327A in 1812 (see note 1). A related tale about Tom Thumb (tale type 327B) was first recorded by Charles Perrault from France in 1697 (Thompson, Folktale 37, 182).

^{4} Consider the example of Sephardic Jews who "converted" to Christianity under duress in Spain in the fifteenth century. Some of them moved to North America, and their descendants continued to practice Christianity openly and Judaism in secret until recently ("Search for the Buried Past").

Margin notes:

Content notes appear at the end of the paper, before Works Cited.

Space included between superscript number and beginning of note

Indent five spaces to superscript number; rest of note is flush left.

Works Cited

Sources arranged alphabetically by author's last name

Aarne, Antti. The Types of the Folklore: Classification and Bibliography. Trans. and ed. Stith Thompson. 2nd rev. ed. FF
Communications 184. Helsinki: Suomalainen Tiedeaka-
temia, 1964.

First line flush left in citation, rest indented five spaces

Bakan, David. Slaughter of the Innocents. Toronto: Canadian
Broadcasting System, 1971.

Bettelheim, Bruno. The Uses of Enchantment: The Meaning
and Importance of Fairy Tales. 1976. New York: Vintage,
1977.

Book

Boswell, John. The Kindness of Strangers: The Abandonment
of Children in Western Europe from Late Antiquity to the
Renaissance. New York: Pantheon, 1988.

Periodical

Brewer, Derek. "The Battleground of Home: Versions of Fairy
Tales." Encounter 54.4 (1980): 52-61.

Encyclopedia article

Denecke, Ludwig. "Grimm, Jacob Ludwig Carl and Wilhelm
Carl." Encyclopaedia Britannica: Micropaedia. 1992 ed.

Interview

Dundes, Alan. Telephone interview. 10 Feb. 1993.

"Fairy tale." Webster's Ninth New Collegiate Dictionary. 1989
ed.

"Hansel and Gretel." Funk & Wagnalls Standard Dictionary of
Folklore, Mythology, and Legend. Ed. Maria Leach. New
York: Funk & Wagnalls, 1949.

Horsley, Richard A. "Who Were the Witches? The Social Roles
of the Accused in the European Witch Trials." Journal of
Interdisciplinary History 9 (1979): 689-715.

Nash, Jesse. "European Witchcraft: The Hidden Tradition."
Human Mosaic 21.1-2 (1987): 10-30.

Radio broadcast

"Search for the Buried Past." The Hidden Jews of New Mexico.
Prod. Nan Rubin. WFCR, Amherst, Mass. 13 Sept. 1992.

Taggart, James M. " 'Hansel and Gretel' in Spain and Mexico."
Journal of American Folklore 99 (1986): 435-60.

Article in an edited anthology

Tatar, Maria. "Folkloristic Phantasies: Grimm's Fairy Tales
and Freud's Family Romance." In Fairy Tales as Ways of
Knowing: Essays on Marchen in Psychology, Society and
Literature. Ed. Michael M. Metzger and Katharina Momm-

Bennett   11

sen. Germanic Studies in America 41. Berne: Lang, 1981.
    75-98.

Thompson, Stith. The Folktale. New York: Holt, 1946.

---. Motif-index of Folk-literature: A Classification of Narrative
    Elements in Folktales, Ballads, Myths, Fables, Mediaeval
    Romances, Exempla, Fabliaux, Jest-books, and Local Leg-
    ends. Rev. ed. 6 vols. plus index. Bloomington: Indiana
    UP, 1957.

Treasure, Geoffrey R. R. "European History and Culture: The
    Emergence of Modern Europe, 1500-1648." Encyclopaedia
    Britannica: Macropaedia. 1992 ed. 657-83.

Weber, Eugen. "Fairies and Hard Facts: The Reality of Folk-
    tales." Journal of the History of Ideas 42 (1981): 93-
    113.

Zipes, Jack. The Brothers Grimm: From Enchanted Forests to
    the Modern World. New York: Routledge, 1988.

Two consecutive works by the same author

Volume in a multi-volume revised edition

APA System for Citing Publications

Instructors in the social sciences might prefer the citation system of the American Psychological Association (APA). Like the MLA system, the APA system calls for a parenthetical citation in the text of the paper. Unlike the MLA system, the APA system includes the year of publication in the parenthetical reference. Here is an example:

> Even though many South American countries rely on the drug trade for their economic survival, the majority of South Americans disapprove of drug use (Gorriti, 1989, p. 72).

The complete publication information for Gorriti's article will appear at the end of your paper, on a page titled "References." (Sample citations for the "References" page appear below.)

If your list of references includes more than one work written by the same author in the same year, cite the first work as *a* and the second as *b*. For example, Gorriti's second article of 1989 would be cited in your paper as (Gorriti, 1989b).

Following are examples of the citation forms you are most likely to use. If you need the format for a type of publication not listed here, consult the third edition of the *Publication Manual of the American Psychological Association* (1983).

A BOOK BY A SINGLE AUTHOR
Briggs, J. (1988). <u>Fire in the crucible: The alchemy of creative genius</u>. New York: St. Martin's Press.

AN ANTHOLOGY OR COMPILATION
Gioseffi, D. (Ed.). (1988). <u>Women on war</u>. New York: Simon & Schuster.

A BOOK BY TWO OR MORE AUTHORS OR EDITORS
Colombo, G., Cullen, R., & Lisle, B. (Eds.). (1989). <u>Rereading America: Cultural contexts for critical thinking and writing</u>. New York: Bedford Books/St. Martin's Press.

Note: List the names of *all* the authors or editors, no matter how many.

A BOOK BY A CORPORATE AUTHOR
International Advertising Association. (1977). <u>Controversy advertising: How advertisers present points of view on public affairs</u>. New York: Hastings House.

WORK IN AN ANTHOLOGY

Mukherjee, B. (1988). The colonization of the mind. In Gioseffi, D. (Ed.) Women on war (pp. 140-142). New York: Simon & Schuster.

AN INTRODUCTION, PREFACE, FOREWORD, OR AFTERWORD

Hemenway, R. (1984). Introduction. In Z. N. Hurston, Dust tracks on a road. Urbana: University of Illinois Press, ix-xxxix.

AN EDITION OTHER THAN THE FIRST

Gumpert, G., & Cathcart, R. (Eds.). (1986). Inter/media: Interpersonal communication in a media world (3rd ed.). New York: Oxford University Press.

A TRANSLATION

Sartre, J. P. (1962). Literature and existentialism. (B. Frechtman, Trans.) New York: Citadel Press. (Original work published 1949.)

A REPUBLISHED BOOK

James, W. (1969). The varieties of religious experience: A study in human nature. London: Collier Books. (Original work published 1961.)

A BOOK IN A SERIES

Berthrong, D. J. (1976). The Cheyenne and Arapaho ordeal: Reservation and agency life in the Indian territory, 1875-1907. Vol. 136. The civilization of the American Indian series. Norman: University of Oklahoma Press.

ARTICLE FROM A DAILY NEWSPAPER

Hottelet, R. C. (1990, March 15). Germany: Why it can't happen again. Christian Science Monitor, p. 19.

ARTICLE FROM A PERIODICAL

Gorriti, G. A. (1989, July). How to fight the drug war. Atlantic Monthly, pp. 70-76.

ARTICLE IN A JOURNAL WITH CONTINUOUS PAGINATION THROUGHOUT VOLUME

Cockburn, A. (1989). British justice, Irish victims. The Nation, 249, 554-555.

ARTICLE FROM A JOURNAL WITH SEPARATE PAGINATION FOR EACH ISSUE

Mukerji, C. Visual language in science and the exercise of power: The case of cartography in early modern Europe. Studies in Visual Communication, 10(3), 30-45.

GOVERNMENT PUBLICATION

United States Dept. of Health, Education, and Welfare. (1973). Current ethical issues in mental health. Washington, DC: U.S. Government Printing Office.

ABSTRACT

Fritz, M. (1990/1991). A comparison of social interactions using a friendship awareness activity. Education and Training in Mental Retardation, 25, 352-359. (From Psychological Abstracts, 1991, 78, Abstract No. 11474)

When the dates of the original publication and of the abstract differ, give both dates separated by a slash.

ANONYMOUS WORK

The status of women: Different but the same. (1992-1993). Zontian, 73(3), 5.

MULTIPLE WORKS BY THE SAME AUTHOR IN THE SAME YEAR

Gardner, H. (1982a). Art, mind, and brain: A cognitive approach to creativity. New York: Basic.

Gardner, H. (1982b). Developmental psychology: An introduction (2nd ed.). Boston: Little, Brown.

MULTIVOLUME WORK

Mussen, Ph. H. (Ed.). (1983). Handbook of child psychology (4th ed., Vols. 1-4). New York: Wiley.

ARTICLE IN A REFERENCE WORK

Frisby, J. P. (1990). Direct perception. In M. W. Eysenck (Ed.), Blackwell dictionary of cognitive psychology (pp. 95-100). Oxford: Basil Blackwell.

COMPUTER SOFTWARE

UnionSquareware (1987). Squarenote, the ideal librarian [Computer program]. Somerville, MA: Author.

If the primary contributors to developing the program are known, begin the reference with those as the author(s) instead of the corporate author. If you are citing a documentation manual rather than the program itself, add the word "manual" before the closing bracket. If there is additional information needed for retrieving the program (such as report and/or acquisition numbers), add this at the end of the entry, in parentheses after the last period.

DATABASE SOURCE (INFORMATION SERVICE)

LeSourd, S. J. (1992, April). The psychology of perspective consciousness. Paper presented at the annual meeting of the American Educational Research Association, San Francisco. (ERIC Document Reproduction Service No. ED 348 296)

Treat an ERIC document as a database source only if the primary or sole place to find it is from ERIC; if the source was previously published and is readily available in printed form, treat it as a journal article or published book.

REVIEW

Harris, I. M. (1991). [Review of Rediscovering masculinity: Reason, language, and sexuality]. Gender and Society, 5, 259-261.

Give the author of the review, not the author of the book being reviewed. Use this form for a film review also. If the review has a title, place it before the bracketed material, and treat it like an article title.

LETTER TO THE EDITOR

Pritchett, J. T., & Kellner, C. H. (1993). Comment on spontaneous seizure activity [Letter to the editor]. Journal of Nervous and Mental Disease, 181, 138-139.

PERSONAL CORRESPONDENCE

B. Ehrenreich (personal communication, August 7, 1992)

(B. Ehrenreich, personal communication, August 7, 1992)

Cite all personal communications to you (such as letters, memos, and telephone conversations) in text only, *without* listing them among the References. The phrasing of your sentences will determine which of the two above forms to use.

UNPUBLISHED MANUSCRIPT

McIntosh, P. (1988). White privilege and male privilege: A personal account of coming to see correspondences through work in women's studies. Working Paper 189. Unpublished manuscript, Wellesley College, Center for Research on Women, Wellesley, MA.

LECTURE

Kagan, J. (1968, April 30). A theoretical look at child development. Albert F. Blakeslee Lecture, Smith College, Northampton, MA.

PROCEEDINGS OF A MEETING, PUBLISHED

Guerrero, R. (1972/1973). Possible effects of the periodic abstinence method. In W. A. Uricchio & M. K. Williams (Eds.), Proceedings of a Research Conference on Natural Family Planning (pp. 96-105). Washington, DC: Human Life Foundation.

If the date of the symposium or conference is different from the date of publication, give both, separated by a slash. If the proceedings are published annually, treat the reference like a periodical article.

FILM

Golden, G. (Producer). (1975). Changing images: Confronting career stereotypes [Film]. Berkeley: University of California.

VIDEOTAPE

Cambridge Video (Producer). (1987). Setting educational/vocational goals [Video]. Charleston, WV: Cambridge Career Products.

SAMPLE RESEARCH PAPER (APA STYLE)

The following paper urges a change in our attitude toward zoos. Arguing the value claim that it is morally wrong for humans to exploit animals for entertainment, the student combines expert opinion gathered from research with her own interpretations of evidence. She is always careful to anticipate and represent the claims of the opposition before going on to refute them.

The student uses the APA style, modified to suit the preferences of her writing instructor. APA style requires a title page with a centered title, author, affiliation, and a short title that can be used as a "running head" on each page. An abstract page follows the title page and includes a one-paragraph abstract or summary of the article. Amanda Repp was told she could omit the title page and abstract recommended by the APA. A full description of APA publication conventions can be found in the *Publication Manual of the American Psychological Association* (1983).

Amanda Repp   Zoos
English 102-G   1
Mr. Kennedy
Fall 1992

                    Why Zoos Should Be Eliminated
    Zoos have come a long way from their grim beginnings.
Once full of tiny cement-block steel cages, the larger zoos now
boast simulated jungles, veldts, steppes, and rain forests, all in
an attempt to replicate the natural habitats of the incarcerated animals. The attempt, however admirable, is misguided.
It is morally wrong to keep wild animals in captivity, and no
amount of replication, no matter how realistic, can compensate for the freedom these creatures are denied.

        Peter Batten (1976) argues that a wild animal's life "is
spent in finding food, avoiding enemies, sleeping, and in mating or other family activities. . . . Deprivation of any of these
fundamentals results in irreparable damage to the individual"
(p. 1). The fact that humans may be stronger or smarter than
beasts does not give them the right to ambush and exploit animals for the purposes of entertainment.

        We humans take our own liberty quite seriously. Indeed,
we consider liberty to be one of our inalienable rights. But too
many of us apparently feel no obligation to grant the same
right to animals, who, because they cannot defend themselves
against our sophisticated methods of capture and because they
do not speak our language, cannot claim it for themselves.

        But the right to liberty is not based on the ability to
claim it, or even on the ability to understand what it is. As
James Rachels (1976) writes:

> Humans have a right to liberty because they have var-
> ious other interests that will suffer if their freedom is
> unduly restricted. The right to liberty--the right to be
> free of external constraints on one's actions--may
> then be seen as derived from a more basic right not to
> have one's interests needlessly harmed. (p. 210)

Animals, like people, have interests that are harmed if they
are kept in captivity: They are separated from their families
and prevented from behaving according to their natural instincts by being removed from the lives they know, which are
the lives they were meant to lead.

Summary of an
opposing argu-
ment

Writer suggests
flaw in compari-
son.

Refutation of op-
posing argument
based on evidence
from personal ex-
perience

Writer summa-
rizes, then points
out a weakness in,
a second oppos-
ing argument.

Writer questions
an unstated war-
rant in the argu-
ment.

Some argue that animals' interests are not being harmed
when they are kept in zoos or aquariums--that no damage is
being done to the individual--but their claims are highly dis-
putable. For example, the Zurich Zoo's Dr. Heini Hediger
(1985) protests that it is absurd to attribute human qualities
to animals at all, but he nevertheless resorts to a human analogy: "Wild animals in the zoo rather resemble estate owners.
Far from desiring to escape and regain their freedom, they are
only bent on defending the space they inhabit and keeping it
safe from invasion" (p. 9). How can Dr. Hediger explain the
actions of the leopards and cheetahs I have seen executing figure eights off the walls and floors of their cages for hours on
end? I have watched, spellbound by their grace but also horrified; it is impossible to believe that these animals do not want
their freedom. An estate owner would not spend his time running frantically around the perimeters of his property. These
cats know they are not lords of any estate. The senseless repetition of their actions suggest that the cats know that they
are caged and that there is nothing to defend against, no "estate" to protect.

Shannon Brownlee (1986) also believes that there is no
concrete evidence that incarcerated animals are suffering or
unhappy, but she weakens her own case in her description of
Jackie, a dolphin in captivity who "spends the day in a seeming stupor" and "chews on the mackerel half-heartedly" at
feeding time (p. 70). Clearly there is something wrong with
Jackie; this becomes apparent when Brownlee contrasts Jackie's lethargic behavior with that of wild dolphins cavorting in
the bay. Brownlee points out that Jackie has never tried to
escape through a hole in his enclosure, although he knows it
is there. But this fact does not necessarily mean that Jackie
enjoys captivity. Instead, it may mean that Jackie's spirit has
been broken, and that he no longer remembers or cares what
his earlier days were like. Granted we have no way of knowing what Jackie is really feeling, but does that give us the
right to assume that he is not feeling anything?

To be fair, Brownlee does not go that far. She does allow
Jackie one emotional state, attributing his malaise to boredom.

Zoos

3

But perhaps if the author were removed from members of her family, as well as all other members of her species, and prevented from engaging in activities that most mattered to her, she would recognize Jackie's problems as something more than boredom. In any case, why should we inflict boredom on Jackie, or any other animal, just because we happen to have the means to do so?

Having registered these basic objections to zoos--that keeping any creature in captivity is a fundamental infringement on that creature's right to liberty and dignity--I want to take a closer look at the zoo as an institution, in order to assess fairly its goals and how it tries to meet them. Most zoo professionals today maintain that zoos exist for two main reasons: to educate humans and to conserve animal species. These are both admirable goals, certainly, but as Seal (1985) notes, "none of these [zoo] budgets is allocated specifically for species preservation. Zoos have been established primarily as recreational institutions and are only sec ndarily developing programs in conservation, education, and research" (p. 74). The fact is most zoos do not have the money, space, or equipment required to make significant contributions in this area. The bulk of their money goes to the upkeep of the animals and exhibits--that is, to put it crudely, to the displays.

On behalf of the education a zoo provides, a common argument is that there is nothing like seeing the real thing. But what you see in the zoo is not a real thing at all. Many zoo and aquarium animals, like Jackie the dolphin, have been domesticated to the point of lethargy, in part because they are being exhibited alone or with only one other member of their species, when what they are used to is traveling in groups and finding their own food, instead of being fed. Anyone who wants to see the real thing would be better off watching some of the excellent programming about nature and wildlife that appears on public television.

As for conservation, it is clearly a worthwhile effort, but zoos are not effective agents of species preservation. It is generally acknowledged that it is difficult to breed zoo animals (Luoma, 1982, p. 104). Animals often do not reproduce at all--

---

Writer shifts to the second half of her argument.

Clarifying word in square brackets

Another opposing argument, with refutation

Summarizes two expert opinions that zoos do not help endangered species

Author, date, page cited parenthetically

quite possibly because of the artificial, and consequently unsettling, circumstances in which they live. When zoo animals do
mate successfully, the offspring is often weakened by inbreeding. According to geneticists, this is because a population of
150 breeder animals is necessary in order to "assure the more

Source with two
authors cited par-
enthetically

or less permanent survival of a species in captivity" (Ehrlich
& Ehrlich, 1981, p. 211). Few zoos have the resources to
maintain populations that size. When zoos rely on smaller
populations for breeding (as many do) the species' gene pool
becomes more and more limited, "vigor and fecundity tend to
decline" (Ehrlich & Ehrlich, 1981, p. 212), and this can eventually lead to extinction. In other words, we are not doing
these animals any favors by trying to conserve them in zoos.
Reserves and preservations, which have room for the larger
populations necessary for successful conservation efforts and
which can concentrate on breeding animals rather than on
displaying them, are much more suitable for these purposes.

For what purposes, then, are zoos suitable? Are they
even necessary? At present, they must house the many generations of animals that have been bred there, since these animals have no place else to go. Most animals in captivity cannot go back to the wild for one of two reasons. The first is
that the creatures would be unable to survive there, since
their instincts for finding their own food and protecting themselves from predators, or even the weather, have been greatly

Paraphrase with
source cited par-
enthetically

diminished during their time spent in captivity (Morton, 1985,
p. 155). Perhaps this is why Jackie the dolphin chooses to
remain in his enclosure.

The other reason animals cannot return to the wild is an
even sadder one: In many cases, their natural habitats no
longer exist. Thanks to deforesting and clearing of land for
homes, highways, factories, and shopping malls--which are
continually being built with no regard for the plant and animal life around them--ecosystems are destroyed constantly,
driving increasing numbers of species from their homes.
Air and water pollution and toxic waste, results of the ever-
increasing urbanization and industrialization throughout the

world, are just some of the agents of this change. It is a problem I wish to address in closing.

Writer closes by proposing a solution of her own.

If zoos were to leave breeding programs to more appropriate organizations and to stop collecting animals, the zoo as an institution would eventually be phased out. Animals would cease to be exhibits and could resume being animals, and the money previously used to run zoos could be put to much better use. Ideally it could be used to investigate why endangered species are endangered, and why so many of the original habitats of these species have disappeared. Most important, it could be used to explore how we can change our habits and reorient our behavior, attitudes, and priorities, so we can begin to address these issues.

The problem of endangered species does not exist in a vacuum; it is a symptom of a much greater predicament. Humankind is responsible for this predicament, and it is up to us to recognize this before it is too late. Saving a selected species here and there will do none of us any good if those species can exist only in isolated, artificial environments, where they will eventually breed themselves into extinction. The money that has been concentrated on such efforts should be devoted instead to educating the public about the endangered planet--not just its animals--or, like the animals, none of us will have any place to go.

References start a
new page.

References

Batten, P. (1976). <u>Living trophies</u>. New York: Crowell.

Brownlee, S. (1986, December). First it was "save the whales,"
now it's "free the dolphins." <u>Discover</u>, pp. 70-72.

Ehrlich, P. & Ehrlich, A. (1981). <u>Extinction: The causes and
consequences of the disappearance of species</u>. New York:
Random House.

Hediger, H. (1968). From cage to territory. In R. Kirchscho-
fer (Ed.), <u>The world of zoos: A survey and gazeteer</u> (pp. 9-
20). New York: Viking.

Luoma, J. (1982, November). Prison or ark? <u>Audubon</u>, pp.
102-109.

Morton, E. S. (1985). The realities of reintroducing species to
the wild. In J. R. Hoage (Ed.), <u>Animal extinctions: What
everyone should know</u> (pp. 147-158). National Zoological
Park Symposia for the Public series. Washington, DC:
Smithsonian Institution.

Rachels, J. (1976). Do animals have a right to liberty? In
T. Regan & P. Singer (Eds.), <u>Animal rights and human
obligations</u> (pp. 205-223). Englewood Cliffs: Prentice
Hall.

Seal, U. S. (1985). The realities of preserving species in captivity. In J. R. Hoage (Ed.), <u>Animal extinctions: What
everyone should know</u> (pp. 147-158). National Zoological
Park Symposia for the Public series. Washington, DC:
Smithsonian Institution.

A book with two authors

A work in an anthology

An article from a periodical

For each reference, flush left on first line, then indent three spaces on subsequent lines

PART THREE

Opposing Viewpoints

THE FOLLOWING SECTION contains a variety of opposing viewpoints on nine controversial questions. These questions generate conflict among experts and laypeople alike for two principal reasons. First, even when the facts are not in dispute, they may be interpreted differently by opposing sides. Example: Do the statistics prove that capital punishment is or is not a deterrent to crime? Second, and certainly more difficult to resolve, equally worthwhile values may be in conflict. Example: In dealing with harmful substances, should we decide in favor of the freedom of the individual to choose or the responsibility of the government to protect?

"Opposing Viewpoints" lends itself to classroom debates, both formal and informal. It can also serve as a useful source of informed opinions which can lead to further research. First, read all of the articles in one of the "Opposing Viewpoints." Then select a topic for your research paper, either one suggested in this book (see "Topics for Research" at the end of each chapter) or another approved by your teacher. You may wish to begin your research by choosing material to support your claim from two or three articles in the text.

In reading, analyzing, and preparing your own responses to the opposing viewpoints, you should ask the following questions about each controversy:

1. Are there two — or more — different points of view on the subject? Do both sides make clear what they are trying to prove? Summarize their claims.

2. Do both sides share the same goals? If not, how are they different?
3. How important is definition of key terms? Do both sides agree on the definitions? If so, what are they? If not, how do they differ? Does definition become a significant issue in the controversy?
4. How important is factual and opinion evidence in support of the claims? Does the support fulfill the appropriate criteria? If not, what are its weaknesses? Is the support conflicting? Do the authorities — both the arguers and the experts they quote — have convincing credentials?
5. Do the arguers base any part of their arguments on needs and values that their readers are expected to share? What are they? Do the arguers provide examples of the ways these values function? Are these values implicit or explicit in the arguments? Is there a conflict of values? If so, which seem more important?
6. What warrants or assumptions underlie the claims? Are they implicit or explicit? Do the arguers examine them for the reader? Are the warrants acceptable? If not, point out their weaknesses.
7. What are the main issues? Is there a genuine debate — that is, does each side try to respond to arguments on the other side?
8. Do the arguers propose solutions to a problem? Are the advantages of their proposals clear? Are there obvious disadvantages to implementation of their solutions?
9. Does each argument follow a clear and orderly organization, one that lends itself to a good outline? If not, what are the weaknesses?
10. Does language play a part in the argument? Are there any examples of misuse of language — slanted or loaded words, clichés, slogans, euphemisms, or other short cuts?
11. Do the arguers show an awareness of audience? How would you describe the audience(s) for whom the various arguments are presented?
12. Do you think that one side won the argument? Explain your answer in detail.

CHAPTER TEN

Abortion

In 1973 the Supreme Court of the United States ruled that a woman's right to an abortion is protected by the Constitution. This decision, *Roe v. Wade,* did not, however, put an end to the controversy over the morality — or the legality — of this right. In the intervening years probably no social issue has ignited so much passion and political activity on both sides. In 1989 (*Webster v. Reproductive Health Services, Inc.*) the Supreme Court voted to allow state legislatures to restrict abortion by imposing limits on the circumstances under which abortion might be performed. Although most Americans favor a woman's right to an abortion, they also favor new legal restrictions on that right — for example, a denial of abortions after viability of the fetus has been established. In other words, abortion should be available but harder to get.

The argument concerning the definition of the fetus, whether or not it is a child entitled to all the rights of a human being, remains crucial, but it is not likely to be resolved in the foreseeable future. In the words of the Supreme Court, "we suppose some [men and women of good conscience] always shall disagree, about the profound moral and spiritual implications of terminating a pregnancy, even in its earliest stage." But other divisive issues, both old and new, also serve to keep the debate alive. In 1992 the Supreme Court, while affirming a constitutional right to an abortion, permitted new restrictions imposed by some states. Among them were the requirements that teenagers obtain the consent of one parent or a judge and that women wait twenty-four hours after being counseled by a medical worker. The Court, however, struck down a law that required a married woman to inform her husband of her decision to have an abortion. In his first week in office, President Clinton overturned several restraining rules imposed by earlier administrations and promised to review the ban on the French abortion pill, RU-486. There is little doubt that these decisions from both the judicial and executive branches will continue to be debated.

Opponents are now grouping for battles that grow out of advances in medical technology. One revolves around the availability of the abortion pill that eliminates the need for surgery. RU-486 is only one of several "morning-after" pills that have been prescribed for more than fifteen years but are still relatively unknown. Most anti-abortionists, however, are also opposed to nonsurgical intervention and have threatened boycotts and disruptive action if abortion pills become easily available. A second source of disagreement flows from the use of early prenatal screening, which now makes it possible to determine the sex and certain mental and physical defects of fetuses during the first trimester. On the basis of these tests, a growing number of women — one survey reports 13 percent — request abortions in order to prevent the birth of "undesirable" children, meaning females and those that are disabled.

Is Abortion Ever Equal to Murder?

HOWARD H. HIATT and CYRUS LEVINTHAL

When does life begin? That value-laden question will come to the forefront of the abortion debate this year, when the Supreme Court is scheduled to take up the case of *Webster v. Reproductive Health Services.*

That case concerns a 1986 Missouri anti-abortion law that declared in its preamble that the "life of each human being begins at conception." In large part, the outcome of *Webster* will hinge on what the Court decides about that assertion. Let's consider some of its implications.

After penetration of the egg by the sperm, the DNA of the egg and the sperm join to form the chromosomes of the fertilized egg, which then begins to divide. As many as half of the fertilized eggs have chromosomal anomalies that will cause them to abort spontaneously early in pregnancy. Some anomalies, such as Down's syndrome, do not always lead to spontaneous abortion. The Down's chromosome can be recognized within weeks of conception, permitting parents to decide whether to abort the defective fetus.

Some would preclude this option by endowing a fertilized egg with

Howard H. Hiatt is a professor of medicine at Harvard Medical School. Cyrus Levinthal is a professor of biology at Columbia University. Their article appeared in the *New York Times* on February 18, 1989.

full legal rights. At the other extreme are a few who deny that even a fully developed fetus just before birth is entitled to full protection. Most pro-choice advocates feel that full rights exist at some time between conception and birth. But when?

Before looking at the possibilities, it helps to think about when life ends. Consider the following.

A two-week-old infant is hospitalized with massive brain injury suffered in an automobile accident. Despite heroic measures, no electrical or other brain activity can be detected during the next two days and he is pronounced dead.

But life for his body parts may continue after his death, as after the death of every person of whatever age. Hair and nails will grow for days. Kidneys, heart, liver, and other organs may go on living for years if transplanted into another individual. Cells taken soon after death and cultured in a laboratory might live well beyond the seventy-two or more years this infant might have lived. But the life of the infant has ended. The conclusion reached in this case — that death of the brain means the end of life — is generally accepted by physicians, courts, and the public.

Returning to the question of when life begins, it is true that the DNA of the fertilized egg has the information necessary to form an individual. But so does virtually every other cell in the body. And nobody would claim full rights for the living cells of the infant killed in the accident, although each has a complete library of DNA. Nor would they for the thousands of living skin cells we lose every time we wash our hands and faces.

Is there some stage in the development of the brain that is critical? Or is it the time at which the fetus can survive outside the womb, either unassisted or with the full support of medical technology? Or should we revert to a criterion used for many years, the time of quickening, when one can feel the fetus moving?

Since none of these criteria can be considered a scientific basis for when life begins, the courts are asked to decide when the products of conception should be endowed with rights. As one considers the relative rights of the pregnant woman and the fetus, three propositions seem reasonable. First, the rights of the fetus for some time before birth are no less than those of the infant immediately following. A fetus born prematurely, as early as the twenty-fourth week, may survive. Technology could shorten that period further. Therefore, thinking should be flexible about what constitutes the period of viability.

Second, as the Supreme Court ruled in the landmark *Roe v. Wade* case of 1973, there is no justification for state interference with the rights of pregnant women in the first three months of a pregnancy, when brain development is still primitive.

Third, after about three months, there should be a gradual increase in fetal rights relative to the rights of the pregnant woman. Some women will choose to bear, for example, a deformed or diseased infant, but others will not. Most will likely wish to terminate pregnancies that result from rape or incest.

In pregnancies beyond three months, the woman considering abortion might turn for advice to groups similar to the multidisciplinary committees that now exist in many hospitals to help advise patients on ethical matters.

The assertion that life begins at conception can be made only on religious, not medical, grounds. No one can prove that the soul does not enter the egg with the DNA from the sperm. However, just as life ends with brain death, so a strong case can be made that human awareness and consciousness emerge only when the brain is well on the way to full development. Since the question of when that occurs cannot now be answered by science or, under our Constitution, by religion, we believe that for abortion decisions in the latter part of pregnancy, the courts should give the states leeway to set guidelines.

Abortion Is Not a Civil Right

GREG KEATH

The battle around the abortion issue has raged for years with the understanding that the major combatants involved are either white liberals, white evangelical Protestants, or white Catholics. Meanwhile, black America — which is affected more profoundly by abortion than is any other group in society — has experienced its own sharp internal division. While most black leaders have favored abortion rights, opinion surveys have found mainstream blacks to be among those most strongly opposed to abortion on demand.

Where does black America really stand on the issue? Statistics from the Department of Health and Human Services suggest that black women are more than twice as likely to abort their children as white women. For every three black babies born, two are aborted. Forty-three percent of all abortions in the United States are performed on black women. From figures supplied by the federal government and the Alan Guttmacher Institute, Richard D. Glasow of National Right to Life has estimated that some 400,000 black pregnancies are aborted each year. At the same time, according to a 1988 poll taken by the National Opinion Research Center, 62 percent of blacks said abortion should be illegal under all circumstances.

How can blacks consistently tell pollsters they oppose abortion while we exercise that right proportionately more than any other group

Greg Keath is the founder and president of Black Alliance for Family. His argument is from the September 27, 1989 issue of the *Wall Street Journal.*

in America? In part, black abortion rates reflect the pressure of social service and private welfare agencies in our communities. A black teenager told me she had asked Planned Parenthood in Detroit for help in carrying her baby to term and putting it up for adoption. But because the baby's father was white, a clinician advised her to abort the baby because, "No one wants to adopt a zebra." Better-educated black women are pushed toward abortion by different forces: the threat to educational hopes or aspirations to economic independence.

As these women struggle with their profound moral choices, many national black leaders have ceased to look at abortion as a moral problem with moral consequences, and have come to see it instead as an opportunity for forging political alliances. At the March for Life rally in 1977 Jesse Jackson said, "The solution to a [crisis pregnancy] is not to kill the innocent baby but to deal with [the mother's] values and her attitudes toward life." Twelve years later, he spoke to the enormous April 1989 abortion rights march in Washington.

The black leadership has succumbed to the temptation to present   5
abortion as a civil-rights issue. By this reasoning, abortion is to women in the 1980s what desegregation was to blacks in the 1960s. Any erosion of abortion rights would accelerate the "move to the right" that black leaders say threatens black progress. At a news conference earlier this year sponsored by Planned Parenthood, Jesse Jackson, Andrew Young, and Julian Bond issued a statement denouncing Operation Rescue, comparing those who participate in abortion clinic sit-ins to "the segregationists who fought desperately to block black Americans from access to their rights."

But many blacks wonder whether black civil rights and abortion fit so neatly together. Black pregnancies have historically been the target of social engineers such as Margaret Sanger, founder of Planned Parenthood. Sanger was convinced that blacks, Jews, Eastern Europeans, and other non-Aryan groups were detracting from the creative intellectual and social potential of America, and she wanted those groups' numbers reduced. In her first book, *Pivot of Civilization,* she warned of free maternity care for the poor: "Instead of decreasing and aiming to eliminate the stocks that are most detrimental to the future of the race and the world it tends to render them to a menacing degree dominant."

In the late 1930s Sanger instituted the Negro Project, a program to gain the backing of black ministers, physicians, and political leaders for birth control and sterilization in the black community. Sanger wrote, "The most successful education approach to the Negro is through a religious appeal. We do not want word to go out that we want to exterminate the Negro population, and the minister is the man who can straighten out that idea if it ever occurs to any of their more rebellious members."

There are disturbing indications that this state of mind has not vanished. Even now, 70 percent of clinics operated by Planned Parenthood — the operator of the largest chain of abortion facilities in the nation — are in black and Hispanic neighborhoods. The schools in which their school-based clinics are located are substantially nonwhite. In a March 1939 letter, Sanger explained why clinics had to be located where the "dysgenic" races lived: "The birth control clinics all over the country are doing their utmost to reach the lower strata of our population . . . but we must realize that there are hundreds of thousands of women who never leave their own vicinity."

Blacks must no longer keep silent on this issue. We cannot permit the public to continue to imagine that we are obediently following our national leaders in endorsing abortion on demand and we must resist the forces that drive black women to seek abortion. The black community in cities such as Baltimore, Chicago, Detroit, and Washington, D.C., has started crisis pregnancy centers to help these women. We are already besieged by homicide, drugs, AIDS, and an alarmingly high infant mortality rate. We do not need to reenact the sterilization programs of the 1930s and 1940s.

Nine Reasons Why Abortions Are Legal

PLANNED PARENTHOOD

I wonder if young women today can fully identify with the situation only two decades ago. When I was a young doctor at a New York hospital, there would scarcely be a week go by that some woman wouldn't be brought to the emergency room near death from an illegal abortion. I saw some wonderful women die, and others reproductively crippled. Then, I too became pregnant, by accident, and though I was a doctor I could not ask any other doctor for help. In those days, if known, it would have cost us both our jobs. So I drove secretly to a Pennsylvania coal-mining town and was led to a secret location. I was lucky. I wasn't injured. But I'm so glad that times have changed. I have five daughters and a son now. I hope they never have to make the agonizing decision about abortion, but if they do, I would hate for them to have to act like criminals and to risk their lives to do what they feel is right for their future.

— Elaine Shaw, M.D., San Francisco, California

I have been married for thirty-five years. I'm the mother of five children, grandmother of three. In the mid-1950s I was brutally raped and left for dead. I later discovered I was pregnant. I was horrified. I would not have that child. Our family doctor couldn't help. An abortion could have cost him and me twenty years in prison. I tried home remedies — like scalding myself and falling down stairs — but they didn't work. Finally I found a

This advertisement from Planned Parenthood, a national pro-choice organization, appeared in the *New York Times* on October 17, 1988.

local abortionist. I will always remember walking up those dark stairs. The incredible filth. The man had a whiskey glass in one hand and a knife in the other. The pain was the worst I have ever felt, but the humiliation was even worse. Hemorrhaging and hospitalization followed. I thought I would never be with my family again. I had no choice, but I resent what I had to go through to terminate that pregnancy. And I resent the people who now say that women should be forced to endure such experiences.

— Sherry Matulis, Peoria, Illinois

Abortion is never an easy decision, but women have been making that choice for thousands of years, for many good reasons. Whenever a society has sought to outlaw abortions, it has only driven them into back alleys where they became dangerous, expensive, and humiliating. Amazingly, this was the case in the United States until 1973 when abortion was legalized nationwide. Thousands of American women died. Thousands more were maimed. For this reason and others, women and men fought for and achieved women's legal right to make their own decisions about abortion.

However, there are people in our society who still won't accept this. Some argue that even the victims of rape or incest should be forced to bear the child. And now, having failed to convince the public or the lawmakers, certain of these people have become violent extremists, engaging in a campaign of intimidation and terror aimed at women seeking abortions and the health professionals who work at family planning clinics.

Some say these acts will stop abortions, but that is ridiculous. When the smoke clears, the same urgent reasons will exist for safe, legal abortions as have always existed. No nation committed to individual liberty could seriously consider returning to the days of back alley abortions; to the revolting specter of a government forcing women to bear children against their will. Still, amid such attacks, it is worthwhile to repeat a few of the reasons *why* our society trusts each woman to make the abortion decision herself.

1. Laws Against Abortion Kill Women

To prohibit abortions does not stop them. When women feel it is absolutely necessary, they will choose to have abortions, even in secret, without medical care, in dangerous circumstances. In the two decades before abortion was legal in the United States it's been estimated that *nearly a million women per year* sought out illegal abortions. Thousands died. Tens of thousands were mutilated. *All* were forced to behave as if they were criminals.

2. Legal Abortions Protect Women's Health

Legal abortion not only protects women's lives, it also protects 5 their health. For tens of thousands of women with heart disease, kidney disease, severe hypertension, sickle-cell anemia, severe diabetes, and other illnesses that can be life-threatening, the availability of legal abortion has helped avert serious medical complications that could have resulted from childbirth. Before legal abortion, such women's choices were limited to dangerous illegal abortion or dangerous childbirth.

3. A Woman Is More Than a Fetus

There's an argument these days that a fetus is a "person" that is "indistinguishable from the rest of us" and that it deserves rights equal to women's. On this question there is a tremendous spectrum of religious, philosophical, scientific, and medical opinion. It's been argued for centuries. Fortunately, our society has recognized that each woman must be able to make this decision, based on her own conscience. To impose a law defining a fetus as a "person," granting it rights equal to or superior to a woman's — a thinking, feeling conscious human being — is arrogant and absurd. It only serves to diminish women.

4. Being a Mother Is Just One Option for Women

Many hard battles have been fought to win political and economic equality for women. These gains will not be worth much if reproductive choice is denied. To be able to choose a safe, legal abortion makes many other options possible. Otherwise an accident or rape can end a woman's economic and personal freedom.

5. Outlawing Abortion Is Discriminatory

Anti-abortion laws discriminate against low-income women, who are driven to dangerous self-induced or back-alley abortions. That is all they can afford. But the rich can travel wherever necessary to obtain a safe abortion.

6. Compulsory Pregnancy Laws Are Incompatible with a Free Society

If there is any matter which is personal and private, then pregnancy is it. There can be no more extreme invasion of privacy than requiring a woman to carry an unwanted pregnancy to term. If government is permitted to compel a woman to bear a child, where will government stop? The concept is morally repugnant. It violates traditional American ideas of individual rights and freedoms.

7. Outlaw Abortion, and More Children Will Bear Children

Forty percent of fourteen-year-old girls will become pregnant before   10
they turn twenty. This could happen to your daughter or someone else
close to you. Here are the critical questions: Should the penalty for lack
of knowledge or even for a moment's carelessness be enforced pregnancy and child-rearing? Or dangerous illegal abortion? Should we
consign a teenager to a life sentence of joblessness, hopelessness, and
dependency?

8. "Every Child a Wanted Child."

If women are forced to carry unwanted pregnancies to term, the
result is unwanted children. Everyone knows they are among society's
most tragic cases, often uncared for, unloved, brutalized, and abandoned. When they grow up, these children are often seriously disadvantaged, and sometimes inclined toward brutal behavior to others.
This is not good for children, for families, or for the country. Children
need love and families who want and will care for them.

9. Choice Is Good for Families

Even when precautions are taken, accidents can and do happen.
For some families, this is not a problem. But for others, such an event
can be catastrophic. An unintended pregnancy can increase tensions,
disrupt stability, and push people below the line of economic survival.
Family planning is the answer. All options must be open.

Bombings and Harassment.   There has been a growing number of
arsons and bombings at family planning and abortion clinics as the
anti-abortion extremists escalate their campaign of intimidation and
terror: Since 1977, over one hundred clinic bombings, arsons, and attempts have occurred. Just as insidious is the harassment inflicted on
women attempting to enter these clinics.

At the most basic level, the abortion issue is not really about
abortion. It is about the value of women in society. Should women make
their own decisions about family, career, and how to live their lives?
Or should government do that for them? Do women have the option of
deciding when or whether to have children? Or is *that* a government
decision?

The anti-abortion leaders really have a larger purpose. They oppose   15
most ideas and programs which can help women achieve equality and
freedom. They also oppose programs which protect the health and well-
being of women *and* their children.

Anti-abortion leaders claim to act "in defense of life." If so, why have they worked to destroy programs which *serve* life, including pre-natal care and nutrition programs for dependent pregnant women? Is this respect for life?

Anti-abortion leaders also say they are trying to save children, but they have fought against health and nutrition programs for children once they are born. The anti-abortion groups seem to believe life begins at conception, but it ends at birth. Is this respect for life?

Then there are programs which diminish the number of unwanted pregnancies *before* they occur: family planning counseling, sex education, and contraception for those who wish it. Anti-abortion leaders oppose those too. And clinics providing such services have been bombed. Is this respect for life?

Such stances reveal the ultimate cynicism of the compulsory pregnancy movement. "Life" is not what they're fighting for. What they want is a return to the days when a woman had few choices in controlling her future. They think that the abortion option gives too much freedom. That even contraception is too liberating. That women cannot be trusted to make their own decisions.

Americans today don't accept that. Women can now select their own paths in society, including when and whether to have children. Family planning, contraception and, if need be, legal abortions are critical to sustaining women's freedom. There is no going back.

If you agree with this, you can help. Circulate this statement among your friends, and support our work by contacting Planned Parenthood in your area. Thank you.

Public Shouldn't Pay
E. L. PATTULLO

To the Editor:

In "Bush and the Zealots" (column, October 19), Anthony Lewis can find no moral basis on which George Bush can deny "the right" to abortion "to poor victims of violence," while allowing it for others. The President denies nothing to the poor that he would grant to the rich; he simply opposes federal financing of abortion in the circumstances concerned.

Lest this seem justice of the kind that gives rich and poor equal freedom to sleep under bridges, Mr. Lewis should examine the economics of the matter. According to ABC's *World News Tonight* of October 25, rape and incest are responsible for about 16,000 pregnancies each

E. L. Pattullo's letter appeared in the *New York Times* on November 17, 1989.

year. The average cost of an abortion, the report added, is $190. Though it would not be necessary — rape and incest not being limited to the poor — only $3.04 million would provide abortions for all these women. Raising such a sum annually would be a minor task for Planned Parenthood and other pro-choice groups. One can only conclude that their concern is not to succor the victims but to score a political victory.

It is not hypocritical for the President and others who reluctantly concede that abortion is sometimes the lesser evil to reject government financing of it. If there be moral fault, it lies with those — is "zealots" too strong a word? — who insist that abortion is a private matter, while denouncing as opportunistic political leaders who resist making the public pay for it.

— E. L. Pattullo

Too Many Abortions
COMMONWEAL

One-and-a-half million abortions a year is a national scandal. Most of these abortions fall outside even the broadest reading of our prevailing ethic that allows taking the life of an assailant in self-defense or the defense of another, that condemns to death individuals guilty of capital crimes, or that authorizes the killing of combatants in time of war or a just revolution. That much we allow the police, the courts, and the armed forces. Physicians and women are allowed greater latitude when it comes to the fetus. That's the law; but it is not moral.

The law rests on the Supreme Court's 1973 decision in *Roe v. Wade,* which ruled that most state laws restricting abortion were a violation of the personal liberty protected by the due process clause of the Fourteenth Amendment. Almost without exception subsequent Court decisions offered the broadest possible interpretation favoring abortion and limiting restrictions. Now many people think the Court's latest abortion decision, *Webster v. Reproductive Health Services,* will shift the balance in the opposite direction.

We are not so sure. First, the Court has not dismantled *Roe.* Second, whatever the law, there is an abortion ethic so deeply rooted in our culture that overturning or narrowing *Roe* may have minimal effect on the number of abortions. What was once unthinkable has become thinkable; indeed, as time passes, the abortion decision is increasingly treated as one almost not worth thinking about at all. A change in law will mean little without a transformation of minds and hearts.

This editorial is from the August 11, 1989 issue of the Roman Catholic magazine *Commonweal.*

One might argue that *Roe* engendered this abortion ethic — this unique exception to our general prohibition of killing innocent others. But in rereading *Roe,* it is hard to find the hard-edged thinking or absolutist language that has come to characterize the way we now speak individually and as a polity on the subject. For example, "abortion on demand" and "the absolute right to privacy" are catchphrases we hear often and loudly, phrases pro-choicers defend and against which pro-lifers rail. But back in 1973, the Court wrote: "Appellants . . . argue that the woman's right is absolute and that she is entitled to terminate her pregnancy at whatever time, in whatever way, and for whatever reason she alone chooses. With this we do not agree." The Court went on: "[T]he right of personal privacy includes the abortion decision, but . . . this right is not unqualified and must be considered against important state interests in regulation." Nor was the decision the woman's alone: "All these are factors [in the abortion decision] the woman and her responsible physician necessarily will consider in consultation." It is not hard to find in these words justification for viability testing at twenty weeks as the Court did in upholding the Missouri law, or, for that matter, for upholding certain counseling and informed consent procedures that were not at issue in *Webster.*

We do not return to *Roe* in order to defend it; its usurpation of the   5 political process in 1973 in favor of judicial fiat is indefensible. And if *Webster* is the prelude to a full, rational, political consideration of abortion at the state level, it is indeed welcome. But we harbor an unhappy premonition that it is not. While the Supreme Court teases the nation with a patchwork process of allowing some restrictions and turning down others, the acrimonious scramble for influence in fifty state houses and state legislatures by pro-life and pro-choice forces will be poisonous to our whole political system. Even worse, as we have suggested above, it is unlikely to help restore a moral perspective of a kind that will help actually to reduce the number of abortions, some of which, under the new dispensation, will be performed illegally. It is indeed a struggle for the minds and hearts of women — and men.

The best, but most difficult, place to begin is with the claim that the fetus is not nothing. *Roe* concluded that the fetus is not considered a "person" under the Fourteenth Amendment, and further on it declined to "resolve the difficult question of when life begins." In most adult humans there arises a sound intuition that somewhere between the period of conception and implantation and a later period when the developing fetus has every aspect of a human being, this is a human being, a human being worthy of protection — and perhaps that sense is nowhere more fully developed than in the pregnant woman herself. Most of us would offer a seat on a crowded train to a pregnant woman; many would offer help if she collapsed on a street or rush to her aid if she was endangered by a speeding car or threatened with a beating. It is not just her comfort or her life that is at stake, but the life of another, our immediate sense is not of one human being deserving of protection, but two. The more obviously pregnant a women is, the more surely we draw that conclusion. The fetus is something.

But so is the woman. And it is the woman contemplating an abortion who must be convinced that the fetus is something, indeed at a certain point becomes someone. Implanting and supporting this conviction has two possible starting points. The most immediate: A pregnant woman considering abortion should receive counseling that fully describes for her what we now know about fetuses and their development; if it is to be an abortion at eight weeks or at twelve weeks, she should see what such a fetus looks like and know its stage of development. Responsible counseling would also offer viable alternatives to the woman if she cannot raise the child; indeed a positive ethic of adoption and the ability of social workers to provide a woman with a serious adoption plan ought to be part of the counseling process. Does that unduly burden the abortion decision as the Court has previously ruled? Perhaps. But it is a burden that the gravity of an abortion decision warrants.

Another and more distant starting point for building the conviction that the fetus deserves maternal consideration and protection lies with a fuller development of the feminist insight that women themselves must take responsibility for their lives, the choices they make, their relationships with others — parallel to the kind of responsibility men must also exercise. Moral agency entails a kind of autonomy, self-esteem, and responsibility in which women and men act instead of merely being acted upon. Feminist thought has generally treated abortion decision as part and parcel of that exercise of autonomy, self-esteem, and responsibility, but the decision for abortion can be read in the opposite way.

Except in extreme cases, the decision to have an abortion can simply be the end point in a series of events in which a woman has failed to take responsibility for her sexual life and become pregnant in a situation in which no family life is possible, or she has allowed herself to be sexually exploited by a man who has no intention of sharing in the care of a child. This starting point for stemming the number of abortions depends on women becoming reproductively responsible moral agents by either saying no to men who will not or cannot share the responsibilities of parenthood or by women becoming effective users of contraception. This is not an ethic that fully expresses the Christian vision of human love, or the care that men and women should express toward one another. But it is a better ethic than the one now expressed in one-and-a-half million abortions. Pro-choice and pro-life advocates, at their best and most sensitive, recognize this: They see that along with the unborn no less victims of this dismal ethic are the women who have abortions. If the coming political struggle can be built on the sense that there are too many abortions, that women and fetuses alike are victims of a shabby ethic, then it will be a struggle that will end not only in better laws, but in a more tolerable moral standard.

I'm Thirty-eight and Running Out of Time
PAULETTE MASON

I need some advice. I'm pregnant — fifteen weeks pregnant. And I'm not married. Please don't think that I don't believe in family values. I do. I'm not promiscuous; it's just that I was lonely and I liked this man a lot. We used birth control but it failed. I didn't know I was pregnant because I didn't have the usual symptoms. Everything that a woman expects to have happen on a monthly basis continued to happen. I never learned that this was possible in high school hygiene; we didn't have sex education, just the seven food groups.

The man I got pregnant by doesn't want to have anything to do with me or the child. I want to have the baby; I'm thirty-eight and I'm running out of time. I've been thinking about how and when and whether I could have a child for a couple of years now. I agree with Marilyn Quayle; for a woman like me, it's an essential part of my nature to make a home with a man and raise a child.

The father of my baby also believes in family values. That's why he wants me to get an abortion. He feels children should be raised in a two-parent home, and since he has no intention of being that other parent, it would be unfair to the child to raise it alone. He's an active Democrat, but he doesn't think Murphy Brown is a good role model.

"You're not Murphy Brown," he said to me. "You're not a rich independent yuppie who can afford to scoff at convention and go it alone. You've been reading too many women's magazines loaded with feminist junk. You barely make a living. How can you support and nurture a child? You don't even have a steady job." (I work freelance.) "I bet you don't even have health insurance," he said. As a matter of fact, I don't have health insurance.

After I got off the phone, I looked into getting insurance. It turned 5 out that no one would insure me; my pregnancy was considered a previous condition. Then I looked into Medicaid and city health clinics. The social worker I talked to said I made too much money to qualify. I called a hospital and found out that if I required a C-section it would

Paulette Mason (a pseudonym) works in the television industry. This article is reprinted from the Op-Ed section of the October 3, 1992 *New York Times.*

cost about $12,000. I didn't have that much in the bank. If the baby were born prematurely, it would cost about $1,000 a day to keep her alive in the hospital nursery. If something was wrong with the baby, I'd be in debt to the hospital for the rest of my life. But I didn't want to let money be the critical factor in this decision.

Finally, I was able to find one insurance company that was willing to insure me and the baby for possible complications. "Boy, am I glad I found you guys," I told the insurance agent. He agreed I was lucky; his company was the only one he knew of that would insure pregnant women.

I thought maybe I could go on welfare so that I could stay at home during those all-important first two years. But when I looked into welfare, it turned out that even with food stamps I wouldn't be able to live on it. The social worker I spoke to said that most women on welfare have some income off the books and live with family members. My parents live on Social Security and small pensions. My brother is unemployed. He says that since the recession, it's been hard to find work.

I made up a budget. After I factored in health insurance for me and the baby ($4,000) and child care help ($300 a week for full-time babysitting), I was many thousands of dollars short.

I looked into child support. The man I got pregnant by lives out of state. The lawyers and court officials I spoke to said that it could easily take two years for me to get a court order. I was at wit's end. Then I got a brainstorm. I called the Catholic church. I figured it was against abortions and so was I. I asked the woman who answered the phone, Can you help me keep my baby? She told me that her agency primarily helped girls from the South Bronx and what they offered them was infant foster care. That was the very day the newspapers in New York were filled with stories about a foster family that had starved a child to death. I mentioned this to the social worker. She said: "We're very careful. All our families are fingerprinted and their records checked."

Things seemed so hopeless by then. I went to a doctor who did 10 second-trimester abortions, which are a good deal more complicated than first-trimester abortions. In the second trimester, the fetus is sufficiently large so that it has to be dismembered to be removed. When I heard the doctor use the word dismember, I started to cry — for myself and my baby and what might have been my future.

If a surgeon isn't skillful, the uterus can be perforated, leading to infection, sterility, even hysterectomy. The procedure takes two days. On the first day, the woman's cervix is dilated. I asked the doctor, "Will it hurt?" The doctor said that sometimes it doesn't hurt but other times it hurts a lot, and women leave sobbing and doubled over in pain. "It's very traumatic to many women," he said, "because they know that they've started a process that will end in termination and there's nothing that can be done to stop it once it starts."

On the second day, the actual procedure is carried out. The woman undresses, puts on a paper gown, is wheeled into an operating room, her legs are put into stirrups and an anesthesiologist puts her under. When she wakes up in the recovery room, her baby is gone. When the doctor explained all this to me, I started to cry again. "I don't know what to do," I told the doctor. The doctor said it was my choice. He said: "Nobody likes to get an abortion, especially a late abortion. I've performed thousands of operations and I've never met a woman who was happy about it. Do you think you can take good care of a child? That's really the question."

This has been agonizing for me. I think about the way I want to have a baby, and about paying someone to act like a mother to my child, and about what I'll say when my child asks why her father didn't want her, and about what I'll feel like during the twenty-four hours my cervix is dilating and I'm waiting for the end. When I think about adoption, I think about spending the rest of my life wondering where my baby, the baby I wanted, is, and if she's happy and how she turned out. And I think, What would Dan Quayle want me to do?

Don't Roll Back Roe

JOHN R. SILBER

The public debate over abortion, already bitter, is likely to become even more so. Indeed, with state legislatures debating new restrictions made possible by the Supreme Court's decision in *Webster v. Reproductive Health Services,* consensus looks further away every day.

This bitter debate grows out of widespread confusion between legal issues and moral ones, between religious issues and political ones. We cannot develop a clear understanding of these difficult issues without considering legal and ethical points of view.

I would oppose any law prohibiting abortion in the first two trimesters. That is, I believe that the states should retain the standard set by the Supreme Court in *Roe v. Wade* even though *Webster* allows them to restrict it.

It is very doubtful, considering past experience, that restrictive legislation would do more than make presently legal abortions illegal. Some of these abortions, involving technologies that enable laymen to perform abortions safely, would be different from current abortions only in their illegality. Others, performed with coat hangers in back

---

John R. Silber is the president of Boston University. This article first appeared in the *New York Times* on January 3, 1990, during Silber's unsuccessful run as the Democratic candidate for governor of Massachusetts.

alleys, will be fatal. I could not in conscience recommend legislation having these effects.

But this is not the same as the "pro-choice" position. It is possible 5 to believe that abortion ought to be legal without believing that it is an unconditional right, or even that it is morally justified in more than a limited number of cases.

Nor is the belief that many abortions are immoral the same as the "pro-life" position. There are instances when the taking of human life is justifiable, legally and morally. Homicide is not equivalent to murder: Some homicides are entirely justified, especially those involving self-defense. A woman whose life is threatened by a pregnancy is justified in terminating the pregnancy that might kill or severely injure her.

So, too, when a woman is raped she is under no obligation morally, and should be under no obligation legally, to accept the consequences of an act of sexual intercourse in which she did not voluntarily participate. She has a right to protect herself from the consequences of assault.

But this does not lead me to conclude that abortions are morally justified when the pregnancy does not threaten the life of the mother and follows from sexual intercourse in which she voluntarily participated. Indiscriminate use of abortion is wrong because the indiscriminate taking of a human life is wrong.

If abortion were not a supercharged issue, it would be apparent to all parties that a fertilized ovum is, in fact, a living human. Obviously it is not a complete human being. But neither is a fetus in the third trimester or, for that matter, a newborn infant or a child of one or two years of age. The value of the life of an infant is based on its potential to become a fulfilled human being, and that potential exists from the time of conception.

Believing firmly as I do in this moral view of abortion, I think it 10 would be a disastrous error to write it into the statute book.

A free society cannot maintain its unity and order unless there is toleration of diverse opinions on which consensus has not been achieved. Without religious toleration, for example, the unity of the thirteen Colonies would have been torn asunder by religious wars of the sort that plagued Europe for centuries. The abortion issue is for many individuals a religious issue, and on such issues we should scrupulously observe the separation of church and state.

By tolerating contrary views, we accept an important fact that is too often overlooked. The instruments of the state and its legal institutions are far too crude and inexact to be used in deciding highly complex issues of personal morality on which persons of good will fundamentally disagree. It is proper to leave such important moral and religious issues to individual moral agents and religious believers.

On the issues of abortion, there is no political, philosophical, moral, or religious consensus. And even though I believe that abortion is, in general, morally wrong, I also believe the state should not enact laws to restrict abortion further. This is an issue that cries out for toleration.

Boys Only

CHARLOTTE ALLEN

There is one Pennsylvania abortion restriction that is not before the Supreme Court right now: the state's 1989 ban on abortions solely for the purpose of destroying a fetus of an unwanted gender. The American Civil Liberties Union, which represents several abortion providers in the case, *Planned Parenthood of Southeastern Pennsylvania v. Casey,* has declined to mount a challenge to the sex-selection ban, so it will remain on Pennsylvania's books regardless of how the Supreme Court rules on other restrictions relating to notice, informed consent, and recordkeeping.

The reason the ACLU gives for its decision not to include the sex-selection ban (which is the only specific one in the country) in its current lawsuit is that it could not find a client claiming injury from the law: a woman who wanted to abort her wrong-sex child (or who was willing to say so). "We couldn't find anyone who was affected," says Kathryn Kolbert, the ACLU lawyer who will argue the case before the Court, probably in April. "It's not a reality in Pennsylvania."

That may be, but elsewhere in the country, sex-selection abortion is becoming an issue among geneticists, medical ethicists, and some feminists. One reason is that sex selection almost always means the abortion of a female fetus. There are other issues as well: trivializing abortion, creating "designer children" or designer birth order (first a boy, then a girl), and as prenatal genetic screening becomes more sophisticated, setting a precedent for aborting on the basis of mild genetic defects, undesirable physiological traits, and conceivably in the future, homosexuality or low IQ.

These are not entirely hypothetical concerns. Interviews with geneticists around the country suggest that there are at least several hundred requests a year from pregnant women to perform amniocentesis or the newer chorionic villus sampling (CVS) of placental tissue to determine fetal sex for reasons unconnected to transmitting a gender-linked disease such as hemophilia. The women are often under age

Charlotte Allen writes for *Insight* magazine. This article is reprinted from the March 9, 1992 issue of *The New Republic.*

thirty-five, the recommended threshold age for screening for medical reasons. According to these geneticists, many of these women go on to abort a wrong-sex fetus. Most, although not all, of the abortions appear to occur among women from Asian countries where preference for male children is exceedingly strong and outright female infanticide not unheard of.

Geneticists are also slowly losing their once-strong aversion to   5 performing prenatal screening to determine fetal sex — 62 percent would do it nowadays or refer a patient to another geneticist, in contrast to only 1 percent in 1973, according to a 1989 book by public health researcher Dorothy C. Wertz and bioethicist John C. Fletcher. Yet public opinion in America appears strongly opposed to sex-selection abortion. A 1989 Gallup Poll revealed that 80 percent of respondents thought it was not just unethical, but should be outright illegal.

The emergence of sex-specific abortion represents not merely a troubling social development, but an acute dilemma for pro-choice feminists. What's at stake is a clash of absolutes: a woman's right to an abortion for any reason versus sex discrimination of the most vicious kind. The response of many feminists, however, is simply denial. "It's an irrelevant issue," says Rosemary Dempsey, a vice president of the National Organization for Women. "It's something that doesn't happen. The mainstream media is being duped by the anti-abortion people." Suppose there were a few women who actually were aborting on the basis of fetal sex? Wouldn't NOW at least have a moral position on the subject? "You're not hearing me," answers Dempsey. "The right to decide whether to terminate a pregnancy belongs to the woman, and I don't think women make decisions of that kind."

"It's a bogus issue," says Judith Lichtman, president of the Women's Legal Defense Fund. "I'm not answering your question because I'm being cute but because it really trivializes a very momentous decision. There are a lot of real problems out there." "We think it's a red herring," says Barbara Radford, executive director of the National Abortion Federation. (The National Abortion Rights Action League wouldn't answer my request for an interview on the topic.) The only dissenter is Judy Norsigian of the Boston Women's Health Book Collective, author of *The New Our Bodies, Ourselves.* "Of course it happens," she says. "It's not a problem if you look at it in terms of numbers, but it still happens. Some are saying that if it happens once, it's a problem. Most of us in this group think of it as a questionable moral position."

Of the several hundred women a year who manage to slip through the ethical net and procure gender tests without medical need, some are referred to abortionists who will terminate otherwise normal pregnancies with no questions asked. "We do a few of these," says Digamber S. Borgaonkar, director of the Delaware Medical Center's genetic screening laboratory and author of several textbooks on human genetics. "Not that we are officially informed [about why the woman wants to terminate the pregnancy]. People are sufficiently discreet about it. But some people will talk about a preferred sex. I was raised in India, and there is a preference for the male sex there. There is also an interest in population control. So if a culture prefers a male child, they prefer a male fetus."

"I personally oppose sex selection," says Mark Evans, director of the prenatal diagnosis program at Wayne State University's medical center. "I believe it is sex discrimination. But you've got to be careful about pointing a finger at a woman. We have had women call us up and ask if we can do a CVS on her for sex selection. We'll say we don't do that. But we'll find out she's thirty-seven years old, so we'll do it. I'll know she's going to have a girl, and we don't do abortions for that reason. But we will help the patient if asked to find someone who will. A doctor has an obligation to present to the patient all her options. We have only a handful of these cases a year. Most people who want it are Third World — Arabs, Indians, Chinese."

John D. Stephens, a geneticist in San Jose, California, last year 10
patented an ultrasound technique that detects a fetus's sex as early as eleven weeks into the pregnancy (conventional ultrasound does not reveal sex until the eighteenth week, when few women are willing to abort). Stephens markets his gender-spotting skills directly to the public via newspaper advertisements. He has built a practice among Sikh émigrés in this country and in Canada, despite the fact, he says, that most Bay Area obstetricians have stopped referring patients to him because he does sex screening. "I don't do abortions, and I don't do any counseling in the area," says Stephens. "What happens is that apparently people will come back to me. I'll see them again. I'll ask about the first pregnancy, and they'll say, 'I've terminated it.' It's almost always a girl. Or else they'll say, 'I've had a lovely little boy.' Who am I to make any moral judgment?"

This reaction from geneticists — disapproval of sex selection but a willingness to tolerate it and even participate passively in the process — has unsavory implications for the future. There have been recent scientific reports suggesting that homosexuality may have a genetic basis. What then? "I may be a Pollyanna, but we think that society's attitudes will be completely changed and parents will warmly accept their lesbian and gay children" by the time screening for homosexuality-linked genes becomes feasible, says Gregory King, spokesman for the Human Rights Campaign Fund, the nation's largest gay-rights organization, which is also pro-choice.

The alternative, of course, is that the more people learn about their genes as times passes, the more picky they could become about the kind of children they want to have. Pre-conception sex selection via sperm separation is a growing business around the world. The public disapproval surrounding Los Angeles newscaster Bree Walker-Lampley's decision to bear, not abort, a child carrying her genes for fused fingers, a mild disability if there ever was one, has led even some pro-choicers to wonder whether there actually might be some moral value to having anti–sex-selection laws like Pennsylvania's, even though a woman could easily bypass them by lying.

"Our members are absolutely pro-choice," says Andrew Kimbrell of the Foundation on Economic Trends, a nonprofit group concerned with the economic and social effects of new technology. "But there's a *Newsweek* poll showing that 9 percent [of the public] would abort for cystic fibrosis and 11 percent if the fetus was predisposed to obesity. This kind of thing is on the increase, and more and more doctors are strongly pushing it." Kimbrell is in favor of laws banning sex-selection abortions, a position others in the pro-choice camp balk at. Part of their reason is that some Third World women face abuse from their husbands if they don't abort daughters; and part is that once it becomes against the law to abort a fetus just because it is female, people may start asking why it should be permissible to abort a fetus just because it is disabled or because its parents do not want it for other reasons.

But almost everyone who has thought seriously about the sex-selection issue believes there is something wrong with the studiously nonjudgmental attitude of many in the medical community. Neither the American College of Obstetricians and Gynecologists nor the American Fertility Society has taken a position on sex selection. The prevailing norm for counseling on the issue among geneticists, abortion clinic personnel, and even many physicians is the "nondirective" variety that is an offshoot of the values-clarification movement, which teaches that people should discover their own values instead of being told what is right and wrong. But his neutrality doesn't always hold sway in practice. "They're taught to try to be nonjudgmental," says Norsigian of the Boston Women's Health Book Collective. "But when it comes to something like Down's syndrome, most physicians have been extremely directive and even obnoxious. They will even say, 'We'll be scheduling an abortion for you.' This happens even when the extent of the disability is very mild."

As sex selection in America moves out of Third World ghettos and becomes an option for the control-obsessed upper middle class, it's worrying that nobody — not doctors, not genetics counselors, not abortion counselors, and not most feminists — seems willing to discourage the practice and some even encourage it. Abortion is not just an abstract dilemma. It takes place in a context of consequences, some of which could eventually prove more harmful to women over the long term than bearing an unwanted child.

Making Painful Choices
on Deformed Fetuses

FLORENCE A. NOLAN

To the Editor:

Re "In Late Abortions, Decisions Are Painful and Options Few" (front page, January 5), your article on the increasing ability of sonograms to detect severely deformed fetuses, and the consequent decision many women make to abort the fetus in the last three months of pregnancy:

I am a pediatrician in private practice, but during my residency I had a great deal of experience with a large intensive-care nursery and many older handicapped children. I had to give very bad news to parents about multiple abnormalities in their newborn children, some gruesome to behold and some invisible to the naked eye, but nevertheless devastating.

Just as there are many styles and characteristics of personality, there are many ways parents deal with tragic news regarding the birth of a child, an event that is usually attended by unrestrained joy. I have found that most parents, however, find emotional resources they would not have predicted they had.

A thorny problem occurs when these parents, in a state of shock and disbelief, are asked to make quick decisions about life-saving or life-prolonging procedures for their children. They are given intricately detailed information rapidly, usually without the experience necessary to know what the long-term outcome of their decision might be.

By this I mean that parents may feel that they are doing the right 5 thing by agreeing to surgery or other interventions, only to find, many years later, that they are essentially still providing intensive care for a child unable to participate in anything close to what most of us would consider a normal human existence.

As you report, this can bring some people emotional and moral fulfillment. For far too many others, it spells marital discord, alcoholism, depression, destitution, and, in some cases, abuse of the affected child.

From the physician's viewpoint, I have sympathetic feelings for the parents who feel themselves left high and dry by the medical establishment, but these same people may very well be the ones to initiate a lawsuit if they or their newborn did not have the outcome desired. It is very difficult for a physician to follow his or her conscience in withholding or withdrawing care options in today's medical and legal climate.

Florence A. Nolan is a pediatrician living in Putnam Valley, New York. This editorial appeared in the *New York Times* on January 28, 1992.

Finally, I have very little sympathy for the couple who said they were petrified and feared for their own well-being in the future if they allowed a child with hydrocephaly to be delivered. This condition is eminently treatable if not curable.

This couple brings me to my ultimate conclusion that abortions of this sort cannot be allowed, especially with scientific advances in pre-natal detection of fetal sex and other body characteristics. It starts to smack of the use of abortion to eliminate any fetus that did not satisfy its parents' idea of perfection.

I had an embryology professor in college who thought that diabetics 10 should not be allowed to have children, believing it would perpetuate the disease. He felt that way about a lot of medical conditions. It frightened me. Your article frightens me anew.

—Florence A. Nolan, M.D.

THINKING AND WRITING ABOUT ABORTION

Questions for Discussion and Writing

1. The Planned Parenthood advertisement lays out nine important reasons in favor of the legality of abortion. Is it possible to tell whether the authors of the ad agree with the proposals in the article by Hiatt and Levinthal? Does the ad address all the issues in the *Commonweal* editorial? How would it respond to the charge in *Commonweal* that abortions result because women have been careless in their responsibilities? What inconsistency does the *Commonweal* editorial find in advocacy of abortion by feminists? Is this argument valid?
2. What arguments in favor of public funding for abortion would pro-choice advocates use to refute Pattullo?
3. Both Nolan, a physician, and Allen argue against abortion to prevent the birth of females and deformed fetuses. Do they make clear the reasons for their opposition? Why do you think some pro-choice feminists refuse to discuss this issue?
4. How many different problems does Mason face in deciding whether or not to have an abortion? Which seem most important? Does her personal anguish influence an argument for or against an abortion? Do you see a solution to her dilemma?
5. Why is Silber, who believes abortion is morally wrong, in favor of its legality? Explain his views on the differences between moral and legal issues.
6. What dangers does Keath see in encouraging blacks to endorse abortion on demand? Why does he feel it necessary to write this warning? Do you think most blacks would agree with him? Why or why not?
7. The satire in the cartoon is based on an analogy. What does it reveal about the cartoonist's opinion of the Supreme Court decision-making process?

Topics for Research

Restrictions that should be imposed by the states; reasons for the restrictions

A review of legislation by the states since the 1989 Supreme Court ruling; significance of the changes

Illegal abortions in the United States before *Roe v. Wade* (1973)

Religious views on abortion

An evaluation of arguments by public officials who personally oppose abortion but publicly support the law permitting abortion

CHAPTER ELEVEN

Animal Rights

Advocates for the rights of animals object to several different kinds of human exploitation of animals — for food, clothing, research, and recreation (as in hunting and bullfighting). In this chapter we confine our discussion to the uses of animals for food and medical research.

Although organized concern for the rights of animals is at least 200 years old in the West, the movement has acquired new momentum, perhaps as a result of human-rights movements, which have succeeded in raising people's consciousness about the rights of women, minorities, homosexuals, the handicapped, and others whose interests have often been ignored by those who are more powerful.

Ethical vegetarianism, based on the belief that the lives of animals are as sacred as those of human beings, is very old. Strict Hindus have practiced vegetarianism for 2,000 years. But it is relatively new in the West. Especially in the last quarter of a century, the growth of factory farming of animals has induced numbers of people to stop eating meat.

Experimentation with animals for medical and other scientific research has proliferated dramatically with immeasurable benefits for human beings, above all in medicine — in the conquest of rabies, bacterial infection, sterile surgical techniques, syphilis, and organ transplants. Less-defensible experimentation has been performed by cosmetic companies.

The advocates of animal rights won an important court victory in February 1993 when a federal judge in Washington found that government rules for the treatment of dogs and primates in laboratory experiments were too lenient. Research groups argue that, if the decision stands and laboratories are required to restrict their use of dogs and primates, new medical research will be severely hampered.

The question is to what extent the welfare of human beings should take precedence over the rights of animals. The answer will rest on religious and philosophical grounds that define the relationship between human beings and their fellow creatures.

Animal Liberation
PETER SINGER

We are familiar with Black Liberation, Gay Liberation, and a variety of other movements. With Women's Liberation some thought we had come to the end of the road. Discrimination on the basis of sex, it has been said, is the last form of discrimination that is universally accepted and practiced without pretense, even in those liberal circles which have long prided themselves on their freedom from racial discrimination. But one should always be wary of talking of "the last remaining form of discrimination." If we have learned anything from the liberation movements, we should have learned how difficult it is to be aware of the ways in which we discriminate until they are forcefully pointed out to us. A liberation movement demands an expansion of our moral horizons, so that practices that were previously regarded as natural and inevitable are now seen as intolerable.

Animals, Men and Morals is a manifesto for an Animal Liberation movement. The contributors to the book may not all see the issue this way. They are a varied group. Philosophers, ranging from professors to graduate students, make up the largest contingent. There are five of them, including the three editors, and there is also an extract from the unjustly neglected German philosopher with an English name, Leonard Nelson, who died in 1927. There are essays by two novelist/critics, Brigid Brophy and Maureen Duffy, and another by Muriel, the Lady Dowding, widow of Dowding of Battle of Britain fame and the founder of "Beauty Without Cruelty," a movement that campaigns against the use of animals for furs and cosmetics. The other pieces are by a psychologist, a botanist, a sociologist, and Ruth Harrison, who is probably best described as a professional campaigner for animal welfare.

Whether or not these people, as individuals, would all agree that they are launching a liberation movement for animals, the book as a whole amounts to no less. It is a demand for a complete change in our attitudes to nonhumans. It is a demand that we cease to regard the exploitation of other species as natural and inevitable, and that, instead, we see it as a continuing moral outrage. Patrick Corbett, Professor of

Peter Singer teaches philosophy at Monash University in Melbourne, Australia. This essay appeared in the April 15, 1973 issue of the *New York Review of Books* as a review of *Animals, Men and Morals,* edited by Stanley and Roslind Godlovitch and John Harris.

Philosophy at Sussex University, captures the spirit of the book in his closing words:

> We require now to extend the great principles of liberty, equality, and fraternity over the lives of animals. Let animal slavery join human slavery in the graveyard of the past.

The reader is likely to be skeptical. "Animal Liberation" sounds more like a parody of liberation movements than a serious objective. The reader may think: We support the claims of blacks and women for equality because blacks and women really are equal to whites and males — equal in intelligence and in abilities, capacity for leadership, rationality, and so on. Humans and nonhumans obviously are not equal in these respects. Since justice demands only that we treat equals equally, unequal treatment of humans and nonhumans cannot be an injustice.

This is a tempting reply, but a dangerous one. It commits the [5] nonracist and nonsexist to a dogmatic belief that blacks and women really are just as intelligent, able, etc., as whites and males — and no more. Quite possibly this happens to be the case. Certainly attempts to prove that racial or sexual differences in these respects have a genetic origin have not been conclusive. But do we really want to stake our demand for equality on the assumption that there are no genetic differences of this kind between the different races or sexes? Surely the appropriate response to those who claim to have found evidence for such genetic differences is not to stick to the belief that there are no differences, whatever the evidence to the contrary; rather one should be clear that the claim to equality does not depend on IQ. Moral equality is distinct from factual equality. Otherwise it would be nonsense to talk of the equality of human beings, since humans, as individuals, obviously differ in intelligence and almost any ability one cares to name. If possessing greater intelligence does not entitle one human to exploit another, why should it entitle humans to exploit nonhumans?

Jeremy Bentham expressed the essential basis of equality in his famous formula: "Each to count for one and none for more than one." In other words, the interests of every being that has interests are to be taken into account and treated equally with the like interests of any other being. Other moral philosophers, before and after Bentham, have made the same point in different ways. Our concern for others must not depend on whether they possess certain characteristics, though just what concern involves may, of course, vary according to such characteristics.

Bentham, incidentally, was well aware that the logic of the demand for racial equality did not stop at the equality of humans. He wrote:

> The day *may* come when the rest of the animal creation may acquire those rights which never could have been withholden from them but by the hand

of tyranny. The French have already discovered that the blackness of the skin is no reason why a human being should be abandoned without redress to the caprice of a tormentor. It may one day come to be recognized that the number of the legs, the villosity of the skin, or the termination of the *os sacrum,* are reasons equally insufficient for abandoning a sensitive being to the same fate. What else is it that should trace the insuperable line? Is it the faculty of reason, or perhaps the faculty of discourse? But a full-grown horse or dog is beyond comparison a more rational, as well as a more conversable, animal than an infant of a day, or a week, or even a month, old. But suppose they were otherwise, what would it avail? The question is not, Can they *reason?* nor Can they *talk?* but, Can they *suffer?*[1]

Surely Bentham was right. If a being suffers, there can be no moral justification for refusing to take that suffering into consideration, and, indeed, to count it equally with the like suffering (if rough comparisons can be made) of any other being.

So the only question is: Do animals other than man suffer? Most people agree unhesitatingly that animals like cats and dogs can and do suffer, and this seems also to be assumed by those laws that prohibit wanton cruelty to such animals. Personally, I have no doubt at all about this and find it hard to take seriously the doubts that a few people apparently do have. The editors and contributors of *Animals, Men and Morals* seem to feel the same way, for although the question is raised more than once, doubts are quickly dismissed each time. Nevertheless, because this is such a fundamental point, it is worth asking what grounds we have for attributing suffering to other animals.

It is best to begin by asking what grounds any individual human has for supposing that other humans feel pain. Since pain is a state of consciousness, a "mental event," it can never be directly observed. No observations, whether behavioral signs such as writhing or screaming or physiological or neurological recordings, are observations of pain itself. Pain is something one feels, and one can only infer that others are feeling it from various external indications. The fact that only philosophers are ever skeptical about whether other humans feel pain shows that we regard such inference as justifiable in the case of humans.

Is there any reason why the same inference should be unjustifiable   10 for other animals? Nearly all the external signs which lead us to infer pain in other humans can be seen in other species, especially "higher" animals such as mammals and birds. Behavioral signs — writhing, yelping, or other forms of calling, attempts to avoid the source of pain, and many others — are present. We know, too, that these animals are biologically similar in the relevant respects, having nervous systems like ours which can be observed to function as ours do.

So the grounds for inferring that these animals can feel pain are nearly as good as the grounds for inferring other humans do. Only

---

[1] *The Principles of Morals and Legislation,* ch. XVII, sec. 1, footnote to paragraph 4.

nearly, for there is one behavioral sign that humans have but nonhumans, with the exception of one or two specially raised chimpanzees, do not have. This, of course, is a developed language. As the quotation from Bentham indicates, this has long been regarded as an important distinction between man and other animals. Other animals may communicate with each other, but not in the way we do. Following Chomsky, many people now make this distinction by saying that only humans communicate in a form that is governed by rules of syntax. (For the purposes of this argument, linguists allow those chimpanzees who have learned a syntactic sign language to rank as honorary humans.) Nevertheless, as Bentham pointed out, this distinction is not relevant to the question of how animals ought to be treated, unless it can be linked to the issue of whether animals suffer.

This link may be attempted in two ways. First, there is a hazy line of philosophical thought, stemming perhaps from some doctrines associated with Wittgenstein, which maintains that we cannot meaningfully attribute states of consciousness to beings without language. I have not seen this argument made explicit in print, though I have come across it in conversation. The position seems to me very implausible, and I doubt that it would be held at all if it were not thought to be a consequence of a broader view of the significance of language. It may be that the use of a public, rule-governed language is a precondition of conceptual thought. It may even be, although personally I doubt it, that we cannot meaningfully speak of a creature having an intention unless that creature can use a language. But states like pain, surely, are more primitive than either of these, and seem to have nothing to do with language.

Indeed, as Jane Goodall points out in her study of chimpanzees, when it comes to the expression of feelings and emotions, humans tend to fall back on nonlinguistic modes of communication which are often found among apes, such as a cheering pat on the back, an exuberant embrace, a clasp of hands, and so on.[2] Michael Peters makes a similar point in his contribution to *Animals, Men and Morals* when he notes that the basic signals we use to convey pain, fear, sexual arousal, and so on are not specific to our species. So there seems to be no reasons at all to believe that a creature without language cannot suffer.

The second, and more easily appreciated way of linking language and the existence of pain is to say that the best evidence that we can have that another creature is in pain is when he tells us that he is. This is a distinct line of argument, for it is not being denied that a non-language-user conceivably could suffer, but only that we could know that he is suffering. Still, this line of argument seems to me to fail, and

---

[2] Jane van Lawick-Goodall, *In the Shadow of Man* (Boston: Houghton Mifflin, 1971), p. 225.

for reasons similar to those just given. "I am in pain" is not the best possible evidence that the speaker is in pain (he might be lying) and it is certainly not the only possible evidence. Behavioral signs and knowledge of the animal's biological similarity to ourselves together provide adequate evidence that animals do suffer. After all, we would not accept linguistic evidence if it contradicted the rest of the evidence. If a man was severely burned, and behaved as if he were in pain, writhing, groaning, being very careful not to let his burned skin touch anything, and so on, but later said he had not been in pain at all, we would be more likely to conclude that he was lying or suffering from amnesia than that he had not been in pain.

Even if there were stronger grounds for refusing to attribute pain 15 to those who do not have a language, the consequences of this refusal might lead us to examine these grounds unusually critically. Human infants, as well as some adults, are unable to use language. Are we to deny that a year-old infant can suffer? If not, how can language be crucial? Of course, most parents can understand the responses of even very young infants better than they understand the responses of other animals, and sometimes infant responses can be understood in the light of later development.

This, however, is just a fact about the relative knowledge we have of our own species and other species, and most of this knowledge is simply derived from closer contact. Those who have studied the behavior of other animals soon learn to understand their responses at least as well as we understand those of an infant. (I am not referring to Jane Goodall's and other well-known studies of apes. Consider, for example, the degree of understanding achieved by Tinbergen from watching herring gulls.)[3] Just as we can understand infant human behavior in the light of adult human behavior, so we can understand the behavior of other species in the light of our own behavior (and sometimes we can understand our own behavior better in the light of the behavior of other species).

The grounds we have for believing that other mammals and birds suffer are, then, closely analogous to the grounds we have for believing that other humans suffer. It remains to consider how far down the evolutionary scale this analogy holds. Obviously it becomes poorer when we get further away from man. To be more precise would require a detailed examination of all that we know about other forms of life. With fish, reptiles, and other vertebrates the analogy still seems strong, with molluscs like oysters it is much weaker. Insects are more difficult, and it may be that in our present state of knowledge we must be agnostic about whether they are capable of suffering.

---

[3] N. Tinbergen, *The Herring Gull's World* (New York: Basic Books, 1961).

If there is no moral justification for ignoring suffering when it occurs, and it does occur in other species, what are we to say of our attitudes toward these other species? Richard Ryder, one of the contributors to *Animals, Men and Morals,* uses the term "speciesism" to describe the belief that we are entitled to treat members of other species in a way in which it would be wrong to treat members of our own species. The term is not euphonious, but it neatly makes the analogy with racism. The nonracist would do well to bear the analogy in mind when he is inclined to defend human behavior toward nonhumans. "Shouldn't we worry about improving the lot of our own species before we concern ourselves with other species?" he may ask. If we substitute "race" for "species" we shall see that the question is better not asked. "Is a vegetarian diet nutritionally adequate?" resembles the slave-owner's claim that he and the whole economy of the South would be ruined without slave labor. There is even a parallel with skeptical doubts about whether animals suffer, for some defenders of slavery professed to doubt whether blacks really suffer in the way whites do.

I do not want to give the impression, however, that the case for Animal Liberation is based on the analogy with racism and no more. On the contrary, *Animals, Men and Morals* describes the various ways in which humans exploit nonhumans, and several contributors consider the defenses that have been offered, including the defense of meat-eating mentioned in the last paragraph. Sometimes the rebuttals are scornfully dismissive, rather than carefully designed to convince the detached critic. This may be a fault, but it is a fault that is inevitable, given the kind of book this is. The issue is not one on which one can remain detached. As the editors state in their Introduction:

> Once the full force of moral assessment has been made explicit there can be no rational excuse left for killing animals, be they killed for food, science, or sheer personal indulgence. We have not assembled this book to provide the reader with yet another manual on how to make brutalities less brutal. Compromise, in the traditional sense of the term, is simple unthinking weakness when one considers the actual reasons for our crude relationships with the other animals.

The point is that on this issue there are few critics who are genuinely detached. People who eat pieces of slaughtered nonhumans every day find it hard to believe that they are doing wrong; and they also find it hard to imagine what else they could eat. So for those who do not place nonhumans beyond the pale of morality, there comes a stage when further argument seems pointless, a stage at which one can only accuse one's opponent of hypocrisy and reach for the sort of sociological account of our practices and the way we defend them that is attempted by David Wood in his contribution to this book. On the other hand, to those unconvinced by the arguments, and unable to accept that they are merely rationalizing their dietary preferences and their fear of being thought peculiar, such sociological explanations can only seem insultingly arrogant.

The logic of speciesism is most apparent in the practice of experimenting on nonhumans in order to benefit humans. This is because the issue is rarely obscured by allegations that nonhumans are so different from humans that we cannot know anything about whether they suffer. The defender of vivisection cannot use this argument because he needs to stress the similarities between man and other animals in order to justify the usefulness to the former of experiments on the latter. The researcher who makes rats choose between starvation and electric shocks to see if they develop ulcers (they do) does so because he knows that the rat has a nervous system very similar to man's, and presumably feels an electric shock in a similar way.

Richard Ryder's restrained account of experiments on animals made me angrier with my fellow men than anything else in this book. Ryder, a clinical psychologist by profession, himself experimented on animals before he came to hold the view he puts forward in his essay. Experimenting on animals is now a large industry, both academic and commercial. In 1969, more than 5 million experiments were performed in Britain, the vast majority without anesthetic (though how many of these involved pain is not known). There are no accurate U.S. figures, since there is no federal law on the subject and in many cases no state law either. Estimates vary from 20 million to 200 million. Ryder suggests that 80 million may be the best guess. We tend to think that this is all for vital medical research, but of course it is not. Huge numbers of animals are used in university departments from Forestry to Psychology, and even more are used for commercial purposes, to test whether cosmetics can cause skin damage, or shampoos eye damage, or to test food additives or laxatives or sleeping pills or anything else.

A standard test for foodstuffs is the "LD50." The object of this test is to find the dosage level at which 50 percent of the test animals will die. This means that nearly all of them will become very sick before finally succumbing or surviving. When the substance is a harmless one, it may be necessary to force huge doses down the animals, until in some cases sheer volume or concentration causes death.

Ryder gives a selection of experiments, taken from recent scientific journals. I will quote two, not for the sake of indulging in gory details, but in order to give an idea of what normal researchers think they may legitimately do to other species. The point is not that the individual researchers are cruel men, but that they are behaving in a way that is allowed by our speciesist attitudes. As Ryder points out, even if only 1 percent of the experiments involve severe pain, that is 50,000 experiments in Britain each year, or nearly 150 every day (and about fifteen times as many in the United States, if Ryder's guess is right). Here then are two experiments:

> O. S. Ray and R. J. Barrett of Pittsburgh gave electric shocks to the feet of 1,042 mice. They then caused convulsions by giving more intense shocks through cup-shaped electrodes applied to the animals' eyes or through pressure spring clips attached to their ears. Unfortunately some of the mice who "successfully completed Day One training were found sick or dead prior to testing on Day Two." [*Journal of Comparative and Physiological Psychology,* vol. 67, 1969, pp. 110–16]

> At the National Institute for Medical Research, Mill Hill, London, W. Feldberg and S. L. Sherwood injected chemicals into the brains of cats — "with a number of widely different substances, recurrent patterns of reaction were obtained. Retching, vomiting, defaecation, increased salivation and greatly accelerated respiration leading to panting were common features." . . .
> The injection into the brain of a large dose of Tubocuraine caused the cat to jump "from the table to the floor and then straight into its cage, where it started calling more and more noisily whilst moving about restlessly and jerkily . . . finally the cat fell with legs and neck flexed, jerking in rapid clonic movements, the condition being that of a major [epileptic] convulsion . . . within a few seconds the cat got up, ran for a few yards at high speed and fell in another fit. The whole process was repeated several times within the next ten minutes, during which the cat lost faeces and foamed at the mouth."
> The animal finally died thirty-five minutes after the brain injection. [*Journal of Physiology,* vol. 123, 1954, pp. 148–67]

There is nothing secret about these experiments. One has only to open any recent volume of a learned journal, such as the *Journal of Comparative and Physiological Psychology,* to find full descriptions of experiments of this sort, together with the results obtained — results that are frequently trivial and obvious. The experiments are often supported by public funds.

It is a significant indication of the level of acceptability of these practices that, although these experiments are taking place at this moment on university campuses throughout the country, there has so far as I know, not been the slightest protest from the student movement. Students have been rightly concerned that their universities should not discriminate on grounds of race or sex, and that they should not serve the purposes of the military or big business. Speciesism continues undisturbed, and many students participate in it. There may be a few qualms at first, but since everyone regards it as normal, and it may even be a required part of a course, the student soon becomes hardened and, dismissing his earlier feelings as "mere sentiment," comes to regard animals as statistics rather than sentient beings with interests that warrant consideration.

Argument about vivisection has often missed the point because it has been put in absolutist terms: Would the abolitionist be prepared to let thousands die if they could be saved by experimenting on a single animal? The way to reply to this purely hypothetical question is to pose another: Would the experimenter be prepared to experiment on a human orphan under six months old, if it were the only way to save many lives? (I say "orphan" to avoid the complication of parental feelings, although in doing so I am being overfair to the experimenter, since the nonhuman subjects of experiments are not orphans.) A negative answer to this question indicates that the experimenter's readiness to use nonhumans is simple discrimination, for adult apes, cats, mice, and other mammals are more conscious of what is happening to them, more self-directing, and, so far as we can tell, just as sensitive to pain as a human infant. There is no characteristic that human infants possess that adult mammals do not have to the same or a higher degree.

(It might be possible to hold that what makes it wrong to experiment on a human infant is that the infant will in time develop into more than the nonhuman, but one would then, to be consistent, have to oppose abortion, and perhaps contraception, too, for the fetus and the egg and sperm have the same potential as the infant. Moreover, one would still have no reason for experimenting on a nonhuman rather than a human with brain damage severe enough to make it impossible for him to rise above infant level.)

The experimenter, then, shows a bias for his own species whenever he carries out an experiment on a nonhuman for a purpose that he would not think justified him in using a human being at an equal or lower level of sentience, awareness, ability to be self-directing, etc. No one familiar with the kind of results yielded by these experiments can have the slightest doubt that if this bias were eliminated the number of experiments performed would be zero or very close to it.

If it is vivisection that shows the logic of speciesism most clearly, 30 it is the use of other species for food that is at the heart of our attitudes toward them. Most of *Animals, Men and Morals* is an attack on meat-eating — an attack which is based solely on concern for nonhumans, without reference to arguments derived from considerations of ecology, macrobiotics, health, or religion.

The idea that nonhumans are utilities, means to our ends, pervades our thought. Even conservationists who are concerned about the slaughter of wild fowl but not about the vastly greater slaughter of chickens for our tables are thinking in this way — they are worried about what we would lose if there were less wildlife. Stanley Godlovitch, pursuing the Marxist idea that our thinking is formed by the activities we undertake in satisfying our needs, suggests that man's first classification of his environment was into Edibles and Inedibles. Most animals came into the first category, and there they have remained.

Man may always have killed other species for food, but he has never exploited them so ruthlessly as he does today. Farming has succumbed to business methods, the objective being to get the highest possible ratio of output (meat, eggs, milk) to input (fodder, labor costs, etc.). Ruth Harrison's essay "On Factory Farming" gives an account of some aspects of modern methods, and of the unsuccessful British campaign for effective controls, a campaign which was sparked off by her *Animal Machines* (London: Stuart, 1964).

Her article is in no way a substitute for her earlier book. This is a pity since, as she says, "Farm produce is still associated with mental pictures of animals browsing in the fields . . . of hens having a last forage before going to roost. . . ." Yet neither in her article nor elsewhere in *Animals, Men and Morals* is this false image replaced by a clear idea of the nature and extent of factory farming. We learn of this only indirectly, when we hear of the code of reform proposed by an advisory committee set up by the British government.

Among the proposals, which the government refused to implement on the grounds that they were too idealistic, were "*Any animal should at least have room to turn around freely.*"

Factory farm animals need liberation in the most literal sense. Veal calves are kept in stalls five feet by two feet. They are usually slaughtered when about four months old, and have been too big to turn in their stalls for at least a month. Intensive beef herds, kept in stalls only proportionately larger for much longer periods, account for a growing percentage of beef production. Sows are often similarly confined when pregnant, which, because of artificial methods of increasing fertility, can be most of the time. Animals confined in this way do not waste food by exercising, nor do they develop unpalatable muscle.

"*A dry bedded area should be provided for all stock.*" Intensively kept animals usually have to stand and sleep on slatted floors without straw, because this makes cleaning easier.

"*Palatable roughage must be readily available to all calves after one week of age.*" In order to produce the pale veal housewives are said to prefer, calves are fed on an all-liquid diet until slaughter, even though they are long past the age at which they would normally eat grass. They develop a craving for roughage, evidenced by attempts to gnaw wood from their stalls. (For the same reason, their diet is deficient in iron.)

"*Battery cages for poultry should be large enough for a bird to be able to stretch one wing at a time.*" Under current British practice, a cage for four or five laying hens has a floor area of twenty inches by eighteen inches, scarcely larger than a double page of the *New York Review of Books*. In this space, on a sloping wire floor (sloping so the eggs roll down, wire so the dung drops through) the birds live for a year or eighteen months while artificial lighting and temperature conditions combine with drugs in their food to squeeze the maximum number of eggs out of them. Table birds are also sometimes kept in cages. More often they are reared in sheds, no less crowded. Under these conditions all the birds' natural activities are frustrated, and they develop "vices" such as pecking each other to death. To prevent this, beaks are often cut off, and the sheds kept dark.

How many of those who support factory farming by buying its produce know anything about the way it is produced? How many have heard something about it, but are reluctant to check up for fear that it will make them uncomfortable? To nonspeciesists, the typical consumer's mixture of ignorance, reluctance to find out the truth, and vague belief that nothing really bad could be allowed seems analogous to the attitudes of "decent Germans" to the death camps.

There are, of course, some defenders of factory farming. Their arguments are considered, though again rather sketchily, by John Harris. Among the most common: "Since they have never known anything else, they don't suffer." This argument will not be put by anyone who knows anything about animal behavior, since he will know that not all behavior has to be learned. Chickens attempt to stretch wings, walk around, scratch, and even dustbathe or build a nest, even though they have never lived under conditions that allowed these activities. Calves can suffer from maternal deprivation no matter at what age they were taken from their mothers. "We need these intensive methods to provide protein for a growing population." As ecologists and famine relief organizations know, we can produce far more protein per acre if we grow the right vegetable crop, soy beans for instance, than if we use the land to grow crops to be converted into protein by animals who use nearly 90 percent of the protein themselves, even when unable to exercise.

There will be many readers of this book who will agree that factory farming involves an unjustifiable degree of exploitation of sentient creatures, and yet will want to say that there is nothing wrong with rearing animals for food, provided it is done "humanely." These people are saying, in effect, that although we should not cause animals to suffer, there is nothing wrong with killing them.

There are two possible replies to this view. One is to attempt to show that this combination of attitudes is absurd. Roslind Godlovitch takes this course in her essay, which is an examination of some common attitudes to animals. She argues that from the combination of "animal suffering is to be avoided" and "there is nothing wrong with killing animals" it follows that all animal life ought to be exterminated (since all sentient creatures will suffer to some degree at some point in their lives). Euthanasia is a contentious issue only because we place some value on living. If we did not, the least amount of suffering would justify it. Accordingly, if we deny that we have a duty to exterminate all animal life, we must concede that we are placing some value on animal life.

This argument seems to me valid, although one could still reply that the value of animal life is to be derived from the pleasures that life can have for them, so that, provided their lives have a balance of pleasure over pain, we are justified in rearing them. But this would imply that we ought to produce animals and let them live as pleasantly as possible, without suffering.

At this point, one can make the second of the two possible replies to the view that rearing and killing animals for food is all right so long as it is done humanely. This second reply is that so long as we think that a nonhuman may be killed simply so that a human can satisfy his taste for meat, we are still thinking of nonhumans as means rather than as ends in themselves. The factory farm is nothing more than the application of technology to this concept. Even traditional methods involve castration, the separation of mothers and their young, the breaking up of herds, branding or ear-punching, and of course transportation to the abattoirs and the final moments of terror when the animal smells blood and senses danger. If we were to try rearing animals so that they lived and died without suffering, we should find that to do so on anything like the scale of today's meat industry would be a sheer impossibility. Meat would become the prerogative of the rich.

I have been able to discuss only some of the contributions to this 45 book, saying nothing about, for instance, the essays on killing for furs and for sport. Nor have I considered all the detailed questions that need to be asked once we start thinking about other species in the radically different way presented by this book. What, for instance, are we to do about genuine conflicts of interest like rats biting slum children? I am not sure of the answer, but the essential point is just that we *do* see this as a conflict of interest, that we recognize that rats have interests too. Then we may begin to think about other ways of resolving the conflict — perhaps by leaving out rat baits that sterilize the rats instead of killing them.

I have not discussed such problems because they are side issues compared with the exploitation of other species for food and for experimental purposes. On these central matters, I hope that I have said enough to show that this book, despite its flaws, is a challenge to every human to recognize his attitudes to nonhumans as a form of prejudice no less objectionable than racism or sexism. It is a challenge that demands not just a change of attitudes, but a change in our way of life, for it requires us to become vegetarians.

Can a purely moral demand of this kind succeed? The odds are certainly against it. The book holds out no inducements. It does not tell us that we will become healthier, or enjoy life more, if we cease exploiting animals. Animal Liberation will require greater altruism on the part of mankind than any other liberation movement, since animals are incapable of demanding it for themselves, or of protesting against their exploitation by votes, demonstrations, or bombs. Is man capable of such genuine altruism? Who knows? If this book does have a significant effect, however, it will be a vindication of all those who have believed that man has within himself the potential for more than cruelty and selfishness.

Vivisection

C. S. LEWIS

It is the rarest thing in the world to hear a rational discussion of vivisection. Those who disapprove of it are commonly accused of "sentimentality," and very often their arguments justify the accusation. They paint pictures of pretty little dogs on dissecting tables. But the other side lies open to exactly the same charge. They also often defend the practice by drawing pictures of suffering women and children whose pain can be relieved (we are assured) only by the fruits of vivisection. The one appeal, quite as clearly as the other, is addressed to emotion, to the particular emotion we call pity. And neither appeal proves anything. If the thing is right — and if right at all, it is a duty — then pity for the animal is one of the temptations we must resist in order to perform that duty. If the thing is wrong, then pity for human suffering is precisely the temptation which will most probably lure us into doing that wrong thing. But the real question — *whether* it is right or wrong — remains meanwhile just where it was.

A rational discussion of this subject begins by inquiring whether pain is, or is not, an evil. If it is not, then the case against vivisection falls. But then so does the case for vivisection. If it is not defended on the ground that it reduces human suffering, on what ground can it be defended? And if pain is not an evil, why should human suffering be reduced? We must therefore assume as a basis for the whole discussion that pain is an evil, otherwise there is nothing to be discussed.

Now if pain is an evil then the infliction of pain, considered in itself, must clearly be an evil act. But there are such things as necessary evils. Some acts which would be bad, simply in themselves, may be excusable and even laudable when they are necessary means to a greater good. In saying that the infliction of pain, simply in itself, is bad, we are not saying that pain ought never to be inflicted. Most of us think that it can rightly be inflicted for a good purpose — as in dentistry or just and reformatory punishment. The point is that it always requires justification. On the man whom we find inflicting pain rests the burden of showing why an act which in itself would be simply bad is, in those particular circumstances, good. If we find a man giving pleasure it is for us to prove (if we criticize him) that his action is wrong. But if we find a man inflicting pain it is for him to prove that his action is right. If he cannot, he is a wicked man.

Clive Staples Lewis (1898–1963) was a professor of English literature at Oxford and Cambridge universities. His writings on Christianity and his moralistic fantasy tales for children continue to be widely popular. "Vivisection" was first published as a pamphlet in 1947 by the New England Anti-Vivisection Society.

Now vivisection can only be defended by showing it to be right that one species should suffer in order that another species should be happier. And here we come to the parting of the ways. The Christian defender and the ordinary "scientific" (i.e., naturalistic) defender of vivisection have to take quite different lines.

The Christian defender, especially in the Latin countries, is very 5 apt to say that we are entitled to do anything we please to animals because they "have no souls." But what does this mean? If it means that animals have no consciousness, then how is this known? They certainly behave as if they had, or at least the higher animals do. I myself am inclined to think that far fewer animals than is supposed have what we should recognize as consciousness. But that is only an opinion. Unless we know on other grounds that vivisection is right we must not take the moral risk of tormenting them on a mere opinion. On the other hand, the statement that they "have no souls" may mean that they have no moral responsibilities and are not immortal. But the absence of "soul" in that sense makes the infliction of pain upon them not easier but harder to justify. For it means the animals cannot deserve pain, nor profit morally by the discipline of pain, nor be recompensed by happiness in another life for suffering in this. Thus all the factors which render pain more tolerable or make it less totally evil in the case of human beings will be lacking in the beasts. "Soullessness," in so far as it is relevant to the question at all, is an argument against vivisection.

The only rational line for the Christian vivisectionist to take is to say that the superiority of man over beast is a real objective fact, guaranteed by Revelation, and that the propriety of sacrificing beast to man is a logical consequence. We are "worth more than many sparrows,"[1] and in saying this we are not merely expressing a natural preference for our own species simply because it is our own but conforming to a hierarchical order created by God and really present in the universe whether anyone acknowledges it or not. The position may not be satisfactory. We may fail to see how a benevolent Deity could wish us to draw such conclusions from the hierarchical order He has created. We may find it difficult to formulate a human right of tormenting beasts in terms which would not equally imply an angelic right of tormenting men. And we may feel that though objective superiority is rightly claimed for men, yet that very superiority ought partly to *consist in* not behaving like a vivisector: that we ought to prove ourselves better than the beasts precisely by the fact of acknowledging duties to them which they do not acknowledge to us. But on all these questions different opinions can be honestly held. If on grounds of our real, divinely ordained, superiority a Christian pathologist thinks it right to vivisect, and does so with scrupulous care to avoid the least dram or scruple of

---

[1] Matthew 10:31.

unnecessary pain, in a trembling awe at the responsibility which he assumes, and with a vivid sense of the high mode in which human life must be lived if it is to justify the sacrifices made for it, then (whether we agree with him or not) we can respect his point of view.

But of course the vast majority of vivisectors have no such theological background. They are most of them naturalistic and Darwinian. Now here, surely, we come up against a very alarming fact. The very same people who will most contemptuously brush aside any consideration of animal suffering if it stands in the way of "research" will also, on another context, most vehemently deny that there is any radical difference between man and the other animals. On the naturalistic view the beasts are at bottom just the same *sort* of thing as ourselves. Man is simply the cleverest of the anthropoids. All the grounds on which a Christian might defend vivisection are thus cut from under our feet. We sacrifice other species to our own not because our own has any objective metaphysical privilege over others, but simply because it is ours. It may be very natural to have this loyalty to our own species, but let us hear no more from the naturalists about the "sentimentality" of antivivisectionists. If loyalty to our own species, preference for man simply because we are men, is not a sentiment, then, what is? It may be a good sentiment or a bad one. But a sentiment it certainly is. Try to base it on logic and see what happens!

But the most sinister thing about modern vivisection is this. If a mere sentiment justifies cruelty, why stop at a sentiment for the whole human race? There is also a sentiment for the white man against the black, for a *Herrenvolk* against the non-Aryans, for "civilized" or "progressive" peoples against "savages" or "backward" peoples. Finally, for our own country, party, or class against others. Once the old Christian idea of a total difference in kind between man and beast has been abandoned, then no argument for experiments on animals can be found which is not also an argument for experiments on inferior men. If we cut up beasts simply because they cannot prevent us and because we are backing our own side in the struggle for existence, it is only logical to cut up imbeciles, criminals, enemies, or capitalists for the same reasons. Indeed, experiments on men have already begun. We all hear that Nazi scientists have done them. We all suspect that our own scientists may begin to do so, in secret, at any moment.

The alarming thing is that the vivisectors have won the first round. In the nineteenth and eighteenth centuries a man was not stamped as a "crank" for protesting against vivisection. Lewis Carroll protested, if I remember his famous letter correctly, on the very same ground which I have just used.[2] Dr. Johnson — a man whose mind had as much *iron*

---

[2] "Vivisection as a Sign of the Times," *The Works of Lewis Carroll,* ed. Roger Lancelyn-Green (London, 1965), pp. 1089–92. See also "Some Popular Fallacies about Vivisection," ibid., pp. 1092–1100.

in it as any man's — protested in a note on *Cymbeline* which is worth quoting in full. In Act I, scene v, the Queen explains to the Doctor that she wants poisons to experiment on "such creatures as We count not worth the hanging, — but none human."[3] The Doctor replies:

> Your Highness
> Shall from this practice but make hard your heart.[4]

Johnson comments: "The thought would probably have been more amplified, had our author lived to be shocked with such experiments as have been published in later times, by a race of men that have practiced tortures without pity, and related them without shame, and are yet suffered to erect their heads among human beings."[5]

The words are his, not mine, and in truth we hardly dare in these 10
days to use such calmly stern language. The reason why we do not dare is that the other side has in fact won. And though cruelty even to beasts is an important matter, their victory is symptomatic of matters more important still. The victory of vivisection marks a great advance in the triumph of ruthless, nonmoral utilitarianism over the old world of ethical law; a triumph in which we, as well as animals, are already the victims, and of which Dachau and Hiroshima mark the more recent achievements. In justifying cruelty to animals we put ourselves also on the animal level. We choose the jungle and must abide by our choice.

You will notice I have spent no time in discussing what actually goes on in the laboratories. We shall be told, of course, that there is surprisingly little cruelty. That is a question with which, at present, I have nothing to do. We must first decide what should be allowed: After that it is for the police to discover what is already being done.

Holding Human Health Hostage

MICHAEL E. DeBAKEY

As a patient-advocate, both in and out of the operating room, I feel a responsibility to protect the rights of patients to medical advances resulting from animal research. Had the animal legislation now pending in Congress been enacted when I began my career, it would have

---

[3] Shakespeare, *Cymbeline,* I, v, 19–20.

[4] Ibid., 23.

[5] *Johnson on Shakespeare: Essays and Notes Selected and Set Forth with an Introduction* by Sir Walter Raleigh (London, 1908), p. 181.

Michael E. DeBakey, M.D., is chancellor, chairman of surgery, and director of the DeBakey Heart Center at Baylor College of Medicine in Houston, Texas. His editorial appeared in the *Journal of Investigative Surgery,* Vol. I, 1988.

prevented me from developing a number of lifesaving procedures in my research laboratory. Instead of restoring thousands of patients to a normal life and a return to productive work, my colleagues and I would have been helpless to offer many of our patients any real hope at all. This legislation, known as the Mrazek bill, seeks to ban the use of pound animals for any research supported by the National Institutes of Health, the chief source of funds for biomedical research in this country. Are we now to hold human health hostage to the rights of abandoned animals to be killed in pounds?

Even with today's technology, I could not have developed on a computer the roller pump that made open-heart surgery possible or the artificial artery that restored to health previously doomed patients with aneurysms. Nor could we have attempted the first successful coronary artery bypass or implanted the first temporary mechanical heart with which we saved a patient's life two decades ago. Would animal-rights activists have objected to the first kidney, heart, or liver transplant? Would they forgo the protection humanity enjoys today against poliomyelitis, tetanus, diphtheria, and whooping cough or the treatment for strep throat, ear infections, bronchitis, and pneumonia — all the products of animal research? Would they have denied the 11 million diabetics the right to life that insulin has given them — or victims of cancer the help they have received from radiation and chemotherapy? It was in monkeys that the deadly AIDS virus was isolated, and that isolation is the initial step in the ultimate development of a vaccine. Would the animal-rights activists halt that research and allow an epidemic to rage unopposed? The truth is that there are no satisfactory insentient models at present for certain types of biomedical research and testing. A computer is not a living system and would not have produced the dramatic medical advances of the past few decades.

Only about 1 percent of abandoned dogs are released for research. If pounds are such a meager source of research animals, you may ask, why am I concerned about losing that source? My reasons are well founded, I believe: Not only are pound animals of particular value in research on heart and kidney disease, brain injury, stroke, blindness, and deafness, but a ban on their use could have grave and far-reaching consequences for human and animal health. In addition, such a ban would impose an extra burden on taxpayers and could price many important research projects out of existence. Each dog and cat bred specifically for research costs hundreds of dollars more than a pound animal. The Mrazek bill makes no accommodation in appropriations for this substantial rise in cost. For many of our most productive researchers, the additional expense would shut down their laboratories. Critical work on inducing tolerance in organ grafts, for example, and on minimizing damage to cardiac muscles after heart attacks has been halted in some research laboratories because of soaring costs of dogs.

Moreover, eliminating the use of pound animals in research would, paradoxically, cause even more animals to die. According to the American Humane Society, 7 million pet dogs are abandoned to pounds or shelters each year, 5 million of which are killed — 600 "trusting pets" killed hourly. Yet some would have you believe that killing animals in a pound is more virtuous than having them help to advance medical knowledge and ultimately benefit human and animal health. I don't like to see life taken from any species unnecessarily, and that would happen if this law is enacted. Every year we would have to breed an additional 138,000 dogs and 50,000 cats for research to replace the pound animals, which would then be put to death anyway because no one wants them. With the current overpopulation of dogs and cats, the logic of such a policy escapes me.

It was humane concerns that led me into medicine. I strongly 5 disapprove of cruelty to animals as well as humans. Medical scientists are not engaged in cockfighting, bullfighting, bull-dogging, calf-roping, or any other "sport" imposing stress or violence on animals. Rather, they are searching for ways to relieve suffering and preserve life. Unquestionably, every precaution should be taken, and enforced, to ensure that laboratory animals are treated humanely. Responsible scientists observe humane guidelines, not only because their search for new medical knowledge is motivated by compassion for the suffering, but because they know that improper treatment adversely affects the quality of their research. Scientists are also obligated to use insentient models when these are satisfactory, but, again, no responsible scientist would incur the substantial expense and devote the considerable space required for housing and caring for animals when other equally satisfactory models were available.

If scientists abandon cat and dog experiments for other models that are not as suitable or as well understood, many potential medical breakthroughs may be severely crippled or halted. Grave diseases such as AIDS, cancer, heart disease, muscular dystrophy, Alzheimer's disease, and other serious conditions will, however, continue to plague our families, friends, and fellow citizens, and those patients will properly expect to receive effective treatments and cures.

Remember, too, that pets have also profited from animal research. It is doubtful that animals could be treated today for heart or kidney disease, leukemia, or other serious disorders if animal research had been prohibited previously. If an animal is seriously ill or injured, would the animal-rights activist deny him a form of treatment potentially beneficial but never used before — and therefore experimental? Until one is faced with a life-threatening condition of a loved one — human or animal — it is difficult to answer that question truthfully.

We have aggressive advocates of the rights of trees, sharks, bats, whales, seals, and other mammals, but what about the rights of ailing humans? Shrill attacks against speciesism are difficult to defend when one observes pit bulldogs mauling and killing children, wolves killing deer, cats consuming rats and birds, and birds consuming worms. And even vegetarians destroy living plants for consumption. Self-preservation is a primary instinct of all members of the animal kingdom, and patients with that instinct deserve our compassion, protection, and assistance as much as other species.

Some animal-rights zealots have been quoted as regarding "the right to human life as a perversion," meat-eating as "primitive, barbaric, and arrogant," and pet ownership as an "absolutely abysmal situation brought about by human manipulation." It is difficult to believe that many animal lovers would embrace such an extreme position. There is a difference, moreover, between animal welfare and antisciencism. Infiltrating laboratories surreptitiously by posing as volunteer workers, destroying research records, vandalizing research facilities, bombing, and threatening scientists are all irrational methods of persuasion. At one research institution, damages amounted to more than a half million dollars when computers were destroyed, blood was poured on files, and liberationist slogans were painted on laboratory walls. Research on infant blindness was halted for eight months while claims of animal abuse were investigated, only to be found baseless. Such harassment, demoralization, and interference divert funds from productive research to security and discourage bright young people from entering research. Once the manpower chain is broken, it will not be easily restored. And where will we then turn for answers to devastating human diseases? Guerrilla tactics, lurid pictures, and sensational headlines may inflame emotions, but they do not lead to rational judgments. More important, should we condone harassment, terrorism, and violence masquerading as concern for animal rights?

As a physician, my greatest concern is, of course, for the suffering 10 human beings who will be denied effective treatment because we took action that seems superficially humane but may ultimately render us powerless against certain diseases. What do I tell dying patients who are waiting for the medical advances that these threatened investigations may produce — that there is no hope because we have been prevented from acquiring the new knowledge needed to correct their conditions? As a human being and physician, I cannot conceive of telling parents their sick child is doomed because we cannot use all the tools at our disposal. Surely those who object to animals in research laboratories must be equally distressed at seeing sick children hooked up to tubes. How will those parents feel about a society that legislates the rights of animals above those of humans?

Through research, we have made remarkable advances in medicine, but we still do not have all the answers. If the animal-rights activists could witness the heartbreaking suffering of patients and families that I encounter daily, I doubt that they would deliberately pose a direct threat to human and animal health by demanding that we abandon some of our most fruitful methods of medical investigation. The American public must decide: Shall we tell hundreds of thousands of victims of heart attacks, cancer, AIDS, and numerous other dread diseases that the right of abandoned animals to die in a pound supersedes the patients' rights to relief from suffering and premature death? In making that decision, let us use not anger and hatred but reason and good will.

Why Worry about the Animals?
JEAN BETHKE ELSHTAIN

The list of cruelties committed in the name of "science" or "research" could be expanded endlessly. "Fully 80 percent of the experiments involving rhesus monkeys are either unnecessary, represent useless duplication of previous work, or could utilize nonanimal alternatives," says John E. McArdle, a biologist and specialist in primates at Illinois Wesleyan University.

Growing awareness of animal abuse is helping to build an increasingly militant animal-welfare movement in this country and abroad — a movement that is beginning to have an impact on public policy. Secretary of Health and Human Services Frederick Goodwin complained recently that complying with new federal regulations on the use — or abuse — of animals will drain off some 17 percent of the research funds appropriated to the National Institutes of Health. (It is cheaper to purchase, use, and destroy animals than to retool for alternative procedures.) One of the institutes, the National Institute of Mental Health, spends about $30 million a year on research that involves pain and suffering for animals.

The new animal-welfare activists are drawing attention in part because of the tactics they espouse. Many preach and practice civil disobedience, violating laws against, say, breaking and entering. Some have been known to resort to violence against property and — on a few occasion — against humans.

Some individuals and groups have always fretted about human responsibility toward nonhuman creatures. In the ancient world, the historian Plutarch and the philosopher Porphyry were among those who insisted that human excellence embodied a refusal to inflict unnecessary suffering on all other creatures, human and nonhuman.

But with the emergence of the Western rationalist tradition, animals 5 lost the philosophic struggle. Two of that tradition's great exponents,

Jean Bethke Elshtain is a professor of political science at Vanderbilt University and the author of many scholarly essays. This article first appeared in the March 1990 issue of *The Progressive*.

René Descartes and Immanuel Kant, dismissed out of hand the moral worth of animals. Descartes's view, which has brought comfort to every human who decides to confine, poison, cripple, infect, or dismember animals in the interest of human knowledge, was the more extreme: He held that animals are simply machines, devoid of consciousness or feeling. Kant, more sophisticated in his ethical reasoning, knew that animals could suffer but denied that they were self-conscious. Therefore, he argued, they could aptly serve as means to human ends.

To make sure that human sensibilities would not be troubled by the groans, cries, and yelps of suffering animals — which might lead some to suspect that animals not only bleed but feel pain — researchers have for a century subjected dogs and other animals to an operation called a centriculocordectomy, which destroys their vocal chords.

Still, there have long been groups that placed the suffering of animals within the bounds of human concern. In the nineteenth and early twentieth centuries, such reform movements as women's suffrage and abolitionism made common cause with societies for the prevention of cruelty to animals. On one occasion in 1907, British suffragettes, trade unionists, and their animal-welfare allies battled London University medical students in a riot triggered by the vivisection of a dog.

Traditionally, such concern has been charitable and, frequently, highly sentimental. Those who perpetrated the worst abuses against animals were denounced for their "beastly" behavior — the farmer who beat or starved his horse; the householder who chained and kicked his dog; the aristocratic hunter who, with his guests, slew birds by the thousands in a single day on his private game preserve.

For the most part, however, animals have been viewed, even by those with "humane" concerns, as means to human ends. The charitable impulse, therefore, had a rather condescending, patronizing air: Alas, the poor creatures deserve our pity.

The new animal-welfare movement incorporates those historic concerns but steers them in new directions. Philosophically, animal-rights activists seek to close the gap between "human" and "beast," challenging the entire Western rationalist tradition which holds that the ability to reason abstractly is *the* defining human attribute. (In that tradition, women were often located on a scale somewhere between "man" and "beast," being deemed human but not quite rational.)

Politically, the new abolitionists, as many animal-welfare activists call themselves, eschew sentimentalism in favor of a tough-minded, insistent claim that animals, too, have rights and that violating those rights constitutes oppression. It follows that animals must be liberated — and since they cannot liberate themselves in the face of overwhelming human hegemony, they require the help of liberators much as slaves did in the last century.

Thus, the rise of vocal movements for animal well-being has strong historic antecedents. What is remarkable about the current proliferation of efforts is their scope and diversity. Some proclaim animal "rights." Others speak of animal "welfare" or "protection." Still others find the term "equality" most apt, arguing that we should have "equal concern" for the needs of all sentient creatures.

When so many issues clamor for our attention, when so many problems demand our best attempts at fair-minded solution, why animals, why now? There is no simple explanation for the explosion of concern, but it is clearly linked to themes of peace and justice. Perhaps it can be summed up this way: Those who are troubled by the question of who is or is not within the circle of moral concern; those who are made queasy by our use and abuse of living beings for our own ends; those whose dreams of a better world are animated by some notion of a peaceable kingdom, *should* consider our relationship with the creatures that inhabit our planet with us — the creatures that have helped sustain us and that may share a similar fate with us unless we find ways to deflect if not altogether end the destruction of our earthly habitat.

Dozens of organizations have sprung up, operating alongside — and sometimes in conflict with — such older mainline outfits as the Humane Society, the Anti-Vivisection League, and the World Wildlife Fund. Among the new groups are People for the Ethical Treatment of Animals (PETA), Trans-Species Unlimited, In Defense of Animals, the Gorilla Foundation, Primarily Primates, Humane Farming Association, Farm Animal Reform, Alliance for Animals, Citizens to End Animal Suffering and Exploitation (CEASE), Whale Adoption Project, Digit Fund — the list goes on and on.

Some organizations focus on the plight of animals on factory farms, 15 especially the condition of anemic, imprisoned veal calves kept in darkness and unable to turn around until they are killed at fourteen weeks. Others are primarily concerned with conditions in the wild, where the habitat of the panda, among others, is being destroyed or where great and wonderful creatures like the black rhinoceros and the African elephant or magnificent cats like the snow leopard or the Siberian tiger are marching toward extinction, victims of greedy buyers of illegal tusks or pelts.

Another group of activists clusters around the use of animals in such profitable pursuits as greyhound racing, where dogs by the hundreds are destroyed once they cease "earning their keep," or in tourist attractions where such wonderfully intelligent social beings as the orca and the dolphin are turned into circus freaks for profit. In the wild, orcas can live for up to 100 years; in captivity, the average, sadly misnamed "killer whale" lasts about five.

Those wonderful chimpanzees that have been taught to speak to us through sign language also arouse concern. If the funding ends or a researcher loses interest, they are sometimes killed, sometimes turned over to the less-than-tender mercies of laboratory researchers to be addicted to cocaine, infected with a virus, or subjected to some other terrible fate. Eugene Linden describes, in his study *Silent Partners,* chimps desperately trying to convey their pain and fear and sadness to uncomprehending experimenters.

Use of animals in war research is an industry in itself, though one usually shielded from public view. Monkeys are the most likely subjects of experiments designed to measure the effects of neutron-bomb radiation and the toxicity of chemical-warfare agents. Beginning in 1957, monkeys were placed at varying distances from ground zero during atomic testing; those that didn't die immediately were encaged so that the "progress" of their various cancers might be noted.

Radiation experiments on primates continue. Monkeys' eyes are irradiated, and the animals are subjected to shocks of up to 1,200 volts. Junior researchers are assigned the "death watch," and what they see are primates so distressed that they claw at themselves and even bite hunks from their own arms or legs in a futile attempt to stem the pain. At a government proving ground in Aberdeen, Maryland, monkeys are exposed to chemical-warfare agents.

Dolphins, animals of exquisite intelligence, have been trained by the military in such scenarios as injecting carbon dioxide cartridges into Vietnamese divers and planting and removing mines. The Navy announced in April 1989 that it would continue its $30 million clandestine program, expanded in the Reagan years, to put dolphins to military use. The aim, the *New York Times* reported, is to use dolphins captured in the Gulf of Mexico to guard the Trident Nuclear Submarine Base at Bangor, Washington.

Several years ago, when I was writing a book on women and war, I came across references to the use of dogs in Vietnam. When I called the Pentagon and was put through to the chief of military history, Southeast Asia Branch, he told me that no books existed on the subject, but he did send me an excerpt from the *Vietnam War Almanac* that stated the U.S. military "made extensive use of dogs for a variety of duties in Vietnam, including scouting, mine detecting, tracking, sentry duty, flushing out tunnels, and drug detecting." Evidently, many of these dogs were killed rather than returned home, since it was feared their military training ill-suited them for civilian life.

Much better known, because of an increasingly successful animal-rights campaign, is the use of animals to test such household products as furniture polish and such cosmetics as shampoo and lipstick.

For years, industry has determined the toxicity of floor wax and detergents by injecting various substances into the stomachs of beagles, rabbits, and calves, producing vomiting, convulsions, respiratory illness, and paralysis. The so-called LD (lethal dose) 50 test ends only when half the animals in a test group have died. No anesthesia or painkillers are administered.

Dr. Andrew Rowan, assistant dean of the Tufts University School of Medicine, has offered persuasive evidence that such testing methods are crude and inaccurate measures of a product's safety. For one thing, a number of potentially significant variables, including the stress of laboratory living, are not taken into account, thus tainting any comparison of the effect of a given substance on human consumers.

The LD50 is notoriously unreproducible; the method for rating 25 irritation is extremely subjective; and interspecies variations make test results highly suspect when applied to the human organism.

Most notorious of the "tests" deployed by the multibillion-dollar cosmetics industry is the Draize, which has been used since the 1940s to measure the potential irritative effects of products. Rabbits — used because their eyes do not produce tears and, therefore, cannot cleanse themselves — are placed into stocks and their eyes are filled with foreign substances. When a rabbit's eyes ulcerate — again, no painkillers are used — the cosmetics testers (who are usually not trained laboratory researchers) report a result. To call this procedure "scientific" is to demean authentic science.

Curiously, neither the LD50 test nor the Draize are required by law. They continue in use because manufacturers want to avoid alarming consumers by placing warning labels on products. More accurate methods available include computer simulations to measure toxicity, cell-culture systems, and organ-culture tests that use chicken-egg membranes.

The disdainful response by corporate America to animal-protection concerns seems, at least in this area, to be undergoing a slow shift toward new laboratory techniques that abandon wasteful, crude, and cruel animal testing. Several large cosmetics manufacturers, including Revlon, have only recently announced that they will phase out animal testing, confirming the claim of animal-welfare groups that the tests are unnecessary.

Among the nastier issues in the forefront of the "animal wars" is the controversy over hunting and trapping.

It's estimated that about 17 million fur-bearing animals (plus "trash" 30 animals — including pets — the trapper doesn't want) are mangled each year in steel-jaw leg-hold traps that tear an animal's flesh and break its bones. Many die of shock or starvation before the trapper returns. Some animals chew off part of a limb in order to escape. More than sixty countries now ban the leg-hold trap, requiring the use of less painful and damaging devices.

Protests against the manufacture, sale, and wearing of fur coats have been aggressively — and successfully — mounted in Western Europe. In Holland, fur sales have dropped 80 percent in the last few years. Radical groups in Sweden have broken into fur farms to release minks and foxes. An effort to shame women who wear fur has had enormous impact in Great Britain.

Similar campaigns have been mounted in the United States, but the fur industry is waging a well-financed counterattack in this country. Curiously, the industry's efforts have been tacitly supported by some rights absolutists within feminism who see wearing a fur coat as a woman's right. It's difficult to think of a greater reductio ad absurdum of the notion of "freedom of choice," but it seems to appeal to certain adherents of upwardly mobile, choice-obsessed political orthodoxy.

Hunting may be the final frontier for animal-welfare groups. Because hunting is tied to the right to bear arms, any criticism of hunting is construed as an attack on constitutional freedoms by hunting and gun organizations, including the powerful and effective National Rifle Association. A bumper sticker I saw on a pickup truck in Northampton, Massachusetts, may tell the tale: MY WIFE, YES. MY DOG, MAYBE. BUT MY GUN, NEVER.

For some animal protectionists, the case against hunting is open and shut. They argue that the vast majority of the estimated 170 million animals shot to death in any given year are killed for blood sport, not for food, and that the offspring of these slaughtered creatures are left to die of exposure or starvation. Defenders of blood sports see them as a skill and a tradition, a lingering relic of America's great frontier past. Others — from nineteenth-century feminists to the Norman Mailer of *Why Are We in Vietnam?* — link the national mania for hunting with a deeper thirst for violence.

I am not convinced there is an inherent connection between animal   35 killing and a more general lust for violence, but some disquieting evidence is beginning to accumulate. Battered and abused women in rural areas often testify, for example, that their spouses also abused animals, especially cows, by stabbing them with pitchforks, twisting their ears, kicking them, or, in one reported incident, using a board with a nail in it to beat a cow to death.

But even people who recoil from hunting and other abuses of animals often find it difficult to condemn such experiments as those cited at the beginning of this article, which are, after all, conducted to serve "science" and, perhaps, to alleviate human pain and suffering. Sorting out this issue is no easy task if one is neither an absolute prohibitionist nor a relentless defender of the scientific establishment. When gross abuses come to light, they are often reported in ways that allow and encourage us to distance ourselves from emotional and ethical involvement. Thus the case of the baboons whose brains were bashed in at the University of Pennsylvania prompted the *New York Times* to editorialize on July 31, 1985, that the animals "seemed" to be suffering. They *were* suffering, and thousands of animals suffer every day.

Reasonable people should be able to agree on this: that alternatives to research that involves animal suffering must be vigorously sought; that there is no excuse for such conditions as dogs lying with open incisions, their entrails exposed, or monkeys with untreated, protruding broken bones, exposed muscle tissue, and infected wounds, living in grossly unsanitary conditions amidst feces and rotting food; that quick euthanasia should be administered to a suffering animal after the conclusion of a pain-inducing procedure; that pre- and postsurgical care must be provided for animals; that research should not be needlessly duplicated, thereby wasting animal lives, desensitizing generations of researchers, and flushing tax dollars down the drain.

What stands in the way of change? Old habits, bad science, unreflective cruelty, profit, and, in some cases, a genuine fear that animal-welfare groups want to stop all research dead in its tracks. "Scientists fear shackles on research," intones one report. But why are scientists so reluctant to promote such research alternatives as modeling, in-vitro techniques, and the use of lower organisms? Because they fear that the public may gain wider knowledge of what goes on behind the laboratory door. Surely those using animals should be able to explain themselves and to justify their expenditure of the lives, bodies, and minds of other creatures.

There is, to be sure, no justification for the harassment and terror tactics used by some animal-welfare groups. But the scientist who is offended when an animal-welfare proponent asks, "How would you feel if someone treated your child the way you treat laboratory animals?" should ponder one of the great ironies in the continuing debate: Research on animals is justified on grounds that they are "so like us."

I *do* appreciate the ethical dilemma here. As a former victim of   40
polio, I have thought long and hard for years about animal research and human welfare. This is where I come down, at least for now:

First, most human suffering in this world cannot be ameliorated in any way by animal experimentation. Laboratory infliction of suffering on animals will not keep people healthy in Asia, Africa, and Latin America. As philosopher Peter Singer has argued, we already know how to cure what ails people in desperate poverty; they need "adequate nutrition, sanitation, and health care. It has been estimated that 250,000 children die each week around the world, and that one-quarter of these deaths are by dehydration due to diarrhea. A simple treatment, already known and needing no animal experimentation, could prevent the deaths of these children."

Second, it is not clear that a cure for terrible and thus far incurable diseases such as AIDS is best promoted with animal experimentation. Some American experts on AIDS admit that French scientists are making more rapid progress toward a vaccine because they are working directly with human volunteers, a course of action Larry Kramer, a gay activist, has urged upon American scientists. Americans have been trying since 1984 to infect chimpanzees with AIDS, but after the expenditure of millions of dollars, AIDS has not been induced in any nonhuman animal. Why continue down this obviously flawed route?

Third, we could surely agree that a new lipstick color, or an even more dazzling floor wax, should never be promoted for profit over the wounded bodies of animals. The vast majority of creatures tortured and killed each year suffer for *nonmedical* reasons. Once this abuse is eliminated, the really hard cases having to do with human medical advance and welfare can be debated, item by item.

Finally, what is at stake is the exhaustion of the eighteenth-century model of humanity's relationship to nature, which had, in the words of philosopher Mary Midgley, "built into it a bold, contemptuous rejection of the nonhuman world."

Confronted as we are with genetic engineering and a new eugenics, 45 with the transformation of farms where animals ranged freely into giant factories where animals are processed and produced like objects, with callous behavior on a scale never before imagined under the rubric of "science," we can and must do better than to dismiss those who care as irrational and emotional animal lovers who are thinking with their hearts (not surprisingly, their ranks are heavily filled with women), and who are out to put a stop to the forward march of rationalism and science.

We humans do not deserve peace of mind on this issue. Our sleep should be troubled and our days riddled with ethical difficulties as we come to realize the terrible toll one definition of "progress" has taken on our fellow creatures.

We must consider our meat-eating habits as well. Meat eating is one of the most volatile, because most personal, of all animal-welfare questions. Meat eaters do not consider themselves immoral, though hard-core vegetarians find meat eating repugnant — the consumption of corpses. Such feminist theorists as Carol Adams insist that there is a connection between the butchering of animals and the historic mal-treatment of women. Certainly, there is a politics of meat that belongs on the agenda along with other animal-welfare issues.

I, for one, do not believe humans and animals have identical rights. But I do believe that creatures who can reason in their own ways, who can suffer, who are mortal beings like ourselves, have a value and dignity we must take into account. Animals are not simply a means to our ends.

When I was sixteen years old, I journeyed on a yellow school bus from LaPorte, Colorado, to Fairbanks, Iowa, on a 4-H Club "exchange trip." On the itinerary was a visit to a meat-packing plant in Des Moines. As vivid as the day I witnessed it is the scene I replay of men in blood-drenched coats "bleeding" pigs strung up by their heels on a slowly moving conveyer belt. The pigs — bright and sensitive creatures, as any person who has ever met one knows — were screaming in terror before the sharp, thin blade entered their jugular veins. They continued to struggle and squeal until they writhed and fell silent.

The men in the slaughter room wore boots. The floor was awash 50 in blood. I was horrified. But I told myself this was something I should remember. For a few months I refused to eat pork. But then I fell back into old habits — this was Colorado farm country in the late 1950s, after all.

But at one point, a few years ago, that scene and those cries of terror returned. This time I decided I would not forget, even though I knew my peace of mind would forever be disturbed.

Animals Have No Rights —
Go Ahead and Lick That Frog

RUSH H. LIMBAUGH III

Rights versus Protection

I'm a very controversial figure to the animal-rights movement. They no doubt view me with some measure of hostility because I am constantly challenging their fundamental premise that animals are superior to human beings. They may deny holding that belief, but the truth is inescapable when you examine the policies they advocate and their invariable preference for the well-being of animals, and their disregard for humans and their livelihoods. It especially bothers them when I state my belief that animals have no fundamental rights. In fact, this statement has bothered more than just animal-rights wackos. Many fellow animal-loving members of my audience misunderstand my point on this as well. But before you jump to the conclusion that I am callous, insensitive, and a heartless animal hater, hear me out. Before beginning the discussion of rights, let me make it perfectly clear that my belief that animals don't have rights is not equivalent to saying that human beings have no moral obligation to protect animals when they can. I am not saying that at all. But this is more, my friends, than a semantical distinction. The animal-rights movement knew what it was doing when it deliberately adopted the label "animal rights." The concept of "rights" is very powerful in the American political lexicon. It carries with it no

Rush H. Limbaugh III is the host of nationally syndicated radio and television programs. This excerpt is from his best-selling book, *The Way Things Ought to Be* (1992).

small amount of clout. If the movement can succeed in drilling into the American psyche the concept that animals have rights, then there will be far less outrage at the antibusiness policies the animal-rights people foist onto the public. If animals have rights, which is after all what we humans have, then what legal or moral basis do we have to protect ourselves in this war for dominance of the planet? Let me try to explain the concept of "rights" and why animals have none.

Rights are either God-given or evolve out of the democratic process. Most rights are based on the ability of people to agree on a social contract, the ability to make and keep agreements. Animals cannot possibly reach such an agreement with other creatures. They cannot respect anyone else's rights. Therefore they cannot be said to have rights.

Thomas Jefferson, in drafting the Declaration of Independence, did not begin by saying, "We hold these truths to be self-evident: that all *animals* are created equal; that they are endowed by their creator with certain unalienable rights; that among these are life, liberty and the pursuit of happiness."

Webster's defines a "right" as "something to which one has a just claim. The power or privilege to which one is justly entitled. A power, privilege, or condition of existence to which one has a natural claim of enjoyment or possession. A power or privilege vested in a person by the law to demand action or forbearance at the hands of another. A legally enforceable claim against another that the other will do or will not do a given act. A capacity or privilege the enjoyment of which is secured to a person by law. A claim recognized and delimited by law for the purpose of securing it."

Notice the words *one, person,* a claim against *another.* All of these words denote human beings, not animals or any other creatures. Inherent in the concept of "rights" is the ability to assert a claim to those rights. Implicit in all of these dictionary definitions is that in order to have rights one must know that he has a just claim to them; one must be able to assert them. Only a moron would argue that an animal has the capacity to assert a claim to any rights. An animal cannot avail himself of legal protection through our judicial system or otherwise. Only if humans intervene on its behalf will it have any protection at all.

In my opinion, at the root of the assertion that animals have rights is the belief that animals and men are equal in creation, that man evolved from apes, and that creation is an allegorical myth contained in that wonderful piece of literature known as the Bible. There is no escaping the connection between secular humanism and animal-rights activism.

The Bible teaches that God created man in His own image and that He placed him on this earth in a position superior to all other creatures, and gave him dominion over animals and nature. God did not create other animals in His own image.

Even if you reject the Bible as the Word of God — even if you believe in evolution and disbelieve in creation — you must still admit that man is the only earthly creature capable of rational thought.

Mortimer Adler, associate editor of the Great Books of the Western World — part of the classics, for those of you in Rio Linda — explains that in the great tradition of Western thought, from Plato right down to the nineteenth century, it was almost universally held that man and man alone is a rational animal. He says that only since the time of Darwin has the opposite view gained any acceptance; and it's mostly among scientists and the educated classes. This relatively new view holds that the difference between man and other mammals is one of degree, not kind. All animals have intelligence, man just has more of it. Adler then goes on to articulate his belief that the traditional view (that man is essentially different from other animals) is undeniable. In support of his belief he cites man's unique ability to make things. Sure, he concedes, bees make hives, birds make nests, and beavers make dams, but those productions are purely instinctive. Man's creations involve reason and free will. "In making houses, bridges, or any other of their artifacts, men invent and select. They are truly artists, as animals are not."

Adler also points out that men build machines which are themselves 10 productive. Animals solve problems when they are confronted with a biological urgency of finding a way of getting what they need. But no animals sit down and ponder things and think through problems as man does. Human thinking, he notes, is discursive and involves language. Animals make sounds and communicate; but they do not communicate thought. No animal ever utters a sentence which asserts something to be true or false. Sorry to offend you porpoise and dolphin worshipers out there.

Finally, Adler posits that man is the only animal with a historical development. Men transmit ideas and institutions, a whole tradition of culture, from one generation to another, and it is this which accounts for the history of the human race. In that regard I should like to pose the question to animal rights purveyors: Who is it that writes books about the history and development of animals? Maybe there is dolphin literature in the depths of the ocean, but I'm not going to enroll in the Kennedy Scuba School to find out. . . .

Human beings are the primary species on this planet. Animals and everything else are subspecies whose position on the planet is subordinate to that of humans. Humans have a responsibility toward lower species and must treat them humanely. *Humanely,* now that's an interesting term. Doesn't that mean as a human would like to be treated? Why not treat them animally? Because that would mean killing them. Can't you see? That's my point exactly. Animals often treat each other with no respect, and they have no redress, absent human intervention on their behalf. . . .

The easiest way for the left to exploit animals politically is to try to play upon this notion that the difference between animals and man is only one of degree. They seem to go even farther by forwarding the notion that the only difference between us and other mammals is that we have the capacity to subjugate other species. An entire myth has evolved that animals have special abilities and deserve to become a new protected class in society. If you don't believe me, here are some examples I've collected showing just how far the movement to accord animals rights that equal, or even exceed, those of humans, has gone. All of these items are completely true.

The *New York Times* science section recently carried a piece on what it seemed to be saying was the most intelligent being roaming the planet today, our good friend, the dolphin. Many people are convinced that human beings would be infinitely better off if they were only smart enough to understand the dolphin. You see, man is the dunce of the planet, according to animal-rights enviro-wackos. The dolphin is a noble, pure creature.

This twaddle has even crept into science reporting. The *New York* 15 *Times* reported, "As much as puppies, or pandas or even children, dolphins are universally beloved. They seem to cavort and frolic at the least provocation, their mouths fixed in what looks like a state of perpetual merriment, and their behavior and enormous brains suggest an intelligence approaching that of human beings or even, some might argue, surpassing it."

I was offended by that. Could somebody please show me one hospital built by a dolphin? Could somebody show me one highway built by a dolphin? Could someone show me one automobile invented by a dolphin?

But vengeance was mine. The *Times* article went on to say that researchers off the coast of Australia have come across male dolphins that engage in very chauvinistic behavior toward female dolphins. This activity is called "herding." "The males will chase after her, bite her, slap her, hit her with their fins, slam into her with their bodies." In other words, Mike Tyson behavioral rules dominate the male dolphin population.

Despite the dolphin's poor dating manners, it's clear that people had better be careful in how *they* approach this noble creature. Consider Allen Cooper, a hapless fellow from Sunderland, England, who last year was accused of "indecent behavior with a dolphin." Animal-rights activists on a pleasure boat testified that they had seen Cooper fondling a dolphin's penis. Cooper was totally humiliated by the resulting publicity, but a court finally cleared him of indecent-assault charges after expert witnesses testified that dolphins often extend their penises to swimmers as a "finger of friendship."

Apparently not all animals are created equal, according to some animal-rights activists. Some animals that have been happily owned by humans turn out to be politically incorrect and presumably have to be curbed. Take the poor cow. The May 1992 edition of *Countryside* magazine has a story called "The Last Roundup for Beef?" In it, liberal ecopest Jeremy Rifkin argues that without cattle, the world would be green, well fed, and peaceful. He claims that 1.28 billion cattle are now taking up 24 percent of the world's land mass, a ridiculous figure that few in the media will ever challenge.

Rifkin is bent out of shape because he says the cattle consume   20 enough grain to feed hundreds of millions of people. The reason the cattle are eating the grain is so they can be fattened and slaughtered, after which they will feed people, who need a high-protein diet. The combined weight of the cattle exceeds that of the world's human population. I presume Rifkin somehow supports curbing the cow population to limit the damage they are inflicting on mankind.

You may recall that Martin Sheen, the actor, once declared Malibu, California, a sanctuary for the homeless when he was honorary mayor. Well, the Malibu City Council recently went him one better by passing a resolution declaring that Malibu was a "human/dolphin shared environment," and urging "warmer relationships between humans and animals." Francis Jeffrey, the cofounder of the Great Whales Foundation, hailed the resolution: "This is a new concept, to say that dolphins are citizens of the community." Mary Frampton, the head of the local Save Our Coast group, told the council that "the dolphins thank you." I wonder how Frampton knows when any dolphins are thanking anyone. Why can't the little talking geniuses communicate this message themselves? After all, Frampton may be lying about what the dolphins told her. We need to hear it from the dolphin's mouth — that is, if we are smart enough to understand what they are trying to tell us. This whole episode just proves what happens when rich people in trendy coastal communities have too much free time on their hands.

Many ski boots are lined with dog fur, and the New York City ASPCA wants to outlaw such boots. Once again, animal-rights activists are lunging for the law rather than examining the facts. Technica US, a ski-boot maker in New Hampshire, says all of its boots are made using dog skin from China, where dogs have been raised for food for thousands of years. At least they aren't using cat hair to line their boots. Then Technica's products would be called "Puss in Boots." . . .

Have you heard of frog licking? Now I know you all lead busy lives, so you probably missed it when it showed up in the papers. But I was amazed when I read that frog licking has become a major preoccupation in Colorado. How could this possibly get started? It had to be this way. An environmentalist is out in the woods communing with nature. Probably some overgrown Boy Scout in little green shorts, a backpack filled with wheat nut mix. He's wearing his Walkman, skipping along some nature trail listening to Madonna music, probably the *Don't Bungle the Jungle* album.

So he's communing with the Nature Goddess and maybe even humming. Ommmmmmm-Ommmmmmm-Ommmmmmmm. He looks at a tree and maybe he says, "Hi, Greg." Maybe he hugs the tree. "Oh, I am at one with this tree." Then he spies a frog and suddenly stops. "Oh, look at that frog. Maybe I should pick it up and lick it." And gets high as a result. You see, the Colorado spotted toad secretes a hallucinogenic substance that can get you high if you lick it near the back of its head. Well, I'm sorry, but most people I know wouldn't lick a frog even if it did give them a buzz. Can you imagine doing that? Well, somebody did it. Somebody had to — otherwise we wouldn't know of this enlightened and marvelous way of turning on. But the amazing thing is that the first person who did it had to tell someone else he did it, who then passed it on for posterity's sake.

Tell me, who would do that kind of thing? I don't know, but they couldn't be considered normal. There may even be a conflict here between environmentalism and animal-rights types. Isn't it a violation of the frog's rights if he is licked? 25

Frogs aren't the only creatures we have to worry about, of course. You know, the sea turtle is an endangered species too. How so, you ask? Well, evil shrimpers happen to nab a couple of sea turtles now and then while murdering zillions of shrimp. Anyway, a guy in Florida was hauled into court for stealing some sea turtle eggs. The judge found him guilty and fined him $106,000. He said, "Wait a minute, these are not sea turtles, these are sea turtle eggs, and there's no law saying I can't steal them." "Sir," the judge replied, "they're going to be sea turtles. Guilty." The guy was stuck with a $106,000 fine. All this makes me wonder about our priorities. When does a sea turtle's life begin? At conception or when it's laid?

By the way, did you ever wonder why people always worry about sea turtles but ignore the lives of the shrimp? Flipper, the dolphin, is high on everybody's protection list. We kill maybe two dolphins for every 1 million tuna, and yet nobody is expressing any concern for the tuna. They're just a bunch of useless creatures. But dolphins are another matter. They're smart and they're cute. They even have a smile on their face! And they try to talk to us. Too bad we're not intelligent enough to understand them.

Conclusion

The point is that animals do not have rights but are accorded protection by human beings. When we establish laws against cruelty to animals, some mistake the laws to be the same as rights. They are not, however.

I received a letter on this subject from a listener, Chris Huson, of

Champaign, Illinois. He agreed with the premise that animals have no rights but are instead accorded protection by humans. He then illustrated the difference by observing that the "right to privacy" is not a right, but rather a protection granted by the government. The "right to privacy" does not allow you to take drugs in your car or home with impunity. The privacy is protected but does not therefore allow you to break the law.

He further stated in his letter that the basic right to life of an ani- 30 mal — which is the source of energy for many animal-rights wackos — must be inferred from the anticruelty laws humans have written, not from any divine source. Our laws do not prevent us from killing animals for food or sport, so the right to life of an animal is nonexistent.

He is right and I don't think it can be stated much better. Yet, we are confronted daily by people who wish to obstruct human progress and individual economic choices by virtue of elevating the importance of animal existence to that of human existence. The only way this can happen is for the force of law to be used to devalue human life.

Well, it is time some of us began to speak up for the sanctity of *human* life and the glories of humankind, which was created in God's image. If the wackos prefer to live in caves, let's provide them with free transportation there. As for the rest of us and our posterity, let's do what we can to treat ourselves with the respect and dignity that God intended.

Animals and Sickness
THE WALL STREET JOURNAL

If it's spring, the "animal-rights movement" can't be far behind. It will be on display today at the National Institutes of Health in Washington, demonstrating on behalf of World Laboratory Animal Liberation Week. On Wednesday, two of this country's most renowned doctors will travel to Washington to try to counteract the demonstration with a news conference. Dr. Michael DeBakey of Baylor is the well-known pioneer in heart surgery. Dr. Thomas Starzl of the University of Pittsburgh has become famous in recent years for his work in providing liver transplants for children. Both consider the animal-rights movement to be one of the greatest threats to continued medical research in the United States.

Polio, drug addiction, cystic fibroids, most vaccines and antibiotics, pacemakers, cancer, Alzheimer's, surgical technique — it's hard to iden-

This editorial is from the April 24, 1989 issue of the *Wall Street Journal.*

tify many breakthroughs in medical progress that don't depend on research using higher animal forms. For most of the past decade, the animal-rights movement hasn't merely opposed animal research; it has tried to destroy it.

On April 2, in an Animal Liberation Front break-in at the University of Arizona, two buildings were set on fire (causing $100,000 damage) and 1,000 animals including mice infected with a human parasite, were stolen. The list of such incidents in the United States is long:

The director of Stanford's animal facility got a bomb threat in December. Intruders stole dogs and records of heart-transplant research at Loma Linda University in August. Indeed, dating back to 1982 there have been break-ins and thefts of animals at medical-research laboratories at Berkeley; Johns Hopkins (rats in Alzheimer's research); the head-injury lab and the veterinary school at Penn (arthritis research, sudden infant death syndrome); University of California, Davis (an arson attack); New York State Psychiatric Institute (Parkinson's research); University of Oregon; and University of California, Irvine (lung research). Currently, a trial is imminent for a woman who allegedly tried to murder the president of U.S. Surgical Corporation in Connecticut with a remote-control bomb.

The animal-rights movement is a textbook example of how many 5 activist groups press their agendas into today's political system. It hardly matters, for instance, that an American Medical Association poll found that 77 percent of adults think that using animals in medical research is necessary. Those people answered the phone and went back to their daily lives, working at real jobs and raising families. Meanwhile the professional activists — animal-rights, antinukers, fringe environmentalists, Hollywood actresses — descend on the people who create "issues" in America.

They elicit sympathetic, free publicity from newspapers and magazines. They do Donahue and Oprah. And they beat on the politicians and bureaucrats. They create a kind of nonstop Twilight Zone of "issues" and "concerns" that most American voters are barely aware of. They do this because it has succeeded so many times.

As an outgrowth of congressional legislation, the U.S. Agriculture Department recently proposed animal-research regulations that would engulf medical scientists in reporting requirements, animal committees, "whistleblower" procedures, and directives to redesign laboratories ("the method of feeding nonhuman primates must be varied daily in order to promote their psychological well-being"). The cost of compliance, in an era of declining funding support for much research, is estimated to be $1.5 billion, and of course this will not satisfy the "movement."

If the United States is forced to work under the constant burden of all these varieties of public-issue nonsense, it can never hope to realize continued gains in either human welfare or its international competitiveness. Happily, evidence is emerging that the scientific community has decided it's time to fight back against all these activist movements.

In what should be the beginning of a countermovement against the animal-rights groups, NIH Director James Wyngaarden, HHS Secretary Louis Sullivan, and drug czar Bill Bennett all issued statements last Friday supporting medical researchers who must work with animals. Dr. David Hubel, of Harvard Medical School and 1981 winner of the Nobel Prize in medicine, has just sent a letter signed by twenty-nine other Nobel laureates, urging U.S. Surgeon General C. Everett Koop to speak out against these groups. Led by a multiple sclerosis victim, there is now a countergroup called Incurably Ill for Animal Research.

And of course, scientists rallied against the National Resources Defense Council's recent assault on the chemicals used to kill insects that prey on the U.S. food supply. The spectacle of schools protecting students from apples was too much even for the gullible. Now perhaps it's time to see through "animal rights," a clear and present danger to the health of us all.

Breakthroughs Don't Require Torture

STEPHEN ZAWISTOWSKI, SUZANNE E. ROY, STEPHEN KAUFMAN, and MARJORIE CRAMER

Your April 24 editorial "Animals and Sickness" perpetuates the false impression that recognition of animal rights will result in catastrophic levels of sickness and disease. Most people who seek protection of animals from abusive treatment would accept a good-faith effort by the biomedical establishment to improve conditions for research animals and increase efforts to develop nonanimal alternatives.

Asking the simplistic question, "Your child's health or a rat's life," is an insult to the many intelligent scientists, doctors, and citizens concerned about the medical-research practices. The real question is whether that rat (or mouse or dog or monkey) should be given a larger cage, better food and postoperative medication to alleviate pain; or whether the same information could have been collected using fewer animals, or none at all.

These letters appeared in the May 19, 1989 issue of the *Wall Street Journal* in response to the editorial "Animals and Sickness." Stephen Zawistowski is science adviser for the American Society for the Prevention of Cruelty to Animals; Suzanne E. Roy is a member of the Physicians Committee for Responsible Medicine; Stephen Kaufman, M.D., is the vice chairman of the Medical Research Modernization Committee; and Marjorie Cramer, M.D., is a fellow of the American College of Surgeons.

Biomedical researchers typically argue that research animals get adequate care as mandated by federal regulations, and that publicized examples of abuse are exceptions. It is difficult to verify such statements when access to animal-care facilities generally is denied to those interested in the well-being of the animals.

— Stephen Zawistowski

Brutal head-trauma experiments at two universities — in which the skulls of thousands of cats and primates were crushed — have been halted. Funding for drug-addiction experiments that subjected cats to the horrors of chemical withdrawal was returned by a researcher. In each case physicians and scientists joined animal advocates in criticizing the studies for their scientific irrelevance and cruelty. A military research project at another university involving hundreds of cats who are shot in the head continues, but it has been condemned by neurosurgeons and trauma experts, and as a result, the U.S. General Accounting Office is investigating.

In the worst cases, animal studies do not just hurt animals and waste money, they harm people too. The drugs thalidomide, Zomex, and DES were tested on animals, but had devastating consequences when humans used them. Just this week, the Food and Drug Administration warned doctors against the use of two heart drugs, Tambocor and Enkaid, which were thought to control irregular heartbeats but were found to actually kill human patients.

— Suzanne E. Roy

You grossly exaggerate the value of animal research. Contrary to scientists' self-serving interpretation of medical history, historian Brandon Reines has found that nearly every important advance in areas such as heart disease and cancer has come from human clinical investigation. While animal experiments had some value in the management of infectious diseases at the turn of the century, they have made little contribution since.

The development of modern research techniques, such as CAT scans, PET scans, needle biopsies, and tissue cultures, permit safe, ethical study of disease with human patients and tissues. This has rendered many uses of animals obsolete.

— Stephen Kaufman, M.D.

Where, may I ask, are the "breakthroughs" in drug addiction, cancer, and Alzheimer's disease that you attribute to animal research? They have not been presented in medical journals nor in the press. Billions are spent each year on medical and scientific "research," most of which is worthless. Many of the real breakthroughs have been a result of clinical work: observations in human patients.

The animal-rights movement is here to stay and has very wide grassroots support. The vast majority of the people involved are also working at "real jobs and raising their families" and are not professional activists as you imply.

While a few animal-rights activists have participated in terrorist attacks, the vast majority are opposed to such tactics.

— Marjorie Cramer, M.D.

"Have a good day at the lab, dear?"

THINKING AND WRITING
ABOUT ANIMAL RIGHTS

Questions for Discussion and Writing

1. What values do the antivivisectionists — Peter Singer and C. S. Lewis — appeal to? Might the same values be held by people on the other side of the issue? If so, which side seems to you to have the better right to make such appeals?

2. Elshtain summarizes all the abuses that animals suffer. Which does she seem to consider the most serious and most in need of elimination? What personal elements does she introduce to strengthen her argument?

3. Which issues do you think DeBakey argues most persuasively? Summarize his attack against animal-rights activists. Does he meet the objections of Elshtain?

4. What support does the *Wall Street Journal* editorial provide in arguing for animal research? Do the letter writers respond effectively to the editorial?

5. What assumptions underlie Limbaugh's contention that animals have no rights? What backing can you find for these assumptions? Would Singer and Lewis argue that animals have rights equal to those of human beings? Decide whether Adler's claims about superior human intelligence are relevant to Limbaugh's argument. What part, if any, does an aside about frog licking play in a debate on animal rights?

6. Some people believe that experimentation on animals unrelated to us, such as rats and rabbits, is acceptable but that experimentation on primates — rhesus monkeys and chimpanzees — is not. (Keep in mind that new rules for treatment of animals in the laboratory would apply only to dogs and primates.) Is there some point on the evolutionary scale when it becomes immoral to continue experimentation? To put it in more specific terms, is there a difference between experimentation on a chimpanzee and on a human being with very low intelligence? Explain your position as fully as possible.

7. If you have ever seen animals slaughtered for food, either on a farm or in a slaughterhouse, describe your reactions and explain whether the experience influenced your attitude toward eating meat.

8. The cartoonist's view of medical experimentation with animals is clear. Why would the opponents of this view regard the cartoon as unfair?

Topics for Research

The case for (or against) ethical vegetarianism

Federal laws governing use of animals in laboratories

Alternatives to animals in medical research

The case for (or against) animal sports — bullfighting, cockfighting, etc.

What the Bible tells us about the rights of animals

CHAPTER TWELVE

Children's Rights

The rights of children have recently climbed to the top of the national agenda. One reason is certainly the long-time advocacy of Hillary Rodham Clinton. But even before her arrival on the national scene, the mounting reports of child abuse and neglect, the increasing numbers of broken and dysfunctional families and teenage pregnancies, and a huge growth in the social work professions focused attention on the problems of our most helpless and vulnerable citizens.

In this country the movement to protect children from abuse, neglect, and exploitation is even older than the founding of the nation. From the days of colonial settlement children have enjoyed legal redress. In the seventeenth century punishment of rebellious children was extreme — the death penalty could be invoked for cursing or striking of parents — but early laws enjoined parents to refrain from undue cruelty to their children and, more important, allowed children to argue in their own defense against charges of insubordination. These laws, the Body of Liberties, based on English law, are described by one historian as "the first code anywhere in the world to offer legal protection of any kind to children."[1] But while they offered children some protection from abuse, they also introduced the power of the state in opposition to that of the parents. Today many of the controversies surrounding the rights of children reflect this often traumatic tug-of-war between the government and the parents in determining the welfare of the child. We see this clearly in the sensational battles that sometimes result when parents are accused — but not convicted — of abuse, and child-welfare officials remove the child from the home.

---

[1] Joseph M. Hawes, *The Children's Rights Movement* (Boston: Twayne, 1991), p. 5.

Perhaps it is not surprising that the movement of women and minorities for civil rights in the 1950s and 1960s should have reached into the world of children. Children, however, have never been regarded as equally entitled with adults to all the rights of citizenship. For the most part, both government and parents have always presumed to act as caretakers, to know the best interests of the child, and to speak on his or her behalf. This philosophy underlies the Fair Labor Standards Act of 1938, which made child labor under the age of sixteen illegal, except in certain nonhazardous occupations.

The presumption that adults know best has recently come under attack. In the 1970s a new movement of so-called child liberationists emerged, calling for relaxation of the distinctions between adults and children. The liberationists support the rights of children to "full participation in society" in every area — that is, the right to make their own choices in regard to education, sex, living arrangements, work, and finance.

Although the child liberationists remain at the extremes of the movement, several court cases have established new legal rights for children. In 1967 the Supreme Court extended to a fifteen-year-old offender the same rights of due process (in this case the right to be defended by a lawyer) available to adults. In 1992 Gregory Kinsley, a twelve-year-old boy, became the first child to hire his own lawyer. After a widely reported court case, he won the right to be adopted by a foster family rather than return to his biological mother, with whom he had spent only seven months of his last eight years. And a small number of states have allowed children to sue for "divorce" from their parents.

The movement for children's rights, while it has greatly increased protection for children who are at risk, has also raised troubling questions. Does the ready intervention of the state undermine the authority of the family and aggravate the very problems intervention is intended to solve? Do children, in fact, want the freedom to behave like adults? If so, at what age should they be empowered to enjoy the freedoms mentioned above? Finally, do expanded rights for children contribute to the well-being of the whole society?

Hillary's Children's Crusade
JOHN LEO

The Republican attempt to demonize Hillary Clinton is a shameful business. She is not a "radical feminist." She did not say that marriage is like slavery or the Indian reservation system. (She wrote that the

John Leo is a contributing editor to *U.S. News & World Report,* where this essay appeared on August 31, 1992.

relationship of child to parent, like that of wife to husband until modern times, has been a legal dependency relationship, in the same category of law as the relationship of slave to master — a prickly, but accurate, statement.)

Still, beneath the partisan attacks there lies an actual issue. It has to do with the conflict of advocates for "children's rights" (the belief that children should have an array of legally enforceable claims against parents and the adult world) versus traditionalists who believe that this is a sure-fire formula for undermining what's left of the American family.

In traditional terms, the family is a politically exempt institution into which the state should not intrude, except in instances of total breakdown (chiefly abuse and custody cases). Once you start talking about "the rights of children," of course, you inevitably arrive at very different conclusions about how families should operate. Parental authority begins to seem like an arbitrary constraint of the powerless by the powerful — something lawyers should step in and rectify, just as they do in other civil-rights cases.

Clinton's three articles on the subject, published between 1973 and 1978, were comparatively mild versions of what the children's rights movement wanted at the time. The midseventies were the high-water mark of the postsixties campaign against adult "oppression." Books like John Holt's *Escape from Childhood* called for the liberation of children from parents. New York University installed a course on children's liberation. A *Youth Liberation* magazine was publishing in Ann Arbor, and a Young People's Liberation movement began resistance to "ageism" at Berkeley High School in California. Children's liberation was widely assumed to be the logical successor to the other anti-authority liberation movements being codified in the seventies.

The Case for Chaos

Amid all this clamor, Clinton turned out three quietly reasoned 5 articles. Writing in the *New York Review of Books*, Garry Wills twice uses the word "radical" to describe Clinton's ideas. But the real radicals of the era were forever pounding the table and demanding full adult rights for all children. Clinton merely argued that courts should stop assuming that all children are legally incompetent until they suddenly become fully competent at age eighteen or twenty-one. She said courts and other tribunals should decide on a case-by-case basis, starting out with the presumption that children are competent to make their own major decisions unless proved otherwise.

Clinton is certainly right in arguing that some older teenagers are locked into dependency relationships long after they are ready to strike out on their own. But there's little sense of the enormous cost and conflict of measuring the competence levels of all children who would wish to haul parents into court. Clinton wants to limit these hearings to major matters, such as surgery, abortion, and school selection: "I prefer that intervention into an ongoing family be limited to decisions that could have long-term and possibly irreparable effects if they were not resolved." But there is no way of stopping ever more trivial cases coming to court. This would, I think, vastly increase the amount of family chaos and virtually guarantee full employment for the nation's lawyers.

Clinton is obviously dedicated and very smart, but there is something overly abstract and unsatisfying about these articles. Margaret O'Brien Steinfels, the editor of *Commonweal,* wrote that the most important of the three pieces was "historically and sociologically naive." Even allowing for the fact that these are law articles, there is no real acknowledgment of how families actually operate. In Clinton's pieces, functioning families are not organisms built around affection, restraint, and sacrifice. They seem to be arbitrary collections of isolated rights bearers chafing to be set free. And there is no real indication in her writing that what children want and what they need are often quite different.

In the world of public policy, the children's rights movement is still alive, but not thriving, largely because it is essentially irrelevant to the current crisis of the family. American children are not suffering from too much parental authority, but from far too little. Rich or poor, children are much more likely to be ignored and psychically abandoned than they are to be "oppressed" by parental fascists.

A great many people now understand that the rights approach will exacerbate friction in the home and open the door for lawyers, judges, bureaucrats, and "the helping professions" to make a further mess of the family. And some are worried about the character children would develop if granted the legal right to go their own way without interference. In her new book, *In Their Best Interest?: The Case Against Equal Rights for Children*, feminist author Laura Purdy argues that they would tend to grow up without self-control and restraint, which come from parental limits. She also thinks compulsory schooling would have to be eliminated. This is a brave new world we can do without. We already have enough problems.

Whose Babies?

THE WALL STREET JOURNAL

In Connecticut and Michigan there are two baby girls whose heart-wrenching stories are worth pondering. Both are caught up in legal battles between their adoptive parents and biological parents, who

---

This editorial appeared in the December 14, 1992 issue of the *Wall Street Journal.*

belatedly decided they wanted custody. In each case the law may be served at the expense of the best interests of the child.

The Connecticut baby is known as Angelica or Megan Marie, depending on which mother you talk to. Last week the state supreme court ruled that the eighteen-month-old youngster belongs to the nineteen-year-old woman who had abandoned her at birth, rather than to the couple with whom she had lived for eight months and who were in the process of adopting her.

Angelica-Megan Marie was born in New Haven on June 26, 1991. Her birth mother, Gina Pellegrino, who said she learned only that day that she was pregnant, walked out of the hospital ten hours after giving birth. In October, child welfare officials placed the abandoned infant for adoption with Cindy and Jerry LaFlamme. Some months later Ms. Pellegrino showed up with a lawyer, demanding her parental "rights," and in June a judge took the child away from the LaFlammes and gave her to Ms. Pellegrino.

Halfway across the country is another baby girl, this one twenty-two months old and known to the public only as "B.G.C." B.G.C. was born in Cedar Rapids, Iowa, on February 8, 1991. Cara Clausen signed away her parental rights, as did the man she named as the birth father. When she was only six days old, B.G.C. went home with her new mother and father, Jan and Roberta DeBoer of Ann Arbor, Michigan, who initiated adoption procedures.

Now, however, a man named Dan Schmidt has come forward, saying   5 he is B.G.C.'s true birth father. Ms. Clausen, whom he has subsequently married, agrees, and a blood test supports the claim. And so the biological parents, who live in Iowa, are suing to get "their" daughter back. An Iowa judge has ordered the DeBoers to give the child to the Schmidts. This is despite charges that Mr. Schmidt has ignored two children from previous marriages. The DeBoers have refused, and a Michigan judge ruled this month that they could keep the baby until January 5, when he will hold a hearing to determine the best interest of the child.

The best interest of the child. That is a concept that so far seems to be absent in both of these custody cases. It is, of course, what all child-welfare cases should be about. Instead, all too often they are about rights rather than responsibilities, about what parent is "entitled" to a child rather than where the child will be happiest and best cared for. The Connecticut judge who changed the life of Angelica-Megan Marie said the case was "narrowly focused on the parent or parents whose parental rights are at stake" and that the adoptive parents "have no right to intervene."

Psychologists counsel adoptive parents to tell their children not that their birth mothers "gave you away" but that they "made another plan for you." There's something to this. It suggests that in choosing adoption, a birth mother acts out of love, that she is taking responsibility for the life of the child she brought into the world.

The adoption option is not a popular one in our society, where 26 in every 100 pregnancies end in abortion. Only about 2 percent of babies born to never-married mothers are placed for adoption. Few pro-life groups have done much to encourage adoption as an alternative to abortion.

And what of Angelica-Megan Marie and B.G.C.? Will the law permit them to be taken from the only parents they have ever known and be placed with birth parents who had previously renounced them? The LaFlammes haven't decided whether to appeal the decision that took Angelica-Megan Marie away from them; they aren't sure they can face another failure. B.G.C. will be the subject of more legal battles in Iowa and Michigan before her case is decided. And so the law grinds on and two more young lives get ground up in it.

Excerpt from Guardianship of Phillip Becker
SUPERIOR COURT OF SANTA CLARA COUNTY

A great criticism of the Beckers has been their refusal of life-prolonging surgery for Phillip. This decision of the Beckers was made while Phillip was [a]n infant. The only ostensible reason for their decision was the parental label that the Beckers applied to him at an early age of incurable defect and family burden. How do children ever escape the labeling of their parents? How do they overcome the life and death decisions parents make for them? How does a child in Phillip's situation ever have a voice on the question of his right to surgery to prolong his life? By the time he is an adult, it is too late. I have written earlier of a neighbor child with cerebral palsy, spasticity, presumed to be mentally retarded. She was cared for at home by her mother and given the best of care. She is reasonably normal, healthy, happy, and in college. An-

---

Phillip Becker, a victim of Down's syndrome, was placed at birth in an institution, rarely visited by his biological parents, and denied surgery for a life-threatening condition. The Heaths, who had met the child in the institution and wanted to provide a loving home for him, sued for custody. The Beckers refused to relinquish their parental rights, and a six-year legal battle ensued before the Heaths were awarded guardianship of Phillip and could permit the surgery to take place. As pointed out elsewhere in the court decision, two legal doctrines were in conflict: "On the one hand, the historically venerated 'parental rights' doctrine, and on the other hand, the more recently emerging doctrine of 'best interests of the child.'"

This excerpt is from the 1981 decision of the *Phillip Becker* case, handed down from the Superior Court of Santa Clara County, California.

other parent close to the court had a son afflicted at birth with an abnormal brain spiking. It took thousands of hours and thousands of dollars and a host of doctors and private schooling to cure him. He is now a normal, healthy adult working and living a socially useful life. Another neighbor has a Down's child. She tried in vain to keep her at home and care for her there but to her ever-lasting grief, her efforts did not succeed and the child had to be institutionalized. In every neighborhood in every city in our country, there are stories like these, and in most of these neighborhoods, the heartwarming part of the story is the same: Dedicated parents are doing the best possible job for their children. No court of any county could have told them what to do or how to do it for their children. What if some parents fail in their efforts? Should they be faulted by some court or judge and their children taken from them? The answer to that is no. There is no court that can make those tough family decisions I have described, and no court should. It is basically for the family and for good parents to make the decisions for the family. Why then deprive the Beckers of custody of Phillip? Is it because of their inattention to the surgical needs of Phillip? The surgery refusal is only a small part of the reason. The primary reason is found in the soul of the case. Whenever a child with the unique problems of Phillip Becker surfaces into the legal system asking for life-prolonging surgery, for habilitation, and a place in society, the court, which is the great moral force of the community and the protector of individual rights and liberty, must make a choice. Do we do as the Spartan Greeks and abandon such infants onto the nearest mountain? Unthinkable. Do we agree with parental decisions to warehouse them and let them rust because mother and father know best, leaving our judicial hands in the waters of parental authority and turning our backs to the developmentally disabled supplicant who is before us like Pontius Pilate? Or do we say that the developmentally disabled are entitled to the same rights as everyone else; that they are entitled to habilitation, entitled to avoid the stigmatization of being mentally ill, entitled to a life worth living, and entitled to a chance at entering into our great society?

The Politics of Child Abuse
WILLIAM NORMAN GRIGG

No impulse is nobler than the desire to protect children. It should come as a surprise to nobody that one of the consequences of moral decline is an increase in the abuse and neglect of children. However,

William Norman Grigg is the author of the forthcoming *The Gospel of Revolt: Feminism versus the Family.* His article appeared in the September 7, 1992 issue of *The New American.*

the escalation of child abuse statistics has been accompanied by an increase in the power and presumption of child "protection" agencies. The American family finds itself bracketed between a degenerate social order that promotes sexual irresponsibility and a growing state that readily disrupts families on the basis of spurious accusations.

There have been many recent episodes that illustrate how the "benevolent" state has used the issue of child abuse to amplify government power and justify the suspension of basic rights. . . .

The Case of Jim Wade

Jim Wade of San Diego is a victim of parent abuse. One evening in 1989, Wade's eight-year-old daughter was abducted from her bed, raped, then returned before dawn. Albert Raymond Carder, a confessed child molester who had haunted Wade's neighborhood, was taken into custody shortly after the incident. Nevertheless, the San Diego County Department of Social Services acted on an almost automatic assumption that Jim Wade had raped his daughter.

The child, who had already endured the unspeakable trauma of abduction and sexual violation, was again forcibly removed from her home — this time by the state. She underwent thirteen months of torturous "therapy" administered by Kathleen Goodfriend of the La Mesa Village counseling group. Finally, the girl relented and accused her father of raping her. After Wade was arrested, a DNA test proved that he could not have been the assailant (although the confessed molester could have been). He was cleared of the charges, but his family was nonetheless burdened with a $260,000 debt for legal services and foster care.

Speaking of Wade's case, Gloria Peters of the San Diego chapter of 5 VOCAL (Victims of Child Abuse Laws) said, "The juvenile court system suspects all parents who come to their attention, even if they don't have evidence. They try to make the children create evidence." Nor does the child "protection" bureaucracy recognize its own fallibility. Remarks Wade, "The people responsible [for his family's trauma] have never even apologized — and they can never apologize enough." . . .

Writing in the March 1992 issue of *Chronicles,* C. Winsor Wheeler offers a chilling synopsis of present circumstances:

> In many of our supposedly "free states," the mere allegation of "child abuse" is now sufficient completely to suspend the constitutional rights of any parent unlucky enough to be so charged. An anonymous phone call is often all it takes to set social services in motion, and in many scenarios the accused is never allowed to face the accuser. The state's inquisition of experts takes over, at times extracting "evidence" from confused children via cruel brainwashing techniques and dragging families through the dungeons of a psychological hell, regardless whether they are really guilty, merely misunderstood, or entirely innocent. . . .

In the July 1992 issue of *Reason,* K. L. Billingsley summarized a report entitled "Families in Crisis" that was produced by a grand jury investigation of the Jim Wade case in San Diego. The report concluded that the child-protection system avails itself of "confidential files, closed courts, gag orders, and statutory immunity" and has "isolated itself to a degree unprecedented in our system of jurisprudence." The grand jury declared that social workers often "lie routinely, even when under oath in court," and frequently disobey court orders. There are also instances in which social workers, with no constitutional mandate or political accountability, retaliate against uncooperative family members with threats of investigations or the denial of visitation privileges.

Many, perhaps most, of those involved in the child-protection movement are animated by a transparently sincere desire to promote the welfare of children. However, some elements of that movement are dominated by feminist assumptions about the "dysfunctional" nature of the traditional family. Further, child-abuse activism has done much to harm the constitutional immunities of the accused — and to expand the reach of the "benevolent" state. . . .

Visionary Pedophiles

Observers of the current child abuse issue may be amazed to learn that some "children's rights" activists have urged the legalization of child sex, including adult-child sexual relations. The arguments submitted by pedophiles and their apologists are rooted in a rejection of the nuclear family. They partake of a sensibility similar to that which characterizes some contemporary child-protection activists.

In the early 1980s, much was made of a group of scholars and 10 activist that composed the "incest lobby." Attention was drawn to this group by a report written by researcher James Ramey for the Sex Information and Education Council of the United States (SIECUS). Ramey's report, which was entitled "Dealing with the Last Taboo," claimed that there were "healthy" situations in which incest is "an obviously appropriate behavior" and that "incest seldom has anything to do with sexually 'perverse' behavior." Ramey claimed to have found several families in which "consent openly allowed active, sophisticated lifestyles which included sexual sharing." . . .

Writing in the March 1980 issue of *Psychology Today,* Benjamin DeMott noted, "Some of the new permissivists seem actually to have succeeded in presenting themselves as defenders of the family — persons with remedies for the divorce rate, runaway children, teenage pregnancy, drunkenness, and the like." The April 14, 1980 issue of *Time* concurred with DeMott's observation, adding, "One strain of [the incest lobby] springs from the fringes of the children's rights movement, which insists that small children be granted all the rights of adults. Some have taken that to mean the right to be sexually active with any partner at all." An example of this "liberationist" concept was provided by Larry Constantine, an assistant clinical psychologist at Tufts University, who asserted, "Children have the right to express themselves sexually, even with members of their own family."

Writing in the Spring 1989 issue of the *Journal of Sex Education and Therapy,* Joan Nelson of the Center for Sexual Concerns proposed a "continuum model" for "participants in intergenerational sexual contact." Peeling away the rind of euphemistic language, we find that Nelson was seeking some way to separate "visionary" child molesters from "pathological" and "pedophilic" ones. Nelson defines the "visionary" pedophile as one who "gives the child love that is not conditional upon sex and participates in sexual contact not for her or his own gratification, but in response to a child's attempts to acquire practical knowledge." Of course, we are required to accept the molester's assessment of his own intentions. Nelson believes that child molestation is "visionary" when placed in the context of "progressive" politics. Visionaries advocate "children's rights to work, to vote, to legal counsel, and to legal emancipation before age eighteen. Many visionaries believe the troubles that characterize our times are rooted in childhood sexual repression that prohibits age-free expression of sexual affection." . . .

Incest and Child Abuse

Even some of those who agitate on behalf of victims of child-sex abuse can support some forms of incest. The book *Conspiracy of Silence* by Sandra Butler is considered a watershed volume by contemporary child-abuse activists. Butler collected first-person accounts from both victims and perpetrators of incestuous assault. But Butler's disapproval of incest is not categorical. She declares: "In the dictionary incest is defined as sexual intercourse between closely related persons where marriage is legally forbidden. This can and does include consensual relationships between adults, most often brothers and sisters, and consensual relationships among children within a family who are engaging in sexual play and experimentation."

Butler concentrated on "nonconsensual" incest, meaning "behavior that an adult family member imposes on a child, who is unable to alter or understand the adult's behavior because of his or her powerlessness in the family and early stage of psychological development. This type of incest is nonconsensual because the child has not yet developed an understanding of sexuality that allows him or her to make a free and fully conscious response to the adult's behavior." This begs the following question: Would Butler consider a sexual liaison between an adult and a "sexually aware" child to be consensual?

Like many secularist child-abuse activists, Butler considers child-sex abuse to be an issue of power relationships, not one of moral principle. Thus, an incestuous assault by a father upon a young daughter is evil not because it violates an eternal principle of the moral law but because it involves the exploitation of a power disparity. Traditionalists object to both the moral violation and the exploitation of the assault; Butler, who is indifferent regarding "consensual" incest, has no use for moral distinctions.

Battling Moral Values

From Butler's perspective, sexual abuse involves "the full range of damaging sexual attitudes and behaviors imposed on children by adults. . . ." Those "damaging" sexual attitudes include the Judeo-Christian principles of sexual fidelity and chastity. For Butler, the task of preventing sexual abuse of children is inseparable from the battle against the "patriarchy":

> I have found it imperative to examine the larger issue of male-dominated family systems in the context of a male-defined society and its assumptions about sex roles and expectations. . . . [M]ale sexual aggression is an outgrowth of the patriarchal nature of male/female relationships in every aspect of our lives. . . . We, too, damage our children when we fail to respect their human rights. . . .

For secular child-abuse agencies and activists, child abuse is wrong because it is "exploitive," not because it is immoral. Much child-abuse activism, whether it takes place among children or adult "survivors," is animated by a desire to "emancipate" children from the "oppressive" nuclear family. Lynne D. Finney, author of *Reach for the Rainbow* (another resource book for "survivors") insists, "Children should be allowed to sue their parents, and the outmoded policy permitting corporal punishment should be eliminated."

Hillary Clinton has long contended that children should be considered legally emancipated and competent to press legal claims against their parents. On July 9, a judge in Orlando, Florida followed a similar line of reasoning in ruling that an eleven-year-old boy can sue to "divorce" his parents.

The destruction of parental authority has been an objective of subversives for centuries. Progressive opinion consistently supports the abolition of "exploitive" parental authority. Such abolitionists are perfectly capable of supporting "visionary" incest on one occasion and persecuting innocent parents through spurious accusations of abuse in the next.

Dignifying Depravity

Contemporary sex education places a premium upon prurience. 20 According to Suetonius, the Roman Emperor Nero "was convinced that nobody could remain chaste . . . but that most people concealed their secret vices; hence, if anyone confessed to obscene practices, Nero forgave him all his other crimes."

Nero's belief was congruent with the approach taken by Alfred Kinsey and his disciples, who have sought to dignify the depraved as perfectly normal. In a society saturated with salaciousness, is it any surprise that children are precociously promiscuous? Is it not predictable that children will "act out sexually" because of exposure to pornographic and sexually abusive "educational" materials? Is it strange that some adults become addicted to deviant sexual practices and seek to become "visionary" child molesters?

Like the "war" against drugs, the crusade against child abuse is a nobel cause conscripted into the service of disreputable ends. We cannot allow our desire to protect children to become perverted into a crusade against the family. Child abusers should be identified, prosecuted, and punished, but constitutional guarantees and immunities must be respected. Empirical evidence, not the ruminations of "experts," must be used to establish guilt. And society must take effective measures against pornography, which includes "educational" efforts of groups like SIECUS.

Child Protection;
Children's Rights

HOWARD COHEN

Children are surely the most vulnerable and powerless people in our society. Although this is in some sense not terribly controversial, we have great difficulty coming to grips with its full meaning. We regularly obscure, minimize, ignore, and even deny this fact. We do so by reminding ourselves that children are loved by adults, cared for, protected, treated specially, guided, prized, and praised. While this is all more or less true for many, perhaps most, children most of the time, it speaks not at all to vulnerability and powerlessness. For children are loved and reared as adults see fit; they are literally at the mercy of adults. (Mercy, after all, is given from love, not obligation.) No matter how much adults do for children — no matter how much kindness and goodwill we express — what is done is done on adult terms. Children may not *demand* anything of us. At most other adults (or the state)

Howard Cohen, a professor of philosophy, is dean of the School of Liberal Arts at the University of Wisconsin–Parkside and the author of *Equal Rights for Children* (1980), from which this excerpt is taken.

may require this or that *for* a child, but children may only request; they may not insist.

The essential powerlessness of children is nowhere more apparent than in the matter of child abuse. Most people see the helplessness of children most clearly and react most strongly when adults — parents especially — are violent toward children or sexually assault them. This has been particularly apparent in official and public reaction to recent reports of child abuse.

In Massachusetts, for example, three recent, widely reported cases in which children died at the hands of their parents have severely shaken the public welfare bureaucracy and the general populace. Although these cases were quite grotesque, and no doubt not typical, examples of child abuse, they nevertheless have helped people to see the larger dimensions of the problem. . . .

What is to be learned from these horrors? First, I suppose, that we may not rely on "parental instinct" to protect children from harm. When we call something an instinct we mean it is ingrained in all parents and it will come through in the end. But if some parents don't have this deep sense of protection and care for their offspring, or if these feelings and impulses break down under stress, then the point of the label "instinct" is lost. The question then becomes who has it and who doesn't — and we'd better find out if our aim is to prevent child abuse. The very existence of parents who have brutalized their children shows that we would be kidding ourselves if we thought that nature has provided for this problem.

A second lesson brought home by these cases is that child abuse 5 is *much* more widespread than we would like to admit. As stories of abused children became public knowledge, people demanded to know why these abusive parents were not detected before their children were dead. Why was there no early warning and intervention? Such questions, coupled with new and stronger abuse reporting laws, lead to closer looks and more discoveries. Case workers are now being trained to find and deal with child abuse; they report that they do not have far to look. In fact the magnitude of the problem is steadily being revised upward as researchers investigate more carefully. A recent report estimated that *2 million* American children are abused each year. The investigator himself regarded this figure as low.)[1] Two million people is roughly the population of Philadelphia.

A third lesson is that child abuse can no longer be treated as merely a psychological problem. Abusive parents have psychological problems to be sure. But it is not enough to say that they are unbalanced, abnormal, weak of will, irresponsible, or whatever. Even if this is all

---

[1]*Boston Globe,* November 21, 1978, p. 14.

true, the fact remains that there are no *structures* in the family, the community, or the larger society to put the brakes on troubled adults. The fact that there are 2 million abused children does not point to a few deviants who slipped through the cracks. It shows that our social institutions do not have adequate structures or mechanisms to keep potential abusers in check or make them change their ways.

This is a very important point, and its full importance is not easy to grasp. If psychological help for abusive parents is not an adequate response to the problem, then we must be ready to accept the idea that dealing with child abuse will mean changing the structures of all relationships between adults and children — not merely the bad ones. If we cannot say in advance which adults are likely to abuse children and which are not, then we cannot reduce child abuse by treating parental problems case by case. We would be too late — and probably do too little as well. To treat the problem seriously, then, we would have to find a way to build checks against child abuse into all our relationships with children. In other words, child abuse would no longer be somebody else's problem; its solution would affect us all. . . .

The dominant thrust of concern for the treatment of children in contemporary America has been for more "care taking." In response to a perceived need for more structure in adult-child relationships, those with the caretaker outlook have sought new ways to protect children from real and potential abuses. Caretakers have been responsible for institutionalizing compulsory education, limitations on child labor, laws prohibiting child abuse and neglect, aid to families with dependent children, school lunch programs, infant health programs, some public support for day care, and so on.

The caretaker conception of child protection has been around for quite some time. Indeed, it was clearly and eloquently expressed by John Locke in the *Second Treatise of Government* (1691). There he characterizes the relationship between parent and child as follows:

> Adam was created a perfect man, his body and mind in full possession of their strength and reason, and so was capable from the first instant of his being to provide for his own support and preservation and govern his actions according to the dictates of the law of reason which God had implanted in him. From him the world is peopled with his descendants who are all born infants, weak and helpless, without knowledge or under-standing; but to supply the defects of this imperfect state till the improve-ment of growth and age has removed them, Adam and Eve, and after them all parents, were by the law of nature "under an obligation to preserve, nourish, and educate the children" they had begotten; not as their own workmanship, but the workmanship of their own Maker, the Almighty, to whom they were to be accountable for them.[2]

---

[2] John Locke, *Second Treatise of Government* (Indianapolis: Bobbs-Merrill, 1952), p. 33.

This passage contains most of the important elements of what we are calling the caretaker conception of child protection.

Children are not merely property. Notice first that the children 10 belong to God. In Locke's view, a view commonly held in the seventeenth century, the fruits of a person's labor were that person's private property. Under the circumstances, it would be quite reasonable to think of one's children as one's property. This is specifically rejected by making children God's property. Parents are to take care of children for God. This is part of the moral and spiritual function of the modern family. The child must be raised to live the sort of life which is pleasing to God. Locke says this is a life in accordance with the "dictates of the law of reason."

Children have their own futures. As God's property, the child has a life of his or her own, for God does not regard us as his commodities. In the first place, I suppose, He has no need of commodities. But more to the point, seventeenth-century spirituality saw God's work as the creation of an orderly, well-governed universe in which each independent part was in harmony with all the others. God's children, then, were destined to take their place in the moral and social order as individuals and not merely in service to some larger unit (the family). This gave them a present status as potential independent beings. But one cannot overstress that the independence was potential.

Children lack human capacities, but not humanity. "Children are born weak and helpless, without knowledge and understanding." In short, they do not yet have what is required to be a being pleasing to God. They do not have the reason which would enable them to live under the law of reason. They are in need of care. Locke says they are born to a state of equality, but not in a state of equality. The point to notice here is that things can turn out well or badly. There are no guarantees that the weak infant will become the reasoning adult. Parents must take steps to see that the "improvement of growth and age" actually come about.

The child's weakness is a source of parental authority which in turn is a source of parental obligation. As a result, parents are under an obligation to "preserve, nourish, and educate" their children. This is not a choice they have. It comes with the job of being a caretaker. The obligation is not to the child, but to God. Therefore, the child may not refuse the services or release them from their obligation. So while the protection of the child is for the child's own good, its principal justification is that God has an interest in order and social harmony. This brings us to the last main element of the caretaker ideology.

Parents can know and do what is best for children. The best interests of the child, the parent, and of the society at large are perceived to be harmony. No doubt, this was easier to believe when people thought that God orchestrated the world order, but the assumption remains a part of the beliefs about child protection. It is in the interest of the child to become a well-developed adult; it is in the interest of society to have a new generation of well-developed adults; and it is in the interest of the parents to bring their caretaking obligations to a satisfactory end and to give a good account of themselves. Thus, there are, in theory, no built-in conflicts in childrearing. Should a parent prove to do a poor job of caretaking, it is never explained by a conflict of interests. Rather, the parent is regarded as unfit: unable to pursue the child's interests, and hence unable to pursue his or her own interests either.

Although the caretaker ideology was clearly articulated by Locke almost three hundred years ago, its acceptance has been quite gradual. The view that Providence still has more to do with a child's life than parental effort does did not disappear easily. Indeed, it is still believed in some quarters today. So the battle for a child's right to protection has been the battle to bring those inclined to leave events to God or the Seasons to recognize and assume their powers over their children's lives. This, I think, helps to account for the moralistic and missionary tone of most child care manuals before Dr. Spock's. They are aimed at parents who are not only presumed to want information, but who are assumed to be unaware of the seriousness of childrearing.

The caretaker approach to children's vulnerability is pretty clearly to structure more responsibility into the parental role. Where parents do not, cannot, or will not assume that responsibility, the state does so (acting in their place as parent). In short, there is no effort to diminish the vulnerability and powerlessness of children, but only to buffer them from the potential consequences of their condition. When things get worse for children, caretakers respond with larger doses of protection.

The caretaker conception of how to relate to children has come under severe attack in the last few years. The problem is that in the course of protecting children we have stunted the fullness of our relationship to them and have slighted them as people. Consider the remarks of three well-known advocates for American youth:

> I wish to pose a question that has preoccupied me for the past couple of years: Do we Americans *really* like children?
>
> After considerable reflection, I suggest that the answer is: Yes, *if* our sentiments are to be taken as evidence. Yes, we do like children, and even love them — if the test is in the values we profess and in the myths we cherish, celebrate, and pass on from generation to generation. However, I am prepared to assert that in spite of our tender sentiments, we do *not* really like children. We do not as a nation really love them in practice, and I am sure that all of you will agree that what we do must finally provide the evidence that answers the question.[3]
>
> — Kenneth Keniston

> Our world is not a good place for children. Every institution in our society severely discriminates against them. We all come to feel that it is

---

[3] Kenneth Keniston, "Change the Victims — Or the Society?," in Beatrice and Ronald Gross, eds., *The Children's Rights Movement* (New York: Anchor Press, 1977), p. 232.

either natural or necessary to cooperate in that discrimination. Unconsciously, we carry out the will of a society which holds a limited and demeaned view of children and which refuses to recognize their right to full humanity.[4]

— Richard Farson

For a long time it never occurred to me to question [modern childhood]. Only in recent years did I begin to wonder whether there might be other or better ways for young people to live. By now I have come to feel that the fact of being a "child," of being seen by older people as a mixture of expensive nuisance, slave, and super-pet, does most young people more harm than good.[5]

— John Holt

These criticisms are grounded in an alternative to the caretaker conception of the treatment of children. We are invited to consider not only the sad stories but also the lot of the typical child. If some children are brutalized, it is partly because all children are demeaned or at least not respected. Improvement for the worst off can not be separated from improvement for the rest. The new child advocates are no longer saying that we do not do enough for our children; they are saying that we are doing the wrong things. Richard Farson divides child advocates into two groups: "On the one hand there are those who are interested in protecting children, and on the other those who are interested in protecting children's rights."[6] He regards the first group as "paternalistic," and places himself in the second, which is more interested in liberation than protection. What it would mean to liberate children is, of course, a long story. But the point here is that it is also a new story. It marks a departure from the aims of more traditional child advocates. The new advocates tend to think of children more as an oppressed minority than as a collection of small and helpless beings, some of whom are, sadly, ill treated. . . .

The new child advocates . . . see the standard, normal, socially acceptable treatment of children as part of the problem. It is the very institution of American childhood which they are attacking. In other words, they are saying that our fundamental ways of relating to children are inadequate, and that we must restructure them. This is a criticism which none of us may escape. We are denied our indignation at the failures of others; we may take no comfort in our own good intentions or kindly feelings toward children. As adults in a society which oppresses children, we are part of the problem.

As a society we have come to understand that there is not only 20 personal bigotry, but institutional racism; not only male chauvinism, but economic and social discrimination against women. We are now being asked to acknowledge that there is not only child abuse, but

---

[4] Richard Farson, *Birthrights* (New York: Macmillan, 1974), p. 1.

[5] John Holt, *Escape from Childhood* (New York: E. P. Dutton, 1974), p. 1.

[6] Farson, op. cit., p. 9.

systematic mistreatment of children. The comparison is harsh and likely to be misunderstood. It is important not to take this as merely an occasion to spread a little blame or to make people feel guilty for their social institutions. If our aim is social change, the real point of comparing children to black people and women is to give "movement status" to the various efforts to change and improve children's lives. . . .

The common threads which unite advocates of a new relationship with children are, first, a deep dissatisfaction with the basic assumptions of the caretaker outlook, and second, a conviction that children must be treated more like adults in certain respects.

Caretakers tend to treat children's rights exclusively in terms of protection. Children's rights advocates, however, see at least three assumptions which the child protectionists make which are regarded as suspect. The first of these is that adults are able to perceive what is in a child's best interest. When we are dealing with other adults, we tend to acknowledge that each individual is the best judge of her or his own best interests. This, of course, is not always true. Some people are hopeless when it comes to seeing their own best interest. They always manage to do the thing which puts them at the greatest disadvantage or makes them most unhappy. But this is the exception; and even for them it is easier to say what is not in their best interest than to say what is. It is very hard to be confident about how another person perceives a situation, and to be sure that you have taken all the factors which are important to them into account. So we tend to take their word for it when they say that something is or is not in their interest. What we lack in knowledge to make those judgments, they compensate for in intuitions about themselves.

We do not make similar concessions to children, however. They are not presumed to have a sufficiently developed set of intuitions about themselves, or a sufficient awareness of what is important to them to make even roughly accurate judgments about their own self-interest. Now while this may be true, and certainly is true for many children, it is not true for all children. But what is more to the point is that a child's ignorance of her or his own self-interest does not improve the adult's knowledge of that child's best interest. The adult is in the same position with respect to the child that he or she is with respect to any other person. All of the difficulties about making a judgment for another remain. While it is not obvious what one should do in this situation, it is at least clear that the child protectionists have assumed that they have a kind of knowledge which it is doubtful that they really do have. And this assumption itself is a potential source of the disintegration of the quality of child care.

The second problem with the caretaker ideology is that it obscures the possibility of a conflict of interest between child and adult. This is partly a consequence of the first point. If the child is disregarded as a judge of her or his own best interest, then expressions of conflict coming from the child will not be taken seriously. Furthermore, the very adults who are engaged in the conflict are usually the adults who determine what the child's best interest is. And it is obviously in *their* interest to deny the conflict. But this is only part of the problem with the assumption of social harmony among adults and children.

What makes the assumption of a community of interest among children and their caretaking adults plausible in the first place is the belief that the interests of both are tied to the interest of a larger unit, for example, the family, which they share in common. Thus, if John Jones acts in his best interest as a father, he is acting in the best interest of all the other family members. If John Jones were only a father, there would be no problem here other than trying to decide what actually is in the best interest of the family. However, John Jones has other social attachments. He is an employee, an organization member, a neighbor, a friend, and so on. In each of these capacities, he has interests — and these interests do not always coincide with his interests as father. Likewise, his children have other social attachments: student, organization member, neighbor, friend. They too have interests which may not coincide with their interests as family members. In complex societies where one's family is not the only or sometimes even the most important group to which one belongs, it is not very plausible to assume that the interests of adults and children will always be in harmony. Again, it is the refusal to recognize these potential conflicts and to think about how to deal with them which children's rights advocates perceive as a source of poor-quality child care inherent in the child-protection ideology.

The third assumption which the new children's rights advocates challenge is the assumption that the quality of care can be improved by passing control over children from adult to adult. In this way, the question of whether the control over the child is itself a problem never arises. Adults as a general rule object to being treated paternalistically — that is, in the ways that parents treat their children. There are instances in which we accept a measure of paternalism, to be sure. Motorcyclists are required to wear helmets for their own protection. But for the most part, we only accept this in cases of serious social concern, or as a last resort. The reason for this is that paternalism tends to undermine one's sense of dignity. The presumption is that the person who is the object of control cannot be reasoned with — cannot be brought to see his or her best interest. And while we agreed that this sometimes happens, to make a regular presumption of it is to deny a person all of the opportunities by which one's dignity is established. Without being able to take control over one's actions, one cannot take credit for them. Here, too, children's rights advocates find the ideology of child protection lacking.

I have outlined these criticisms not so much to establish the deficiencies of child protection as to explain the context in which child advocates are now demanding equal rights for children. The debate over the accuracy of the assumptions still lies before us. And it is clear that we will have to evaluate the virtues and defects of protection as they arise in the discussion of particular rights. For it is fairly specific rights which the child advocates have in mind. Two of the writers who have been clearest about this are Richard Farson and John Holt. Farson makes self-determination the basic right: "Children should have the right to decide matters that affect them most directly." Whatever is needed to make this possible — to reduce the control that adults have over the lives of children — Farson would specify as a child's right. Holt takes the position that children should have "the right to do, in general, what any adult may legally do." Since adults are presumed to be self-determining in this society, this way of putting it comes to pretty much the same thing.

What child advocates want is an end of legal and social discrimination against children in most areas of life. The extent of the program is best captured in one of the numerous bills of rights which have been proposed for children. The rights enumerated by Farson in *Birthrights* typify the sorts of things that the advocates have in mind:

1. The Right to Self-determination. Children should have the right to decide matters that affect them most directly.
2. The Right to Alternate Home Environments. Self-determining children should be able to choose from among a variety or arrangements: residences operated by children, child-exchange programs, twenty-four-hour child-care centers, and various kinds of schools and employment opportunities.
3. The Right to Responsive Design. Society must accommodate itself to children's size and to their need for safe space.
4. The Right to Information. A child must have the right to all information ordinarily available to adults — including, and perhaps especially, information that makes adults uncomfortable.
5. The Right to Educate Oneself. Children should be free to design their own education, choosing from among many options the kinds of learning experiences they want, including the option not to attend any kind of school.
6. The Right to Freedom from Physical Punishment. Children should live free of physical threat from those who are larger and more powerful than they.
7. The Right to Sexual Freedom. Children should have the right to conduct their sexual lives with no more restriction than adults.
8. The Right to Economic Power. Children should have the right to work, to acquire and manage money, to receive equal pay for equal work, to choose trade apprenticeship as an alternative to school, to gain promotion to leadership positions, to own property, to develop a credit record, to enter into binding contracts, to engage in enterprise, to obtain guaranteed support apart from the family, to achieve financial independence.
9. The Right to Justice. Children must have the guarantee of a fair

trial with due process of law, an advocate to protect their rights against parents as well as the system, and a uniform standard of detention.[7]

There is no denying that these are radical proposals which would have far-reaching consequences for American society. There is an overwhelming temptation to plunge into the list and try to imagine what life would be like if children had such rights. This temptation is only a little less powerful than the temptation to reject these suggestions out of hand as the product of a hopeless idealist. I think for the present we should resist both of these temptations, and ask instead what it means to demand these things for children as *rights*.

Juvenile Justice
Is Delinquent

RITA KRAMER

Anyone who reads newspapers or watches TV is familiar with scenes of urban violence in which the faces of those who rob and rape, maim and kill get younger and younger. On the streets, in the subways, and even in the schools, juvenile crime has taken on a character unthinkable when the present justice system was set up to deal with it. That system, like so many of the ambitious social programs designed in the sixties, has had unintended results. Instead of solving society's ills, it has added to them.

The juvenile justice system now in place in most parts of the country is not very different from New York's Family Court. Originally conceived to protect children (defined by different states as those under age sixteen, seventeen, or eighteen) who ran afoul of the law, it was designed to function as a kind of wise parent providing rehabilitation.

The 1950s delinquent, who might have been a shoplifter, a truant, or a car thief, would not be treated like an adult criminal. He was held to be, in the wording of the New York statute, "not criminally responsible . . . by reason of infancy." He would be given a hearing (not a trial) closed to the press and public and the disposition (not a sentence) would remain sealed, so the juvenile would not be stigmatized by youthful indiscretion. The optimistic belief was that under the guidance of social workers he would undergo a change of character.

---

[7]Richard Farson, "A Child's Bill of Rights," in Gross and Gross, op. cit., pp. 325–28.

Rita Kramer, author of *At a Tender Age: Violent Youth and Juvenile Justice* (1988), is a frequent contributor to the *Wall Street Journal,* where this article appeared on May 27, 1992.

Legal Aid Lawyers

It was a dream destined to become a nightmare. In the early 1960s, the character of juvenile court proceedings underwent a radical transformation. Due process was interpreted to grant youthful "respondents" (not defendants) not only the services of a lawyer, but also the protections the criminal justice system affords adults, who are liable to serious penalties if found guilty.

In the hands of Legal Aid Society lawyers (and sometimes sympathetic judges), the juvenile system focuses on the minutiae of procedural technicalities at the expense of fact-finding, in order to achieve the goal of "getting the kid off." The question is not whether a teenage boy has beaten up a homeless old man, shot a storekeeper, or sodomized a little girl. He may even admit the act. The question is whether his admission can be invalidated because a police officer forgot to have him initial his responses to the Miranda warnings in the proper place or whether the arresting officer had probable cause to search him for the loaded gun that was found on him.

It has become the lawyer's job not only to protect his young client from punishment but from any possibility of rehabilitation in the system's various facilities. The best interests of the child or adolescent have been reinterpreted to mean his legal rights, even when the two are in opposition. He now has the right to continue the behavior that brought him into the juvenile court, which he leaves with the knowledge that his behavior had no real negative consequences to him.

Even when there are consequences, they are mild indeed, a fact not lost on his peers. Eighteen months in a facility that usually has TV, a basketball court, and better food and medical care than at home is the worst that all but the most violent repeat offenders have to fear in New York. The system, based on a person's age and not his crimes, fails either to restrain or retrain him.

As juvenile courts were changing, so were juvenile criminals. As recently as the early seventies, the majority of cases before children's and family courts were misdemeanors. In New York City, the most common charge was "jostling," pickpocketing without physical contact. By 1991, robbery — a charge that involves violence against people — had outpaced drug-related offenses as the largest category of crimes by juveniles. Between 1987 and 1991, the fastest-growing crime by juveniles was loaded-gun possession, and metal detectors and spot police checks had become routine in some inner-city high schools.

Cases of violent group assault — "kids" causing serious physical injury "for fun" — had increased dramatically. Predatory behavior was becoming a form of entertainment for some of the urban young, white as well as black and Hispanic. Last year, according to Peter Reinharz, chief of New York City's Family Court Division, 85 percent of the young offenders brought into Family Court were charged with felonies. "These are dangerous people," Mr. Reinharz says. "We hardly ever see the nonviolent any more."

Nationwide figures compiled by the FBI's Uniform Crime Reporting 10 Program in 1990 showed the highest number of arrests of youth for violent offenses — homicide, armed robbery, rape, aggravated assault — in the more than twenty-five years that the statistics have been compiled. Juvenile arrest rates, after rising steadily from the mid-1960s through the 1970s, remained relatively constant until the 1989–1990 statistics revealed a 26 percent increase in the number of youths arrested for murder and nonnegligent manslaughter, while arrests for robbery had increased by 16 percent, and those for aggravated assault by 17 percent.

But the system still defines juveniles as children rather than as criminals, a distinction that makes little sense to their victims or to the rest of the public. Family Court turns the worst juvenile offenders over to the adult system for trial, but they are still sentenced as juveniles.

When anything does happen it's usually so long after the event, so short in duration, and so ineffective that it's no wonder the young men who rob, maim, rape, and terrorize don't perceive those actions as having any serious consequences. Eighty percent of chronic juvenile offenders (five or more arrests) go on to adult criminal careers.

Is it possible to change these young criminals? And what should be done to protect the community from them?

The first necessity is legislation to open juvenile court proceedings to the public and the press. It makes no sense to protect the privacy of those who are a palpable menace to their neighbors or scruple about "stigmatizing" them. A repeat offender should know the authorities will make use of his past record in deciding what to do with him next time. At present, a young habitual criminal is born again with a virgin record when he reaches the age to be dealt with by the adult system.

Opening court records would also make it possible to undertake 15 follow-up studies to find out what works and what doesn't in the various detention facilities and alternative programs designed to rehabilitate. Taxpayers have a right to know what outcomes they are getting for the $85,000 a year it costs to keep a juvenile offender in a secure facility in New York state.

Intervention should occur early, while there is still time to try measures that might make a difference. First offenders should be required to make restitution to their victims or perform community service. A second arrest should be followed by stronger measures. For those who have families who undertake to be responsible for them, there should be intensive supervision by well-trained probation officers with manageable caseloads. For those who require placement out of the home, it should include intensive remedial schoolwork and practical training in some job-related skill. The youth should remain long enough for such efforts to have some hope of proving effective.

Sanctions should be swift and sure. Once arrested, a court appearance should follow without delay, preferably on the same day, so that there is a clear connection made between behavior and its consequences. Placement in appropriately secure institutions, locked away from the community for definite periods of time, should be the immediate and inevitable response to repeated acts of violence. And incarceration should involve some form of work that helps defray its cost to the community, not just a period of rest and recreation. Young criminals should know that is what they can expect.

Arrested While on Parole

A growing cadre of violent teenage boys are growing up with mothers who are children and no resident fathers. What they need most of all is structure and supervision. We may not be able to change attitudes, but we can change behavior. While there is no evidence that any form of therapy can really change a violent repeat offender into someone with empathy for others, it has been demonstrated that the one thing that can result in impulse control is the certainty of punishment.

The present system actually encourages the young to continue their criminal behavior by showing them that they can get away with it. No punishment means a second chance at the same crimes. A significant number of boys arrested for violent crimes were out on parole at the time of the arrest.

They think of the system as a game they can win. "They can't do   20 nothing to me, I ain't sixteen yet" is a repeated refrain in a system that breeds contempt for the law and for the other institutions of society. It is time to acknowledge its failure and restructure the system so that "juvenile justice" ceases to be an oxymoron. We owe it to the law-abiding citizens who share the streets and schools with the violent few to protect the rights of the community and not just those of its victimizers.

Heeding the Cry for Family
ELLEN GOODMAN

This is what passes for a happy ending after a sequence of family disasters: A twelve-year-old boy has gotten what he wants.

Gregory Kingsley, sturdy and unshakable in the face of courtroom

Ellen Goodman is a Pulitzer Prize–winning columnist based at the *Boston Globe,* where this article was published on October 1, 1992.

lawyers in Florida, has a new family, a new name, and a new life. The boy who went from mother to father to pillar to post in the foster-care system is now permanently home as Shawn Russ.

More to the point, the child who will be forever known as the son who "divorced" his parents has grabbed a chance to reach his own goal: "I'm doing this for me so I can be happy."

Happiness is not guaranteed, of course, and happy endings do not always stay that way. It doesn't take a seer to wonder how he will wrestle over his lifetime with his new-old identity and new-old families.

But in its extended form, this was a story ripe enough for a Dick- 5 ensian novel. There was enough family pathos to make the term "dys-functional family" sound like an antiseptic label in the dictionary of psychobabble. And everything has changed.

Now George Russ — a man neglected by his own father, a lawyer with eight children who met Gregory at a home for abused and ne-glected boys — has a new adopted son.

Now Rachel Kingsley — a high school dropout who gave birth at nineteen to a premature Gregory, a divorced mother, poor, perhaps abused, certainly neglectful — has been legally severed from her son.

And now Jeremiah and Zachariah Kingsley — who also did time in foster care and live with the mother whom the court ruled neglectful — no longer have a brother named Gregory.

The importance of the case is not that it granted one boy a so-called divorce. It's that for once, the sound of a child's voice was heard above the din of adult concerns. For once, when the family and the state both miserably failed him, a child was allowed to sue and speak for his own best interests.

The case, even more than the judgment, cast light on some hard 10 dilemmas about families that fall apart and a child welfare system with so many cracks that it lets the kids keep on falling.

It raised questions about when to support biological families and when to give up on them. About how much time a troubled parent may need to get his or her life together again and how little time a child has. About the damage done when the state prematurely severs the ties between parent and child and the damage done when it takes too long.

These are not new issues. When Rachel Kingsley portrayed herself as a mother whose chief crime was poverty, it struck a chord. She is not the first parent to express bewildered anger that the state would pay money for foster care when she could have used it for parent care.

When a stream of witnesses described her as a woman who drank and smoked marijuana, slept with men for money, and left the kids for days on end, it struck a nerve. They are not the first neighbors, friends, or family members who want to rescue children.

When the state workers described the rock and hard place of their foster-care mandate, it had a dismal familiarity. On the one hand, they are supposed to give priorities to biological families, allow parents time to restore their ties. On the other hand they are told that children should not languish in foster families.

But this time, the deciding voice belonged to the one person who [15] was an expert on his life. It was Gregory who cut through the debate about neglect.

Whatever his mother's troubles or intentions, for eighteen months of foster care, he testified, she never phoned or wrote. "I thought she forgot about me. I thought she didn't care about me." Whatever the pros and cons about biological families and adoption, he said with remarkably emotional clarity: "I just want a place to be."

I don't know how much of a legal precedent he has set. There are some 420,000 children in foster care. How many of those children can wend their way to or through the legal system? How many adults want to adopt them?

In some ways, Gregory's story is a foster child's favorite fantasy. But it may have a greater impact on our national consciousness than our law.

We live in a time of renewed emphasis on the importance of the traditional family, the biological family, parental authority. Children's rights are often dismissed as the dangerous and disruptive tools of people who want to destroy families.

In Florida however, we met a boy who wanted the right to create a [20] family. He reminded us that every family story is different. What matters most is not biology, but belonging. This time, it was the child who knew best. Just call him Shawn.

"Philip has questioned my stewardship."

Drawing by Weber; © *1992 The New Yorker Magazine, Inc.*

THINKING AND WRITING ABOUT CHILDREN'S RIGHTS

Questions for Discussion and Writing

1. Leo agrees with Hillary Clinton on some issues, disagrees with her on others. Point out the areas of agreement and disagreement. What is his principal objection to the children's rights movement?
2. What agencies and movements does Grigg regard as enemies of children? To what does he attribute the rise in child abuse? Do his charges seem valid? What principles should govern a society that wishes to protect its children against abuse?
3. What reasons does Cohen give for thinking it might be necessary to change "the structure of all relationships between adults and children — not merely the bad ones"? Why should "good" ones be changed? Enumerate Cohen's criticisms of the caretaker approach. In what essential ways does the philosophy of "child liberation" differ from that of child caretaking? Evaluate the possible effects of the freedoms listed by the children's rights advocates. Cite the assumptions on which Grigg and Cohen base their differing views on the child-parent relationship. Can the validity of these assumptions be tested?

4. How does Kramer explain the idea that "legal rights" of the child and "the best interests of the child" may be in conflict? What reasons does she give for arguing that the juvenile justice system must be reformed? Who would benefit most from the reforms? Do her solutions seem feasible?

5. What issues does Goodman raise in the Gregory Kingsley case about "families that fall apart"? Does she offer a solution? Can you think of other areas of their lives in which children, aged twelve, should be given equality with adults to make decisions?

6. In the three cases involving conflicts between the biological and adoptive or foster parents, what principles guided the courts in their differing decisions? (In June 1993 the Michigan Supreme Court awarded "B.G.C." to her biological parents.) Do you think the "best interests of the child" prevailed in all three cases? Explain your views.

7. If you are familiar with a case of alleged child abuse in which the government intervened, tell whether that experience taught you anything about how children's rights are protected or denied.

8. What does the word *stewardship* in the cartoon suggest about the parent-child relationship in this family? Can you tell how the cartoonist feels about it?

Topics for Research

The Walter Polovchak case, 1982: Walter Polovchak, a fourteen-year-old Russian boy, refused to return to the Soviet Union with his parents after a visit to the United States. The Supreme Court granted him the right to remain in the States when his parents returned to Russia. The American Civil Liberties Union unsuccessfully defended the right of the parents to force their son to return with them.

Religious objections of parents to medical care for their children

Corporal punishment in our schools: the law and the practice

The facts about child abuse

The disappearance of American childhood: Have children already been "liberated"?

CHAPTER THIRTEEN

Endangered Species

Saving endangered species would appear to be one environmental issue with almost universal appeal. Although we may not be familiar with nor care much about snail darters or salt marsh harvest mice, millions of us can be roused to protective action by threats to well-known birds and mammals — falcons and eagles, whales, gorillas, and elephants. Those who advocate the rescue and preservation of endangered species cite both esthetic and practical reasons. Endangered animals — and plants — may be beautiful, interesting, and intellectually satisfying as representatives of the earth's astounding biological diversity. But living things may also contribute, both directly and indirectly, to the health and survival of the human species on this planet.

Unfortunately, the area inhabited by an endangered species cannot always support both the survival of the species and the immediate needs of human beings. The gravest conflicts arise when jobs of loggers and fishermen are lost, when access to housing, water, farmland, and recreational development is thwarted because a particular animal or plant must be protected.

In the United States the Endangered Species Act, first passed in 1973 and reauthorized in 1992, lists as endangered more than six-hundred animals and plants. But so far only five species have been "delisted" — that is, restored to population levels that ensure survival — and about 3,500 additional species have been proposed for inclusion. In December 1992 the number of plants and animals to be protected increased by 53 percent.

Both those who support the Endangered Species Act and those who oppose it in its present form can agree on the answers to some questions. But others are more difficult. For example, are the animals on the endangered list truly endangered? Should every plant and animal on the list be saved? And if some species become extinct because of human activities, will the result be seriously detrimental to human survival? Some extremists value wildness for its own sake and consider survival of the human species irrelevant and even undesirable. (David M. Graber, in his *Los Angeles Times* book review of Bill McKibben's *The End of Nature* says, "We are not interested in the utility of a particular species, or free-flowing river, or ecosystem to mankind. They have intrinsic value, more value — to me — than another human body, or a billion of them.")

If it is agreed that saving most or all of an endangered species is both morally and practically desirable, how shall it be done? By saving each listed species or by saving the habitat, which can mean millions of acres? And who shall bear the cost? The worker who is displaced? It has been estimated that saving one spotted owl may cost 100,000 jobs. The U.S. taxpayer? Saving the Hawaiian monk seal has cost the U.S. government $2.8 million.

In other parts of the world, especially in poor countries, where human beings and animals compete for scarce resources, a form of wildlife preservation called *sustainable utilization* is being practiced. That means that human beings become partners in protecting the endangered species and stand to profit from treating game parks as tourist attractions, even encouraging hunting as a way of "saving" the animals.

To limit the area of debate, the articles in this section deal almost entirely with animals.

Species Extinction
HELEN CALDICOTT

> In my book, a "pioneer" is a man who turned all the grass upside down, strung barbed wire over the dust that was left, poisoned the water and cut down the trees, killed the Indian who owned the land and called it progress. If I had my way, the land would be like God made it, and none of you sons of bitches would be here at all.
>
> — Charlie Russell, cowboy artist, 1923

We have taken over the planet as if we owned it, and we call it progress because we think we are making it better, but in fact we are regressing. Species are dying in the wake of this "progress," and we

---

Helen Caldicott, M.D., although trained as a physician, now works full time as an antinuclear activist and is the cofounder of the group Physicians for Social Responsibility. This essay is reprinted from her 1992 book *If You Love This Planet: A Plan to Heal the Earth.*

seem not to realize that our life depends upon theirs. Peter Raven, director of the Missouri Botanical Gardens in St. Louis, says that the destruction of species is more critical for the world than the greenhouse effect and ozone depletion, because it is moving faster and is inevitable. He predicts that over the next thirty years human beings will cause the extinction of a hundred species per day.[1] For fifteen years, I traveled the world warning people about the medical and ecological consequences of nuclear war, not aware that life was already dying quietly and unobtrusively from man's ongoing activities. Now I see that the threat of species extinction is as serious as the threat of nuclear war.

Life began on the planet 4 billion years ago, and over time an astounding array of diverse forms have gradually emerged. But the advance of evolution has not always been smooth. There was a rapid increase in the numbers of species up to 600 million years ago, with a subsequent decrease in diversification for the next 200 million years. In the last 400 million years, the numbers slowly increased, with the interruption of five significant extinction phases. The largest of these was the Permian era, 240 million years ago, when 77 to 96 percent of all marine animal species became extinct. It took another 5 million years for species diversity to recover. About 65 million years ago, another significant era of species extinction began when the dinosaurs, which had previously ruled the earth, disappeared and mammals gained global hegemony. Thus the evolutionary stage was set for the appearance of *Homo sapiens.* Since that time, the numbers of species have continued to increase to the present all-time high.[2]

Human beings first appeared in a primitive form some three million years ago. That species lived in relative harmony with other life forms until only ten thousand years ago, when it began to have a devastating effect upon the diversity of other species. Humans hunted animals and birds and chopped down or burned forests and plants. To give two examples, in Polynesia, in an isolated island environment, one-half of the bird species are extinct because of human hunting and forest destruction, and more recently, during the 1800s, almost all the unique shrubs and trees were destroyed on the small island of St. Helena, in the North Atlantic. Of the 30 million species estimated to be extant today, we may now be losing 17,500 each year.[3]

In this time frame, the span of *Homo sapiens*'s existence seems trivial. Yet we now threaten to exterminate most of the world's species, which have taken four billion years to evolve. Although the dinosaurs disappeared, they did not, as we may well be doing, bring about their own extinction.

---

[1] Eugene Linden, "The Death of Birth," *Time,* January 2, 1989, pp. 32–35.
[2] Edward O. Wilson, "Threats to Biodiversity," *Scientific American,* September 1989, pp. 108–16.
[3] Ibid.

Unlike the dinosaurs, we clearly have almost total dominion and control over the planet. The development of the opposing thumb gave us the ability to make and hold instruments, weapons, and tools of mass destruction. Our abnormally large neocortex — the thinking part of the brain, which developed in a very short evolutionary time frame — has enabled us to communicate thoughts, by speech and writing, and to destroy, dominate, and subdue all other species, for our own benefit, as we perceive it. We are shortsighted and egocentric, little realizing that our survival is intimately related to and depends upon the survival of 30 million other species. This behavior may, in the long run, be a kind of suicide. The behavior of most other species is conditioned for their long-term survival. For example, humans stand at the apex of the pyramid of the food chain. Bacteria in the soil break down the fallen leaves to produce humus and compost to feed the plants to feed us. If we kill the bacteria with chemical toxins and change of climate, we will indirectly kill ourselves. We have a similar relationship with many other species.

We really "came into our own" with the dawn of the industrial age, early in the 1800s. As we harnessed nature and worked with the natural laws of science, we learned to destroy forests and pollute the air, water, and soil very efficiently, and this efficiency has, over the last two centuries, increased exponentially. In the grand scheme of evolution, our obsession with interpersonal, national, and religious conflicts and our wars are meaningless.

Although 30 million species of plants and animals have not been systematically documented, scientists arrive at this number by extrapolation, having analyzed the number of new species in a small area of rain forest. Within each of these 30 million species, there is a huge degree of genetic diversity that is terribly important. Let me use the species of *Homo sapiens* as an example. Each person carries a unique set of genes that was derived from a particular sperm that fertilized a particular egg. Each sperm and egg was genetically different from any other sperm or egg, and this unique gene structure (genotype) determines all the facial and bodily characteristics, personality, and mental abilities of an individual. The process of evolution depends upon genetic diversity, because as the environment changes, only those organisms with specific characteristics that allow them to survive the change will reproduce. This is what Charles Darwin called survival of the fittest. Without genetic diversity, evolution could not have happened. To give a simple example, some breeds of maize are able to survive better in climatically unfavorable conditions than are others. Scientists are finding that by mating one variety of wild maize with a domestic type, a better cropping plant can be produced. So instead of concentrating on saving a few individuals within a particular species, we must save all the variants of life forms within each species.

There are thousands or even millions of varieties of plants that we have not yet even identified, but as we destroy the environment, we will be needing special strains of wild maize, wheat, rice, and other species that will grow in difficult terrains and climates. Over thousands of years, the human race has utilized about 7,000 different plant species for food, but the present generation tends to rely upon only about twenty species to provide 80 percent of the world's food. These twenty include rice, wheat, millet, and maize.[4]

We consume less than 0.1 percent of naturally occurring species. But we do know that more than 75,000 plant species are edible and that some are far more appropriate than those we now use. Edward O. Wilson has described a plant called the winged bean, or *Psophocarpus tetragonolobus,* from New Guinea, which is at present ignored by the world's food manufacturers and farmers. The whole plant is edible — roots, seeds, flowers, stems, and leaves — and a coffeelike drink can be made from the juice. It grows rapidly, to a height of fifteen feet in several weeks, and exhibits a nutritional value equivalent to that of the soy bean.[5]

At a time when the human population is growing explosively and needs an enormous amount of food, it seems imperative that we start preserving and cultivating different plant and food varieties that will provide efficient sources of nutrition.

Ironically, as other species become extinct, we are proliferating. In 1800, we numbered 1 billion; in 1990, 5.2 billion. Over the next ten years, we will add another 1 billion. By the end of the next century, if present trends continue, we may reach 14 billion, or three times our present number.[6] Clearly, the ecosphere cannot sustain 5.2 billion, let alone 14 billion.

Let me now introduce the varieties of ways in which species are being destroyed.

Tropical Forests. . . . These special ecosystems probably contain 15 to 24 million of the 30 million planetary species. Within twenty-five to fifty years, the trees and those species may well be gone, destroyed because of Third World debt and First World greed.

Wetlands. These serve as crucial breeding grounds for fish, crustaceans, and other sea-dwelling creatures. Until very recently, though, mangrove swamps and reedy wetlands were not valued as habitats for species. Rather, they were seen as ugly, muddy, difficult areas that were best cleared for "canal developments" or filled in for real estate investment. Although some people now understand the ecological significance

---

[4] Ibid.

[5] Ibid., p. 114.

[6] World Commission on Environment and Development, *Our Common Future* (New York: Oxford University Press, 1987), p. 4.

of wetlands, most "developers" are still uneducated, and indeed the majority of people in the Western world are deeply ignorant about the biological meaning of species extinction. Some 25 to 50 percent of the global wetlands have so far been destroyed. In the United States, this number is 54 percent.[7] As the human population increases, it decreases the number of fish by eliminating their breeding nurseries. Yet fish are a key source of first-class protein for millions of people.

Coral Reefs. These are a rich source of species and are very complex ecosystems in their own right. An area of 400,000 square kilometers of coral reef is estimated to contain 500,000 species. Many of these animals and fish engage in a kind of biological warfare with one another, and they have therefore evolved a large number of specific toxins that can be harnessed for medical treatment and possibly other advantageous uses. But coral reefs are mysteriously dying all around the world. It seems that coral polyps (the living organisms that provide the vivid colors and that create the solid coral structure as their protective habitat) are very sensitive to temperature change, so their death could signify early global warming from the greenhouse effect. Worldwide temperatures in the 1980s were 4°F above those of any previous decade on record. Toxic chemicals derived from agriculture, industrial waste discharged into rivers, and urban runoff from houses (pesticides, cleaners, fertilizers, and sewage) could also be killing the coral. These magnificent reefs, true wonders of nature, must be preserved at all costs, and no change in climate or human "development" should be allowed to threaten their existence.[8]

Arid Zones or Deserts. These are habitats to many fragile species of plants and animals. Australian deserts were once filled with tiny exotic marsupials that looked like delicate, forlorn, scaled-down kangaroos, as well as other unique and precious life forms.[9] Of the seventy-two different mammalian species that once lived in the desert, eleven are now extinct, five are found only on isolated "safe" islands, and fifteen are threatened. These indigenous animals were decimated by the introduction of foreign species of what are called feral animals. Foxes prey on small animals, as do wild cats and dogs, while grass-eating rabbits, pigs, goats, camels, buffalo, rodents, wild horses (called

---

[7] Walter H. Corson, ed., *The Global Ecology Handbook: What You Can Do about the Environmental Crisis* (Boston: Beacon Press, 1990), p. 102.

[8] Ibid.; Robert Lamb, "The Displeased Coral Diver Was Small Beer," *International Herald Tribune,* January 19, 1989; Mike Seccombe, "Government Divided over Reef Oil Exploration Plans," *Sydney Morning Herald,* July 18, 1990; Greg Roberts, "Resort Sewerage Killing Coral Says Expert," *Sydney Morning Herald,* March 7, 1989; Deborah Smith, "30 Years Isn't Long to Save the Species," *Sydney Morning Herald,* August 19, 1990.

[9] Michael Kennedy, "Endangered," *Habitat,* August 29, 1990.

brumbies), and cattle have destroyed thousands of square miles of fragile plant ecosystems.[10]

Introduced Species. I have . . . described the devastation wrought by introduced species that have no natural predators. But sometimes foreign animals are brought into a country specifically to prey upon a natural pest that needs to be eradicated. For instance, the South American cane toad was brought to Australia in order to eradicate a beetle that was destroying sugarcane crops in Queensland. Not only did it not kill the beetle, which lived out of reach on tall sugarcanes, but, having no natural predators, it has multiplied out of control and spread like a creeping plague over much of the east coast of Australia. I live on the east coast hundreds of miles south of the point of introduction, and at night my paths and gardens are alive with silent, hopping, slimy cane toads, which are brown, warty, and ugly. They not only look repulsive but have poisonous glands located in the area of their head. If they are eaten by animals such as snakes, goannas, lizards, cats, or dogs, the animal is poisoned and dies. The cane toad plague is now so serious that many of our indigenous reptiles and other creatures are threatened with extinction. (I may sound somewhat judgmental in regard to the cane toad, but I would have none of these feelings if it were located in its original environment.)

Savannas and Grasslands. The wildlife of these regions is also under threat, particularly in Africa, because human beings enjoy displaying exotic animal skins on their floors, hanging animal heads on their walls, grinding rhinoceros horns for aphrodisiacs, wearing shoes and belts made from crocodiles and snakes, and making jewelry and piano keys from elephant tusks.

In Africa in the 1930s, there were ten million elephants; now there are fewer than three-quarters of a million. Eighty thousand elephants are killed each year by poachers who hack off their tusks with chain saws and leave the huge carcass to rot in the midday sun, while they make a living from their illegal bounty.[11] These poachers are often poor, and because the world supports an unequal distribution of wealth, this is their one mode of survival, the destruction of nature. Lions, tigers, leopards, zebras, giraffes, and other wonderful exotic animals are all endangered. Soon, these animals will exist only in zoos, and eventually these few remaining specimens will become extinct.

The total population of other creatures is also diminishing. For instance, blue whales have decreased in number from 200,000 to 15,000, 20

---

[10] Roger Beckman and Steven Morten, "Where Have All the Desert Mammals Gone?" *Wildlife* (Wildlife Preservation Society of Queensland, Brisbane), Spring 1990.

[11] Corson, op. cit., p. 103.

and humpback whales from 50,000 to 8,000.[12] The number of southern white rhinoceroses in Zaire dwindled from 400 in the 1970s to 15 in 1984; the population is now up to 28.[13]

Wildlife Smugglers. There exists a very lucrative international trade in wild animals and their component parts. As a member of the South Australian National Parks and Wildlife Council in the 1970s, I learned how our beautiful indigenous cockatoos were being drugged and smuggled in socks packed in suitcases aboard international flights. Australian snakes, birds, and marsupials are also part of this international commerce.

On a trip to Crete in 1987, I was walking along a side street when I heard a familiar scream — it was a sulfur-crested cockatoo looking very bedraggled and dirty in a cage outside someone's shop. Annoyed to see this smuggled bird, I grew even more incensed when I realized that it should by rights be flying free with a flock of hundreds of others in the Australian bush. How much did its captors pay for it? In all likelihood, $2,500 on the black market.

The international trade in wildlife and its products is now worth $4 billion to $5 billion a year (excluding fish and timber). Bangkok is used as an international transit station by dealers who "launder" illegally obtained wildlife, which is poached in Indonesia, Laos, Vietnam, and Cambodia. This international Mafia is threatening the extinction of the great panda, crocodiles, alligators, snakes, cacti, and orchids. Recently, a traveler from Mali was intercepted in Paris, and his luggage was found to contain fifty pythons, twenty tortoises, twenty lizards, and several vipers. A Japanese tourist arriving in Bangkok had eleven rare monkeys jammed into a carry-on bag, five of them had suffocated. Monkeys' teeth are often extracted with pliers and cut with clippers to make their bites harmless, and leopards' fur is dyed black to make it look like a house cat's. Americans have created a huge demand in rare parrots and dangerous snakes, while the Japanese like monkeys.[14]

Chemical Destruction of Wildlife. Some of the most important, and yet seemingly insignificant, species in the world are threatened by toxic chemical sprays used on crops. These creatures are the worms, fungi, insects, and bacteria that maintain a healthy soil base and root system for plants. They form the base of the pyramid of the food chain. Bees

---

[12] Ibid.

[13] "Help WWF Stop the Rhino Horn Trade," World Wildlife Fund Campaign Report, April 1991.

[14] CITES The Convention on International Trade in Endangered Species of Wild Fauna and Flora, United Nations Environment Program, UNEP Environment Brief no. 8, P.O. Box 30552, Nairobi, Kenya; Smith, op. cit.; Charles P. Wallace, "A Wildlife Smuggler's Paradise," *Los Angeles Times,* October 20, 1990.

and other insects that pollinate crops and disperse seeds are also undervalued but are vital to our survival. Bats, which represent one-quarter of all mammalian species, also scatter seeds. We probably do not realize that 90 percent of the most valuable U.S. crops, worth a total of $4 billion, are fertilized by insects, and the catch-22 is obvious. Pesticides and weedicides used to protect the crops from predatory insects and weeds kill the very organisms upon which the crops depend.[15]

Wild birds, bats, and parasitic insects have another function. They eat insect pests and therefore act as natural insecticides. So nature is clearly best left to itself. It has all the inbuilt mechanisms and feedback loops to ensure its ongoing health and survival. To put it crudely, we humans just screw things up. Organic natural farming is the only sensible alternative to chemically destructive farming.

The Domino Effect. If we upset the balance of nature by eliminating large predatory animals, we produce a reactionary overpopulation of smaller predators that are normally kept in check. These in turn then eat and render extinct the lower-order animals upon which they feed. We must not disturb the hierarchical balance of nature and the food chain.

Frogs — The New Canaries. Years ago, canaries were used as sensitive indicators in coal mines to determine whether the air was safe for the miners to breathe. When the canary died from toxic fumes, it was time for the miners to leave. For the last decade, biologists have noticed an alarming decline in the numbers and species of amphibians — frogs, toads, and salamanders. These creatures were the first vertebrates ever to inhabit the land. They appeared 400 million years ago and evolved into present-day species some 200 million years ago. Because their bodies are acutely sensitive to the environment, they are our canaries, our barometer of global environmental poisoning.

Frog species are disappearing from Australia, the United States, Japan, Canada, Puerto Rico, and Costa Rica. This phenomenon is particularly worrisome because they are disappearing from national parks and from some of the best-protected areas of the world, where they should be safe.

What is threatening them? Many theories have been proposed: (a) frogs' eggs are very sensitive to UV light; (b) foreign predator fish introduced into frog habitats, such as ponds and lakes, eat the tadpoles and baby frogs; (c) toxic chemicals and heavy metals are poisoning the frogs because frogs naturally absorb large amounts of water, some of which is now polluted, through their skin; (d) habitat damage caused

---

[15] Corson, op. cit., p. 103.

by logging, pesticide pollution, and dam construction threatens frogs' survival; (e) frogs are so sensitive to variations in temperature and moisture that if the rainfall and climate change, the frogs die — and these changes seem to be occurring as the greenhouse effect becomes manifest.

Frogs are an important link in the ecological chain. Tadpoles consume large quantities of algae, so streams are kept clean and flowing, and adult frogs eat enormous numbers of insects, including mosquitoes. The Everglades, in Florida, offer a good example of the ecological necessity of frogs. Scientists recently recorded a 90 percent reduction in the number of wading birds, possibly caused by the demise of pig frogs, which provided the birds' food.[16] If frogs are the new canaries, the situation is very serious and we had better act fast.

Destruction of Habitats by Trapping and Mining. The Gouldian finch is an exquisitely colored bird once found throughout the grassy woodlands of tropical Australia. Fifty years ago, flocks of thousands used to swarm through the air, but the swarming has stopped. Now flocks of only fifty or fewer are seen, because the finch was extensively trapped for the birdcage industry and because its habitat was destroyed by the regular, intentional burning of the grasslands. The bird nests were vulnerable to destruction since they were located in termite and ant mounds close to the ground, or in the hollows of old gum trees. A recent survey found only two intact breeding colonies in the whole country, and one of these is at present threatened by a gold-mining company. The company plans to mine at the site of the breeding colony and to construct tailings dams close by. These dams will hold cyanide-contaminated water, so when the birds drink their daily fill of water, they will die. Is this the epitaph of the Gouldian finch?[17]

Antarctica. One of the last bastions of pristine wilderness is now under threat. The Antarctic is an ecosystem delicately balanced and teeming with life. No land plants grow on the icy waste, but the sea supports all the life forms. The base of the food chain consists of single-celled plants called phytoplankton, which trap energy from the sun. Billions of tiny crustaceans known as krill eat the plankton, which in turn forms the food base of whales, penguins, crabeater seals, and large seabirds such as the petrel. Small fish and squid also eat the krill and

---

[16] Richard Cole, "Amphibians in Global Decline Say Scientists," *Northern Star,* June 20, 1990; Stan Ingram, "Of Fire, Water, Earth and Air — The Mystery of the Disappearing Frog," *Wildlife,* Spring 1990.

[17] David Charley, "Famous Finches Feel the Pressure," *Northern Star,* June 30, 1990.

in turn feed emperor penguins, albatrosses, large fish, seals, and sperm whales.[18]

Although the climate of Antarctica is not conducive to human habitation, we have nevertheless devised many ways to intrude and damage this unique and fragile biosphere:

- Large-scale international commercial fishing is depleting the sea.

- In February 1989, an oil spill from an Argentinean tanker killed thousands of penguins, skuas, and their chicks.

- The tourist industry recently decided that the habitat of the South Pole is a nice place to take its customers. They leave a trail of desolation as tons of garbage are dumped from tourist ships into the sea. Incidentally, most ship captains in the world still believe that the oceans are a universal sewage disposal system and act accordingly.

- For fifty years, scientists established research stations in the Antarctic, but they did not build adequate sewage systems and left hundreds of cans of toxic waste and garbage when they departed. How could they research the delicate web of life and then so insensitively threaten it, or were they interested only in their research papers?

- Ozone destruction is an extraordinary threat. Remember that in the winter the ozone over the South Pole decreases to only 6 percent of its original 100 percent. Remember, too, that life cannot exist without the ozone layer. Plankton is extremely sensitive to UV light. As it dies, so will the rest of the life cycle.

- Mining corporations have been pressuring their governments for the right to dig up minerals in the Antarctic. That activity would lead to the ecological devastation of much of the area. Accordingly, an international treaty called the Convention on the Regulation of Antarctic Marine Resource Activities has been drafted and was agreed upon by thirty-three nations in Wellington in June 1988. Fortunately, Australia, Britain, and, probably, France have decided not to sign it. The treaty will not be valid unless all nations agree to it. Since then, Australia has proposed that the world declare the Antarctic a park to be left in its original, pristine state. This may well be the favorable outcome.[19]

---

[18] Jane Brody, "Studies Point to Food Web Danger," *Sydney Morning Herald,* February 15, 1989; "A Strategy for Antarctic Conservation: International Union for Conservation of Nature and Natural Resources, IUCN — The World Conservation Union" (Proceedings of the Eighteenth Session of the IUCN General Assembly, Perth, Australia, November 28–December 5, 1990).

[19] Ibid.

The Fish and the Sea. World market forces have helped destroy the ecology of the sea. New efficient techniques and excessive fishing have so depleted some fish species that they may never recover. Market forces are also responsible for pollution of the oceans by toxic sewage and poisons, plastic disposal, radioactive pollution, acid rain, and oil spills. Much of the oceanic life is still a mystery to us, because we cannot really explore the deepest layers of the oceans. Strange and wonderful life forms have, however, been dredged from great depths, but even these species are not immune to the danger of sunken nuclear submarines and land-based poisons that we tip into the sea.

Pollution of the sea by plastic kills large numbers of marine animals. [35] The fish eat pieces of indigestible Styrofoam and plastic, which causes intestinal obstruction or blockage of the bowel, and they die a slow death from starvation. Seabirds also eat plastic, because it resembles fish, and they suffer similar deaths. Birds and fish often get caught up and trapped in the conjoined plastic rings that hold together a six-pack of beer or soda cans. These rings strangle birds and fish. I once found a dead albatross with one of these disposable obscenities wrapped around its neck, on the ninety-mile beach in South Australia. What a symbol of the industrial consumerist age! The National Academy of Sciences estimated that up to two million birds, ten thousand sea mammals, and countless fish die each year in American waters because of internal damage caused by plastics.[20]

Fishing ships have become fishing factories. Instead of catching tuna with rods, fishers now use huge seining nets to scoop up tuna and all other associated fish from large sea volumes. (Thousands of dolphins are also caught in these nets and die unnecessarily.) International quotas must be placed upon certain fish species in order to protect them. Tuna, for example, should be regarded as a luxury item and harvested accordingly, in relatively small numbers.

The Japanese and Taiwanese, whose diets consist almost solely of fish and rice, are profligate fishers. At present, they deploy drift nets made of finely meshed, colorless, invisible nylon sixty kilometers long that hang fifteen meters below the surface of the sea. The nets catch anything swimming in either direction along this barrier. They also trap seabirds that dive into the water to catch fish, and they ensnare whales, dolphins, sharks, turtles, and seals as well as the target fish, salmon and tuna. U.S. environmentalists estimate that more than three-quarters of a million seabirds are killed in drift nets each season, plus tens of thousands of dolphins.[21] . . .

---

[20] Peter Pringle, "The Green Bottles Don't Accidently Fall on a U.S. Heap," *Sydney Morning Herald,* July 28, 1989.

[21] Paul Grigson, "Wall of Death Headed for Southern Waters," *Sydney Morning Herald,* July 8, 1989.

Whales. The Japanese are still whaling despite an international law that bans the killing of whales. This country continues to catch 1,800 whales per year for "scientific purposes." Their carcasses are cut up and sold for meat for sushi, sashimi, and other delicacies. However, whale meat in fact provides less than 1 percent of the protein in Japan. Since the international ban in 1985, the Japanese have killed 13,650 whales.[22] The blue, sperm, and right whales have been hunted to commercial extinction, and the fin and minke whales are threatened.

The Soviets stopped whaling in 1987, but they announced that they would take thirty fin whales and seventy minke whales a year in 1990 from the Okhotsk Sea — to broaden their "knowledge and understanding of the marine ecosystem." That means they will kill them to learn that they are becoming extinct.

Dolphins. Dolphins are highly intelligent, having very large brains, 40 and capable of communicating with human beings. They can count, repeat words in a primitive phonetic form, and communicate emotionally when they have befriended certain people. In addition to being slaughtered as a side effect of the large-scale fishing industry, they are dying spontaneously of mysterious causes, which may well be related to ocean pollution. For instance, scientists reported that an examination of 260 dead dolphins washed up on the beaches in Spain in August 1990 revealed that they were suffering from a viral infection similar to distemper in dogs. But they also had liver lesions caused by toxic substances in their blood that apparently entered their bodies from the contaminated water. Scientists believe that poisons in the sea are inhibiting their immune system, thus making them more susceptible to viral infections. This mechanism is very similar to the pathophysiology of AIDS, where the immune system is depleted by the AIDS virus and patients die of massive bacterial or viral infections and cancer.[23]

Tourists are encouraged to feed dolphins with fish on certain organized cruises in the States, but this practice has been discouraged by the Center for Marine Conservation, because the fish themselves may be infected.[24] Bottle-nosed dolphins and sea lions have been used for sinister purposes. The Reagan administration spent $30 million in a clandestine program to train these highly intelligent animals to guard the Trident submarine base at Bangor, Washington. While navy officials said that the dolphins and sea lions are somewhat unreliable during training and occasionally go "absent without leave or refuse to obey orders," they admitted that what the animals lack in discipline, they

---

[22] Brian Woodley, "Moratorium Fails to Stop Killing of Whales," *Weekend Australian,* June 30–July 1, 1990.

[23] Dianne Dumanowski, "Measles-like Virus Reported in Dolphins," *Boston Globe,* October 24, 1990.

[24] Ibid.

make up for in sonar and speed: "Their sonar system is better than any radar and they can pick up objects with incredible accuracy." The Naval Ocean Systems Center, in San Diego, is a sort of "boot camp" for a hundred dolphins and twenty-five California sea lions.[25] Funding for this program has been cut, but the training program continues.[26]

Sea Turtles. These creatures are under threat in the South Pacific. Fiji exports turtle shells, and 2,025 kilos of shell are exported to Japan each year. This figure represents a total of two thousand hawksbill turtles. The trouble is that only the large, mature turtles are captured and killed, and since these mature creatures are the breeders, the future of the whole population is in jeopardy. Turtles live for more than a hundred years. Five of the six sea turtle species are in serious danger of becoming extinct, according to the World Wildlife Fund.[27]

Turtles are fascinating creatures. William, my son, and I stayed on Heron Island, on the Great Barrier Reef in Queensland, several years ago. As we lay luxuriating on the sand, huge female turtles clambered up the beach from the sea, laboriously dug a hole in the warm sand with their flippers, and proceeded to lay several hundred eggs. When the eggs hatched at night, the tiny baby turtles dug their way through the sand and headed toward the nearest light, mistaking it for the moon reflected in the sea. In this case, it was toward streetlights, and the baby turtles became lost. In the morning, the beach was still alive with turtles, but the sea gulls snapped them up. Some eventually got to the water, where big fish waited to devour them. Thus, out of thousands of hatchlings, few survive. When they disappear into the ocean, no one knows where they go. They reappear years later as giant adults. . . .

Once upon a time, the whole North American continent abounded with millions of animals and birds, as did Europe, the Middle East, Australia, and all other regions. Not only are we losing species, but we are killing millions of genetically unique individuals within single species. As someone recently said, cutting down a forest is equivalent to shooting the animals and birds that live within.

I refuse to contemplate a world devoid of diverse life forms. Is our development so important and sacrosanct that we must destroy all other species in our drive toward domination of the planet? Such behavior is anthropocentric. Let us instead develop a sense of humility and a deep love for our fellow creatures, recognizing that their value is equal to our own.

45

[25] Timothy Egan, "Environmentalists Flipping over Dolphins Use as Navy Guard Dogs," *Sydney Morning Herald,* April 15, 1989.

[26] Personal communication from the Naval Oceans Systems Center, San Diego.

[27] Associated Press, "Greenpeace Wants Ban on Fiji Turtle Shells," *Northern Star,* July 5, 1990.

Saving the Species

RICHARD MINITER

To hear them talk in Rio, you might suppose that the Treaty on Biodiversity — which President Bush refused to sign because of its threat to the U.S. biotechnology industry, but which he half endorsed in his speech — is essential to save some thousands of species from extinction at the hands of economic development. And this apocalyptic environmentalism is the only respectable view on the subject.

Every major institution has its resident doomster. Stanford biologist Paul Ehrlich — fresh from paying up to Julian Simon after losing his 1970 bet that various raw material shortages would send their prices skyrocketing (in fact there were no shortages; prices fell) — says as many as 3 percent of living organisms could be extinct by the end of the decade and urged Americans to immediately "cease 'developing' any more relatively undisturbed land."

"The Earth is nearing a stage of extinction of species unequaled since that of the age of the dinosaurs," cries a 1989 General Accounting Office report.

Dark predictions about an impending loss of species go back to Norman Myers's 1979 book *The Sinking Ark*. The world could "lose one-quarter of all species by the year 2000," Myers warns, at which time, development would trigger "an extinction spasm accounting for one million species."

These predictions are all flawed at the outset by one fundamental 5 fact — no one knows how many species actually exist. As recently as the 1960s, scientists thought there were about 4 million species. Then estimates exploded when biologists realized how numerous and diverse life was in tropical rain forests. Estimates of global species counts range as high as 100 million, but taxonomists have catalogued only a little fewer than 1.4 million. The rest is guesswork.

Almost every estimate of species loss is based on computer models. These models rely upon assumptions that overstate potential extinction rates. Modelers assume that habitats are like islands which shrink as development spreads. But the analogy is faulty. On islands, animals can't adapt to rising seas, but many animals can adapt to human development, especially when the development in question is light farming or low-density housing. Another flaw is that the computer models are based on thirty-year-old tropical-island research. Since tropical areas have more life per square foot than temperature areas, habitat

Richard Miniter is an independent television producer who writes on environmental issues. This article is reprinted from the July 6, 1992 issue of *National Review*, a conservative journal.

loss is bound to take a larger toll in the tropics. By extrapolating from tropical data, some models overstate the human impact on wildlife.

If there were a major problem of disappearing species, would the U.N. Biodiversity Treaty solve it? Fortunately, we have a precedent to examine here. The Biodiversity Treaty's American ancestor is the Endangered Species Act, which is currently up for reauthorization. The 1973 Act was a Nixon-era nod to the greens. It requires that federal agencies preserve "the ecosystems upon which endangered species and threatened species depend." But the law is murky in several key provisions. An "endangered" species is one near extinction throughout all or most of its range. How this is determined is largely at the discretion of the U.S. Fish and Wildlife Service (FWS), which is regularly petitioned by environmentalists and antidevelopment activists to add still more species to the more than 1,140 already on the endangered list.

Even the term "species" is vaguely defined by law. "Species" includes "any subspecies of fish or wildlife or plants and any other group of fish or wildlife of the same species or smaller taxa in common spatial arrangement." In other words, any plant or animal living in a definable region can be legally called "endangered." If the FWS wanted to list the squirrels in the park across from the White House as an "endangered" subspecies, they could do it.

"Never mind that the Lafayette Park grey squirrel is indistinguishable from the grey squirrels in any other park in Washington," Eric Felton wrote recently in *Insight* magazine. "The Lafayette Park squirrels are geographically divided from their relatives, separated by blocks of urban jungle, and so can be considered as a distinct subspecies to be listed for protection." Felton asked John Fay, an FWS biologist, if the agency really had the discretion to list the squirrels in Lafayette Park as endangered. Fay says he thinks it unlikely the FWS would act that way, but he acknowledges, "In a very narrow legal sense, it's true."

Perhaps the best example of the misuse of the Endangered Species 10 Act is what enthusiasts call "the salt marsh harvest mouse story."

Federal officials told a man owning both marshland and upland property in California that he could develop neither piece of land, because of the salt marsh harvest mouse, a small animal that lives in briny estuaries close to the sea. The owner challenged the officials, pointing out that the mouse liked wet, salty areas, not dry uplands. Ah, said the officials, you're right. But if global warming occurs, the polar ice caps will melt, and if the ice caps melt, the seas will rise, and if the seas rise, the mouse will be forced to seek new habitat. And the most likely habitat would be your uplands.

"I used to tell that story at conferences. I'd get a few laughs, but I was sure it was apocryphal," says Mark Pollot, author of the forthcoming book *Grand Theft & Petit Larceny: Property Rights in America.* "Then I told it once and a man said, 'That's my client.'"

Furthermore, the act doesn't even do what it's supposed to do. Of the more than 1,140 species listed as endangered, only seventeen have ever been taken off the list. Out of the seventeen, seven were "delisted" because of extinction and four more because of what the FWS calls "original data error." And three more species recovered because of natural factors unrelated to the act, according to the National Wilderness Institute in Virginia.

The FWS in its 1990 report to Congress admits the American alligator is its only "success story," and it's not much of a showpiece. The American alligator lost most of its habitat in the first place because the Army Corps drained the Kissimmee river basin. Then, when the time came to reverse government policies and protect the alligator, the FWS may have undercounted the surviving alligators. "It now appears that the animal never should have been placed on the endangered species list," said the National Wildlife Federation.

The FWS seems less interested in rescuing species from extinction than in placing them on the list. Of the 1,140 listed species, the FWS has completed recovery plans for only 275. It seems that "almost all of the emphasis of environmental groups and government agencies is on the listing end of the process, and there is practically nothing happening on the recovery end," writes Utah State University professor Randy T. Simmons, who is researching a book on endangered species, bureaucracy, and property rights.

Listing and recovering all of the 4,197 species environmentalists want could cost taxpayers some $32.3 billion, according to the Interior Department. "And that figure excludes the cost of compensating property owners, lost jobs, and lost tax revenues," says Ike Sugg, an analyst at the Competitive Enterprise Institute. There has to be a better way.

Public Slaughter, Private Conservation

Hawk Mountain claws its way into the sky above eastern Pennsylvania's Kittatinny Ridge. Geography and wind patterns combine to funnel some 20,000 birds, mostly hawks, ospreys, falcons, and eagles, past the mountain on an average fall day. Until 1934 it was site of an annual slaughter of tens of thousands of birds. Bowing to political pressure, the Pennsylvania legislature placed a bounty on the goshawk, which was said to kill chickens.

It would have been cheaper for the state to simply reimburse farmers who lost chickens. At the peak of the bounty period, Pennsylvania paid out more than $90,000 for hawks that may have killed a total of $1,875 worth of chickens. And by subsidizing hawk slayings, the state encouraged an explosion of rodents which caused an estimated $4 million worth of crop damage in 1934 alone.

When Rosalie Edge, a conservationist and suffragette, learned of the hawk killings, she urged the Audubon Society to buy Hawk Mountain.

When it refused, she took matters into her own hands, buying the 1,398 acre mountain property in 1935.

It's a situation some environmentalists might consider ironic. By exercising her property rights, Miss Edge prevented state-sponsored ecological destruction. Hawk Mountain is now a world renowned bird-watching site and hosts more than fifty thousand visitors every year. "Property rights hold everyone accountable and provide niches for off-beat groups [to try new approaches] in a setting where majority rules," says Richard Stroup, with the Political Economy Research Center in Bozeman, Montana.

Hawk Mountain points the way to a new approach to endangered species. Landowners can do extraordinary things to save species that are in jeopardy. Falconer organizations saved the peregrine falcon from extinction. North American bluebird populations rebounded thanks to the efforts of the North American Bluebird Society. The Nature Conservancy owns or manages more than 2 million acres of habitat. The National Audubon Society owns more than eighty bird sanctuaries. Ducks Unlimited, a nonprofit organization founded by hunters and conservationists in 1935, buys and protects duck habitat throughout North America. Trout Unlimited, the Elk Foundation, and other groups perform similarly.

In short, humans are central to preserving and protecting wildlife. That's why privately owned species like chickens, cows, and horses — all of which were foreign to North America — outnumber publicly owned native species like bison, alligators, and passenger pigeons. No privately owned or managed species has ever been driven to extinction.

To own a species, one doesn't have to cage or fence it; ownership means that the owner is the sole steward. Owners have a direct, personal, and long-term interest in their property which government bureaucrats lack. They will fund research to learn, for example, how to combat diseases that afflict the wildlife they own.

And protecting endangered species can be financially rewarding. Timber companies are fencing off their land, limiting access to paying hunters. This is called "fee hunting." Controlled access and changes in logging practices improve the land significantly. "Lands that were once an eyesore with no game are now a showcase with abundant herds," William Wall, a wildlife ecology manager with IP Timberlands, told *Forbes.* IP Timberlands, a limited partnership mostly owned by International Paper, protects bald eagles and cockaded woodpeckers while allowing recreational use of its 6.3 million acres for a small fee. The recreation program generated about $10 million in 1990.

Private ownership and management — whether not-for-profit like Hawk Mountain or decidedly profitable like IP Timberlands — succeeds because of property rights. An owner has a stake in his property and will work to improve it. Take the case of the Gulf of Mexico redfish. In the 1980s the redfish population dwindled drastically. Accusing fishermen of greed, several governments banned all commercial fishing in certain waters. Meanwhile, the population of Mississippi catfish increased 500 percent during the same period. Why are redfish headed for extinction and catfish thriving?

The main reason, surely, is that no one owns the redfish; therefore, there is no incentive for any one fisherman to reduce his catch or snitch on those who overfish. On the other hand, catfish are owned. Owners ensure that catfish ponds have optimum oxygen levels and are kept free of disease.

Experience suggests that government control encourages environmentally unsound behavior, while ownership leads to environmental responsibility. But the Endangered Species Act and the Biodiversity Treaty operate on exactly opposite principles.

The Great Spotted Owl War

RANDY FITZGERALD

One afternoon last November, Donald Walker, Jr., got a four-page letter from an attorney for an environmental group calling itself the Forest Conservation Council. The organization threatened to sue, seeking heavy fines and imprisonment, if Walker cut down a single tree on his 200 acres of Oregon timberland.

Walker, his wife Kay, and two daughters live in central Oregon on land that has been in the family for three generations. Since being laid off from his lumbermill job in 1989, Walker had cut a few trees each year for income to help support the family.

Barely able to control his mounting anger, Walker called his seventy-seven-year-old father, who lives nearby. He had received a similar letter. Then Walker talked to a neighbor, a retired log-truck driver, who cut timber on his land just to pay his property taxes every year. The same threat had been mailed to him.

Kay Walker reacted with disbelief. "Here we are caught up in this owl mess again," she fumed.

This article was published in the November 1992 issue of *Reader's Digest*, where Randy Fitzgerald is a staff writer. He is also a freelance writer whose books include *Porkbarrel: The Unexpurgated Grace Commission Story of Congressional Profligacy* (with Gerald Lipson, 1984) and *The Quiet Revolution: Emerging Alternatives to Government* (1986).

The "mess" had begun when environmentalists challenged the In-   5
terior Department's decision not to list the northern spotted owl as a
threatened or endangered species under the Endangered Species Act.
The act permits anyone to sue to enforce provisions protecting a species in peril and its suspected habitat.

As a result of this and related court action, most timber sales on
federal forest land in the Pacific Northwest have been halted, throwing
thousands of loggers and mill employees out of work.

Now the act is being used against private landowners. Besides the
Walkers, about 190 other landowners in Oregon have received legal
threats from the same environmental group. Most are small private
landowners or modest local logging companies. "We can't afford to fight
this in court," Walker says. "I'm out of work, and last year our property taxes nearly doubled. Our tree farm is the last hope we have to survive."

The hardships visited on logging families by the spotted-owl controversy will eventually touch all Americans through higher prices for
wood products. But these problems could have been avoided — and
still can be — if environmentalists, timber owners, and federal officials
would compromise.

The Real Agenda. In 1987, a Massachusetts group called Green-
world petitioned the U.S. Fish and Wildlife Service to list the northern
spotted owl as an endangered species. After a review, the FWS ruled
that the owl was not in danger of extinction. In retaliation, twenty-two
environmental groups — ranging from the Seattle Audubon Society to
the Sierra Club — sued to reverse the decision.

A number of these groups had another agenda — to outlaw logging   10
in old-growth forests throughout much of the Northwest — and were
using the owl as a tool. "The northern spotted owl is the wildlife species
of choice to act as a surrogate for old-growth forest protection," explained Andy Stahl, staff forester for the Sierra Club Legal Defense Fund,
at a 1988 law clinic for other environmentalists. "Thank goodness the
spotted owl evolved in the Pacific Northwest," he joked, "for if it hadn't,
we'd have to genetically engineer it."

Old-growth forests are often defined as stands of trees at least 200
years of age that have never been exposed to cutting. There are 9
million acres of old-growth forest on federal lands in Oregon, California,
and Washington. Of this, some 6 million acres — enough to form a
three-mile-wide band of trees from New York to Seattle — are already
off-limits to logging, preserved mostly in national parks and federal
wilderness areas.

So the fight came down to the remaining 3 million acres, which
were being cut at the rate of some 60,000 acres a year. By the time this
old growth was harvested, foresters for the Northwest Forestry Asso-

ciation argued, a like amount of acreage in other forests would have matured into old growth. Environmental groups countered that the spotted owl would be extinct by then because it can't survive in sufficient numbers in younger forests.

Responding to the environmentalists' petition, U.S. District Judge Thomas Zilly ordered the FWS to take a second look. Then, U.S. District Judge William Dwyer stopped most Pacific Northwest timber sales on U.S. Forest Service land. And last June, U.S. District Judge Helen Frye banned old-growth timber sales on most of the Bureau of Land Management's Pacific Northwest land.

In June 1990, the FWS reversed course and listed the owl as threatened, after a committee representing four federal agencies concluded that the owl population was declining. The estimated 2,000 owl pairs still alive, the committee decided, were dependent primarily on the old-growth timberland. The FWS has since proposed a critical spotted-owl habitat in the three states, with suggested sizes ranging from 11.6 million to 6.9 million acres.

Later academic studies have challenged the government's conclu-   15
sions. A timber-industry group, the American Forest Resource Alliance, summarized fifteen studies by forest experts at major universities and discovered that, as more land is surveyed, the known owl population continues to increase. Even the FWS's current projections show 3,500 known pairs, nearly twice the number federal bureaucrats first estimated.

Furthermore, the Alliance contends that the owls do not require old-growth forest; they can adapt to younger forests. Northern spotted owls thrive in Boise Cascade's 50,000 acre forest near Yakima, Washington, which has been harvested and regrown repeatedly. The same situation exists on 70,000 acres of Weyerhaeuser timberland near Eugene, Oregon.

Despite the evidence, the wheels of government and the federal courts have been set in motion to protect the owl. The result has been havoc for people.

"Alaska Widows."   Nestled in a picturesque river valley at the foot of Oregon's Cascade Mountains, the town of Oakridge calls itself the tree-planting capital of the world. Its 3,400 residents are surrounded by the Willamette National Forest, which teems with elk and deer, bear and cougar.

After timber-sale restrictions began to take effect, logging companies started laying off workers, and truckers who had hauled the wood were idled. Mill workers who had been making as much as $17 an hour found that the few jobs available were sacking groceries or pumping gas at minimum wage, and even those soon disappeared.

Local unemployment shot up to 25 percent. For-sale signs sprouted   20 like mushrooms. Business began to go bankrupt — first the variety store and the animal-feed store, then three gas stations, two clothing stores, several restaurants, and the town's only movie theater.

To survive financially, several dozen Oakridge men sought employment in the only section of the West Coast still hiring loggers — Alaska. Separated from their families ten months at a time, they live on rafts in a region accessible only by floatplane or boat. Left behind in Oakridge are the wives, who call themselves Alaska Widows.

Cheryl Osborne, who has three children, rises each morning at 5:30 to cook breakfast in the restaurant she and her husband opened in the building next to their house. The house is up for sale, and the restaurant is barely making it. In the afternoons Osborne works as a bookkeeper for a small logging company that's just making ends meet.

Linda Cutsforth hasn't been able to find full-time work since she lost her mill job after twenty-five years of employment. She has seen the strain take its toll on timber families. "Loggers look like whipped dogs," she says. "My husband feels like he's sentenced to prison in Alaska."

Jill Silvey works at the local elementary school, where she has seen the economic casualties up close. One fourth-grade boy lived in a tent on the river with his family after they lost their home. Several children from another family live in a campground and arrive hungry at school each day.

In timber towns across the Pacific Northwest, families and entire [25] communities that had once been close-knit are disintegrating. Loggers in towns with names like Happy Camp and Sweet Home, who had taken pride in their self-sufficiency and hard work, now feel abandoned and betrayed.

Adding Up Costs.   "Environmentalists predicted in 1990 that only 2,300 jobs would be affected in the three states," remembers Chris West, vice president of the Northwest Forestry Association.

Earlier this year, the FWS projected the loss of 32,100 jobs. As compiled by timber-industry groups and labor unions, the ultimate figure, taking privately owned woodlands into account, may exceed 100,000.

Ripple effects have begun to reach consumers nationwide. Pacific Northwest states supply more than one-third of all the softwood lumber and plywood produced in America. In 1991 the volume of wood withdrawn from harvest because of owl restrictions was enough to construct 270,000 new homes. The scarcity drove up lumber prices at least 30 percent, adding more than $3,000 to the cost of building a $150,000 home.

If the restrictions on cutting continue, most economists expect a further sharp rise in timber prices. For every 20 percent increase in wood costs, up to 65,000 American families are priced out of houses they could have afforded previously. Prices will also rise on paper products and furniture.

Short-term relief would be available if the Forest Service could 30 salvage wood presently rotting on the ground. Major storms, for example, have blown down 195 million board feet of timber in Oregon's spotted-owl habitat, enough to keep more than 1,300 people employed for up to a year and provide enough timber to construct some 16,000 American homes.

But environmental groups have blocked the Forest Service from salvaging the wood — this despite the government and industry contention that not all of the blow-downs are essential to the owl's habitat.

Striking a Balance. "There have certainly been forest abuses," admits Cheryl Osborne, herself a former member of the Audubon Society. Clear-cutting, for example, leaves large, ugly bald spots sprinkled with the charred remains of stumps and debris. Congress, too, is to blame, having directed the overcutting of trees in the national forests to increase federal revenues. "But you can't wipe out the livelihoods of tens of thousands of people just to accommodate the spotted owl," declares Osborne. "Why can't there be a balance?"

There can be, if loggers use a range of techniques known as New Forestry. At Collins Pine Company's 91,500-acre forest in northeastern California, no clear-cutting is permitted. Old-growth-forest trees such as ponderosa pine are mingled with other species of new growth. Most trees killed by insects, burned, or blown down are weeded out, but vigorous ones are left to help replenish the forest with seed.

At Collins, more trees are always growing than are being cut. The result is a thriving wildlife population, including bald eagles, ospreys, and California spotted owls.

"We should be able to manage forests for spotted owls," says wild- 35 life biologist Larry Irwin. "We know of hundreds of cases where owl habitat was created by accident as a result of management practices. Surely, then, we can do it by design."

Most environmental groups are skeptical of New Forestry: It still means cutting trees. Many timber companies resist it, claiming it is a less efficient way to harvest fewer trees. A growing number of foresters and wildlife biologists, however, are accepting New Forestry as a bridge to cross the deep chasm that separates most environmental groups from most timber growers.

Spotted owls and logging are not incompatible — and Congress must take this controversy away from the courts and carve out a compromise that serves the national interest. "The reign of terror against private landowners must end," says Donald Walker, Jr. "Loggers need their jobs back, the Alaska Widows need their husbands, and the nation needs the renewable resource that this group of hard-working Americans provides."

The Case for Preservation

PETER KORN

In 1973 Congress unwittingly passed the most effective and benevolent piece of environmental legislation ever enacted in the United States. It took about fifteen years before environmentalists began to recognize and make full use of the Endangered Species Act, but now that they have, the natural resources of the West, and the battles over their development and protection, will never be the same.

From a conservationist viewpoint, the difference is between fighting battles and fighting wars. The history of conservationism in this country is marked by small victories that, over the length of time, usually yield to development interests. A river may be cleaned up here, a shoreline protected there, but over time the march of what we once unabashedly called progress would triumph. President Jimmy Carter's landmark legislation establishing the Arctic National Wildlife Refuge appeared to lock up a sizable portion of wilderness; more than a decade later the refuge still exists, but it appears oil drilling is about to begin there.

The Endangered Species Act has proved to be a much more definitive piece of conservation legislation. For one thing, it works. The act has changed the ground rules of environmentalism, finally giving the environmentalists a weapon with which to battle development interests to a standoff. Because of the act, as many as 8 million acres of untouched, ancient forests in the Pacific Northwest might be made off-limits to the relentless crackle of chain saws. Development projects such as dams and subdivisions have been discarded or delayed.

But now the development interests have begun to amass their political forces to reverse this shift in power. They are planning a frontal assault on the law when it comes up for renewal in this session of Congress. The outcome of the battle will determine the potency of environmentalism for decades to come, not to mention the fate of thousands of endangered plant and animal species.

First, some history. What most distinguishes the act as a piece of   5 environmental legislation is how far it goes. It puts protection of species ahead of all considerations — a highly moral position (or perhaps an oversight). When H.R. 37 became the Endangered Species Act in 1973 it encountered little opposition. Promoters of the act spoke of saving eagles, buffaloes, and grizzly bears. Who could vote against such high-profile beneficiaries? Nobody mentioned spotted owls and snail darters, or the thousands of species of plants and insects also facing extinction. And nobody considered that the act might work retroactively. It's one thing for a snail darter to hold up construction of a dam, another for

Peter Korn writes on environmental topics. This article is reprinted from the March 30, 1992 issue of *The Nation,* a liberal journal.

an owl or salmon to alter an already established infrastructure — the Pacific Northwest's logging industry, in the owl's case.

Oregon Senator Bob Packwood voted for the act in 1973 but is now leading the efforts to modify it. "It just never occurred to us the extraordinary ramifications of the act," Packwood says. "We were thinking projects, we were thinking site specifics. We were not thinking ecosystems." But ecosystems are what they've got. Three years ago the spotted owl gained listing as a threatened species. The owl lives only in old-growth forests. Preserving the species has meant preserving the owl's lumber-rich ecosystem — the ancient forests.

Controversy has dogged the law since its inception. In 1977 construction was delayed on Tellico Dam in Tennessee with the discovery of the snail darter, a tiny fish that existed only in the Little Tennessee River and would vanish if the dam were completed. The Tennessee Congressional delegation subsequently led an assault on section 7 of the act, which requires the federal government to prevent destruction of endangered species' habitats. Arguing before the Supreme Court, Griffin Bell, attorney for the Tennessee Valley Authority, held up a small glass jar containing a snail darter and asked the Court how a three-inch fish could be valued more highly than a multimillion-dollar dam. The Court ruled for the fish. The act's preeminent power was upheld, though in 1979 the fish were transplanted and the dam constructed under a rare legislative exception passed by Congress.

The key to the act's draconian effect is its insistence, in section 4, that listings be made solely on the basis of scientific evidence. Economic impact can be considered only during implementation of the measures recommended to preserve the species.

Sometimes the law yields tremendous results — the bald eagle, alligator, brown pelican, and peregrine falcon all recovered after gaining the act's protection. But there have been losses: In 1987 the last dusky seaside sparrow died in captivity. The losses continue in the United States partly because there is a backlog of more than 4,000 candidates for listing. Well under a quarter of the threatened species in this country are officially listed and protected, and 40 percent of those listed still await recovery plans. The reluctance of federal agencies to list species without pressure from environmental lawsuits indicates a political motivation for some of the delay. But most often the cause is an overburdened government agency. The act does not set a firm deadline for action by the secretary of the interior on a petition for listing. Some declining species may wait decades before receiving a ruling, and some species perish waiting for listing.

Nevertheless, the act represents a gold mine of possibilities for 10 environmentalists and their attorneys. Government agencies have tended to interpret the law narrowly, but time after time in court, environmentalists have found the weapon they need in the act's language.

Which brings us to the recently listed Snake River coho and chinook salmon runs. The cost of the owl rulings has been borne primarily by the logging community. The number of jobs lost in the timber industry because of habitat preservation ranges from 10,000 to 100,000, depending on who supplies the figures. But the recovery plan for the salmon would affect an entire region: Farmers, fishermen, loggers, and the aluminum and transportation industries all benefit from the rivers in one way or another, and will have to give up some of their interests to save the Salmon. Thanks to the hydroelectric dams on the Columbia River, electricity rates in the Northwest are 40 percent of the national average. Those same dams, however, are responsible for death rates as high as 80 percent for juvenile salmon migrating to sea. So the general public may have to pay higher electric rates if dams are shut down during salmon migration months [see Clay Hathorn, "Save Our Salmon, Save Our Soul," *The Nation,* January 6/13/91].

Salmon once thrived in rivers in the lower forty-eight states: up and down the East Coast and on the West Coast well down into California. Now, with a few exceptions, they are limited to rivers in the Northwest. The American Fisheries Society, an organization primarily comprising fisheries scientists, lists 214 wild runs of West Coast salmon, and steelhead and cutthroat trout in some danger of extinction. The society found 159 of these at high or moderate risk of extinction, yet only one is protected under the act. So more listings could follow.

All of which has a lot of people asking, Why go to such lengths to preserve a species? The Global 2000 Report, issued during the Carter administration, predicts that as many as 20 percent of the earth's species will become extinct by the turn of the century — that's approximately 2 million life forms. There is no way to measure the worth of those species. But every now and then, we learn the value of maintaining the genetic diversity of the earth's ecosystem.

The rosy periwinkle, a tropical flower, is used to treat leukemia. Tree poachers have been stripping Pacific yews since scientists discovered that the tree's bark offers new hope in the treatment of ovarian cancer. Ironically, the yew, which is found in the Northwest's old-growth forests, might be extinct if not for protection afforded those ecosystems; now some cancer sufferers are willing to drive the tree to extinction in order to obtain treatment. There are other reasons for saving endangered species. The most obvious is simply that by preserving the earth's genetic pool we keep open future options for nature and science to maintain a healthy environment. There is a growing understanding that all life forms are part of one interdependent ecosystem, and the declining health of one species signals danger for all species, including humans. For "glamour" species, such as grizzly bears, there is an aesthetic argument to be made. And there are moral considerations: Humans should not try to play God by deciding which species are more important than others.

Every few years the Endangered Species Act comes up for renewal. 15

It has been amended five times, but the coming battle promises to be the most heated. The effects of the owl and salmon listings have motivated some to seek changes, and the ranks of the dissatisfied have grown.

Timber interests in the Southeast have been hurt by the listing of the red cockaded woodpecker. Construction of a dam for the Animas La Plata water project in Colorado has been delayed by a dispute over the Colorado River squawfish, sending water interests into the legislative fray. In Southern California, listing of the Stevens kangaroo rat as endangered has held up Riverside County housing development, pushing real estate developers and home builders into the camp of those who would amend the act. In fact, a report issued recently by a White House advisory commission singled out the Endangered Species Act as a primary regulatory program adding to the cost of housing.

In response, conservationists have formed a coalition to fight efforts to weaken the law. Their numbers run the gamut of environmental organizations, from Greenpeace to the Garden Club of America. Michael Bean, an attorney with the Environmental Defense Fund who serves as a strategist for the coalition, calls the act "fundamentally sound." Bean knows the most significant battle will be whether to introduce economic considerations into the decision to list a species. A secondary front will focus on the act's protection of subspecies and populations. Currently, it protects some endangered species — for example, the bald eagle — in the contiguous United States, even though the species may thrive elsewhere in the country. Indeed, the bald eagle and grizzly bear were never endangered in Alaska, but this did not deter protection in the Lower Forty-eight. The same holds for the act's protection of endangered subspecies of salmon, even though a few salmon runs remain healthy.

One of the most controversial elements of the act is the exemption process, which was added in 1978 in response to the snail darter episode. This allows the president to convene a panel, dubbed the "god squad," to exempt protected species from coverage of the act. Recently the god squad reassembled to consider overruling a number of spotted-owl forest set-asides in favor of logging. For his part, Bean favors improvements in dealing with the backlog of candidate species, either by expediting the listing process or by extending some protection to species while they await a listing decision. Senator Packwood is confident he will be able to push through changes dictating that economic impact be considered in the listing process. "I think the momentum is growing, saying we ought to have a balance," he says.

On the environmentalists' side, Andy Kerr of the Oregon Natural Resources Council says, "We all know we're going to have to empty the benches for this one." Kerr says the act has become "the law of last resort." What he would like is to have an early warning system built into the legislation in order to target species that are declining but not yet endangered. Others have suggested that the Endangered Species Act misses the point, and that what is needed is an Endangered Eco-systems Act.

Hidden behind the debate that will rage in Congress this session are two unanswerable questions: How much is a species worth, and how much dominion over those species should humans have? It's one thing to save a species of animal or plant from extinction because it may one day provide a technological use to people, as with the yew tree. But opponents of the act as it now stands question whether a species of owl is worth 20,000 jobs, or whether maintaining wild salmon in our rivers is worth higher electric rates.

Congress will debate the language of the act, but probably not its morality. And if Packwood and his colleagues are able to change the law so that economic factors are taken into consideration before a species can be listed, the act's entire underpinning will have been compromised. Then, saving species will become a matter for bureaucratic rule, a weighing of conflicting interests.

The uniqueness of the act is that government agencies are virtually unable to contravene its clear intent — to save species at all costs. "We aren't so poor that we have to drive species into extinction, nor are we so rich that we can afford to," says Kerr. If the Endangered Species Act itself becomes endangered, more species will surely follow.

No Red Squirrels? Mother Nature May Be Better Off

MICHAEL D. COPELAND

A mountain near Tucson, Arizona, has become the latest battle-ground in the war between environmentalists and developers. Opponents of a proposed $200 million observatory on Mount Graham claim that its construction threatens the existence of the Mount Graham red squirrel, which lives only at the summit of this mountain. The diminutive squirrels, totaling slightly more than 100 in number, were listed as endangered in 1987 under the Endangered Species Act. They are being used in an attempt to halt this project, just as the snail darter, the northern spotted owl, and the dusky seaside sparrow have been used to interfere with previous construction or resource-use decisions.

Michael D. Copeland is executive director of the Montana-based organization Political Economy Research Center. This article was published in the June 7, 1990 issue of the *Wall Street Journal.*

Interior Secretary Manuel Lujan recently questioned whether the interference on behalf of a single species is worth the cost, and suggested that Congress consider increasing the flexibility of the Endangered Species Act. His remarks, which included the statement, "Nobody's told me the difference between a red squirrel, a black one, or a brown one," may not earn high marks from environmental groups. But they make considerable sense to much of the scientific community.

The view that the loss of a single species can have disastrous consequences represents a misguided notion about the significance of individual animal or plant categories. The Endangered Species Act assumes that preserving one species has enormous value or benefit. But this assumption is not warranted.

Suppose we lost a species. How devastating would that be? "Mass extinctions have been recorded since the dawn of paleontology," writes Harvard paleontologist Stephen Gould. These evolutionary disruptions delineated the major boundaries of geologic time. The most severe of these occurred approximately 250 million years ago, at the end of the Permian Period, with an estimated 96 percent extinction of species, says Mr. Gould. The cause of these extinctions is uncertain, but possibilities include global cooling, radiation, and sea-level fluctuations. There is general agreement among scientists that today's species represent a small proportion of all those that have ever existed — probably less than 1 percent. This means that more than 99 percent of all species ever living have become extinct.

Yet, in spite of these extinctions, both Mr. Gould and University of 5 Chicago paleontologist Jack Sepkoski say that the actual number of living species has probably increased over time. The "niches" created by extinctions provide an opportunity for a vigorous development of new species, a process called speciation. Periods of mass extinctions have been followed by increases in the number of species, as when small mammals expanded rapidly after dinosaurs disappeared.

Thus, evolutionary history appears to have been characterized by millions of species extinctions and subsequent increases in species numbers. Indeed, by attempting to preserve species living on the brink of extinction, we may be wasting time, effort, and money on animals that will disappear over time regardless of our efforts.

Advocates of preservation often contend that the process of evolution has endowed each species with a genetic accumulation of characteristics that enhance its chances of survival. If a species becomes extinct, this genetic history disappears forever and cannot be passed along to future species. The loss of any single species detracts from the genetic pool, this argument goes, and reduces the range of possibilities for future adaptation.

But Mr. Gould challenges this view. In his book *Wonderful Life* he writes that traits that enhance survival "do so in ways that are incidental and unrelated to the causes of their evolution in the first place. . . . A trait with no previous significance, one that had just hitchhiked along for the developmental ride as a side consequence of another adaptation, may now hold the key to your survival."

In other words, traits that have helped a species survive in the past are not particularly important to the future survival of that species or to its offshoots. The evolved survival traits of an endangered species are no more valuable than the traits of the new species that will eventually evolve after its extinction. Preserving a species will not necessarily increase the survival chances of future generations.

Why, then, are environmentalists so concerned with strict enforce- 10 ment of the Endangered Species Act? The answer is that saving species is often a subterfuge for achieving other goals, such as the prevention of development. When the Sierra Club's Legal Defense Fund attempted to delay a federal sale of old-growth timber in the Pacific Northwest, Andy Stahl, one of its analysts, made this fact quite clear. He called the northern spotted owl "the wildlife species of choice to act as a surrogate for old-growth protection, and I've often thought that thank goodness the spotted owl evolved in the Northwest, for if it hadn't we'd have to genetically engineer it . . . we can use it to protect a lot of old-growth." Evidently, Mr. Stahl is more concerned with old-growth timber than with the spotted owl.

Opinion is divided on whether the Mount Graham red squirrel will actually become extinct if the observatory is built; some say that the squirrel will have no trouble existing in the thousands of acres of nearby coniferous forests. But even if we lose this small population, we can rest assured that the consequence will not be evolutionary Armageddon. Whether the telescope should be built is a question to be decided by careful weighing of costs and benefits by the owners and developers. They should consider the potential loss of the squirrel as a possible cost, but not measure it as a disaster.

Creature Comfort: The Revitalization of American Wildlife

ROBERT GORDON, JR., and GEORGE DUNLOP

One of America's great untold stories is the remarkable comeback of many species of wildlife. Public attention focuses on the 259 species and subspecies of animals classified as endangered by the U.S. Fish and

Robert Gordon, Jr., is director of the National Wilderness Institute in Washington,

Wildlife Service. It is less often observed that hundreds of species —
from moose in New Hampshire to black bear in Pennsylvania to mountain lions in California — are increasing in population, demonstrating
the resiliency and dynamism of nature.

One of the most dramatic stories of recovery involves our national
symbol, the bald eagle. A decade ago, it was on the verge of extinction.
Thanks to substitutes for the pesticide DDT (which was damaging eagle
eggs) and harsh penalties for poaching, the bird's population has tripled
in fifteen years, and it may soon be taken off the endangered species
list. In northern California sixteen adults and one juvenile eagle were
recently counted in a single tree. In Montana the number of observed
nesting pairs has risen from twelve to ninety-six.

Temporary restrictions on hunting have similarly led to an explosion of the American alligator population. This reptile was on the first
federal endangered species list when the Endangered Species Act
passed in 1973, although it probably wouldn't have been included by
current standards. Dennis David of the Florida Game and Fresh Water
Commission estimates that there are now as many as one million
alligators in his state alone, and alligators are not limited to Florida.
The range of the species extends in an arc from North Carolina to
Oklahoma. The creature has been downgraded from the endangered to
the threatened species list, which allows a certain leeway in harvesting.
The fees collected from egg collectors, hunters, and others virtually
offset Florida's management costs.

Some species have recovered because their habitats have improved
as the unintended consequence of human activity. The population of
white-tailed deer, for instance, has risen nearly thirtyfold from 500,000
in the 1920s to 14 million today, partially because of reforestation in
the Northeast. (Because industry and farming have moved westward,
there are now 26 million more acres of forest in Maine, New Hampshire,
Vermont, and New York than there were at the turn of the century.)

Similarly, the chestnut-sided warbler was sighted only once by [5]
Audubon in all his peregrinations across America. It is now a more
common songbird because its habitats of forest edges, slashings, and
brushy pastures have expanded in the past century — though there has
recently been a slight decline.

But many of the most remarkable recoveries have occurred as the
result of deliberate human efforts. Specially designed birdhouses have
helped the Eastern bluebird make a comeback since it faced extinction
in 1930 as a result of competition from the European starling. Setting
aside land for state and national parks and forests, as well as private

D.C. George Dunlop, formerly assistant secretary for natural resources and environment
in the U.S. Department of Agriculture, is now an official of the National Wilderness
Institute. Their article is reprinted from Summer 1990 issue of *Policy Review,* a quarterly
journal published by the Heritage Foundation.

wildlife sanctuaries, has preserved valuable natural habitat for hundreds of species.

Sheepshape

Simply setting land aside for nature, however, is not always enough for species recovery; many of the comebacks in the animal world have required careful management of the habitat. It has become fashionable in much of the environmental movement to support a let-nature-take-its-course approach to the regulation of park and wilderness lands, a philosophy that led to the great Yellowstone fire of 1988. However, many of the success stories in wildlife recovery result from a contrary view, in which government agencies or private organizations take an active, managerial role in support of species that people care a great deal about. . . .

Giant Goose Chase

Hunters, fishermen, and farmers have played an important role in the revival of many species. The Pittman-Robertson Act, enacted in the 1930s with the support of hunters, levies an excise tax on firearms and ammunition that provided $100 million in 1989 alone to state wildlife programs for restoration of habitat, restocking, and development of wildlife resources. A similar program, the Dingell-Johnson Act, does the same for game fish.

In Missouri, hunters help wildlife managers by collecting information about the population density of the wild turkey. There are now as many as 20,000 wild turkeys in the state's Mark Twain Forest. The hunters' cooperation pays off in another way: Officials from the Missouri Department of Conservation capture the bird with cannon nets, and then exchange one wild turkey for four ruffed grouse from Indiana. Now eight counties in Missouri have a grouse season they didn't have before.

The wild turkey had been reduced to a few southern states by the early 1900s, but today can be found throughout the continental United States. Its numbers have risen to between two million and three million, thanks to cooperative efforts by hunters and game commissions, as well as restocking by private property owners.

Farmers and hunters saved another big bird from extinction. The giant Canada goose is similar in appearance to other Canada geese, but much larger. While a typical male Canada goose might weigh nine pounds, a male giant could weigh fourteen to fifteen pounds.

During the 1950s, giant Canada geese were believed to be extinct. However, in 1962, goose specialist Harold Hansen discovered some of the giants in Rochester, Minnesota, and afterwards at other locations. Farmers and hunters, among others, had been collecting giant Canada goose eggs and rearing goslings in captivity for food and for farm or decoy flocks. The stock reared by these farmers and hunters, and their knowledge of how to care for the geese, greatly benefited subsequent restoration programs. Current estimates of the giant Canada goose population run as high as 150,000.

Profits of Game

Like farmers, hunters, and fishermen, ranchers can play a positive role in recovering wildlife. A good example is the Deseret Ranch in Woodruff, Utah. The 200,000-acre ranch is home to pronghorn antelope, buffalo, mule deer, moose, red fox, coyote, bobcat, mountain lion, and Rocky Mountain elk, as well as 7,000 to 8,000 head of cattle. Currently the ranch is working to establish healthy populations of Bear Lake cutthroat trout. It is conducting a study for reintroduction of an upland game bird, the sharp-tailed grouse, and it is participating in an experimental antelope harvest strategy with the Utah Division of Wildlife Resources.

Hunters are willing to pay higher fees for Deseret trophies, because the ranch's managers work hard to enhance the health and quality of wildlife on the property. A case in point is the elk herd, which has grown from around 350 in 1979 to between 1,200 and 1,400 today. Nationally, the elk population has grown fivefold since the 1920s — from approximately 100,000 to about half a million today. Deseret elk are exceptionally healthy. Their calving rate is high — about 65 calves to 100 cows, and about 90 percent of the calves are a result of the first heat. First-heat calves are more mature and have a higher survival rate during the winter than calves born after the second or third heat, as is more common on state and federal lands near the ranch.

In accounting for the excellent health of Deseret's elk, general 15 manager Gregg Simonds stresses the quality of grazing lands. Cattle grazing is strictly monitored to insure ample high-quality graze and forage for other species. Deseret's wildlife biologist Shane Davis stresses the minimal disturbance to elk herds during the rutting season and a high ratio of healthy, mature elk bulls to cows for breeding.

Nature's Resiliency

There are several lessons from these stories of species recovery. One is that humans can care for and expand wildlife populations not just through negative means — such as bans on pesticides or restrictions on hunting until the population stabilizes — but through sound management techniques such as prescribed fires, improvement of food and water sources, and other enhancements of habitat. Most of these management techniques are site and situation specific, not conducive to administration by a central state or federal bureaucracy. They involve trial-and-error experiments tailored to conditions in local ecosystems. Wildlife biologists can easily tell whether their techniques actually benefit the species they are trying to help. If not, they try something else.

A second lesson is that ranchers, farmers, outdoor sportsmen, and others from the private sector play an important role in effective wildlife policies, sometimes on their own, sometimes in association with government wildlife authorities. Sportsmen naturally have an incentive to care for and expand the species they like to hunt and fish. Increasingly, property owners are discovering the attractions of enhancing habitat on their lands, either for their own enjoyment or for the hunting income offered by rich and diverse animal populations.

Perhaps the most important lesson is that nature itself is dynamic and resilient. Natural forces, of course, are the cause of the majority of extinctions. Other species have been devastated by human action, such as encroachments on habitat and overhunting; the passenger pigeon and the Carolina parakeet are among the most prominent man-caused extinctions on the American continent. But one of the glories of nature is how strong and renewable it is. Many of our threatened species can regain their numbers. Through careful management of their habitat, man can help.

"It's made from an endangered species for that one person in a thousand who couldn't care less."

Drawing by Weber; © *1992 The New Yorker Magazine, Inc.*

THINKING AND WRITING ABOUT ENDANGERED SPECIES

Questions for Discussion and Writing

1. What purpose is served by Caldicott's long introduction to the origin of life on this planet? Does Caldicott seem to place a higher value on the endangered species for their own sake or for their contribution to human life on earth? What people and agencies does she blame for the destruction of species? What point is she making in describing the lives of sea turtles?

2. What assumption about endangered species does Copeland attack? How does he support his attack? Does his evidence effectively refute Caldicott's grim scenario?

3. Does Korn effectively answer the question he poses: Why go to such lengths to preserve a species? Both Korn and Copeland refer to "development interests" in conflict with environmental protection. Both writers are concerned with the morality of the conflict as well as the practical consequences. Describe their differing views of the moral component.

4. How does Miniter refute data supplied by environmentalists? Which kinds of evidence are most convincing? Least convincing? What is Miniter's solution for the problem of loss of species?

5. Fitzgerald emphasizes the adverse economic impact of saving endangered species on individuals and their families. How does he attempt to persuade his readers that the environmentalists are the villains in this drama? How successful is he?

6. Why do Gordon and Dunlop think that central state and federal bureaucracies are not the appropriate agencies for managing species recovery? Can the data in their article be used to refute Caldicott and Korn?

7. What use of emotional appeals do you find in these articles? Are the examples of personal experience more or less effective than statistical data? Do you find evidence of exaggeration, selective use of data, inappropriate appeals, loaded words, controversial definitions? What compromises are suggested for resolving the debate between environmentalists and commercial interests? Can nonexperts evaluate the proposals?

8. Who or what is the object of the cartoonist's sarcasm?

Topics for Research

Endangered plants and medical research

Saving the elephant and the rhinoceros in Africa

Reintroducing the wolf into the American West

Conservation by private ownership and management

The doctrine of biocentrism, nature's intrinsic value apart from its contribution to human life. (An influential source: *The End of Nature* by Bill McKibben)

CHAPTER FOURTEEN

Euthanasia

Euthanasia means "good death" or "mercy killing," that is, causing the death of one who is so ill or disabled that continued existence will produce intolerable suffering. Euthanasia may be active or passive; in the first case, death is deliberately inflicted, sometimes by a relative; in the second case, life-support systems are withdrawn and the patient dies naturally.

Controversy surrounding the morality of euthanasia has been heightened enormously in recent years because of advances in medical technology that make it possible for human beings, both newborn and old, to be kept alive almost indefinitely, even when severely impaired. As our life span lengthens, more and more people will reach an age when illness and disability create the possibility for euthanasia.

In those cases in which the patient cannot make a rational choice, decisions to prolong or terminate life must be left to families, doctors, and, not infrequently, the courts. Even the definition of *life* is at issue. A person may be declared "brain dead" while vital functions persist. Other problems of definition have become increasingly important. Where a patient has signed a living will, a physician may nevertheless refuse to remove the feeding tube, arguing that continuing to provide nourishment does not constitute "medication, artificial means, or heroic measures." In June 1990 the Supreme Court ruled that a state may pass laws allowing patients to refuse unwanted life-sustaining treatment, provided that the patient has previously expressed "clear and convincing evidence" of such a desire. As a consequence, legal initiatives for and against euthanasia have appeared on state ballots in the last two years. So far, euthanasia has failed to win many converts. In 1992 California voters turned back Initiative 161, which would have allowed doctors to assist in death requested by terminally ill patients. Also in

1992, after several doctor-assisted suicides by the inventor of a "self-execution machine," Michigan became the first state to make doctor-assisted suicide illegal.

On one side are those who regard the problems posed by euthanasia as essentially religious: Life is sacred, no matter how severely disabled the patient may be, and no human being can arrogate to him- or herself a decision reserved for God. On the other side are those who insist that it is the quality of life that should influence the decision and that death may be preferable to a severely impaired life. Euthanasia thus becomes an act of charity. In one widely publicized case which tested the limits of the quality-of-life criterion, parents approved denial of food and water to their severely retarded newborn son rather than allow a stomach operation for him.

One final problem confronts us in all the discussions about euthanasia. Will increasingly widespread acceptance of such deaths lead to a more relaxed attitude toward the taking of life in general and toward taking the lives of those in need of constant and lifelong attention in particular? One writer asks if the same principle of withholding food and water from a woman in a coma should be extended "to the thousands of others who fall into a coma every year, and to the many more mentally retarded or deranged, and sufferers of Alzheimer's disease who are a 'burden' on their families."

Death by Choice

DANIEL C. MAGUIRE

Who would dare arrogate to himself the decision to impose death on a child or unconscious person who is not in a position to assent or dissent to the action? What right does any person have to make decisions about life and death in any way that assumes absolute and ultimate authority over another human being? Could a doctor make such a decision? It would seem that he could not. His medical skills are one thing, the moral decision to end a life is another. How would a family feel who learned that a doctor had reached an independent decision to terminate their father's life?

Could the family make such a decision? It would seem not, for several good reasons. There might be a conflict of interest arising from avarice, spite, or impatience with the illness of the patient. And even if these things were not present, the family might be emotionally trau-

---

Daniel Maguire is a professor of ethics at Marquette University and a former Roman Catholic priest. This excerpt is from his book, *Death by Choice* (1974).

matized when their pain of loss is complicated by the recollection of their decision. Also, the family might constitute a split and therefore a hung jury. Then what?

Could a court-appointed committee of impartial persons make the decision? No, it would seem not. They would not only be impartial but also uninformed about the personal realities of the patient. The decision to terminate life requires a full and intimate knowledge of all the reality-constituting circumstances of the case. Strangers would not have this.

The conclusion, therefore, would seem inescapable that there is no moral way in which death could be imposed on a person who is incapable of consent because of youth or irreversible loss of consciousness.

This objection contains so much truth that my reply to it will 5 contain much agreement as well as disagreement. To begin with, it should be noted that we are discussing not the legality but the morality of terminating life without the consent of the patient. Terminating life by a deliberate act of commission in the kinds of cases here discussed is illegal in this country. By an ongoing fiction of American law it would be classified as murder in the first degree. Terminating by calculated omission is murky at best and perilous at worst under current law. Therefore, it can be presumed that any conclusion we reach here will probably be illegal. This is a morally relevant fact; it is not to be presumed morally decisive, however, since there may be good moral grounds to assume the risk of illegality. As we have stated, morality and legality are not identical.

With this said, then, let us face up to the objection. There are two parts to my response. First, holding the question of *who should decide* in abeyance for the moment, I would suggest that there are cases where, if that difficult question could be satisfactorily answered, it would seem to be a morally good option (among other morally good options) to terminate a life. In other words, there are cases where the termination of a life could be defended as a moral good if the proper authority for making the decision could be located. Of course, if the objections raised against all those who could decide are decisive, then this otherwise morally desirable act would be immoral by reason of improper agency.

There are cases where it would appear to be arguably moral to take the necessary action (or to make the necessary omission) to end a life. Dr. Ruth Russell tells this story:

> I used to annually take a class of senior students in abnormal psychology to visit the hospital ward in a training school for medical defectives. There was a little boy about four years old the first time we visited him in the hospital. He was a hydrocephalic with a head so immensely large that he had never been able to raise it off the pillow and he never would. He had a tiny little body with this huge head and it is very difficult to keep him from developing sores. The students asked, "Why do we keep a child like that alive?"

The next year we went back with another class. This year the child's hands had been padded to keep him from hitting his head. Again the students asked, "Why do we do this?" The third year we went back and visited the same child. Now the nurses explained that he had been hitting his head so hard that in spite of the padding he was injuring it severely and they had tied his arms down to the sides of his crib.[1]

What are the defensible moral options in this kind of case? One might be to keep the child alive in the way that was being done. This might show a great reverence for life and reinforce society's commitment to weak and defective human life. It may indeed be the hallmark of advancing civilization that continuing care would be taken of this child. Termination of this child's life by omission or commission might set us on the slippery slope that has led other societies to the mass murder of physically and mentally defective persons.

All of this is possibly true but it is by no means self-evidently true to the point that other alternatives are apodictically excluded. This case is a singularly drastic one. Given its special qualities, action to end life here is not necessarily going to precipitate the killing of persons in distinguishably different circumstances.

Furthermore, keeping this child alive might exemplify the materi- 10 alistic error of interpreting the sanctity of life in merely physical terms. This interpretation, of course, is a stark oversimplification. It is just as wrong as the other side of the simplistic coin, which would say that life has no value until it attains a capacity for distinctively personal acts such as intellectual knowledge, love, and imagination. A fetus, while not yet capable of intellectual and other distinctively personal activity, is on a trajectory toward personhood and already shares in the sanctity of human life. (This does not mean that it may never be terminated when other sacred values outweigh its claim to life in a conflict situation.)

The sanctity of life is a generic notion that does not yield a precisely spelled-out code of ethics. Deciding what the sanctity of life requires in conflict situations, such as the case of the hydrocephalic child described by Dr. Russell, may lead persons to contradictory judgments. To say that the sanctity of life requires keeping that child alive regardless of his condition, and that all other alternatives impeach the perception of life as sacred, is both arrogant and epistemologically unsound. In this case, maintaining this child in this condition might be incompatible with its sacred human dignity. It might not meet the minimal needs of human physical existence. In different terms, the sanctity of death might here take precedence over a physicalist inter-

---

[1] See *Dilemmas of Euthanasia,* a pamphlet containing excerpts, papers, and discussions from the Fourth Euthanasia Conference, held in New York on December 4, 1971; this is a publication of the Euthanasia Educational Council, Inc. [now called Concern for Dying], New York, p. 35.

pretation of the sanctity of life. There is a time when human death befits human life, when nothing is more germane to the person's current needs. This conclusion appears defensible in the case of the hydrocephalic boy.

Also, to keep this child alive to manifest and maintain society's respect for life appears to be an unacceptable reduction of this child to the status of means. Society should be able to admit the value of death in this case and still maintain its respect for life. Our reverence for life should not be dependent on this sort of martyrdom.

The decision, therefore, that it is morally desirable to bring on this boy's death is a defensible conclusion from the facts and prognosis of this case. (We are still holding in abeyance the question of who should make that decision.) There are two courses of action that could flow from that decision. The decision could be made to stop all special medication and treatment and limit care to nourishment, or the decision could be made in the light of all circumstances to take more direct action to induce death.

There is another case, a famous one . . . , where the life of a radically deformed child was ended. This is the tragic case of Corinne van de Put, who was a victim of thalidomide, a drug that interfered with the limb buds between the sixth and eighth weeks of pregnancy. Corinne was born on May 22, 1962, with no arms or shoulder structure and with deformed feet. It would not even be possible to fit the child with artificial limbs since there was no shoulder structure, but only cartilage. Some experts said the chances for survival were 1 in 10 and a Dr. Hoet, a professor of pathological embryology at the Catholic University of Louvain, was of the opinion that child had only a year or two to live. Eight days after the baby was born, the mother, Madame Suzanne van de Put, mixed barbiturates with water and honey in the baby's bottle and thus killed her daughter.

During the trial, Madame van de Put was asked why she had not followed the gynecologist's advice to put the child in a home. "I did not want it," she replied. "Absolutely not. For me, as an egoist, I could have been rid of her. But it wouldn't have given her back her arms." The president of the court pointed out that the child appeared to be mentally normal. "That was only worse," said Madame van de Put. "If she had grown up to realize the state she was in, she would never have forgiven me for letting her live."[2]

Is Madame van de Put's decision to be seen as one of the several morally defensible options available in this case? I think that it is. Again, this does not say that other solutions have no moral probability. As Norman St. John-Stevas points out in his discussion of this case, there

---

[2]For an account of this case and a negative judgment on Madame van de Put's action, see Norman St. John-Stevas, *The Right to Life* (New York, Chicago, San Francisco: Holt, Rinehart & Winston, 1964), pp. 3–24.

are individuals who, though terribly disadvantaged, live fruitful and apparently happy lives. He speaks of Arthur Kavanagh, who was born in 1831 without limbs. No mechanical mechanism could be devised to help him. According to St. John-Stevas, however, Kavanagh managed to achieve some mystifying successes.

> Yet throughout his life he rode and drove, traveled widely, shot and fished. From 1868 until 1880 he sat as Member for Carlow and spoke in the Commons. In addition, he was a magistrate, a grand juror, a poor-law guardian, and he organized a body to defend the rights of landlords.[3]

St. John-Stevas, however, does admit that "Not everyone can be an Arthur Kavanagh. . . ." Neither could everyone be a Helen Keller. The problem is that no one knows this when these decisions are made. The option to let the person live and find out is not necessarily safe. The person may not have the resources of a Kavanagh or a Keller and may rue both the day of birth and the decision to let him live. As Madame van de Put said, Corinne may "never have forgiven me for letting her live." The decision to let live is not inherently safe. It may be a decision for a personal disaster. There are persons living who have found their lives a horror, who do not think they have the moral freedom to end their lives, and who ardently wish someone had ended life for them before they reached consciousness. It is little consolation to these people to be told that they were let live on the chance that they might have been a Beethoven. The presumption that the decision to let live will have a happy moral ending is gratuitous and is not a pat solution to the moral quandary presented by such cases.

Interestingly, in the van de Put case, the defense counsel told the jury that he did not think Madame van de Put's solution was the only one, but that it was not possible to condemn her for having chosen it.[4] It could have been moral also to muster all possible resources of imagination and affection and give Corinne the ability to transcend her considerable impairments and achieve fullness of life. In this very un-clear situation, this could have been a defensible option. It was not, however, one without risks. It could have proved itself wrong.

The decision to end Corinne's life was also arguably moral, though, again, not without risks. It could not be called immoral on the grounds that it is better to live than not to live regardless of the meaning of that life. This is again a physicalist interpretation of the sanctity of life. It also could not be called immoral on the grounds that this kind of killing is likely to spill over and be used against unwanted children, etc., since this case has its own distinguishing characteristics which make it quite exceptional. It could not be called immoral because it is

---

[3] Ibid., p. 16.
[4] Ibid., pp. 7–8.

direct killing since . . . the issue is not directness or indirectness, but whether there is proportionate reason.

In this case, then, as in the case of the hydrocephalic boy, we have a situation where the imposition of death could seem a moral good, prescinding still from the question of who should decide. There could be other cases, too, where death could be seen as a good. Suppose someone suffers severe cerebral damage in an accident but due to continuing brainstem activity can be kept alive almost indefinitely through tubal nourishing and other supportive measures. Would it not seem a clear good if a decision could be made to withdraw support and allow death to have its final say? The spectacle of living with the breathing but depersonalized remains of a loved one could make death seem a needed blessing. In conclusion, then, there are cases where the imposition of death would seem a good. It was logically indicated to state that conclusion before going to the main thrust of the objection, the question of who could decide when the person in question can give no consent.

In Defense of Voluntary Euthanasia

SIDNEY HOOK

A few short years ago, I lay at the point of death. A congestive heart failure was treated for diagnostic purposes by an angiogram that triggered a stroke. Violent and painful hiccups, uninterrupted for several days and nights, prevented the ingestion of food. My left side and one of my vocal cords became paralyzed. Some form of pleurisy set in, and I felt I was drowning in a sea of slime. At one point, my heart stopped beating; just as I lost consciousness, it was thumped back into action again. In one of my lucid intervals during those days of agony, I asked my physician to discontinue all life-supporting services or show me how to do it. He refused and predicted that someday I would appreciate the unwisdom of my request.

A month later, I was discharged from the hospital. In six months, I regained the use of my limbs, and although my voice still lacks its old resonance and carrying power I no longer croak like a frog. There remain some minor disabilities and I am restricted to a rigorous, low-sodium diet. I have resumed my writing and research.

This essay by Sidney Hook (1902–1989), former professor of philosophy at New York University and senior research fellow at the Hoover Institution on War, Revolution, and Peace, was published in the *New York Times* on March 1, 1987.

My experience can be and has been cited as an argument against honoring requests of stricken patients to be gently eased out of their pain and life. I cannot agree. There are two main reasons. As an octogenarian, there is a reasonable likelihood that I may suffer another "cardiovascular accident" or worse. I may not even be in a position to ask for the surcease of pain. It seems to me that I have already paid my dues to death — indeed, although time has softened my memories they are vivid enough to justify my saying that I suffered enough to warrant dying several times over. Why run the risk of more?

Secondly, I dread imposing on my family and friends another grim round of misery similar to the one my first attack occasioned.

My wife and children endured enough for one lifetime. I know that   5 for them the long days and nights of waiting, the disruption of their professional duties, and their own familial responsibilities counted for nothing in their anxiety for me. In their joy at my recovery they have been forgotten. Nonetheless, to visit another prolonged spell of helpless suffering on them as my life ebbs away, or even worse, if I linger on into a comatose senility, seems altogether gratuitous.

But what, it may be asked, of the joy and satisfaction of living, of basking in the sunshine, listening to music, watching one's grandchildren growing into adolescence, following the news about the fate of freedom in a troubled world, playing with ideas, writing one's testament of wisdom and folly for posterity? Is not all that one endured, together with the risk of its recurrence, an acceptable price for the multiple satisfactions that are still open even to a person of advanced years?

Apparently those who cling to life no matter what think so. I do not.

The zest and intensity of these experiences are no longer what they used to be. I am not vain enough to delude myself that I can in the few remaining years make an important discovery useful for mankind or can lead a social movement or do anything that will be historically eventful, no less event-making. My autobiography, which describes a record of intellectual and political experiences of some historical value, already much too long, could be posthumously published. I have had my fill of joys and sorrows and am not greedy for more life. I have always thought that a test of whether one had found happiness in one's life is whether one would be willing to relive it — whether, if it were possible, one would accept the opportunity to be born again.

Having lived a full and relatively happy life, I would cheerfully accept the chance to be reborn, but certainly not to be reborn again as an infirm octogenarian. To some extent, my views reflect what I have seen happen to the aged and stricken who have been so unfortunate as to survive crippling paralysis. They suffer, and impose suffering on others, unable even to make a request that their torment be ended.

I am mindful too of the burdens placed upon the community, with   10 its rapidly diminishing resources, to provide the adequate and costly services necessary to sustain the lives of those whose days and nights are spent on mattress graves of pain. A better use could be made of these resources to increase the opportunities and qualities of life for the young. I am not denying the moral obligation the community has to look after its disabled and aged. There are times, however, when an individual may find it pointless to insist on the fulfillment of a legal and moral right.

What is required is no great revolution in morals but an enlargement of imagination and an intelligent evaluation of alternative uses of community resources.

Long ago, Seneca observed that "the wise man will live as long as he ought, not as long as he can." One can envisage hypothetical circumstances in which one has a duty to prolong one's life despite its costs for the sake of others, but such circumstances are far removed from the ordinary prospects we are considering. If wisdom is rooted in knowledge of the alternatives of choice, it must be reliably informed of the state one is in and its likely outcome. Scientific medicine is not infallible, but it is the best we have. Should a rational person be willing to endure acute suffering merely on the chance that a miraculous cure might presently be at hand? Each one should be permitted to make his own choice — especially when no one else is harmed by it.

The responsibility for the decision, whether deemed wise or foolish, must be with the chooser.

Active and Passive Euthanasia

JAMES RACHELS

The distinction between active and passive euthanasia is thought to be crucial for medical ethics. The idea is that it is permissible, at least in some cases, to withhold treatment and allow a patient to die, but it is never permissible to take any direct action designed to kill the patient. This doctrine seems to be accepted by most doctors, and it is endorsed in a statement adopted by the House of Delegates of the American Medical Association on December 4, 1973:

> The intentional termination of the life of one human being by another — mercy killing — is contrary to that for which the medical profession stands and is contrary to the policy of the American Medical Association.

James Rachels, a professor at the University of Miami, is editor of *Moral Problems,* a reader on the ethical aspects of contemporary social issues. "Active and Passive Euthanasia" was published in the *New England Journal of Medicine,* Vol. 292, in 1975.

The cessation of the employment of extraordinary means to prolong the life of the body when there is irrefutable evidence that biological death is imminent is the decision of the patient and/or his immediate family. The advice and judgment of the physician should be freely available to the patient and/or his immediate family.

However, a strong case can be made against this doctrine. In what follows I will set out some of the relevant arguments, and urge doctors to reconsider their views on this matter.

To begin with a familiar type of situation, a patient who is dying of incurable cancer of the throat is in terrible pain, which can no longer be satisfactorily alleviated. He is certain to die within a few days, even if present treatment is continued, but he does not want to go on living for those days since the pain is unbearable. So he asks the doctor for an end to it, and his family joins in the request.

Suppose the doctor agrees to withhold treatment, as the conventional doctrine says he may. The justification for his doing so is that the patient is in terrible agony, and since he is going to die anyway, it would be wrong to prolong his suffering needlessly. But now notice this. If one simply withholds treatment, it may take the patient longer to die, and so he may suffer more than he would if more direct action were taken and a lethal injection given. This fact provides strong reason for thinking that, once the initial decision not to prolong his agony has been made, active euthanasia is actually preferable to passive euthanasia, rather than the reverse. To say otherwise is to endorse the option that leads to more suffering rather than less, and is contrary to the humanitarian impulse that prompts the decision not to prolong his life in the first place.

Part of my point is that the process of being "allowed to die" can be relatively slow and painful, whereas being given a lethal injection is relatively quick and painless. Let me give a different sort of example. In the United States about one in 600 babies is born with Down's syndrome. Most of these babies are otherwise healthy — that is, with only the usual pediatric care, they will proceed to an otherwise normal infancy. Some, however, are born with congenital defects such as intestinal obstructions that require operations if they are to live. Sometimes, the parents and the doctor will decide not to operate, and let the infant die. Anthony Shaw describes what happens then:

> . . . When surgery is denied [the doctor] must try to keep the infant from suffering while natural forces sap the baby's life away. As a surgeon whose natural inclination is to use the scalpel to fight off death, standing by and watching a salvageable baby die is the most emotionally exhausting experience I know. It is easy at a conference, in a theoretical discussion, to decide that such infants should be allowed to die. It is altogether different to stand by in the nursery and watch as dehydration and infection wither a tiny being over hours and days. This is a terrible ordeal for me and the

hospital staff — much more so than for the parents who never set foot in the nursery.[1]

I can understand why some people are opposed to all euthanasia, and insist that such infants must be allowed to live. I think I can also understand why other people favor destroying these babies quickly and painlessly. But why should anyone favor letting "dehydration and infection wither a tiny being over hours and days"? The doctrine that says that a baby may be allowed to dehydrate and wither, but may not be given an injection that would end its life without suffering, seems so patently cruel as to require no further refutation. The strong language is not intended to offend, but only to put the point in the clearest possible way.

My second argument is that the conventional doctrine leads to 5 decisions concerning life and death made on irrelevant grounds.

Consider again the case of the infants with Down's syndrome who need operations for congenital defects unrelated to the syndrome to live. Sometimes there is no operation, and the baby dies, but when there is no such defect, the baby lives on. Now, an operation such as that to remove an intestinal obstruction is not prohibitively difficult. The reason why such operations are not performed in these cases is, clearly, that the child has Down's syndrome and the parents and doctor judge that because of that fact it is better for the child to die.

But notice that this situation is absurd, no matter what view one takes of the lives and potential of such babies. If the life of such an infant is worth preserving, what does it matter if it needs a simple operation? Or, if one thinks it better that such a baby should not live on, what difference does it make that it happens to have an unobstructed intestinal tract? In either case, the matter of life and death is being decided on irrelevant grounds. It is the Down's syndrome, and not the intestines, that is the issue. The matter should be decided, if at all, on that basis, and not be allowed to depend on the essentially irrelevant question of whether the intestinal tract is blocked.

What makes this situation possible, of course, is the idea that when there is an intestinal blockage, one can "let the baby die," but when there is no such defect there is nothing that can be done, for one must not "kill" it. The fact that this idea leads to such results as deciding life or death on irrelevant grounds is another good reason why the doctrine should be rejected.

One reason why so many people think that there is an important moral difference between active and passive euthanasia is that they think killing someone is morally worse than letting someone die. But is it? Is killing, in itself, worse than letting die? To investigate this issue,

---

[1] A. Shaw, "Doctor, Do We Have a Choice?" *New York Times Magazine*, January 30, 1972, p. 54.

two cases may be considered that are exactly alike except that one involves killing whereas the other involves letting someone die. Then, it can be asked whether this difference makes any difference to the moral assessments. It is important that the cases be exactly alike, except for this one difference, since otherwise one cannot be confident that it is this difference and not some other that accounts for any variation in the assessments of the two cases. So, let us consider this pair of cases:

In the first, Smith stands to gain a large inheritance if anything 10 should happen to his six-year-old cousin. One evening while the child is taking his bath, Smith sneaks into the bathroom and drowns the child, and then arranges things so that it will look like an accident.

In the second, Jones also stands to gain if anything should happen to his six-year-old cousin. Like Smith, Jones sneaks in planning to drown the child in his bath. However, just as he enters the bathroom Jones sees the child slip and hit his head, and fall face down in the water. Jones is delighted; he stands by, ready to push the child's head back under if it is necessary, but it is not necessary. With only a little thrashing about, the child drowns all by himself, "accidentally," as Jones watches and does nothing.

Now Smith killed the child, whereas Jones "merely" let the child die. That is the only difference between them. Did either man behave better, from a moral point of view? If the difference between killing and letting die were in itself a morally important matter, one should say that Jones's behavior was less reprehensible than Smith's. But does one really want to say that? I think not. In the first place, both men acted from the same motive, personal gain, and both had exactly the same end in view when they acted. It may be inferred from Smith's conduct that he is a bad man, although that judgment may be withdrawn or modified if certain further facts are learned about him — for example, that he is mentally deranged. But would not the very same thing be inferred about Jones from his conduct? And would not the same further considerations also be relevant to any modification of this judgment? Moreover, suppose Jones pleaded, in his own defense, "After all, I didn't do anything except just stand there and watch the child drown. I didn't kill him; I only let him die." Again, if letting die were in itself less bad than killing, this defense should have at least some weight. But it does not. Such a "defense" can only be regarded as a grotesque perversion of moral reasoning. Morally speaking, it is no defense at all.

Now, it may be pointed out, quite properly, that the cases of euthanasia with which doctors are concerned are not like this at all. They do not involve personal gain or the destruction of normal, healthy children. Doctors are concerned only with cases in which the patient's life is of no further use to him, or in which the patient's life has become or will soon become a terrible burden. However, the point is the same in these cases: The bare difference between killing and letting die does not, in itself, make a moral difference. If a doctor lets a patient die, for humane reasons, he is in the same moral position as if he had given the patient a lethal injection for humane reasons. If his decision was wrong — if, for example, the patient's illness was in fact curable — the decision would be equally regrettable no matter which method was used to carry it out. And if the doctor's decision was the right one, the method used is not in itself important.

The AMA policy statement isolates the crucial issue very well; the crucial issue is "the intentional termination of the life of one human being by another." But after identifying this issue, and forbidding "mercy killing," the statement goes on to deny that the cessation of treatment is the intentional termination of a life. This is where the mistake comes in, for what is the cessation of treatment, in these circumstances, if it is not "the intentional termination of the life of one human being by another"? Of course it is exactly that, and if it were not, there would be no point to it.

Many people will find this judgment hard to accept. One reason, I think, is that it is very easy to conflate the question of whether killing is, in itself, worse than letting die, with the very different question of whether most actual cases of killing are more reprehensible than most actual cases of letting die. Most actual cases of killing are clearly terrible (think, for example, of all the murders reported in the newspapers), and one hears of such cases every day. On the other hand, one hardly ever hears of a case of letting die, except for the actions of doctors who are motivated by humanitarian reasons. So one learns to think of killing in a much worse light than of letting die, for it is not the bare difference between killing and letting die that makes the difference in these cases. Rather, the other factors — the murderer's motive of personal gain, for example, contrasted with the doctor's humanitarian motivation — account for different reactions to the different cases.

I have argued that killing is not in itself any worse than letting die; if my contention is right, it follows that active euthanasia is not any worse than passive euthanasia. What arguments can be given on the other side? The most common, I believe, is the following:

"The important difference between active and passive euthanasia is that, in passive euthanasia, the doctor does not do anything to bring about the patient's death. The doctor does nothing, and the patient dies of whatever ills already afflict him. In active euthanasia, however, the doctor does something to bring about the patient's death: He kills him. The doctor who gives the patient with cancer a lethal injection has himself caused his patient's death; whereas if he merely ceases treatment, the cancer is the cause of the death."

A number of points need to be made here. The first is that it is not exactly correct to say that in passive euthanasia the doctor does nothing, for he does do one thing that is very important: He lets the patient die. "Letting someone die" is certainly different in some respects, from other types of action — mainly in that it is a kind of action that one

15

may perform by way of not performing certain other actions. For example, one may let a patient die by way of not giving medication, just as one may insult someone by way of not shaking his hand. But for any purpose of moral assessment, it is a type of action nonetheless. The decision to let a patient die is subject to moral appraisal in the same way that a decision to kill him would be subject to moral appraisal: It may be assessed as wise or unwise, compassionate or sadistic, right or wrong. If a doctor deliberately let a patient die who was suffering from a routinely curable illness, the doctor would certainly be to blame for what he had done, just as he would be to blame if he had needlessly killed the patient. Charges against him would then be appropriate. If so, it would be no defense at all for him to insist that he didn't "do anything." He would have done something very serious indeed, for he let his patient die.

Fixing the cause of death may be very important from a legal point of view, for it may determine whether criminal charges are brought against the doctor. But I do not think that this notion can be used to show a moral difference between active and passive euthanasia. The reason why it is considered bad to be the cause of someone's death is that death is regarded as a great evil — and so it is. However, if it had been decided that euthanasia — even passive euthanasia — is desirable in a given case, it has also been decided that in this instance death is no greater an evil than the patient's continued existence. And if this is true, the usual reason for not wanting to be the cause of someone's death simply does not apply.

Finally, doctors may think that all of this is only of academic interest — the sort of thing that philosophers may worry about but that has no practical bearing on their own work. After all, doctors must be concerned about the legal consequences of what they do, and active euthanasia is clearly forbidden by the law. But even so, doctors should also be concerned with the fact that the law is forcing upon them a moral doctrine that may well be indefensible and has a considerable effect on their practices. Of course, most doctors are not now in the position of being coerced in this matter, for they do not regard themselves as merely going along with what the law requires. Rather, in statements such as the AMA policy statement that I have quoted, they are endorsing this doctrine as a central point of medical ethics. In that statement, active euthanasia is condemned not merely as illegal but as "contrary to that for which the medical profession stands," whereas passive euthanasia is approved. However, the preceding considerations suggest that there is really no moral difference between the two, considered in themselves (there may be important moral differences in some cases in their *consequences,* but, as I pointed out, these differences may make active euthanasia, and not passive euthanasia, the morally preferable option). So, whereas doctors may have to discriminate between active and passive euthanasia to satisfy the law, they

20

should not do any more than that. In particular, they should not give the distinction any added authority and weight by writing it into official statements of medical ethics.

That Right Belongs Only to the State

MORTIMER OSTOW

To the Editor:

Nine members of the Kennedy Institute for the Study of Human Reproduction and Bioethics commented on May 18 on your May 2 editorial "Who Shall Make the Ultimate Decision?" Their assertion that it is important to establish precise criteria to guide the judgment of reasonable people cannot be faulted.

I believe comment is called for, however, on your argument that vital decisions respecting life and death belong to the patient or, when he is incompetent to make them, to those who are presumed to have his best interests at heart. The members of the Kennedy Institute concur.

It is a basic assumption of our society that individual members possess no right to determine matters of life and death respecting other individuals, or even themselves. That right belongs only to the state. The prohibition of murder, suicide, and, until recently, abortion, has rested on this assumption. The right to determine whether life-preserving efforts are to be continued or discontinued therefore belongs neither to the physician nor to the patient or his guardian, but to the state.

In practical terms, when such a decision is called for, the decision is to be made only by some agency or agent of the state, and it is to be made only by due process. To cede the right to the individuals involved is to license murder.

Aside from the philosophic argument, which not everyone will find 5 cogent, there are two practical reasons for requiring due process in such instances. In discussion of matters of continuing or withholding life-support systems and euthanasia, the arguments usually offered relate to the best interests of the patient or to the economic cost to society. Abortion, too, is discussed in these terms. A far more important consideration, it seems to me, is what making life-and-death decisions does to the individuals who decide.

While most of us will doubt that having made a decision to termi-

Dr. Ostow's letter appeared in the *New York Times* on June 1, 1971.

nate life support to a suffering relative will then incline one to commit murder, still, making such a decision does condition the unconditional respect for life, and does weaken the concept of the distinction between what is permitted and what is forbidden.

One can see a tendency to pass from withdrawing life support from the moribund to facilitating the death of the suffering, and from there to the neglect or even abandonment of the profoundly defective, and from there to the degradation or liquidation of any whom society might consider undesirable. The undisciplined making of life-and-death decisions tends to corrupt the individual who makes them, and corrupted individuals tend to corrupt society.

Second, it is not necessarily true that the individual himself has his own interests at heart. Afflicted with a painful and long-drawn-out illness, many individuals will wish for death, even when objectively there is a reasonable possibility of recovery. Permitting the patient to make the decision to die may amount to encouraging his suicide. Anyone familiar with the ambivalence which prevails in family relationships will not take it for granted that family members will necessarily represent the patient's best interests.

It is important for the morale and morality of our society that "the ultimate decision" be made only by a disinterested agent or agency of our society, and only by due process.

— Mortimer Ostow, M.D.

Cozy Little Homicides

JOHN LEO

Many dying people exhibit the symptom of "half knowledge": Though aware that death is near, they suppress the thought and talk with perfect sincerity about plans for the future.

If you read *Regulating Death,* the very sobering book about euthanasia in the Netherlands, you may think the Dutch people are suffering from a tribal case of half knowledge on the subject. As the author, Carlos Gomez, tells it, the Dutch seem to know that something is wrong with their euthanasia regulations, or nonregulations, but they also seem content with what they regard as a humane and rational system.

Mercy killing is technically illegal in the Netherlands, but for almost two decades Dutch doctors have been allowed to kill patients, on the understanding that the cases will be reported to a district prosecutor,

---

John Leo is the author of *How the Russians Invented Baseball: And Other Essays of Enlightenment* (1989) and a contributing editor to *U.S. News & World Report,* where this article was published on November 11, 1991.

who will permit the doctors to plead mitigating circumstances. Thus euthanasia is positioned as a socially approved crime that requires some sort of vague pro forma public airing.

Gomez shows that this airing is usually nonexistent. Most killings go unreported and uninvestigated. Almost everyone admits that the 200 cases reported in 1987 represented only a tiny fraction of the actual number of cases. A great deal of blurring and fudging takes place. The Dutch public blurs the crucial distinction between pulling the plug (withdrawing life-sustaining medical intervention) and killing the patient outright. Doctors blur details and lie on death certificates, so no one really knows how many are being killed or whether the killings are confined to terminal patients of sound mind who ask to die. Gomez reports that of a sample of twenty-six killings, there were four cases in which the patient was in no position to give consent or in which "it was doubtful that consent could have been obtained properly."

This means that in all likelihood, at least every sixth or seventh   5 case of euthanasia in the Netherlands is not "physician-assisted suicide" but homicide, approved by no one, reported to no one.

It also means that the alleged model problem in the Netherlands is, in effect, shot through with dishonesty, totally unregulated and wide open to the worst-case scenario of euthanasia — the dispatching of the troublesome or the vulnerable or the medically expensive elderly on the whim of anyone with a medical degree.

Here is the kicker: Gomez warns that Initiative 119, the euthanasia proposition on the ballot this week in the state of Washington, "is *very* like the current Dutch arrangement." It gives doctors permission to perform what has been an illegal act, but it sets up no credible system of oversight. As in the Netherlands, the fudgers and blurrers are hard at work. Wording of the bill, apparently inserted to protect doctors from any kind of criminal prosecution, invites fudging on the cause of death: "respiratory arrest," for example, and not the drugs injected to induce that arrest. This means statistics and studies will be unreliable, and, as Gomez argues, "cases of euthanasia would blend imperceptibly into the larger background of deaths resulting from natural causes." As in the Netherlands, the incidence of mercy killing, presented as little more than a statistical blip, could increase to a substantial number with little or no public awareness.

The worst feature of 119 is the lack of strong guarantees that all deaths will be truly voluntary. There are no safeguards to make sure that the patient is fully informed and that the death decision is not affected by clinical depression or outside pressure. Subtle and not-so-subtle coercion by hospital staff and family upon the vulnerable elderly can be substantial, particularly when care is an obvious economic burden on relatives. A letter from handicapped residents of a Dutch nursing home, quoted in anti-119 campaign literature, says, "We realize that we cost the community a good deal of money. . . . Many times we notice that we are talked into wishing death."

The first results of a major study of Dutch euthanasia, appearing in the September 14 issue of *The Lancet,* blithely mention that patients were "hardly ever" coerced into requesting death, then drop the subject. The study estimates that 0.8 percent of all deaths in the Netherlands are "life-terminating acts without explicit and persistent request." That's just less than a third of all life-ending medical decisions. Many of these involve patients "near to death and suffering grievously," but many others apparently don't. Carlos Gomez, who has looked at the raw data behind *The Lancet*'s article, charges that the study misleads the public by excluding from the totals 2,000 to 3,000 additional deaths with improper consent or no consent at all.

Once doctors are legally positioned as agents of death, the temp- 10 tation to cut corners on voluntariness will grow. In his book, Gomez says he was plagued by the sense that some Dutch doctors "felt that certain patients were better off dead, that it was a humane act to kill them." If Initiative 119 passes, we can expect the same moral problem: how to protect our most vulnerable patients from high-minded doctors who think it's time for them to die.

Consequences of Imposing the Quality-of-Life Ethic

EILEEN DOYLE

Under the American Constitution, all who belong to the human species *are persons* and are guaranteed the protection of their inalienable right to life (and other inalienable rights).

(The only exceptions are living human beings before birth who have unjustly been denied their right to life by the 1973 Supreme Court abortion decisions, *Roe v. Wade* and *Doe v. Bolton.*)

The Constitution adheres to the sanctity of life ethic and the theory of natural rights which state that human beings by their very nature are of intrinsic value — they do not have to earn their value; it belongs to them simply because they are human.

Therefore they are endowed with inalienable rights to life and other rights. The state cannot bestow or take away these·inalienable rights because they do not belong to the state to dispose of, but rather to each individual human being. The state exists to protect these rights.

The problem for euthanasia proponents is that under our Consti- 5 tution, euthanasia (killing human beings who are innocent of unjust

---

Eileen Doyle, R.N., is president of New York State Nurses for Life. This selection is from *A Pro-Life Primer on Euthanasia* (1985).

aggression on others' lives) cannot be legalized. It is obvious that the American people would not permit them to tear up the Constitution and write a new one to fit their purposes, so they have devised a clever strategy to make it appear that we would be abiding by the Constitution even while violating it.

First they attack the sanctity-of-life ethic as a religious doctrine because it is based on the religious belief that human beings are created by God in His Image. They fail to realize that whatever the religious beliefs upon which it was founded, its principles embodied in our Constitution are right now held dear by the vast majority of American people.

They propose to replace this sanctity-of-life ethic with a new one which we call the quality-of-life ethic. But underlying this new ethic is another religious belief of secular humanism, which believes that human life is the result of random evolution and denies or questions the existence of God or at least God's involvement in human affairs — a remote God.

The Supreme Court has declared that secular humanism as a world view is a religion in the First Amendment sense (*Torasco v. Watkins, United States v. Seeger, Welsh v. United States*).

Redefining Some People

This quality-of-life ethic proposes that some human beings have a quality of life so poor that they ought not be classified as legal persons with inalienable rights. To be declared a person with human rights, a human being must be able to pass certain tests. The tests vary according to who is proposing them but in general, it requires that to be declared a person (with inalienable rights) a human being must be able to: think and reason; give or receive love; be useful in some way; be capable of meaningful life, i.e., able to enjoy or appreciate life.

Those who fail the test would lose legal personhood and have no inalienable rights. Therefore, these human beings could be killed without violating anyone's inalienable rights. 10

This is precisely what the Court did in the abortion decisions in declaring the unborn as not persons, thus allowing them to be killed. The whole idea is pure legal fiction, a subterfuge to quiet the consciences of the American people who have a horror of killing innocent people.

Killing a "nonperson" demoted to a less-than-human status by legal fiat seems then to be more like killing a dog or a cat to put it out of its misery. Then all can pretend that no evil, unjust deed has been done.

This quality-of-life ethic also holds that even among those who pass the tests of personhood, there may be many who have a quality of life so poor because of grave illness or birth defects that life itself is no longer a value to be preserved for these people. So to take these lives would not be an injustice but a benefit for them.

And finally (as discussed last month), this quality-of-life ethic allows that there is a compelling state interest sufficient to deny the inalienable right to life to a class of citizens: permanently dependent, institution-alized people who put an inordinate burden on the state to provide public funds and medical resources for their care.

The Awesome Result

If the proponents of this quality-of-life ethic succeed in having it   15
replace the sanctity of life ethic, what would be the consequences?

1. It would destroy the underlying principles embodied in our Con-stitution, reducing it to a worthless, ineffective, hypocritical document. A new constitution would have to be written to replace it.

2. It would be an injustice to the vast majority of the Americans who adhere to the principles of the Constitution and who treasure our Constitution to have those principles overridden and the Constitution destroyed by a small elite who wish to impose their own set of prin-ciples, not accepted by most people.

3. Large numbers of people whose inalienable right to life is now protected by the law of homicide would be killed without their consent because somebody else had decided they are not persons. These could include newborn infants with birth defects, autistic children, psychotic people, senile aged, comatose people, those with severe drug or alcohol addiction, and so on. All these could easily fail the tests of personhood.

Then there are the huge numbers of people who by somebody's definition other than their own have lives not worth living, who could be disposed of.

And finally there are those millions of dependent, institutionalized   20
people on the public dole eating up the valuable resources of the powerful, so-called nondependent taxpayers. To dispose of them — the dependents — would become a "patriotic duty."

Equal protection of the law would become a mockery.

4. The psychological and spiritual damage to those who do the killing and to those who permit it would corrupt our entire nation. All would be a party to killing and to the lying to ourselves that we are doing good rather than admitting the crimes.

5. Inordinate power, tyrannical power, would be vested in the Su-preme Court. For it would be the Court that would ultimately decide who is and who is not a legal person; who has and who has not a sufficient quality of life to give it value worth preserving; and at what point there is a compelling state interest sufficient to override the inalienable right to life of dependent citizens.

As with the concept of a constitutional right to die, the concept of a quality of life ethic becomes absurd as well, when analyzed to its logical conclusions. For we would literally be handing over our priceless freedom and all inalienable rights to an oligarchy of nine Justices on the Supreme Court.

And for what? To give power to an elite few to create their idea of a "brave new world" — for themselves, who in turn might become their own victims should misfortune make them dependent and powerless. 25

In the Face of Death:
Rights, Choices, Beliefs

JAMES M. WALL

A book about how to commit suicide has vaulted to the top of the bestseller lists. *New York Times* columnist Anna Quindlen admits that she picked up *Final Exit* out of curiosity, but kept it for another reason. The day may come when she will want to know how to die with a minimum of pain and anguish. And if that day does come, "whose business is it, really, but my own and that of those I love?" Derek Humphry's little volume, published in the spring, went unnoticed until it was highlighted in the *Wall Street Journal.* Then media coverage was immediate and widespread, pushing the book to the top of the *Times* bestseller list.

Most commentators make the usual demurs, reminding us that the choice to die should be made in discussions with loved ones and professional counselors. And they point out that teenagers and adults despondent over temporary — or even permanent — burdens are not the book's intended audience. Only the terminally ill who face pro-longed and painful suffering should be encouraged to prepare for the time when, as Quindlen says, "I may feel so bereft of strength, purpose, stamina, and the will to live that I may want to know what constitutes a lethal dose of Seconal."

The issue here is clearly one of controlling how and when one dies — the understandable longing of the human spirit to name the time and place for a final exit. In our secular culture this seems an entirely reasonable desire, one which deserves fulfillment. But the desire to take one's own life is the epitome of modern individualism. If one thinks ultimate reality is located no higher than human personality, what one does with one's life is one's own affair. Betty Rollin, who wrote an introduction to *Final Exit,* is a television journalist who assisted in the suicide of her mother, who was terminally ill from ovarian cancer. Rollin argues that "some people want to eke out every second of life —

This argument appeared in the August 21, 1991 issue of *The Christian Century,* a journal of which James M. Wall is an editor.

no matter how grim — and that is their right." But others, she insists, do not, and "that should be their right."

But is it? When Quindlen maintains that her death is her business and that of "those I love," she does not consider the significance of suicide on the wider circles of life that surround her. John Donne's reminder that none of us is an island speaks to the point: The death of each individual has a ripple effect in the present and into the future.

If, as modernity dictates, the individual is supreme, then our re- 5 sponsibility is only to ourselves, since there is no God who gave us life or who awaits us in death. But if we believe that life derives from a loving Creator, then suicide must be considered within a larger context. In a nonreligious culture, *Final Exit* assures people that, in the face of death, individual choice is all that matters. Only someone who accepts individualism as the highest good would be so confident that there is an obvious qualitative difference between the "freely chosen" decision to die made by a person facing a terminal illness and a decision made by a physically healthy but mentally tormented individual.

In considering the "right to die," it is important to distinguish between the comatose patient being kept alive by mechanical means and the person still capable of making decisions. When consciousness disappears permanently, a decision to die becomes the responsibility of others, who may reach the judgment that for all practical purposes life for an individual has concluded and that therefore artificial supports need not be maintained.

Richard Lamm, the former governor of Colorado who has campaigned against excessive medical costs, recently cited the case of a patient in a Washington, D.C. hospital who had been in a comatose state since Lamm was a high school student. The patient has survived entirely through artificial means in a condition which benefits neither that person nor society. In this case, the larger community has not acted in the best interest of either the individual or the community. Fear of political and legal retribution from "right-to-life" activists has forced the medical community to preserve the person's life. That decision reflects a narrow definition of "life" held by a small but politically strong group of activists.

An individual does not have the "right to die" when individual choice has disappeared and the decision of life or death has fallen to the community (primarily the family). That is why it is so important to instruct one's family in advance not to employ excessive means to sustain life when there is no prospect of recovering consciousness.

But what about a conscious decision to commit suicide? Though an individual may rationalize that his or her death would be to everyone's advantage, suicide leaves a void in a network of close relationships. Its impact does not stop with "those I love." Friends, former teachers, colleagues, distant family relations, even casual acquaintances are all affected by suicide. The web of life, as Joseph Sittler so aptly put it, is like a spider web: Touch any part, and the entire web shimmers.

Despite Humphry's caveats and warnings, his book is irresponsible. There is, admittedly, a difference between the elderly terminal patient in horrible pain who wants all pain to cease and the despondent teenager whose pain is one of low self-esteem. But the difference is finally one of degree. The terminally ill person, out of personal suffering and a concern for the impact a lingering illness has on family and the immediate human circle, may turn to suicide. But the emotionally distraught teenager or adult may reach the same conclusion: My pain is too great, and my presence is detrimental to those around me. To make that decision before life involuntarily leaves us is a decision we are free to make, but it is a choice that is ultimately selfish. It is not surprising that our culture, which regards individual choice as inviolable, would find so much merit in a book like *Final Exit.*

Euthanasia: Can We Keep It a Special Case?

LAWRENCE J. SCHNEIDERMAN

Should physicians be permitted to offer death among their therapeutic options? Should they be licensed to kill — not inadvertently or negligently but willfully, openly, and compassionately? This, on the most superficial level, is the euthanasia debate.

In California, a petition to put this matter before the voters failed to gain sufficient signatures. Perhaps this was because too many of those life-affirming hedonists cringed at the thought of signing their own death warrants, or — more likely in this land where almost everything has a price — because the sponsoring Hemlock Society did not hire enough solicitors.

In any case, euthanasia is being performed.

As a medical ethicist, when I give talks on this subject to physicians, I always ask: "How many of you have ever hastened death to alleviate the suffering of your patients?" Many hands are raised — uneasily; I can offer them no legal immunity. Of all the humane acts physicians perform, euthanasia is the one we do most furtively.

But this is an old story. In 1537, while serving in the army of Francis I, the troubled surgeon Ambroise Paré confided in his diary:

Lawrence J. Schneiderman is a professor at the University of California–San Diego School of Medicine, where he is a clinician and researcher and director of the Program in Medical Ethics. His article is reprinted from the May–June 1990 issue of *The Humanist.*

We thronged into the city and passed over the dead bodies and some that were not yet dead, hearing them cry under the feet of our horses, which made a great pity in my heart, and truly I repented that I had gone forth from Paris to see so pitiful a spectacle. Being in the city, I entered a stable, thinking to lodge my horse and that of my man, where I found four dead soldiers and three who were propped against the wall, their faces wholly disfigured, and they neither saw, nor heard, nor spoke, and their clothes yet flaming from the gun powder, which had burnt them. Beholding them with pity there came an old soldier who asked me if there was any means of curing them. I told him no. At once he approached them and cut their throats gently and without anger. Seeing this great cruelty I said to him that he was an evil man. He answered me that he prayed God that when he should be in such a case, he might find someone that would do the same for him, to the end that he might not languish miserably.

Today, the euthanasia debate takes place under the shadow of Nazi doctors who appropriated the term to describe the "special treatment" given first to the physically and mentally handicapped, then to the weak and elderly, and, finally, to Jews, gypsies, and other "undesirables" as part of the Final Solution — all in the name of social hygiene. In that monstrous orgy of evil, numbers replaced names, bodies replaced souls; all were hauled by the trainload to work or to death, then converted to ashes or merely dumped in such profusion that the very earth bubbled. That was no *euthanasia* — no easy, pleasant death. That was ugly, debasing death.

But we are different, are we not? Not like *them.* And yet, and yet . . . didn't we American physicians commit atrocities of our own, such as allowing untreated blacks to succumb to the "natural course" of syphilis; misleading Spanish-speaking women into thinking they were obtaining contraceptives, when in fact they were receiving inactive dummy tablets to distinguish drug side-effects, resulting in unwanted pregnancies; and injecting cancer cells into unwitting elderly patients? All for the sake of medical progress . . . we can only look back and shake our heads.

Worthy colleagues — with whom I respectfully disagree — are so fearful of the "Naziness" in us all that they oppose withholding life-sustaining treatment from *anyone:* the malformed newborn with no hope of survival, the permanently unconscious patient, the terminal cancer patient who begs to be allowed to die. Who would be next? they argue. The physically and mentally handicapped? The weak and the elderly? And then? And then? This, of course, is the familiar "slippery slope" argument. Start with one exception and you inevitably skid down the moral slope of ever more exceptions. This also is the euthanasia debate, on a deeper level. What will become of a society that permits — indeed promotes — death as a social good?

An ethics consultation is where we ponder such questions at the bedside of a patient who perhaps is hopelessly ill. Not infrequently, back in the doctor's conference room, a harried resident will burst out:

"What good is it for us to keep him alive anyway?" I don't regard this as a callous question for the simple reason that it is phrased intimately and in the singular: Why do *we* keep *him* alive? In contrast, you'd be surprised how often decent people who possess the most humane and compassionate sensibilities demand: "Why do *they* keep *them* alive?" That question, in my view, is morally indistinguishable from: "Why do *they* let *them* die?"

For, you see, the first question arises from *this* patient, this special 10
case, *here.* The second question arises from a state of mind — *those* people. *There.* It is a state of mind that provides a dehumanizing abstraction appealing to both extremes of the political spectrum, and it has been applied to both ends of life. It can lead to the demand that *all* handicapped newborns be kept alive without regard to their specific agonies and that life-prolonging treatment be denied to *all* the elderly beyond a certain age.

What is so special about the special case? For those of us in medicine, it exerts a palpable moral power; the special case is our daily news, our gossip, a shaping force in our culture. Case studies and case reports are basic teaching tools. *Case* (from *casus,* "happening," "accident") in its original meaning refers to a unique person in unique circumstances. Physicians are molded by their particular autobiography of cases, by their own singular distressing experiences. My first physical diagnosis teacher said, "Make sure you examine the neck veins. Always. Once I missed a patient with congestive heart failure because I neglected to do so." Since then, I have heard many such honest confessions — covertly, for in the litigious world of contemporary medicine, it is almost treachery to reveal that this is how we learn best, by being wrong. To help my compulsively driven and terrified students get on with their duties, I tell them that, if it is true you learn from your mistakes, someday I will know everything.

And we do learn from our special cases, one by one — sometimes badly and incompletely, but each time the lesson is so painful that ultimately we do learn. For example, as a medical student, I was monitoring the blood pressure of a man dying of acute pulmonary edema and myocardial infarction. The end of a gala evening for him. Next to me was the man's wife — coiffed and elegantly gowned, cradling his head and crooning her love while the man blanched into death. It was a good death, since his physician, who was controlling the intravenous infusion on the other side of the bed, had made sure that the man was heavily sedated with morphine. It was a lesson I took with me to my internship, when I treated my first patient with terminal cancer of the bowel. She was tough, this woman, crusty, white-haired, and quite prepared to die. The searing looks she leveled at me made me very much aware of my youth, my health, my innocence.

Alas, she was right about my innocence. I had not yet learned everything there was to know about morphine. Pumping in large doses to control her pain, I failed to deal with its paralytic effects on the intestine. As a result, her last day was a horror of acute intestinal obstruction. I shall never forget the curses she hurled at me between squalls of sewage. I doubt there was a soul in the world who knew or cared that she died, but, of course, she was for me immemorial, a special case. Am I forgiven now that countless others have received the blessing of her curses? — for you can be sure that I never fail to teach the importance of keeping the bowels open when caring for a cancer patient. Am I forgiven? I do not know.

Yet, you can see how easy it is to corrupt this experience, to slide from the special case to a state of mind based upon dehumanizing abstractions. For it was a failure in mechanics that led to the poor woman's suffering, and it is merely with the hope of better attending to such mechanics that we have developed the powerful technology that now pervades medicine. Now we can better manage not only the bowels but also the hearts, livers, kidneys, lungs, and all combinations thereof. How do we know we manage them better? We do randomized, double-blind, prospective experimental trials in which patients are aggregated into treatment groups, outcomes are analyzed, and their differences compared by statistics — another state of mind (a related word, in fact), another set of abstractions. Bearing the weight of these massive studies like armies of pharaonic slaves, we plod step by step up federally funded pyramids of therapeutic progress. Read any good medical journal: It is filled with multiauthored, multi-institutional papers. Modern medicine; how dehumanizing, we are told.

And lo and behold, we are repelled into an opposite state of mind, 15 a sentimental longing to escape such cold-blooded modernity. We applaud the hit play *Whose Life Is It Anyway?,* which ends with the quadriplegic hero rejecting life-sustaining technology and going home to die. As the lights come up, we are left to assume that offstage he will effervesce nobly, wittily, free of hunger, thirst, and embarrassing bodily products — fulfilling Milan Kundera's definition of kitsch.

But the facts are not so vaporous, and the truth is not so clean-shaven. For the truth is: Death is not an artist many of us admire. This artist's work is often messy. Pretending otherwise is sentimentality — a state of mind that we define as reaching sentiments too cheaply and easily. Of course, there is also the opposite state of mind, the reaction to sentimentality: cynicism, which can also be arrived at too cheaply and easily. Both of these states of mind are false. It is against both of these states of mind that the special case protests.

This, I submit, is what the euthanasia debate is about: theoretical and statistical abstractions versus the anguishing, messy particulars of the special case. In illness, we are made exquisitely aware of what it means to be ourselves, no other, alone — this is happening to *me.* Those of us still healthy, if we are compassionate, acknowledge and even honor the unbreachable solitude of those who are ill. It joins us in a *community* of human feeling — notice that I do not use the word *state.* Because it is truly human, such a community — unlike the totalitarian state (of politics or of mind) — is as varied and unpredictable as the beings within it. And so, the argument goes, if we honor our fellow human beings — their variety, each and every life — it follows that we must honor how each person chooses to live that life, so long as it causes no harm to others. We must also honor — if fate so grants — whatever coda each person sees fit to put on that life. In euthanasia, as in abortion, this issue of choice gets lost in the rhetorical smoke. No one is really *pro*-abortion. Similarly, no one claims to *like* euthanasia. Proponents merely want to have these options available in desperate circumstances.

But what will happen then? my worthy colleagues ask. Will things fall apart? Is Nazi Germany our malign destiny? Or could it be, rather, that peaceable kingdom, the Netherlands, where an estimated five to ten thousand patients are administered euthanasia on request (and illegally) every year? Explicitly defined violations simply are not prosecuted. The physician is permitted to administer painless death only when a fully informed, rational patient voluntarily and repeatedly requests it in a medical situation that is considered intolerable and hopeless and unresponsive to any other means of medical relief. As a further safeguard, two physicians must concur with a patient's request. At no time are social goals considered. Each patient is treated as a special case, and in each case the act is voluntary.

But is it necessary to kill? my worthy colleagues argue, dubious that a person in such extremity is capable of any voluntary act and drawing a distinction between "active" and "passive" euthanasia. Can't we simply allow such a case to die? Such a distinction, in my view, makes no sense, now that medicine has become so powerful that almost *any* life can be prolonged, however briefly. And once a decision is made that death is preferable to existence, *any* choice — whether giving or withholding treatment, whether it be surgery or antibiotics or narcotics — is an act toward or against that end. So, the only relevant moral questions become *why* (the motive) and *how* (the method). One can have the cruelest motive and employ the kindest method; for example, slipping Gramps an overdose of sleeping medicine to get rid of him and get at his money. Or, one can have the kindest motive and employ the cruelest method: letting him "languish miserably" (in the words of Paré) out of a loving reluctance to hasten his death. Neither of these acts is as morally defensible, in my opinion, as the bloody dagger-thrust performed "gently and without anger" by that old unknown soldier.

And so, while the cautious Dutch carry on, several states — including California, once again — are preparing euthanasia initiatives. And the difficult questions will have to be faced. Can we be both merciful 20 and just in matters of medically administered death? How? Do we keep the laws the way they are and grant no exceptions, thus publicly condemning (while at the same time insidiously perpetuating) unsupervised euthanasia? Or should we change the laws? And if we do so, can we craft them in such a way so as not to destroy hallowed and fragile values? Should we explicitly define and sanction certain acts of humane suicide assisted by physicians? Should we allow patients direct legal access to the necessary drugs? Or should we not attempt to change the laws but only openly acknowledge (as in the Netherlands) certain permissible violations — thus cautioning physicians to weigh each act as one they may have to defend in criminal court? The approach we take will reveal much about ourselves as a society. Are our moral cousins the Nazis or the Dutch? Can we keep our anguish fresh each time we contemplate the end of a fellow human being? Or will our anguish grow stale, allowing us to slide down the slope from "easy death" to "useful death," heaping *them* into nameless, faceless piles, saying there go *they,* not *I,* and discovering too late — as others have before — that if yesterday *they* were the retarded, the handicapped, the Jews, the blacks; and if today *they* are the elderly, the AIDS patient; then tomorrow *they* will be ourselves, wondering where all the others are — common waste requiring special treatment rather than special cases sharing a common fate.

"This is a surprise—he doesn't want any extraordinary measures taken to resuscitate him."

Drawing by Ed Fisher; © 1992 The New Yorker Magazine, Inc.

THINKING AND WRITING ABOUT EUTHANASIA

Questions for Discussion and Writing

1. Ostow argues that only the state should be allowed to make a decision concerning the lives of the terminally ill. What reasons, including analogies,

does Ostow offer in support of his argument? Do you agree with his conclusion? Why or why not? What other writers in this chapter might disagree?

2. Does Rachels prove that there is no moral difference between active and passive euthanasia? Is his attempt to meet the arguments of the opposition a convincing tactic? Which of his arguments do you find most persuasive? Why?

3. What is Hook's principal reason for regretting that his request to discontinue the life support was denied? What qualities in the author are reflected in this article? Does the fact that the article is written by the patient himself make the argument more or less powerful? Can Hook's argument for voluntary euthanasia be used to answer Doyle's arguments?

4. Explain the title of Schneiderman's article. Would Schneiderman agree or disagree with Wall and Doyle? Schneiderman poses a number of difficult questions at the end of his article. Do you have answers, however tentative, to some of the questions?

5. What are Leo's principal objections to euthanasia as practiced by the Dutch? (Notice that Schneiderman treats Dutch euthanasia favorably.) The American Academy of Neurology states that "a physician's duty aggressively to promote the well-being of the patient presumes that some chance of improvement or recovery remains." In other words, if a treatment cannot *cure* or improve, it should be discontinued. What is your view of such a policy?

6. Under what circumstances would Maguire sanction euthanasia? Based on the cases he describes, how would he define the sanctity of life?

7. Define the "quality-of-life ethic," as Doyle sees it. According to the author, how does the Constitution of the United States prevent the legalization of euthanasia? What consequences does the author foresee if euthanasia is permitted by law, as abortion is? Do you think her predictions are soundly based?

8. An article in the *New York Times,* subtitled "My grandmother didn't want to end in a nursing home," argues for the right of the author's terminally ill grandmother to refuse life support. Is there a similar case in your family experience? What decisions were made, and how were they arrived at?

9. Readers have been familiar with Dracula for almost one hundred years, but the cartoon might not have been so clearly understood a generation ago. What circumstances have changed?

Topics for Research

The case of Dr. Jack Kevorkian, the Michigan "suicide doctor"

The hospice solution

Handicapped newborns: Who should decide?

Euthanasia in the Netherlands

Noteworthy cases involving the right to die

CHAPTER FIFTEEN

Freedom of Speech

The First Amendment to the Constitution of the United States reads, "Congress shall make no laws respecting an establishment of religion, or prohibiting the free expression thereof; or abridging the freedom of speech, or of the press; or the right of the people peaceably to assemble, and to petition the Government for a redress of grievances." (The first ten amendments were ratified on December 15, 1791, and form what is known as the "Bill of Rights.") The arguments in this section will consider primarily the issue of "abridging the freedom of speech, or of the press."

The limits of free speech in the United States are constantly being adjusted as social values change and new cases testing those limits emerge. Several prominent areas of controversy are emphasized in the following selection of essays.

One of the most hotly debated issues has been played out on college campuses. A number of colleges and universities have formulated codes of speech conduct which define the "correct" ways of naming certain persons, groups, or activities in order to avoid offense to those who have historically been most vulnerable to "hate" speech — African Americans, Jews, women, and gays and lesbians. These policies have frequently provoked opposition from members of the college community on both sides of the political spectrum. Their disagreement is based on a principle enunciated in 1929 by Justice Oliver Wendell Holmes: "the principle of free thought — not free thought for those who agree with us but freedom for the thought that we hate." A few students who have been harshly punished for using "racist, sexist, and homophobic" speech have taken their cases to court. In several cases the courts decided that the policies enforcing strict speech codes were in violation of the First Amendment. College and university officials are now drafting new codes that would define the prohibited language and conduct in narrower and more specific terms.

Freedom of speech is also a central issue in arguments over the lyrics of rap songs, which have been accused of advocating violence against police officers and women. Parents have raised concerns about the effects of such lyrics on young listeners and proposed rating labels for some albums. The language in one recent rap song, calling for the murder of police officers, has led to appeals for censorship and boycotts of the record company.

Even nonverbal art forms whose creators express views that offend large groups of people are not immune to issues of free speech. Controversial movies, photography, painting, and sculpture, as well as religious displays on public land, and even nude dancing have all been defended as forms of speech protected by the Constitution.

In Praise of Censure
GARRY WILLS

Rarely have the denouncers of censorship been so eager to start practicing it. When a sense of moral disorientation overcomes a society, people from the least expected quarters begin to ask, "Is nothing sacred?" Feminists join reactionaries to denounce pornography as demeaning to women. Rock musician Frank Zappa declares that when Tipper Gore, the wife of Senator Albert Gore from Tennessee, asked music companies to label sexually explicit material, she launched an illegal "conspiracy to extort." A *Penthouse* editorialist says that housewife Terry Rakolta, who asked sponsors to withdraw support from a sitcom called *Married . . . with Children,* is "yelling fire in a crowded theater," a formula that says her speech is not protected by the First Amendment.

But the most interesting movement to limit speech is directed at defamatory utterances against blacks, homosexuals, Jews, women, or other stigmatizable groups. It took no Terry Rakolta of the left to bring about the instant firing of Jimmy the Greek and Al Campanis from sports jobs when they made racially denigrating comments. Social pressure worked far more quickly on them than on *Married . . . with Children,* which is still on the air.

The rules being considered on college campuses to punish students for making racist and other defamatory remarks go beyond social and

---

Garry Wills is the author of many books on politics including *Nixon Agonistes* and *Reagan's America.* His essay appeared in *Time* on July 31, 1989.

commercial pressure to actual legal muzzling. The right-wing *Dartmouth Review* and its imitators have understandably infuriated liberals, who are beginning to take action against them and the racist expressions they have encouraged. The American Civil Liberties Union considered this movement important enough to make it the principal topic at its biennial meeting last month in Madison, Wisconsin. Ironically, the regents of the University of Wisconsin had passed their own rules against defamation just before the ACLU members convened on the university's campus. Nadine Strossen, of New York University School of Law, who was defending the ACLU's traditional position on free speech, said of Wisconsin's new rules, "You can tell how bad they are by the fact that the regents had to make an amendment at the last minute exempting classroom discussion! What is surprising is that Donna Shalala [chancellor of the university] went along with it." So did constitutional lawyers on the faculty.

If a similar code were drawn up with right-wing imperatives in mind — one banning unpatriotic, irreligious, or sexually explicit expressions on campus — the people framing Wisconsin-type rules would revert to their libertarian pasts. In this competition to suppress, is regard for freedom of expression just a matter of whose ox is getting gored at the moment? Does the left just get nervous about the Christian cross when Klansmen burn it, while the right will react only when Madonna flirts crucifixes between her thighs?

The cries of "un-American" are as genuine and as frequent on either side. Everyone is protecting the country. Zappa accuses Gore of undermining the moral fiber of America with the "sexual neuroses of these vigilant ladies." He argues that she threatens our freedoms with "connubial insider trading" because her husband is a senator. Apparently her marital status should deprive her of speaking privileges in public — an argument Westbrook Pegler used to make against Eleanor Roosevelt. *Penthouse* says Rakolta is taking us down the path toward fascism. It attacks her for living in a rich suburb — the old "radical chic" argument that rich people cannot support moral causes.

There is a basic distinction that cuts through this free-for-all over freedom. It is the distinction, too often neglected, between censorship and censure (the free expression of moral disapproval). What the campuses are trying to do (at least those with state money) is use the force of government to contain freedom of speech. What Donald Wildmon, the freelance moralist from Tupelo, Mississippi, does when he gets Pepsi to cancel its Madonna ad is censure the ad by calling for a boycott. Advocating boycotts is a form of speech protected by the First Amendment. As Nat Hentoff, journalistic custodian of the First Amendment, says, "I would hate to see boycotts outlawed. Think what that would do to Cesar Chavez." Or, for that matter, to Ralph Nader. If one disapproves of a social practice, whether it is racist speech or unjust hiring in lettuce fields, one is free to denounce that and to call on others to express their disapproval. Otherwise there would be no form of persuasive speech except passing a law. This would make the law coterminous with morality.

Equating morality with legality is in effect what people do when they claim that anything tolerated by law must, in the name of freedom, be approved by citizens in all their dealings with one another. As Zappa says, "Masturbation is not illegal. If it is not illegal to do it, why should it be illegal to sing about it?" He thinks this proves that Gore, who is not trying to make raunch in rock illegal, cannot even ask distributors to label it. Anything goes, as long as it's legal. The odd consequence of this argument would be a drastic narrowing of the freedom of speech. One could not call into question anything that was not against the law — including, for instance, racist speech.

A false ideal of tolerance has not only outlawed censorship but discouraged censoriousness (another word for censure). Most civilizations have expressed their moral values by mobilization of social opprobrium. That, rather than specific legislation, is what changed the treatment of minorities in films and TV over recent years. One can now draw opprobrious attention by gay bashing, as the Beastie Boys rock group found when their distributor told them to cut out remarks about "fags" for business reasons. Or by anti-Semitism, as the just disbanded rap group Public Enemy has discovered.

It is said that only the narrow-minded are intolerant or opprobrious. Most of those who limited the distribution of Martin Scorsese's movie *The Last Temptation of Christ* had not even seen the movie. So do we guarantee freedom of speech only for the broad-minded or the better educated? Can one speak only after studying whatever one has reason, from one's beliefs, to denounce? Then most of us would be doing a great deal less speaking than we do. If one has never seen any snuff movies, is that a bar to criticizing them?

Others argue that asking people not to buy lettuce is different from 10 asking them not to buy a rocker's artistic expression. Ideas (carefully disguised) lurk somewhere in the lyrics. All the more reason to keep criticism of them free. If ideas are too important to suppress, they are also too important to ignore. The whole point of free speech is not to make ideas exempt from criticism but to expose them to it.

One of the great mistakes of liberals in recent decades has been the ceding of moral concern to right-wingers. Just because one opposes censorship, one need not be seen as agreeing with pornographers. Why should liberals, of all people, oppose Gore when she asks that labels be put on products meant for the young, to inform those entrusted by law with the care of the young? Liberals were the first to promote "healthy" television shows like *Sesame Street* and *The Electric Company.* In the 1950s and 1960s they were the leading critics of television, of its mindless violence, of the way it ravaged the attention span needed for reading. Who was keeping kids away from TV sets then? How did promoters of Big Bird let themselves be cast as champions of the Beastie Boys — not just of their *right* to perform but of their performance itself? Why should it be left to Gore to express moral disapproval of a group calling itself Dead Kennedys (sample lyric: "I kill children, I love to see them die")?

For that matter, who has been more insistent that parents should "interfere" in what their children are doing, Tipper Gore or Jesse Jackson? All through the 1970s, Jackson was traveling the high schools, telling parents to turn off TVs, make the kids finish their homework, check with teachers on their performance, get to know what the children are doing. This kind of "interference" used to be called education.

Belief in the First Amendment does not preempt other beliefs, making one a eunuch to the interplay of opinions. It is a distortion to turn "You can express any views" into the proposition "I don't care what views you express." If liberals keep equating equality with approval, they will be repeatedly forced into weak positions.

A case in point is the Corcoran Gallery's sudden cancellation of an exhibit of Robert Mapplethorpe's photographs. The whole matter was needlessly confused when the director, Christina Owr-Chall, claimed she was canceling the show to *protect* it from censorship. She meant that there might be pressure to remove certain pictures — the sadomasochistic ones or those verging on kiddie porn — if the show had gone on. But she had in mind, as well, the hope of future grants from the National Endowment for the Arts, which is under criticism for the Mapplethrope show and for another show that contained Andres Serrano's *Piss Christ,* the photograph of a crucifix in what the title says is urine. Owr-Chall is said to be yielding to censorship, when she is clearly yielding to political and financial pressure, as Pepsi yielded to commercial pressure over the Madonna ad.

What is at issue here is not government suppression but government subsidy. Mapplethorpe's work is not banned, but showing it might have endangered federal grants to needy artists. The idea that what the government does not support it represses is nonsensical, as one can see by reversing the statement to read: "No one is allowed to create anything without the government's subvention." What pussycats our supposedly radical artists are. They not only want the government's permission to create their artifacts, they want federal authorities to supply the materials as well. Otherwise they feel "gagged." If they are not given government approval (and money), they want to remain an avant-garde while being bankrolled by the Old Guard.

What is easily forgotten in this argument is the right of citizen taxpayers. They send representatives to Washington who are answerable for the expenditure of funds exacted from them. In general these voters want to favor their own values if government is going to get into the culture-subsidizing area at all (a proposition many find objectionable in itself). Politicians, insofar as they support the arts, will tend to favor conventional art (certainly not masochistic art). Anybody who doubts that has no understanding of a politician's legitimate concern for his or her constituents' approval. Besides, it is quaint for those familiar with the politics of the art world to discover, with a shock, that there is politics in politics.

Luckily, cancellation of the Mapplethorpe show forced some artists back to the flair and cheekiness of unsubsidized art. Other results of pressure do not turn out as well. Unfortunately, people in certain regions were deprived of the chance to see *The Last Temptation of Christ* in the theater. Some, no doubt, considered it a loss that they could not buy lettuce or grapes during a Chavez boycott. Perhaps there was even a buyer perverse enough to miss driving the unsafe cars Nader helped pressure off the market. On the other hand, we do not get sports analysis made by racists. These mobilizations of social opprobrium are not examples of repression but of freedom of expression by committed people who censured without censoring, who expressed the kinds of belief the First Amendment guarantees. I do not, as a result, get whatever I approve of subsidized, either by Pepsi or the government. But neither does the law come in to silence Tipper Gore or Frank Zappa or even that filthy rag, the *Dartmouth Review.*

On Racist Speech
CHARLES R. LAWRENCE III

I have spent the better part of my life as a dissenter. As a high school student, I was threatened with suspension for my refusal to participate in a civil-defense drill, and I have been a conspicuous consumer of my First Amendment liberties ever since. There are very strong reasons for protecting even racist speech. Perhaps the most important of these is that such protection reinforces our society's commitment to tolerance as a value, and that by protecting bad speech from government regulation, we will be forced to combat it as a community.

But I also have a deeply felt apprehension about the resurgence of racial violence and the corresponding rise in the incidence of verbal and symbolic assault and harassment to which blacks and other traditionally subjugated and excluded groups are subjected. I am troubled by the way the debate has been framed in response to the recent surge of racist incidents on college and university campuses and in response to some universities' attempts to regulate harassing speech. The prob-

Charles R. Lawrence III is a professor of law at Stanford University. His article, which appeared in the October 25, 1989 *Chronicle of Higher Education,* is adapted from a speech to a conference of the American Civil Liberties Union.

lem has been framed as one in which the liberty of free speech is in conflict with the elimination of racism. I believe this has placed the bigot on the moral high ground and fanned the rising flames of racism.

Above all, I am troubled that we have not listened to the real victims, that we have shown so little understanding of their injury, and that we have abandoned those whose race, gender, or sexual preference continues to make them second-class citizens. It seems to me a very sad irony that the first instinct of civil libertarians has been to challenge even the smallest, most narrowly framed efforts by universities to provide black and other minority students with the protection the Constitution guarantees them.

The landmark case of *Brown v. Board of Education* is not a case that we normally think of as a case about speech. But *Brown* can be broadly read as articulating the principle of equal citizenship. *Brown* held that segregated schools were inherently unequal because of the *message* that segregation conveyed — that black children were an untouchable caste, unfit to go to school with white children. If we understand the necessity of eliminating the system of signs and symbols that signal the inferiority of blacks, then we should hesitate before proclaiming that all racist speech that stops short of physical violence must be defended.

University officials who have formulated policies to respond to   5 incidents of racial harassment have been characterized in the press as "thought police," but such policies generally do nothing more than impose sanctions against intentional face-to-face insults. When racist speech takes the form of face-to-face insults, catcalls, or other assaultive speech aimed at an individual or small group of persons, it falls directly within the "fighting words" exception to First Amendment protection. The Supreme Court has held that words which "by their very utterance inflict injury or tend to incite an immediate breach of the peace" are not protected by the First Amendment.

If the purpose of the First Amendment is to foster the greatest amount of speech, racial insults disserve that purpose. Assaultive racist speech functions as a preemptive strike. The invective is experienced as a blow, not as a proffered idea, and once the blow is struck, it is unlikely that a dialogue will follow. Racial insults are particularly undeserving of First Amendment protection because the perpetrator's intention is not to discover truth or initiate dialogue but to injure the victim. In most situations, members of minority groups realize that they are likely to lose if they respond to epithets by fighting and are forced to remain silent and submissive.

Courts have held that offensive speech may not be regulated in public forums such as streets where the listener may avoid the speech by moving on, but the regulation of otherwise protected speech has been permitted when the speech invades the privacy of the unwilling listener's home or when the unwilling listener cannot avoid the speech.

Racist posters, fliers, and graffiti in dormitories, bathrooms, and other common living spaces would seem to clearly fall within the reasoning of these cases. Minority students should not be required to remain in their rooms in order to avoid racial assault. Minimally, they should find a safe haven in their dorms and in all other common rooms that are a part of their daily routine.

I would also argue that the university's responsibility for ensuring that these students receive an equal educational opportunity provides a compelling justification for regulations that ensure them safe passage in all common areas. A minority student should not have to risk becoming the target of racially assaulting speech every time he or she chooses to walk across campus. Regulating vilifying speech that cannot be anticipated or avoided would not preclude announced speeches and rallies — situations that would give minority-group members and their allies the chance to organize counterdemonstrations or avoid the speech altogether.

The most commonly advanced argument against the regulation of racist speech proceeds something like this: We recognize that minority groups suffer pain and injury as the result of racist speech, but we must allow this hate mongering for the benefit of society as a whole. Freedom of speech is the lifeblood of our democratic system. It is especially important for minorities because often it is their only vehicle for rallying support for the redress of their grievances. It will be impossible to formulate a prohibition so precise that it will prevent the racist speech you want to suppress without catching in the same net all kinds of speech that it would be unconscionable for a democratic society to suppress.

Whenever we make such arguments, we are striking a balance on the one hand between our concern for the continued free flow of ideas and the democratic process dependent on that flow, and, on the other, our desire to further the cause of equality. There can be no meaningful discussion of how we should reconcile our commitment to equality and our commitment to free speech until it is acknowledged that there is real harm inflicted by racist speech and that this harm is far from trivial. 10

To engage in a debate about the First Amendment and racist speech without a full understanding of the nature and extent of that harm is to risk making the First Amendment an instrument of domination rather than a vehicle of liberation. We have not all known the experience of victimization by racist, misogynist, and homophobic speech, nor do we equally share the burden of the societal harm it inflicts. We are often quick to say that we have heard the cry of the victims when we have not.

The *Brown* case is again instructive because it speaks directly to the psychic injury inflicted by racist speech by noting that the symbolic message of segregation affected "the hearts and minds" of negro chil-

dren "in a way unlikely ever to be undone." Racial epithets and harassment often cause deep emotional scarring and feelings of anxiety and
fear that pervade every aspect of a victim's life.

Brown also recognized that black children did not have an equal
opportunity to learn and participate in the school community if they
bore the additional burden of being subjected to the humiliation and
psychic assault contained in the message of segregation. University
students bear an analogous burden when they are forced to live and
work in an environment where at any moment they may be subjected
to denigrating verbal harassment and assault. The same injury was
addressed by the Supreme Court when it held that sexual harassment
that creates a hostile or abusive work environment violates the ban on
sex discrimination in employment of Title VII of the Civil Rights Act of
1964.

Carefully drafted university regulations would bar the use of words
as assault weapons and leave unregulated even the most heinous of
ideas when those ideas are presented at times and places and in manners that provide an opportunity for reasoned rebuttal or escape from
immediate injury. The history of the development of the right to free
speech has been one of carefully evaluating the importance of free
expression and its effects on other important societal interests. We
have drawn the line between protected and unprotected speech before
without dire results. (Courts have, for example, exempted from the
protection of the First Amendment obscene speech and speech that
disseminates official secrets, that defames or libels another person, or
that is used to form a conspiracy or monopoly.)

Blacks and other people of color are skeptical about the argument 15
that even the most injurious speech must remain unregulated because,
in an unregulated marketplace of ideas, the best ones will rise to the
top and gain acceptance. Our experience tells us quite the opposite.
We have seen too many demagogues elected by appealing to America's
racism. We have seen too many good liberal politicians shy away from
the issues that might brand them as being too closely allied with us.

Whenever we decide that racist speech must be tolerated because
of the importance of maintaining societal tolerance for all unpopular
speech, we are asking blacks and other subordinated groups to bear
the burden for the good of all. We must be careful that the ease with
which we strike the balance against the regulation of racist speech is
in no way influenced by the fact that the cost will be borne by others.
We must be certain that those who will pay that price are fairly represented in our deliberations and that they are heard.

At the core of the argument that we should resist all government
regulation of speech is the ideal that the best cure for bad speech is
good, that ideas that affirm equality and the worth of all individuals
will ultimately prevail. This is an empty ideal unless those of us who
would fight racism are vigilant and unequivocal in that fight. We must

look for ways to offer assistance and support to students whose speech and political participation are chilled in a climate of racial harassment.

Civil-rights lawyers might consider suing on behalf of blacks whose right to an equal education is denied by a university's failure to ensure a nondiscriminatory educational climate or conditions of employment. We must embark upon the development of a First Amendment jurisprudence grounded in the reality of our history and our contemporary experience. We must think hard about how best to launch legal attacks against the most indefensible forms of hate speech. Good lawyers can create exceptions and narrow interpretations that limit the harm of hate speech without opening the floodgates of censorship.

Everyone concerned with these issues must find ways to engage actively in actions that resist and counter the racist ideas that we would have the First Amendment protect. If we fail in this, the victims of hate speech must rightly assume that we are on the oppressors' side.

Free Speech on the Campus
NAT HENTOFF

A flier distributed at the University of Michigan some months ago proclaimed that blacks "don't belong in classrooms, they belong hanging from trees."

At other campuses around the country, manifestations of racism are becoming commonplace. At Yale, a swastika and the words WHITE POWER! were painted on the building housing the University's Afro-American Cultural Center. At Temple University, a White Students Union has been formed with some 130 members.

Swastikas are not directed only at black students. The Nazi symbol has been spray-painted on the Jewish Student Union at Memphis State University. And on a number of campuses, women have been singled out as targets of wounding and sometimes frightening speech. At the law school of the State University of New York at Buffalo, several women students have received anonymous letters characterized by one professor as venomously sexist.

These and many more such signs of the resurgence of bigotry and know-nothingism throughout the society — as well as on campus — have to do solely with speech, including symbolic speech. There have also been physical assaults on black students and on black, white, and Asian women students, but the way to deal with physical attacks is

Nat Hentoff is the author of *The First Freedom* and is an editor for the *Village Voice*. This article appeared in the May 1989 issue of the *Progressive*.

clear: Call the police and file a criminal complaint. What is to be done, however, about speech alone — however disgusting, inflammatory, and rawly divisive that speech may be?

At more and more colleges, administrators — with the enthusiastic 5 support of black students, women students, and liberal students — have been answering that question by preventing or punishing speech. In public universities, this is a clear violation of the First Amendment. In private colleges and universities, suppression of speech mocks the secular religion of academic freedom and free inquiry.

The Student Press Law Center in Washington, D.C. — a vital source of legal support for student editors around the country — reports, for example, that at the University of Kansas, the student host and producer of a radio news program was forbidden by school officials from interviewing a leader of the Ku Klux Klan. So much for free inquiry on that campus.

In Madison, Wisconsin, *The Capital Times* ran a story in January about Chancellor Sheila Kaplan of the University of Wisconsin branch at Parkside, who ordered her campus to be scoured of "some anonymously placed white-supremacist hate literature." Sounding like the legendary Mayor Frank ("I am the law") Hague of Jersey City, who booted "bad speech" out of town, Chancellor Kaplan said, "This institution is not a lamppost standing on the street corner. It doesn't belong to everyone."

Who decides what speech can be heard or read by everyone? Why, the chancellor, of course. That's what George III used to say, too.

University of Wisconsin political science professor Carol Tebben thinks otherwise. She believes university administrators "are getting confused when they are acting as censors and trying to protect students from bad ideas. I don't think students need to be protected from bad ideas. I think they can determine for themselves what ideas are bad."

After all, if students are to be "protected" from bad ideas, how are 10 they going to learn to identify and cope with them? Sending such ideas underground simply makes them stronger and more dangerous.

Professor Tebben's conviction that free speech means just that has become a decidedly minority view on many campuses. At the University of Buffalo Law School, the faculty unanimously adopted a "Statement Regarding Intellectual Freedom, Tolerance, and Political Harassment." Its title implies support of intellectual freedom, but the statement warned students that once they enter "this legal community," their right to free speech must become tempered "by the responsibility to promote equality and justice."

Accordingly, swift condemnation will befall anyone who engages in "remarks directed at another's race, sex, religion, national origin, age, or sex preference." Also forbidden are "other remarks based on prejudice and group stereotype."

This ukase is so broad that enforcement has to be alarmingly subjective. Yet the University of Buffalo Law School provides no due-process procedures for a student booked for making any of these prohibited remarks. Conceivably, a student caught playing a Lenny Bruce, Richard Pryor, or Sam Kinison album in his room could be tried for aggravated insensitivity by association.

When I looked into this wholesale cleansing of bad speech at Buffalo, I found it had encountered scant opposition. One protester was David Gerald Jay, a graduate of the law school and a cooperating attorney for the New York Civil Liberties Union. Said the appalled graduate: "Content-based prohibitions constitute prior restraint and should not be tolerated."

You think that the law professors and administration at this public 15
university might have known that. But hardly any professors dissented, and among the students only members of the conservative Federalist Society spoke up for free speech. The fifty-strong chapter of the National Lawyers Guild was on the other side. After all, it was more important to go on record as vigorously opposing racism and sexism than to expose oneself to charges of insensitivity to these malignancies.

The pressures to have the "right" attitude — as proved by having the "right" language in and out of class — can be stifling. A student who opposes affirmative action, for instance, can be branded a racist.

At the University of California at Los Angeles, the student newspaper ran an editorial cartoon satirizing affirmative action. (A student stops a rooster on campus and asks how the rooster got into UCLA. "Affirmative action," is the answer.) After outraged complaints from various minority groups, the editor was suspended for violating a publications policy against running "articles that perpetuate derogatory or cultural stereotypes." The art director was also suspended.

When the opinion editor of the student newspaper at California State University at Northridge wrote an article asserting that the sanctions against the editor and art director at UCLA amounted to censorship, he was suspended too.

At New York University Law School, a student was so disturbed by the pall of orthodoxy at that prestigious institution that he wrote to the school newspaper even though, as he said, he expected his letter to make him a pariah among his fellow students.

Barry Endick described the atmosphere at NYU created by "a host 20
of watchdog committees and a generally hostile classroom reception regarding any student comment right of center." This "can be arguably viewed as symptomatic of a prevailing spirit of academic and social intolerance of . . . any idea which is not 'politically correct.'"

He went on to say something that might well be posted on campus bulletin boards around the country, though it would probably be torn down at many of them:

> We ought to examine why students, so anxious to wield the Fourteenth Amendment, give short shrift to the First. Yes, Virginia, there are racist assholes. And you know what, the Constitution protects them, too.

Not when they engage in violence or vandalism. But when they speak or write, racist assholes fall right into this Oliver Wendell Holmes definition — highly unpopular among bigots, liberals, radicals, feminists, sexists, and college administrators:

> If there is any principle of the Constitution that more imperatively calls for attachment than any other, it is the principle of free thought — not free only for those who agree with us, but freedom for the thought we hate.

The language sounds like a pietistic Sunday sermon, but if it ever falls wholly into disuse, neither this publication nor any other journal of opinion — Right or Left — will survive.

Sometimes, college presidents and administrators sound as if they fully understand what Holmes was saying. Last year, for example, when *The Daily Pennsylvanian* — speaking for many at the University of Pennsylvania — urged that a speaking invitation to Louis Farrakhan be withdrawn, University President Sheldon Hackney disagreed.

"Open expression," said Hackney, "is the fundamental principle of a university." Yet consider what the same Sheldon Hackney did to the free-speech rights of a teacher at his own university. If any story distills the essence of the current decline of free speech on college campuses, it is the Ballad of Murray Dolfman.

For twenty-two years, Dolfman, a practicing lawyer in Philadelphia, had been a part-time lecturer in the Legal Studies Department of the University of Pennsylvania's Wharton School. For twenty-two years, no complaint had ever been made against him; indeed, his student course evaluations had been outstanding. Each year students competed to get into his class.

On a November afternoon in 1984, Dolfman was lecturing about personal-service contracts. His style somewhat resembles that of Professor Charles Kingsfield in *The Paper Chase*. Dolfman insists that students he calls on be prepared — or suffer the consequences. He treats all students this way — regardless of race, creed, or sex.

This day, Dolfman was pointing out that no one can be forced to work against his or her will — even if a contract has been signed. A court may prevent the register from working for someone else so long as the contract is in effect but, Dolfman said, there can "be nothing that smacks of involuntary servitude."

Where does this concept come from? Dolfman looked around the room. Finally, a cautious hand was raised: "The Constitution?"

"Where in the Constitution?" No hands. "The Thirteenth Amend- 30 ment," said the teacher. So, what does *it* say? The students were looking everywhere but at Dolfman.

"We will lose our liberties," Dolfman often told his classes, "if we don't know what they are."

On this occasion, he told them that he and other Jews, as ex-slaves, spoke at Passover of the time when they were slaves under the Pharaohs so that they would remember every year what it was like not to be free.

"We have ex-slaves here," Dolfman continued, "who should know about the Thirteenth Amendment." He asked black students in the class if they could tell him what was in that amendment.

"I wanted them to really think about it," Dolfman told me recently, "and know its history. You're better equipped to fight racism if you know all about those post–Civil War amendments and civil-rights laws."

The Thirteenth Amendment provides that "neither slavery nor in- 35 voluntary servitude . . . shall exist within the United States."

The black students in his class did not know what was in that amendment, and Dolfman had them read it aloud. Later, they complained to university officials that they had been hurt and humiliated by having been referred to as ex-slaves. Moreover, they said, they had no reason to be grateful for a constitutional amendment which gave them rights which should never have been denied them — and gave them precious little else. They had not made these points in class, although Dolfman — unlike Professor Kingsfield — encourages rebuttal.

Informed of the complaint, Dolfman told the black students he had intended no offense, and he apologized if they had been offended.

That would not do — either for the black students or for the administration. Furthermore, there were mounting black-Jewish tensions on campus, and someone had to be sacrificed. Who better than a part-time Jewish teacher with no contract and no union? He was sentenced by — George Orwell would have loved this — the Committee on Academic Freedom and Responsibility.

On his way to the stocks, Dolfman told President Sheldon Hackney that if a part-time instructor "can be punished on this kind of charge, a tenured professor can eventually be booted out, then a dean, and then a president."

Hackney was unmoved. Dolfman was banished from the campus 40 for what came to be a year. But first he was forced to make a public apology to the entire university and then he was compelled to attend a "sensitivity and racial awareness" session. Sort of like a Vietnamese reeducation camp.

A few conservative professors objected to the stigmatization of Murray Dolfman. I know of no student dissent. Indeed, those students most concerned with making the campus more "sensitive" to diversity exulted in Dolfman's humiliation. So did most liberals on the faculty.

If my children were still of college age and wanted to attend the University of Pennsylvania, I would tell them this story. But where else could I encourage them to go?

Politically Correct Speech and the First Amendment

NADINE STROSSEN and J. PETER BYRNE

Nadine Strossen: For the past several years I have been traveling around the country talking to audience after audience about free speech on campus and the extent to which we should tolerate racist, sexist, homophobic, and other forms of what is called "hate speech." I was bemused the first time I was asked recently whether the First Amendment should protect hate speech, because I thought that issue had been definitively settled in 1978 by the two *Skokie* cases (appellate court of Illinois and federal court), in which the American Civil Liberties Union valiantly defended the right to free speech of a group of American neo-Nazis who wanted to march through the town of Skokie, Illinois, which has a large Jewish population and a large population of Holocaust survivors.

At great trauma to itself, the ACLU took the case, and as a result, our membership dropped off enormously, by about 10 percent around the country. That to me is astonishing. We're talking about 10 percent of an organization whose cardinal principle is dedication to the Bill of Rights, and of course, that includes free speech. As a constitutional law professor, I thought it was clearly understood that the central principle of the Bill of Rights is the indivisibility of rights. That is, if any person or any group is deprived of any right, then all rights are endangered for all people and all groups. That was the principle the ACLU was defending in *Skokie.*

That is not a position that just the ACLU and the Cato Institute have advocated; it is a position that has been accepted by the entire spectrum of Supreme Court justices from left to right, from conservative to liberal, or however you want to describe them. I think that is striking when we look at a Court that now is so divided on so many issues. I

Nadine Strossen is a professor at New York Law School and president of the American Civil Liberties Union. J. Peter Byrne is a professor at Georgetown University Law Center. Their views were presented at a Cato Institute Policy Forum and are reprinted from the March–April 1991 issue of the *Cato Policy Report.*

mean, how many decisions are 5–4 with fragmentary opinions within them? First Amendment protection for offensive or hateful speech is one of the few individual rights issues on which the Court is unanimous.

Hustler Magazine v. Falwell (1988) is a good example. In 1983 the magazine published a phony ad that purported to be a description by the Reverend Jerry Falwell of his first sexual experience. Falwell sued the magazine, and eventually the case reached the Supreme Court. In a unanimous opinion written by Chief Justice Rehnquist, hardly the most staunch advocate of free speech, the Court took a very strong stand. It held that despite the fact that the ad was offensive, or indeed, because it was offensive, it had to be protected and could not be the basis for a civil damages suit. I use that example to put what I am talking about in context; it is not just the ACLU position; it is the accepted position of American constitutional law.

Many colleges and universities have either adopted or are in the   5
process of adopting speech codes that restrict what students can say on the basis of content. Some of those codes have gotten a lot of publicity. At Stanford University, for example, the speech code was very hotly debated by Charles Lawrence, a law school professor who favored restrictions on hate speech, and the great constitutional law scholar Gerald Gunther, who opposed them. Gunther ultimately lost. What many people do not realize is that in a quieter, less controversial fashion — because there are not Gunthers opposing them — those codes are being adopted by schools all over the country.

Even at my own law school, a couple of months ago the faculty was considering a proposal to curb sexual harassment on campus. The proposal defined sexual harassment in sweeping terms to include everything from jokes about sex to comments on a person's appearance. Some faculty members advocated rules that would have prohibited a professor from having any kind of intimate relationship not only with a present student but also with anyone who had ever been a student, on the theory that we professors have continuing power over students because we may be asked to write letters of recommendation. I come from a faculty that includes many members of the ACLU; in fact the chair of the committee that drafted the rules is an active member of the ACLU. The problem was that the faculty just wasn't thinking in terms of free speech.

I think it is only rather recently that people have started to realize how endangered free speech is by some otherwise seemingly noble goals that, considered in their own right, in the abstract, nobody could quarrel with. Who's in favor of sexual harassment? Who's in favor of undermining equality of educational opportunity on the basis of sex and race? It's only recently that some people have started to see the adverse impact on free speech of attempts to attain those goals by imposing speech codes. The bad news is that we have the academics, including some well-respected constitutional law professors, advocating revisionist views of free speech. The good news is that the courts are steadfastly resisting efforts to rethink the First Amendment in this context.

The one case that has been decided so far was quite definitive. A student at the University of Michigan, who felt his speech was chilled by the University's anti-hate-speech rule, was so worried about being called a racist or a sexist because of what he wanted to say that he proceeded anonymously. In the course of his graduate studies in psychobiology he had come across some evidence that there might be genetic distinction among races and between sexes that might affect their intelligence. He felt he couldn't discuss those ideas in his graduate seminar without running afoul of the anti-hate-speech rule, and indeed, the judge agreed that it was a serious problem that raised a justiciable issue and proceeded to strike down the rule.

There was also a suit brought against the University of Connecticut by a woman named Nina Wu. She had put a sign on her door saying, "The following categories are not allowed into this room," and one was "homos." She explained that she meant *Homo sapiens;* but it was not surprisingly assumed that she meant homosexuals, and she was, therefore, not only reprimanded or chastised but also barred from university facilities. The Connecticut Civil Liberties Union brought a suit on her behalf that resulted in a very favorable resolution consistent with the First Amendment.

Wu is an Asian-American woman. I think it's striking that the very minority group members who think that they are going to benefit from anti-hate-speech rules are the ones who are disproportionately victimized by them. Efforts to regulate group defamation or hate speech are always offered as a vehicle for protecting oppressed groups. Yet what anti-hate-speech rules are doing is handing over to government, in this case to university officials, the power to enforce codes that are inevitably vague and subjective and leave an enormous amount of discretion to the decision maker. For example, the Michigan code talks about words that create a "hostile" or "intimidating" environment. Well, I think each one of us in this room would interpret those words differently, so it's not surprising that the power structure that is being challenged as oppressive interprets the rules in a way that oppresses those who felt they were being oppressed in the first place.

In the Michigan case the university had to open its files and reveal what the actual enforcement record had been — who had brought complaints under the rule, and how the rule had been enforced. The only two students who had been punished for racist speech (there were other categories of hate speech) were both black. One was a law student who got into an argument during which she used the term "white trash," and that was held to be a violation of the code. The other student was enrolled in a preclinical course in the dentistry school — a course considered so difficult that there was an orientation session so students could air their concerns and get acculturated to the rigors of the course. The black student said, "I heard that this course is particularly difficult for minority students." It happened that the instructor was a black woman who took the student's expression of concern as a racist attack on her; she accused the student of racism, and he was punished. I think it's striking that in a university that has tens of thousands of students, in a year and a half of enforcement, those were the only cases of racism. I think that's hardly a coincidence; indeed, if we look through history, we find that pattern repeated over and over.

I think it's also striking that the student who received the harshest penalty under the University of Michigan's rule was a black student accused of homophobia. He was a graduate student in social work who believed that homosexuality was a curable disease; as part of his clinical experience in social work he wanted to design a program for curing the disease. Whether or not you agree with the student's approach, I hope you would agree that his is the kind of idea that should be allowed to be expressed and should not be punished. In his petition for clemency to the president of the university, the student said he thought that he had been singled out for punishment on account of his race and his political views.

There is an ultimate irony in the "politically correct" movement; its root notion is that everything in life is political and all academic subjects reflect the power struggle between those who are oppressed and their perceived oppressors. In that sense, the movement seems to be calling for a more politically aware view of the world. Yet to think that granting the oppressive, as they say, power structure the additional power to sanction certain speech is somehow going to improve the lot of the oppressed strikes me as politically naive.

I think campus speech codes reflect a more widespread problem, a problem that has to do not only with what you can't say but with what you can't think — and even worse, what you must say, what you must think, what you must teach, and what you must study.

When the ACLU national board recently unanimously opposed campus hate-speech codes on free-speech grounds, one of the examples given of an appropriate corrective for such speech was required courses on multiculturalism and diversity. Now, that's no panacea for First Amendment problems, because the way those courses are taught can raise free-speech problems. I'm proud to say that I moved an amendment, which was adopted, that cautions that any such course would have to be taught in a way that respected the individual rights of conscience and belief of the students. I think there is a great danger that that kind of course could degenerate into a reeducation camp. Pressure to be "politically correct" in such a course poses an insidious danger that we have to be alert to as universities all over the country make seemingly benevolent efforts to adopt multicultural curricula.

I could not feel more strongly that we have a serious and very disturbing problem of racism, sexism, homophobia, and other forms of group hatred on our campuses; there is no doubt about it. All organizations that keep statistics on incidents of hate-based violence report a dramatic increase, and I think that's tragic. A major reason I feel so strongly that we must adhere to the principle of free speech when we try to combat group hatred is that free speech is the only effective route. We are never going to eliminate group hatred, oppression, or bigotry by silencing its most crass expressions and forcing them to go underground; that is counterproductive.

Some people argue that there is a conflict between civil liberties on the one hand and civil rights on the other. I reject that argument. I think it is clear that the goal of equality in education, as well as civil-rights goals generally, is more effectively pursued by allowing free speech — even racist speech. Many of the responses to the recent epidemic of racist incidents have proven that point. The country as a whole is now very conscious of problems of racism. That consciousness has led to constructive steps, including counseling, educational programs, information, counterspeech, and counterdemonstrations. I think that is the only way to eradicate, or at least counter, the racist attitudes that erupt in hate speech.

It's encouraging that many scholars, activists, and commentators recently have challenged the politically correct speech line and warned of its dangers. We have reached a turning point when we see a cover story in *Newsweek* entitled "Thought Police: Watch What You Say; There Is a Politically Correct Way to Talk about Race, Sex, and Ideas; Is This the New Enlightenment or the New McCarthyism?" That article, as well as most coverage that I have seen in the mass media, criticizes rules that would dictate "correct" speech not only as violations of free speech but also as unproductive in terms of advancing equality.

J. Peter Byrne: Professor Strossen has elided two aspects of the problem that are best kept separate. I would disassociate myself from all of the silly forms of politically correct speech, but there is a real concern that manifests itself in the simple but offensive hypothetical of the words "niggers suck" spray painted on the side of a student union. There's nothing cute about that; it's not funny. Clearly, those words are speech. And many administrators and faculty members around the country are sincerely trying to determine the appropriate response to that form of speech. Obviously that kind of speech — and it's not directed at just blacks but at other racial minority groups, religious minorities, and homosexuals as well — has to do with broad cultural changes in American universities. The fact is that you are seeing, for the first time, multiracial, multicultural universities, and that situation presents challenges.

I agree with a great deal of what Professor Strossen says about the 20 necessity of protecting speech that is vulgar, stupid, and generally inhibiting of intelligent thought throughout society as a whole. We are all citizens under the Constitution, and the government has no transcendent criteria for deciding which forms of speech are acceptable and which are not. I think, however, that on university campuses different principles can apply.

Universities are not entirely open institutions. Our system of academic freedom assumes that only people who are qualified to speak on a particular topic will hold forth in the classroom, and if their speech is inadequate, they will be penalized — they will not be rehired, be tenured, or get raises. Even admission to most of our universities requires some showing of aptitude. Our whole system of education is based on the idea that we can have a more productive educational discourse if we adhere to fundamental standards of competence and courtesy.

The main objective of scholarship at universities is the establishment of a form of speech that aspires to a degree of credibility to which we are comfortable applying the word "knowledge." The struggle to say something worthwhile, to collectively address very hard problems, requires a certain degree of tolerance and courtesy, and the type of racial insult that I gave as an illustration is fundamentally at odds with that attitude. Liberal education means very little unless it equips students with the capacity to master difficult forms of thought and expression and the ability to express themselves with some degree of persuasiveness.

Although I believe that universities can, in principle, penalize members of the academic community for voicing racial insults, I do not believe that any member of the academic community can be penalized for expressing a substantive view, however offensive it may be, in a form that is subject to rational contradiction through the adducement of evidence or through open debate.

The types of insults we are talking about are not forms of speech that further debate; they are forms of speech that burden debate and cause people to retreat into a form of tribal safety that engenders a closing in rather than an opening out. That approach to speech permits universities to penalize members of their communities who abuse their fellow students in a way that is subrational. It's worth saying, I suppose, that I think that that view of the authority of universities is encompassed within the First Amendment. What the Supreme Court has said about academic freedom establishes that universities, acting to further academic values, have more discretion in the regulation of their members than the government does with regard to society as a whole.

Having said that, I certainly do not want to gloss over the difficulties 25 there may be in administering a program that requires university officials to distinguish between gross insults and the expression of substantive views that are offensive but have to be protected. That task requires a great deal of care and good faith. The effort of separating those two kinds of speech is part and parcel of what it means to be a member of an intellectual community. Speech calls our attention to significant ethical questions about the way we treat each other, about our need to hear things that are uncomfortable, and about our need to transcend our own prejudices.

Strossen: We are indeed entering an era of multiculturalism in our universities, perhaps even in advance of the rest of society, and there is a challenge to bridging gaps that have separated people. One of the reasons there have been outbursts of racism and other forms of group hatred on campuses is that many students grew up in de facto segregated neighborhoods, went to de facto segregated schools, and were not thrown together with people of other ethnic, racial, or religious groups until they went to college. We have to start addressing the problem not by looking at its most crude and superficial manifestation — the blatant racist insult — but by dealing with the root causes of racism and segregation in our society. It's a politically appealing solution to a government official or to a university administrator to say, "Aha, I am doing something about this problem; I'm stopping one student from calling another a nigger."

One of my profound bases for opposing that kind of "solution" is that it deters people from pursuing a serious strategy to deal with the real problem. About a year ago I debated law professor Charles Lawrence of Stanford — the primary proponent of anti-hate-speech codes not only at Stanford but all over the country. He agreed with me that those codes have always been used to punish disproportionately the speech of minority groups. His way around that admitted problem was to make an exception to the rule: The rule will not apply to speech about "members of dominant majority groups."

That raises some questions. At Howard University is a white person part of a dominant majority? Is a Jew part of a dominant majority group at Yeshiva University? One of the law students in the audience asked, "Can I, as a woman, a white woman, make a racist remark to a black male?" Lawrence said, "No; you can to a white male because you are oppressed vis-à-vis him, but you can't to a black male, and you can't to a gay male." At that point I said, "But what if she's a lesbian?" and the audience burst out laughing. I didn't mean to be funny, but Lawrence never answered the question. One faculty member asked a proponent of the Stanford rule, "Does this mean that a black student could be punished for calling a white student a honky?" The answer from the chair of the committee that drafted the rule was "No, because in our society whites are dominant, and therefore they inherently can't feel oppressed or victimized when they are called those names by blacks." I could give you many more examples from the politically correct movement that raise shades of the Nuremberg laws and apartheid.

Colleges and universities are opening the door to increased racism and other forms of group-based hatred and suspicion by adopting anti-hate-speech codes.

Ice-T: The Issue Is Social Responsibility

MICHAEL KINSLEY

How did the company that publishes this magazine come to produce a record glorifying the murder of police?

> I got my 12-gauge sawed off
> I got my headlights turned off
> I'm 'bout to bust some shots off
> I'm 'bout to dust some cops off . . .
> Die, Die, Die Pig, Die!

So go the lyrics to "Cop Killer" by the rapper Ice-T on the album *Body Count.* The album is released by Warner Brothers Records, part of the Time Warner media and entertainment conglomerate.

In a *Wall Street Journal* op-ed piece laying out the company's position, Time Warner co-CEO Gerald Levin makes two defenses. First, Ice-T's "Cop Killer" is misunderstood. "It doesn't incite or glorify violence. . . . It's his fictionalized attempt to get inside a character's head. . . . 'Cop Killer' is no more a call for gunning down the police than 'Frankie and Johnny' is a summons for jilted lovers to shoot one another." Instead of "finding ways to silence the messenger," we should be "heeding the anguished cry contained in his message."

This defense is self-contradictory. "Frankie and Johnny" does not pretend to have a political "message" that must be "heeded." If "Cop Killer" has a message, it is that the murder of policemen is a justified response to police brutality. And not in self-defense, but in premeditated acts of revenge against random cops. ("I know your family's grievin' — f____ 'em.")

Killing policemen is a good thing — that is the plain meaning of the 5 words, and no "larger understanding" of black culture, the rage of the streets or anything else can explain it away. This is not Ella Fitzgerald telling a story in song. As in much of today's popular music, the line between performer and performance is purposely blurred. These are political sermonettes clearly intended to endorse the sentiments being expressed. Tracy Marrow (Ice-T) himself has said, "I scared the police, and they need to be scared." That seems clear.

The company's second defense of "Cop Killer" is the classic one of free expression: "We stand for creative freedom. We believe that the worth of what an artist or journalist has to say does not depend on preapproval from a government official or a corporate censor."

Michael Kinsley is a senior editor at *The New Republic,* where he writes the weekly column *TRB.* This essay appeared in *Time* magazine on June 20, 1992.

Of course Ice-T has the right to say whatever he wants. But that doesn't require any company to provide him an outlet. And it doesn't relieve a company of responsibility for the messages it chooses to promote. Judgment is not "censorship." Many an "anguished cry" goes unrecorded. This one was recorded, and promoted, because a successful artist under contract wanted to record it. Nothing wrong with making money, but a company cannot take the money and run from the responsibility.

The founder of *Time,* Henry Luce, would snort at the notion that his company should provide a value-free forum for the exchange of ideas. In Luce's system, editors were supposed to make value judgments and promote the truth as they saw it. *Time* has moved far from its old Lucean rigidity — far enough to allow for dissenting essays like this one. That evolution is a good thing, as long as it's not a handy excuse for abandoning all standards.

No commercial enterprise need agree with every word that appears under its corporate imprimatur. If Time Warner now intends to be "a global force for encouraging the confrontation of ideas," that's swell. But a policy of allowing diverse viewpoints is not a moral free pass. Pro and con on national health care is one thing; pro and con on killing policemen is another.

A bit of sympathy is in order for Time Warner. It is indeed a "global 10 force" with media tentacles around the world. If it imposes rigorous standards and values from the top, it gets accused of corporate censorship. If it doesn't, it gets accused of moral irresponsibility. A dilemma. But someone should have thought of that before deciding to become a global force.

And another genuine dilemma. Whatever the actual merits of "Cop Killer," if Time Warner withdraws the album now the company will be perceived as giving in to outside pressure. That is a disastrous precedent for a global conglomerate.

The Time-Warner merger of 1989 was supposed to produce corporate "synergy": The whole was supposed to be more than the sum of the parts. The "Cop Killer" controversy is an example of negative synergy. People get mad at "Cop Killer" and start boycotting the movie *Batman Returns.* A reviewer praises "Cop Killer" ("Tracy Marrow's poetry takes a switchblade and deftly slices life's jugular," etc.), and *Time* is accused of corruption instead of mere foolishness. Senior Time Warner executives find themselves under attack for — and defending — products of their company they neither honestly care for nor really understand, and doubtless weren't even aware of before controversy hit.

Anyway, it's absurd to discuss "Cop Killer" as part of the "confrontation of ideas" — or even as an authentic anguished cry of rage from the ghetto. "Cop Killer" is a cynical commercial concoction, designed to titillate its audience with imagery of violence. It merely exploits the authentic anguish of the inner city for further titillation. Tracy Marrow is in business for a buck, just like Time Warner. "Cop Killer" is an excellent joke on the white establishment, of which the company's anguished apologia ("Why can't we hear what rap is trying to tell us?") is the punch line.

Ice-T: The Issue
Is Creative Freedom
BARBARA EHRENREICH

Ice-T's song "Cop Killer" is as bad as they come. This is black anger — raw, rude, and cruel — and one reason the song's so shocking is that in postliberal America, black anger is virtually taboo. You won't find it on TV, not on the *McLaughlin Group* or *Crossfire,* and certainly not in the placid features of Arsenio Hall or Bernard Shaw. It's been beaten back into the outlaw subcultures of rap and rock, where, precisely because it is taboo, it sells. And the nastier it is, the faster it moves off the shelves. As Ice-T asks in another song on the same album, "Goddamn what a brotha gotta do/ To get a message through/ To the red, white, and blue?"

But there's a gross overreaction going on, building to a veritable paroxysm of white denial. A national boycott has been called, not just of the song or Ice-T, but of all Time Warner products. The president himself has denounced Time Warner as "wrong" and Ice-T as "sick." Ollie North's Freedom Alliance has started a petition drive aimed at bringing Time Warner executives to trial for "sedition and anarchy."

Much of this is posturing and requires no more courage than it takes to stand up in a VFW hall and condemn communism or crack. Yes, "Cop Killer" is irresponsible and vile. But Ice-T is as right about some things as he is righteous about the rest. And ultimately, he's not even dangerous — least of all to the white power structure his songs condemn.

The "danger" implicit in all the uproar is of empty-headed, suggestible black kids, crouching by their boom boxes, waiting for the word. But what Ice-T's fans know and his detractors obviously don't is that "Cop Killer" is just one more entry in pop music's long history of macho hyperbole and violent boast. Flip to the classic-rock station, and you might catch the Rolling Stones announcing "the time is right for violent revoloo-shun!" from their 1968 hit "Street Fighting Man." And where

---

Barbara Ehrenreich, co-chair of Democratic Socialists of America, is the author of *The Worst Years of Our Lives: Irreverent Notes from a Decade of Greed* (1990).

were the defenders of our law-enforcement officers when a white British group, the Clash, taunted its fans with the lyrics: "When they kick open your front door/ How you gonna come/ With your hands on your head/ Or on the trigger of your gun?"

"Die, Die, Die Pig" is strong speech, but the Constitution protects 5 strong speech, and it's doing so this year more aggressively than ever. The Supreme Court has just downgraded cross burnings to the level of bonfires and ruled that it's no crime to throw around verbal grenades like "nigger" and "kike." Where are the defenders of decorum and social stability when prime-time demagogues like Howard Stern deride African Americans as "spear chuckers"?

More to the point, young African-Americans are not so naive and suggestible that they have to depend on a compact disc for their sociology lessons. To paraphrase another song from another era, you don't need a rap song to tell which way the wind is blowing. Black youths know that the police are likely to see them through a filter of stereotypes as miscreants and potential "cop killers." They are aware that a black youth is seven times as likely to be charged with a felony as a white youth who has committed the same offense, and is much more likely to be imprisoned.

They know, too, that in a shameful number of cases, it is the police themselves who indulge in "anarchy" and violence. The U.S. Justice Department has received 47,000 complaints of police brutality in the past six years, and Amnesty International has just issued a report on police brutality in Los Angeles, documenting forty cases of "torture or cruel, inhuman, or degrading treatment."

Menacing as it sounds, the fantasy in "Cop Killer" is the fantasy of the powerless and beaten down — the black man who's been hassled once too often ("A pig stopped me for nothin'!"), spread-eagled against a police car, pushed around. It's not a "responsible" fantasy (fantasies seldom are). It's not even a very creative one. In fact, the sad thing about "Cop Killer" is that it falls for the cheapest, most conventional image of rebellion that our culture offers: the lone gunman spraying fire from his AK-47. This is not "sedition"; it's the familiar, all-American, Hollywood-style pornography of violence.

Which is why Ice-T is right to say he's no more dangerous than George Bush's pal Arnold Schwarzenegger, who wasted an army of cops in *Terminator 2*. Images of extraordinary cruelty and violence are marketed every day, many of far less artistic merit than "Cop Killer." This is our free market of ideas and images, and it shouldn't be any less free for a black man than for other purveyors of "irresponsible" sentiments, from David Duke to Andrew Dice Clay.

Just, please, don't dignify Ice-T's contribution with the word *sedi-* 10 *tion*. The past masters of sedition — men like George Washington, Toussaint-Louverture, Fidel Castro, or Mao Zedong, all of whom led and won armed insurrections — would be unimpressed by "Cop Killer" and probably saddened. They would shake their heads and mutter words like "infantile" and "adventurism." They might point out that the cops are hardly a noble target, being, for the most part, honest working stiffs who've got stuck with the job of patrolling ghettos ravaged by economic decline and official neglect.

There is a difference, the true seditionist would argue, between a revolution and a gesture of macho defiance. Gestures are cheap. They feel good, they blow off some rage. But revolutions, violent or otherwise, are made by people who have learned how to count very slowly to 10.

Freedom of Speech and Holocaust Revisionism

DAVID M. OSHINSKY and MICHAEL CURTIS

College newspapers are facing a dilemma that pits free speech against historical deception. A group calling itself the Committee for Open Debate on the Holocaust has sent an advertisement to at least a dozen leading campus dailies. The ad contends that the Holocaust never occurred.

Newspapers at Harvard, Yale, Brown, the University of Pennsylvania, and the University of Southern California have refused to run it. Those at Northwestern, Cornell, Duke, and the University of Michigan have published it amid protests from students, faculty, and members of their own editorial boards. At Rutgers, the ad was printed free of charge on December 3 as a "guest commentary," surrounded by rebuttals.

The ad attempts to prey on students' ignorance about the Holocaust. It insists, without evidence, that there were no mass killings of Jews and no "execution gas chambers in any camp in Europe that was under German control." It claims the so-called execution chambers were "fumigation chambers," used "to delouse clothing . . . and prevent disease." It is "from this life-*saving* procedure," the ad says, "that the myth of extermination gas chambers emerged."

The slickly done ad does not use the violent language common to the literature of racist and nativist groups. It wraps itself in concepts of free speech and open inquiry, arguing that all points of view deserve to be heard. Timed to exploit the controversy about political correctness, the ad says "elitist" and "Zionist" groups have stifled debate on

David M. Oshinsky is a professor of history at Rutgers University. Michael Curtis, also at Rutgers, is a professor of political science. Their article was published in the *New York Times* on December 11, 1991.

the Holocaust in order "to drum up world sympathy" for Jewish causes and Israel.

The ad was written by Bradley R. Smith, a political soulmate of the California-based Institute for Historical Review, the principal promoter of "Holocaust revisionism." Its founder, Willis A. Carto, was described by the Anti-Defamation League last year as "perhaps the leading anti-Semite in the United States." He has been associated with the Populist Party, whose presidential candidate in 1988 was David Duke; the Liberty Lobby, a hate group; and the Noontide Press, which distributes such tracts as "The Testing of Negro Intelligence" and "The International Jew."

In 1980, Mr. Carto's institute offered $50,000 to anyone who could "prove" that Jews were exterminated at Auschwitz. Mel Mermelstein, a Holocaust survivor, submitted sworn declarations from people who had been in the camp. When the institute refused to pay up, he took its officers to court in Los Angeles. That Jews were gassed to death at Auschwitz "is not reasonably subject to dispute," the presiding judge declared. "It is simply a fact." In 1985, Mr. Mermelstein was awarded the $50,000, plus $40,000 for pain and suffering.

Bradley Smith's committee apparently believes that its theories will be tolerated by some on First Amendment grounds and accepted by others out of ignorance or worse. The Duke student newspaper naively repeated the committee's description of itself as a group of revisionist scholars. Duke's history department was appalled and responded with a statement that distinguished between those who revise history and those who deny it.

Most college editors seem aware of the committee's intentions. Their decision to print its ad is based on principle: An aversion to censorship or a belief that hate material should be aired and publicly refuted. Surely their right to publish such ads should not be questioned. They alone must decide what good purpose, if any, is served by printing ads that are intentionally hurtful and obviously false.

The ads should be rejected. If one group advertises that the Holocaust never happened, another can buy space to insist that American blacks were never enslaved. The stakes are high because college newspapers may soon be flooded with ads that present discredited assertions as if they were part of normal historical debate. If the Holocaust is not a fact, then nothing is a fact, and truth itself will be diminished.

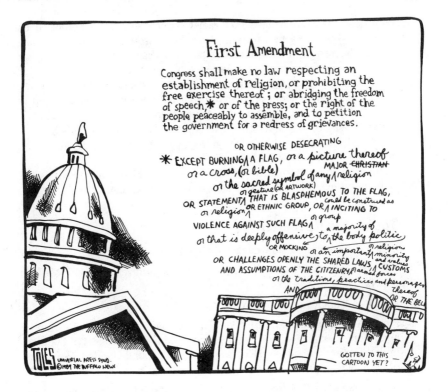

THINKING AND WRITING ABOUT FREEDOM OF SPEECH

Questions for Discussion and Writing

1. According to Garry Wills, why is "censure" superior to censorship? (Look up or ask about the specific references in his essay if you aren't familiar with them.) Would he agree with Kinsley that a refusal to produce "Cop Killer" is not an act of censorship?

2. Can you think of circumstances in which creative freedom should bow to social responsibility? What does Kinsley mean when he says, "Judgment is not censorship"? What evidence does Ehrenreich use to prove that "Cop Killer" is not dangerous? Is it convincing?

3. How does Lawrence relate *Brown v. Board of Education* to issues of free speech? What principles does he invoke in defense of restrictive speech codes on campus?

4. Hentoff argues for exposure of students to bad ideas as well as good ones. (See pp. 5–6 for a quotation from *Aeropagitica,* in which John Milton makes the same point.) What bad ideas does Hentoff have in mind? Spell out the educational advantages of such exposure. What is Hentoff's main criticism of university officials? Do you think it is justified?

   Hentoff uses examples freely to argue his case. Do all his examples support the points he wants to make?

5. Why does Strossen believe that racist speech should be permitted on campus? What is Byrne's response? Are his reasons for objecting to hate speech different from Lawrence's? What is Strossen trying to prove in her exchange with Lawrence as recounted in the last paragraph of the debate?

6. Oshinsky and Curtis raise the question of media responsibility to the truth. Does a belief in freedom of speech mean that newspapers have a right to publish "discredited assertions as if they were part of normal historical debate"? Why or why not? Are "discredited assertions" the same as Hentoff's bad ideas? Has the college newspaper on your campus ever been guilty of publishing nontruths?

7. Summarize the cartoonist's wry claim about the First Amendment. Is the same point expressed in any of the essays in this chapter?

Topics for Research

Lyrics in rock music: How dangerous are they?

Codes of speech conduct at some colleges and universities: purpose and effect

Religious displays on public land

Public funds for offensive art. (Look up the cases of Robert Mapplethorpe and Andres Serrano, whose works scandalized some members of Congress in the summer and fall of 1989.) Is withdrawal of public funds a "regulation of the imagination"?

Recent extensions of freedom of speech by the courts (e.g., burning the American flag, begging on the street, cursing people on the street)

CHAPTER SIXTEEN

Gay and Lesbian Rights

In the last decade homosexual men and women have mounted an increasingly active campaign for a legal revolution that would extend their civil rights and forbid discrimination. They have called for passage of new laws and repeal of old rules regarding marriage, adoption, housing, employment, medical insurance, and military service.

Gays and lesbians define themselves as members of an identifiable group entitled, like other groups in our society who have not enjoyed full equality and freedom, to special protection that would enable them to live openly as homosexuals and to participate more fully in American life. They argue that special laws are necessary because homosexual men and women are more vulnerable than heterosexuals to rejection and discrimination. Beyond protection from wrong, the National Gay and Lesbian Task Force also seeks the majority's acceptance of homosexual activity and relationships. One spokesperson says, "We also have a right — as heterosexual Americans already have — to see government and society affirm our lives." The Task Force is seeking passage of a federal gay rights bill.

Opposition to homosexual rights is based in part on religious and moral beliefs as well as long-standing social conventions governing relations between the sexes. But some objections flow from a refusal to accept sexuality as a basis for so-called special rights or legal protection beyond what is already on the books in most states, designed to protect every citizen, regardless of sexual orientation. Civil rights for gays and lesbians are, in the words of one critic, "one more division in a fragmented society. To race, creed, sex, and class we must now add sexuality."

A *Newsweek* poll in August 1992 showed widespread support for some rights demanded by gays and lesbians — health insurance, inheritance rights, and social security for homosexual spouses — but equally widespread disapproval of legally sanctioned gay marriages and adoption rights. Legislation and court decisions have reflected a similar ambivalence. A number of cities now allow homosexual partners to register as domestic partners with accompanying benefits. Several states also permit adoption by same-sex couples. In at least six states and 110 towns and cities gays and lesbians are protected by law against job discrimination. But the courts and the public have been reluctant to accede to all demands for change. In 1980 the U.S. Supreme Court upheld Georgia's sodomy law, forbidding sexual intercourse between adults of the same sex. In 1992 the voters of Colorado approved a ballot initiative that denied homosexuals preferential treatment or protection against discrimination. At least seven other states plan to introduce similar ballot initiatives in 1994. In January 1993 President Clinton announced that he would lift the ban, imposed in 1982, on gays and lesbians in the military services. But opposition from military officials, influential senators and representatives, and vocal segments of the public forced the president to postpone repeal of the ban for six months while a specific plan is formulated. The argument about military service seems likely to become only one part of a national debate about homosexual rights in all areas of American life.

Majority Opinion of the Supreme Court on Homosexual Relations

BYRON R. WHITE

Sodomy was a criminal offense at common law and was forbidden by the laws of the original 13 states when they ratified the Bill of Rights. In 1868, when the Fourteenth Amendment was ratified, all but 5 of the 37 states in the Union had criminal sodomy laws. In fact, until 1961, all 50 states outlawed sodomy, and today, 24 states and the District of Columbia continue to provide criminal penalties for sodomy performed in private and between consenting adults. Against this background, to claim that a right to engage in such conduct is "deeply rooted in this

---

These excerpts, representing the majority opinion of the Supreme Court of the United States in the case of *Bowers v. Hardwick* (1986), were written by Associate Justice Byron R. White. They were reprinted in the *New York Times,* July 5, 1986.

nation's history and tradition" or "implicit in the concept of ordered liberty" is, at best, facetious.

Privacy of the Home

Respondent, however, asserts that the result should be different where the homosexual conduct occurs in the privacy of the home. He relies on *Stanley v. Georgia* (1969), where the Court held that the First Amendment prevents conviction for possessing and reading obscene material in the privacy of his home: "If the First Amendment means anything, it means that a state has no business telling a man, sitting alone in his house, what books he may read or what films he may watch."

Stanley did protect conduct that would not have been protected outside the home, and it partially prevented the enforcement of state obscenity laws; but the decision was firmly grounded in the First Amendment. The right pressed upon us here has no similar support in the text of the Constitution, and it does not qualify for recognition under the prevailing principles for construing the Fourteenth Amendment. Its limits are also difficult to discern. Plainly enough, otherwise illegal conduct is not always immunized whenever it occurs in the home. Victimless crimes, such as the possession and use of illegal drugs do not escape the law where they are committed at home. *Stanley* itself recognized that its holding offered no protection for the possession in the home of drugs, firearms, or stolen goods. And if respondent's submission is limited to the voluntary sexual conduct between consenting adults, it would be difficult, except by fiat, to limit the claimed right to homosexual conduct while leaving exposed to prosecution adultery, incest, and other sexual crimes even though they are committed in the home. We are unwilling to start down that road.

Even if the conduct at issue here is not a fundamental right, respondent asserts that there must be a rational basis for the law and that there is none in this case other than the presumed belief of a majority of the electorate in Georgia that homosexual sodomy is immoral and unacceptable. This is said to be an inadequate rationale to support the law. The law, however, is constantly based on notions of morality, and if all laws representing essentially moral choices are to be invalidated under the Due Process Clause, the courts will be very busy indeed. Even respondent makes no such claim, but insists that majority sentiments about the morality of homosexuality should be declared inadequate. We do not agree, and are unpersuaded that the sodomy laws of some twenty-five states should be invalidated on this basis.

Accordingly, the judgment of the Court of Appeals is reversed.

An Open Letter to the U.S. Supreme Court Re: Bowers v. Hardwick

GAY & LESBIAN ALLIANCE AGAINST DEFAMATION

Michael Hardwick was arrested in the bedroom of his Georgia apartment when a police officer entered his home and observed him engaging in sexual activity with another man. He was charged with violating Georgia's sodomy statute.

Hardwick's case reached the U.S. Supreme Court, where, on June 30, 1986, a 5–4 majority ruled in *Bowers v. Hardwick* that private sexual conduct between consenting adults of the same sex is not protected by the Constitution.

In this bicentennial year of the Constitution, with its emphasis on liberty and equal rights, all Americans should consider the ominous implications of the *Hardwick* decision.

- The Court side-stepped the issue of heterosexual sodomy, leaving the door open for legal intrusions into all people's bedrooms.

- *Hardwick* could lay the groundwork for reversing earlier decisions based on the right of privacy, such as those guaranteeing the freedom of choice to have an abortion and the right to use contraceptives.

- *Hardwick* could signal the end of the federal judiciary's concern with individual rights and the beginning of an era of judicial deference to state control of our private conduct.

In *Hardwick,* the Supreme Court called "facetious" the claim that gay and lesbian people have equal rights under the Constitution — a hostile, defamatory dismissal of the rights of 10 percent or more of all Americans. On the first anniversary of the *Hardwick* decision, nearly 300 law professors and professionals have joined with the Gay & Lesbian Alliance Against Defamation, Inc. (GLAAD) in an open letter deploring the grave injustice of the Court's decision. . . .

The undersigned members of the academic and legal communities 5 deplore the Supreme Court's 5–4 holding that the Constitution does

---

This letter from the Gay & Lesbian Alliance Against Defamation, Inc. (GLAAD) was published in the *New York Times* on June 18, 1987 as an open letter to the U.S. Supreme Court regarding the *Bowers v. Hardwick* case.

not protect the private sexual conduct of consenting adults of the same sex.

We believe that this nation was founded upon principles of limited government and respect for diverse individual choice which compel the protection of every American's freedom of intimate association. Offering little or no legal analysis, however, the Court elected to attack the gay and lesbian segment of our population. Ignoring precedent, the Court referred only to "history and tradition," logic which would have left miscegenation statutes in place, schools still segregated, children still toiling in sweatshops, women still subordinate to their husbands, and all Americans less free to lead their own lives.

The majority failed to explain how the Constitution can be deemed, as it has, to protect the liberty to use contraceptives, to have an abortion if one chooses, to use pornography in one's home, and to live with whom one wishes — but not the liberty to engage in the most intimate and personal human relations with another consenting adult. Instead, the Court inexplicably left in place repugnant and intrusive laws rejected by more than half the states and most of Europe and the free world. The existence of these statutes and their selective enforcement not only offend the Constitution, but breed contempt for the law and provide a pretext for harassment and discrimination.

We agree with the dissent that:

> Only the most willful blindness could obscure the fact that sexual intimacy is "a sensitive, key relationship of human existence, central to family life, community welfare, and the development of human personality. . . ." The fact that individuals define themselves in a significant way through their intimate sexual relationships with others suggests, in a Nation as diverse as ours, that there may be many "right" ways of conducting those relationships, and that much of the richness of a relationship will come from the freedom an individual has to *choose* the form and nature of these intensely personal bonds.

We were pleased to see the polls which indicated that a substantial majority of the American people correctly perceived the issues of freedom here and disagreed with the Supreme Court's decision.

Because we believe the majority opinion poses a grave threat to the constitutional freedoms of all Americans, gay and nongay alike, we wish to register our strong disagreement.

Bogus Sex: Reflections on Homosexual Claims

JOSEPH SOBRAN

In August 1977 a New York public official named Adam Walinsky wrote a short newspaper article arguing against the proposals of militant homosexuals for legislation in their favor. It was not a memorable article: I read it and found it neither distinguished for insight nor tainted by malice. Probably it would have caused no stir except that Walinsky held a minor municipal post, which caused some readers to suppose that his private views somehow represented (or at least could influence) public policy.

A few nights after his article appeared, a mob of homosexuals gathered outside his home, equipped with bullhorns and chanting slogans. Among other things they threatened to burn down the house, then and there, with Walinsky and his family inside it. No doubt this was mere bravado, but all the same it was an ugly incident.

It brought an editorial rebuke from the *New York Times*. The editorial, in turn, moved one reader to write the following letter:

> This is in response to the statement in an August 16 Topics item in your editorial page that the zap of the home of Adam Walinsky by homosexual activists was an intolerable violation of "privacy and safety."
>
> As a homosexual citizen, I cannot walk the streets of New York City or the suburbs thereof without being subject to derogatory comments by perfect strangers regarding my homosexuality. My privacy and safety are thereby violated.
>
> Mr. Walinsky is one individual who would stir up hatred against a large class (group) of people. If on one night he is subjected to some of the hatred which he has forced on large numbers of other citizens on a constant basis by his ill-informed writing, then my sympathy does not lie with him.
>
> The *Times* would do well to concern itself with the privacy and safety of a large group of citizens (homosexuals) rather than that of one bigot.

Now one would think that the incident, so reminiscent of a Ku Klux Klan rally (except that it occurred not in a secluded rural hideaway but at the urban home of its intended victim), would mortify any civilized partisan of the cause in whose name it occurred. Yet the writer virtually says that Walinsky had it coming to him (as did his wife and children, one presumes). Even more remarkable, he accuses Walinsky of wanting to "stir up hatred" and of being a "bigot."

Joseph Sobran is a critic-at-large for the *National Review*. The essay reprinted here first appeared in his 1983 book *Single Issues*.

But this should not amaze us. Man is vengeful, and never crueler 5
than when he fancies that he has been insulted. Hitler did not think he
was persecuting Jews; he thought the Jews had been persecuting him
and his fellow Aryans. I once saw a televised interview with a young
man who had murdered eight or ten young women, and he spoke of
them, their bad manners and self-centeredness and insensitivity to
others' feelings, with a tone of genuine grievance; what is more, he was
strikingly intelligent and articulate. It may be that he only killed particularly annoying young women. For that matter, Hitler may have been
singularly unfortunate in his Jewish acquaintances. Perhaps they merely
(as we say) overreacted — like the young fellow who thinks threatening
to incinerate a family is justified by occasional "derogatory comments"
about homosexuals.

Militant minorities frequently cultivate a morbidly exaggerated
sense of the wrongs done them. Often there is much truth in their
complaints, which makes it awkward to gainsay them: The degree of
their victimization can never be exactly determined, and one risks
seeming unfeeling if one points out that the wrongs are, after all, finite.
But failure to say this may encourage violence. For if all of society is
engaged in oppression, then any victim of that oppression may excus-
ably strike out at any member of that society. That proposition was
most vividly expressed a few years ago by Bill Walton, the basketball
player, who said that, given the history of racism, he wouldn't blame
any black man who took up a gun and shot him, Bill Walton, at random,
simply because he happened to be white.

Such secular theodicies, which come to terms with the ugly facts
of crime by deducing that society has brought death and destruction
on itself, have resulted in a whole strategy of intimidation in politics.
James Baldwin warned of "the fire next time," and even Martin Luther
King, though carefully confining his explicit advocacy to nonviolence,
used to predict "a long, hot summer" if Negro demands were not met.
Even the women's liberation movement issues such threats from time
to time, and male hecklers have been beaten up at rallies. One young
feminist went so far as to shoot and wound Andy Warhol. She was
thought to be deranged, though perhaps she was merely ahead of her
time.

But feminist and homosexual movements, which consist of relatively affluent and well-educated people, are unlikely to resort to physical assaults on any large scale. As urban rioting has disappeared, even
spokesmen for the Negro causes have been unable to sound plausibly
ominous. Instead the strategy of intimidation has depended, increasingly, on accusations. The putative victims now resort to charging their
opponents with evil motives: "racism," "sexism," "bigotry," and so forth.
In a word, he who resists the claims of these groups, for whatever
reason, is threatened with opprobrium. It has not been sufficiently
realized that this familiar tactic has seriously damaged our public dis-

cussion, making it difficult to consider issues of public policy and morality impersonally and on their merits. The civilized presumption of the goodwill of one's adversary is rapidly eroding. The homosexual's letter, appearing in the pages of our greatest newspaper, is a vivid illustration of this process. It shows how the fanatic may attempt to browbeat the well-meaning but weak-minded citizen into acquiescence.

To define as a "bigot" anyone who disagrees with you is itself a bigoted way of thinking, and a form of rhetorical terrorism as well. But such question-begging tactics are common enough. James Q. Wilson has pointed out the tendentious use of the word "reform." Is permitting women to have their unborn children killed in their wombs a step forward for civilization? Well, it is known as "abortion reform." There are now people advocating the destruction at birth of seriously deformed children. Perhaps this will soon be known as "infanticide reform." We call people "civil-rights advocates" when the measures they espouse actually diminish civil rights, in the sense that they weaken the individual citizen vis-à-vis the state.

The phrase "gay rights" is full of ambiguity and confusion. Does it 10 refer to rights (a) peculiarly due to homosexuals, and not to others, or (b) due to all alike, but peculiarly withheld from homosexuals? Now (a) is obviously repugnant to our political ethos: everybody has the same rights, and a "right" enjoyed by some but not others is no right at all, but a privilege (literally a private law). As for (b), that is closer to what is meant by those who advocate so-called gay rights: Present laws and even informal mores "discriminate," it is held, against homosexuals. But this is only to say that we as a culture disapprove of homosexuality. Laws prohibiting homosexual behavior "discriminate" against homosexuals only in the Pickwickian sense that laws prohibiting theft discriminate against thieves. The law condemns acts, not a class of persons. Sodomy laws, after all, are like most other laws in that respect: They do not even recognize violators as constituting a distinct class of persons. They have to do only with discrete offenses, regardless of the general inclinations of the offender. Discrimination has to do with the intent to single out persons. Such an intent might be present where the law punished as illicit only sexual acts committed with a partner of one's own sex; however, this is not a typical homosexual complaint. Prosecution of homosexual acts nowadays is rare, and homosexuals admit this.

Sometimes homosexuals protest discrimination in nonsexual matters like housing and employment. Though they typically insist that they are asking only for acceptance, not approval, they demand that everyone else act as if homosexuality were perfectly respectable. Probably respectability is their ultimate goal, as the outraged complaint about "derogatory remarks" suggests. In any case, we all recognize many kinds of discrimination as legitimate and even noninvidious. A man may have nothing against students, yet prefer not to rent an apartment to them or hire them in his shop because they tend not to stick around long. These are matters of discretion; and if he makes a misjudgment in the case of a given student, well, that is his business; just as it is his business if he marries the wrong woman, or goes to the wrong church, or votes for the wrong candidate. Why homosexuals should be specially protected among all the possible subjects of discrimination is not clear.

That partly explains why militant homosexuals like to compare their woes with those of historically persecuted groups like Jews and blacks. The trouble is that these minorities were made to suffer for circumstances beyond their control, and independent of the individual choices and behavior of their members. They were persecuted, in fact, for membership itself. It is disingenuous for homosexuals to insinuate that they have suffered group persecution, when it is hard to see how they can have been regarded as a group at all until their recent efforts to band together for political reasons. Even granting that they have been persecuted, a group of persecuted people is not the same thing as a persecuted group.

But whether they are in fact "persecuted," even as individuals, depends on whether they are singled out for pursuit and dealt heavier penalties than those who commit offenses of comparable gravity. There was a time when pickpockets were hanged in England. To say that the penalty was too severe is not, however, to say that pickpockets were persecuted, since the severity was not animated by a malice uniquely directed against pickpockets. Perhaps gentlemen of that trade were given, in private, to condoling with one another on the law's rigors, and to agreeing that their sufferings were rivaled only by those of the early Christians; but their contemporaries would have thought them bathetic had they said so openly, and they knew it, which distinguishes them creditably from today's organized homosexuals.

It is true that those whom society defines as deviants are prone to band together for companionship and consolation. Thus we frequently hear about the sentiments of the "homosexual community" of this or that city. But in what sense does such a community exist? Communities usually consist of such constituent parts as are almost by definition impossible where homosexuality prevails: families, tribes, lines of descent, and associations based on and incorporating these, like religious and fraternal bodies, charitable organizations, clubs, and so forth. Their mark is continuity and permanence. Homosexuality, on the other hand, is centrifugal, seeking transitory pleasures and generally resisting long and stable relations. Propagandists for homosexuality are unconvincing on this point, especially when their assertions are set against the personal ads in the *Village Voice.* Homosexual pornography features an inordinate amount of sadomasochism, if the ads are any indication. Furthermore, while heterosexual pornography exists in profusion, it is protested by many heterosexuals as debasing to proper sexuality. It is a striking fact that homosexuals seldom (to my knowledge, never) object to homosexual pornography on similar grounds; from which it would seem that the homosexual subculture makes no value distinctions among kinds of sexual relations but is, in principle, promiscuous.

This point is of some importance because the arguments for the legitimation of homosexuality seem to require the rejection of any sexual norms. This is implicit in the false opposition between heterosexuality and homosexuality characteristic of homosexual polemics. One would think, to listen to them, that the law simply permits all voluntary heterosexual relations while forbidding all homosexual acts. Obviously this is not so. Such sex laws as exist tend to favor a particular norm of intercourse that is heterosexual, yes, and much more besides: monogamous, for instance. Fornication and adultery were punishable offenses for a long time (and still are, in some places). One does not perceive an alternative ideal of sexual relations animating homosexual protest; on the contrary, it is the absence of ideals that is striking. Hence the homosexual movement is essentially one of revolt, not reform. Its social organization is based on a lower common denominator than "straight" society; its tendency is not toward integration and community, but, on the contrary, toward decreased responsibility.

This false duality also enables homosexuals to skip over a difficulty raised by their claims. If homosexuality is not to be regarded as deviant behavior, what is? Anything at all? What about intercourse with animals? Shall we forbid the landlord to refuse to rent to the man whose partner in sex is his pet? If not, are we granting a special status to heterosexuals and homosexuals who prefer human partners, and thereby "discriminating" against others? What about sex with children? With the dead? Are these too "valid life-styles"? The homosexual is annoyed when such questions are posed, but there is no reason in principle why he should be. As Dr. Johnson observed, the levelers always want to level *down* to themselves, but can't bear leveling *up* to themselves. Their assault on standards is ambiguous: For all their rhetorical relativism, they really want some positive value ascribed to *their* preference. They want it to be accepted as a complement to "straight" sex in normality and dignity. They want the stigma removed. They want to be told there is nothing wrong with them, and they want to force the larger society to say it. This view has already been more or less accepted by the American Psychiatric Association, which recently voted to declare that homosexuality is not a mental illness. Whatever the truth of this matter, it is odd (as Edith Efron remarks) to find members of an allegedly scientific discipline settling such a question by a show of hands.

The progress of the homosexual cause is interesting. For centuries the general Western view was that homosexuality was a sin; a willful and therefore punishable perversion. Then modern psychology was invoked on behalf of homosexuals to convince the public that their inclination was a maladjustment, more to be pitied than censured — involuntary, and therefore not subject to punishment; a view which was accepted as enlightened for some years. The current view, sponsored by homosexual pressure groups, has reverted in part to the view that it is indeed voluntary (as the old morality held), but (contrary to erstwhile "enlightenment") nonpathological: a mere "preference."

Since there is little prospect of punishment, it is now safe for homosexuals to take this position — the same one St. Paul has lately been derided for taking, though of course he held that it was not an innocent preference. The important point, for our purposes, is that the word "preference" is meant to suggest that homosexuality is a matter of sheer personal predilection, beyond objective value judgment, and, moreover, that it is a matter of choice rather than of compulsion and neurosis. Articulate homosexuals are now waspish toward that kind of tolerance that regards them as helplessly afflicted. One gets the impression that they could be "straight" if they wanted to be, only they don't want to be. But of course this sounds suspiciously like sour grapes. As Ernest van den Haag has observed, it is incredible that anybody would willingly pay the immense social costs of being a homosexual if he could easily avoid it. If not an erotic disorder, it is surely a social maladjustment.

The great uproar in Dade County, Florida, this year centered around whether homosexuals were worthy models for children. Though homosexuals accused their adversaries of demagogy for raising this issue, it is surely a vital one. For the homosexual claims of normality necessarily imply that it is a matter of indifference whether social influences tend to make a child grow up homo- or heterosexual. This is an inherently implausible proposition for the simple reason that eros is too near the center of life *not* to matter. I, for one, would find it easier to believe that homosexuality was preferable than that neither was.

There is no area of life in which we are not willing to affirm norms: 20 ethics, health, beauty, literature, music — we discuss all these things on their merits, confident that it is possible to discriminate intelligently. Of course there are fashions and shifts of taste, but we discuss and reason and argue about even these. Some differences don't matter very much. But it does matter whether Shakespeare is more worthwhile than Mickey Spillane, just as it matters whether we habitually eat a balanced diet or junk food.

Sex matters too, and (as I have observed before) one sign of this is the grisly form it takes in war, where victors often mutilate their adversaries and rape the women, these abuses being the ultimate annihilations of the dignity and integrity of the defeated: Nothing could more horribly violate their dignity; death and agony do not suffice. This is a cross-cultural phenomenon, reflecting the universal perception that sexual order is at the heart of social order.

Even if there were no real reason to prefer heterosexuality, the fact of its prevalence in our culture would be a reason to encourage the young to prefer it, just, as, in a smaller way, the prevalence of right-handedness makes it more convenient to be right-handed. And when a whole civilization is based on the presumption that one should have an erotic preference for the opposite sex, the homosexual is denied full enjoyment of a vast range of cultural activities and works of art, lofty and popular. The estrangement is too pervasive to be dismissed.

As Chesterton remarks, the old songs do not celebrate lovers; they celebrate true lovers. The ability to fully enjoy sexual rapture and yet to subordinate it to the discipline of fidelity is a genuine human achievement — and a fruitful one. It gives resonance to individual lives and health to whole societies. This kind of permanence is not typical of homosexuality — or, more accurately, of male sexuality except when, as George Gilder has put it, the abrupt male impulses are subordinated to the deeper, more long-term sexual rhythms of woman. Our literature testifies to the sense of transfiguration men feel in devoting themselves to a single permanent union, and women, though perhaps somewhat less ecstatic, are perhaps more naturally adapted to it, as their aversion to casual and promiscuous sex shows (even in lesbian relationships). There are simply and obviously few greater forms of human happiness, few richer satisfactions, than are found in such abiding erotic complementarity. The appreciation of, and hence capacity for, this kind of union is surely one of the finest things we can hope to bequeath to children. It can hardly coexist with a readiness to indulge in casual intercourse, based on shallow congenialities, with either sex. One must be either disingenuous or egocentric to confuse the propagation of erotic norms with specific persecution of homosexuals.

Of course the plainest reason of all for encouraging heterosexual monogamy is simply to give children the capacity and disposition to enjoy responsibly one of the basic and perennially satisfying human experiences: parenthood. This is not to say that everyone should be a parent; or that everyone will succeed as a parent; or that people who are incapable of successfully begetting and rearing children should not frankly face the facts. It *is* to say that among all human potentialities, this one should be fostered by the community, because most will choose the vocation of parenthood anyway, and because it can do no harm to help see that it is within reach and among the options even of those who may not choose it. We do not refrain from teaching children to read merely because some of them, as adults, may choose never to crack a book. That adults have a certain freedom to turn their backs on the norms of the community does not oblige the community to relinquish those norms; most particularly it does not require the community to stop upholding those norms pedagogically, as guides to the young. The textbook institutionalization of sodomy is a greater perversion than the toleration of sodomy. One might almost say that it is a greater perversion than the practice of sodomy.

When homosexual spokesmen make common cause with feminists 25 of the contemporary kind and with abortion advocates, on grounds that they have "the same enemies," they are right. The enemies of both are those who believe that the family is the harbor of earthly happiness, and that sexual intercourse is best subordinated to community and futurity. Feminists who scorn family satisfactions in favor of jobs forget that most jobs are not "rewarding" — or, as Gilder has more accurately pointed out, that men find them rewarding principally as sources of self-validation *within* the family, in that jobs help make men valuable to the family, giving them roles of importance, i.e., as providers complementary to the childbearing and nurturing roles of mothers. Abortion advocates who categorically and uncritically affirm abortion as a "right" regardless of morality or circumstance are, like homosexual polemicists, guilty of nihilism in the area of sexual morality, since they too fail to suggest a positive norm to govern and delimit the demands they so vociferously advance. Would they admit there are circumstances in which a woman may be unjustified in getting an abortion? It is frustrating even to try to get ideologues of this sort to face such questions.

If I may repeat myself once more, it is a little odd to speak of having "sex" with one's own sex, just as it is a little odd to speak of talking to oneself as "conversation." Perhaps, by analogy with junk food, we can speak of junk sex. Obviously that applies to other vices (to use the old-fashioned term, which I choose not only for its moral bias but also precisely for its lack of pathological implication) besides homosexuality. But to speak of that vice in such terms is to risk offending homosexuals, since homosexuality, in the present state of things, is widely regarded as a kind of quasi-ethnic category, so that to derogate *it* is to insult *them*. This in itself is a tribute to the success with which the propagandists have sown confusion.

Of course homosexuals are people who possess rights and dignity like the rest of us. Often they are otherwise good people, capable of achievement and even heroism — like the rest of us. But we distinguish between the sin and the sinner; and if a man chooses to identify himself with what others regard as his defect, he must bear the consequence of that, and not accuse others of violating his dignity when they disagree with him and disapprove of his "life-style." We should not encourage homosexuals in their weakness; nor harass them for their peculiar temptation.

Still, it is precisely because of their human dignity that we should be concerned about that temptation, whatever form our concern (always charitable, one hopes) may take. It would be a victory of humanity to undo the damage of the gay rights movement by persuading its members, without humiliating them, that they need not pretend that their vice is a virtue in order to belong to the moral community. To put it another way, homosexuals should be encouraged to realize that homosexuality is unworthy of them.

Excerpts from "Gay Politics: Sixteen Propositions"

MICHAEL DENNENY

Political reflection must begin with and remain loyal to our primary experience of ourselves and the world or it degenerates into nonsense, the making of idle theory of which there is no end (and consequently, no seriousness). These thoughts begin with the fact — somewhat startling when I think about it — that I find my identity as a gay man as basic as any other identity I can lay claim to. Being gay is a more elemental aspect of who I am than my profession, my class, or my race. This is new but not unheard of. It corresponds to what Isherwood[1] was getting at in *Christopher and His Kind,* when he frankly confesses his loyalty to his "tribe" in contrast to his desertion of his class and his troubling realization that he had less in common with his countrymen than with his German lover who had been drafted to fight against them in the Second World War. Obviously being gay was not Isherwood's sole claim to identity. Nor is it mine, but it *is* of enormous significance to how I find and feel myself in the world. Those who do not find this to be the case with themselves will probably find these reflections pointless. And since they are based on the experiences of a gay man, it is unclear how much of this discussion would be relevant to lesbians, if indeed any.

Proposition 1

Homosexuality and gay are not the same thing; gay is when you decide to make an issue of it.

Homosexual is properly an adjective; it describes something you do. *Gay* is a noun; it names something you are. Gore Vidal, who prefers the adjectively intensified word *homosexualist,* insists on this distinction tirelessly; one assumes he is right in his own case. For him, being homosexual is not a central part of his identity; it merely describes some of his behavior, in which case the adjective homosexualist is probably more precise, if inelegant.

Whether or not being gay is a central part of one's identity — one's felt sense of self in everyday life, who I am — *is not a theoretical*

Michael Denneny is a senior editor at St. Martin's Press, founder of the *Christopher Street Magazine,* and an editor of the *Christopher Street Reader* (1983), from which this essay is reprinted.

[1] Christopher Isherwood (1904–1986), British-born author of the gay classic *Berlin Stories* (1935). — ED.

question. It is a fact and can be ascertained by fairly elemental self-reflection. There are Jews for whom that fact is an accident of birth and nothing more; blacks for whom the most monstrous aspect of racism is its bewildering irrelevance to who they are. But there are also gays, Jews, and blacks who know themselves as this particular gay man, this particular Jew, this particular black. Such people experience their humanness *through* being gay, Jewish, or black; they do not experience their humanity apart from its concrete manifestation in the world. The following analogy can illustrate, not prove, this position: One can be an athlete *through* being a pole-vaulter, football player, or swimmer; one cannot be simply an athlete without taking part in some sport.

One can argue about whether one *should* gain a significant part of one's identity in this way; whether one actually *does,* however, is a *fact.* Facts, of course, can change. Eight years ago I did not experience myself *primarily* as a gay man; today, if I spend more than four days in a totally straight environment, I feel like climbing the walls. I experience myself as a fish out of water, as a "homosexual alien," in the words of the Immigration Service.

Proposition 2

Gays insofar as they are gay are ipso facto *different* from straights.

Merle Miller entitled his courageous pamphlet *On Being Different,* 5 which was both accurate and apt. The liberal line that gays are no different from anyone else is less to the point than Richard Goldstein's observation that gays are different from other people in every way *except* in bed. Liberals assert that we are *essentially* the same as them and therefore our oppression is unjust. This passes for tolerance. However, tolerance can only be tolerance of real diversity and difference. The liberal position is not really tolerant — although it is subtle — because it denies that we are different, which at bottom is another way of denying that we exist *as gays.* This position is absurd — if we are not different, why all this fuss in the first place?

By relegating homosexuality to the realm of privacy — that which is not spoken about or seen and is therefore unimportant politically (consequently "no different") — liberal "tolerance" becomes a perfect example of what Herbert Marcuse called "repressive tolerance" (a concept that seemed to me idiotic as applied in the sixties). The way liberals have of not noticing that one is gay or, if forced to notice, of not wanting to hear about it or, if forced to hear about it, of asserting that "that's your private life and no concern of mine or of anyone else" is an extremely insidious tactic that in practice boils down to "let's all act straight and what you do in the bedroom is your own business."

This is the source of the liberals' famous lament: Why *must* you flaunt your homosexuality? (Flaunt is the antigay buzzword as *shrill* and *strident* were the antifeminist buzzwords.) This position is identical to that of Anita Bryant, who repeatedly made it clear that she was no dummy, she knew that many of those "bachelors" and "spinsters" in the schools were gay, and she was not advocating a McCarthy-like witch hunt to have them rooted out and fired; all she wanted was that gay teachers not hold hands and kiss in public, that gay adults not "recruit" impressionable youngsters for the "gay life-style." In other words, get back in the closet and we won't bother you. Anita Bryant was not your traditional bigot; she was something new, a direct response to the emergence of gay liberation. As such, we can expect more of her ilk.

When you point out that this is also the essence of the liberals' position, for all its tolerance, they sometimes get infuriated. They have an odd animus against the very idea of gay oppression. People who are otherwise perfectly sensible get uncomfortable and sometimes hostile when you suggest that even *they* might have internalized some of the pervasive antigay hostility and prejudice of the larger society. It is hard to know how to respond when they act like you have insulted their honor, but I suspect the best answer is Curtis Thornton's simple observation about white people: "I understand why they don't want us to think they are prejudiced. But if most of them were not prejudiced, it wouldn't be a prejudiced country" (in John Gwaltney's marvelous book *Drylongso*).

Liberals in general tend to get upset if one tries to make an issue of being gay or if one says that being gay is an important and central part of one's life and identity. One feels like asking them whether their own heterosexuality is not an important part of *their* lives. But, of course, they do not talk about heterosexuality, they talk about sexuality. Which is the whole point.

Proposition 9

Gay politics (using politics in its narrow meaning) is a politics of pure principle.

For us there is no "social question." We are not asking for a bigger   10
slice of the pie but for justice. We do not require social programs, jobs, day-care centers, educational and professional quotas, or any of the other legitimate demands of previously exploited minority groups. Our demands will not cost the body politic one cent. We demand only the freedom to be who we are. The fact that this demand, which takes away nothing from anyone else, is met with such obstinate resistance is a noteworthy indication of how deep-seated is the hostility against us.

On the other hand, we could expect that gay politics has its best chance in countries that are constitutional republics, where the belief that justice is the ultimate source of authority and legitimacy for the government gives us a powerful lever against the prejudice of society.

It seems to me no accident that gay politics and gay culture have arisen first and most strongly in the United States. This is the only "nation" I know of that was brought into being by dissidents; whatever revisionist history may teach us are the facts of the case, the enormous authority the image of the Pilgrims and the Founding Fathers has for this country should not be underestimated. It often seems that non-American observers simply cannot understand our feeling that *as Americans* it is our *right* to be faggots if we choose — or as historian and lesbian novelist Noretta Koertge puts it: "Being American means being able to paint my mailbox purple if I want." Invoking the ultimate principles — if not realities — of this country is one of our most promising tactics, and should be explored and emphasized.

Proposition 12

The only remedy for powerlessness is power.
                                    — Charles Ortleb

Economic exploitation, one of the great nineteenth-century themes of political discourse, has largely been replaced in our own day by the discussion of oppression. Exploitation means basically that someone is stealing from you; oppression is essentially a matter of invisibility, of feeling weightless and insubstantial, without voice or impact in the world. Blacks, the colonized, women, and gays all share this experience of being a ghost in their own country, the disorienting alienation of feeling they are not actually there. This psychological experience is the subjective correlate to the objective fact of powerlessness.

It is odd that the desire for power has for many an unpleasant aura about it, for powerlessness is a true crime against the human spirit and undercuts the possibility of justice among people. In his *Inquiry Concerning the Principles of Morals,* David Hume lays this out quite clearly, albeit without being aware of it, when he speculates that "were there a species intermingled with men which, though rational, were possessed of such inferior strength, both of body and mind, that they were incapable of all resistance and could never, upon the highest provocation, make us feel the effects of their resentment, the necessary consequence, I think, is that we . . . should not, properly speaking, lie under any restraint of justice with regard to them. . . . Our intercourse with them could not be called society, which supposes a degree of equality, but absolute command on the one side, and servile obedience on the other. . . . Our permission is the only tenure by which they hold their possessions, our compassion and kindness the only check by which they [*sic*] curb our lawless will . . . the restraints of justice . . . would never have place in so unequal a confederacy."

Well, we know there are such "creatures intermingled with men" — women first of all, and the colonized races, as well as homosexuals,

Jews, and mental patients. It is truly strange that this philosopher, who seems to think he is idly speculating, was quite clearly laying out the premises of the power structure that at that very moment was subjugating so many groups of people. And with two centuries of hindsight, it should be clear to all of us just how effective their "compassion and kindness" is as a check against their "lawless will." If we have to rely on "the laws of humanity" to convince them "to give gentle usage to these creatures," we will stay precisely where we have been, under their heel being stomped on.

I do not pretend to understand the origin and mechanics of this 15 strange social system in which we live. But it seems to me it should be abundantly clear to even the dimmest wit that without power you will not get justice. How anybody could rely on "compassion and kindness" after looking around at the world we live in is beyond me. "Moderate" gays who think we can achieve tolerance by respectability seem to me willfully ignorant of our own history, as well as the history of other oppressed groups. They are the court Jews of our time, however good their subjective intentions.

Straights who object to our daily increasing visibility are basically objecting to the assertion of power implicit in that phenomenon. They would prefer that we continue to rely on their "compassion and kindness" and correctly sense that our refusal to do so directly insults them. With their record on the matter it is hard to imagine why they are surprised. In fact, our extraordinary explosion into visibility, the spontaneous and visible assertion of our sexual identity that constitutes the clone look is politically valuable. Not only are we more visible to each other, we are more visible to them. Of course, one would naturally expect a backlash at this point; it is virtually unknown in history for any group to give up power over any other without a struggle. . . .

It has been known for well over a century now that something is drastically wrong with our culture; our values seem to be working in reverse. Western civilization looks more and more like the sorcerer's apprentice: It has unleashed powers that threaten to overwhelm it. Nihilism is the name usually applied to this phenomenon. Our values have turned against us and threaten devastation if not extinction. This sounds rhetorical. It is not. It is a simple description of the current state of affairs, as a moment's uncomfortable reflection on the Holocaust, the threat of nuclear annihilation, the consequences of pollution and irreversible ecological intervention, genetic engineering, or a dozen other phenomena reported daily in the papers, makes quite clear. We need a revaluation of all our values, but how can this be accomplished if there is no Archimedian point on which to stand? If the salt has lost its savor, wherewith shall it be salted?

I suggest that the complex, subtle, everyday transformation of values that we gays have been engaged in for the last ten years, the self-renewal that constitutes gay liberation, is a creative response to the viciously negative values of our culture. As such, it would be *a part* of that urgently necessary revaluation of all values and could serve not as a historical catalyst that will save anybody else but as an example of what is necessary and as a welcome ally to those already engaged by this challenge. In the struggle for gay liberation we come home to ourselves and our world and take our place among the ranks of decent and responsible people everywhere who stand together at this decisive moment in humanity's career on the planet.

Why Heterosexuals Need to Support Gay Rights

DONNA MINKOWITZ

This is an article addressed to heterosexuals. Almost all mainstream *and* radical media are implicitly addressed to you, but this article has a more urgent agenda than most hetero apostrophes. Twenty years after lesbians and gay men threw coins, bottles, and an uprooted parking meter at the cops who were attempting to arrest them for being queer, many of you still don't think our rights are anything to fight for. Most of you still aren't by our side when we need you.

There is a myth that the gay community isn't oppressed any more. On the TV news, we are a powerful minority beginning to flex its perversely huge muscles. But that image ignores much of our experience. Young people, taught by their pop culture heroes to hate fags and dykes, are beating gay men and lesbians in the streets with a frightening frequency.

Beyond the violence and the hate-mongering, our enemies have used AIDS and an infestation of Reaganite judges to deal us serious civil-rights setbacks. If you see us putting our bodies on the line in increasingly brave and confrontational street demonstrations, that's because there are almost as many reasons for us to riot as there were twenty years ago. I am referring to much more than AIDS.

Officially sanctioned homophobia is now more common and more vicious than when I came out in the late seventies. The first rumblings of a new exuberance in antigay bigotry came in 1985, when syndicated columnists began to call for the quarantining or tattooing of HIV-positive gay men, and the *New York Post* gleefully used headlines like GAY

This excerpt is taken from the April–May 1991 edition of *UTNE Reader.* The full article appeared in the June 27, 1989 *Village Voice,* where Donna Minkowitz is a contributor.

AIDS DEN. Violence against us rose 41 percent that year in New York, and there is a connection. When "progressive" shows like *Saturday Night Live* use antigay routines, when superstars like Eddie Murphy go on about how much they hate bulldykes and fags, they send a message that we are expendable. So do preachers who hurl concepts of sin with the overt intention to destroy. More than one fundamentalist minister has called for the execution of homosexuals. In a 1986 pastoral letter that declared homosexual desire intrinsically immoral, the Vatican said that antigay violence was "only to be expected" if we press for civil rights.

Even lesbians and gay men who have never been assaulted are 5 affected by the threat of violence. It controls the way we dress, who we walk with, even whether we feel free to hold hands in public. The thought that someone might sock me for looking too dykey used to make me throw on earrings whenever my hair was clipped too short for Jerry Falwell's comfort. I don't wear earrings any more, but I spend a lot of time looking over my shoulder.

The Supreme Court did its share to legitimize gay-bashing by affirming discrimination against us with its 1986 *Hardwick* ruling. Gays and lesbians, the justices said, could be arrested for sex that involved the genitals of one partner and the mouth or anus of the other. Although the ruling only addressed the legal status of sodomy, many courts have interpreted *Hardwick* as denying gays and lesbians the right to sue for equal protection under the law.

If you're like most straight liberals or leftists, the phrase "life-style issues" began springing to your lips several paragraphs ago. Straights have always used this phrase to trivialize our movement, as though all we were fighting for were better couches and end tables from Bloomingdale's. But when a woman is denied the right to see her lover of five years, now incapacitated from a car accident, that is not a life-style issue. When a man is thrown out of his apartment after the death of his lover of many years (because New York's rent-control laws do not consider same-sex couples "family members"), you should be out on the streets with us calling it an outrage.

If you believe in civil rights, don't follow in the footsteps of the NAACP, whose chief lobbyist recently remarked that they had "no position" on gay and lesbian rights; don't imitate the B'nai B'rith Anti-Defamation League, which insisted on keeping the issue of antigay discrimination out of its videos ostensibly documenting prejudice against all groups. If you're a human-rights activist, don't pour shame on your cause like Amnesty International, which still refuses to plead the cases of gays and lesbians imprisoned or tortured for their sexual preference.

There's another reason to help us win our liberation. Homophobia hurts you almost as much as it hurts us. Smears against "mannish women" played a large roll in quelling the U.S. women's movement after the vote was won in 1920. Homophobia has been a weapon to enforce assigned gender roles: that women submit to male prerogatives, and that men exercise them. Feminists have sometimes been the last to understand this: In 1970, the National Organization for Women purged many dedicated activists after Betty Friedan sparked a "lavender menace" scare. Mainstream feminism is still noticeably cool to gay and lesbian liberation. The inevitable result is a straight, white, male elite dividing and conquering us once again.

There's a lot you can do beyond refusing to bash us yourselves. 10 Take to the streets whenever our rights are being threatened (which is frequently). Don't back local political candidates who oppose domestic partnership rights for gay and lesbian couples; that's like supporting a candidate who isn't sure blacks should sit in the front of the bus. If you have children, teach them from an early age that both homosexuality and heterosexuality are paths open to them, and that they will grow to be wonderful adults in either case. When a radio announcer or a columnist or a politician says gays and lesbians should be punished, don't sit idly by. Don't sell us out.

Against Gay Marriage

JEAN BETHKE ELSHTAIN

Every society embraces an image of a body politic. This complex symbolism incorporates visions and reflections on who is inside and who is outside; on what counts as order and disorder; on what is cherished and what is despised. This imagery is fluid but not, I will argue, entirely up for grabs. For without some continuity in our imagery and concern, we confront a deepening nihilism. In a world of ever more transgressive enthusiasms, the individual — the self — is more, not less, in thrall to whatever may be the reigning ethos. Ours is a culture whose reigning ethic is surely individualism and freedom. Great and good things have come from this stress on freedom and from the insistence that there are things that cannot and must not be done for me and to me in the name of some overarching collective. It is, therefore, unsurprising that anything that comes before us in the name of "rights" and "freedom" enjoys a prima facie power, something akin to political grace.

But perhaps we have reached the breaking point. When Madonna

Jean Bethke Elshtain, a professor of political science at Vanderbilt University, is the author of many scholarly essays. This essay is one side of a debate reprinted from the November 22, 1991 issue of *Commonweal.*

526 Opposing Viewpoints

proclaims, in all sincerity, that mock masturbation before tens of thousands is "freedom of expression" on a par, presumably, with the right to petition, assemble, and protest, something seems a bit out of whack — distorted, quirky, not-quite-right. I thought about this sort of thing a lot when I listened to the stories of the "Mothers of the Disappeared" in Argentina and to their invocation of the language of "human rights" as a fundamental immunity — the right not to be tortured and "disappeared." I don't believe there is a slippery slope from queasiness at, if not repudiation of, public sexual acts for profit, orchestrated masturbation, say, and putting free speech as a fundamental right of free citizens in peril. I don't think the body politic has to be nude and sexually voracious — getting, consuming, demanding pleasure. That is a symbolism that courts nihilism and privatism (however publicly it may be trumpeted) because it repudiates intergenerational, familial, and communal contexts and believes history and tradition are useful only to be trashed. Our culture panders to what social critic John O'Neill calls the "libidinal body," the body that titillates and ravishes and is best embodied as young, thin, antimaternal, calculating, and disconnected. Make no mistake about it: Much of the move to imagery of the entitled self and the aspirations to which it gives rise are specifically, deeply, and troublingly antinatal — hostile to the regenerative female body and to the symbolism of social regeneration to which this body is necessarily linked and has, historically, given rise.

Don't get me wrong: Not every female body must be a regenerative body. At stake here is not mandating and coercing the lives of individuals but pondering the fate of a society that, more and more, repudiates generativity[1] as an animating image in favor of aspiration without limit of the contractual and "wanting" self. One symbol and reality of the latter is the search for intrusive intervention in human reproducing coming from those able to command the resources of genetic engineers and medical reproduction experts, also, therefore, those who have more clout over what gets lifted up as our culture's dominant sense of itself. One finds more and more the demand that babies can and must be made whenever the want is there. This demandingness, this transformation of human procreation into a technical operation, promotes a project Oliver O'Donovan calls "scientific self-transcendence." The technologizing of birth is antiregenerative, linked as it is to a refusal to accept any natural limits. What technology "can do," and the law permits, we seem ready to embrace. Our ethics rushes to catch up with the rampant rush of our forged and incited desires.

These brief reflections are needed to frame my equally brief comments on the legality, or not, of homosexual marriage. I have long

---

[1] The power or function of producing offspring. — ED.

favored domestic partnership possibilities — ways to regularize and stabilize commitments and relationships. But marriage is not, and never has been, primarily about two people — it is and always has been about the possibility of generativity. Although in any given instance, a marriage might not have led to the raising of a family, whether through choice or often unhappy recognition of, and final reconciliation to, the infertility of one or another spouse, the symbolism of marriage-family as social regenesis is fused in our centuries-old experience with marriage ritual, regulation, and persistence.

The point of criticism and contention runs: In defending the family 5 as framed within a horizon of intergenerationality, one privileges a restrictive ideal of sexual and intimate relations. There are within our society, as I already noted, those who believe this society can and should stay equally open to all alternative arrangements, treating "lifestyles" as so many identical peas in a pod. To be sure, families in modernity coexist with those who live another way, whether heterosexual and homosexual unions that are by choice or by definition childless; communalists who diminish individual parental authority in favor of the preeminence of the group; and so on.

But the recognition and acceptance of plural possibilities does not mean each alternative is equal to every other with reference to specific social goods. No social order has ever existed that did not endorse certain activities and practices as preferable to others. Ethically responsible challenges to our terms of exclusion and inclusion push toward a loosening but not a wholesale negation in our normative endorsement of intergenerational family life. Those excluded by, or who exclude themselves from, the familial intergenerational ideal, should not be denied social space for their own practices. And it is possible that if what were at stake were, say, seeking out and identifying those creations of self that enhance an aesthetic construction of life and sensibility, the romantic bohemian or rebel would get higher marks than the Smith family of Remont, Nebraska. Nevertheless, we should be cautious about going too far in the direction of a wholly untrammeled pluralism lest we become so vapid that we are no longer capable of distinguishing between the moral weightiness of, say, polishing one's Porsche and sitting up all night with an ill child. The intergenerational family, as symbolism of social regenesis, as tough and compelling reality, as defining moral norm, remains central and critical in nurturing recognitions of human frailty, mortality, and finitude and in inculcating moral limits and constraints. To resolve the untidiness of our public and private relations by either reaffirming unambiguously a set of unitary, authoritative norms or eliminating all such norms as arbitrary is to jeopardize the social goods that democratic and familial authority, paradoxical in relation to one another, promise — to men and women as parents and citizens and to their children.

Here Comes the Groom
ANDREW SULLIVAN

A (Conservative) Case for Gay Marriage

Last month in New York, a court ruled that a gay lover had the right to stay in his deceased partner's rent-control apartment because the lover qualified as a member of the deceased's family. The ruling deftly annoyed almost everybody. Conservatives saw judicial activism in favor of gay rent control: three reasons to be appalled. Chastened liberals (such as the *New York Times* editorial page), while endorsing the recognition of gay relationships, also worried about the abuse of already stretched entitlements that the ruling threatened. What neither side quite contemplated is that they both might be right, and that the way to tackle the issue of unconventional relationships in conventional society is to try something both more radical and more conservative than putting courts in the business of deciding what is and is not a family. That alternative is the legalization of civil gay marriage.

The New York rent-control case did not go anywhere near that far, which is the problem. The rent-control regulations merely stipulated that a "family" member had the right to remain in the apartment. The judge ruled that to all intents and purposes a gay lover is part of his lover's family, inasmuch as a "family" merely means an interwoven social life, emotional commitment, and some level of financial inter-dependence.

It's a principle now well established around the country. Several cities have "domestic partnership" laws, which allow relationships that do not fit into the category of heterosexual marriage to be registered with the city and qualify for benefits that up till now have been reserved for straight married couples. San Francisco, Berkeley, Madison, and Los Angeles all have legislation, as does the politically correct Washington, D.C., suburb, Takoma Park. In these cities, a variety of interpersonal arrangements qualify for health insurance, bereavement leave, insurance, annuity and pension rights, housing rights (such as rent-control apartments), adoption and inheritance rights. Eventually, according to gay lobby groups, the aim is to include federal income tax and veterans' benefits as well. A recent case even involved the right to use a family member's accumulated frequent-flier points. Gays are not the only beneficiaries; heterosexual "live-togethers" also qualify.

There's an argument, of course, that the current legal advantages extended to married people unfairly discriminate against people who've

---

Andrew Sullivan is editor of *The New Republic,* where this essay appeared on August 28, 1989.

shaped their lives in less conventional arrangements. But it doesn't take a genius to see that enshrining in the law a vague principle like "domestic partnership" is an invitation to qualify at little personal cost for a vast array of entitlements otherwise kept crudely under control.

To be sure, potential DPs have to prove financial interdependence, 5 shared living arrangements, and a commitment to mutual caring. But they don't need to have a sexual relationship or even closely mirror old-style marriage. In principle, an elderly woman and her live-in nurse could qualify. A couple of uneuphemistically confirmed bachelors could be DPs. So could two close college students, a pair of seminarians, or a couple of frat buddies. Left as it is, the concept of domestic partnership could open a Pandora's box of litigation and subjective judicial decision-making about who qualifies. You either are or are not married; it's not a complex question. Whether you are in a "domestic partnership" is not so clear.

More important, the concept of domestic partnership chips away at the prestige of traditional relationships and undermines the priority we give them. This priority is not necessarily a product of heterosexism. Consider heterosexual couples. Society has good reason to extend legal advantages to heterosexuals who choose the formal sanction of marriage over simply living together. They make a deeper commitment to one another and to society; in exchange, society extends certain benefits to them. Marriage provides an anchor, if an arbitrary and weak one, in the chaos of sex and relationships to which we are all prone. It provides a mechanism for emotional stability, economic security, and the healthy rearing of the next generation. We rig the law in its favor not because we disparage all forms of relationships other than the nuclear family, but because we recognize that not to promote marriage would be to ask too much of human virtue. In the context of the weakened family's effect upon the poor, it might also invite social disintegration. One of the worst products of the New Right's "family values" campaign is that its extremism and hatred of diversity has disguised this more measured and more convincing case for the importance of the marital bond.

The concept of domestic partnership ignores these concerns, indeed directly attacks them. This is a pity, since one of its most important objectives — providing some civil recognition for gay relationships — is a noble cause and one completely compatible with the defense of the family. But the way to go about it is not to undermine straight marriage; it is to legalize old-style marriage for gays.

The gay movement has ducked this issue primarily out of fear of division. Much of the gay leadership clings to notions of gay life as essentially outsider, antibourgeois, radical. Marriage, for them, is co-optation into straight society. For the Stonewall generation, it is hard to see how this vision of conflict will ever fundamentally change. But for many other gays — my guess, a majority — while they don't deny the importance of rebellion twenty years ago and are grateful for what was done, there's now the sense of a new opportunity. A need to rebel has quietly ceded to a desire to belong. To be gay and to be bourgeois no longer seems such an absurd proposition. Certainly since AIDS, to be gay and to be responsible has become a necessity.

Gay marriage squares several circles at the heart of the domestic partnership debate. Unlike domestic partnership, it allows for recognition of gay relationships, while casting no aspersions on traditional marriage. It merely asks that gays be allowed to join in. Unlike domestic partnership, it doesn't open up avenues for heterosexuals to get benefits without the responsibilities of marriage, or a nightmare of definitional litigation. And unlike domestic partnership, it harnesses to an already established social convention the yearnings for stability and acceptance among a fast-maturing gay community.

Gay marriage also places more responsibilities upon gays: It says 10 for the first time that gay relationships are not better or worse than straight relationships, and that the same is expected of them. And it's clear and dignified. There's a legal benefit to a clear, common symbol of commitment. There's also a personal benefit. One of the ironies of domestic partnership is that it's not only more complicated than marriage, it's more demanding, requiring an elaborate statement of intent to qualify. It amounts to a substantial invasion of privacy. Why, after all, should gays be required to prove commitment before they get married in a way we would never dream of asking of straights?

Legalizing gay marriage would offer homosexuals the same deal society now offers heterosexuals: general social approval and specific legal advantages in exchange for a deeper and harder-to-extract-yourself-from commitment to another human being. Like straight marriage, it would foster social cohesion, emotional security, and economic prudence. Since there's no reason gays should not be allowed to adopt or be foster parents, it could also help nurture children. And its introduction would not be some sort of radical break with social custom. As it has become more acceptable for gay people to acknowledge their loves publicly, more and more have committed themselves to one another for life in full view of their families and their friends. A law institutionalizing gay marriage would merely reinforce a healthy social trend. It would also, in the wake of AIDS, qualify as a genuine public health measure. Those conservatives who deplore promiscuity among some homosexuals should be among the first to support it. Burke could have written a powerful case for it.

The argument that gay marriage would subtly undermine the unique legitimacy of straight marriage is based upon a fallacy. For heterosexuals, straight marriage would remain the most significant — and only legal — social bond. Gay marriage could only delegitimize straight marriage if it were a real alternative to it, and this is clearly not true. To put it bluntly, there's precious little evidence that straights could be persuaded by any law to have sex with — let alone marry — someone of their own sex. The only possible effect of this sort would be to persuade gay men and women who force themselves into heterosexual marriage (often at appalling cost to themselves and their families) to find a focus for their family instincts in a more personally positive environment. But this is clearly a plus, not a minus: Gay marriage could both avoid a lot of tortured families and create the possibility for many happier ones. It is not, in short, a denial of family values. It's an extension of them.

Of course, some would claim that any legal recognition of homosexuality is a de facto attack upon heterosexuality. But even the most hardened conservatives recognize that gays are a permanent minority and aren't likely to go away. Since persecution is not an option in a civilized society, why not coax gays into traditional values rather than rail incoherently against them?

There's a less elaborate argument for gay marriage: It's good for gays. It provides role models for young gay people who, after the exhilaration of coming out, can easily lapse into short-term relationships and insecurity with no tangible goal in sight. My own guess is that most gays would embrace such a goal with as much (if not more) commitment as straights. Even in our society as it is, many lesbian relationships are virtual textbook cases of monogamous commitment. Legal gay marriage could also help bridge the gulf often found between gays and their parents. It could bring the essence of gay life — a gay couple — into the heart of the traditional straight family in a way the family can most understand and the gay offspring can most easily acknowledge. It could do as much to heal the gay-straight rift as any amount of gay rights legislation.

If these arguments sound socially conservative, that's no accident. 15 It's one of the richest ironies of our society's blind spot toward gays that essentially conservative social goals should have the appearance of being so radical. But gay marriage is not a radical step. It avoids the mess of domestic partnership; it is humane; it is conservative in the best sense of the word. It's also practical. Given the fact that we already allow legal gay relationships, what possible social goal is advanced by framing the law to encourage those relationships to be unfaithful, undeveloped, and insecure?

The Case for a
Military Gay Ban

DAVID HACKWORTH

Representative Pat Schroeder of Colorado wanted to give women "equality and opportunity" by making them rucksack-toting grunts. Now she aims at putting homosexuals in the foxholes to "end the final bastion of discrimination."

I cannot think of a better way to destroy fighting spirit and gut U.S. combat effectiveness. My credentials for saying this are over four decades' experience as a soldier or military reporter.

Despite the ban on service by homosexuals, gays have long served in the armed forces, some with distinction. Many perhaps felt no sexual inclination toward their heterosexual fellow soldiers. If they did, they had their buddies' attitudes and the Uniform Code of Military Justice hanging over their heads. Still, I have seen countless examples of inappropriate and morale-busting behavior.

In Italy, for example, in the postwar occupation, a gay soldier could not keep his hands off other soldiers in my squad. He disrupted discipline, mangled trust among squad members, and zeroed out morale. In the same unit, the personnel major was gay. He had affairs with ambitious teenage soldiers in exchange for kicking up their test scores. This corrupted the command's promotion system and led to the commissioning of William Calley–like lieutenants[1] not fit to lead combat soldiers.

During my second tour in the Korean War, a gay commanding officer gave combat awards to his lovers, who had never been on the line. In Vietnam, a young captain in my unit was asked by the commander to go to bed with him. This almost destroyed the esprit of a fine parachute unit.

These are not isolated incidents: During my army career I saw countless officers and NCOs who couldn't stop themselves from hitting on soldiers. The absoluteness of their authority, the lack of privacy, enforced intimacy, and twenty-four-hour duty day made sexual urges difficult to control. The objects of their affection were impressionable lads who, searching for a caring role model, sometimes ended up in a gay relationship they might not have sought.

A majority of American citizens, according to polls, support Schroeder's bill. Many people look at the armed forces as they do the post

---

David Hackworth, a retired colonel of the U.S. Army and the most decorated living American veteran, is a contributing editor at *Newsweek*. This article appeared in the June 28, 1992 issue of the *Washington Post*.

[1] U.S. Army Lieutenant William Calley was convicted in 1971 of murdering twenty-two unarmed Vietnamese civilians in the 1968 My Lai massacre. — ED.

office, the Bank of America, or General Motors — an 8-to-5 institution where discrimination on the basis of sexual orientation is against basic freedom, human rights, and the American way of life. If these polls are true, a lot of people don't understand what war is about.

Sure, banning gays from defending their country is discriminatory. But discriminations are necessary when a larger public purpose is being served. Civilian standards of fairness and equality don't apply down where the body bags are filled.

On the battlefield, what allows men to survive is combat units made up of disciplined team players, who are realistically trained and led by caring skippers who set the example and know their trade. When all of these factors are in synch, a unit has the right stuff. It becomes tight, a family, and clicks like a professional football team. Spirited men who place their lives in their buddies' hands are the most essential element in warfare. The members of such combat teams trust one another totally.

One doesn't need to be a field marshal to understand that sex 10 between service members undermines those critical factors that produce discipline, military orders, spirit, and combat effectiveness. Mix boys and girls, gays and straights in close quarters such as the barracks or the battlefield, and both sexual contact and the consequent breakdown of morale are inevitable.

Many bright people are pushing for the ban to be lifted. I suspect that few if any have been down in the trenches, but I have no doubt their psychological/sociological/political clout will have considerable influence even if they don't have a clue what combat is about.

Unfortunately, most of the top brass won't sound off. They duck and weave and offer hollow and spurious Pentagonese double-talk reasons for continuing the ban — reasons that only fuel the pro-gay argument. But they have told me in the "G" ring of the Pentagon that they're "against it, but sounding off would be the kiss of death, like opposing women in combat — a career killer, you know."

I hope that our lawmakers will visit Quantico and Fort Benning before they vote, and ask Marine gunnery sergeants and Army platoon sergeants what a few gays would do to the fighting spirit of units. These pros told me: Gays are not wanted by straight men or women in their showers, toilets, foxholes, or fighting units. They say that in combat young men face death constantly, and what allows them to make it through the hell of it all is a feeling of toughness, invincibility, and total trust in their buddies.

My experience with warriors in over eight years of roaming the killing fields in seven wars confirms what these old salts are saying.

A serving lieutenant general recently wrote to me, "Ask Pat Schroe- 15 der if she'd like her kids under a gay first sergeant who might use his rank and authority to demand sexual favors from his subordinate eighteen-year-old kids. We just had that occur in my command."

No doubt advocates of gays in combat units will argue that they don't approve of demanding sexual favors and that the first sergeant deserved what he got — a court-martial. The problem is, all the court-martials and regulations in the world can't prevent the kind of morale problems that a change in the law is bound to create. Sure, the first sergeant is serving hard time at Fort Leavenworth, but Pat Schroeder and the two dozen lawmakers who support her bill must also ask themselves what happened to the morale and fighting spirit of his unit.

Have the Guts to Accept Gay Soldiers
LUCIAN TRUSCOTT III

"A Gay Young Cavalryman."

How times change. Those words appear as the title of a song opposite Page 1 of the brief memoir my father wrote of his service in the Army between the world wars. Can you imagine a song today called "A Gay Young Fighter Pilot" or ". . . Infantryman" or ". . . Leatherneck?"

I commanded an infantry rifle company in the first year of the Korean War. Among the 150 or so men I had with me on the tops of those mean mountains in that bitter cold was at least one gay soldier. All of the other 149 of us knew that, if nothing else, he was effeminate. That and his red hair are probably why I remember him so well after all these years.

I saw men ridicule him to his face on occasion, as men will. You know: one hand on a hip, the other waving in the air with a limp wrist as the mimic took prim, mincing steps around him. And the first sergeant approached me one day and said, "Sir, I think Wilson [not his name] is a goddam queer." About all I could say was, "Well, Top, I guess there's no damn law against it as long he's doing his job."

His job was BAR-man; the initials stand for Browning Automatic 5 Rifle. It is a big weapon, weighing more than 20 pounds, but even at his size — about 5 feet 7 inches and 140 pounds — he carried the BAR in his squad. The weapon was so reliable and deadly that the Chinese invariably went for the BAR-man first.

But he did that job, which few men wanted, until a wet spring day in 1951, when I knelt and looked at the small, round hole dead center in his wet, greenish-gray forehead below the line of his red hair. I noticed some of the men in his squad turning away from me so I wouldn't see

---

Lucian Truscott III is a retired infantry officer of the U.S. Army. This article is reprinted from the November 29, 1992 edition of the *Boston Sunday Globe*.

them crying softly as they put him on a litter so we could carry him with us. He was one of us, a soldier.

I am as sure of the fact that he was gay as I am that he wasn't the only one in the company, that he was a damned good soldier, and that there were gays in the infantry battalion I commanded in Vietnam in 1967 and 1968. There are probably homosexuals in any group of a hundred or so men you assemble anyplace, anytime.

A few years ago my son wrote a novel about a gay cadet at West Point and brought down the wrath of many graduates upon his (and my) head for even intimating that West Point ever had a homosexual cadet. Now, looking back from the vantage point of forty or fifty years of knowledge and experience and with society finally having allowed gays out of the closet, I'm certain that four general officers I knew (two of them very well) were gay; one was a highly decorated infantry officer in World War II.

I am surprised that the chairman of the Joint Chiefs of Staff, General Colin Powell, takes a stance against gays in the military. As a black officer, he must be more intimate with discrimination than most of us.

The argument seems to be that integration of gays will disrupt the 10 discipline of an organization. Of course it will! Did the integration of blacks? You're damned right it did! And still does to a degree. But the armed forces have controlled any disruption and will continue to do so until the last of the bigots is gone and we finally have equality.

Why don't we have the guts to admit that there always have been and always will be gays in our society? Admit it and treat them as men. They are, you know.

"*Still, the Trojan War might well have gone the other way if the Greeks had excluded gays from their armed forces.*"

Drawing by Handelsman; © 1992 The New Yorker Magazine, Inc.

THINKING AND WRITING ABOUT GAY AND LESBIAN RIGHTS

Questions for Discussion and Writing

1. How do Truscott and Hackworth use their authority and experience as soldiers to persuade the reader? How would you characterize the evidence on both sides? Are the two authors engaged in a debate, responding to or rebutting each other's arguments? Can you think of other issues that might have been raised by either side? If you think that one argument is stronger than another, tell why.

2. Explain Sullivan's view of gay marriage as "conservative." Would you agree with his definition? (Sullivan has also argued that accepting gays in the military represents a conservative, not radical, approach.) Why does he think that "domestic partnership" is not a substitute for marriage?

3. What is Elshtain's principal objection to gay and lesbian marriage? Why does she think that her long opening discussion of freedom and individualism is necessary to her thesis that gay and lesbian marriages will not produce socially desirable results? Do you think that Elshtain and Sullivan share any goals?

4. What is Sobran's criticism of the idea of "gay rights"? Define the "ambiguity" and "confusion" that he refers to. Why does he think that homosexual men and women have no right to compare their problems to those of Jews and African Americans?

5. Does Denneny argue any of the issues that Sobran discusses? Why does Denneny object to "relegating homosexuality to the realm of privacy"? Do you think he would agree with Sullivan about the conservative case for gay marriage?

6. Summarize the arguments of the majority and minority Supreme Court decisions concerning the sodomy law in Georgia. What issues were stressed on each side? This decision was rendered in 1980. Do you think the same decision would be arrived at today? Explain why.

7. What, according to Minkowitz, are the two principal reasons that heterosexuals should support gay rights? Which of the two reasons emerges as more persuasive? Why?

8. Denneny speaks of his view as a significant contribution to solving much larger problems. Denneny says that the drive for gay-rights means a revaluation of Western civilization. Enlarge on the meaning of this claim. Is it valid?

9. The cartoonist assumes that the reader knows a little about the Trojan War, a long conflict recounted by Homer in *The Iliad,* in which the Greeks defeated the Trojans. Can you guess the meaning of the remark in the cartoon and its relevance to the debate in our own country about gays in the military?

Topics for Research

The Stonewall riots in Greenwich Village, New York City, 1969 (birth of the gay rights movement)

Conservatives and radicals in the gay rights movement: goals and strategies

Religious attitudes toward homosexual rights

A decade of polls regarding attitudes toward homosexual rights

Homosexuality: choice or biology?

CHAPTER SEVENTEEN

Multicultural Studies

In 1908 a playwright coined the phrase "melting pot" to describe the extraordinary amalgam of races and cultures that characterized the United States, a nation of immigrants. For generations the national goal was assimilation by all people to a shared language, culture, and values, and its chief vehicle was the public school. Here students learned the English language, a common history dating from the first European settlements in the sixteenth and seventeenth centuries, and a celebration of American values and American achievements.

Despite its success, the goal of assimilation was never perfectly realized, and in recent years we have witnessed an explosion of interest in and defense of ethnic identity that demands to be reflected in the school curriculum. Multicultural studies, say its supporters, should stress the "pluribus" in the motto of the United States, "E Pluribus Unum" (out of many, one), the parts not of a melting pot but of a mosaic in which separate groups retain their identities.

Today more and more textbooks and curricula include the contributions of those who have been left out of the American story. Few people would deny that such a correction was badly needed. Although most school curricula from the elementary grades through college have for generations exposed students to many cultures, the treatment has sometimes overlooked or trivialized significant aspects of those cultures.

But the debate has revealed that there are really several kinds of multicultural studies under discussion. To name a few, one calls for the inclusion of history, literature, and the arts from the diversity of groups represented in our population, with emphasis on the values of Western civilization. Another advocates a curriculum based on cultural relativism, in which all cultures are presumed to be morally and intellectually equal. Still another calls for multicultural education that will not merely make available a selection of ethnically or racially specific courses but will instill rejection of Western civilization as a source of oppression. (At Stanford University a few years ago the chant of some partisans was, "Hey! Hey! Ho! Ho! Western Culture's Gotta Go!")

The advocates of multicultural studies argue that such education, however defined, will, as a matter of justice, emphasize the contributions of minority groups whose histories have been neglected, especially those of African Americans and Hispanics, as well as the history of women. One of the assumptions underlying this argument is that a lack of self-esteem among minority students has been the cause of school failure and that a study of ethnic history and culture will instill pride and encourage learning.

Opposition to multicultural studies focuses on those programs that would devalue Western culture and individual achievement. They point to the dangers of separateness and heightened ethnic identity which in other parts of the world have led to the appalling tragedies of "ethnic cleansing." They point out that not all histories are admirable — including that of our own nation — and that knowledge of ethnic or racial history, if honestly taught, will not necessarily produce self-esteem or improved performance in school. In addition, some critics fear that the "new multiculturalism" is bent not only on celebrating minority cultures but on "putting down everything American."

Before the opposing sides in this debate can decide whether there is a basis for consensus, they must answer several hard questions. Will greater exposure to a variety of minority cultures contribute to a more liberal education? That is, will it broaden the intellectual and moral perspectives of all students? Or, given the time constraints of a four-year undergraduate education, will it result in fragmentation and superficiality? Perhaps more important, will an emphasis on group differences strengthen or threaten the national identity that has distinguished American life, and grave problems notwithstanding, has contributed to its success as a nation?

Multiculturalism: E Pluribus Plures

DIANE RAVITCH

Questions of race, ethnicity, and religion have been a perennial source of conflict in American education. The schools have often attracted the zealous attention of those who wish to influence the future,

Diane Ravitch, former assistant U.S. secretary of education, is the author of several books, including *The Troubled Crusade: American Education, 1945–1980* (1985) and as well as those who wish to change the way we view the past. In our history, the schools have been not only an institution in which to teach young people skills and knowledge but an arena where interest groups fight to preserve their values, or to revise the judgments of history, or to bring about fundamental social change. In the nineteenth century, Protestants and Catholics battled over which version of the Bible should be used in school, or whether the Bible should be used at all. In recent decades, bitter racial disputes — provoked by policies of racial segregation and discrimination — have generated turmoil in the streets and in the schools. The secularization of the schools during the past century has prompted attacks on the curricula and textbooks and library books by fundamentalist Christians, who object to whatever challenges their faith-based views of history, literature, and science.

Given the diversity of American society, it has been impossible to insulate the schools from pressures that result from differences and tensions among groups. When people differ about basic values, sooner or later those disagreements turn up in battles about how schools are organized or what the schools should teach. Sometimes these battles remove a terrible injustice, like racial segregation. Sometimes, however, interest groups politicize the curriculum and attempt to impose their views on teachers, school officials, and textbook publishers. Across the country, even now, interest groups are pressuring local school boards to remove myths and fables and other imaginative literature from children's readers and to inject the teaching of creationism in biology. When groups cross the line into extremism, advancing their own agenda without regard to reason or to others, they threaten public education itself, making it difficult to teach any issues honestly and making the entire curriculum vulnerable to political campaigns.

For many years, the public schools attempted to neutralize controversies over race, religion, and ethnicity by ignoring them. Educators believed, or hoped, that the schools could remain outside politics; this was, of course, a vain hope since the schools were pursuing policies based on race, religion, and ethnicity. Nonetheless, such divisive questions were usually excluded from the curriculum. The textbooks minimized problems among groups and taught a sanitized version of history. Race, religion, and ethnicity were presented as minor elements in the American saga; slavery was treated as an episode, immigration as a sidebar, and women were largely absent. The textbooks concentrated on presidents, wars, national politics, and issues of state. An occasional "great black" or "great woman" received mention, but the main narrative paid little attention to minority groups and women.

With the ethnic revival of the 1960s, this approach to the teaching

American Reader (1990). This essay was originally published in the Summer 1990 issue of *The American Scholar.*

of history came under fire, because the history of national leaders —
virtually all of whom were white, Anglo-Saxon, and male — ignored the
place in American history of those who were none of the above. The
traditional history of elites had been complemented by an assimilationist view of American society, which presumed that everyone in the
American melting pot would eventually lose or abandon those ethnic
characteristics that distinguished them from mainstream Americans.
The ethnic revival demonstrated that many groups did not want to be
assimilated or melted. Ethnic studies programs popped up on campuses
to teach not only that "black is beautiful" but also that every other
variety of ethnicity is "beautiful" as well; everyone who had "roots"
began to look for them so that they too could recover that ancestral
part of themselves that had not been homogenized.

As ethnicity became an accepted subject for study in the 1960s, 5
textbooks were assailed for their failure to portray blacks accurately;
within a few years, the textbooks in wide use were carefully screened
to eliminate bias against minority groups and women. At the same time,
new scholarship about the history of women, blacks, and various ethnic
minorities found its way into the textbooks. At first, the multicultural
content was awkwardly incorporated as little boxes on the side of the
main narrative. Then some of the new social historians (like Stephan
Thernstrom, Mary Beth Norton, Gary Nash, Winthrop Jordan, and Leon
Litwack) themselves wrote textbooks, and the main narrative itself
began to reflect a broadened historical understanding of race, ethnicity,
and class in the American past. Consequently, today's history textbooks
routinely incorporate the experiences of women, blacks, American Indians, and various immigrant groups.

Although most high school textbooks are deeply unsatisfactory
(they still largely neglect religion, they are too long, too encyclopedic,
too superficial, and lacking in narrative flow), they are far more sensitive
to pluralism than their predecessors. For example, the latest edition of
Todd and Curti's *Triumph of the American Nation,* the most popular
high school history text, has significantly increased its coverage of
blacks in America, including profiles of Phillis Wheatley, the poet; James
Armistead, a revolutionary war spy for Lafayette; Benjamin Banneker, a
self-taught scientist and mathematician; Hiram Revels, the first black to
serve in the Congress; and Ida B. Wells-Barnett, a tireless crusader
against lynching and racism. Even better as a textbook treatment is
Jordan and Litwack's *The United States,* which skillfully synthesizes the
historical experiences of blacks, Indians, immigrants, women, and other
groups into the mainstream of American social and political history.
The latest generation of textbooks bluntly acknowledges the racism of
the past, describing the struggle for equality by racial minorities while
identifying individuals who achieved success as political leaders, doctors, lawyers, scholars, entrepreneurs, teachers, and scientists.

As a result of the political and social changes of recent decades, cultural pluralism is now generally recognized as an organizing principle of this society. In contrast to the idea of the melting pot, which promised to erase ethnic and group differences, children now learn that variety is the spice of life. They learn that America has provided a haven for many different groups and has allowed them to maintain their cultural heritage or to assimilate, or — as is often the case — to do both; the choice is theirs, not the state's. They learn that cultural pluralism is one of the norms of a free society; that differences among groups are a national resource rather than a problem to be solved. Indeed, the unique feature of the United States is that its common culture has been formed by the interaction of its subsidiary cultures. It is a culture that has been influenced over time by immigrants, American Indians, Africans (slave and free) and by their descendants. American music, art, literature, language, food, clothing, sports, holidays, and customs all show the effects of the commingling of diverse cultures in one nation. Paradoxical though it may seem, the United States has a common culture that is multicultural.

Our schools and our institutions of higher learning have in recent years begun to embrace what Catharine R. Stimpson of Rutgers University has called "cultural democracy," a recognition that we must listen to a "diversity of voices" in order to understand our culture, past and present. This understanding of the pluralistic nature of American culture has taken a long time to forge. It is based on sound scholarship and has led to major revisions in what children are taught and what they read in school. The new history is — indeed, must be — a warts-and-all history; it demands an unflinching examination of racism and discrimination in our history. Making these changes is difficult, raises tempers, and ignites controversies, but gives a more interesting and accurate account of American history. Accomplishing these changes is valuable, because there is also a useful lesson for the rest of the world in America's relatively successful experience as a pluralistic society. Throughout human history, the clash of different cultures, races, ethnic groups, and religions has often been the cause of bitter hatred, civil conflict, and international war. The ethnic tensions that now are tearing apart Lebanon, Sri Lanka, Kashmir, and various republics of the Soviet Union remind us of the costs of unfettered group rivalry. Thus, it is a matter of more than domestic importance that we closely examine and try to understand that part of our national history in which different groups competed, fought, suffered, but ultimately learned to live together in relative peace and even achieved a sense of common nationhood.

Alas, these painstaking efforts to expand the understanding of American culture into a richer and more varied tapestry have taken a new turn, and not for the better. Almost any idea, carried to its extreme, can be made pernicious, and this is what is happening now to multiculturalism. Today, pluralistic multiculturalism must contend with a new, particularistic multiculturalism. The pluralists seek a richer common culture; the particularists insist that no common culture is possible or desirable. The new particularism is entering the curriculum in a number of school systems across the country. Advocates of particularism propose an ethnocentric curriculum to raise the self-esteem and academic achievement of children from racial and ethnic minority backgrounds. Without any evidence, they claim that children from minority backgrounds will do well in school *only* if they are immersed in a positive, prideful version of their ancestral culture. If children are of, for example, Fredonian ancestry, they must hear that Fredonians were important in mathematics, science, history, and literature. If they learn about great Fredonians and if their studies use Fredonian examples and Fredonian concepts, they will do well in school. If they do not, they will have low self-esteem and will do badly.

At first glance, this appears akin to the celebratory activities asso- 10 ciated with Black History Month or Women's History Month, when schoolchildren learn about the achievements of blacks and women. But the point of those celebrations is to demonstrate that neither race nor gender is an obstacle to high achievement. They teach all children that everyone, regardless of their race, religion, gender, ethnicity, or family origin, can achieve self-fulfillment, honor, and dignity in society if they aim high and work hard.

By contrast, the particularistic version of multiculturalism is unabashedly filiopietistic and deterministic. It teaches children that their identity is determined by their "cultural genes." That something in their blood or their race memory or their cultural DNA defines who they are and what they may achieve. That the culture in which they live is not their own culture, even though they were born here. That American culture is "Eurocentric," and therefore hostile to anyone whose ancestors are not European. Perhaps the most invidious implication of particularism is that racial and ethnic minorities are not and should not try to be part of American culture; it implies that American culture belongs only to those who are white and European; it implies that those who are neither white nor European are alienated from American culture by virtue of their race or ethnicity; it implies that the only culture they do belong to or can ever belong to is the culture of their ancestors, even if their families have lived in this country for generations.

The war on so-called Eurocentrism is intended to foster self-esteem among those who are not of European descent. But how, in fact, is self-esteem developed? How is the sense of one's own possibilities, one's potential choices, developed? Certainly, the school curriculum plays a relatively small role as compared to the influence of family, community, mass media, and society. But to the extent that curriculum influences what children think of themselves, it should encourage children of all racial and ethnic groups to believe that they are part of this society and that they should develop their talents and minds to the fullest. It is enormously inspiring, for example, to learn about men and women from diverse backgrounds who overcame poverty, discrimination, physical handicaps, and other obstacles to achieve success in a variety of fields. Behind every such biography of accomplishment is a story of heroism, perseverance, and self-discipline. Learning these stories will encourage a healthy spirit of pluralism, of mutual respect, and of self-respect among children of different backgrounds. The children of American society today will live their lives in a racially and culturally diverse nation, and their education should prepare them to do so.

The pluralist approach to multiculturalism promotes a broader interpretation of the common American culture and seeks due recognition for the ways that the nation's many racial, ethnic, and cultural groups have transformed the national culture. The pluralists say, in effect, "American culture belongs to us, all of us; the U.S. is us, and we remake it in every generation." But particularists have no interest in extending or revising American culture; indeed, they deny that a common culture exists. Particularists reject any accommodation among groups, any interactions that blur the distinct lines between them. The brand of history that they espouse is one in which everyone is either a descendant of victims or oppressors. By doing so, ancient hatreds are fanned and recreated in each new generation. Particularism has its intellectual roots in the ideology of ethnic separatism and in the black nationalist movement. In the particularist analysis, the nation has five cultures: African American, Asian American, European American, Latino/Hispanic, and Native American. The huge cultural, historical, religious, and linguistic differences within these categories are ignored, as is the considerable intermarriage among these groups, as are the linkages (like gender, class, sexual orientation, and religion) that cut across these five groups. No serious scholar would claim that all Europeans and white Americans are part of the same culture, or that all Asians are part of the same culture, or that all people of Latin-American descent are of the same culture, or that all people of African descent are of the same culture. Any categorization this broad is essentially meaningless and useless.

Several districts — including Detroit, Atlanta, and Washington, D.C. — are developing an Afrocentric curriculum. *Afrocentricity* has been described in a book of the same name by Molefi Kete Asante of Temple University. The Afrocentric curriculum puts Africa at the center of the student's universe. African Americans must "move away from an [*sic*] Eurocentric framework" because "it is difficult to create freely when you use someone else's motifs, styles, images, and perspectives." Because they are not Africans, "white teachers cannot inspire in our children the visions necessary for them to overcome limitations." Asante recommends that African Americans choose an African name (as he did), reject European dress, embrace African religion (not Islam or Christianity), and love "their own" culture. He scorns the idea of universality as a form of Eurocentric arrogance. The Eurocentrist, he says, thinks of Beethoven or Bach as classical, but the Afrocentrist thinks of Ellington or Coltrane as classical; the Eurocentrist lauds Shakespeare or Twain, while the Afrocentrist prefers Baraka, Shange, or Abiola. Asante is critical of black artists like Arthur Mitchell and Alvin Ailey who ignore Afrocentricity. Likewise, he speaks contemptuously of a group of black university students who spurned the Afrocentrism of the local Black Student Union and formed an organization called Inter-race: "Such madness is the direct consequence of self-hatred, obligatory attitudes, false assumptions about society, and stupidity."

The conflict between pluralism and particularism turns on the issue 15 of universalism. Professor Asante warns his readers against the lure of universalism: "Do not be captured by a sense of universality given to you by the Eurocentric viewpoint; such a viewpoint is contradictory to your own ultimate reality." He insists that there is no alternative to Eurocentrism, Afrocentrism, and other ethnocentrisms. In contrast, the pluralist says, with the Roman playwright Terence, "I am a man: nothing human is alien to me." A contemporary Terence would say "I am a person" or might be a woman, but the point remains the same: You don't have to be black to love Zora Neale Hurston's fiction or Langston Hughes's poetry or Duke Ellington's music. In a pluralist curriculum, we expect children to learn a broad and humane culture, to learn about the ideas and art and animating spirit of many cultures. We expect that children, whatever their color, will be inspired by the courage of people like Helen Keller, Vaclav Havel, Harriet Tubman, and Feng Lizhe. We expect that their response to literature will be determined by the ideas and images it evokes, not by the skin color of the writer. But particularists insist that children can learn only from the experiences of people from the same race.

Particularism is a bad idea whose time has come. It is also a fashion spreading like wildfire through the education system, actively promoted by organizations and individuals with a political and professional interest in strengthening ethnic power bases in the university, in the education profession, and in society itself. One can scarcely pick up an educational journal without learning about a school district that is converting to an ethnocentric curriculum in an attempt to give "self-esteem" to children from racial minorities. A state-funded project in a Sacramento high school is teaching young black males to think like Africans and to develop the "African Mind Model Technique," in order to free themselves of the racism of American culture. A popular black rap singer, KRS-One, complained in an op-ed article in the *New York Times* that the schools should be teaching blacks about their cultural heritage, instead of trying to make everyone Americans. "It's like trying to teach a dog to be a cat," he wrote. KRS-One railed about having to learn about Thomas Jefferson and the Civil War, which had nothing to do (he said) with black history.

Pluralism can easily be transformed into particularism, as may be seen in the potential uses in the classroom of the Mayan contribution to mathematics. The Mayan example was popularized in a movie called *Stand and Deliver,* about a charismatic Bolivian-born mathematics teacher in Los Angeles who inspired his students (who are Hispanic) to learn calculus. He told them that their ancestors invented the concept of zero; but that wasn't all he did. He used imagination to put across mathematical concepts. He required them to do homework and to go to school on Saturdays and during the Christmas holidays, so that they might pass the Advanced Placement mathematics examination for college entry. The teacher's reference to the Mayans' mathematical genius was a valid instructional device: It was an attention-getter and would have interested even students who were not Hispanic. But the Mayan example would have had little effect without the teacher's insistence that the class study hard for a difficult examination.

Ethnic educators have seized upon the Mayan contribution to mathematics as the key to simultaneously boosting the ethnic pride of Hispanic children and attacking Eurocentrism. One proposal claims that Mexican-American children will be attracted to science and mathematics if they study Mayan mathematics, the Mayan calendar, and Mayan astronomy. Children in primary grades are to be taught that the Mayans were first to discover the zero and that Europeans learned it long afterwards from the Arabs, who had learned it in India. This will help them see that Europeans were latecomers in the discovery of great ideas. Botany is to be learned by study of the agricultural techniques of the Aztecs, a subject of somewhat limited relevance to children in urban areas. Furthermore, "ethnobotanical" classifications of plants are to be substituted for the Eurocentric Linnaean system. At first glance, it may seem curious that Hispanic children are deemed to have no cultural affinity with Spain; but to acknowledge the cultural tie would confuse the ideological assault on Eurocentrism.

This proposal suggests some questions: Is there any evidence that the teaching of "culturally relevant" science and mathematics will draw Mexican-American children to the study of these subjects? Will Mexican-American children lose interest or self-esteem if they discover that their ancestors were Aztecs or Spaniards, rather than Mayans? Are children who learn in this way prepared to study the science and mathematics that are taught in American colleges and universities and that are needed for advanced study in these fields? Are they even prepared to study the science and mathematics taught in *Mexican* universities? If the class is half Mexican-American and half something else, will only the Mexican-American children study in a Mayan and Aztec mode or will all the children? But shouldn't all children study what is culturally relevant for them? How will we train teachers who have command of so many different systems of mathematics and science?

The efficacy of particularist proposals seems to be less important 20
to their sponsors than their value as ideological weapons with which
to criticize existing disciplines for their alleged Eurocentric bias. In a
recent article titled "The Ethnocentric Basis of Social Science Knowledge Production" in the *Review of Research in Education,* John Stanfield
of Yale University argues that neither social science nor science are
objective studies, that both instead are "Euro-American" knowledge
systems which reproduce "hegemonic racial domination." The claim
that science and reason are somehow superior to magic and witchcraft,
he writes, is the product of Euro-American ethnocentrism. According
to Stanfield, current fears about the misuse of science (for instance,
"the nuclear arms race, global pollution") and "the power-plays of Third
World nations (the Arab oil boycott and the American-Iranian hostage
crisis) have made Western people more aware of nonscientific cognitive
styles. These last events are beginning to demonstrate politically that
which has begun to be understood in intellectual circles: namely, that
modes of social knowledge such as theology, science, and magic are
different, not inferior or superior. They represent different ways of
perceiving, defining, and organizing knowledge of life experiences." One
wonders: If Professor Stanfield broke his leg, would he go to a theologian, a doctor, or a magician?

Every field of study, it seems, has been tainted by Eurocentrism,
which was defined by a professor at Manchester University, George
Ghevarughese Joseph, in *Race and Class* in 1987, as "intellectual racism." Professor Joseph argues that the history of science and technology — and in particular, of mathematics — in non-European societies was distorted by racist Europeans who wanted to establish the
dominance of European forms of knowledge. The racists, he writes,
traditionally traced mathematics to the Greeks, then claimed that it
reached its full development in Europe. These are simply Eurocentric
myths to sustain an "imperialist/racist ideology," says Professor Joseph,
since mathematics was found in Egypt, Babylonia, Mesopotamia, and
India long before the Greeks were supposed to have developed it.
Professor Joseph points out too that Arab scientists should be credited
with major discoveries traditionally attributed to William Harvey, Isaac
Newton, Charles Darwin, and Sir Francis Bacon. But he is not concerned
only to argue historical issues; his purpose is to bring all of these
different mathematical traditions into the school classroom so that
children might study, for example, "traditional African designs, Indian
rangoli patterns, and Islamic art" and "the language and counting systems found across the world."

This interesting proposal to teach ethnomathematics comes at a
time when American mathematics educators are trying to overhaul
present practices, because of the poor performance of American children on national and international assessments. Mathematics educators
are attempting to change the teaching of their subject so that children

can see its uses in everyday life. There would seem to be an incipient conflict between those who want to introduce real-life applications of mathematics and those who want to teach the mathematical systems used by ancient cultures. I suspect that most mathematics teachers would enjoy doing a bit of both, if there were time or student interest. But any widespread movement to replace modern mathematics with ancient ethnic mathematics runs the risk of disaster in a field that is struggling to update existing curricula. If, as seems likely, ancient mathematics is taught mainly to minority children, the gap between them and middle-class white children is apt to grow. It is worth noting that children in Korea, who score highest in mathematics on international assessments, do not study ancient Korean mathematics.

Particularism is akin to cultural Lysenkoism,[1] for it takes as its premise the spurious notion that cultural traits are inherited. It implies a dubious, dangerous form of cultural predestination. Children are taught that if their ancestors could do it, so could they. But what happens if a child is from a cultural group that made no significant contribution to science or mathematics? Does this mean that children from that background must find a culturally appropriate field in which to strive? How does a teacher find the right cultural buttons for children of mixed heritage? And how in the world will teachers use this technique when the children in their classes are drawn from many different cultures, as is usually the case? By the time that every culture gets its due, there may be no time left to teach the subject itself. This explosion of filiopietism (which, we should remember, comes from adults, not from students) is reminiscent of the period some years ago when the Russians claimed that they had invented everything first; as we now know, this nationalistic braggadocio did little for their self-esteem and nothing for their economic development. We might reflect, too, on how little social prestige has been accorded in this country to immigrants from Greece and Italy, even though the achievements of their ancestors were at the heart of the classical curriculum.

Filiopietism and ethnic boosterism lead to all sorts of odd practices. In New York State, for example, the curriculum guide for eleventh grade American history lists three "foundations" for the U.S. Constitution, as follows:

A. Foundations
1. Seventeenth- and eighteenth-century Enlightenment thought
2. Haudenosaunee political system
   a. Influence upon colonial leadership and European intellectuals (Locke, Montesquieu, Voltaire, Rousseau)

---

[1] Trofim Denisovich Lysenko (1898–1976) was a Soviet agronomist and geneticist who believed that physical and environmental factors influenced heredity. — ED.

b. Impact on Albany Plan of Union, Articles of Confederation, and U.S. Constitution
3. Colonial experience

Those who are unfamiliar with the Haudenosaunee political system 25 might wonder what it is, particularly since educational authorities in New York State rank it as equal in importance to the European Enlightenment and suggest that it strongly influenced not only colonial leaders but the leading intellectuals of Europe. The Haudenosaunee political system was the Iroquois confederation of five (later six) Indian tribes in upper New York State, which conducted war and civil affairs through a council of chiefs, each with one vote. In 1754, Benjamin Franklin proposed a colonial union at a conference in Albany; his plan, said to be inspired by the Iroquois Confederation, was rejected by the other colonies. Today, Indian activists believe that the Iroquois Confederation was the model for the American Constitution, and the New York State Department of Education has decided that they are right. That no other state sees fit to give the American Indians equal billing with the European Enlightenment may be owing to the fact that the Indians in New York State (numbering less than forty thousand) have been more politically effective than elsewhere or that other states have not yet learned about this method of reducing "Eurocentrism" in their American history classes.

Particularism can easily be carried to extremes. Students of Fredonian descent must hear that their ancestors were seminal in the development of all human civilization and that without the Fredonian contribution, we would all be living in caves or trees, bereft of art, technology, and culture. To explain why Fredonians today are in modest circumstances, given their historic eminence, children are taught that somewhere, long ago, another culture stole the Fredonians' achievements, palmed them off as their own, and then oppressed the Fredonians.

I first encountered this argument almost twenty years ago, when I was a graduate student. I shared a small office with a young professor, and I listened as she patiently explained to a student why she had given him a D on a term paper. In his paper, he argued that the Arabs had stolen mathematics from the Nubians in the desert long ago (I forget in which century this theft allegedly occurred). She tried to explain to him about the necessity of historical evidence. He was unconvinced, since he believed that he had uncovered a great truth that was beyond proof. The part I couldn't understand was how anyone could lose knowledge by sharing it. After all, cultures are constantly influencing one another, exchanging ideas and art and technology, and the exchange usually is enriching, not depleting.

Today, there are a number of books and articles advancing controversial theories about the origins of civilization. An important work,

The African Origin of Civilization: Myth or Reality, by Senegalese scholar Cheikh Anta Diop, argues that ancient Egypt was a black civilization, that all races are descended from the black race, and that the achievements of "Western" civilization originated in Egypt. The views of Diop and other Africanists have been condensed into an everyman's paperback titled *What They Never Told You in History Class* by Indus Khamit Kush. This latter book claims that Moses, Jesus, Buddha, Mohammed, and Vishnu were Africans; that the first Indians, Chinese, Hebrews, Greeks, Romans, Britains, and Americans were Africans; and that the first mathematicians, scientists, astronomers, and physicians were Africans. A debate currently raging among some classicists is whether the Greeks "stole" the philosophy, art, and religion of the ancient Egyptians and whether the ancient Egyptians were black Africans. George G. M. James's *Stolen Legacy* insists that the Greeks "stole the Legacy of the African Continent and called it their own." James argues that the civilization of Greece, the vaunted foundation of European culture, owed everything it knew and did to its African predecessors. Thus, the roots of Western civilization lie not in Greece and Rome but in Egypt and, ultimately, in black Africa.

Similar speculation was fueled by the publication in 1987 of Martin Bernal's *Black Athena: The Afroasiatic Roots of Classical Civilization,* Volume 1, *The Fabrication of Ancient Greece, 1785–1985,* although the controversy predates Bernal's book. In a fascinating foray into the politics of knowledge, Bernal attributes the preference of Western European scholars for Greece over Egypt as the fount of knowledge to nearly two centuries of racism and "Europocentrism," but he is uncertain about the color of the ancient Egyptians. However, a review of Bernal's book last year in the *Village Voice* began, "What color were the ancient Egyptians? Blacker than Mubarak, baby." The same article claimed that white racist archeologists chiseled the noses off ancient Egyptian statues so that future generations would not see the typically African facial characteristics. The debate reached the pages of the *Biblical Archeology Review* last year in an article titled "Were the Ancient Egyptians Black or White?" The author, classicist Frank J. Yurco, argues that some Egyptian rulers were black, others were not, and that "the ancient Egyptians did not think in these terms." The issue, wrote Yurco, "is a chimera, cultural baggage from our own society that can only be imposed artificially on ancient Egyptian society."

Most educationists are not even aware of the debate about whether the ancient Egyptians were black or white, but they are very sensitive to charges that the schools' curricula are Eurocentric, and they are eager to rid the schools of the taint of Eurocentrism. It is hardly surprising that America's schools would recognize strong cultural ties with Europe since our nation's political, religious, educational, and economic institutions were created chiefly by people of European descent, our government was shaped by European ideas, and nearly 80 percent of the people who live here are of European descent. The particularists treat all of this history as a racist bias toward Europe, rather than as the matter-of-fact consequences of European immigration. Even so, American education is not centered on Europe. American education, if it is centered on anything, is centered on itself. It is "Americentric." Most American students today have never studied any world history; they know very little about Europe, and even less about the rest of the world. Their minds are rooted solidly in the here and now. When the Berlin Wall was opened in the fall of 1989, journalists discovered that most American teenagers had no idea what it was, nor why its opening was such a big deal. Nonetheless, Eurocentrism provides a better target than Americentrism.

In school districts where most children are black and Hispanic, there has been a growing tendency to embrace particularism rather than pluralism. Many of the children in these districts perform poorly in academic classes and leave school without graduating. They would fare better in school if they had well-educated and well-paid teachers, small classes, good materials, encouragement at home and school, summer academic programs, protection from the drugs and crime that ravage their neighborhoods, and higher expectations of satisfying careers upon graduation. These are expensive and time-consuming remedies that must also engage the larger society beyond the school. The lure of particularism is that it offers a less complicated anodyne, one in which the children's academic deficiencies may be addressed — or set aside — by inflating their racial pride. The danger of this remedy is that it will detract attention from the real needs of schools and the real interests of children, while simultaneously arousing distorted race pride in children of all races, increasing racial antagonism and producing fresh recruits for white and black racist groups.

The particularist critique gained a major forum in New York in 1989, with the release of a report called "A Curriculum of Inclusion," produced by a task force created by the State Commissioner of Education, Thomas Sobol. In 1987, soon after his appointment, Sobol appointed a Task Force on Minorities to review the state's curriculum for instances of bias. He did this not because there had been complaints about bias in the curriculum, but because — as a newly appointed state commissioner whose previous job had been to superintend the public schools of a wealthy suburb, Scarsdale — he wanted to demonstrate his sensitivity to minority concerns. The Sobol task force was composed of representatives of African-American, Hispanic, Asian-American, and American Indian groups.

The task force engaged four consultants, one from each of the aforementioned racial or ethnic minorities, to review nearly one hundred teachers' guides prepared by the state. These guides define the state's curriculum, usually as a list of facts and concepts to be taught, along with model activities. The primary focus of the consultants, not surprisingly, was the history and social studies curriculum. As it happened, the history curriculum had been extensively revised in 1987 to make it multicultural, in both American and world history. In the 1987 revision the time given to Western Europe was reduced to one-quarter of one year, as part of a two-year global studies sequence in which equal time was allotted to seven major world regions, including Africa and Latin America.

As a result of the 1987 revisions in American and world history, New York State had one of the most advanced multicultural history–social studies curricula in the country. Dozens of social studies teachers and consultants had participated, and the final draft was reviewed by such historians as Eric Foner of Columbia University, the late Hazel Hertzberg of Teachers College, Columbia University, and Christopher Lasch of the University of Rochester. The curriculum was overloaded with facts, almost to the point of numbing students with details and trivia, but it was not insensitive to ethnicity in American history or unduly devoted to European history.

But the Sobol task force decided that this curriculum was biased and Eurocentric. The first sentence of the task force report summarizes its major thesis: "African Americans, Asian Americans, Puerto Ricans/Latinos, and Native Americans have all been the victims of an intellectual and educational oppression that has characterized the culture and institutions of the United States and the European American world for centuries." [35]

The task force report was remarkable in that it vigorously denounced bias without identifying a single instance of bias in the curricular guides under review. Instead, the consultants employed harsh, sometimes inflammatory, rhetoric to treat every difference of opinion or interpretation as an example of racial bias. The African-American consultant, for example, excoriates the curriculum for its "White Anglo-Saxon (WASP) value system and norms," its "deep-seated pathologies of racial hatred," and its "white nationalism"; he decries as bias the fact that children study Egypt as part of the Middle East instead of as part of Africa. Perhaps Egypt should be studied as part of the African unit (geographically, it is located on the African continent); but placing it in one region rather than the other is not what most people think of as racism or bias. The "Latino" consultant criticizes the use of the term "Spanish-American War" instead of "Spanish-Cuban-American War." The Native American consultant complains that tribal languages are classified as "foreign languages."

The report is consistently Europhobic. It repeatedly expresses negative judgments on "European-Americans" and on everything Western and European. All people with a white skin are referred to as "Anglo-Saxons" and "WASPs." Europe, says the report, is uniquely responsible for producing aggressive individuals who "were ready to 'discover, invade, and conquer' foreign land because of greed, racism, and national egoism." All white people are held collectively guilty for the historical crimes of slavery and racism. There is no mention of the "Anglo-Saxons" who opposed slavery and racism. Nor does the report acknowledge that some whites have been victims of discrimination and oppression. The African-American consultant writes of the Constitution, "There is something vulgar and revolting in glorifying a process that heaped undeserved rewards on a segment of the population while oppressing the majority."

The New York task force proposal is not merely about the reconstruction of what is taught. It goes a step further to suggest that the history curriculum may be used to ensure that "children from Native American, Puerto Rican/Latino, Asian-American, and African-American cultures will have higher self-esteem and self-respect, while children from European cultures will have a less arrogant perspective of being part of the group that has 'done it all.'"

In February 1990 Commissioner Sobol asked the New York Board of Regents to endorse a sweeping revision of the history curriculum to make it more multicultural. His recommendations were couched in measured tones, not in the angry rhetoric of his task force. The board supported his request unanimously. It remains to be seen whether New York pursues the particularist path marked out by the commissioner's advisory group or finds its way to the concept of pluralism within a democratic tradition.

The rising tide of particularism encourages the politicization of all curricula in the schools. If education bureaucrats bend to the political and ideological winds, as is their wont, we can anticipate a generation of struggle over the content of the curriculum in mathematics, science, literature, and history. Demands for "culturally relevant" studies, for ethnostudies of all kinds, will open the classroom to unending battles over whose version is taught, who gets credit for what, and which ethno-interpretation is appropriate. Only recently have districts begun to resist the demands of fundamentalist groups to censor textbooks and library books (and some have not yet begun to do so). 40

The spread of particularism throws into question the very idea of American public education. Public schools exist to teach children the general skills and knowledge that they need to succeed in American society, and the specific skills and knowledge that they need in order to function as American citizens. They receive public support because they have a public function. Historically, the public schools were known as "common schools" because they were schools for all, even if the children of all the people did not attend them. Over the years, the courts have found that it was unconstitutional to teach religion in the common schools or to separate children on the basis of their race in the common schools. In their curriculum, their hiring practices, and their general philosophy, the public schools must not discriminate against or give preference to any racial or ethnic group. Yet they are permitted to accommodate cultural diversity by, for example, serving food that is culturally appropriate or providing library collections that emphasize the interests of the local community. However, they should not be expected to teach children to view the world through an ethnocentric perspective that rejects or ignores the common culture. For generations, those groups that wanted to inculcate their religion or their ethnic heritage have instituted private schools — after school, on weekends, or on a full-time basis. There, children learn with lovers of the same group — Greeks, Poles, Germans, Japanese, Chinese, Jews, Lutherans, Catholics, and so on — and are taught by people from the same group. Valuable as this exclusive experience has been for those who choose it, this has not been the role of public education. One of the primary purposes of public education has been to create a national community, a definition of citizenship and culture that is both expansive and *inclusive.*

The curriculum in public schools must be based on whatever knowledge and practices have been determined to be best by professionals — experienced teachers and scholars — who are competent to make these judgments. Professional societies must be prepared to defend the integrity of their disciplines. When called upon, they should establish review committees to examine disputes over curriculum and to render judgment, in order to help school officials fend off improper political pressure. Where genuine controversies exist, they should be taught and debated in the classroom. Was Egypt a black civilization? Why not raise the question, read the arguments of the different sides in the debate, show slides of Egyptian pharaohs and queens, read books about life in ancient Egypt, invite guest scholars from the local university, and visit museums with Egyptian collections? If scholars disagree, students should know it. One great advantage of this approach is that students will see that history is a lively study, that textbooks are fallible, that historians disagree, that the writing of history is influenced by the historian's politics and ideology, that history is written by people who make choices among alternative facts and interpretations, and that history changes as new facts are uncovered and new interpretations win adherents. They will also learn that cultures and civilizations constantly interact, exchange ideas, and influence one another, and that the idea of racial or ethnic purity is a myth. Another advantage is that students might once again study ancient history, which has all but disappeared from the curricula of American schools. (California recently introduced a required sixth grade course in ancient civilizations, but ancient history is otherwise *terra incognita* in American education.)

The multicultural controversy may do wonders for the study of history, which has been neglected for years in American schools. At this time, only half of our high school graduates ever study any world history. Any serious attempt to broaden students knowledge of Africa, Europe, Asia, and Latin America will require at least two, and possibly three years of world history (a requirement thus far only in California). American history, too, will need more time than the one-year high-school survey course. Those of us who have insisted for years on the importance of history in the curriculum may not be ready to assent to its redemptive power, but hope that our new allies will ultimately join a constructive dialogue that strengthens the place of history in the schools.

As cultural controversies arise, educators must adhere to the principle of "E Pluribus Unum." That is, they must maintain a balance between the demands of the one — the nation of which we are common citizens — and the many — the varied histories of the American people. It is not necessary to denigrate either the one or the many. Pluralism is a positive value, but it is also important that we preserve a sense of an American community — a society and a culture to which we all belong. If there is no overall community with an agreed-upon vision of liberty and justice, if all we have is a collection of racial and ethnic cultures, lacking any common bonds, then we have no means to mobilize public opinion on behalf of people who are not members of our particular group. We have, for example, no reason to support public education. If there is no larger community, then each group will want to teach its own children in its own way, and public education ceases to exist.

History should not be confused with filiopietism. History gives no   45 grounds for race pride. No race has a monopoly on virtue. If anything, a study of history should inspire humility, rather than pride. People of every racial group have committed terrible crimes, often against others of the same group. Whether one looks at the history of Europe or Africa or Latin America or Asia, every continent offers examples of inhumanity. Slavery has existed in civilizations around the world for centuries. Examples of genocide can be found around the world, throughout history, from ancient times right through to our own day. Governments and cultures, sometimes by edict, sometimes simply following tradition, have practiced not only slavery but human sacrifice, infanticide, cliterodectomy, and mass murder. If we teach children this, they might recognize how absurd both racial hatred and racial chauvinism are.

What must be preserved in the study of history is the spirit of inquiry, the readiness to open new questions and to pursue new understandings. History, at its best, is a search for truth. The best way to portray this search is through debate and controversy, rather than through imposition of fixed beliefs and immutable facts. Perhaps the most dangerous aspect of school history is its tendency to become Official History, a sanctified version of the Truth taught by the state to captive audiences and embedded in beautiful mass-market textbooks as holy writ. When Official History is written by committees responding to political pressures, rather than by scholars synthesizing the best available research, then the errors of the past are replaced by the politically fashionable errors of the present. It may be difficult to teach children that history is both important and uncertain, and that even the best historians never have all the pieces of the jigsaw puzzle, but it is necessary to do so. If state education departments permit the revision of their history courses and textbooks to become an exercise in power politics, then the entire process of state-level curriculum-making becomes suspect, as does public education itself.

The question of self-esteem is extraordinarily complex, and it goes well beyond the content of the curriculum. Most of what we call self-esteem is formed in the home and in a variety of life experiences, not only in school. Nonetheless, it has been important for blacks — and for other racial groups — to learn about the history of slavery and of the civil-rights movement; it has been important for blacks to know that their ancestors actively resisted enslavement and actively pursued equality; and it has been important for blacks and others to learn about black men and women who fought courageously against racism and who provide models of courage, persistence, and intellect. These are instances where the content of the curriculum reflects sound scholarship, and at the same time probably lessens racial prejudice and provides inspiration for those who are descendants of slaves. But knowing about the travails and triumphs of one's forebears does not necessarily translate into either self-esteem or personal accomplishment. For most children, self-esteem — the self-confidence that grows out of having reached a goal — comes not from hearing about the monuments of their ancestors but as a consequence of what they are able to do and accomplish through their own efforts.

As I reflected on these issues, I recalled reading an interview a few years ago with a talented black runner. She said that her model is Mikhail Baryshnikov. She admires him because he is a magnificent athlete. He is not black; he is not female; he is not American-born; he is not even a runner. But he inspires her because of the way he trained and used his body. When I read this, I thought how narrow-minded it is to believe that people can be inspired *only* by those who are exactly like them in race and ethnicity.

Response to Diane Ravitch

MOLEFI KETE ASANTE

We are all implicated in the positions we hold about society, culture, and education. Although the implications may take quite different forms in some fields and with some scholars, such as the consequences and

Molefi Kete Asante is a professor and the chair of the African-American studies department at Temple University and the author of more than thirty books, including *The Afrocentric Idea* (1987). This article, a response to Diane Ravitch, first appeared in *The American Scholar* in Spring 1991.

our methods and inquiry on our systems of values, we are nevertheless captives of the positions we take, that is, if we take those positions honestly.

In a recent article in *The American Scholar* (Summer 1990), Diane Ravitch reveals the tensions between scholarship and ideological perspectives in an exceedingly clear manner. The position taken in her article "Multiculturalism: E. Pluribus Plures" accurately demonstrates the thesis that those of us who write are implicated in what we choose to write. This is not a profound announcement since most fields of inquiry recognize that a researcher's presence must be accounted for in research or a historian's relationship to data must be examined in seeking to establish the validity of conclusions. This is not to say that the judgment will be invalid because of the intimacy of the scholar with the information but rather that in accounting for the scholar's or researcher's presence we are likely to know better how to assess the information presented. Just as a researcher may be considered an intrusive presence in an experiment, the biases of a scholar may be just as intrusive in interpreting data or making analysis. The fact that a writer seeks to establish a persona of a noninterested observer means that such a writer wants the reader to assume that an unbiased position is being taken on a subject. However, we know that as soon as a writer states a proposition, the writer is implicated and such implication holds minor or extreme consequences.

The remarkable advantage of stating aims and objectives prior to delivering an argument is that the reader knows precisely to what the author is driving. Unfortunately, too many writers on education either do not know the point they are making or lose sight of their point in the making. Such regrettably is the case with Diane Ravitch's article on multicultural education.

Among writers who have written on educational matters in the last few years, Professor Ravitch of Columbia University's Teacher's College is considered highly quotable and therefore, in the context of American educational policy, influential. This is precisely why her views on multiculturalism must not remain unchallenged. Many of the positions taken by Professor Ravitch are similar to the positions taken against the Freedmen's Bureau's establishment of black schools in the South during the 1860s. Then, the white conservative education policymakers felt that it was necessary to control the content of education so that the recently freed Africans would not become self-assured. An analysis of Ravitch's arguments will reveal what Martin Bernal calls in *Black Athena* "the neo-Aryan" model of history. Her version of multiculturalism is not multiculturalism at all, but rather a new form of Eurocentric hegemonism.

People tend to do the best they can with the information at their 5 disposal. The problem in most cases where intellectual distortions arise is ignorance rather than malice. Unlike in the political arena where oratory goes a long way, in education, sooner or later the truth must come out. The proof of the theory is in the practice. What we have seen in the past twenty-five years is the gradual dismantling of the educational kingdom built to accompany the era of white supremacy. What is being contested is the speed of its dismantling. In many ways, the South African regime is a good parallel to what is going on in American education. No longer can the structure of knowledge which supported white hegemony be defended; whites must take their place, not above or below, but alongside the rest of humanity. This is a significantly different reality than we have experienced in American education and there are several reasons for this turn of events.

The first reason is the accelerating explosion in the world of knowledge about cultures, histories, and events seldom mentioned in American education. Names of individuals and their achievements, views of historiography, and alternatives to European perspectives have proliferated due to international interaction, trade, and computer technology. People from other cultures, particularly non-Western people, have added new elements into the educational equation. A second reason is the rather recent intellectual liberation of large numbers of African-descended scholars. While there have always been African scholars in every era, the European hegemony, since the 1480s, in knowledge about the world, including Africa, was fairly complete. The domination of information, the naming of things, the propagation of concepts, and the dissemination of interpretations were, and still are in most cases in the West, a Eurocentric hegemony. During the twentieth century, African scholars led by W. E. B. Du Bois began to break from the intellectual shackles of Europe and make independent inquiries into history, science, origins, and Europe itself. For the first time in years, a cadre of scholars, trained in the West, but largely liberated from the hegemonic European thinking began to expose numerous distortions, often elevated to "truth" in the works of Eurocentric authors. A third reason for the current assault on the misinformation spread by white hegemonic thinkers is the conceptual inadequacy of simply valorizing Europe. Few whites have ever examined their culture critically. Those who have done so have often been severely criticized by their peers: the cases of Sidney Willhelm, Joe Feagin, Michael Bradley, and Basil Davidson are well known.

As part of the Eurocentric tradition, there seems to be silence on questions of hegemony, that is, the inability to admit the mutual conspiracy between race doctrine and educational doctrine in America. Professor Ravitch and others would maintain the facade of reasonableness even in the face of arguments demonstrating the irrationality of both white supremacist ideas on race and white hegemonic ideas in education. They are corollary and both are untenable on genetic and intellectual grounds.

Eurocentric Hegemonism

Let us examine the argument of the defenders of the Eurocentric hegemony in education more closely. The status quo always finds its best defense in territoriality. Thus, it is one of the first weapons used by the defenders of the white hegemonic education. Soon after my book *The Afrocentric Idea* was published, I was interviewed on "The Today Show" along with Herb London, the New York University professor/politician who is one of the founders of the National Association of Scholars. When I suggested the possibility of schools weaving information about other cultures into the fabric of the teaching-learning process, Professor London interrupted that "there is not enough *time* in the school year for what Asante wants." Of course there is, if there is enough for the Eurocentric information, there is enough time for cultural information from other groups. Professor Ravitch uses the same argument. Her strategy is to cast serious examinations of the curriculum as pressure groups, much like creationists in biology. Of course the issue is neither irrational nor sensational; it is preeminently a question of racial dominance, the maintenance of which, in any form, I oppose. On the contrary, the status quo defenders, like the South African Boers, believe that it is possible to defend what is fundamentally anti-intellectual and immoral: the dominance and hegemony of the Eurocentric view of reality on a multicultural society. There is space for Eurocentrism in a multicultural enterprise so long as it does not parade as universal. No one wants to banish the Eurocentric view. It is a valid view of reality where it does not force its way. Afrocentricity does not seek to replace Eurocentricity in its arrogant disregard for other cultures.

The Principal Contradictions

A considerable number of white educators and some blacks have paraded in single file and sometimes in concert to take aim at multiculturalism. In her article Professor Ravitch attempts to defend the indefensible. Believing, I suspect, that the best defense of the status quo is to attack, she attacks diversity, and those that support it, with gusto, painting straw fellows along the way. Her claim to support multiculturalism is revealed to be nothing more than an attempt to apologize for white cultural supremacy in the curriculum by using the same logic as white racial supremacists used in trying to defend white racism in previous years. She assumes falsely that there is little to say about the rest of the world, particularly about Africa and African Americans. Indeed, she is willing to assert, as Herbert London has claimed, that the school systems do not have enough time to teach all that Afrocentrists believe ought to be taught. Nevertheless, she assumes that all that is not taught about the European experience is valid and necessary. There are some serious flaws in her line of reasoning. I shall attempt to locate the major flaws and ferret them out.

Lip service is paid to the evolution of American education from the days of racial segregation to the present when "new social historians" routinely incorporate the experiences of other than white males. Nowhere does Professor Ravitch demonstrate an appreciation for the role played by the African-American community in overcoming the harshest elements of racial segregation in the educational system. Consequently, she is unable to understand that more fundamental than eliminating racial segregation has to be the removal of racist thinking, assumptions, symbols, and materials in the curriculum.

However, there is no indication that Professor Ravitch is willing to grant an audience to this reasoning because she plods deeper into the same quagmire by attempting to conceptualize multiculturalism, a simple concept in educational jargon. She posits a *pluralist* multiculturalism — a redundancy — then suggests a *particularistic* multiculturalism — an oxymoron — in order to beat a dead horse. The ideas are nonstarters because they have no reality in fact. I wrote the first book in this country on transracial communication and edited the first handbook on intercultural communication, and I am aware of the categories Professor Ravitch seeks to forge. She claims that the pluralist multiculturalist believes in pluralism and the particularistic multiculturalist believes in particularism. Well, multiculturalism in education is almost self-defining. It is simply the idea that the educational experience should reflect the diverse cultural heritage of our system of knowledge. I have contended that such is not the case and cannot be the case until teachers know more about the African-American, Native American, Latino, and Asian experiences. This position obviously excites Professor Ravitch to the point that she feels obliged to make a case for "mainstream Americans."

The Myth of Mainstream

The idea of "mainstream American" is nothing more than an additional myth meant to maintain Eurocentric hegemony. When professor Ravitch speaks of mainstream, she does not have Spike Lee, Aretha Franklin, or John Coltrane in mind. Bluntly put, "mainstream" is a code word for "white." When a dean of a college says to a faculty member, as one recently said, "You ought to publish in mainstream journals," the dean is not meaning *Journal of Black Studies* or *Black Scholar.* As a participant in the racist system of education, the dean is merely carrying out the traditional function enlarging the white hegemony over scholarship. Thus, when the status quo defenders use terms like "mainstream," they normally mean "white." In fact, one merely has to substitute the words "white-controlled" to get at the real meaning behind the code.

Misunderstanding Multiculturalism

Misunderstanding the African-American struggle for education in the United States, Professor Ravitch thinks that the call to multiculturalism is a matter of anecdotal references to outstanding individuals or descriptions of civil rights. But neither acknowledgment of achievements per se, nor descriptive accounts of the African experience adequately convey the aims of the Afrocentric restructuring, as we shall see. From the establishment of widespread public education to the current emphasis on massaging the curriculum toward an organic and systemic recognition of cultural pluralism, the African-American concept of nationhood has been always central. In terms of Afrocentricity, it is the same. We do not seek segments or modules in the classroom but rather the infusion of African-American studies in every segment and in every module. The difference is between "incorporating the experiences" and "infusing the curriculum with an entirely new life." The real unity of the curriculum comes from infusion, not from including African Americans in what Ravitch would like to remain a white contextual hegemony she calls mainstream. No true mainstream can ever exist until there is knowledge, understanding, and acceptance of the role Africans have played in American history. One reason the issue is debated by white scholars such as Ravitch is because they do not believe there is substantial or significant African information to infuse. Thus, ignorance becomes the reason for the strenuous denials of space for the cultural infusion. If she knew or believed that it was possible to have missed something, she would not argue against it. What is at issue is her own educational background. Does she know classical Africa? Did she take courses in African-American studies from qualified professors? Those who know do not question the importance of Afrocentric or Latino infusion into the educational process.

The Misuse of Self-esteem

Professor Ravitch's main critique of the Afrocentric, Latinocentric, or Americentric (Native American) project is that it seeks to raise "self-esteem and self-respect" among Africans, Latinos, and Native Americans. It is important to understand that this is not only a self-serving argument, but a false argument. In the first place, I know of no Afrocentric curriculum planner — Asa Hilliard, Wade Nobles, Leonard Jeffries, Don McNeely being the principal ones — who insists that the primary aim is to raise self-esteem. The argument is a false lead to nowhere because the curriculum planners I am familiar with insist that the fundamental objective is to provide *accurate* information. A secondary effect of accuracy and truth might be the adjustment of attitudes by both black and white students. In several surveys of college students, research has demonstrated that new information changes attitudes in both African-American and white students. Whites are not so apt to take a superior attitude when they are aware of the achievements of other cultures. They do not lose their self-esteem, they adjust their views. On the other hand, African Americans who are often as ignorant as whites about African achievements adjust their attitudes about themselves once they are exposed to new information. There is no great secret in this type of transformation. Ravitch, writing from the point of view of those whose cultural knowledge is reinforced every hour, not just in the curriculum, but in every media, smugly contends that she cannot see the value of self-esteem. Since truth and accuracy will yield by-products of attitude adjustments, the Afrocentrists have always argued for the accurate representation of information.

Afrocentricity does not seek an ethnocentric curriculum. Unfortu-   15
nately, Diane Ravitch chose to ignore two books that explain my views on this subject, *The Afrocentric Idea* (1987) and *Kemet, Afrocentricity and Knowledge* (1990) and instead quotes from *Afrocentricity* (1980), which was not about education but about personal and social transformation. Had she read the later works she would have understood that Afrocentricity is not an ethnocentric view in two senses. In the first place, it does not valorize the African view while downgrading others. In this sense, it is unlike the Eurocentric view, which is an ethnocentric view because it valorizes itself and parades as universal. It becomes racist when the rules, customs, and/or authority of law or force dictate it as the proper view. This is what often happens in school curricula. In the second place, as to method, Afrocentricity is not a naive racial theory. It is a systematic approach to presenting the African as subject rather than object. Even Ravitch might be taught the Afrocentric Method!

American Culture

There is no common American culture as is claimed by the defenders of the status quo. There is a hegemonic culture to be sure, pushed as if it were a common culture. Perhaps Ravitch is confusing concepts here. There is a common American *society*, which is quite different from a common American culture. Certain cultural characteristics are shared by those within the society but the meaning of *multicultural* is many cultures. To believe in multicultural education is to assume that there are "many cultures." The reason Ravitch finds confusion is because the only way she can reconcile the "many cultures" is to insist on many "little" cultures under the hegemony of the "big" white culture. Thus, what she means by multiculturalism is precisely what I criticized in *The Afrocentric Idea,* the acceptance of other cultures within a European framework.

In the end, the neat separation of pluralist multiculturalists and particularistic multiculturalists breaks down because it is a false, straw separation developed primarily for the sake of argument and not for clarity. The real division on the question of multiculturalism is between those who truly seek to maintain a Eurocentric hegemony over the curriculum and those who truly believe in cultural pluralism without hierarchy. Ravitch defends the former position.

Professor Ravitch's ideological position is implicated in her misreading of several scholars' works. When Professor John Stanfield writes that modes of social knowledge such as theology, science, and magic are different, not inferior or superior, Ravitch asks, "If Professor Stanfield broke his leg, would he go to a theologian, a doctor, or a magician?" clearly she does not understand the simple statement Stanfield is making. He is not writing about *uses* of knowledge, but about *ranking* of knowledge. To confuse the point by providing an answer for a question never raised is the key rhetorical strategy in Ravitch's case. Thus, she implies that because Professor George Gheverughese Joseph argues that mathematics was developed in Egypt, Babylonia, Mesopotamia, and India long before it came to Europe, he seeks to replace modern math with "ancient ethnic mathematics." This is a deliberate misunderstanding of the professor's point: Mathematics in its modern form owes debts to Africans and Asians.

Another attempt to befuddle issues is Ravitch's gratuitous comment that Koreans "do not study ancient mathematics" and yet they have high scores. There are probably several variables for the Koreans making the highest scores "in mathematics on international assessments." Surely one element would have to be the linkage of Korean traditions in mathematics to present mathematical problems. Koreans do not study European theorists prior to their own; indeed they are taught to honor and respect the ancestral mathematicians. This is true for Indians, Chinese, and Japanese. In African traditions, the *European* slave trade broke the linkage, and the work of scholars such as Ahmed Baba and Hypathia remains unknown to the African American and thus does not take its place in the family of world mathematics.

Before Professor Ravitch ends her assault on ethnic cultures, she 20 fires a volley against the Haudenosaunee political system of Native Americans. As a New Yorker, she does not like the fact that the state's curriculum guide lists the Haudenosaunee Confederation as an inspiration for the U.S. Constitution alongside the Enlightenment. She says readers "might wonder what it is." Bluntly put, a proper education would acquaint students with the Haudenosaunee Confederation, and in that case Professor Ravitch's readers would know the Haudenosaunee as a part of the conceptual discussion that went into the development of the American political systems. Only a commitment to white hegemony would lead a writer to assume that whites could not obtain political ideas from others.

Finally, she raises a "controversy" that is no longer a controversy among reputable scholars: Who were the Egyptians? Most scholars accept a simple answer: They were Africans. The question of whether or not they were black was initially raised by Eurocentric scholars in the nineteenth century seeking to explain the testimony of the ancient Greeks, particularly Herodotus and Diodorus Siculus, who said that Egyptians were "Black with woolly hair." White hegemonic studies that sought to maintain the false notion of white racial supremacy during the nineteenth century fabricated the idea of a European or an Asian Egyptian to deny Africa its classical past and to continue the Aryan myth. It is shocking to see Professor Ravitch raise this issue in the 1990s. It is neither a controversial issue nor should it be to those familiar with the evidence.

The debate over the curriculum is really over a vision of the future of the United States. Keepers of the status quo, such as Professor Ravitch, want to maintain a "white framework" for multiculturalism because they have no faith in cultural pluralism without hierarchy. A common culture does not exist, but this nation is on the path toward it. Granting all the difficulties we face in attaining this common culture, we are more likely to reach it when we allow the full participation of all ethnic groups in a quest for a usable curriculum. In the end, we will find that such a curriculum, like inspiration, will not come from this or that individual model but from integrity and accuracy.

Value Free?

ALBERT SHANKER

It's easy to be in favor of multicultural and global education, in principle. The trouble comes when you try to say exactly what you mean by the term so you can put it into action.

If you want to feel convinced about the value of multicultural and global education, all you have to do is to look at the strife that is bred by ethnic, racial, and religious differences. Look at Eastern Europe, at India, at some of our own cities. If only we understood where other people were coming from — if only we had more sensitivity to their cultures — we might not be so wedded to our own points of view. And

---

Albert Shanker is president of the American Federation of Teachers. This article is from the January 6, 1991 issue of the *New York Times,* where Shanker's column appears weekly.

we might have a better chance of avoiding the conflicts that come from ethnocentrism.

However, when we come to apply this principle, there are some serious problems. The New York State Regents' goal for global education, which has also been taken up by multiculturalists, makes some of these problems very clear. According to the goal, "Each student will develop the ability to understand, respect, and accept people of different races; sex; cultural heritage; national origin; religion; and political, economic, and social background, and their values, beliefs, and attitudes."

The goal, expressed in a lot of positive words ("understand, respect, and accept"), sounds very broad-minded, very reasonable. And up to a point, it expresses what we'd hope for from a multicultural and global education. An educated person is not narrow-minded or provincial. So of course we don't want students to be prejudiced — to prejudge the correctness or desirability of some idea or action before they know anything about it. We want them to be open to new ideas and ways of doing things.

But do we really want them to "respect and accept" the "values, 5 beliefs, and attitudes" of other people, no matter what they are? Is every value, belief, and attitude as good as every other?

Do we want them to respect and accept the beliefs that led Chinese leaders to massacre dissenting students in Tiananmen Square? And what about the values and beliefs that allowed the Ayatollah Khomeini to pronounce a death sentence on Salman Rushdie and the current leaders in Iran to confirm this sentence? Is it okay to condemn an author to death because he wrote something that offends against your religious beliefs?

Is exposing unwanted children to the elements and certain death, a custom still widely practiced in some countries in Asia and Africa, to be respected and accepted because it is part of somebody else's culture? Is female circumcision?

Must we respect the custom of forcing young children in the Philippines or Thailand to work in conditions of virtual slavery? And must we look respectfully on Hitler's beliefs and actions?

Should we teach students to accept the sexism of the Japanese or their racist attitudes toward immigrants just because they're part of the Japanese culture? And should we encourage students, in the name of open-mindedness and cultural sensitivity, to accept Afrikaner values and the racist beliefs that undergird apartheid? (If the United States and other nations had been so "open-minded" over the years, would these values and beliefs now be changing in South Africa?)

People who support this kind of approach to multicultural and 10 global education may think they are being objective — even scientific. They may think they're freeing themselves from the limitations of their own culture and its values. But by not taking a position, they are taking one. They are saying that apartheid is okay; that there is nothing wrong with murdering someone who has committed blasphemy.

They're also teaching their students not to make moral judgments. If any custom or law of people in any culture is as defensible as any other, what kind of judgment is possible? So, without intending to, they encourage students in prejudice of a different sort: Instead of mindlessly assuming that other ways of doing things have to be wrong, students will mindlessly assume these ways of doing things have to be right — or at least as good as anyone else's. And by approving practices that would not be tolerated here or in any other democracy, they are saying that some people should be held to lower standards than others — a kind of moral superiority that is hardly consistent with multicultural and global education.

It's important that we teach our children about each other's and other people's customs and values. We are unlikely to survive if we don't. But this does not mean teaching students that they need not hold other people's practices — and our own — up to moral scrutiny. If we do this, we confuse objectivity with neutrality. And how can we possibly justify neutrality about the difference between being able to speak and write as we please and having to restrain our tongues and our pens on pain of death?

Whose Culture Is It Anyway?
HENRY LOUIS GATES, JR.

I recently asked the dean of a prestigious liberal arts college if his school would ever have, as Berkeley has, a 70 percent nonwhite enrollment. "Never," he replied. "That would completely alter our identity as a center of the liberal arts."

The assumption that there is a deep connection between the shape of a college's curriculum and the ethnic composition of its students reflects a disquieting trend in education. Political representation has been confused with the "representation" of various ethnic identities in the curriculum.

The cultural right wing, threatened by demographic changes and the ensuing demands for curricular change, has retreated to intellectual protectionism, arguing for a great and inviolable "Western tradition," which contains the seeds, fruit, and flowers of the very best thought or uttered in history. (Typically, Mortimer Adler has ventured that blacks

Henry Louis Gates, Jr., is currently head of the Afro-American studies department at Harvard University. This article was published in the May 4, 1991 issue of the *New York Times*.

"wrote no good books.") Meanwhile, the cultural left demands changes to accord with population shifts in gender and ethnicity. Both are wrongheaded.

I am just as concerned that so many of my colleagues feel that the rationale for a diverse curriculum depends on the latest Census Bureau report as I am that those opposed see pluralism as forestalling the possibility of a communal "American" identity. To them, the study of our diverse cultures must lead to "tribalism" and "fragmentation."

The cultural diversity movement arose partly because of the frag- 5 mentation of society by ethnicity, class, and gender. To make it the culprit for this fragmentation is to mistake effect for cause. A curriculum that reflects the achievement of the world's great cultures, not merely the West's, is not "politicized"; rather it situates the West as one of a community of civilizations. After all, culture is always a conversation among different voices.

To insist that we "master our own culture" before learning others — as Arthur Schlesinger, Jr., has proposed — only defers the vexed question: What gets to count as "our" culture? What has passed as "common culture" has been an Anglo-American regional culture, masking itself as universal. Significantly different cultures sought refuge underground.

Writing in 1903, W. E. B. Du Bois expressed his dream of a high culture that would transcend the color line: "I sit with Shakespeare and he winces not." But the dream was not open to all. "Is this the life you grudge us," he concluded, "O knightly America?" For him, the humanities were a conduit into a republic of letters enabling escape from racism and ethnic chauvinism. Yet no one played a more crucial role than he in excavating the long-buried heritage of Africans and African Americans.

The fact of one's ethnicity, for any American of color, is never neutral: One's public treatment, and public behavior, are shaped in large part by one's perceived ethnic identity, just as by one's gender. To demand that Americans shuck their cultural heritages and homogenize themselves into a "universal" WASP culture is to dream of an America in cultural whiteface, and that just won't do.

So it's only when we're free to explore the complexities of our hyphenated culture that we can discover what a genuinely common American culture might actually look like.

Is multiculturalism un-American? Herman Melville didn't think so. 10 As he wrote: "We are not a narrow tribe, no. . . . We are not a nation, so much as a world." We're all ethnics; the challenge of transcending ethnic chauvinism is one we all face.

We've entrusted our schools with the fashioning and refashioning of a democratic polity. That's why schooling has always been a matter of political judgment. But in a nation that has theorized itself as plural from its inception, schools have a very special task.

Our society won't survive without the values of tolerance, and cultural tolerance comes to nothing without cultural understanding. The challenge facing America will be the shaping of a truly common public culture, one responsive to the long-silenced cultures of color. If we relinquish the ideal of America as a plural nation, we've abandoned the very experiment America represents. And that is too great a price to pay.

Report on Minority Cultures in the Classroom

NEW YORK STATE SOCIAL STUDIES SYLLABUS REVIEW AND DEVELOPMENT COMMITTEE

The United States is a microcosm of humanity today. No other country in the world is peopled by a greater variety of races, nationalities, and ethnic groups. But although the United States has been a great asylum for diverse peoples, it has not always been a great refuge for diverse cultures. The country has opened its doors to a multitude of nationalities, but often their cultures have not been encouraged to survive or, at best, have been kept marginal to the mainstream.

Since the 1960s, however, a profound reorientation of the self-image of Americans has been under way. Before this time the dominant model of the typical American has been conditioned primarily by the need to shape a unified nation out of a variety of contrasting and often conflicting European immigrant communities. But following the struggles for civil rights, the unprecedented increase in non-European immigration over the last two decades, and the increasing recognition of the nation's indigenous heritage, there has been a fundamental change in the image of what a resident of the United States is.

The Challenge

With this change, which necessarily highlights the racial and ethnic pluralism of the nation, previous ideals of assimilation to an Anglo-American model have been put in question and are now slowly and sometimes painfully being set aside. Many people in the United States today are no longer comfortable with the requirement, common in the

These excerpts from *One Nation, Many Peoples: A Declaration of Cultural Interdependence,* a report submitted to the New York State Board of Regents by the Social Studies Syllabus Review and Development Committee of New York State, appeared in the *New York Times* on June 21, 1991.

past, that they shed their specific cultural differences in order to be considered American. Instead . . . many in the United States from European and non-European backgrounds have been encouraging a more tolerant, inclusive, and realistic vision of American identity than any that has existed in the past. . . .

It is fitting for New York State, host to the Statue of Liberty, to inaugurate a curriculum that reflects the rich cultural diversity of the nation. The beacon of hope welcomes not just the "wretched and poor" individuals of the world, but also the dynamic and rich cultures all people bring with them.

Two centuries after this country's founders issued a Declaration of 5 Independence . . . the time has come to recognize cultural interdependence. We propose the principle of respect for diverse cultures is critical to our nation, and we affirm that a right to cultural diversity exists. We believe that the schoolroom is one of the places where this cultural interdependence must be reflected. . . .

Multicultural education is often viewed as divisive and even as destructive to the values which hold us together as Americans. . . . But national unity does not require that we eliminate the very diversity that is the source of our uniqueness. . . . If the United States is to continue to prosper in the twenty-first century, then all of its citizens, whatever their race or ethnicity, must believe that they and their ancestors have shared in the building of the country and have a stake in its success. . . .

To improve teaching and learning in the social studies, it will not suffice to change the listing of content and topics to be taught, nor to change the emphasis on history or any other field. The perceived goal itself must change, for it has become the teaching of large and ever-increasing amounts of information without adequate organizing and supporting frameworks. . . .

The Recommended Tack

With regard to diversity, the tendency has been to tell the story of the United States and global history from the perspective of males and whites, and we quickly began to add important information about women and people of color. But then we must in fairness go to lists of contributions of the many other national, ethnic, religious and cultural, and other groups, and as we did so, it became clear that this encyclopedic approach would never fit in the syllabus, let alone the classroom. . . .

It is recommended that the approach to the social studies, kindergarten through twelve, shift the emphasis from the mastery of information to the development of fundamental tools, concepts and intellectual processes that make people learners who can approach knowledge in a variety of ways and struggle with the contradictions. . . .

There needs to be a significant expansion of in-service education 10
for teachers. . . . Just to cite one example of the way in which sound
scholarship can inform practice, it is still commonplace to hear teachers
in social studies classes talk about "races" of people. . . . Students need
to see race as a cultural phenomenon, not a physical description, and
need to be able to examine history and how it is used. . . . Until this
kind of scholarship is explicitly made part of teachers' knowledge
base, it will not be reflected in classrooms; whole generations of children will continue to be miseducated on this fundamental concept,
and information which is essential . . . to heal our society will be largely
unknown. . . .

For school improvement, the State Education Department must
become an agency to encourage, support, and lead the schools to carry
out their decentralized day-to-day work in imaginative, reflective, and
carefully evaluated ways.

Toward a Divisive Diversity
ARTHUR SCHLESINGER, JR.

It is unquestionably necessary to diversify the syllabus in order to
meet the needs of a more diversified society. It is unquestionably necessary to provide for global education in an increasingly interdependent
world. Our students should by all means be better acquainted with
women's history, with the history of ethnic and racial minorities, with
Latin American, Asian, and African history. Debate, alternative interpretations, "multiple perspectives" are all essential to the educational
enterprise. I welcome changes that would adapt the curriculum to these
purposes. If that is what the report means by multicultural education,
I am all for it.

But I fear that the report implies much more than this. The underlying philosophy of the report, as I read it, is that ethnicity is the defining
experience for most Americans, that ethnic ties are permanent and
indelible, that the division into ethnic groups establishes the basic
structure of American society and that a main objective of public
education should be the protection, strengthening, celebration, and per-

Arthur Schlesinger, Jr., a professor of humanities at the City University of New York,
has received Pulitzer Prizes in both history and biography. This dissent from New York
state's Social Studies Syllabus Review and Development Committee's report on diversifying the curriculum (see p. 568) is reprinted from the June 25, 1991 *Wall Street Journal.*

petuation of ethnic origins and identities. Implicit in the report is the classification of all Americans according to ethnic and racial criteria.

These propositions are assumed rather than argued in the report. They constitute an ethnic interpretation of American history that, like the economic interpretation, is valid up to a point but misleading and wrong when presented as the whole picture.

The ethnic interpretation, moreover, reverses the historic theory of America — which has been, not the preservation and sanctification of old cultures and identities, but the creation of a new national culture and a new national identity. As Secretary of State John Quincy Adams told a German contemplating migration to these shores, those who would settle in America must recognize one necessity: "They must cast off the European skin, never to resume it. They must look forward to their posterity rather than backward to their ancestors."

A Society Divided

Of course students should learn more about the rich variety of 5 peoples and cultures that have forged this new American identity. They also should understand the curse of racism — the great failure of the American experiment, the glaring contradiction of American ideals and the still crippling disease of American society. But we should also be alert to the danger of a society divided into distinct and immutable ethnic and racial groups, each taught to cherish its own apartness from the rest.

The republic has survived and grown because it has maintained a balance between *pluribus* and *unum*. The report, it seems to me, is saturated with *pluribus* and neglectful of *unum*.

The first paragraph of the preamble notes that "no other country in the world is peopled by a greater variety of races, nationalities, and ethnic groups." It continues: "But although the United States has been a great asylum for diverse peoples, it has not always been a great refuge for diverse cultures." Both points are correct — but the report is oblivious to the historical fact that the second sentence explains the first.

Why has the United States been exempt from the "trends toward separation and dissolution" that, as the report later notes, are having such destructive effects in the Soviet Union, Canada, and elsewhere? Obviously the reason the United States is still the most successful large multiethnic nation is because, instead of emphasizing and perpetuating ethnic separatism, it has assimilated immigrant cultures into a new American culture.

Most immigrants came to America precisely in order to escape their pasts. They wanted to participate in the making of an American culture and an American national identity. Even black Americans, who came as involuntary immigrants and have suffered — still suffer —

awful persecution and discrimination, have made vital contributions to the American culture.

The preamble rejects "previous ideals of assimilation to an Anglo-American model." Of course America derives its language and its primary political purposes and institutions from Britain. To pretend otherwise is to falsify history. To teach otherwise is to mislead our students. But the British legacy has been modified, enriched, and reconstituted by the absorption of non-Anglo cultures and traditions as well as by the distinctive experiences of American life. That is why America is so very different a nation from Britain.

The report does on occasion refer in general terms to the need for *unum* as well as for *pluribus*. The preamble observes, "Special attention will need to be given to those values, characteristics, and traditions which we share in common." I do not, however, find this concern much reflected in the body of the report or in the proposals for syllabus revision. Part II begins by describing "the search for common cultural grounds" as "more important than ever." This comment, if true, should give that search a much higher priority than it receives in the report. Buried toward the end is a comment on the importance of examining with care "what the elements are that hold together a nation or culture in spite of what are often great differences. This surely is one of the central questions to be considered in any course in American history." It surely is, but it receives practically no attention in the proposals for curricular revision.

A basic question is involved: Should public education seek to make our young boys and girls contributors to a common American culture? Or should it strengthen and perpetuate separate ethnic and racial subcultures? The report places its emphasis on cultivating and reinforcing ethnic differences. Students, the report says, should be "continually" encouraged to ask themselves what their cultural heritage is, why they should be proud of it, "why should I develop an understanding of and respect for my own culture(s), language(s), religion, and national origin(s)." Would it not be more appropriate for students to be "continually" encouraged to understand the American culture in which they are growing up and to prepare for an active role in shaping that culture?

Am I wrong in sensing a certain artificiality and inauthenticity in all this? If the ethnic subcultures had genuine vitality, they would be sufficiently instilled in children by family, church, and community. It is surely not the office of the public school to promote ethnic separatism and heighten ethnic tensions. The bonds of national cohesion in the republic are sufficiently fragile already. Public education should aim to strengthen, not weaken, them.

Our democratic ideals have been imperfectly realized, but the long labor to achieve them and to move the American experiment from exclusion to participation has been a central theme of American history. It should be a central theme of the New York social studies curriculum.

And it is important for students to understand where these demo- 15
cratic ideals come from. They come of course from Europe. Indeed,
Europe is the unique source of these ideals — ideals that today empower people in every continent and to which today most of the world
aspires. That is why it is so essential (in my view) to acquaint students
with the Western history and tradition that created our democratic
ideals — and why it is so wrong to tell students of non-European origin
that Western ideals are not for them.

I regret the note of Europhobia that sometimes emerges in vulgar
attacks on "Eurocentric" curriculums. Certainly Europe, like every other
culture, has committed its share of crimes. But, unlike most cultures,
it has also generated ideals that have opposed and exposed those
crimes.

The report, however, plays up the crimes and plays down the ideals.
Thus, when it talks about the European colonization of Africa and India,
it deplores "the eradication of many varieties of traditional culture
and knowledge." Like infanticide? slavery? polygamy? subjugation of
women? suttee? veil-wearing? foot-binding? clitorectomies? Nothing is
said about the influence of European ideas of democracy, human rights,
self-government, rule of law.

The Schools' Function

I also am doubtful about the note occasionally sounded in the
report that "students must be taught social criticism" and "see themselves as active makers and changers of culture and society" and "promote economic fairness and social justice" and "bring about change in
their communities, the nation, and the world." I very much hope that,
as citizens, students will do all these things, but I do not think it is the
function of the schools to teach students to become reformers any
more than I ever thought it the function of the schools to teach them
the beauty of private enterprise and the sanctity of the status quo. I
will be satisfied if we can teach children to read, write, and calculate.
If students understand the nature of our Western democratic tradition,
they will move into social criticism on their own. But let us not politicize
the curriculum on behalf either of the left or of the right.

I recognize that I am very much in the minority in these comments.
But I cannot conscientiously go along with my colleagues. I respect
their serious concern and devoted labor, and I have enjoyed my association with them. I would only beg them to consider what kind of
nation we will have if we press further down the road to cultural
separatism and ethnic fragmentation, if we institutionalize the classification of our citizens by ethnic and racial criteria, and if we abandon
our historic commitment to an American identity. What will hold our
people together then?

In Defense of Multiculturalism

NATHAN GLAZER

I served as a member of the committee appointed by New York's commissioner of education, Thomas Sobol, to review the social studies syllabi in the state's elementary and high schools. Our committee, composed of academics and teachers, was not particularly biased toward strong advocates of multiculturalism. It included critics of the multicultural trend — Arthur Schlesinger, Kenneth Jackson, Paul Gagnon, and myself. Nevertheless, the report that emerged, "One Nation, Many Peoples: A Declaration of Cultural Interdependence," called for further acknowledgment of American diversity, and was severely attacked by some members of the committee, and in many editorials (see "Mr. Sobol's Planet," *The New Republic,* July 15 and 22, 1991), for further dissolving the common bonds that make us a nation. I also appended critical remarks to the report, yet had reservations in joining in a frontal attack. The report needs its sharp critics (it was undoubtedly the criticism that subsequently led Mr. Sobol to make recommendations to the Regents of New York State that most critics of multiculturalism would agree with). But we also need to see why the demand for something called multiculturalism is now so widespread, and why American education will have to respond to it.

Multiculturalism can mean many things, and no one argues with a curriculum that gives proper weight to the role of American Indians, blacks, Asians, and European immigrant and ethnic groups in American history. But as currently used, the word "multiculturalism" is something of a misnomer. It suggests a general desire or need for students to have something in the curriculum that relates to their own ethnic traits, if these exist, or to those of their parents or ancestors. I don't think this desire is particularly widespread among many ethnic groups. "We are all immigrants" is nice rhetoric, but in fact we are not all immigrants. Some of us came in the last decade, some of our parents came long before that, many millions of us have only the haziest idea of how many ancestors came from where. Since 1980 the census has included a new question, "What is your ancestry?" The great majority of respondents report two, three, or more ancestries. Tens of millions simply insist on being "American," and nothing else.

Nor does multiculturalism reflect the increased immigration of recent decades, particularly to some of our largest cities, such as New

Nathan Glazer is a professor of education and sociology at Harvard University and the author of numerous books, including *Affirmative Discrimination: Ethnic Inequality and Public Policy* (1987). This article appeared in the September 2, 1991 edition of *The New Republic.*

York, Los Angeles, San Francisco, and Miami. It is not the new immigrants who are arguing for multiculturalism. Most of them would be content with the education provided to the previous waves of European immigrants, which paid not a whit of attention to their ethnic or racial background, or to their distinct culture or language. A product of that kind of education, I was also quite content with it.

But if it is not the new immigration that is driving the multicultural demands, what is? Multiculturalism in its present form derives basically from black educators. It is one of the longest settled elements in the American population that makes the sharpest case for multiculturalism. Asians, who make up half of current immigrants, are not much concerned. Nor are Spanish-speaking immigrants from Central and South America. Puerto Ricans and Mexican Americans do tend to support bilingual education and the maintenance of the Spanish language. But they are definitely junior partners in the fight for multiculturalism.

I'm convinced that were it not for the pattern of poor achievement   5 among blacks in the schools, the multicultural movement would lose much of its force. Even taking into account recent progress among blacks, shown in NAEP (National Assessment of Educational Progress) scores, SAT scores, and high school graduation rates, blacks still regularly score below whites, often below Hispanics and Native Americans, and far below Asians. Multiculturalism, and one of its variants, Afrocentrism, is presented to us by black educators and leaders as one of the means whereby this deficiency may be overcome.

It is not a new proposal, though it has achieved greater force and notoriety in the past few years. Many of us are simply not aware how far advanced our schools already are on the road to a black-oriented version of multiculturalism. The SATs, according to David Reich in the *New York Times,* are now thoroughly multicultural, the questions requiring knowledge of Zora Neale Hurston, Ralph Ellison, Richard Wright, Gwendolyn Brooks, Lorraine Hansberry, and Jackie Robinson (he comes up twice). The fiction reading is from Maya Angelou. Diane Ravitch and Chester Finn, in *What Do Our 17-Year-Olds Know?,* report that in a national sample of seventeen-year-olds more could identify Harriet Tubman than Winston Churchill or Joseph Stalin, more knew Tubman than knew that George Washington commanded the American army during the Revolution, or that Lincoln wrote the Emancipation Proclamation.

The mass of materials that flowed in on us as we worked on our report showed how established multiculturalism was in New York state. One of the documents listed teachers' guides available from the State Education Department, in addition to the social studies syllabi. Of the seven publications available, four dealt with minorities and women. One of them, the most substantial, was a three-volume publication on the teaching of the Holocaust. A survey of in-service workshops completed by New York state teachers in 1990–1991 showed that far more had taken workshops on African history, black studies, ethnic studies, multicultural education, and cultural diversity than on American and European history.

One of the reasons all this is so agitating to so many is historical. After all, when Jewish and Italian-American students dominated the public schools of New York City, George Washington and Abraham Lincoln were still on the walls, not Herzl and Garibaldi, and students were told that the Anglo-American forefathers of the American commonwealth were their forefathers. The students and their parents did not object, and most embraced the new identity. This background dominates much of the argument over multiculturalism. "We didn't get it, why should they? We didn't need it, why do they? We didn't want it, why do they?" But things change. They — and by that I mean primarily American blacks — may need it. I say "may" because we don't know. Nor are we clear on how many want it, but there are certainly a good number.

Multiculturalism today is in the same class as the proposals for schools for black boys, another desperate try to help black high school achievement. Or vouchers to permit black students to attend private black schools. In view of the extensive failure among low-income blacks, it is not easy to stand four-square against these proposals particularly when advanced by black advocates aiming to overcome black school failure.

I do not see how school systems with a majority of black and Latino 10 students, with black or Latino leadership at the top, as is true of almost all our big-city school systems, can stand firmly against the multicultural thrust. The new president of the New York City Board of Education, H. Carl McCall, is reported by the *New York Times* as saying he could support a school "focusing primarily, but not exclusively, on black male students" and that "an Afrocentric curriculum . . . can be positive." One could add other testimonials, from members of other big-city school boards, and from school superintendents. In the big cities, in many schools, an unbalanced, indeed distorted view of American and world history and culture is prevailing. We should fight its excesses. Yet when set against the reality of majorities of blacks and Latino students in these schools, the political dominance of black and Latino administrators, the weak preparation of teachers and administrators in history, and the responsiveness of textbook publishers to organized pressure, the weight of the truth of history, as determined by the best scholars, is reduced to only one interest.

This may appear shocking, but it is not an entirely new phenomenon. In the elementary and high schools, a properly nuanced historical truth based on the best available evidence has always been only one interest among many. History in the schools has always played a socializing, nationalizing function (sometimes a regional pride function, as in the Southern versions of some texts). That function was the inculcation of patriotism in immigrants, and their assimilation to a culture deriving from England, and the experience of English-speaking colonists.

Some recent trends, even without the pressure of multiculturalists, are already changing that pattern. The most important is the general challenge to an unquestioning, simple, and direct American patriotism. After the past twenty years, with the relative decline of American power and the doubts about an unblemished American virtue, we will not have the triumphalist history that prevailed until a few decades ago. Our little war in Iraq will not turn around this tendency to be skeptical about the American past and present. (The worst of all histories, except for all the others, we might say.)

What does one do in the face of these trends? One thing is to fight the errors, distortions, untruths, imbalances. Some of the comments attached to the report did that, and the report fortunately did not add further weight to the more extreme claims. But the sharper critics of the report, I believe, have failed to recognize that demographic and political pressures change the history that is to be taught. They direct us to look for things we could not have noticed before. Assertions that are at first glance fantastic may have to be given some modest acquiescence. Yes, it seems that there were some Egyptian pharaohs who were racially black. (What one makes of it is another matter.) Yes, it seems that some ancient Greeks believed that they got their gods, myths, mystical knowledge from ancient Egypt. Martin Bernal's *Black Athena* will eventually leave some deposit in textbook accounts. (It will be ironic if one consequence of Afrocentrism is that our students, who know nothing of ancient Greece and less of ancient Egypt, will now be forced to learn something in order to accommodate the argument of African influences!) Yes, there is another side to the story of the expansion of Europe and imperialism. Yes, it is possible that, as the economic historian Barbara Solow argues, the weight of slave-produced plantation products was much greater in shaping the economy of the American colonies than is generally understood. Yes, there is a Mexican perspective on the Mexican-American War, and when one deals with classes that are dominantly Latin American it would be best to know it. And so on.

Black and Hispanic advocates will call for these new perspectives; historians, attracted by new ideas, politicized by new trends, looking for new topics, will explore them, and their researches will over time change weight and nuance in the treatment of various issues in the textbooks. It's happened before; it will happen again.

Yet another development bears on the multicultural problem. This is the push for more choice in the public school system. That effort, supported by conservatives today, was first introduced as a policy alternative in American education in the late 1960s by liberals and radicals. Choice bears upon this debate because it implies diversity of curricula, because there should be something to choose among. It implies that quite a range of emphases may be offered, from Afrocentrism to Eurocentrism — perhaps, some have noted in alarm, the spectrum will run all the way from black Muslims to white racists.

In Milwaukee today hundreds of low-income black students attend, with state grants, inner-city black private schools, some of which emphasize Afrocentrism or black nationalism in their curricula. This program, under strong attack by the local teachers' union and others, has been adopted less because Milwaukee black leaders want to promote Afrocentrism than because they are fed up with the poor education their children receive in the public schools and hope that private schools, whatever their orientation, will do better — a view bolstered by the researches of James Coleman, John Chubb, and Terry Moe.

The movement for choice means the acceptance of more diversity in school curricula. At the margin, this diversity can be limited, if public funds are to be provided to assist choice. But there seems to me a kind of contradiction in simultaneously insisting on a strong, common, assimilationist curriculum in the public schools and accepting a wide range of diversity in the non-public school system. The line between the two systems and the two functions will not be easily maintained.

Inevitably, the current debate is focused on high-profile reports, large statements. But much of it ignores the reality of what goes on in American schooling. While multiculturalism and Afrocentrism race ahead in some schools and systems, others may happily continue to be the schools many of us remember and approve of, with only some modest modifications to prepare students for tests with a surprisingly high content of questions dealing with blacks and women, and particularly black women. The New York state report is only one step in a process that is far from concluded. The syllabi we reviewed are not required or imposed. The specific curricula of the classrooms are developed by hundreds of school districts, thousands of schools, many thousands of administrators and teachers. The syllabi are themselves broad outlines with examples. Many schools in the state already do more in the way of "multiculturalism" than the syllabi call for, many do less, and this ragged pattern will continue.

Whatever the strength of the multicultural thrust, I believe that American history in its main lineaments will have to be what it has been, and will not become completely alien to those of us educated in another time. We will find the story of the settlement by the English, but students will also be told that the Spaniards got to New Mexico and Florida first. The description of colonial America will place more emphasis on blacks, slave and free. The War for Independence will still play a large role, but we will now certainly find the blacks who fought in the war, along with Pulaski, von Steuben, Lafayette, and Haym Solomon. The Constitution will maintain its centrality, but we will now emphasize the argument over slavery, the references to the Indians.

The expansion westward will emphasize how nasty we were to the Indians and the Mexicans. The struggle over slavery leading to the Civil War will emphasize even more strongly the criminal failure of Reconstruction and the importance of the postwar amendments and their role. The story of industrialization and the rise of the city will include more about the immigrants and the black migration north. And so on.

The skeletal structure will remain, because we still live under the polity established by the Constitution, and it is in that polity, under that Constitution, that racial and ethnic and minority groups and women seek to expand their rights. It will be quite a job to keep nonsense and exaggeration and mindless ethnic and racial celebration out of the schools, but the basic structure of instruction in history will survive.

In my own comments, attached to the report, I took issue with the attempt to turn the United States into a congeries of ethnic and racial groups, and nothing more. Assimilation is a reality; scores of millions of unhyphenated Americans, who owe no allegiance to any identity other than American, are evidence of that. And assimilation continues to work its way, through the processes of work and of entertainment, with less help from the schools than before.

In this respect, present-day immigrants will not be very different from previous immigrants. They will assimilate. But one group, because of its experience of cruel, centuries-long ill treatment, is not yet fully incorporated in this generally successful process of nation building. Present-day multiculturalism is a product of that apartness. Most of those who embrace it, I believe, do so in the hope that it will overcome that apartness. They want, in some key respects, to become more like other Americans — for example, in educational achievement — not different from them, and believe that the way to becoming more like them, is to take more account of difference, and yes, of ill treatment, of past and current achievement, even if exaggerated.

That is where we stand, and while some parts of this phenomenon are alarming enough, the proper parallel is not with Serbia and Croatia, or even Quebec. It is with our own American past, and the varying ways over time in which people of different race, religion, and ethnic background have become one nation.

Ugh! Oops.
FRED SIEGEL

The following are some of the multicultural no-nos, which appear in the *Dictionary of Cautionary Words and Phrases.* According to its foreword, the dictionary was the brainchild of the 1989 Multicultural

Fred Siegel is an associate professor of humanities at Cooper Union in New York

Management Program Fellows, a group of journalists from, among other newspapers, the *Baltimore Sun, New York Newsday, Dallas Times Herald, Chicago Tribune, Atlanta Journal-Constitution,* and *Miami Herald.* Their aim? Politically correct journalism. It is not a parody.

African-American: Also used for black. Preferred by some, but not universally accepted. May be objectionable to those persons preferring black.

Articulate: Can be considered offensive when referring to a minority, particularly a black person, and his or her ability to handle the English language. The usage suggests that "those people" are not considered well educated, articulate, and the like.

Banana: An offensive term referring to Asian Americans who allegedly have abandoned their culture. Objectionable because no person or group can appropriately attach judgmental terms to others. Just as objectionable: Coconut for Mexican Americans and Oreo for black Americans.

Barracuda: A negative generalization of persons without morals   5 and/or ethical standards or judgments. Many times directed at forceful women. Do not use.

Beauty: Avoid descriptive terms of beauty when not absolutely necessary. For instance, do not use "blond and blue-eyed" unless you would also use "brown-haired and brown-eyed" as a natural measure of attractiveness.

Beefcake: Objectionable when referring to male physical attractiveness.

Burly: An adjective too often associated with large black men, implying ignorance, and considered offensive in this context.

Buxom: Offensive reference to a woman's chest. Do not use. See "Woman."

Codger: Offensive reference to a senior citizen. See "Senior Citi-   10 zens."

Community: Implies a monolithic culture in which people act, think, and vote in the same way. Do not use, as in Asian, Hispanic, black, or gay community. Be more specific as to what the group is: e.g., black residents in a northside neighborhood.

Coot: Offensive reference to senior citizen. See "Senior Citizens."

City. He has written for many magazines, including *Commonweal, The Atlantic, Tikkun, Dissent,* and *The New Republic,* where this excerpt appeared on February 28, 1991, as part of Siegel's article "The Cult of Multiculturalism."

Dear: A term of endearment objectionable to some. Usage such as "He was a dear man" or "She is a dear" should be avoided.

Dutch treat: To share the cost, as in a date. Implies that Dutch people are cheap.

Fried chicken: A loaded phrase when used carelessly and as a stereotype, referring to the cuisine of black people. Also applies to watermelon. 15

Gay: Refers only to homosexual men. See "Homosexual."

Geezer: An objectionable reference to a senior citizen. Avoid using. See "Senior Citizens."

Homosexual: The preferred term for people attracted to members of the same sex. Gay refers only to homosexual men; lesbian refers only to homosexual women. Derisive terms such as dyke, fruit, fairy, or queer are highly objectionable.

Illegal alien: Often used to refer to Mexicans and Latin Americans believed to be in the United States without visas; the preferred term is undocumented worker or undocumented resident.

Impotent: A clinical term referring to male sexual dysfunction. Not proper when used to stereotype or characterize males. 20

Inscrutable: An adjective often carelessly applied to Asian Americans. Avoid all terms that stereotype entire groups.

Ivan: A common and offensive substitute for a Soviet person.

Jew: Refers to people of the Jewish faith. Some people find use of Jew alone offensive and prefer Jewish person. Not a synonym for stingy. Always used as a noun, never a verb.

Johns: Men who frequent prostitutes, but not a proper generic term for men or bathrooms.

Leader: Use with caution. Be more specific: black politician, black activist. Implies person has approval of an entire group of people. 25

Man: May be used when both men and women are involved and a more clearly defined term is not available. Frequently the best choice is a substitute, such as "humanity," "a person," or "an individual."

Man, the: A reference to the establishment, mainly white. Could be offensive.

"The Myth": Avoid any word, description, or phrase that contributes to the stereotype of black males as strictly athletic, well proportioned, or having high sexual drives and exaggerated sex organs.

Oriental: Unacceptable to some Asian Americans. Use Asian American or Asian(s), the specific term.

Peg leg: Use prosthesis or artificial limb. Also avoid hook. 30

Qualified minorities: Do not use in stories about affirmative action. Unnecessary description that indicates minorities are generally unqualified.

Retarded: An adjective meaning slow or backward in mental or emotional development. Refer to specific medical condition. Do not use retard, stupid, or ignorant.

Rubbing noses: Allegedly an Eskimo kiss. However, Eskimos don't rub noses and object to the characterization. Do not use.

Senior citizens: Do not use for anyone under sixty-five. In general, avoid ageism by giving ages where relevant. Do not describe people as elderly, senile, matronly, or well preserved. Also do not identify people as grandparents unless it is relevant to the story. Do not use dirty old man, codger, coot, geezer, silver fox, old-timers, Pop, old buzzard. Blue-haired is objectionable when used to characterize older people.

Soulful: Can be an objectionable adjective when applied strictly to 35 blacks. Another potentially objectionable adjective: articulate. See "Articulate."

Stunning: Avoid physical description. See "Woman."

Swarthy: Refers to darkened skin color. Avoid all unnecessary references to skin color, such as yellow. Other objectionable terms are paleface, redskin, and lily-white.

Sweetie: Objectionable term of endearment. Do not use.

Ugh: A guttural sound used to mimic American Indian speech. Highly offensive.

Watermelon: See "Fried chicken." 40

White bread: A term denoting blandness. Could have racial connotation.

Whore: Derogatory, along with trollop, tart, loose woman, hussy.

Without rhythm: A stereotype about whites. Implies that others have rhythm, also a stereotype.

Woman: The preferred term for a female adult. Girl is appropriate only for those seventeen years old and under. Avoid gal and lady. Also avoid derogatory terms for women, such as skirt, broad, chick, bimbo, bumbo, babe, ball and chain, and little woman. Also avoid adjectives describing female physical attributes or mannerisms such as pert, petite, foxy, buxom, fragile, feminine, stunning, gorgeous, statuesque, or full-figured.

THINKING AND WRITING ABOUT
MULTICULTURAL STUDIES

Questions for Discussion and Writing

1. Can you find references to different versions of multicultural studies among the selections in this chapter? What elements, if any, do they share?

2. In what ways do the authors who argue *for* multicultural studies agree? Do Glazer, Gates, Asante, and the panel of educators who wrote "Report on Minority Cultures in the Classroom" cite the same reasons for their advocacy?

3. What distinction does Ravitch develop between "pluralistic multiculturalism" and "particularistic multiculturalism"? What specific dangers does she see in the latter?

4. Why does Schlesinger say that the "ethnic interpretation of American history" is "valid up to a point but misleading and wrong when presented as the whole picture"? Asante says that "the debate over the curriculum is really over a vision of the future of the United States." How does he characterize his own vision? Does his vision differ significantly from the one defined by Schlesinger?

5. Shanker warns that educators must not confuse "objectivity with neutrality." Explain the meaning of this phrase and tell how Shanker relates it to the study of the values and practices of different cultures.

6. How do you respond to the list of "cautionary words and phrases" quoted by Siegel? Do you think that the use of the "correct" words leads to desirable or undesirable social and political consequences? Or perhaps both? Be specific about any results you describe. Are some designations more useful than others?

7. Many cartoons make fun of current preoccupations, especially those which are treated with great seriousness. The cartoonist in this chapter aims at several familiar targets. What are they? Do you think he has made some hits? Or is he off the mark?

Topics for Research

A multicultural curriculum at a selected public school: its strengths and shortcomings

Evaluation of the curriculum of a day school devoted to keeping alive a particular group identity (e.g., Japanese, Hebrew, Muslim, Hindu)

Evaluation of changes in a course syllabus at this college: cultural pluralism or divisive diversity?

How movies and TV treat minority peoples and cultures

The historical significance of Christopher Columbus

CHAPTER EIGHTEEN

Sex Education

Sex education in school has always occasioned some controversy even when courses were devoted only to the facts of reproduction and boys and girls were instructed in separate classes. Although many parents may have been unable or unwilling to discuss such facts with their children, they were nevertheless convinced that home or church should be the place of instruction. And if values were to be taught, premarital chastity, marriage, and sexual fidelity in marriage were to be emphasized above all others. Now changing mores and increased sexual activity among teenagers have produced sweeping reforms in the subject matter of sex education courses, especially in big-city schools, and an ongoing debate between those who favor the reforms and those who oppose them. The debate about subject matter remains, however, essentially a debate about values: the freedom of teenagers to choose when and how they engage in sexual activity, the rights of parents and community to control the moral content of their children's education, the right of educators to introduce controversial material that reflects a changing society.

The advocates of the new curriculum argue that it is intended primarily to reduce an alarmingly high number of teenage pregnancies and to teach sexually active teenagers how to protect themselves against AIDS. Advocates are convinced that it is unrealistic to assume that teenagers will practice abstinence even when confronted by disease or unwanted pregnancy. For this reason they have supported the distribution of condoms and instruction in their use, sometimes in the classroom. Equally controversial is the inclusion in some school curricula of a "diversity" component that treats homosexuality as an acceptable alternative to heterosexuality and urges respect for gay families.

Those who oppose the distribution of the new materials believe that, however well intentioned, it will appear to sanction greater sexual activity and lead to further weakening of the traditional heterosexual family. They insist that the curriculum of a sex education course should emphasize abstinence as the only morally and medically acceptable approach. In part, objections to the changes by both parents and community are based on deeply held religious beliefs.

In addition to questions about the content of the curriculum, there are questions about the administration of the programs. Should sex education be mandatory? Or should parents have the option of withdrawing their children from some parts of the course? At what age should sex education begin? (According to a recent Roper Organization poll, the average recommended age was nine.) By whom should it be taught? (Peer education has proven effective in some schools. Would it be appropriate everywhere?)

One troubling aspect of the debate is that not much is known about the effectiveness of the proposed changes. Whether information alone will induce teenagers to refrain from risky sexual activity is doubtful. Both sides have offered data to support their claims that sex education does or does not work, but most studies have been inconclusive.

"We Give Up."
WILLIAM J. BENNETT

Another example: teenage, out-of-wedlock pregnancy. We have now seen in places around the country what I regard as a classic bureaucratic response to this problem: setting up birth-control clinics in schools. Now this is obviously a local decision, but I would say this to any locality considering it: You had better be sure — really sure — that you have consulted fully and thoroughly with parents and the community. Or you may find that you have created a full enrollment policy for private schools.

And let me say more, if I may. Of course this is a local decision and not a decision for the secretary of education. It is a judgment not about birth control in general but about birth control in the schools. First of all, in my view, this is not what school is for. School should be predominantly and overwhelmingly about learning — about math and English and history and science. But even as an additional function of the school, it is my view that this response to teenage pregnancy — what I've described and talked about — is the wrong kind of response

---

This excerpt was taken from a speech given by former U.S. secretary of education William J. Bennett to the Education Writers Association in Baltimore on April 11, 1986.

to the problem. It offers a bureaucratic solution — a highly questionable, if not offensive one — in place of the exercise of individual responsibility, not just by the children but by the adults around them. Further, it tends to legitimate the very behavior whose natural consequences it intends to discourage. And further yet, it encourages those children who do not have sexual intimacy on their minds to have it on their minds, to be mindful of it. Or it suggests to these young people that they're somehow behind the times. It thrusts upon those young people with scruples about sexual intimacy a new publicly legitimated possibility. And it does this in school. The child sees those in authority over him or over her acknowledging as commonplace what ought not to be commonplace and what parents do not wish, with good reason, to be commonplace. If individual parents wish, there are many places to which they can take their children for professional help and guidance. But the wholesale use of the school is not the way to do it.

Birth-control clinics in school may prevent some births. That I wouldn't deny. The question is: What lessons do they teach, what attitudes do they encourage, what behaviors do they foster? I believe there are certain kinds of surrender that adults may not declare in the presence of the young. One such surrender is the abdication of moral authority. Schools are the last place this should happen. To do what is being done in some schools, I think, is to throw up one's hands and say "We give up. We give up. We give up on teaching right and wrong to you, there is nothing we can do. Here, take these things and limit the damage done by your actions." If we revoke responsibility, if we fail to treat young people as moral agents, as people responsible for moral actions, we fail to do the job of nurturing our youth.

School Birth-Control Clinics: A Necessary Evil

CHARLES KRAUTHAMMER

The latest outrage of American life: The pill goes to school. There are now seventy-two "comprehensive health clinics" in or near the nation's public high schools.

Very comprehensive. More than a quarter dispense and more than half prescribe birth-control devices. When the New York City Board of

The former chief resident in psychiatry at Harvard Medical School, Charles Krauthammer is now a well-known writer on public policy and contributes regularly to such publications as *The New Republic* and *Time* magazine. This article is reprinted from the December 3, 1986 *Washington Post.*

Education found out that two of its clinics were in the dispensing business, it ordered them to cease and desist.

Secretary of Education William Bennett has waxed eloquent on the subject. He is surely right that birth control in the schools makes sexual activity legitimate and represents an "abdication of moral authority." Clinics are not only an admission by adults that they cannot control teenage sexuality, but also tacit consent, despite the "just say no" rhetoric.

Unfortunately, there are two problems: not just sex, but pregnancy. As in all social policy, there is a choice to be made. Is it worth risking the implicit message that sex is OK in order to decrease pregnancies?

(Clinic opponents sometimes argue that birth-control dispensaries 5 do not decrease the number of pregnancies, a contention that defies both intuition and the evidence.)

Bennett is right about the nature of the message. But he vastly overestimates its practical effect. Kids do not learn their morals at school. (Which is why the vogue for in-school drug education will prove an expensive failure.) They learn at home. Or they used to.

Now they learn from the culture, most notably from the mass media. Your four-eyed biology teacher and your pigeon-toed principal say don't. The Pointer Sisters say do. To whom are you going to listen?

My authority for the image of the grotesque teacher and moronic principal is *Porky's,* the wildly popular teen sex flick that has spawned imitators and sequels. My authority for the fact that teenage sex control is an anachronism is Madonna. "Papa don't preach," she sings. "I'm gonna keep my baby."

The innocent in the song is months — nine months, to be precise — beyond the question of sex. Her mind is already on motherhood.

Kids are immersed in a mass culture that relentlessly says yes. A 10 squeak from the schools saying no, or a tacit signal saying maybe, is not going to make any difference. To pretend otherwise is grossly to misread what shapes popular attitudes.

What a school can credibly tell kids depends a lot on whether they grew up on the Pillsbury dough boy or on a grappling group of half-nudes frenzied with Obsession.

Time to face facts. Yes, birth-control clinics are a kind of surrender. But at Little Big Horn, surrender is the only sound strategy. Sex oozes from every pore of the culture, and there's not a kid in the world who can avoid it. To shut down school birth-control clinics in order to imply the contrary is a high-minded but very costly exercise in message sending. Costly because the message from the general culture will prevail anyway, and sex without contraception means babies.

The sex battle is lost. The front-line issue is pregnancy. Some situations are too far gone to be reversed. They can only be contained. Containment here means trying at least to prevent some of the personal agony and social pathology that invariably issue from teenage pregnancy.

Not that the sexual revolution can never be reversed. It can, in principle. In our time, the vehicle might be AIDS. The association of sex and sin elicits giggles. The association of sex and death elicits terror. Nevertheless, the coming counterrevolution, like all cultural revolutions, will not be made in the schools. It will happen outside — in movies and the newsmagazines, on the soaps and MTV — and then trickle down to the schools. As usual, they will be the last to find out.

I am no more pleased than the next parent to think that in ten years' time my child's path to math class will be adorned with a tasteful display of condoms in the school's clinic window. But by then it will be old hat.

The very word "condom" has broken through into the national consciousness, i.e., network TV. It was uttered for the first time ever on a prime-time entertainment show, "Cagney and Lacey." Condoms will now find their place beside bulimia, suicide, incest, and spouse murder in every child's mental world.

If the schools ignore that world, it will not change a thing. Neglect will make things worse. In a sex-soaked culture, school is no shelter from the storm. Only a monastery is, if it doesn't have cable.

Should Children Have Sex?

DALE O'LEARY

To the Editor:

In the debate over condoms in the schools, condom advocates have been avoiding the central question: Should children have sex? This is a legitimate issue. Saying "Children are having sex, and adults have to accept it" is not responsive. Children take drugs, shoplift, use guns, get drunk, and skip school, and no one suggests adults should blithely accept such behavior or aid and abet it.

Implicit in the argument for condoms in the schools is the assumption that the only thing wrong with children having sex is the possibility they could become pregnant or contract a sexually transmitted disease.

If these were the only concerns, condoms, with their 14 percent user failure rate, would still be a poor solution. Condom advocates may feel that with abortion as a backup this is an acceptable risk, but the acquired immune deficiency syndrome (AIDS) virus cannot be aborted.

Yet pregnancy and disease are not the only effects of child sex. People who are outraged over child molesting wink at child sex. How can those handing out condoms know whether or not the users are

Dale O'Leary is a freelance writer who lectures on methods of argument. She has contributed articles to the Boston *Pilot,* the Providence *Visitor,* and the Providence *Journal.* This letter to the editor appeared in the October 10, 1991 *New York Times.*

psychologically equipped to deal with sexuality? Indeed, many experts believe that no child is ready to deal with sex, no matter how eager he or she may be to engage in it.

The girls who seem willing and ready for sexual encounters may have already been victims. "A so-called precocious, provocative, or seductive child," according to Beverly Engel, an expert on sexual child abuse, "appears so because of prior sexual abuse." Early sexualization leaves children with the "dysfunctional message — that they are important because of their sexuality."

We have only to look around the malls and teenage gathering places to see sexualized eleven- and twelve-year-old girls who are ready to prostitute themselves for attention, affection, and popularity. What will be the price to their self-esteem, their self-worth, their future relationships with men?

And what is the effect on young men? Are we creating a generation of men who believe that any woman will be willing to satisfy their demands if they produce a condom? Has male respect for women increased? Hardly. What has increased is acts of violence against women, date rape, abusive rap music, and pornography.

Condom advocates say sex is responsible, as long as no one gets hurt. In child sex someone always gets hurt.

— Dale O'Leary

Protect Our Children

CAROL F. ROYE

To the Editor:

The AIDS education battle in New York City is deeply disturbing. Our adolescents are contracting the human immunodeficiency virus, which causes AIDS, at an alarming rate. It is believed that at least 20 percent of new patients with AIDS were infected during teenage or early adult years.

Further, the male-to-female ratio of HIV seroprevalence in teenagers and young adults is much lower than for adults, emphasizing the heterosexual transmission in this age group. They will die from this disease. Yet, some of our school leaders are trying to foil AIDS education — the best means we have of preventing the disease among teenagers.

AIDS cannot be cured. Why then are we loath to teach our children

Carol F. Roye is a nurse practitioner in New York City. This article, which appeared as an editorial in the September 12, 1992 *New York Times,* responds to Dale O'Leary's October 10, 1991 editorial in that publication.

how to prevent AIDS? We must get beyond our personal discomfort about discussing sexuality and get on with protecting our children.

Opponents of comprehensive AIDS education have not presented documentation showing that discussion of AIDS prevention leads to increased sexual activity. They just think it is so. The literature on adolescent sexuality suggests that frank discussion of sexuality and AIDS prevention, even in a setting where condoms and other forms of birth control are distributed, results in lower rates of sexual activity. Also, national surveys show that parents overwhelmingly want their children protected, and endorse education on sexuality and family life in schools. As a mother of five, I agree.

My experience as a nurse practitioner in New York City adolescent   5 clinics bears this out. When teenagers who are sexually active or at high risk for sexual activity come to the clinic, I counsel them about all aspects of sexuality. Even those who are considered "problem children" listen wide-eyed to an honest, frank discussion of sexuality. They ask for clarification of potentially fatal misperceptions. And, of course, abstinence is presented as the safest option. However, abstinence is not a realistic option for many teenagers.

Yet after such a discussion and the dispensing of birth-control devices (or instructions on obtaining them, depending on the type of clinic), a number of patients come to their follow-up appointment and state that they have not been sexually active since their last clinic visit. Kids respond to honesty, respect, and genuine concern. They understand that teaching about AIDS prevention does not mean we condone their sexual activity, but that we care about them.

The rates of teenage pregnancy (approximately 1 million a year in the United States), sexually transmitted diseases (which are increasing at alarming rates with the highest rates for teenagers and young adults), and HIV seroprevalence in teenagers all attest to the prevalence of adolescent sexual activity in New York City and the country. Denying that social reality so that we adults can avoid facing uncomfortable discussions with our children will not protect them from AIDS.

— Carol F. Roye

Sex Ed, Up to Date

JOHN P. HALE

The first day in the first grade is always a milestone for parent and child. It is the start of an adventure which parents welcome with mixed emotions, knowing babyhood has ended and real student days have

John P. Hale is a former member of the New York State Board of Social Welfare. His article appeared in the *National Review* on May 25, 1992.

begun, with work to be done, tests to be taken, and skills to be acquired to help the child grow into a self-sufficient adult. While parents of a first grader almost always leave their child at the schoolhouse door with a twinge of regret, that regret would be converted to horror for New York City parents if they realized what new lessons await their child.

"If teachers do not discuss lesbian/gay issues, they are not likely to come up," says the new teachers' manual *Children of the Rainbow — First Grade,* on page 372. No parent would argue with that, since five- and six-year-olds are not known for any level of interest in such topics. What would startle the parents is that that statement is the jumping-off point for instructions to the teacher on how to introduce the subject.

"At least 10 percent of each class will grow up to be homosexual," continues the manual, and "It is also common for them to be thrown out of their homes once their parents find out their child is gay." "Classes," the teachers are advised, "should include references to les-bian/gay people in all curricular areas and should avoid exclusionary practices by presuming a person's sexual orientation."

The manual continues: "Challenging sexual myths can begin on the first day of school." And if the boys tend to play with trucks and the girls with dolls and the children do not themselves suggest switching after a couple of sessions, teacher should suggest that the switch take place.

What's going on? The New York City school system has made 5 reshaping children's attitudes and behavior its number-one goal. But the reshaping is not toward self-restraint and discipline, but rather toward all forms of hedonism, hetero- as well as homosexual. And the process involves driving a wedge between children and their parents, both by telling the children not to accept their parents' values, and by *not* telling the parents what the schools are doing.

One factor is the enlarged role that homosexuals are playing in molding New York City school policy. When the federal government made a grant to New York's schools to support education in drug prevention, $500,000 of that money was awarded to the Gay and Lesbian Community Center to run Youth Enrichment Services!

The volunteers who will staff condom distribution rooms in city high schools and who will be available to counsel the children on sexuality include delegates from the Gay Men's Health Crises (GMHC) and the Hetrick Martin Institute for Gay and Lesbian Youth, both of which have been designated as official resources of the New York City school system.

GMHC has a new illustrated color brochure that outlines safe-sex practices and advises, "If you have sex with women these guidelines still apply." One of the guidelines is to wear a latex surgical glove when you insert your fist into your partner's rectum. The pamphlet has circulated unofficially in at least one city high school. So far the Board of Education has been silent as to whether it will make surgical gloves available to the children as a health measure.

The Hetrick Martin Institute has published its own sex ed curriculum, which states the course has been given in area high schools. One portion of the curriculum is a detailed instruction on anal intercourse with the admonition, "Do it. Have fun!"

Of even greater significance to parents are three excerpts from the 10 January 1992 training manual. Some background is in order. When the New York State Board of Regents issued guidelines on the new AIDS curriculum to be adopted by all local school districts, it recognized that parents had the ultimate right to determine what type of instruction their children should receive. The Regents mandated that parents be given the right to opt their children out of a portion of the course. New York City schools raised the question whether parents should be told that they could opt out. Here is the answer given in the manual.

> *Question:* How are children withdrawn from prevention lessons of the AIDS instruction program?
> *Answer:* According to New York State Regulations, parents and/or guardians have the right to withdraw their children from the prevention lessons of the AIDS instruction program. *The school is not under an affirmative obligation to inform parents of this right. . . .* [Emphasis added.]

Put bluntly, you don't have to tell them. That will certainly eliminate the inconvenience of parents opting out.

Look at a second question and answer in the same manual:

> *Question:* If a parent has told me explicitly that he/she does not want his/her child to have a condom, am I still permitted to give that child a condom if he/she requests it?
> *Answer:* Yes. . . .

That's consistent, if you have reached the conclusion that parental rights have flickered out in the arena of sexuality training. Whether the schools have the right to ignore the parents' explicit instruction is currently being challenged in a suit pending in the Supreme Court of Richmond County (Staten Island).

The manual also deals with the thorny problem of what to do if the children themselves object to something being taught because of their "religious beliefs." The schools are currently distributing a City Board of Health pamphlet called *Teens Have the Right,* which tells the children that they have the "right to decide to have sex and who to have it with." It is the clear teaching of several major religious bodies in the city that unmarried people, which includes most teenagers, do not have the right to have sexual intercourse. They teach that sexual intercourse out of wedlock is wrong. One can be sure that this is one "religious belief" the volunteers are being trained to cope with.

We are talking about a school system that has exhibited an impaired ability to carry out basic instruction in reading, writing, and mathematics; a system which now has a corps of security officers larger than the police force of the city of Boston to attempt to protect the students from physical harm. Instead of dealing with either of those problems, the school system is worried about molding first graders' attitude toward lesbianism.

A crucial element in the schools' strategy is hiding from parents the details of their children's sex ed courses. And by the same token, the starting point for topping the damage is a recognition that the primary right to determine what a child is exposed to in school rests with parents. We have watched with fascination the disintegration of a political system, the Soviet one, built on the concept that the child belongs to the state. Now we see the concept taking root in our own schools. To stop it, we must press for two reforms: mandating that parents be informed of all course content to which their child will be exposed, and adopting a voucher system to give parents freedom of choice as to where to send their child.

If it is not already too late.   15

Sex Education: How Well Does It Work?

SARAH GLAZER

Should the United States Follow Sweden's Example?

Encouraging abstinence is an important goal of most sex education programs in the United States; 86 percent of the sex education teachers responding to the Guttmacher Institute survey said they taught their students that abstinence is the best way to prevent pregnancy and to avoid sexually transmitted diseases. Most of the teachers said they tried to help students avoid intercourse by providing instruction on how to resist peer pressure and how to say no to a boyfriend or girlfriend.

But most sex educators believe it's unrealistic to focus exclusively on abstinence. They point out that the mean age at which American women now start menstruation is twelve-and-a-half, approximately three years younger than it was in the late 1800s. Not only are women entering puberty earlier, they are waiting longer to get married. This has created "an extended period of time in which people are able and interested in having sex," notes Rosoff of the Guttmacher Institute.

Sarah Glazer is a staff writer for *Editorial Research Reports* (formerly *The Congressional Quarterly*), where this article appeared on June 23, 1989.

"Nobody's ever died from not having sex," counters Kathleen Sullivan. "It's the one appetite that's not necessary to fulfill." Sullivan is director of Project Respect in Glenview, Illinois, which, with the help of federal grants, has developed a sex education curriculum promoting abstinence. Sullivan claims the program — which she says is being used in twenty-six schools in six Midwestern states — has changed students' attitudes. For example, students were asked whether they agreed with the statement, "It is important for me not to have sex before I get married." Before participating in the program, 38 percent of the students agreed with the statement; after completing the program, 56 percent agreed with it. Sullivan, however, admits she does not yet have any data indicating what effect, if any, her program's curriculum has had on students' sexual behavior or pregnancy rates.

Zella Luria, a professor of psychology at Tufts University, believes that sex education programs that focus exclusively on abstinence could be counterproductive and, ultimately, psychologically damaging. Luria criticizes what she calls the traditional American "antipleasure" approach to sex. "In our country, hellfire is still close to sexuality and thus shapes our education and services related to sexuality. Who pays the price? Our children do." Telling girls that their bodies are an enemy within lays the groundwork for "sexual guilt . . . and avoidance of birth control, which requires acknowledgment of a sexual body." When girls think it is improper to seek sexual pleasure, Luria writes, they are "swept away" by passion as a way of dealing with society's double standard. "The script has no room for contraception."[1]

Luria maintains that her positive views of sex can and should be 5 accompanied with a moral message: "I think the message should be [that] sex is part of intimacy and you're not intimate with just anybody."

Luria and sex educators who share her philosophy point to Sweden's sex education program as one that has produced lower teen pregnancy rates without the "hellfire." In 1975, when a new Swedish law went into effect legalizing abortion on demand, the government intensified its mandatory sex education program at all grade levels and added free distribution of contraceptives for adolescents. From the age of twelve or thirteen, Swedish children receive formal education in contraception, which may include demonstrations of contraceptives in a classroom or at a family planning clinic. Teachers are trained to answer questions about sexual matters from children from preschool on.

Between 1975 and 1984, Sweden's teenage pregnancy rate declined by about one-third. The number of abortions also declined, another sign that contraceptives were being used more widely. "The effectiveness [of the country's sex education program] can be measured by the

---

[1] Zella Luria, "The Adolescent Years and Sexuality," *Independent School* (Spring 1989): 45–49.

fact that today no child is born in Sweden unless it's planned for," says Christina Engfeldt, deputy director of the Swedish Information Service in New York.

Sweden's sex education program is generally characterized by a nonmoralistic tone. Rather than preaching abstinence, Engfeldt says, Swedish teachers present sexuality as a stage of development in becoming an adult. Since 1977, however, Swedish educators have added a new emphasis on ethics to the curriculum. They have incorporated such ethical principles in the teachers' manual as "Nobody is entitled to regard and treat another human being simply as a means of selfish gratification" and "Fidelity toward a person with whom one has a permanent relationship is a duty." But the principles make no mention of marriage, reflecting the greater prevalence and social acceptance in Sweden of unmarried couples living together and of children born out of wedlock.

Perhaps because of Sweden's more liberal attitude toward sex, Swedish teenagers have their first sexual relations at an earlier age than American teenagers. By the age of fifteen, for example, 33 percent of Swedish boys and 41 percent of girls have had their first sexual experience. By contrast, fewer than 17 percent of American boys and 6 percent of American girls report having had intercourse by that age.[2] (Recent surveys show significantly higher U.S. figures. S. L. Hofferth, J. R. Kahn, and W. Baldwin reported in *Family Planning Perspectives* in 1987 that about 15 percent of white American females and about 20 percent of black American females said they had engaged in sexual activity by the age of fifteen. Still, these numbers are lower than their Swedish counterparts.) Yet the trend toward sexual relations at younger ages is not viewed as a social problem in Sweden. "They're having it earlier because they've learned how to handle it," says Engfeldt. "That's one way of showing your feelings. The risk of getting pregnant is minimal."[3]

Ronald Moglia, director of the Human Sexuality Program at New York University, says Swedish teenagers actually receive fewer hours of formal sex education than do American students who attend one of the more comprehensive sex education programs in this country. He believes the widespread use of contraceptives by Swedish teens can be attributed more to values in Swedish society than to its sex education

10

---

[2] Carl Gustaf Boethius, "Swedish Sex Education and Its Results," *Current Sweden,* (March 1984), and National Research Council, *Risking the Future,* 1987, p. 97.

[3] Like Sweden, most developed countries in Europe experienced a pronounced decline in teenage birthrates during the late 1970s and 1980s. One explanation for the decline has nothing to do with sex education. It is that women in these countries are marrying and having children later in life in order to take advantage of wider career and educational options. Because of similar social influences in the United States, teenage birthrates here declined steadily between 1960 and 1976, but the teenage birthrate has since leveled out. . . .

program. There is also a big difference in the way the governments of the two countries view their role in making social policies. "Here our government sees itself passing laws that the people want," says Moglia. "Sweden sees the government as passing laws people should have. That doesn't go over in Washington, D.C. No one would get elected."

For example, many Swedes express astonishment at the "opt-out" option many American school systems offer parents who find sex education courses so objectionable that they prefer to keep their children out of them. Sweden's growing immigrant population, the main source of opposition to sex education in that country, is given no such alternative. "Your parents wouldn't say, 'My child isn't going to take mathematics.' The rest of the curriculum shouldn't be optional either," says Engfeldt.

Can Americans Agree on a Sex Ed Curriculum?

The wide diversity of views about sexual matters in the United States raises problems that are hard to imagine in a society like Sweden, with its widely shared values. For example, as part of the new Virginia sex education mandate, state regulations require students to be taught that sex outside of marriage violates state laws. Jacquelyn Henneberg of Falls Church is among those who support this approach: "We feel sex is really for marriage, and for marriage alone. Thus, sex should be taught in this context."[4] But another Falls Church citizen, Barbara R. Jasny, finds this part of the curriculum objectionable. For one thing, she says, it doesn't match reality. "By the time students reach the eighth grade, many will be brought face-to-face with a conflict: Despite the curriculum, not all single parents or unmarried adults are celibate." In addition, Jasny believes the approach may create problems of its own: "A consequence of the curriculum as written is that some of our children, when faced with mounting sexual urges, will be driven into too-early marriages — one reason for the high divorce rate."[5]

Virginia, like other states, finds itself struggling with a difficult dilemma. Claude Sandy, director of the division of sciences and elementary education for the state's Department of Education, believes "it is virtually impossible" to teach sex education without discussing values, as some Virginia citizens have proposed. "What we have stressed is those values should not be the teacher's own values. They should be core values we can agree upon."

But since Virginia's citizens have important disagreements about

---

[4] Quoted in "Minority Members Concerned about Family Prerogatives," *Lasso* (newspaper published by students at George Mason Junior Senior High School in Falls Church, Va.), June 6, 1989, p. 8.

[5] *Ad Hoc Committee's Recommendations on Family Life and Sex Education,* January 20, 1989.

such issues as abortion, homosexuality, and premarital sex, the teacher can be put in the awkward position of trying to represent a common consensus that may not exist. "I don't think these things can be taught without going into some explanation of their perspective," says the Reverend Yates of the Episcopal Church in Falls Church. The best a teacher can do, he suggests, is to reveal his or her perspective and to explain that there are other perspectives so that children from families of different persuasions do not feel uncomfortable in the classroom.

The difficulty in reaching common ground has surfaced even in 15
debates over the opt-out alternative, which Virginia regulations require all schools to offer. According to Virginia education official Sandy, "That has been controversial from the standpoint of whether you can just opt out of sensitive areas. We have difficulty defining what are sensitive areas."

Those Virginia citizens who support a facts-only sex education approach argue that the curriculum should consciously avoid controversial issues like abortion in order to spare children from religious and ethical conflicts within the classroom. But teacher Mary Lee Tatum says the problem with a stripped-down curriculum is in deciding what you select to teach. She expresses the concern that when sex education is taught outside of a broad discussion of values, sex is presented as a mechanical act. "It gives kids a false message," she says. The right message, in her view, is that sex is "part of who we are instead of what we do."

Even in an area as polarized as sex education there are some areas of agreement. Everyone seems disturbed by the nation's high teenage pregnancy rate and the possibility that young people are exposing themselves to a fatal disease like AIDS through early, unprotected sexual activity. Experts on both sides of the debate seem to agree that parents can be the most important force in transmitting healthy values about sexuality to their children — even if those values vary somewhat — but that many parents are not doing it.

Michael Carrera[6] of Hunter College has urged his fellow sex education proponents to pare down their expectations about what sex education can hope to achieve within the schools. "Everyone is so frightened by the sexual tragedies that we face in our society that they look for some educational remedy. I'm sorry, but . . . sex education is not it. Mommies and daddies are it."

Unfortunately, the most invidious sex education messages children receive are those that are beamed over the airwaves every day. Television, Carrera says, portrays women as "getting what they want by

---

[6]Michael Carrera is a Hunter College professor who also directs adolescent sexuality programs for the Children's Aid Society in New York City. — ED.

using seduction, not by using their brains" and men as "getting what they want by using force, coercion, money, and power." To prevent such messages from becoming the only sexual reality young people ever know will require an intensive effort on the part of parents, religious leaders, and educators.

Sex Is for Adults

ELLEN HOPKINS

Remember how drunken driving used to be kind of funny? Or if not funny, inevitable, especially for the young. When I was in high school (I'm thirty-five), only losers worried about the alcoholic consumption of the person behind the wheel. Fourteen years later, when my sister made her way through the same suburban high school, designated drivers had become the norm and only losers swerved off into the night.

I was reminded of this remarkable evolution in attitude when I began to explore the idea that teaching abstinence to teenagers need not be the province of right-wing crazies. Could it be that teenage sex is no more inevitable than we once thought teenage drunken driving? Is it possible to make a liberal, feminist argument for pushing abstinence in the schools? I believe it is.

The argument goes like this:

Sex education doesn't work.

There are lots of nice things to be said for sex education. It makes 5 kids more knowledgeable, more tolerant, and maybe even more skillful lovers. But it does not do the one thing we all wish it would: make them more responsible.

In a landmark study of ten exemplary programs published by the Centers for Disease Control in 1984, no evidence was found that knowledge influenced teenagers' behavior significantly. Supporters of sex education point to studies that show that educated teenagers are slightly more likely to use birth control. Opponents point to studies that show they are slightly more likely to have sex at a younger age. No one points to the many studies that compare the pregnancy rates of the educated and the ignorant: depressingly similar.

Even if sex education worked, birth control doesn't.

At least it doesn't work often enough. The Alan Guttmacher Insti-

---

Ellen Hopkins is a contributing editor to *Rolling Stone.* This article appeared in the December 26, 1992 *New York Times.*

tute, a research organization that specializes in reproductive health, estimates that up to 36 percent of women in their early twenties will get pregnant while relying on male use of condoms in the first year; and with the supposedly foolproof pill, up to 18 percent of teenage girls get pregnant in the first year. (The more effective and more expensive contraceptive Norplant is not widely available to young women.) If you project these failure rates a few years ahead, unintended pregnancy begins to look uncomfortably close to an inevitability.

So let's follow one sexually active teenager who does just what she's statistically likely to do. Her options are bleak.

If she wants an abortion, good luck to her if she's poor, under   10
eighteen, or doesn't live near a big city. The simplest abortion costs about $300. Only twelve states have no laws requiring parental consent or notification for minors seeking an abortion. And 83 percent of America's counties don't even have an abortion provider.

What if our teenager chose to have the baby and give it up for adoption? While there's a dearth of solid follow-up research on birth mothers, surrendering the flesh of your flesh is obviously wrenching. Suppose our teenager keeps the baby. She may be ruining her life. Only 50 percent of women who have their first child at seventeen or younger will have graduated from high school by the age of thirty. And many of those who do have merely gotten a General Education Development degree, which is of such dubious worth that the army no longer accepts recruits with it.

Even a ruined life may be better than a life cut short by AIDS.

If condoms — or young condom users — are so unreliable that up to 36 percent of young women get pregnant in a single year of use, what does that say about our teenager's chances of being exposed to HIV as she "protects" herself with a latex sheath?

Our teenager, though, leads a charmed life. Or so she thinks. Even if she doesn't get pregnant and none of her boyfriends is HIV positive, she still puts herself at substantial risk for later infertility.

More than 12 million episodes of sexually transmitted diseases   15
occur each year in the United States, and two-thirds of those afflicted are under twenty-five. Most such diseases can damage the female and male reproductive systems. Infectious-disease experts estimate that after just one episode of pelvic inflammatory disease (a common result of contracting sexually transmitted disease), 35 percent of women become infertile. After three episodes, the odds of becoming infertile soar to more than 75 percent. Many infertility specialists believe that one of the prime causes of today's high infertility rate is that so many baby boomers had sex early and with multiple partners.

Current recommendations for "safer" sex are unrealistic.

Our teenager knows that before going to bed with someone, she and the guy are supposed to exchange detailed sexual histories. Tandem AIDS test are next, and if both can forge a monogamy pact, they will use condoms (and a more reliable form of birth control like the pill) for six months and then get tested again.

Does our teenager hammer out these elaborate social contracts every time Cupid calls? Of course not.

I had always assumed that abstinence lessons were synonymous with Sex Respect, the religious right's curriculum that uses fear to pressure kids to avoid all sexual activity — including necking — until marriage. While supporters claim success, their evaluation techniques are problematic. Plus, imagine those poor kids having to chant silly Sex Respect slogans ("control your urgin', be a virgin" is my favorite).

But studies of a program in Atlanta's public schools suggest that promoting abstinence can be done intelligently and effectively. Eighth graders are taught by peer counselors (popular, reasonably chaste kids from the upper grades — kids who look like they *could* have sex if they wanted it). Their message is simple: Sex is for grown-ups. Weirdly, it works. By the end of eighth grade, girls who weren't in the program were as much as fifteen times more likely to have begun having sex as those who were. 20

While the program in Atlanta is backed up by contraceptive counseling, kids who choose to have sex are erratic birth-control users and just as likely to get pregnant as sexually active kids who aren't in the program.

In other words, sex is for grown-ups. I feel strange writing this. Then I remember my first heady experimentations (at a relatively geriatric age) and contrast them with those of a sixteen-year-old girl who recently visited Planned Parenthood in Westchester county. Three boys were with her, their relationship to her unclear. On the admittance form, the girl wrote that she wasn't in a relationship and had been sexually active for some time. An exam proved her pregnant. Her entire being was joyless.

I once thought I'd tell my young son that anything goes — so long as he used condoms. Now I'm not so sure. Not only do I want my son to live, I don't want him to miss out on longing — longing for what he isn't yet ready to have.

"Guess who's been made condom monitor?"

THINKING AND WRITING ABOUT SEX EDUCATION

Questions for Discussion and Writing

1. The writer Norman Cousins coined the term "cop-out realism" to describe our reluctant acceptance of antisocial behavior that seems difficult or impossible to control. Would this definition apply to the decision to distribute condoms in school? Do any of the writers in this chapter support such an interpretation?

2. In the articles by O'Leary and Hopkins, what are the main issues supporting the argument that sex is for adults only? Do the two authors agree on the issues? Which ones seem most important? (See the article "Equal Rights for Children" in Chapter 12, which argues that children have the right to make their own decisions about sexual practice.)

3. How do the various writers treat parental rights in the sex education debate? Specify the warrants on which the different claims are grounded. What is your own position on the degree to which parents should intervene?

4. Summarize the most important attributes of sex education in Sweden. Would such education be appropriate or possible in the United States?

What cultural influence might spell success or failure for such a program here?

5. One educator in "Sex Education: How Well Does It Work?" says that "it is virtually impossible to teach sex education without discussing values. . . ." Do other writers in this section agree with him? What values are mentioned? Are other values implicit in the arguments?

6. In these articles what support — statistics, factual data, expert opinion, examples — do the authors provide for their conclusions? What kinds of support are most effective? Why? What conflicts of evidence can you find?

7. Do you think the cartoonist objects to all sex education in schools or only some aspects of it? How did you arrive at your interpretation?

Topics for Research

A sex education program in the United States that has worked

Why some sex education courses don't work

The conflict over values in sex education programs

Sex education messages in the media

Reasons for the rise in sexual activity among children

PART FOUR

Classic Arguments

From Crito

PLATO

Plato, who died in 347 B.C., was one of the greatest Greek philosophers. He was a student of the Greek philosopher Socrates, whose teachings he recorded in the form of dialogues between Socrates and his pupils. In the dialogue below, Crito visits Socrates in prison — condemned to death for corrupting the youth of Athens — and tries to persuade him to escape. Socrates, however, refuses, basing his decision on his definition of justice and virtue.

Socrates: . . . Ought a man to do what he admits to be right, or ought he to betray the right?

Crito: He ought to do what he thinks right.

Socrates: But if this is true, what is the application? In leaving the prison against the will of the Athenians, do I wrong any? Or rather do I not wrong those whom I ought least to wrong? Do I not desert the principles which are acknowledged by us to be just — what do you say?

Crito: I cannot tell, Socrates; for I do not know.

Socrates: Then consider the matter in this way: — Imagine that I 5 am about to play truant (you may call the proceeding by any name which you like), and the laws of the government come and interrogate me: "Tell us, Socrates," they say: "what are you about? Are you not going by an act of yours to overturn us — the laws, and the whole state, as far as in you lies? Do you imagine that a state can subsist and not be overthrown, in which the decisions of law have no power, but are set aside and trampled upon by individuals?" What will be our answer, Crito, to these and the like words? Any one, and especially a rhetorician, will have a good deal to say on behalf of the law which requires a sentence to be carried out. He will argue that this law should not be set aside; and shall we reply, "Yes, but the state has injured us and given an unjust sentence." Suppose I say that?

Crito: Very good, Socrates.

Socrates: "And was that our agreement with you?" the law would answer; "or were you to abide by the sentence of the state?" And if I were to express my astonishment at their words, the law would probably add: "Answer, Socrates, instead of opening your eyes — you are in the habit of asking and answering questions. Tell us, — What complaint have you to make against us which justifies you in attempting to destroy us and the state? In the first place did we not bring you into existence? Your father married your mother by our aid and begat you. Say whether you have any objection to urge against those of us who regulate mar-

---

From Plato's *Crito,* translated by Benjamin Jowett (3rd edition, 1982).

riage?" None, I should reply. "Or against those of us who after birth regulate the nurture and education of children, in which you also were trained? Were not the laws, which have the charge of education, right in commanding your father to train you in music and gymnastics?" Right, I should reply. "Well then, since you were brought into the world and nurtured and educated by us, can you deny in the first place that you are our child and slave, as your fathers were before you? And if this is true you are not on equal terms with us; nor can you think that you have a right to do to us what we are doing to you. Would you have any right to strike or revile or do any other evil to your father or your master, if you had one, because you have been struck or reviled by him, or received some other evil at his hands? — you would not say this? And because we think right to destroy you, do you think that you have any right to destroy us in return, and your country as far as in you lies? Will you, O professor of true virtue, pretend that you are justified in this? Has a philosopher like you failed to discover that our country is more to be valued and higher and holier far than mother or father or any ancestor, and more to be regarded in the eyes of the gods and of men of understanding? Also to be soothed, and gently and reverently entreated when angry, even more than a father, and either to be persuaded, or if not persuaded, to be obeyed? And when we are punished by her, whether with imprisonment or stripes, the punishment is to be endured in silence, and if she leads us to wounds or death in battle, thither we follow as is right; neither may any one yield or retreat or leave his rank, but whether in battle or in a court of law, or in any other place, he must do what his city and his country order him; or he must change their view of what is just: and if he may do no violence to his father or mother, much less may he do violence to his country." What answer shall we make to this, Crito? Do the laws speak truly, or do they not?

Crito: I think that they do.

Socrates: Then the laws will say, "Consider, Socrates, if we are speaking truly that in your present attempt you are going to do us an injury. For, having brought you into the world, and nurtured and educated you, and given you and every other citizen a share in every good which we had to give, we further proclaim to any Athenian by the liberty which we allow him, that if he does not like us when he has become of age and has seen the ways of the city, and made our acquaintance, he may go where he pleases and take his goods with him. None of us laws will forbid him or interfere with him. Any one who does not like us and the city, and who wants to emigrate to a colony or to any other city, may go where he likes, retaining his property. But he who has experience of the manner in which we order justice and administer the state, and still remains, has entered into an implied contract that he will do as we command him. And he who disobeys us is, as we maintain, thrice wrong; first, because in disobeying us he is disobeying his parents; secondly, because we are the authors of his education; thirdly, because he has made an agreement with us that he will duly obey our commands; and he neither obeys them nor convinces us that our commands are unjust; and we do not rudely impose them, but give him the alternative of obeying or convincing us; — that is what we offer, and he does neither.

"These are the sort of accusations to which, as we were saying, you, Socrates, will be exposed if you accomplish your intentions; you, above all other Athenians." Suppose now I ask, why I rather than anybody else? They will justly retort upon me that I above all other men have acknowledged the agreement. "There is clear proof," they will say, "Socrates, that we and the city were not displeasing to you. Of all Athenians you have been the most constant resident in the city, which, as you never leave, you may be supposed to love. For you never went out of the city either to see the games, except once when you went to the Isthmus, or to any other place unless when you were on military service; nor did you travel as other men do. Nor had you any curiosity to know other states or their laws: your affections did not go beyond us and our state; we were your special favorites, and you acquiesced in our government of you; and here in this city you begat your children, which is a proof of your satisfaction. Moreover, you might in the course of the trial, if you had liked, have fixed the penalty at banishment; the state which refuses to let you go now would have let you go then. But you pretended that you preferred death to exile, and that you were not unwilling to die. And now you have forgotten these fine sentiments, and pay no respect to us the laws, of whom you are the destroyer; and are doing what only a miserable slave would do, running away and turning your back upon the compacts and agreements which you made as a citizen. And first of all answer this very question: Are we right in saying that you agreed to be governed according to us in deed, and not in word only? Is that true or not?" How shall we answer, Crito? Must we not assent?

Crito: We cannot help it, Socrates.

Socrates: Then will they not say: "You, Socrates, are breaking the covenants and agreements which you made with us at your leisure, not in any haste or under any compulsion or deception, but after you have had seventy years to think of them, during which time you were at liberty to leave the city, if we were not to your mind, or if our covenants appeared to you to be unfair. You had your choice, and might have gone either to Lacedaemon or Crete, both which states are often praised by you for their good government, or to some other Hellenic or foreign state. Whereas you, above all our Athenians, seemed to be so fond of the state, or, in other words, of us her laws (and who would care about a state which has no laws?), that you never stirred out of her; the halt, the blind, the maimed were not more stationary in her than you were. And now you run away and forsake your agreements. Not so, Socrates, if you will take our advice; do not make yourself ridiculous by escaping out of the city.

"For just consider, if you transgress and err in this sort of way, what good will you do either to yourself or to your friends? That your friends will be driven into exile and deprived of citizenship, or will lose their property, is tolerably certain; and you yourself, if you fly to one of the neighboring cities, as, for example, Thebes or Megara, both of which are well governed, will come to them as an enemy, Socrates, and their government will be against you, and all patriotic citizens will cast an evil eye upon you as a subverter of the laws, and you will confirm in the minds of the judges the justice of their own condemnation of you. For he who is a corrupter of the laws is more than likely to be a corrupter of the young and foolish portion of mankind. Will you then flee from well-ordered citizens and virtuous men? and is existence worth having on these terms? Or will you go to them without shame, and talk to them, Socrates? And what will you say to them? What you say here about virtue and justice and institutions and laws being the best things among men? Would that be decent of you? Surely not. But if you go away from well-governed states to Crito's friends in Thessaly, where there is a great disorder and licence, they will be charmed to hear the tale of your escape from prison, set off with ludicrous particulars of the manner in which you were wrapped in a goatskin or some other disguise, and metamorphosed as the manner is of runaways; but will there be no one to remind you that in your old age you were ashamed to violate the most sacred laws from a miserable desire of a little more life? Perhaps not, if you keep them in a good temper; but if they are out of temper you will hear many degrading things; you will live, but how? — as the flatterer of all men, and the servant of all men; and doing what? — eating and drinking in Thessaly, having gone abroad in order that you may get a dinner. And where will be your fine sentiments about justice and virtue? Say that you wish to live for the sake of your children — you want to bring them up and educate them — will you take them into Thessaly and deprive them of Athenian citizenship? Is this the benefit which you will confer upon them? Or are you under the impression that they will be better cared for and educated here if you are still alive, although absent from them; for your friends will take care of them? Do you fancy that if you are an inhabitant of Thessaly they will take care of them, and if you are an inhabitant of the other world that they will not take of them? Nay: but if they who call themselves friends are good for anything, they will — to be sure they will.

"Listen, then, Socrates, to us who have brought you up. Think not of life and children first, and of justice afterwards, but of justice first, that you may be justified before the princes of the world below. For neither will you nor any that belong to you be happier or holier or juster in this life, or happier in another, if you do as Crito bids. Now you depart in innocence, a sufferer and not a doer of evil; a victim, not of the laws of men. But if you go forth, returning evil for evil, and injury for injury, breaking the covenants and agreements which you have made with us, and wronging those whom you ought least of all to wrong, that is to say, yourself, your friends, your country, and us, we shall be angry with you while you live, and our brethren, the laws in the world below, will receive you as an enemy; for they will know that you have done your best to destroy us. Listen, then, to us and not to Crito."

This, dear Crito, is the voice which I seem to hear murmuring in 15 my ears, like the sound of the flute in the ears of the mystic; that voice, I say, is humming in my ears, and prevents me from hearing any other. And I know that anything more which you may say will be vain. Yet speak, if you have anything to say.

Crito: I have nothing to say, Socrates.

Socrates: Leave me then, Crito, to fulfill the will of God, and to follow whither he leads.

Discussion Questions

1. What debt to the law and his country does Socrates acknowledge? Mention the specific reasons for which he owes obedience. Is the analogy of the country to parents a plausible one? Why or why not?
2. Explain the nature of the "implied contract" that exists between Socrates and the state. According to the state, how has Socrates forfeited his right to object to punishment?
3. What appeal does that state make to Socrates' sense of justice and virtue?

Writing Suggestions

1. Socrates bases his refusal to escape the death penalty on his definition of justice and virtue. Basing your own argument on other criteria, make a claim for the right of Socrates to try to escape his punishment. Would some good be served by his escape?
2. The analogy between one's country and one's parents is illustrated at great length in Socrates' argument. In the light of modern ideas about the relationship between the state and the individual in a democracy, write a refutation of the analogy. Perhaps you can think of a different and more fitting one.

To His Coy Mistress

ANDREW MARVELL

Andrew Marvell (1621–1678) was a long-time member of the British Parliament and a writer of political satires. Today, however, he is remembered for two splendid poems, "The Garden" and the one that appears below. "To His Coy Mistress" is a noteworthy expression of an idea familiar in the love poems of many languages — carpe diem in Latin, meaning "seize the day," the idea that life is fleeting and love and other pleasures should be enjoyed while the lovers are still young and beautiful.

Had we but world enough, and time,
This coyness, lady, were no crime.
We would sit down, and think which way
To walk, and pass our long love's day.
Thou by the Indian Ganges' side   5
Should'st rubies find; I by the tide
Of Humber¹ would complain. I would
Love you ten years before the Flood;
And you should, if you please, refuse
Till the conversion of the Jews.   10
My vegetable love should grow
Vaster than empires, and more slow.
An hundred years should go to praise
Thine eyes, and on thy forehead gaze;
Two hundred to adore each breast;   15
But thirty thousand to the rest:
An age at least to every part,
And the last age should show your heart.
For, lady, you deserve this state,
Nor would I love at lower rate.   20
But at my back I always hear
Time's winged chariot hurrying near;
And yonder all before us lie
Deserts of vast eternity.
Thy beauty shall no more be found,   25
Nor in thy marble vault shall sound
My echoing song; then worms shall try
That long-preserved virginity;
And your quaint honor turn to dust,
And into ashes all my lust.   30

---

¹An estuary in England. — ED.

The grave's a fine and private place,
But none, I think, do there embrace.
Now, therefore, while the youthful hue
Sits on thy skin like morning dew,
And while thy willing soul transpires   35
At every pore with instant fires,
Now let us sport us while we may;
And now, like amorous birds of prey,
Rather at once our time devour,
Than languish in his slow-chapped² power.   40
Let us roll all our strength and all
Our sweetness up into one ball;
And tear our pleasures with rough strife
Thorough the iron gates of life.
Thus, though we cannot make our sun   45
Stand still, yet we will make him run.

Discussion Questions

1. One critic notes that "To His Coy Mistress" is an argument in the form of a poem, which can be outlined as a syllogism. What are the major and minor premises and the conclusion?
2. What witty images in the first half of the poem suggest "world enough, and time" for love?
3. There is a change in the tone of the lover's exhortation in the middle of the poem. At what point does it occur? What words and images convey a different mood?
4. Why is the "*carpe diem*" sentiment more likely to have been taken seriously in earlier times?

Writing Suggestions

1. Address a letter or an essay to Marvell, wherever he is, telling him how some circumstances surrounding love among the young have changed since he wrote his poem more than 300 years ago.
2. Look at some other poems that express the "*carpe diem*" idea — for example, Robert Herrick's "To the Virgins to Make Much of Time," Omar Khayyám's "The Rubáiyát," works by Catullus, a Latin Poet — and write a paper analyzing their concerns (what do they most wish to enjoy while they are young?) and their acceptance of or resistance to the end of youth and pleasure.

---

²Slow-jawed. — ED.

A Modest Proposal

JONATHAN SWIFT

*This essay is acknowledged by almost all critics to be the most powerful
example of irony in the English language. (Irony means saying one thing
but meaning another.) In 1729 Jonathan Swift, prolific satirist and dean of
St. Patrick's Cathedral in Dublin, was moved to write in protest against
the terrible poverty in which the Irish were forced to live under British
rule. Notice that the essay is organized according to one of the patterns
outlined in Part Two of this book (see "Presenting the Stock Issues,"
p. 259). First, Swift establishes the need for a change, then he offers his
proposal, and finally, he lists its advantages.*

It is a melancholy object to those who walk through this great
town[1] or travel in the country, when they see the streets, the roads,
and cabin doors, crowded with beggars of the female sex, followed by
three, four, or six children, all in rags and importuning every passenger
for an alms. These mothers, instead of being able to work for their
honest livelihood, are forced to employ all their time in strolling to beg
sustenance for their helpless infants, who, as they grow up, either turn
thieves for want of work, or leave their dear native country to fight for
the Pretender in Spain, or sell themselves to the Barbados.[2]

I think it is agreed by all parties that this prodigious number of
children in the arms, or on the backs, or at the heels of their mothers,
and frequently of their fathers, is in the present deplorable state of the
kingdom a very great additional grievance; and therefore whoever could
find out a fair, cheap, and easy method of making these children sound,
useful members of the commonwealth would deserve so well of the
public as to have his statue set up for a preserver of the nation.

But my intention is very far from being confined to provide only
for the children of professed beggars; it is of a much greater extent,
and shall take in the whole number of infants at a certain age who are
born of parents in effect as little able to support them as those who
demand our charity in the streets.

As to my own part, having turned my thoughts for many years upon
this important subject, and maturely weighed the several schemes of
other projectors,[3] I have always found them grossly mistaken in their

---

From *A Tale of a Tub and Other Stories,* edited by Kathleen Williams (1975).

[1] Dublin. — ED.

[2] The Pretender was James Stuart, who was exiled to Spain. Many Irishmen had
joined an army attempting to return him to the English throne in 1715. Others had
become indentured servants, agreeing to work for a set number of years in Barbados or
other British colonies in exchange for their transportation out of Ireland. — ED.

[3] Planners. — ED.

computation. It is true, a child just dropped from its dam may be supported by her milk for a solar year, with little other nourishment; at most not above the value of two shillings, which the mother may certainly get, or the value in scraps, by her lawful occupation of begging; and it is exactly at one year that I propose to provide for them in such a manner as instead of being a charge upon their parents or the parish, or wanting food and raiment for the rest of their lives, they shall on the contrary contribute to the feeding, and partly to the clothing, of many thousands.

There is likewise another great advantage in my scheme, that it will prevent those voluntary abortions, and that horrid practice of women murdering their bastard children, alas, too frequent among us, sacrificing the poor innocent babes, I doubt, more to avoid the expense than the shame, which would move tears and pity in the most savage and inhuman breast.

The number of souls in this kingdom being usually reckoned one million and a half, of these I calculate there may be about two hundred thousand couples whose wives are breeders; from which number I subtract thirty thousand couples who are able to maintain their own children, although I apprehend there cannot be so many under the present distress of the kingdom; but this being granted, there will remain an hundred and seventy thousand breeders. I again subtract fifty thousand for those women who miscarry, or whose children die by accident or disease within the year. There only remain an hundred and twenty thousand children of poor parents annually born. The question therefore is, how this number shall be reared and provided for, which, as I have already said, under the present situation of affairs, is utterly impossible by all the methods hitherto proposed. For we can neither employ them in handicraft or agriculture; we neither build houses (I mean in the country) nor cultivate land. They can very seldom pick up a livelihood by stealing till they arrive at six years old, except where they are of towardly parts[4]; although I confess they learn the rudiments much earlier, during which time they can however be looked upon only as probationers, as I have been informed by a principal gentleman in the county of Cavan, who protested to me that he never knew above one or two instances under the age of six, even in a part of the kingdom so renowned for the quickest proficiency in that art.

I am assured by our merchants that a boy or a girl before twelve years old is no salable commodity; and even when they come to this age they will not yield above three pounds, or three pounds and a half a crown at most on the Exchange; which cannot turn to account either to the parents or the kingdom, the charge of nutriment and rags having been at least four times that value.

---

[4] Innate talents. — ED.

I shall now therefore humbly propose my own thoughts, which I hope will not be liable to the least objection.

I have been assured by a very knowing American of my acquaintance in London, that a young healthy child well nursed is at a year old a most delicious, nourishing, and wholesome food, whether stewed, roasted, baked, or boiled; and I make no doubt that it will equally serve in a fricassee or a ragout.[5]

I do therefore humbly offer it to public consideration that of the hundred and twenty thousand children, already computed, twenty thousand may be reserved for breed, whereof only one fourth part to be males, which is more than we allow to sheep, black cattle, or swine; and my reason is that these children are seldom the fruits of marriage, a circumstance not much regarded by our savages, therefore one male will be sufficient to serve four females. That the remaining hundred thousand may at a year old be offered in sale to the persons of quality and fortune through the kingdom, always advising the mother to let them suck plentifully in the last month, so as to render them plump and fat for a good table. A child will make two dishes at an entertainment for friends; and when the family dines alone, the fore or hind quarter will make a reasonable dish, and seasoned with a little pepper or salt will be very good boiled on the fourth day, especially in winter.

I have reckoned upon a medium that a child just born will weigh twelve pounds, and in a solar year if tolerably nursed increaseth to twenty-eight pounds.

I grant this food will be somewhat dear, and therefore very proper for landlords, who, as they have already devoured most of the parents, seem to have the best title to the children.

Infant's flesh will be in season throughout the year, but more plentiful in March, and a little before and after. For we are told by a grave author, an eminent French physician,[6] that fish being a prolific diet, there are more children born in Roman Catholic countries about nine months after Lent than at any other season; therefore, reckoning a year after Lent, the markets will be more glutted than usual, because the number of popish infants is at least three to one in this kingdom; and therefore it will have one other collateral advantage, by lessening the number of Papists among us.

I have already computed the charge of nursing a beggar's child (in which list I reckon all cottagers, laborers, and four-fifths of the farmers) to be about two shillings per annum, rags included; and I believe no gentleman would repine to give ten shillings for the carcass of a good fat child, which, as I have said, will make four dishes of excellent nutritive meat, when he hath only some particular friend or his own

---

[5] Stew. — ED.

[6] A reference to Swift's favorite French writer, François Rabelais (1494?–1553), who was actually a broad satirist known for his coarse humor. — ED.

family to dine with him. Thus the squire will learn to be a good landlord, and grow popular among the tenants; the mother will have eight shillings net profit, and be fit for work till she produces another child.

Those who are more thrifty (as I must confess the times require) may flay the carcass; the skin of which artificially[7] dressed will make admirable gloves for ladies, and summer boots for fine gentlemen. 15

As to our city of Dublin, shambles[8] may be appointed for this purpose in the most convenient parts of it, and butchers we may be assured will not be wanting; although I rather recommend buying the children alive, and dressing them hot from the knife as we do roasting pigs.

A very worthy person, a true lover of his country, and whose virtues I highly esteem, was lately pleased in discoursing on this matter to offer a refinement upon my scheme. He said that many gentlemen of his kingdom, having of late destroyed their deer, he conceived that the want of venison might be well supplied by the bodies of young lads and maidens, not exceeding fourteen years of age nor under twelve, so great a number of both sexes in every county being now ready to starve for want of work and service; and these to be disposed of by their parents, if alive, or otherwise by their nearest relations. But with due deference to so excellent a friend and so deserving a patriot, I cannot be altogether in his sentiments; for as to the males, my American acquaintance assured me from frequent experience that their flesh was generally tough and lean, like that of our schoolboys, by continual exercise, and their taste disagreeable; and to fatten them would not answer the charge. Then as to the females, it would, I think with humble submission, be a loss to the public, because they soon would become breeders themselves; and besides, it is not improbable that some scrupulous people might be apt to censure such a practice (although indeed very unjustly) as a little bordering upon cruelty; which, I confess, hath always been with me the strongest objection against any project, how well soever intended.

But in order to justify my friend, he confessed that this expedient was put into his head by the famous Psalmanazar,[9] a native of the island Formosa, who came from thence to London above twenty years ago, and in conversation told my friend that in his country when any young person happened to be put to death, the executioner sold the carcass to persons of quality as a prime dainty; and that in his time the body of a plump girl of fifteen, who was crucified for an attempt to poison the emperor, was sold to his Imperial Majesty's prime minister of state,

---

[7]With art or craft. — ED.

[8]Butcher shops or slaughterhouses. — ED.

[9]Georges Psalmanazar was a Frenchman who pretended to be Japanese and wrote an entirely imaginary *Description of the Isle Formosa*. He had become well known in gullible London society. — ED.

and other great mandarins of the court, in joints from the gibbet, at four hundred crowns. Neither indeed can I deny that if the same use were made of several plump young girls in this town, who without one single groat to their fortunes cannot stir abroad without a chair, and appear at the playhouse and assemblies in foreign fineries which they never will pay for, the kingdom would not be the worse.

Some persons of a desponding spirit are in great concern about that vast number of poor people who are aged, diseased, or maimed, and I have been desired to employ my thoughts what course may be taken to ease the nation of so grievous an encumbrance. But I am not in the least pain upon that matter, because it is very well known that they are every day dying and rotting by cold and famine, and filth and vermin, as fast as can be reasonably expected. And as to the younger laborers, they are now in almost as hopeful a condition. They cannot get work, and consequently pine away for want of nourishment to a degree that if any time they are accidentally hired to common labor, they have not strength to perform it; and thus the country and themselves are happily delivered from the evils to come.

I have too long digressed, and therefore shall return to my subject. 20 I think the advantages by the proposal which I have made are obvious and many, as well as of the highest importance.

For first, as I have already observed, it would greatly lessen the number of Papists, with whom we are yearly overrun, being the principal breeders of the nation as well as our most dangerous enemies; and who stay at home on purpose to deliver the kingdom to the Pretender, hoping to take their advantage by the absence of so many good Protestants, who have chosen rather to leave their country than to stay at home and pay tithes against their conscience to an Episcopal curate.

Secondly, the poorer tenants will have something valuable of their own, which by law may be made liable to distress,[10] and help to pay their landlord's rent, their corn and cattle being already seized and money a thing unknown.

Thirdly, whereas the maintenance of an hundred thousand children, from two years old and upwards, cannot be computed at less than ten shillings a piece per annum, the nation's stock will be thereby increased fifty thousand pounds per annum, besides the profit of a new dish introduced to the tables of all gentlemen of fortune in the kingdom who have any refinement in taste. And the money will circulate among ourselves, the goods being entirely of our own growth and manufacture.

Fourthly, the constant breeders, besides the gain of eight shillings sterling per annum by the sale of their children, will be rid of the charge of maintaining them after the first year.

Fifthly, this food would likewise bring great custom to taverns, 25 where the vintners will certainly be so prudent as to procure the best

---

[10] Subject to possession by lenders. — ED.

receipts for dressing it to perfection, and consequently have their houses frequented by all the fine gentlemen, who justly value themselves upon their knowledge in good eating; and a skillful cook, who understands how to oblige his guests, will contrive to make it as expensive as they please.

Sixthly, this would be a great inducement to marriage, which all wise nations have either encouraged by rewards or enforced by laws and penalties. It would increase the care and tenderness of mothers toward their children, when they were sure of a settlement for life to the poor babes, provided in some sort by the public, to their annual profit instead of expense. We should see an honest emulation among the married women, which of them could bring the fattest child to the market. Men would become as fond of their wives during the time of their pregnancy as they are now of their mares in foal, their cows in calf, or sows when they are ready to farrow; nor offer to beat or kick them (as is too frequent a practice) for fear of a miscarriage.

Many other advantages might be enumerated. For instance, the addition of some thousand carcasses in our exportation of barreled beef, the propagation of swine's flesh, and improvements in the art of making good bacon, so much wanted among us by the great destruction of pigs, too frequent at our tables, which are no way comparable in taste or magnificence to a well-grown, fat, yearling child, which roasted whole will make a considerable figure at a lord mayor's feast or any other public entertainment. But his and many others I omit, being studious of brevity.

Supposing that one thousand families in this city would be constant customers for infants' flesh, besides others who might have it at merry meetings, particularly weddings and christenings, I compute that Dublin would take off annually about twenty thousand carcasses, and the rest of the kingdom (where probably they will be sold somewhat cheaper) the remaining eighty thousand.

I can think of no one objection that will possibly be raised against this proposal, unless it should be urged that the number of people will be thereby much lessened in the kingdom. This I freely own, and it was indeed one principal design in offering it to the world. I desire the reader will observe, that I calculate my remedy for this one individual kingdom of Ireland and for no other that ever was, is, or I think ever can be upon earth. Therefore let no man talk to me of other expedients: of taxing our absentees at five shillings a pound: of using neither clothes nor household furniture except what is of our own growth and manufacture: of utterly rejecting the materials and instruments that promote foreign luxury: of curing the expensiveness of pride, vanity, idleness, and gaming in our women: of introducing a vein of parsimony, prudence, and temperance: of learning to love our country, in the want of which we differ even from Laplanders and the inhabitants of Topinamboo:[11]

---

[11] District of Brazil inhabited by primitive natives. — ED.

of quitting our animosities and factions, nor acting any longer like the Jews, who were murdering one another at the very moment their city was taken:[12] of being a little cautious not to sell our country and conscience for nothing: of teaching landlords to have at least one degree of mercy toward their tenants: lastly, of putting a spirit of honesty, industry, and skill into our shopkeepers; who, if a resolution could now be taken to buy only our native goods, would immediately unite to cheat and exact upon us in the price, the measure, and the goodness, nor could ever yet be brought to make one fair proposal of just dealing, though often and earnestly invited to it.

Therefore I repeat, let no man talk to me of these and the like 30 expedients, till he hath at least some glimpse of hope that there will ever be some hearty and sincere attempt to put them in practice.

But as to myself, having been wearied out for many years with offering vain, idle, visionary thoughts, and at length utterly despairing of success, I fortunately fell upon this proposal, which, as it is wholly new, so it hath something solid and real, of no expense and little trouble, full in our own power, and whereby we can incur no danger in disobliging England. For this kind of commodity will not bear exportation, the flesh being of too tender a consistence to admit a long continuance in salt, although perhaps I could name a country which would be glad to eat up our whole nation without it.

After all, I am not so violently bent upon my own opinion as to reject any offer proposed by wise men, which shall be found equally innocent, cheap, easy, and effectual. But before something of that kind shall be advanced in contradiction to my scheme, and offering a better, I desire the author or authors will be pleased maturely to consider two points. First, as things now stand, how they will be able to find food and raiment for an hundred thousand useless mouths and backs. And secondly, there being a round million of creatures in human figure throughout this kingdom, whose sole subsistence put into a common stock would leave them in debt two millions of pounds sterling, adding those who are beggars by profession to the bulk of farmers, cottagers, and laborers, with their wives and children who are beggars in effect; I desire those politicians who dislike my overture, and may perhaps be so bold to attempt an answer, that they will first ask the parents of these mortals whether they would not at this day think it a great happiness to have been sold for food at a year old in this manner I prescribe, and thereby have avoided such a perpetual scene of misfortunes as they have since gone through by the oppression of landlords, the impossibility of paying rent without money or trade, the want of common sustenance, with neither house nor clothes to cover them

---

[12]During the Roman siege of Jerusalem (A.D. 70), prominent Jews were charged with collaborating with the enemy and put to death. — ED.

from the inclemencies of the weather, and the most inevitable prospect of entailing the like of greater miseries upon their breed forever.

I profess, in the sincerity of my heart, that I have not the least personal interest in endeavoring to promote this necessary work, having no other motive than the public good of my country, by advancing our trade, providing for infants, relieving the poor, and giving some pleasure to the rich. I have no children by which I can propose to get a single penny; the youngest being nine years old, and my wife past childbearing.

Discussion Questions

1. What implicit assumption about the treatment of the Irish underlies Swift's proposal? Do expressions such as "just dropped from its dam" and "whose wives are breeders" give the reader a clue?
2. In this essay Swift assumes a persona; that is, for the purposes of the proposal he makes, he pretends to be a different person. Describe the characteristics of that person. Point out the places in the essay that reveal them.
3. In several places, however, Swift reveals himself as the outraged witness of English cruelty and indifference. Note the language that seems to reflect his own feelings.
4. Throughout the essay Swift recites lists of facts, many of them in the form of statistics. How do these facts contribute to the persuasiveness of his argument? How do they affect the reader?
5. What social practices and attitudes of both the Irish and the English does Swift condemn?
6. Does Swift offer any solutions for the problems he attacks? How do you know?
7. When this essay first appeared in 1729, some readers took it seriously and accused Swift of monstrous cruelty. Can you think of reasons why these readers failed to recognize the ironic intent?

Writing Suggestions

1. Try an ironical essay of your own. Choose a subject that clearly lends itself to such treatment. As Swift did, use logic and restraint in your language.
2. Choose a problem for which you think you have a solution. Defend your solution by using the stock issues as your pattern of organization.

An End to Blind Obedience

MARY WOLLSTONECRAFT

*Mary Wollstonecraft (1759–1797) was an Anglo-Irish writer who in her life
and writing anticipated the nineteenth-century women's movement. As a
publisher's assistant, she became acquainted with several eminent radical
writers and thinkers of her day, including Thomas Paine and William
Blake. She earned a reputation as an original and courageous thinker
with the publication of* A Vindication of the Rights of Women *in 1792.
The excerpt that follows, with a new title, is from the second chapter of
that work.*

To account for, and excuse the tyranny of man, many ingenious
arguments have been brought forward to prove, that the two sexes, in
the acquirement of virtue, ought to aim at attaining a very different
character: or, to speak explicitly, women are not allowed to have sufficient strength of mind to acquire what really deserves the name of
virtue. Yet it should seem, allowing them to have souls, that there is
but one way appointed by Providence to lead *mankind* to either virtue
or happiness.

If then women are not a swarm of ephemeron triflers, why should
they be kept in ignorance under the specious name of innocence? Men
complain, and with reason, of the follies and caprices of our sex, when
they do not keenly satirize our headstrong passions and groveling
vices. — Behold, I should answer, the natural effect of ignorance! The
mind will ever be unstable that has only prejudices to rest on, and the
current will run with destructive fury when there are no barriers to
break its force. Women are told from their infancy, and taught by the
example of their mothers, that a little knowledge of human weakness,
justly termed cunning, softness of temper, *outward* obedience, and a
scrupulous attention to a puerile kind of propriety, will obtain for them
the protection of man; and should they be beautiful, every thing else is
needless, for, at least, twenty years of their lives.

Thus Milton describes our first frail mother; though when he tells
us that women are formed for softness and sweet attractive grace, I
cannot comprehend his meaning, unless, in the true Mahometan strain,
he meant to deprive us of souls, and insinuate that we were beings only
designed by sweet attractive grace, and docile blind obedience, to
gratify the senses of man when he can no longer soar on the wing of
contemplation.

How grossly do they insult us who thus advise us only to render
ourselves gentle, domestic brutes! For instance, the winning softness
so warmly, and frequently, recommended, that governs by obeying.
What childish expressions, and how insignificant is the being — can it

be an immortal one? who will condescend to govern by such sinister methods! 'Certainly,' says Lord Bacon, 'man is of kin to the beasts by his body; and if he be not of kin to God by his spirit, he is a base and ignoble creature!' Men, indeed, appear to me to act in a very unphilosophical manner when they try to secure the good conduct of women by attempting to keep them always in a state of childhood. Rousseau was more consistent when he wished to stop the progress of reason in both sexes, for if men eat of the tree of knowledge, women will come in for a taste; but, from the imperfect cultivation which their understanding now receive, they only attain a knowledge of evil.

Children, I grant, should be innocent; but when the epithet is applied 5 to men, or women, it is but a civil term for weakness. For if it be allowed that women were destined by Providence to acquire human virtues, and by the exercise of their understandings, that stability of character which is the firmest ground to rest our future hopes upon, they must be permitted to turn to the fountain of light, and not forced to shape their course by the twinkling of a mere satellite. Milton, I grant, was of a very different opinion; for he only bends to the indefeasible right of beauty, though it would be difficult to render two passages which I now mean to contrast, consistent. But into similar inconsistencies are great men often led by their senses.

> To whom thus Eve with *perfect beauty* adorn'd.
> My Author and Disposer, what thou bidst
> *Unargued* I obey; So God ordains;
> God is *thy law, thou mine:* to know no more
> Is Woman's *happiest* knowledge and her *praise.*

These are exactly the arguments that I have used to children; but I have added, your reason is now gaining strength, and, till it arrives at some degree of maturity, you must look up to me for advice — then you ought to *think,* and only rely on God.

Yet in the following lines Milton seems to coincide with me; when he makes Adam thus expostulate with his Maker.

> Hast thou not made me here thy substitute,
> And these inferior far beneath me set?
> Among *unequals* what society
> Can sort, what harmony or true delight?
> Which must be mutual, in proportion due
> Giv'n and receiv'd; but in *disparity*
> The one intense, the other still remiss
> Cannot well suit with either, but soon prove
> Tedious alike: of *fellowship* I speak
> Such as I seek, fit to participate
> All rational delight —

In treating, therefore, of the manners of women, let us, disregarding sensual arguments, trace what we should endeavour to make them in order to co-operate, if the expression be not too bold, with the supreme Being.

By individual education, I mean, for the sense of the word is not precisely defined, such an attention to a child as will slowly sharpen the senses, form the temper, regulate the passions as they begin to ferment, and set the understanding to work before the body arrives at maturity; so that the man may only have to proceed, not to begin, the important task of learning to think and reason.

To prevent any misconstruction, I must add, that I do not believe   10
that a private education can work the wonders which some sanguine writers have attributed to it. Men and women must be educated, in a great degree, by the opinions and manners of the society they live in. In every age there has been a stream of popular opinion that has carried all before it, and given a family character, as it were, to the century. It may then fairly be inferred, that, till society be differently constituted, much cannot be expected from education. It is, however, sufficient for my present purpose to assert, that, whatever effect circumstances have on the abilities, every being may become virtuous by the exercise of its own reason; for if but one being was created with vicious inclinations, that is positively bad, what can save us from atheism? or if we worship a God, is not that God a devil?

Consequently, the most perfect education, in my opinion, is such an exercise of the understanding as is best calculated to strengthen the body and form the heart. Or, in other words, to enable the individual to attain such habits of virtue as will render it independent. In fact, it is a farce to call any being virtuous whose virtues do not result from the exercise of its own reason. This was Rousseau's opinion respecting men: I extend it to women, and confidently assert that they have been drawn out of their sphere by false refinement, and not by an endeavour to acquire masculine qualities. Still the regal homage which they receive is so intoxicating, that till the manners of the times are changed, and formed on more reasonable principles, it may be impossible to convince them that the illegitimate power, which they obtain, by degrading themselves, is a curse, and that they must return to nature and equality, if they wish to secure the placid satisfaction that unsophisticated affections impart. But for this epoch we must wait — wait, perhaps, till kings and nobles, enlightened by reason, and, preferring the real dignity of man to childish state, throw off their gaudy hereditary trappings: and if then women do not resign the arbitrary power of beauty — they will prove that they have *less* mind than man. . . .

Many are the causes that, in the present corrupt state of society, contribute to enslave women by cramping their understandings and sharpening their senses. One, perhaps, that silently does more mischief than all the rest, is their disregard of order.

To do every thing in an orderly manner, is a most important precept, which women, who, generally speaking, receive only a disorderly kind of education, seldom attend to with that degree of exactness that men, who from their infancy are broken into method, observe. This negligent kind of guess-work, for what other epithet can be used to point out the random exertions of a sort of instinctive common sense, never brought to the test of reason? prevents their generalizing matters of fact — so they do to-day, what they did yesterday, merely because they did it yesterday.

This contempt of the understanding in early life has more baneful consequences than is commonly supposed; for the little knowledge which women of strong minds attain, is, from various circumstances, of a more desultory kind than the knowledge of men, and it is acquired more by sheer observations on real life, than from comparing what has been individually observed with the results of experience generalized by speculation. Led by their dependent situation and domestic employ-ments more into society, what they learn is rather by snatches; and as learning is with them, in general, only a secondary thing, they do not pursue any one branch with that persevering ardour necessary to give vigour to the faculties, and clearness to the judgment. In the present state of society, a little learning is required to support the character of a gentleman; and boys are obliged to submit to a few years of discipline. But in the education of women, the cultivation of the understanding is always subordinate to the acquirement of some corporeal accomplish-ment; even while enervated by confinement and false notions of mod-esty, the body is prevented from attaining that grace and beauty which relaxed half-formed limbs never exhibit. Besides, in youth their faculties are not brought forward by emulation; and having no serious scientific study, if they have natural sagacity it is turned too soon on life and manners. They dwell on effects, and modifications, without tracing them back to causes; and complicated rules to adjust behaviour are a weak substitute for simple principles.

As a proof that education gives this appearance of weakness to   15 females, we may instance the example of military men, who are, like them, sent into the world before their minds have been stored with knowledge or fortified by principles. The consequences are similar; soldiers acquire a little superficial knowledge, snatched from the muddy current of conversation, and, from continually mixing with society, they gain, what is termed a knowledge of the world; and this acquaintance with manners and customs has frequently been confounded with a knowledge of the human heart. But can the crude fruit of casual obser-vation, never brought to the test of judgment, formed by comparing speculation and experience, deserve such a distinction? Soldiers, as well as women, practice the minor virtues with punctilious politeness. Where is then the sexual difference, when the education has been the same? All the difference that I can discern, arises from the superior advantage of liberty, which enables the former to see more of life.

It is wandering from my present subject, perhaps, to make a political remark; but, as it was produced naturally by the train of my reflections, I shall not pass it silently over.

Standing armies can never consist of resolute, robust men; they may be well disciplined machines, but they will seldom contain men under the influence of strong passions, or with very vigorous faculties. And as for any depth of understanding, I will venture to affirm, that it is as rarely to be found in the army as amongst women; and the cause, I maintain, is the same. It may be further observed, that officers are also particularly attentive to their persons, fond of dancing, crowded rooms, adventures, and ridicule. Like the *fair* sex, the business of their lives is gallantry. — They were taught to please, and they only live to please. Yet they do not lose their rank in the distinction of sexes, for they are still reckoned superior to women, though in what their superiority consists, beyond what I have just mentioned, it is difficult to discover.

The great misfortune is this, that they both acquire manners before morals, and a knowledge of life before they have, from reflection, any acquaintance with the grand ideal outline of human nature. The consequence is natural; satisfied with common nature, they become a prey to prejudices, and taking all their opinions on credit, they blindly submit to authority. So that, if they have any sense, it is a kind of instinctive glance, that catches proportions, and decides with respect to manners; but fails when arguments are to be pursued below the surface, or opinions analyzed.

May not the same remark be applied to women? Nay, the argument may be carried still further, for they are both thrown out of a useful station by the unnatural distinctions established in civilized life. Riches and hereditary honours have made cyphers of women to give consequence to the numerical figure; and idleness has produced a mixture of gallantry and despotism into society, which leads the very men who are the slaves of their mistresses to tyrannize over their sisters, wives, and daughters. This is only keeping them in rank and file, it is true. Strengthen the female mind by enlarging it, and there will be an end to blind obedience; but, as blind obedience is ever sought for by power, tyrants, and sensualists are in the right when they endeavor to keep women in the dark, because the former only want slaves, and the latter a play-thing. The sensualist, indeed, has been the most dangerous of tyrants, and women have been duped by their lovers, as princes by their ministers, whilst dreaming that they reigned over them.

Discussion Questions

1. What lessons in behavior are women taught in infancy, according to Wollstonecraft? Why are these lessons unsatisfactory? Are they detrimental only to women?
2. What is her criticism of the education of women? What should be the purpose of the education that Wollstonecraft wants women to receive? In

what respects are women and soldiers alike? Would such an analogy be valid today?

3. What qualities does Wollstonecraft value in both men and women? What qualities does she condemn? Some of these qualities are made explicit, but others must be inferred from her general discussion.

Writing Suggestions

1. Do you think that the lessons in behavior learned by women in the eighteenth century persist today in any form? Be specific in your references both to Wollstonecraft's list and to the examples of changes or lack of changes today.

2. Wollstonecraft, who has been called an early feminist, devoted most of her efforts to demands for a sound education for women. (She wrote an earlier treatise on this subject entitled "Thoughts on the Education of Daughters.") Feminists today express many other concerns. Select some of the problems that receive most public attention, and comment on their importance to women and the whole society. Are other problems receiving too little attention?

Civil Disobedience

HENRY DAVID THOREAU

*Henry David Thoreau (1817–1862), philosopher and writer, is best known
for* Walden, *an account of his solitary retreat to Walden Pond, near Concord, Massachusetts. Here he remained for more than two years in an
effort to "live deliberately, to front only the essential facts of life." "Civil
Disobedience" was first given as a lecture in 1848 and published in 1849.
It was widely read and influenced both Mahatma Gandhi in the passive-
resistance campaign he led against the British in India and Martin Luther
King, Jr., in the civil-rights movement.*

I heartily accept the motto, — "That government is best which governs least"; and I should like to see it acted up to more rapidly and
systematically. Carried out, it finally amounts to this, which also I
believe, — "That government is best which governs not at all"; and when
men are prepared for it, that will be the kind of government which they
will have. Government is at best but an expedient; but most governments are usually, and all governments are sometimes, inexpedient.
The objections which have been brought against a standing army, and
they are many and weighty, and deserve to prevail, may also at
last be brought against a standing government. The standing army is
only an arm of the standing government. The government itself,
which is only the mode which the people have chosen to execute their
will, is equally liable to be abused and perverted before the people
can act through it. Witness the present Mexican war, the work of
comparatively a few individuals using the standing government as
their tool; for, in the outset, the people would not have consented
to this measure.

This American government, — what is it but a tradition, though a
recent one, endeavoring to transmit itself unimpaired to posterity, but
each instant losing some of its integrity? It has not the vitality and force
of a single living man; for a single man can bend it to his will. It is a
sort of wooden gun to the people themselves. But it is not the less
necessary for this; for the people must have some complicated machinery or other, and hear its din, to satisfy that idea of government
which they have. Governments show thus how successfully men can
be imposed on, even impose on themselves, for their own advantage.
It is excellent, we must all allow. Yet this government never of itself
furthered any enterprise, but by the alacrity with which it got out of its
way. *It* does not keep the country free. *It* does not settle the West. *It*
does not educate. The character inherent in the American people has
done all that has been accomplished; and it would have done somewhat

more, if the government had not sometimes got in its way. For government is an expedient by which men would fain succeed in letting one another alone; and, as has been said, when it is most expedient, the governed are most let alone by it. Trade and commerce, if they were not made of India-rubber, would never manage to bounce over the obstacles which legislators are continually putting in their way; and, if one were to judge these men wholly by the effects of their actions, and not partly by their intentions, they would deserve to be classed and punished with those mischievous persons who put obstructions on the railroads.

But, to speak practically and as a citizen, unlike those who call themselves no-government men, I ask for, not at once no government, but *at once* a better government. Let every man make known what kind of government would command his respect, and that will be one step toward obtaining it.

After all, the practical reason why, when the power is once in the hands of the people, a majority are permitted, and for a long period continue, to rule, is not because they are most likely to be in the right, nor because this seems fairest to the minority, but because they are physically the strongest. But a government in which the majority rule in all cases cannot be based on justice, even as far as men understand it. Can there not be a government in which majorities do not virtually decide right and wrong, but conscience? — in which majorities decide only those questions to which the rule of expediency is applicable? Must the citizen ever for a moment, or in the least degree, resign his conscience to the legislator? Why has every man a conscience, then? I think that we should be men first, and subjects afterward. It is not desirable to cultivate a respect for the law, so much as for the right. The only obligation which I have a right to assume, is to do at any time what I think right. It is truly enough said, that a corporation has no conscience; but a corporation of conscientious men is a corporation *with* a conscience. Law never made men a whit more just; and, by means of their respect for it, even the well-disposed are daily made the agents of injustice. A common and natural result of an undue respect for law is, that you may see a file of soldiers, colonel, captain, corporal, privates, powder-monkeys, and all, marching in admirable order over hill and dale to the wars, against their wills, aye, against their common sense and consciences, which makes it very steep marching indeed, and produces a palpitation of the heart. They have no doubt that it is a damnable business in which they are concerned; they are all peaceably inclined. Now, what are they? Men at all? or small moveable forts and magazines, at the service of some unscrupulous man in power? Visit the Navy-Yard, and behold a marine, such a man as an American government can make, or such as it can make a man with its black arts, — a mere shadow and reminiscence of humanity, a man laid out alive and standing, and already, as one may say, buried under arms with funeral accompaniments, though it may be, —

> Not a drum was heard, nor a funeral note,
> As his corse to the rampart we hurried;
> Not a soldier discharged his farewell shot
> O'er the grave where our hero we buried.

The mass of men serve the state thus, not as men mainly, but as machines, with their bodies. They are the standing army, and the militia, jailers, constables, posse comitatus, &c. In most cases there is no free exercise whatever of the judgment or of the moral sense; but they put themselves on a level with wood and earth and stones; and wooden men can perhaps be manufactured that will serve the purpose as well. Such command no more respect than men of straw, or a lump of dirt. They have the same sort of worth only as horses and dogs. Yet such as these even are commonly esteemed good citizens. Others, — as most legislators, politicians, lawyers, ministers, and office-holders, — serve the State chiefly with their heads; and, as they rarely make any moral distinctions, they are as likely to serve the Devil, without *intending* it, as God. A very few, as heroes, patriots, martyrs, reformers in the great sense, and *men,* serve the state with their consciences also, and so necessarily resist it for the most part, and they are commonly treated as enemies by it. A wise man will only be useful as a man, and will not submit to be "clay," and "stop a hole to keep the wind away," but leave that office to his dust at least: —

> I am too high-born to be propertied,
> To be a secondary at control,
> Or useful serving-man and instrument
> To any sovereign state throughout the world.

He who gives himself entirely to his fellow-men appears to them useless and selfish; but he who gives himself partially to them is pronounced a benefactor and philanthropist.

How does it become a man to behave toward this American government today? I answer that he cannot without disgrace be associated with it. I cannot for an instant recognize that political organization as *my* government which is the *slave's* government also.

All men recognize the right of revolution; that is, the right to refuse allegiance to, and to resist, the government, when its tyranny or its inefficiency are great and unendurable. But almost all say that such is not the case now. But such was the case, they think, in the Revolution of '75. If one were to tell me that this was a bad government because it taxed certain foreign commodities brought to its ports, it is most probable that I should not make an ado about it, for I can do without them. All machines have their friction; and possibly this does enough good to counterbalance the evil. At any rate, it is a great evil to make a stir about it. But when the friction comes to have its machine, and oppression and robbery are organized, I say, let us not have such a machine any longer. In other words, when a sixth of the population of a nation which has undertaken to be the refuge of liberty are slaves, and a whole country is unjustly overrun and conquered by a foreign army, and subjected to military law, I think that it is not too soon for honest men to rebel and revolutionize. What makes this duty the more urgent is the fact, that the country so overrun is not our own, but ours is the invading army.

Paley, a common authority with many on moral questions, in his chapter on the "Duty of Submission to Civil Government," resolves all civil obligation into expediency; and he proceeds to say, "that so long as the interest of the whole society requires it, that is, so long as the established government cannot be resisted or changed without public inconveniency, it is the will of God that the established government be obeyed, and no longer. . . . This principle being admitted, the justice of every particular case of resistance is reduced to a computation of the quantity of the danger and grievance on the one side, and of the probability and expense of redressing it on the other." Of this, he says, every man shall judge for himself. But Paley appears never to have contemplated those cases to which the rule of expediency does not apply, in which a people, as well as an individual, must do justice, cost what it may. If I have unjustly wrested a plank from a drowning man, I must restore it to him though I drown myself. This, according to Paley, would be inconvenient. But he that would save his life, in such a case, shall lose it. This people must cease to hold slaves, and to make war on Mexico, though it cost them their existence as a people.

In their practice, nations agree with Paley; but does any one think 10 that Massachusetts does exactly what is right at the present crisis?

> A drab of state, a cloth-'o-silver slut,
> To have her train borne up, and her soul trail in the dirt.

Practically speaking, the opponents to a reform in Massachusetts are not a hundred thousand politicians at the South, but a hundred thousand merchants and farmers here, who are more interested in commerce and agriculture than they are in humanity, and are not prepared to do justice to the slave and to Mexico, *cost what it may.* I quarrel not with far-off foes, but with those who, near at home, cooperate with, and do the bidding of, those far away, and without whom the latter would be harmless. We are accustomed to say, that the mass of men are unprepared; but improvement is slow, because the few are not materially wiser or better than the many. It is not so important that many should be as good as you, as that there be some absolute goodness somewhere; for that will leaven the whole lump. There are thousands who are *in opinion* opposed to slavery and to the war, who yet in effect do nothing to put an end to them; who, esteeming themselves children of Washington and Franklin, sit down with their hands in their pockets, and say that they know not what to do, and do nothing; who even postpone the question of freedom to the question of free-trade, and quietly read the prices-current along with the latest advice from Mexico, after dinner, and, it may be, fall asleep over them both. What is the price-current of an honest man and patriot today? They hesitate, and they regret, and sometimes they petition; but they do nothing in earnest and with effect. They will wait, well disposed, for others to remedy the evil, that they may no longer have it to regret. At most, they give only a cheap vote, and a feeble countenance and God-speed, to the right, as it goes by them. There are nine hundred and ninety-nine patrons of virtue to one virtuous man; but it is easier to deal with the real possessor of a thing than with the temporary guardian of it.

All voting is a sort of gaming, like checkers or backgammon, with a slight moral tinge to it, a playing with right and wrong, with moral questions; and betting naturally accompanies it. The character of the voters is not staked. I cast my vote, perchance, as I think right; but I am not vitally concerned that that right should prevail. I am willing to leave it to the majority. Its obligation, therefore, never exceeds that of expediency. Even voting *for the right* is *doing* nothing for it. It is only expressing to men feebly your desire that it should prevail. A wise man will not leave the right to the mercy of chance, nor wish it to prevail through the power of the majority. There is but little virtue in the action of masses of men. When the majority shall at length vote for the abolition of slavery, it will be because they are indifferent to slavery, or because there is but little slavery left to be abolished by their vote. *They* will then be the only slaves. Only *his* vote can hasten the abolition of slavery who asserts his own freedom by his vote.

I hear of a convention to be held at Baltimore, or elsewhere, for the selection of a candidate for the presidency, made up chiefly of editors, and men who are politicians by profession; but I think, what is it to any independent, intelligent, and respectable man what decision they may come to? Shall we not have the advantage of his wisdom and honesty, nevertheless? Can we not count upon some independent votes? Are there not many individuals in the country who do not attend conventions? But no: I find that the respectable man, so called, has immediately drifted from his position, and despairs of his country, when his country has more reason to despair of him. He forthwith adopts one of the candidates thus selected as the only *available* one, thus providing that he is himself *available* for any purposes of the demagogue. His vote is of no more worth than that of any unprincipled foreigner or hireling native, who may have been bought. O for a man who is *a man*, and, as my neighbor says, has a bone in his back which you cannot pass your hand through! Our statistics are at fault: The population has been returned too large. How many *men* are there to a square thousand miles in this country? Hardly one. Does not America offer any inducement for men to settle here? The American has dwindled into an Odd Fellow, — one who may be known by the development of his organ of gregariousness, and a manifest lack of intellect and cheerful self-reliance; whose first and chief concern, on coming into the world, is to see that the Almshouses are in good repair; and, before yet he has lawfully donned the virile garb, to collect a fund for the support of the widows and orphans that may be; who, in short, ventures to live only by the aid of the Mutual Insurance company, which has promised to bury him decently.

It is not a man's duty, as a matter of course, to devote himself to the eradication of any, even the most enormous wrong; he may still properly have other concerns to engage him; but it is his duty, at least, to wash his hands of it, and, if he gives it no thought longer, not to give it practically his support. If I devote myself to other pursuits and contemplations, I must first see, at least, that I do not pursue them sitting upon another man's shoulders. I must get off him first, that he may pursue his contemplations too. See what gross inconsistency is tolerated. I have heard some of my townsmen say, "I should like to have them order me out to help put down an insurrection of the slaves, or to march to Mexico; — see if I would go"; and yet these very men have each, directly by their allegiance, and so indirectly, at least, by their money, furnished a substitute. The soldier is applauded who refuses to serve in an unjust war by those who do not refuse to sustain the unjust government which makes the war; is applauded by those whose own act and authority he disregards and sets at nought; as if the State were penitent to that degree that it hired one to scourge it while it sinned, but not to that degree that it left off sinning for a moment. Thus, under the name of Order and Civil Government, we are all made at last to pay homage to and support our own meanness. After the first blush of sin, comes its indifference; and from immoral it becomes, as it were, *un*moral, and not quite unnecessary to that life which we have made.

The broadest and most prevalent error requires the most disinterested virtue to sustain it. The slight reproach to which the virtue of patriotism is commonly liable, the noble are most likely to incur. Those who, while they disapprove of the character and measures of a government, yield to it their allegiance and support, are undoubtedly its most conscientious supporters, and so frequently the most serious obstacles to reform. Some are petitioning the State to dissolve the Union, to disregard the requisitions of the President. Why do they not dissolve it themselves, — the union between themselves and the State, — and refuse to pay their quota into its treasury? Do not they stand in the same relation to the State, that the State does to the Union? And have not the same reasons prevented the State from resisting the Union which have prevented them from resisting the State?

How can a man be satisfied to entertain an opinion merely, and 15 enjoy *it*? Is there any enjoyment in it, if his opinion is that he is aggrieved? If you are cheated out of a single dollar by your neighbor, you do not rest satisfied with knowing that you are cheated, or with saying that you are cheated, or even with petitioning him to pay you your due; but you take effectual steps at once to obtain the full amount, and see that you are never cheated again. Action from principle, the perception and the performance of right, changes things and relations; it is essentially revolutionary, and does not consist wholly with anything which was. It not only divides states and churches, it divides families; ay, it divides the *individual,* separating the diabolical in him from the divine.

Unjust laws exist: Shall we be content to obey them, or shall we endeavor to amend them, and obey them until we have succeeded, or shall we transgress them at once? Men generally, under such a government as this, think that they ought to wait until they have persuaded the majority to alter them. They think that, if they should resist, the remedy would be worse than the evil. But it is the fault of the government itself that the remedy *is* worse than the evil. *It* makes it worse. Why is it not more apt to anticipate and provide for reform? Why does it not cherish its wise minority? Why does it cry and resist before it is hurt? Why does it not encourage its citizens to be on the alert to point out its faults, and *do* better than it would have them? Why does it always crucify Christ, and excommunicate Copernicus and Luther, and pronounce Washington and Franklin rebels?

One would think, that a deliberate and practical denial of its authority was the only offence never contemplated by government; else, why has it not assigned its definite, its suitable and proportionate penalty? If a man who has no property refuses but once to earn nine shillings for the State, he is put in prison for a period unlimited by any law that I know, and determined only by the discretion of those who placed him there; but if he should steal ninety times nine shillings from the State, he is soon permitted to go at large again.

If the injustice is part of the necessary friction of the machine of government, let it go, let it go: Perchance it will wear smooth, — certainly the machine will wear out. If the injustice has a spring, or a pulley, or a rope, or a crank, exclusively for itself, then perhaps you may consider whether the remedy will not be worse than the evil; but if it is of such a nature that it requires you to be the agent of injustice to another, then, I say, break the law. Let your life be a counter friction to stop the machine. What I have to do is to see, at any rate, that I do not lend myself to the wrong which I condemn.

As for adopting the ways which the State has provided for remedying the evil, I know not of such ways. They take too much time, and a man's life will be gone. I have other affairs to attend to. I came into this world, not chiefly to make this a good place to live in, but to live in it, be it good or bad. A man has not everything to do, but something; and because he cannot do *everything,* it is not necessary that he should do *something* wrong. It is not my business to be petitioning the Governor or the Legislature any more than it is theirs to petition me; and, if they should not hear my petition, what should I do then? But in this case the State has provided no way: Its very Constitution is the evil. This may seem to be harsh and stubborn and unconciliatory; but it is to treat with the utmost kindness and consideration the only spirit that can appreciate or deserves it. So is all change for the better, like birth and death, which convulse the body.

I do not hesitate to say, that those who call themselves Abolitionists 20 should at once effectually withdraw their support, both in person and property, from the government of Massachusetts, and not wait till they constitute a majority of one, before they suffer the right to prevail through them. I think that it is enough if they have God on their side, without waiting for that other one. Moreover, any man more right than his neighbors, constitutes a majority of one already.

I meet this American government, or its representative, the State government, directly, and face to face, once a year — no more — in the person of its tax-gatherer; this is the only mode in which a man situated as I am necessarily meets it; and it then says distinctly, Recognize me; and the simplest, the most effectual, and, in the present posture of affairs, the indispensablest mode of treating with it on this head, of expressing your little satisfaction with and love for it, is to deny it then. My civil neighbor, the tax-gatherer, is the very man I have to deal with, — for it is, after all, with men and not with parchment that I quarrel, — and he has voluntarily chosen to be an agent of the government. How shall he ever know well what he is and does as an officer of the government, or as a man, until he is obliged to consider whether he shall treat me, his neighbor, for whom he has respect, as a neighbor and well-disposed man, or as a maniac and disturber of the peace, and see if he can get over this obstruction to his neighborliness without a ruder and more impetuous thought or speech corresponding with his action? I know this well, that if one thousand, if one hundred, if ten men whom I could name, — if ten *honest* men only, — aye, if *one* HONEST man, in this State of Massachusetts, *ceasing to hold slaves,* were actually to withdraw from this copartnership, and be locked up in the county jail therefor, it would be the abolition of slavery in America. For it matters not how small the beginning may seem to be: What is once well done is done forever. But we love better to talk about it: That we say is our mission. Reform keeps many scores of newspapers in its service, but not one man. If my esteemed neighbor, the State's ambassador, who will devote his days to the settlement of the question of human rights in the Council Chamber, instead of being threatened with the prisons of Carolina, were to sit down the prisoner of Massachusetts, that State which is so anxious to foist the sin of slavery upon her sister, — though at present she can discover only an act of inhospitality to be the ground of a quarrel with her, — the Legislature would not wholly waive the subject the following winter.

Under a government which imprisons any unjustly, the true place for a just man is also a prison. The proper place today, the only place which Massachusetts has provided for her freer and less desponding spirits, is in her prisons, to be put out and locked out of the State by her own act, as they have already put themselves out by their principles. It is there that the fugitive slave, and the Mexican prisoner on parole, and the Indian come to plead the wrongs of his race, should find them; on that separate, but more free and honorable ground, where the State places those who are not *with* her, but *against* her, — the only house in a slave State in which a free man can abide with honor. If any think that their influence would be lost there, and their voices no longer afflict the ear of the State, that they would not be as an enemy within its walls, they do not know by how much truth is stronger than error, nor how much more eloquently and effectively he can combat injustice who has experienced a little in his own person. Cast your whole vote, not a strip of paper merely, but your whole influence. A minority is powerless while it conforms to the majority; it is not even a minority then; but it is irresistible when it clogs by its whole weight. If the alternative is to keep all just men in prison, or give up war and slavery, the State will not hesitate which to choose. If a thousand men were not to pay their tax-bills this year, that would not be a violent and bloody measure, as it would be to pay them, and enable the State to commit violence and shed innocent blood. This is, in fact, the definition of a peaceable revolution, if any such is possible. If the tax-gatherer, or any other public officer, asks me, as one has done, "But what shall I do?" my answer is, "If you really wish to do any thing, resign your office." When the subject has refused allegiance, and the officer has resigned his office, then the revolution is accomplished. But even suppose blood should flow. Is there not a sort of blood shed when the conscience is wounded? Through this wound a man's real manhood and immortality flow out, and he bleeds to an everlasting death. I see this blood flowing now.

I have contemplated the imprisonment of the offender, rather than the seizure of his goods, — though both will serve the same purpose, — because they who assert the purest right, and consequently are most dangerous to a corrupt State, commonly have not spent much time in accumulating property. To such the State renders comparatively small service, and a slight tax is wont to appear exorbitant, particularly if they are obliged to earn it by special labor with their hands. If there were one who lived wholly without the use of money, the State itself would hesitate to demand it of him. But the rich man, — not to make any invidious comparison, — is always sold to the institution which makes him rich. Absolutely speaking, the more money, the less virtue; for money comes between a man and his objects, and obtains them for him; and it was certainly no great virtue to obtain it. It puts to rest many questions which he would otherwise be taxed to answer; while the only new question which it puts is the hard but superfluous one, how to spend it. Thus his moral ground is taken from under his feet. The opportunities of living are diminished in proportion as what are called the "means" are increased. The best thing a man can do for his culture when he is rich is to endeavor to carry out those schemes which he entertained when he was poor. Christ answered the Herodians according to their condition. "Show me the tribute-money," said he; — and one took a penny out of his pocket; — if you use money which has the image of Cæsar on it, and which he has made current and valuable, that is, *if you are men of the State,* and gladly enjoy the advantages of Cæsar's government, then pay him back some of his own when he demands it; "Render therefore to Cæsar that which is Cæsar's, and to God those things which are God's," — leaving them no wiser than before as to which was which; for they did not wish to know.

When I converse with the freest of my neighbors, I perceive that, whatever they may say about the magnitude and seriousness of the question, and their regard for the public tranquility, the long and the short of the matter is, that they cannot spare the protection of the existing government, and they dread the consequences to their property and families of disobedience to it. For my own part, I should not like to think that I ever rely on the protection of the State. But, if I deny the authority of the State when it presents its tax-bill, it will soon take and waste all my property, and so harass me and my children without end. This is hard. This makes it impossible for a man to live honestly, and at the same time comfortably, in outward respects. It will not be worth the while to accumulate property; that would be sure to go again. You must hire or squat somewhere, and raise but a small crop, and eat that soon. You must live within yourself, and depend upon yourself always tucked up and ready for a start, and not have many affairs. A man may grow rich in Turkey even, if he will be in all respects a good subject of the Turkish government. Confucius said: "If a state is governed by the principles of reason, poverty and misery are subjects of shame; if a state is not governed by the principles of reason, riches and honors are the subjects of shame." No: Until I want the protection of Massachusetts to be extended to me in some distant southern port, where my liberty is endangered, or until I am bent solely on building up an estate at home by peaceful enterprise, I can afford to refuse allegiance to Massachusetts, and her right to my property and life. It costs me less in every sense to incur the penalty of disobedience to the State, than it would to obey. I should feel as if I were worth less in that case.

Some years ago, the State met me in behalf of the Church, and 25 commanded me to pay a certain sum toward the support of a clergyman whose preaching my father attended, but never I myself. "Pay," it said, "or be locked up in the jail." I declined to pay. But, unfortunately, another man saw fit to pay it. I did not see why the schoolmaster should be taxed to support the priest, and not the priest the schoolmaster; for

I was not the State's schoolmaster, but I supported myself by voluntary subscription. I did not see why the lyceum should not present its tax-bill, and have the State to back its demand, as well as the Church. However, at the request of the selectmen, I condescended to make some such statement as this in writing: — "Know all men by these presents, that I, Henry Thoreau, do not wish to be regarded as a member of any incorporated society which I have not joined." This I gave to the town clerk; and he has it. The State, having thus learned that I did not wish to be regarded as a member of that church, has never made a like demand on me since; though it said that it must adhere to its original presumption that time. If I had known how to name them, I should then have signed off in detail from all the societies which I never signed on to; but I did not know where to find a complete list.

I have paid no poll-tax for six years. I was put into a jail once on this account, for one night; and, as I stood considering the walls of solid stone, two or three feet thick, the door of wood and iron, a foot thick, and the iron grating which strained the light, I could not help being struck with the foolishness of that institution which treated me as if I were mere flesh and blood and bones, to be locked up. I wondered that it should have concluded at length that this was the best use it could put me to, and had never thought to avail itself of my services in some way. I saw that, if there was a wall of stone between me and my townsmen, there was a still more difficult one to climb or break through, before they could get to be as free as I was. I did not for a moment feel confined, and the walls seemed a great waste of stone and mortar. I felt as if I alone of all my townsmen had paid my tax. They plainly did not know how to treat me, but behaved like persons who are underbred. In every threat and in every compliment there was a blunder; for they thought that my chief desire was to stand the other side of that stone wall. I could not but smile to see how industriously they locked the door on my meditations, which followed them out again without let or hinderance, and *they* were really all that was dangerous. As they could not reach me, they had resolved to punish my body; just as boys, if they cannot come at some person against whom they have a spite, will abuse his dog. I saw that the State was half-witted, and it was timid as a lone woman with her silver spoons, and that it did not know its friends from its foes, and I lost all my remaining respect for it, and pitied it.

Thus the State never intentionally confronts a man's sense, intellectual or moral, but only his body, his senses. It is not armed with superior wit or honesty, but with superior physical strength. I was not born to be forced. I will breathe after my own fashion. Let us see who is the strongest. What force has a multitude? They only can force me who obey a higher law than I. They force me to become like themselves. I do not hear of *men* being *forced* to live this way or that by masses of men. What sort of life were that to live? When I meet a government which says to me, "Your money or your life," why should I be in haste to give it my money? It may be in a great strait, and not know what to do: I cannot help that. It must help itself; do as I do. It is not worth the while to snivel about it. I am not responsible for the successful working of the machinery of society. I am not the son of the engineer. I perceive that, when an acorn and a chestnut fall side by side, the one does not remain inert to make way for the other, but both obey their own laws, and spring and grow and flourish as best they can, till one, perchance, overshadows and destroys the other. If a plant cannot live according to its nature, it dies; and so a man.

The night in prison was novel and interesting enough. The prisoners in their shirt-sleeves were enjoying a chat and the evening air in the doorway, when I entered. But the jailer said, "Come, boys, it is time to lock up"; and so they dispersed, and I heard the sound of their steps returning into the hollow apartments. My roommate was introduced to me by the jailer, as "a first-rate fellow and a clever man." When the door was locked, he showed me where to hang my hat, and how he managed matters there. The rooms were white-washed once a month; and this one, at least, was the whitest, most simply furnished, and probably the neatest apartment in the town. He naturally wanted to know where I came from, and what brought me there; and, when I had told him, I asked him in my turn how he came there, presuming him to be an honest man, of course; and, as the world goes, I believe he was. "Why," said he, "they accuse me of burning a barn; but I never did it." As near as I could discover, he had probably gone to bed in a barn when drunk, and smoked his pipe there; and so a barn was burnt. He had the reputation of being a clever man, had been there some three months waiting for his trial to come on, and would have to wait as much longer; but he was quite domesticated and contented, since he got his board for nothing, and thought that he was well-treated.

He occupied one window, and I the other; and I saw, that if one stayed there long, his principal business would be to look out the window. I had soon read all the tracts that were left there, and examined where former prisoners had broken out, and where a grate had been sawed off, and heard the history of the various occupants of that room; for I found that even here there was a history and a gossip which never circulated beyond the walls of the jail. Probably this is the only house in the town where verses are composed, which are afterward printed in a circular form, but not published. I was shown quite a long list of verses which were composed by some young men who had been detected in an attempt to escape, who avenged themselves by singing them.

I pumped my fellow-prisoner as dry as I could, for fear I should 30 never see him again; but at length he showed me which was my bed, and left me to blow out the lamp.

It was like travelling into a far country, such as I had never expected to behold, to lie there for one night. It seemed to me that I never had heard the town-clock strike before, nor the evening sounds of the village; for we slept with the windows open, which were inside the grating. It was to see my native village in the light of the Middle Ages, and our Concord was turned into a Rhine stream, and visions of knights and castles passed before me. They were the voices of old burghers that I heard in the streets. I was an involuntary spectator and auditor of whatever was done and said in the kitchen of the adjacent village-inn, — a wholly new and rare experience to me. It was a closer view of my native town. I was fairly inside of it. I never had seen its institutions before. This is one of its peculiar institutions; for it is a shire town. I began to comprehend what its inhabitants were about.

In the morning, our breakfasts were put through the hole in the door, in small oblong-square tin pans, made to fit, and holding a pint of chocolate, with brown bread, and an iron spoon. When they called for the vessels again, I was green enough to return what bread I had left; but my comrade seized it, and said that I should lay that up for lunch or dinner. Soon after, he was let out to work at haying in a neighboring field, whither he went every day, and would not be back till noon; so he bade me good-day, saying that he doubted if he should see me again.

When I came out of prison, — for some one interfered, and paid that tax, — I did not perceive that great changes had taken place on the common, such as he observed who went in a youth, and emerged a tottering and gray-headed man; and yet a change had to my eyes come over the scene, — the town, and State, and country, — greater than any that mere time could effect. I saw yet more distinctly the State in which I lived. I saw to what extent the people among whom I lived could be trusted as good neighbors and friends; that their friendship was for summer weather only; that they did not greatly propose to do right; that they were a distinct race from me by their prejudices and superstitions, as the Chinamen and Malays are; that, in their sacrifices to humanity, they ran no risks, not even to their property; that, after all, they were not so noble but they treated the thief as he had treated them, and hoped, by a certain outward observance and a few prayers, and by walking in a particular straight though useless path from time to time, to save their souls. This may be to judge my neighbors harshly; for I believe that many of them are not aware that they have such an institution as the jail in their village.

It was formerly the custom in our village, when a poor debtor came out of jail, for his acquaintances to salute him, looking through their fingers, which were crossed to represent the grating of a jail window, "How do ye do?" My neighbors did not thus salute me, but first looked at me, and then at one another, as if I had returned from a long journey. I was put into jail as I was going to the shoemaker's to get a shoe which was mended. When I was let out the next morning, I proceeded to finish my errand, and having put on my mended shoe, joined a huckleberry party, who were impatient to put themselves under my conduct; and in half an hour, — for the horse was soon tackled, — was in the midst of a huckleberry field, on one of our highest hills, two miles off, and then the State was nowhere to be seen.

This is the whole story of "My Prisons." 35

I have never declined paying the highway tax, because I am as desirous of being a good neighbor as I am of being a bad subject; and, as for supporting schools, I am doing my part to educate my fellow-countrymen now. It is for no particular item in the tax-bill that I refuse to pay it. I simply wish to refuse allegiance to the State, to withdraw and stand aloof from it effectually. I do not care to trace the course of my dollar, if I could, till it buys a man, or a musket to shoot one with, — the dollar is innocent, — but I am concerned to trace the effects of my allegiance. In fact, I quietly declare war with the State, after my fashion, though I will still make what use and get what advantage of her I can, as is usual in such cases.

If others pay the tax which is demanded of me, from a sympathy with the State, they do but what they have already done in their own case, or rather they abet injustice to a greater extent than the State requires. If they pay the tax from a mistaken interest in the individual taxed, to save his property or prevent his going to jail, it is because they have not considered wisely how far they let their private feelings interfere with the public good.

This, then, is my position at present. But one cannot be too much on his guard in such a case, lest his action be biased by obstinacy, or an undue regard for the opinions of men. Let him see that he does only what belongs to himself and to the hour.

I think sometimes, Why, this people mean well; they are only ignorant; they would do better if they knew how: why give your neighbors this pain to treat you as they are inclined to? But I think again, this is no reason why I should do as they do, or permit others to suffer much greater pain of a different kind. Again, I sometimes say to myself, When many millions of men, without heat, without ill will, without personal feelings of any kind, demand of you a few shillings only, without the possibility, such is their constitution, of retracing or altering their present demand, and without the possibility, on your side, of appeal to any other millions, why expose yourself to this overwhelming brute force? You do not resist cold and hunger, the winds and the waves, thus obstinately; you quietly submit to a thousand similar necessities. You do not put your head into the fire. But just in proportion as I regard this as not wholly a brute force, partly a human force, and consider that I have relations to those millions as to so many millions of men, and not of mere brute or inanimate things, I see that appeal is possible, first and instantaneously, from them to the Maker of them, and, secondly, from them to themselves. But, if I put my head deliberately into the fire, there is no appeal to fire or to the Maker of fire, and I have only myself to blame. If I could convince myself that I have any right to be satisfied with men as they are, and to treat them according, and not according, in some respects, to my requisitions and expectations of what they and I ought to be, then, like a good Mussulman and fatalist, I should endeavor to be satisfied with things as they are, and say it is the will of God. And, above all, there is this difference between resisting this and a purely brute or natural force, that I can resist this with some effect; but I cannot expect, like Orpheus, to change the nature of the rocks and trees and beasts.

I do not wish to quarrel with any man or nation. I do not wish to   40
split hairs, to make fine distinctions, or set myself up as better than my neighbors. I seek rather, I may say, even an excuse for conforming to the laws of the land. I am but too ready to conform to them. Indeed, I have reason to suspect myself on this head; and each year, as the tax-gatherer comes round, I find myself disposed to review the acts and position of the general and State governments, and the spirit of the people, to discover a pretext for conformity.

> We must affect our country as our parents;
> And if at any time we alienate
> Our love or industry from doing it honor,
> We must respect effects and teach the soul
> Matter of conscience and religion,
> And not desire of rule or benefit.

I believe that the State will soon be able to take all my work of this sort out of my hands, and then I shall be no better a patriot than my fellow-countrymen. Seen from a lower point of view, the Constitution, with all its faults, is very good; the law and the courts are very respect-able; even this State and this American government are, in many re-spects, very admirable and rare things, to be thankful for, such as a great many have described them; but seen from a point of view a little higher, they are what I have described them; seen from a higher still, and the highest, who shall say what they are, or that they are worth looking at or thinking of at all?

However, the government does not concern me much, and I shall bestow the fewest possible thoughts on it. It is not many moments that I live under a government, even in this world. If a man is thought-free, fancy-free, imagination-free, that which *is not* never for a long time appearing *to be* to him, unwise rulers or reformers cannot fatally inter-rupt him.

I know that most men think differently from myself; but those whose lives are by profession devoted to the study of these or kindred subjects, content me as little as any. Statesmen and legislators, standing so completely within the institution, never distinctly and nakedly behold it. They speak of moving society, but have no resting-place without it. They may be men of a certain experience and discrimination, and have no doubt invented ingenious and even useful systems, for which we sincerely thank them; but all their wit and usefulness lie within certain not very wide limits. They are wont to forget that the world is not governed by policy and expediency. Webster never goes behind government, and so cannot speak with authority about it. His words are wisdom to those legislators who contemplate no essential reform in the existing government; but for thinkers, and those who legislate for all time, he never once glances at the subject. I know of those whose serene and wise speculations on this theme would soon reveal the limits of his mind's range and hospitality. Yet, compared with the cheap professions of most reformers, and the still cheaper wisdom and eloquence of politicians in general, his are almost the only sensible and valuable words, and we thank Heaven for him. Comparatively, he is always strong, original, and, above all, practical. Still his quality is not wisdom, but prudence. The lawyer's truth is not Truth, but consistency, or a consistent expediency. Truth is always in harmony with herself, and is not concerned chiefly to reveal the justice that may consist with wrong-doing. He well deserves to be called, as he has been called, the Defender of the Constitution. There are really no blows to be given by him but defensive ones. He is not a leader, but a follower. His leaders are the men of '87. "I have never made an effort," he says, "and never propose to make an effort; I have never countenanced an effort, and never mean to countenance an effort, to disturb the arrangement as originally made, by which the various States came into the Union." Still thinking of the sanction which the Constitution gives to slavery, he says, "Because it was a part of the original compact, — let it stand." Notwithstanding his special acuteness and ability, he is unable to take a fact out of its merely political relations, and behold it as it lies absolutely to be disposed of by the intellect, — what, for instance, it behooves a man to do here in America today with regard to slavery, but ventures, or is driven, to make some such desperate answer as the following, while professing to speak absolutely, and as a private man, — from which what new and singular code of social duties might be inferred? "The manner," says he, "in which the governments of those States where slavery exists are to regulate it, is for their own consideration, under their responsibility to their constituents, to the general laws of propriety, humanity, and justice, and to God. Associations formed elsewhere, springing from a feeling of humanity, or any other cause, have nothing whatever to do with it. They have never received any encouragement from me, and they never will."[1]

They who know of no purer sources of truth, who have traced up

---

[1] These extracts have been inserted since the Lecture was read.

its stream no higher, stand, and wisely stand, by the Bible and the Constitution, and drink at it there with reverence and humility; but they who behold where it comes trickling into this lake or that pool, gird up their loins once more, and continue their pilgrimage toward its fountain-head.

No man with a genius for legislation has appeared in America. They are rare in the history of the world. There are orators, politicians, and eloquent men, by the thousand; but the speaker has not yet opened his mouth to speak, who is capable of settling the much-vexed questions of the day. We love eloquence for its own sake, and not for any truth which it may utter, or any heroism it may inspire. Our legislators have not yet learned the comparative value of free-trade and of freedom, of union, and of rectitude, to a nation. They have no genius or talent for comparatively humble questions of taxation and finance, commerce and manufactures and agriculture. If we were left solely to the wordy wit of legislators in Congress for our guidance, uncorrected by the seasonable experience and the effectual complaints of the people, America would not long retain her rank among the nations. For eighteen hundred years, though perchance I have no right to say it, the New Testament has been written; yet where is the legislator who has wisdom and practical talent enough to avail himself of the light which it sheds on the science of legislation?

The authority of government, even such as I am willing to submit 45 to, — for I will cheerfully obey those who know and can do better than I, and in many things even those who neither know nor can do so well, — is still an impure one: To be strictly just, it must have the sanction and consent of the governed. It can have no pure right over my person and property but what I concede to it. The progress from an absolute to a limited monarchy, from a limited monarchy to a democracy, is a progress toward a true respect for the individual. Even the Chinese philosopher was wise enough to regard the individual as the basis of the empire. Is a democracy, such as we know it, the last improvement possible in government? Is it not possible to take a step further towards recognizing and organizing the rights of man? There will never be a really free and enlightened State, until the State comes to recognize the individual as a higher and independent power, from which all its own power and authority are derived, and treats him accordingly. I please myself with imagining a State at last which can afford to be just to all men, and to treat the individual with respect as a neighbor; which even would not think it inconsistent with its own repose, if a few were to live aloof from it, not meddling with it, nor embraced by it, who fulfilled all the duties of neighbors and fellowmen. A State which bore this kind of fruit, and suffered it to drop off as fast as it ripened, would prepare the way for a still more perfect and glorious State, which also I have imagined, but not yet anywhere seen.

Discussion Questions

1. Summarize briefly Thoreau's reasons for arguing that civil disobedience is sometimes a *duty*.
2. Thoreau, like Martin Luther King, Jr., in "Letter from Birmingham Jail" (p. 663), speaks of "unjust laws." Do they agree on the positions that citizens should take in response to these laws? Are Thoreau and King guided by the same principles? In Plato's "Crito" (p. 607), what does Socrates say about obedience to unjust laws?
3. What examples of government policy and action does Thoreau use to prove that civil disobedience is a duty? Explain why they are — or are not — effective.
4. Why do you think Thoreau provides such a detailed account of one day in prison? (Notice that King does not give a description of his confinement.) What observation about the community struck Thoreau when he emerged from jail?

Writing Suggestions

1. Choose a government policy or law with which you are familiar, and argue that civil disobedience to it is justified. (Examples might include the Vietnam War, the draft, dangers to the environment, a university regulation.) Be specific about the injustice of the law or policy and the values that underlie the resistance.
2. Under what circumstances might civil disobedience prove to be dangerous and immoral? Can you think of cases of disobediences when *conscience*, as Thoreau uses the term, did not appear to be the guiding principle? Try to identify what you think is the true motivation for the resistance.

Professions for Women

VIRGINIA WOOLF

*Virginia Woolf (1882–1941) was a novelist and essayist and a leading
member of the Bloomsbury group, a celebrated circle of writers, artists,
and intellectuals that flourished in London in the early part of the century.
Her novels, among them* Mrs. Dalloway, To the Lighthouse, *and* The
Waves, *were brilliant technical experiments. Her essays and literary criticism were highly original, distinguished by wit and spontaneity. All her
life she suffered from nervous depression, and in 1941 she committed
suicide. "Professions for Women" was a paper read to the Women's Service League in London in 1931.*

When your secretary invited me to come here, she told me that
your Society is concerned with the employment of women and she
suggested that I might tell you something about my own professional
experiences. It is true I am a woman; it is true I am employed; but what
professional experiences have I had? It is difficult to say. My profession
is literature; and in that profession there are fewer experiences for
women than in any other, with the exception of the stage — fewer, I
mean, that are peculiar to women. For the road was cut many years
ago — by Fanney Burney, by Aphra Behn, by Harriet Martineau, by Jane
Austen, by George Eliot — many famous women, and many more unknown and forgotten, have been before me, making the path smooth,
and regulating my steps. Thus, when I came to write, there were very
few material obstacles in my way. Writing was a reputable and harmless
occupation. The family peace was not broken by the scratching of a
pen. No demand was made upon the family purse. For ten and sixpence
one can buy paper enough to write all the plays of Shakespeare — if
one has a mind that way. Pianos and models, Paris, Vienna and Berlin,
masters and mistresses, are not needed by a writer. The cheapness of
writing paper is, of course, the reason why women have succeeded as
writers before they have succeeded in the other professions.

But to tell you my story — it is a simple one. You have only got to
figure to yourselves a girl in a bedroom with a pen in her hand. She
had only to move that pen from left to right — from ten o'clock to one.
Then it occurred to her to do what is simple and cheap enough after
all — to slip a few of those pages into an envelope, fix a penny stamp
in the corner, and drop the envelope into the red box at the corner. It
was thus that I became a journalist; and my effort was rewarded on the
first day of the following month — a very glorious day it was for me —
by a letter from an editor containing a check for one pound ten shillings

---

From *The Death of the Moth and Other Essays* (1942).

and sixpence. But to show you how little I deserve to be called a professional woman, how little I know of the struggles and difficulties of such lives, I have to admit that instead of spending that sum upon bread and butter, rent, shoes, and stockings, or butcher's bills, I went out and bought a cat — a beautiful cat, a Persian cat, which very soon involved me in bitter disputes with my neighbors.

What could be easier than to write articles and to buy Persian cats with the profits? But wait a moment. Articles have to be about something. Mine, I seem to remember, was about a novel by a famous man. And while I was writing this review, I discovered that if I were going to review books I should need to do battle with a certain phantom. And the phantom was a woman, and when I came to know her better I called her after the heroine of a famous poem, the Angel in the House. It was she who used to come between me and my paper when I was writing reviews. It was she who bothered me and wasted my time and so tormented me that at last I killed her. You who come of a younger and happier generation may not have heard of her — you may not know what I mean by the Angel in the House. I will describe her as shortly as I can. She was intensely sympathetic. She was immensely charming. She was utterly unselfish. She excelled in the difficult arts of family life. She sacrificed herself daily. If there was a chicken, she took the leg; if there was a draft she sat in it — in short she was so constituted that she never had a mind or a wish of her own, but preferred to sympathize always with the minds and wishes of others. Above all — I need not say it — she was pure. Her purity was supposed to be her chief beauty — her blushes, her great grace. In those days — the last of Queen Victoria — every house had its Angel. And when I came to write I encountered her with the very first words. The shadow of her wings fell on my page; I heard the rustling of her skirts in the room. Directly, that is to say, I took my pen in my hand to review that novel by a famous man, she slipped behind me and whispered: "My dear, you are a young woman. You are writing about a book that has been written by a man. Be sympathetic; be tender; flatter; deceive; use all the arts and wiles of our sex. Never let anybody guess that you have a mind of your own. Above all, be pure." And she made as if to guide my pen. I now record the one act for which I take some credit to myself, though the credit rightly belongs to some excellent ancestors of mine who left me a certain sum of money — shall we say five hundred pounds a year? — so that it was not necessary for me to depend solely on charm for my living. I turned upon her and caught her by the throat. I did my best to kill her. My excuse, if I were to be had up in a court of law, would be that I acted in self-defense. Had I not killed her she would have killed me. She would have plucked the heart out of my writing. For, as I found, directly I put pen to paper, you cannot review even a novel without having a mind of your own, without expressing what you think to be the truth about human relations, morality, sex. And all these questions, according to the Angel of the House, cannot be dealt with freely and openly by women; they must charm, they must conciliate, they must — to put it bluntly — tell lies if they are to succeed. Thus, whenever I felt the shadow of her wing or the radiance of her halo upon my page, I took up the inkpot and flung it at her. She died hard. Her fictitious nature was of great assistance to her. It is far harder to kill a phantom than a reality. She was always creeping back when I thought I had dispatched her. Though I flatter myself that I killed her in the end, the struggle was severe; it took much time that had better have been spent upon learning Greek grammar; or in roaming the world in search of adventures. But it was a real experience; it was an experience that was bound to befall all women writers at this time. Killing the Angel in the House was part of the occupation of a woman writer.

But to continue my story. The Angel was dead; what then remained? You may say that what remained was a simple and common object — a young woman in a bedroom with an inkpot. In other words, now that she had rid herself of falsehood, that young woman had only to be herself. Ah, but what is "herself"? I mean, what is a woman? I assure you, I do not know. I do not believe that you know. I do not believe that anybody can know until she has expressed herself in all the arts and professions open to human skill. That indeed is one of the reasons why I have come here — out of respect for you, who are in process of showing us by your experiments what a woman is, who are in process of providing us, by your failures and successes, with that extremely important piece of information.

But to continue the story of my professional experiences, I made 5 one pound ten and six by my first review; and I bought a Persian cat with the proceeds. Then I grew ambitious. A Persian cat is all very well, I said; but a Persian cat is not enough. I must have a motor car. And it was thus that I became a novelist — for it is a very strange thing that people will give you a motor car if you will tell them a story. It is a still stranger thing that there is nothing so delightful in the world as telling stories. It is far pleasanter than writing reviews of famous novels. And yet, if I am to obey your secretary and tell you my professional experiences as a novelist, I must tell you about a very strange experience that befell me as a novelist. And to understand it you must try first to imagine a novelist's state of mind. I hope I am not giving away professional secrets if I say that a novelist's chief desire is to be as unconscious as possible. He has to induce in himself a state of perpetual lethargy. He wants life to proceed with the utmost quiet and regularity. He wants to see the same faces, to read the same books, to do the same things day after day, month after month, while he is writing, so that nothing may break the illusion in which he is living — so that nothing may disturb or disquiet the mysterious nosings about, feelings round, darts, dashes, and sudden discoveries of that very shy and illusive spirit, the imagination. I suspect that this state is the same both for men and women. Be that as it may, I want you to imagine me writing a novel in a state of trance. I want you to figure to yourselves a girl sitting with a pen in her hand, which for minutes, and indeed for hours, she never dips into the inkpot. The image that comes to my mind when I think of this girl is the image of a fisherman lying sunk in dreams on the verge of a deep lake with a rod held out over the water. She was letting her imagination sweep unchecked round every rock and cranny of the world that lies submerged in the depths of our unconscious being. Now came the experience, the experience that I believe to be far commoner with women writers than with men. The line raced through the girl's fingers. Her imagination had rushed away. It had sought the pools, the depths, the dark places where the largest fish slumber. And then there was a smash. There was an explosion. There was foam and confusion. The imagination had dashed itself against something hard. The girl was roused from her dream. She was indeed in a state of the most acute and difficult distress. To speak without figure she had thought of something, something about the body, about the passions which it was unfitting for her as a woman to say. Men, her reason told her, would be shocked. The consciousness of what men will say of a woman who speaks the truth about her passions had roused her from her artist's state of unconsciousness. She could write no more. The trance was over. Her imagination could work no longer. This I believe to be a very common experience with women writers — they are impeded by the extreme conventionality of the other sex. For though men sensibly allow themselves great freedom in these respects, I doubt that they realize or can control the extreme severity with which they condemn such freedom in women.

These then were two very genuine experiences of my own. These were two of the adventures of my professional life. The first — killing the Angel in the House — I think I solved. She died. But the second, telling the truth about my own experiences as a body, I do not think I solved. I doubt that any woman has solved it yet. The obstacles against her are still immensely powerful — and yet they are very difficult to define. Outwardly, what is simpler than to write books? Outwardly, what obstacles are there for a woman rather than for a man? Inwardly, I think, the case is very different; she has still many ghosts to fight, many prejudices to overcome. Indeed it will be a long time still, I think, before a woman can sit down to write a book without finding a phantom to be slain, a rock to be dashed against. And if this is so in literature, the freest of all professions for women, how is it in the new professions which you are now for the first time entering?

Those are the questions that I should like, had I time, to ask you. And indeed, if I have laid stress upon these professional experiences of mine, it is because I believe that they are, though in different forms, yours also. Even when the path is nominally open — when there is nothing to prevent a woman from being a doctor, a lawyer, a civil servant — there are many phantoms and obstacles, as I believe, looming in her way. To discuss and define them is I think of great value and importance; for thus only can the labor be shared, the difficulties be solved. But beside this, it is necessary also to discuss the ends and the aims for which we are fighting, for which we are doing battle with these formidable obstacles. Those aims cannot be taken for granted; they must be perpetually questioned and examined. The whole position, as I see it — here in this hall surrounded by women practicing for the first time in history I know not how many different professions — is one of extraordinary interest and importance. You have won rooms of your own in the house hitherto exclusively owned by men. You are able, though not without great labor and effort, to pay the rent. You are earning your five hundred pounds a year. But this freedom is only a beginning; the room is your own, but it is still bare. It has to be furnished; it has to be decorated; it has to be shared. How are you going to furnish it, how are you going to decorate it? With whom are you going to share it, and upon what terms? These, I think are questions of the utmost importance and interest. For the first time in history you are able to ask them; for the first time you are able to decide for yourselves what the answers should be. Willingly would I stay and discuss those questions and answers — but not tonight. My time is up; and I must cease.

Discussion Questions

1. How does Woolf explain the attraction of writing as a profession for women in the eighteenth and nineteenth centuries?
2. Who is the Angel in the House? What advice did she give to Woolf? Why did Woolf think it necessary to kill her?
3. What other experience constituted an adventure in her professional life? Is such an experience relevant for women writers today?
4. What questions does Woolf pose at the end to her audience of professional women? Why does she leave them vague and undefined?

Writing Suggestions

1. Woolf says, "Even when the path is nominally open — when there is nothing to prevent a woman from being a doctor, a lawyer, a civil servant — there are many phantoms and obstacles . . . looming in her way." Choose a specific profession, describe it, and try to explain the "many phantoms and obstacles" in it for women. Or make a case for an opposing view — that women no longer experience the problems described by Woolf in 1931.
2. Some critics argue that men entering professions generally practiced only by women suffer the same "phantoms and obstacles." Choose one or more vocations and spell out the prejudices that such men might encounter. Or, if you disagree with the critics, argue that these men do not experience difficulties.

Politics and the English Language

GEORGE ORWELL

This essay, written after World War II, develops George Orwell's claim that careless and dishonest use of language contributes to careless and dishonest thought and political corruption. Political language, he argues, is "largely the defense of the indefensible." But Orwell, novelist, critic, and political satirist — best known for his book 1984 — believes that bad language habits can be reversed, and he lists rules for getting rid of some of the most offensive.

Most people who bother with the matter at all would admit that the English language is in a bad way, but it is generally assumed that we cannot by conscious action do anything about it. Our civilization is decadent and our language — so the argument runs — must inevitably share in the general collapse. It follows that any struggle against the abuse of language is a sentimental archaism, like preferring candles to electric light or hansom cabs to aeroplanes. Underneath this lies the half-conscious belief that language is a natural growth and not an instrument which we shape for our own purposes.

Now, it is clear that the decline of a language must ultimately have political and economic causes: It is not due simply to the bad influence of this or that individual writer. But an effect can become a cause, reinforcing the original cause and producing the same effect in an intensified form, and so on indefinitely. A man may take to drink because he feels himself to be a failure, and then fail all the more completely because he drinks. It is rather the same thing that is happening to the English language. It becomes ugly and inaccurate because our thoughts are foolish, but the slovenliness of our language makes it easier for us to have foolish thoughts. The point is that the process is reversible. Modern English, especially written English, is full of bad habits which spread by imitation and which can be avoided if one is willing to take the necessary trouble. If one gets rid of these habits one can think more clearly, and to think clearly is a necessary first step towards political regeneration: so that the fight against bad English is not frivolous and is not the exclusive concern of professional writers. I will come back to this presently, and I hope that by that time the meaning of what I have said here will have become clearer. Meanwhile, here are five specimens of the English language as it is now habitually written.

These five passages have not been picked out because they are

---

From *Horizon*, April 1946.

especially bad — I could have quoted far worse if I had chosen — but because they illustrate various of the mental vices from which we now suffer. They are a little below the average, but are fairly representative samples. I number them so that I can refer back to them when necessary:

(1) I am not, indeed, sure whether it is not true to say that the Milton who once seemed not unlike a seventeenth-century Shelley had not become out of an experience ever more bitter in each year, more alien [*sic*] to the founder of that Jesuit sect which nothing could induce him to tolerate.
Professor Harold Laski (Essay in *Freedom of Expression*)

(2) Above all, we cannot play ducks and drakes with a native battery of idioms which prescribes such egregious collocations of vocables as the Basic *put up with* for *tolerate* or *put at a loss* for *bewilder.*
Professor Lancelot Hogben (*Interglossa*)

(3) On the one side we have the free personality: By definition it is not neurotic, for it has neither conflict nor dream. Its desires, such as they are, are transparent, for they are just what institutional approval keeps in the forefront of consciousness; another institutional pattern would alter their number and intensity; there is little in them that is natural, irreducible, or culturally dangerous. But *on the other side,* the social bond itself is nothing but the mutual reflection of these self-secure integrities. Recall the definition of love. Is not this the very picture of a small academic? Where is there a place in this hall of mirrors for either personality or fraternity?
Essay on psychology in *Politics* (New York)

(4) All the "best people" from the gentlemen's clubs, and all the frantic fascist captains, united in common hatred of Socialism and bestial horror of the rising tide of the mass revolutionary movement, have turned to acts of provocation, to foul incendiarism, to medieval legends of poisoned wells, to legalize their own destruction of proletarian organizations, and rouse the agitated petty-bourgeoisie to chauvinistic fervor on behalf of the fight against the revolutionary way out of the crisis.
Communist pamphlet

(5) If a new spirit *is* to be infused into this old country, there is one thorny and contentious reform which must be tackled, and that is the humanization and galvanization of the BBC. Timidity here will bespeak cancer and atrophy of the soul. The heart of Britain may be sound and of strong beat, for instance, but the British lion's roar at present is like that of Bottom in Shakespeare's *Midsummer Night's Dream* — as gentle as any sucking dove. A virile new Britain cannot continue indefinitely to be traduced in the eyes or rather ears, of the world by the effete languors of Langham Place, brazenly masquerading as "standard English." When the Voice of Britain is heard at nine o'clock, better far and infinitely less ludicrous to hear aitches honestly dropped than the present priggish,

inflated, inhibited, school-ma'amish arch braying of blameless bashful mewing maidens!

Letter in Tribune

Each of these passages has faults of its own, but, quite apart from avoidable ugliness, two qualities are common to all of them. The first is staleness of imagery: The other is lack of precision. The writer either has a meaning and cannot express it, or he inadvertently says something else, or he is almost indifferent as to whether his words mean anything or not. The mixture of vagueness and sheer incompetence is the most marked characteristic of modern English prose, and especially of any kind of political writing. As soon as certain topics are raised, the concrete melts into the abstract and no one seems to think of turns of speech that are not hackneyed: Prose consists less and less of *words* chosen for the sake of their meaning, and more and more of *phrases* tacked together like the sections of a prefabricated hen-house. I list below, with notes and examples, various of the tricks by means of which the work of prose-construction is habitually dodged:

Dying Metaphors. A newly invented metaphor assists thought by 5 evoking a visual image, while on the other hand a metaphor which is technically "dead" (e.g., *iron resolution*) has in effect reverted to being an ordinary word and can generally be used without loss of vividness. But in between these two classes there is a huge dump of worn-out metaphors which have lost all evocative power and are merely used because they save people the trouble of inventing phrases for themselves. Examples are: *ring the changes on, take up the cudgels for, toe the line, ride roughshod over, stand shoulder to shoulder with, play into the hands of, no axe to grind, grist to the mill, fishing in troubled waters, rift within the lute, on the order of the day, Achilles' heel, swan song, hotbed.* Many of these are used without knowledge of their meaning (what is a "rift," for instance?), and incompatible metaphors are frequently mixed, a sure sign that the writer is not interested in what he is saying. Some metaphors now current have been twisted out of their original meaning without those who use them even being aware of the fact. For example, *toe the line* is sometimes written *tow the line.* Another example is *the hammer and the anvil,* now always used with the implication that the anvil gets the worst of it. In real life it is always the anvil that breaks the hammer, never the other way about: A writer who stopped to think what he was saying would be aware of this, and would avoid perverting the original phrase.

Operators or Verbal False Limbs. These save the trouble of picking out appropriate verbs and nouns, and at the same time pad each sentence with extra syllables which give it an appearance of symmetry.

Characteristic phrases are: *render inoperative, militate against, make contact with, be subjected to, give rise to, give grounds for, have the effect of, play a leading part (role) in, make itself felt, take effect, exhibit a tendency to, serve the purpose of,* etc., etc. The keynote is the elimination of simple verbs. Instead of being a single word, such as *break, stop, spoil, mend, kill,* a verb becomes a *phrase,* made up of a noun or adjective tacked on to some general-purpose verb such as *prove, serve, form, play, render.* In addition, the passive voice is wherever possible used in preference to the active, and noun constructions are used instead of gerunds (*by examination of* instead of *by examining*). The range of verbs is further cut down by means of the *-ize* and *de-* formation, and the banal statements are given an appearance of profundity by means of the *not un-* formation. Simple conjunctions and prepositions are replaced by such phrases as *with respect to, having regard to, the fact that, by dint of, in view of, in the interests of, on the hypothesis that;* and the ends of sentences are saved from anticlimax by such resounding commonplaces as *greatly to be desired, cannot be left out of account, a development to be expected in the near future, deserving of serious consideration, brought to a satisfactory conclusion,* and so on and so forth.

Pretentious Diction. Words like *phenomenon, element, individual* (as noun), *objective, categorical, effective, virtual, basic, primary, promote, constitute, exhibit, exploit, utilize, eliminate, liquidate,* are used to dress up simple statements and give an air of scientific impartiality to biased judgments. Adjectives like *epoch-making, epic, historic, unforgettable, triumphant, age-old, inevitable, inexorable, veritable,* are used to dignify the sordid processes of international politics, while writing that aims at glorifying war usually takes on an archaic color, its characteristic words being: *realm, throne, chariot, mailed fist, trident, sword, shield, buckler, banner, jackboot, clarion.* Foreign words and expressions such as *cul de sac, ancien régime, deus ex machina, mutatis mutandis, status quo, gleichshaltung, weltanschauung,* are used to give an air of culture and elegance. Except for the useful abbreviations *i.e., e.g.,* and *etc.,* there is no real need for any of the hundreds of foreign phrases now current in English. Bad writers, and especially scientific, political, and sociological writers, are nearly always haunted by the notion that Latin or Greek words are grander than Saxon ones, and unnecessary words like *expedite, ameliorate, predict, extraneous, deracinated, clandestine, subaqueous,* and hundreds of others constantly gain ground from their Anglo-Saxon opposite numbers.[1] The jargon

---

[1]An interesting illustration of this is the way in which the English flower names which were in use till very recently are being ousted by Greek ones, *snapdragon* becoming *antirrhinum, forget-me-not* becoming *myosotis,* etc. It is hard to see any practical reason

peculiar to Marxist writing (*hyena, hangman, cannibal, petty bourgeois, these gentry, lackey, flunkey, mad dog, White Guard,* etc.) consists largely of words and phrases translated from Russian, German, or French; but the normal way of coining a new word is to use a Latin or Greek root with the appropriate affix and, where necessary, the *-ize* formation. It is often easier to make up words of this kind (*deregionalize, impermissible, extramarital, nonfragmentatory,* and so forth) than to think up the English words that will cover one's meaning. The result, in general, is an increase in slovenliness and vagueness.

Meaningless Words. In certain kinds of writing, particularly in art criticism and literary criticism, it is normal to come across long passages which are almost completely lacking in meaning.[2] Words like *romantic, plastic, values, human, dead, sentimental, natural, vitality,* as used in art criticism, are strictly meaningless in the sense that they not only do not point to any discoverable object, but are hardly ever expected to do so by the reader. When one critic writes, "The outstanding feature of Mr. X's work is its living quality," while another writes, "The immediately striking thing about Mr. X's work is its peculiar deadness," the reader accepts this as a simple difference of opinion. If words like *black* and *white* were involved, instead of the jargon words *dead* and *living,* he would see at once that language was being used in an improper way. Many political words are similarly abused. The word *fascism* has now no meaning except in so far as it signifies "something not desirable." The words *democracy, socialism, freedom, patriotic, realistic, justice,* have each of them several different meanings which cannot be reconciled with one another. In the case of a word like *democracy,* not only is there no agreed definition, but the attempt to make one is resisted from all sides. It is almost universally felt that when we call a country democratic we are praising it: Consequently the defenders of every kind of regime claim that it is a democracy, and fear that they might have to stop using the word if it were tied down to any one meaning. Words of this kind are often used in a consciously dishonest way. That is, the person who uses them has his own private definition, but allows his hearer to think he means something quite different. Statements like *Marshal Pétain was a true patriot, The Soviet Press is the freest in the world, The Catholic Church is opposed to*

---

for this change of fashion: It is probably due to an instinctive turning-away from the more homely word and a vague feeling that the Greek word is scientific.

[2] Example: "Comfort's catholicity of perception and image, strangely Whitmanesque in range, almost the exact opposite in aesthetic compulsion, continues to evoke that trembling atmospheric accumulative hinting at a cruel, an inexorably serene timelessness . . . Wrey Gardiner scores by aiming at simple bull's-eyes with precision. Only they are not so simple, and through this contended sadness runs more than the surface bittersweet of resignation" (*Poetry Quarterly*).

persecution, are almost always made with intent to deceive. Other words used in variable meanings, in most cases more or less dishonestly, are: *class, totalitarian, science, progressive, reactionary, bourgeois, equality.*

Now that I have made this catalog of swindles and perversions, let me give another example of the kind of writing that they lead to. This time it must of its nature be an imaginary one. I am going to translate a passage of good English into modern English of the worst sort. Here is a well-known verse from *Ecclesiastes:*

> I returned and saw under the sun, that the race is not to the swift, nor the battle to the strong, neither yet bread to the wise, nor yet riches to men of understanding, nor yet favor to men of skill; but time and chance happeneth to them all.

Here it is in modern English:

> Objective consideration of contemporary phenomena compels the conclusion that success or failure in competitive activities exhibits no tendency to be commensurate with innate capacity, but that a considerable element of the unpredictable must invariably be taken into account.

This is a parody, but not a very gross one. Exhibit (3), above, for 10 instance, contains several patches of the same kind of English. It will be seen that I have not made a full translation. The beginning and ending of the sentence follow the original meaning fairly closely, but in the middle the concrete illustrations — race, battle, bread — dissolve into the vague phrase "success or failure in competitive activities." This had to be so, because no modern writer of the kind I am discussing — no one capable of using phrases like "objective consideration of contemporary phenomena" — would ever tabulate his thoughts in that precise and detailed way. The whole tendency of modern prose is away from concreteness. Now analyze these two sentences a little more closely. The first contains forty-nine words but only sixty syllables, and all its words are those of everyday life. The second contains thirty-eight words of ninety syllables: Eighteen of its words are from Latin roots, and one from Greek. The first sentence contains six vivid images, and only one phrase ("time and chance") that could be called vague. The second contains not a single fresh, arresting phrase, and in spite of its ninety syllables it gives only a shortened version of the meaning contained in the first. Yet without a doubt it is the second kind of sentence that is gaining ground in modern English. I do not want to exaggerate. This kind of writing is not yet universal, and outcrops of simplicity will occur here and there in the worst-written page. Still, if you or I were told to write a few lines on the uncertainty of human fortunes, we should probably come much nearer to my imaginary sentence than to the one from *Ecclesiastes.*

As I have tried to show, modern writing at its worst does not consist in picking out words for the sake of their meaning and inventing images in order to make the meaning clearer. It consists in gumming together long strips of words which have already been set in order by someone else, and making the results presentable by sheer humbug. The attraction of this way of writing is that it is easy. It is easier — even quicker once you have the habit — to say *In my opinion it is a not unjustifiable assumption that* than to say *I think.* If you use ready-made phrases, you not only don't have to hunt about for words; you also don't have to bother with the rhythms of your sentences, since these phrases are generally so arranged as to be more or less euphonious. When you are composing in a hurry — when you are dictating to a stenographer, for instance, or making a public speech — it is natural to fall into a pretentious, Latinized style. Tags like a *consideration which we should do well to bear in mind* or *a conclusion to which all of us would readily assent* will save many a sentence from coming down with a bump. By using stale metaphors, similes, and idioms, you save much mental effort, at the cost of leaving your meaning vague, not only for your reader but for yourself. This is the significance of mixed metaphors. The sole aim of a metaphor is to call up a visual image. When these images clash — as in *The Fascist octopus has sung its swan song, the jackboot is thrown into the melting pot* — it can be taken as certain that the writer is not seeing a mental image of the objects he is naming; in other words he is not really thinking. Look again at the examples I gave at the beginning of this essay. Professor Laski (1) uses five negatives in fifty-three words. One of these is superfluous, making nonsense of the whole passage, and in addition there is the slip *alien* for akin, making further nonsense, and several avoidable pieces of clumsiness which increase the general vagueness. Professor Hogben (2) plays ducks and drakes with a battery which is able to write prescriptions, and, while disapproving of the everyday phrase *put up with,* is unwilling to look *egregious* up in the dictionary and see what it means. (3), if one takes an uncharitable attitude towards it, is simply meaningless: Probably one could work out its intended meaning by reading the whole of the article in which it occurs. In (4), the writer knows more or less what he wants to say, but an accumulation of stale phrases chokes him like tea leaves blocking a sink. In (5), words and meaning have almost parted company. People who write in this manner usually have a general emotional meaning — they dislike one thing and want to express solidarity with another — but they are not interested in the detail of what they are saying. A scrupulous writer, in every sentence that he writes, will ask himself at least four questions, thus: What am I trying to say? What words will express it? What image or idiom will make it clearer? Is this image fresh enough to have an effect? And he will probably ask himself two more: Could I put it more shortly? Have I said anything that is avoidably ugly? But you are not obliged to go to all this trouble. You can shirk it by simply throwing your mind open and letting the ready-made phrases come crowding in. They will construct your sentences for you — even think your thoughts for you, to a certain extent — and at need they will perform the important service of partially concealing your meaning even from yourself. It is at this point that the special connection between politics and the debasement of language becomes clear.

In our time it is broadly true that political writing is bad writing. Where it is not true, it will generally be found that the writer is some kind of rebel, expressing his private opinions and not a "party line." Orthodoxy, of whatever color, seems to demand a lifeless, imitative style. The political dialects to be found in pamphlets, leading articles, manifestos, White Papers, and the speeches of undersecretaries do, of course, vary from party to party, but they are all alike in that one almost never finds in them a fresh, vivid, home-made turn of speech. When one watches some tired hack on the platform mechanically repeating the familiar phrases — *bestial atrocities, iron heel, bloodstained tyranny, free peoples of the world, stand shoulder to shoulder* — one often has a curious feeling that one is not watching a live human being but some kind of dummy; a feeling which suddenly becomes stronger at moments when the light catches the speaker's spectacles and turns them into blank discs which seem to have no eyes behind them. And this is not altogether fanciful. A speaker who uses that kind of phraseology has gone some distance towards turning himself into a machine. The appropriate noises are coming out of his larynx, but his brain is not involved as it would be if he were choosing his words for himself. If the speech he is making is one that he is accustomed to make over and over again, he may be almost unconscious of what he is saying, as one is when one utters the responses in church. And this reduced state of consciousness, if not indispensable, is at any rate favorable to political conformity.

In our time, political speech and writing are largely the defense of the indefensible. Things like the continuance of British rule in India, the Russian purges and deportations, the dropping of the atom bombs on Japan, can indeed be defended, but only by arguments which are too brutal for most people to face, and which do not square with the professed aims of political parties. Thus political language has to consist largely of euphemism, question-begging, and sheer cloudy vagueness. Defenseless villages are bombarded from the air, the inhabitants driven out into the countryside, the cattle machine-gunned, the huts set on fire with incendiary bullets: This is called *pacification*. Millions of peasants are robbed of their farms and sent trudging along the roads with no more than they can carry; this is called *transfer of population or rectification of frontiers*. People are imprisoned for years without trial, or shot in the back of the neck, or sent to die of scurvy in Arctic lumber camps: This is called *elimination of unreliable elements*. Such phraseology is needed if one wants to name things without calling up mental pictures of them. Consider for instance some comfortable English professor defending Russian totalitarianism. He cannot say outright, "I believe in killing off your opponents when you can get good results by doing so." Probably, therefore, he will say something like this:

> While freely conceding that the Soviet régime exhibits certain features which the humanitarian may be inclined to deplore, we must, I think, agree that a certain curtailment of the right to political opposition is an unavoidable concomitant of transitional periods, and that the rigors which the Russian people have been called upon to undergo have been amply justified in the sphere of concrete achievement.

The inflated style is itself a kind of euphemism. A mass of Latin words fall upon the facts like soft snow, blurring the outlines and covering up all the details. The great enemy of clear language is insincerity. When there is a gap between one's real and one's declared aims, one turns as it were instinctively to long words and exhausted idioms, like a cuttlefish squirting out ink. In our age there is no such thing as "keeping out of politics." All issues are political issues, and politics itself is a mass of lies, evasions, folly, hatred, and schizophrenia. When the general atmosphere is bad, language must suffer. I should expect to find — this is a guess which I have not sufficient knowledge to verify — that the German, Russian, and Italian languages have all deteriorated in the last ten or fifteen years, as a result of dictatorship.

But if thought corrupts language, language can also corrupt thought. 15 A bad usage can spread by tradition and imitation, even among people who should and do know better. The debased language that I have been discussing is in some ways very convenient. Phrases like *a not unjustifiable assumption, leaves much to be desired, would serve no good purpose, a consideration which we should do well to bear in mind,* are a continuous temptation, a packet of aspirins always at one's elbow. Look back through this essay, and for certain you will find that I have again and again committed the very faults I am protesting against. By this morning's post I have received a pamphlet dealing with conditions in Germany. The author tells me that he "felt impelled" to write it. I open it at random, and here is almost the first sentence that I see: "(The Allies) have an opportunity not only of achieving a radical transformation of Germany's social and political structure in such a way as to avoid a nationalistic reaction in Germany itself, but at the same time of laying the foundations of a cooperative and unified Europe." You see, he "feels impelled" to write — feels, presumably, that he has something new to say — and yet his words, like cavalry horses answering the bugle, group themselves automatically into the familiar dreary pattern. This invasion of one's mind by ready-made phrases (*lay the foundations, achieve a radical transformation*) can only be prevented if one is constantly on guard against them, and every such phrase anesthetizes a portion of one's brain.

I said earlier that the decadence of our language is probably curable. Those who deny this would argue, if they produced an argument at all, that language merely reflects existing social conditions, and that we cannot influence its development by any direct tinkering with words and constructions. So far as the general tone or spirit of a language goes, this may be true, but it is not true in detail. Silly words and expressions have often disappeared, not through any evolutionary process but owing to the conscious action of a minority. Two recent examples were *explore every avenue* and *leave no stone unturned,* which were killed by the jeers of a few journalists. There is a long list of flyblown metaphors which could similarly be got rid of if enough people would interest themselves in the job; and it should also be possible to laugh the *not un-* formation out of existence,[3] to reduce the amount of Latin and Greek in the average sentence, to drive out foreign phrases and strayed scientific words, and, in general, to make pretentiousness unfashionable. But all these are minor points. The defense of the English language implies more than this, and perhaps it is best to start by saying what it does *not* imply.

To begin with it has nothing to do with archaism, with the salvaging of obsolete words and turns of speech, or with the setting up of a "standard English" which must never be departed from. On the contrary, it is especially concerned with the scrapping of every word or idiom which has outworn its usefulness. It has nothing to do with correct grammar and syntax, which are of no importance so long as one makes one's meaning clear, or with the avoidance of Americanisms, or with having what is called a "good prose style." On the other hand it is not concerned with fake simplicity and the attempt to make written English colloquial. Nor does it even imply in every case preferring the Saxon word to the Latin one, though it does imply using the fewest and shortest words that will cover one's meaning. What is above all needed is to let the meaning choose the word, and not the other way about. In prose, the worst thing one can do with words is to surrender to them. When you think of a concrete object, you think wordlessly, and then, if you want to describe the thing you have been visualizing you probably hunt about till you find the exact words that seem to fit. When you think of something abstract you are more inclined to use words from the start, and unless you make a conscious effort to prevent it, the existing dialect will come rushing in and do the job for you, at the expense of blurring or even changing your meaning. Probably it is better to put off using words as long as possible and get one's meaning as

---

[3] One can cure oneself of the *not un-* formation by memorizing this sentence: *A not unblack dog was chasing a not unsmall rabbit across a not ungreen field.*

clear as one can through pictures or sensations. Afterwards one can choose — not simply *accept* — the phrases that will best cover the meaning, and then switch round and decide what impression one's words are likely to make on another person. This last effort of the mind cuts out all stale or mixed images, all prefabricated phrases, needless repetitions, and humbug and vagueness generally. But one can often be in doubt about the effect of a word or a phrase, and one needs rules that one can rely on when instinct fails. I think the following rules will cover most cases:

(i)   Never use a metaphor, simile, or other figure of speech which you are used to seeing in print.
(ii) Never use a long word where a short one will do.
(iii) If it is possible to cut a word out, always cut it out.
(iv) Never use the passive where you can use the active.
(v)   Never use a foreign phrase, a scientific word, or a jargon word if you can think of an everyday English equivalent.
(vi) Break any of these rules sooner than say anything outright barbarous.

These rules sound elementary, and so they are, but they demand a deep change in attitude in anyone who has grown used to writing in the style now fashionable. One could keep all of them and still write bad English, but one could not write the kind of stuff that I quoted in those five specimens at the beginning of this article.

I have not here been considering the literary use of language, but merely language as an instrument for expressing and not for concealing or preventing thought. Stuart Chase and others have come near to claiming that all abstract words are meaningless, and have used this as a pretext for advocating a kind of political quietism. Since you don't know what Fascism is, how can you struggle against Fascism? One need not swallow such absurdities as this, but one ought to recognize that the present political chaos is connected with the decay of language, and that one can probably bring about some improvement by starting at the verbal end. If you simplify your English, you are freed from the worst follies of orthodoxy. You cannot speak any of the necessary dialects, and when you make a stupid remark its stupidity will be obvious, even to yourself. Political language — and with variations this is true of all political parties, from Conservatives to Anarchists — is designed to make lies sound truthful and murder respectable, and to give an appearance of solidity to pure wind. One cannot change this all in a moment, but one can at least change one's own habits, and from time to time one can even, if one jeers loudly enough, send some worn-out and useless phrase — some *jackboot, Achilles' heel, hotbed, melting pot, acid test, veritable inferno,* or other lump of verbal refuse — into the dustbin where it belongs.

Discussion Questions

1. Orwell disagrees with a common assumption about language. What is it? Where in the essay does he attack this assumption directly?
2. What faults do his five samples of bad language have in common? Select examples of these faults in each passage.
3. What "tricks" for avoiding good prose does Orwell list? Do you think that some are more dangerous or misleading than others? Explain the reasons for your answer.
4. What different reasons does Orwell suggest for the slovenliness of much political writing and speaking? What examples does he give to support these reasons? Are they persuasive?
5. How does Orwell propose that we get rid of our bad language habits? Do you think his recommendations are realistic? Can the teaching of writing in school assist in the remedy?
6. Why does Orwell urge the reader to "look back through this essay" to find "the very faults I am protesting against"? Can you, in fact, find any?

Writing Suggestions

1. Choose a speech or an editorial whose meaning seems to be obscured by pretentious diction, meaningless words, euphemism, or "sheer cloudy vagueness." Point out the real meaning of the piece. If you think that its purpose is deceptive, expose the unpleasant truth that the author is concealing. Use Orwell's device, giving concrete meaning to any abstractions. (One source of speeches is a publication called *Vital Speeches of the Day.* Another is the *New York Times,* which often prints in full, or excerpts major portions of, speeches by leading figures in public life.)
2. Orwell's essay appeared before the widespread use of television. Do you think that TV makes it harder for politicians to be dishonest? Choose a particular public event — a war, a street riot, a terrorist activity, a campaign stop — and argue either for or against the claim that televised coverage makes it harder for a politician to engage in "sheer cloudy vagueness." Or does it make no difference at all? Be specific in your use of evidence.

Letter from Birmingham Jail

MARTIN LUTHER KING, JR.

Martin Luther King, Jr., (1929–1968) was a clergyman, author, distin-guished civil-rights leader, and winner of the Nobel Peace Prize in 1964 for his contributions to racial harmony and his advocacy of nonviolent response to aggression. He was assassinated in 1968. In the following se-lections we meet King in two of his various roles. In "Letter from Birming-ham Jail," he appears as historian and philosopher. He wrote the letter from a jail cell on April 16, 1963, after his arrest for participation in a demonstration for civil rights for blacks. The letter was a reply to eight Alabama clergymen who, in a public statement, had condemned demon-strations in the streets.

My dear Fellow Clergymen,

While confined here in the Birmingham city jail, I came across your recent statement calling our present activities "unwise and untimely." Seldom, if ever, do I pause to answer criticism of my work and ideas. If I sought to answer all of the criticisms that cross my desk, my secre-taries would be engaged in little else in the course of the day, and I would have no time for constructive work. But since I feel that you are men of genuine good will and your criticisms are sincerely set forth, I would like to answer your statement in what I hope will be patient and reasonable terms.

I think I should give the reason for my being in Birmingham, since you have been influenced by the argument of "outsiders coming in." I have the honor of serving as president of the Southern Christian Lead-ership Conference, an organization operating in every southern state, with headquarters in Atlanta, Georgia. We have some eighty-five affiliate organizations all across the South — one being the Alabama Christian Movement for Human Rights. Whenever necessary and possible we share staff, educational, and financial resources with our affiliates. Sev-eral months ago our local affiliate here in Birmingham invited us to be on call to engage in a nonviolent direct-action program if such were deemed necessary. We readily consented and when the hour came we lived up to our promises. So I am here, along with several members of my staff, because we were invited here. I am here because I have basic organizational ties here.

Beyond this, I am in Birmingham because injustice is here. Just as the eighth-century prophets left their little villages and carried their "thus saith the Lord" far beyond the boundaries of their hometowns;

From *A Testament of Hope* (1986).

and just as the Apostle Paul left his little village of Tarsus and carried the gospel of Jesus Christ to practically every hamlet and city of the Graeco-Roman world, I too am compelled to carry the gospel of freedom beyond my particular hometown. Like Paul, I must constantly respond to the Macedonian call for aid.

Moreover, I am cognizant of the interrelatedness of all communities and states. I cannot sit idly by in Atlanta and not be concerned about what happens in Birmingham. Injustice anywhere is a threat to justice everywhere. We are caught in an inescapable network of mutuality, tied in a single garment of destiny. Whatever affects one directly affects all indirectly. Never again can we afford to live with the narrow, provincial "outside agitator" idea. Anyone who lives in the United States can never be considered an outsider anywhere in this country.

You deplore the demonstrations that are presently taking place in Birmingham. But I am sorry that your statement did not express a similar concern for the conditions that brought the demonstrations into being. I am sure that each of you would want to go beyond the superficial social analyst who looks merely at effects, and does not grapple with underlying causes. I would not hesitate to say that it is unfortunate that so-called demonstrations are taking place in Birmingham at this time, but I would say in more emphatic terms that it is even more unfortunate that the white power structure of this city left the Negro community with no other alternative.

In any nonviolent campaign there are four basic steps: (1) collection of the facts to determine whether injustices are alive, (2) negotiation, (3) self-purification, and (4) direct action. We have gone through all of these steps in Birmingham. There can be no gainsaying of the fact that racial injustice engulfs this community.

Birmingham is probably the most thoroughly segregated city in the United States. Its ugly record of police brutality is known in every section of this country. Its unjust treatment of Negroes in the courts is a notorious reality. There have been more unsolved bombings of Negro homes and churches in Birmingham than any city in this nation. These are the hard, brutal, and unbelievable facts. On the basis of these conditions Negro leaders sought to negotiate with the city fathers. But the political leaders consistently refused to engage in good faith negotiation.

Then came the opportunity last September to talk with some of the leaders of the economic community. In these negotiating sessions certain promises were made by the merchants — such as the promise to remove the humiliating racial signs from the stores. On the basis of these promises Reverend Shuttlesworth and the leaders of the Alabama Christian Movement for Human Rights agreed to call a moratorium on any type of demonstrations. As the weeks and months unfolded we realized that we were the victims of a broken promise. The signs remained. Like so many experiences of the past we were confronted with blasted hopes, and the dark shadow of a deep disappointment settled upon us. So we had no alternative except that of preparing for direct action, whereby we would present our very bodies as a means of laying our case before the conscience of the local and national community. We were not unmindful of the difficulties involved. So we decided to go through a process of self-purification. We started having workshops on nonviolence and repeatedly asking ourselves the questions, "Are you able to accept blows without retaliating?" "Are you able to endure the ordeals of jail?" We decided to set our direct-action program around the Easter season, realizing that with the exception of Christmas, this was the largest shopping period of the year. Knowing that a strong economic withdrawal program would be the by-product of direct action, we felt that this was the best time to bring pressure on the merchants for the needed changes. Then it occurred to us that the March election was ahead and so we speedily decided to postpone action until after election day. When we discovered that Mr. Connor was in the run-off, we decided again to postpone action so that the demonstrations could not be used to cloud the issues. At this time we agreed to begin our nonviolent witness the day after the run-off.

This reveals that we did not move irresponsibly into direct actions. We too wanted to see Mr. Connor defeated; so we went through postponement after postponement to aid in this community need. After this we felt that direct action could be delayed no longer.

You may well ask, "Why direct action? Why sit-ins, marches, etc.? 10 Isn't negotiation a better path?" You are exactly right in your call for negotiation. Indeed, this is the purpose of direct action. Nonviolent direct action seeks to create such a crisis and establish such creative tension that a community that has constantly refused to negotiate is forced to confront the issue. It seeks so to dramatize the issue that it can no longer be ignored. I just referred to the creation of tension as a part of the work of the nonviolent resister. This may sound rather shocking. But I must confess that I am not afraid of the word tension. I have earnestly worked and preached against violent tension, but there is a type of constructive nonviolent tension that is necessary for growth. Just as Socrates felt that it was necessary to create a tension in the mind so that individuals could rise from the bondage of myths and half-truths to the unfettered realm of creative analysis and objective appraisal, we must see the need of having nonviolent gadflies to create the kind of tension in society that will help men to rise from the dark depths of prejudice and racism to the majestic heights of understanding and brotherhood. So the purpose of the direct action is to create a situation so crisis-packed that it will inevitably open the door to negotiation. We, therefore, concur with you in your call for negotiation. Too long has our beloved Southland been bogged down in the tragic attempt to live in monologue rather than dialogue.

One of the basic points in your statement is that our acts are untimely. Some have asked, "Why didn't you give the new administration time to act?" The only answer that I can give to this inquiry is that the new administration must be prodded about as much as the outgoing one before it acts. We will be sadly mistaken if we feel that the election of Mr. Boutwell will bring the millennium to Birmingham. While Mr. Boutwell is much more articulate and gentle than Mr. Connor, they are both segregationists, dedicated to the task of maintaining the status quo. The hope I see in Mr. Boutwell is that he will be reasonable enough to see the futility of massive resistance to desegregation. But he will not see this without pressure from the devotees of civil rights. My friends, I must say to you that we have not made a single gain in civil rights without determined legal and nonviolent pressure. History is the long and tragic story of the fact that privileged groups seldom give up their privileges voluntarily. Individuals may see the moral light and voluntarily give up their unjust posture; but as Reinhold Niebuhr has reminded us, groups are more immoral than individuals.

We know through painful experience that freedom is never voluntarily given by the oppressor; it must be demanded by the oppressed. Frankly, I have never yet engaged in a direct action movement that was "well-timed," according to the timetable of those who have not suffered unduly from the disease of segregation. For years now I have heard the words "Wait!" It rings in the ear of every Negro with a piercing familiarity. This "Wait" has almost always meant "Never." It has been a tranquilizing thalidomide, relieving the emotional stress for a moment, only to give birth to an ill-formed infant of frustration. We must come to see with the distinguished jurist of yesterday that "justice too long delayed is justice denied." We have waited for more than 340 years for our constitutional and God-given rights. The nations of Asia and Africa are moving with jetlike speed toward the goal of political independence, and we still creep at horse and buggy pace toward the gaining of a cup of coffee at a lunch counter. I guess it is easy for those who have never felt the stinging darts of segregation to say, "Wait." But when you have seen vicious mobs lynch your mothers and fathers at will and drown your sisters and brothers at whim; when you see hate-filled policemen curse, kick, brutalize, and even kill your black brothers and sisters with impunity; when you see the vast majority of your 20 million Negro brothers smothering in an airtight cage of poverty in the midst of an affluent society; when you suddenly find your tongue twisted and your speech stammering as you seek to explain to your six-year-old daughter why she can't go to the public amusement park that has just been advertised on television, and see tears welling up in her little eyes when she is told that Funtown is closed to colored children, and see the depressing clouds of inferiority begin to form in her little mental sky, and see her begin to distort her little personality by unconsciously developing a bitterness toward white people; when you have to concoct an answer for a five-year-old son asking in agonizing pathos: "Daddy, why do white people treat colored people so mean?"; when you take a cross-country drive and find it necessary to sleep night after night in the uncomfortable corners of your automobile because no motel will accept you; when you are humiliated day in and day out by nagging signs reading "white" and "colored"; when your first name becomes "nigger" and your middle name becomes "boy" (however old you are) and your last name becomes "John," and when your wife and mother are never given the respected title "Mrs."; when you are harried by day and haunted by night by the fact that you are a Negro, living constantly at tiptoe stance never quite knowing what to expect next, and plagued with inner fears and outer resentments; when you are forever fighting a degenerating sense of "nobodiness"; then you will understand why we find it difficult to wait. There comes a time when the cup of endurance runs over, and men are no longer willing to be plunged into an abyss of injustice where they experience the blackness of corroding despair. I hope, sirs, you can understand our legitimate and unavoidable impatience.

You express a great deal of anxiety over our willingness to break laws. This is certainly a legitimate concern. Since we so diligently urge people to obey the Supreme Court's decision of 1954 outlawing segregation in the public schools, it is rather strange and paradoxical to find us consciously breaking laws. One may well ask, "How can you advocate breaking some laws and obeying others?" The answer is found in the fact that there are two types of laws: There are *just* and there are *unjust* laws. I would agree with Saint Augustine that "An unjust law is no law at all."

Now what is the difference between the two? How does one determine when a law is just or unjust? A just law is a man-made code that squares with the moral law or the law of God. An unjust law is a code that is out of harmony with the moral law. To put it in the terms of Saint Thomas Aquinas, an unjust law is a human law that is not rooted in eternal and natural law. Any law that uplifts human personality is just. Any law that degrades human personality is unjust. All segregation statutes are unjust because segregation distorts the soul and damages the personality. It gives the segregator a false sense of superiority, and the segregated a false sense of inferiority. To use the words of Martin Buber, the great Jewish philosopher, segregation substitutes an "I-it" relationship for the "I-thou" relationship, and ends up relegating persons to the status of things. So segregation is not only politically, economically, and sociologically unsound, but it is morally wrong and sinful. Paul Tillich has said that sin is separation. Isn't segregation an existential expression of man's tragic separation, an expression of his awful estrangement, his terrible sinfulness? So I can urge men to disobey segregation ordinances because they are morally wrong.

Let us turn to a more concrete example of just and unjust laws. An unjust law is a code that a majority inflicts on a minority that is not binding on itself. This is difference made legal. On the other hand, a just law is a code that a majority compels a minority to follow that it is willing to follow itself. This is sameness made legal.

Let me give another explanation. An unjust law is a code inflicted upon a minority which that minority had no part in enacting or creating because they did not have the unhampered right to vote. Who can say that the legislature of Alabama which set up the segregation laws was democratically elected? Throughout the state of Alabama all types of conniving methods are used to prevent Negroes from becoming registered voters, and there are some counties without a single Negro registered to vote despite the fact that the Negro constitutes a majority of the population. Can any law set up in such a state be considered democratically structured?

These are just a few examples of unjust and just laws. There are some instances when a law is just on its face and unjust in its application. For instance, I was arrested Friday on a charge of parading without a permit. Now there is nothing wrong with an ordinance which requires a permit for a parade, but when the ordinance is used to preserve segregation and to deny citizens the First Amendment privilege of peaceful assembly and peaceful protest, then it becomes unjust.

I hope you can see the distinction I am trying to point out. In no sense do I advocate evading or defying the law as the rabid segregationist would do. This would lead to anarchy. One who breaks an unjust law must do it *openly, lovingly* (not hatefully as the white mothers did in New Orleans when they were seen on television screaming, "nigger, nigger, nigger"), and with a willingness to accept the penalty. I submit that an individual who breaks a law that conscience tells him is unjust, and willingly accepts the penalty by staying in jail to arouse the conscience of the community over its injustice, is in reality expressing the very highest respect for law.

Of course, there is nothing new about this kind of civil disobedience. It was seen sublimely in the refusal of Shadrach, Meshach, and Abednego to obey the laws of Nebuchadnezzar because a higher moral law was involved. It was practiced superbly by the early Christians who were willing to face hungry lions and the excruciating pain of chopping blocks, before submitting to certain unjust laws of the Roman Empire. To a degree academic freedom is a reality today because Socrates practiced civil disobedience.

We can never forget that everything Hitler did in Germany was [20] "legal" and everything the Hungarian freedom fighters did in Hungary was "illegal." It was "illegal" to aid and comfort a Jew in Hitler's Germany. But I am sure that if I had lived in Germany during that time I would have aided and comforted my Jewish brothers even though it was illegal. If I lived in a Communist country today where certain principles dear to the Christian faith are suppressed, I believe I would openly advocate disobeying these antireligious laws. I must make two honest confessions to you, my Christian and Jewish brothers. First, I must confess that over the last few years I have been gravely disappointed with the white moderate. I have almost reached the regrettable conclusion that the Negro's great stumbling block in the stride toward freedom is not the White Citizen's Counciler or the Ku Klux Klanner, but the white moderate who is more devoted to "order" than to justice; who prefers a negative peace which is the absence of tension to a positive peace which is the presence of justice; who constantly says, "I agree with you in the goal you seek, but I can't agree with your methods of direct action"; who paternalistically feels that he can set the timetable for another man's freedom; who lives by the myth of time and who constantly advises the Negro to wait until a "more convenient season." Shallow understanding from people of good will is more frustrating than absolute misunderstanding from people of ill will. Lukewarm acceptance is much more bewildering than outright rejection.

I had hoped that the white moderate would understand that law and order exist for the purpose of establishing justice, and that when they fail to do this they become dangerously structured dams that block the flow of social progress. I had hoped that the white moderate would understand that the present tension of the South is merely a necessary phase of the transition from an obnoxious negative peace, where the Negro passively accepted his unjust plight, to a substance-filled positive peace, where all men will respect the dignity and worth of human personality. Actually, we who engage in nonviolent direct action are not the creators of tension. We merely bring to the surface the hidden tension that is already alive. We bring it out in the open where it can be seen and dealt with. Like a boil that can never be cured as long as it is covered up but must be opened with all its pus-flowing ugliness to the natural medicines of air and light, injustice must likewise be exposed, with all the tension its exposing creates, to the light of human conscience and the air of national opinion before it can be cured.

In your statement you asserted that our actions, even though peaceful, must be condemned because they precipitate violence. But can this assertion be logically made? Isn't this like condemning the robbed man because his possession of money precipitated the evil act of robbery? Isn't this like condemning Socrates because his unswerving commitment to truth and his philosophical delvings precipitated the misguided popular mind to make him drink the hemlock? Isn't this like condemning Jesus because His unique God-consciousness and never-ceasing devotion to his will precipitated the evil act of crucifixion? We must come to see, as federal courts have consistently affirmed, that it is immoral to urge an individual to withdraw his efforts to gain his basic constitutional rights because the quest precipitates violence. Society must protect the robbed and punish the robber.

I had also hoped that the white moderate would reject the myth of time. I received a letter this morning from a white brother in Texas which said: "All Christians know that the colored people will receive equal rights eventually, but it is possible that you are in too great of a religious hurry. It has taken Christianity almost two thousand years to accomplish what it has. The teachings of Christ take time to come to earth." All that is said here grows out of a tragic misconception of time. It is the strangely irrational notion that there is something in the very flow of time that will inevitably cure all ills. Actually time is neutral. It can be used either destructively or constructively. I am coming to feel that the people of ill will have used time much more effectively than the people of good will. We will have to repent in this generation not merely for the vitriolic words and actions of the bad people, but for the appalling silence of the good people. We must come to see that human progress never rolls in on wheels of inevitability. It comes through the tireless efforts and persistent work of men willing to be co-workers with God, and without this hard work time itself becomes an ally of the forces of social stagnation. We must use time creatively, and forever realize that the time is always ripe to do right. Now is the time to make real the promise of democracy, and transform our pending national elegy into a creative psalm of brotherhood. Now is the time to lift our national policy from the quicksand of racial injustice to the solid rock of human dignity.

You spoke of our activity in Birmingham as extreme. At first I was rather disappointed that fellow clergymen would see my nonviolent efforts as those of the extremist. I started thinking about the fact that I stand in the middle of two opposing forces in the Negro community. One is a force of complacency made up of Negroes who, as a result of long years of oppression, have been so completely drained of self-respect and a sense of "somebodiness" that they have adjusted to segregation, and of a few Negroes in the middle class who, because of a degree of academic and economic security, and because at points they profit by segregation, have unconsciously become insensitive to the problems of the masses. The other force is one of bitterness and hatred, and comes perilously close to advocating violence. It is expressed in the various black nationalist groups that are springing up over the nation, the largest and best known being Elijah Muhammad's Muslim movement. This movement is nourished by the contemporary frustration over the continued existence of racial discrimination. It is made up of people who have lost faith in America, who have absolutely repudiated Christianity, and who have concluded that the white man is an incurable "devil." I have tried to stand between these two forces, saying that we need not follow the "do-nothingism" of the complacent or the hatred and despair of the black nationalist. There is the more excellent way of love and nonviolent protest. I'm grateful to God that, through the Negro church, the dimension of nonviolence entered our struggle. If this philosophy had not emerged, I am convinced that by now many streets of the South would be flowing with floods of blood.

And I am further convinced that if our white brothers dismiss us as "rabble-rousers" and "outside agitators" those of us who are working through the channels of nonviolent direct action and refuse to support our nonviolent efforts, millions of Negroes, out of frustration and despair, will seek solace and security in black nationalist ideologies, a development that will lead inevitably to a frightening racial nightmare.

Oppressed people cannot remain oppressed forever. The urge for 25 freedom will eventually come. This is what happened to the American Negro. Something within has reminded him of his birthright of freedom; something without has reminded him that he can gain it. Consciously and unconsciously, he has been swept in by what the Germans call the *Zeitgeist,* and with his black brothers of Africa, and his brown and yellow brothers of Asia, South America, and the Caribbean, he is moving with a sense of cosmic urgency toward the promised land of racial justice. Recognizing this vital urge that has engulfed the Negro community, one should readily understand public demonstrations. The Negro has many pent-up resentments and latent frustrations. He has to get them out. So let him march sometime; let him have his prayer pilgrimages to the city hall; understand why he must have sit-ins and freedom rides. If his repressed emotions do not come out in these nonviolent ways, they will come out in ominous expressions of violence. This is not a threat; it is fact of history. So I have not said to my people "get rid of your discontent." But I have tried to say that this normal and healthy discontent can be channelized through the creative outlet of nonviolent direct action. Now this approach is being dismissed as extremist. I must admit that I was initially disappointed in being so categorized.

But as I continued to think about the matter I gradually gained a bit of satisfaction from being considered an extremist. Was not Jesus an extremist in love — "Love your enemies, bless them that curse you, pray for them that despitefully use you." Was not Amos an extremist for justice — "Let justice roll down like waters and righteousness like a mighty stream." Was not Paul an extremist for the gospel of Jesus Christ — "I bear in my body the marks of the Lord Jesus." Was not Martin Luther an extremist — "Here I stand; I can do none other so help me God." Was not John Bunyan an extremist — "I will stay in jail to the end of my days before I make a butchery of my conscience." Was not Abraham Lincoln an extremist — "This nation cannot survive half slave and half free." Was not Thomas Jefferson an extremist — "We hold these truths to be self-evident, that all men are created equal." So the question is not whether we will be extremist but what kind of extremist will we be. Will we be extremists for hate or will we be extremists for love? Will we be extremists for the preservation of injustice — or will we be extremists for the cause of justice? In that dramatic scene on Calvary's hill, three men were crucified. We must not forget that all three were crucified for the same crime — the crime of extremism. Two were extremists for immorality, and thusly fell below their environment. The other,

Jesus Christ, was an extremist for love, truth, and goodness, and thereby rose above his environment. So, after all, maybe the South, the nation, and the world are in dire need of creative extremists.

I had hoped that the white moderate would see this. Maybe I was too optimistic. Maybe I expected too much. I guess I should have realized that few members of a race that has oppressed another race can understand or appreciate the deep groans and passionate yearnings of those that have been oppressed and still fewer have the vision to see that injustice must be rooted out by strong, persistent, and determined action. I am thankful, however, that some of our white brothers have grasped the meaning of this social revolution and committed themselves to it. They are still all too small in quantity, but they are big in quality. Some like Ralph McGill, Lillian Smith, Harry Golden, and James Dabbs have written about our struggle in eloquent, prophetic, and understanding terms. Others have marched with us down nameless streets of the South. They have languished in filthy roach-infested jails, suffering the abuse and brutality of angry policemen who see them as "dirty nigger-lovers." They, unlike so many of their moderate brothers and sisters, have recognized the urgency of the moment and sensed the need for powerful "action" antidotes to combat the disease of segregation.

Let me rush on to mention my other disappointment. I have been so greatly disappointed with the white church and its leadership. Of course, there are some notable exceptions. I am not unmindful of the fact that each of you has taken some significant stands on this issue. I commend you, Reverend Stallings, for your Christian stance on this past Sunday, in welcoming Negroes to your worship service on a non-segregated basis. I commend the Catholic leaders of this state for integrating Springhill College several years ago.

But despite these notable exceptions I must honestly reiterate that I have been disappointed with the church. I do not say that as one of the negative critics who can always find something wrong with the church. I say it as a minister of the gospel, who loves the church; who was nurtured in its bosom; who has been sustained by its spiritual blessings, and who will remain true to it as long as the cord of life shall lengthen.

I had the strange feeling when I was suddenly catapulted into the leadership of the bus protest in Montgomery several years ago that we would have the support of the white church. I felt that the white ministers, priests, and rabbis of the South would be some of our strongest allies. Instead, some have been outright opponents, refusing to understand the freedom movement and misrepresenting its leaders; all too many others have been more cautious than courageous and have remained silent behind the anesthetizing security of the stained-glass windows.

In spite of my shattered dreams of the past, I came to Birmingham with the hope that the white religious leadership of this community would see the justice of our cause, and with deep moral concern, serve as the channel through which our just grievances would get to the power structure. I had hoped that each of you would understand. But again I have been disappointed. I have heard numerous religious leaders of the South call upon their worshipers to comply with a desegregation decision because it is the *law,* but I have longed to hear white ministers say, "Follow this decree because integration is morally *right* and the Negro is your brother." In the midst of blatant injustices inflicted upon the Negro, I have watched white churches stand on the sideline and merely mouth pious irrelevancies and sanctimonious trivialities. In the midst of a mighty struggle to rid our nation of racial and economic injustice, I have heard so many ministers say, "Those are social issues with which the gospel has no real concern," and I have watched so many churches commit themselves to a completely otherworldly religion which made a strange distinction between body and soul, the sacred and the secular.

So here we are moving toward the exit of the twentieth century with a religious community largely adjusted to the status quo, standing as a taillight behind other community agencies rather than a headlight leading men to higher levels of justice.

I have traveled the length and breadth of Alabama, Mississippi, and all the other southern states. On sweltering summer days and crisp autumn mornings I have looked at her beautiful churches with their lofty spires pointing heavenward. I have beheld the impressive outlay of her massive religious education buildings. Over and over again I have found myself asking: "What kind of people worship here? Who is their God? Where were their voices when the lips of Governor Barnett dripped with words of interposition and nullification? Where were they when Governor Wallace gave the clarion call for defiance and hatred? Where were their voices of support when tired, bruised, and weary Negro men and women decided to rise from the dark dungeons of complacency to the bright hills of creative protest?"

Yes, these questions are still in my mind. In deep disappointment, I have wept over the laxity of the church. But be assured that my tears have been tears of love. There can be no deep disappointment where there is not deep love. Yes, I love the church; I love her sacred walls. How could I do otherwise? I am in the rather unique position of being the son, the grandson, and the great-grandson of preachers. Yes, I see the church as the body of Christ. But, oh! How we have blemished and scarred that body through social neglect and fear of being nonconformists.

There was a time when the church was very powerful. It was during 35 that period when the early Christians rejoiced when they were deemed worthy to suffer for what they believed. In those days the church was not merely a thermometer that recorded the ideas and principles of popular opinion; it was a thermostat that transformed the mores of society. Wherever the early Christians entered a town the power structure got disturbed and immediately sought to convict them for being "disturbers of the peace" and "outside agitators." But they went on with the conviction that they were "a colony of heaven," and had to obey God rather than man. They were small in number but big in commitment. They were too God-intoxicated to be "astronomically intimidated." They brought an end to such ancient evils as infanticide and gladiatorial contest.

Things are different now. The contemporary church is often a weak, ineffectual voice with an uncertain sound. It is so often the arch-supporter of the status quo. Far from being disturbed by the presence of the church, the power structure of the average community is consoled by the church's silent and often vocal sanction of things as they are.

But the judgment of God is upon the church as never before. If the church of today does not recapture the sacrificial spirit of the early church, it will lose its authentic ring, forfeit the loyalty of millions, and be dismissed as an irrelevant social club with no meaning for the twentieth century. I am meeting young people every day whose disappointment with the church has risen to outright disgust.

Maybe again, I have been too optimistic. Is organized religion too inextricably bound to the status quo to save our nation and the world? Maybe I must turn my faith to the inner spiritual church, the church within the church, as the true *ecclesia* and the hope of the world. But again I am thankful to God that some noble souls from the ranks of organized religion have broken loose from the paralyzing chains of conformity and joined us as active partners in the struggle for freedom. They have left their secure congregations and walked the streets of Albany, Georgia, with us. They have gone through the highways of the South on tortuous rides for freedom. Yes, they have gone to jail with us. Some have been kicked out of their churches, and lost support of their bishops and fellow ministers. But they have gone with the faith that right defeated is stronger than evil triumphant. These men have been the leaven in the lump of the race. Their witness has been the spiritual salt that has preserved the true meaning of the gospel in these troubled times. They have carved a tunnel of hope through the dark mountain of disappointment.

I hope the church as a whole will meet the challenge of this decisive hour. But even if the church does not come to the aid of justice, I have no despair about the future. I have no fear about the outcome of our struggle in Birmingham, even if our motives are presently misunderstood. We will reach the goal of freedom in Birmingham and all over the nation, because the goal of America is freedom. Abused and scorned though we may be, our destiny is tied up with the destiny of America. Before the Pilgrims landed at Plymouth we were here. Before the pen of Jefferson etched across the pages of history the majestic words of the Declaration of Independence, we were here. For more than two centuries our foreparents labored in this country without wages; they made cotton king; and they built the homes of their masters in the midst of brutal injustice and shameful humiliation — and yet out of a bottomless vitality they continued to thrive and develop. If the inexpressible cruelties of slavery could not stop us, the opposition we now face will surely fail. We will win our freedom because the sacred heritage of our nation and the eternal will of God are embodied in our echoing demands.

I must close now. But before closing I am impelled to mention one 40 other point in your statement that troubled me profoundly. You warmly commended the Birmingham police force for keeping "order" and "preventing violence." I don't believe you would have so warmly commended the police force if you had seen its angry violent dogs literally biting six unarmed, nonviolent Negroes. I don't believe you would so quickly commend the policemen if you would observe their ugly and inhuman treatment of Negroes here in the city jail; if you would watch them push and curse old Negro women and young Negro girls; if you would see them slap and kick old Negro men and young boys; if you will observe them, as they did on two occasions, refuse to give us food because we wanted to sing our grace together. I'm sorry that I can't join you in your praise for the police department.

It is true that they have been rather disciplined in their public handling of the demonstrators. In this sense they have been rather publicly "nonviolent." But for what purpose? To preserve the evil system of segregation. Over the last few years I have consistently preached that nonviolence demands that the means we use must be as pure as the ends we seek. So I have tried to make it clear that it is wrong to use immoral means to attain moral ends. But now I must affirm that it is just as wrong, or even more so, to use moral means to preserve immoral ends. Maybe Mr. Connor and his policemen have been rather publicly nonviolent, as Chief Pritchett was in Albany, Georgia, but they have used the moral means of nonviolence to maintain the immoral end of flagrant racial injustice. T. S. Eliot has said that there is no greater treason than to do the right deed for the wrong reason.

I wish you had commended the Negro sit-inners and demonstrators of Birmingham for their sublime courage, their willingness to suffer, and their amazing discipline in the midst of the most inhuman provocation. One day the South will recognize its real heroes. They will be the James Merediths, courageously and with a majestic sense of purpose facing jeering and hostile mobs and the agonizing loneliness that characterizes the life of the pioneer. They will be old, oppressed, battered Negro women, symbolized in a seventy-two-year-old woman of Montgomery, Alabama, who rose up with a sense of dignity and with her people decided not to ride the segregated buses, and responded to one who inquired about her tiredness with ungrammatical profundity: "My feet is tired, but my soul is rested." They will be the young high school and college students, young ministers of the gospel, and a host of their elders courageously and nonviolently sitting-in at lunch counters and willingly going to jail for conscience's sake. One day the South will know that when these disinherited children of God sat down at lunch counters they were in reality standing up for the best in the American dream and the most sacred values in our Judeo-Christian heritage, and thusly, carrying our whole nation back to those great wells of democracy which were dug deep by the Founding Fathers in the formulation of the Constitution and the Declaration of Independence.

Never before have I written a letter this long (or should I say a book?). I'm afraid that it is much too long to take your precious time. I can assure you that it would have been much shorter if I had been writing from a comfortable desk, but what else is there to do when you are alone for days in the dull monotony of a narrow jail cell other than write long letters, think strange thoughts, and pray long prayers?

If I have said anything in this letter that is an overstatement of the truth and is indicative of an unreasonable impatience, I beg you to forgive me. If I have said anything in this letter that is an understatement of the truth and is indicative of my having a patience that makes me patient with anything less than brotherhood, I beg God to forgive me.

I hope this letter finds you strong in the faith. I also hope that 45 circumstances will soon make it possible for me to meet each of you, not as an integrationist or a civil-rights leader, but as a fellow clergyman and a Christian brother. Let us all hope that the dark clouds of racial prejudice will soon pass away and the deep fog of misunderstanding will be lifted from our fear-drenched communities and in some not too distant tomorrow the radiant stars of love and brotherhood will shine over our great nation with all of their scintillating beauty.

Yours for the cause of Peace and Brotherhood,
Martin Luther King, Jr.

Discussion Questions

1. As in "I Have a Dream" (p. 678), King uses figurative language in his letter. Find some particularly vivid passages and evaluate their effect in the context of this letter.
2. Explain King's distinction between just and unjust laws. Are there dangers in attempting to make such a distinction?
3. What characteristics of mind and behavior does King exhibit in the letter? Select the specific passages that provide proof.
4. Why does King say that "the white moderate" is a greater threat to Negro progress than the outspoken racist? Is his explanation convincing?
5. How does King justify his philosophy of nonviolence in the face of continued aggression against the Negro?

Writing Suggestions

1. Can you think of a law against which defiance would be justified? Explain why the law is unjust and why refusal to obey is morally defensible.
2. In paragraph 12 King lists the grievances of Negroes in this country. King's catalog is similar to the lists in the Declaration of Independence. Can you think of any other group who might compile a list of grievances? If so, choose a group and draw up such a list, making sure that your list is as clear and specific as those you have read.

I Have a Dream

MARTIN LUTHER KING, JR.

In the widely reprinted "I Have a Dream" speech, Martin Luther King, Jr., appears as the charismatic leader of the civil-rights movement. This inspirational address was delivered on August 28, 1963, in Washington, D.C., at a demonstration by two hundred thousand people for civil rights for blacks.

Five score years ago, a great American, in whose symbolic shadow we stand, signed the Emancipation Proclamation. This momentous decree came as a great beacon light of hope to millions of Negro slaves who had been seared in the flames of withering injustice. It came as a joyous daybreak to end the long night of captivity.

But one hundred years later, we must face the tragic fact that the Negro is still not free. One hundred years later, the life of the Negro is still sadly crippled by the manacles of segregation and the chains of discrimination. One hundred years later, the Negro lives on a lonely island of poverty in the midst of a vast ocean of material prosperity. One hundred years later, the Negro is still languishing in the corners of American society and finds himself an exile in his own land. So we have come here today to dramatize an appalling condition.

In a sense we have come to our nation's capital to cash a check. When the architects of our republic wrote the magnificent words of the Constitution and the Declaration of Independence, they were signing a promissory note to which every American was to fall heir. This note was a promise that all men would be guaranteed the unalienable rights of life, liberty, and the pursuit of happiness.

It is obvious today that America has defaulted on this promissory note insofar as her citizens of color are concerned. Instead of honoring this sacred obligation, America has given the Negro people a bad check; a check which has come back marked "insufficient funds." But we refuse to believe that the bank of justice is bankrupt. We refuse to believe that there are insufficient funds in the great vaults of opportunity of this nation. So we have come to cash this check — a check that will give us upon demand the riches of freedom and the security of justice. We have also come to this hallowed spot to remind America of the fierce urgency of *now*. This is no time to engage in the luxury of cooling off or to take the tranquilizing drugs of gradualism. *Now* is the time to make real the promises of Democracy. *Now* is the time to rise from the dark and desolate valley of segregation to the sunlit path of racial justice. *Now* is the time to open the doors of opportunity to all of God's children.

From *A Testament of Hope* (1986).

Now is the time to lift our nation from the quicksands of racial injustice to the solid rock of brotherhood.

It would be fatal for the nation to overlook the urgency of the 5 moment and to underestimate the determination of the Negro. This sweltering summer of the Negro's legitimate discontent will not pass until there is an invigorating autumn of freedom and equality. Nineteen sixty-three is not an end, but a beginning. Those who hope that the Negro needed to blow off steam and will now be content will have a rude awakening if the nation returns to business as usual. There will be neither rest nor tranquillity in America until the Negro is granted his citizenship rights. The whirlwinds of revolt will continue to shake the foundations of our nation until the bright day of justice emerges.

But there is something that I must say to my people who stand on the warm threshold which leads into the palace of justice. In the process of gaining our rightful place we must not be guilty of wrongful deeds. Let us not seek to satisfy our thirst for freedom by drinking from the cup of bitterness and hatred. We must forever conduct our struggle on the high plane of dignity and discipline. We must not allow our creative protest to degenerate into physical violence. Again and again we must rise to the majestic heights of meeting physical force with soul force. The marvelous new militancy which has engulfed the Negro community must not lead us to a distrust of all white people, for many of our white brothers, as evidenced by their presence here today, have come to realize that their destiny is tied up with our destiny and their freedom is inextricably bound to our freedom. We cannot walk alone.

And as we walk, we must make the pledge that we shall march ahead. We cannot turn back. There are those who are asking the devotees of civil rights, "When will you be satisfied?" We can never be satisfied as long as the Negro is the victim of the unspeakable horrors of police brutality. We can never be satisfied as long as our bodies, heavy with the fatigue of travel, cannot gain lodging in the motels of the highways and the hotels of the cities. We cannot be satisfied as long as the Negro's basic mobility is from a smaller ghetto to a larger one. We can never be satisfied as long as a Negro in Mississippi cannot vote and a Negro in New York believes he has nothing for which to vote. No, no, we are not satisfied, and we will not be satisfied until justice rolls down like waters and righteousness like a mighty stream.

I am not unmindful that some of you have come here out of great trials and tribulations. Some of you have come fresh from narrow jail cells. Some of you have come from areas where your quest for freedom left you battered by the storms of persecution and staggered by the winds of police brutality. You have been the veterans of creative suffering. Continue to work with the faith that unearned suffering is redemptive.

Go back to Mississippi, go back to Alabama, go back to South Carolina, go back to Georgia, go back to Louisiana, go back to the slums and ghettos of our northern cities, knowing that somehow this situation can and will be changed. Let us not wallow in the valley of despair.

I say to you today, my friends, that in spite of the difficulties and frustrations of the moment I still have a dream. It is a dream deeply rooted in the American dream. 10

I have a dream that one day this nation will rise up and live out the true meaning of its creed: "We hold these truths to be self-evident; that all men are created equal."

I have a dream that one day on the red hills of Georgia the sons of former slaves and the sons of former slaveowners will be able to sit down together at the table of brotherhood.

I have a dream that one day even the state of Mississippi, a desert state sweltering with the heat of injustice and oppression, will be transformed into an oasis of freedom and justice.

I have a dream that my four little children will one day live in a nation where they will not be judged by the color of their skin but by the content of their character.

I have a dream today. 15

I have a dream that one day the state of Alabama, whose governor's lips are presently dripping with the words of interposition and nullification, will be transformed into a situation where little black boys and black girls will be able to join hands with little white boys and white girls and walk together as sisters and brothers.

I have a dream today.

I have a dream that one day every valley shall be exalted, every hill and mountain shall be made low, the rough places will be made plain, and the crooked places will be made straight, and the glory of the Lord shall be revealed, and all flesh shall see it together.

This is our hope. This is the faith with which I return to the South. With this faith we will be able to hew out of the mountain of despair a stone of hope. With this faith we will be able to transform the jangling discords of our nation into a beautiful symphony of brotherhood. With this faith we will be able to work together, to pray together, to struggle together, to go to jail together, to stand up for freedom together, knowing that we will be free one day.

This will be the day when all of God's children will be able to sing with new meaning 20

My country, 'tis of thee,
Sweet land of liberty,
    Of thee I sing:
Land where my fathers died,
Land of the pilgrims' pride,
From every mountain-side
    Let freedom ring.

And if America is to be a great nation this must become true. So let freedom ring from the prodigious hilltops of New Hampshire. Let freedom ring from the mighty mountains of New York. Let freedom ring from the heightening Alleghenies of Pennsylvania!

Let freedom ring from the snowcapped Rockies of Colorado!

Let freedom ring from the curvaceous peaks of California!

But not only that; let freedom ring from Stone Mountain of Georgia!

Let freedom ring from Lookout Mountain of Tennessee!   25

Let freedom ring from every hill and molehill of Mississippi. From every mountainside, let freedom ring.

When we let freedom ring, when we let it ring from every village and every hamlet, from every state and every city, we will be able to speed up that day when all of God's children, black men and white men, Jews and Gentiles, Protestants and Catholics, will be able to join hands and sing in the words of the old Negro spiritual, "Free at last! free at last! thank God almighty, we are free at last!"

Discussion Question

1. King's style alternates between the abstract and the concrete, between the grandiloquent and the simple, with abundant use of metaphors. Find examples of these qualities. Are all the stylistic strategies equally effective? Explain your answer.
2. What specific injustices suffered by black people does King mention? Why does he interrupt his series of "Let freedom ring" imperatives at the end with the statement, "But not only that"?
3. What values does the speech stress? Would these values be equally appealing to both blacks and whites? Why or why not?
4. More than thirty years later, how much of King's indictment of conditions remains true? Mention specific changes or lack of changes. If conditions have improved, does that make his speech less meaningful today?

Writing Suggestions

1. Using the same material as the original, rewrite this speech for an audience that is not impressed with the inspirational style. Think carefully about the changes in language you would make to convince this audience that, despite your dispassionate treatment, injustices exist and should be rectified.
2. Choose another highly emotional subject — for example, women's rights, child pornography, nuclear power — and write an inspirational speech or advertisement urging your audience to change their views. Be passionate, but try to avoid sentimentality or corniness. (You may want to look at other examples of the inspirational or hortatory style in a collection of speeches, among them speeches made in favor of the abolition of slavery and women's suffrage, declarations of war, and inaugural addresses.)

ACKNOWLEDGMENTS (continued from page iv)

Dave Barry, "Bring Back Carl's Plaque." Copyright © 1985 by the author. Reprinted by permission.

William J. Bennett, "We Give Up." From speech given to the Education Writers Association in April, 1986. Reprinted by permission of the author.

Ellen Bravo and Ellen Cassedy, "What Sexual Harrassment Is — and Is Not." From *The 9 to 5 Guide to Combatting Sexual Harrassment: Candid Advice from 9to5, the National Association of Working Women*. Copyright © 1992 John Wiley. Reprinted by permission of John Wiley & Sons, Inc.

Armin Brott, "Not All Men Are Sly Foxes." From *Newsweek*, July 1992 and © 1992, Newsweek, Inc. All rights reserved. Reprinted by permission.

Warren E. Burger, "The Right to Bear Arms." From *Parade*, January 14, 1990. Reprinted with permission from *Parade*, copyright © 1990, and the author.

Helen Caldicott, "Species Extinction." From *If You Love This Planet: A Plan to Heal the Earth*, copyright © 1992 W. W. Norton. Reprinted by permission.

Howard Cohen, "Equal Rights for Children." From *Equal Rights for Children*. Copyright © 1980 by Littlefield, Adams & Co. Reprinted by permission of Rowman & Littlefield Publishers.

Michael D. Copeland, "No Red Squirrels? Mother Nature May Be Better Off." Reprinted with permission of the *Wall Street Journal* © 1990 Dow Jones and Company, Inc. All rights reserved.

Louis L. Cregler and Herbert Mark, "Cocaine Is Even Deadlier Than We Thought." From the *New York Times*, July 30, 1986. Reprinted by permission of the authors.

Michael E. DeBakey, "Holding Human Health Hostage." Reprinted by permission of the author.

Harry A. DeMell, "Immigration Still Makes America What It Is." From the *New York Times*, August 8, 1992. Reprinted by permission of the author.

Michael Denneny, "Gay Politics." Reprinted from *The Christopher Street Reader*, copyright © 1983, with permission of the author.

Barbara Ehrenreich, "Ice-T: The Issue Is Creative Freedom." From *Time*, July 20, 1992. Copyright © 1992 Time Inc. Reprinted by permission.

Jean Bethke Elshtain, "Against Gay Marriage." From *Commonweal*, November 22, 1991. Copyright © 1991 Commonweal Foundation. Reprinted with permission. "Why Worry about the Animals" reprinted by permission from *The Progressive*, 409 East Main Street, Madison, WI 53703.

Suzanne Fields, "Deconstructing Date Rape." From *Heterodoxy*, April 1992. Reprinted with permission from *Heterodoxy* and the author.

"First Amendment." Toles copyright © 1989 The Buffalo News. Reprinted with permissin of Universal Press Syndicate. All rights reserved.

Randy Fitzgerald, "The Great Spotted Owl War." Reprinted with permission from the November 1992 *Reader's Digest*. Copyright © 1992 by The Reader's Digest Assn., Inc.

Henry Louis Gates, Jr., "Whose Culture Is It Anyway?" Copyright © 1991 by Henry Louis Gates, Jr. First appeared in the *New York Times* (May 4, 1991). Reprinted by permission of Brandt & Brandt Literary Agents, Inc.

General Electric advertisement, "GE: The initials of a friend." Reprinted by permission of General Electric.

Barbara Gerbasi, "Mainstreaming My Son." From the *New York Times*, April 14, 1985. Copyright © 1985 by The New York Times Company. Reprinted by permission.

GLAAD, "An Open Letter to the Supreme Court Re: *Bowers v. Hardwick*." From the *New York Times*, June 18, 1987. Reprinted by permission.

Nathan Glazer, "In Defense of Multiculturalism." Reprinted by permission of *The New Republic*, © 1991, The New Republic, Inc.

Sarah Glazer, "Sex Education: How Well Does It Work?" Reprinted with permission from *Editorial Research Reports*, Vol. 1, 1989 published by Congressional Quarterly, Inc.

Rita Kramer, "Juvenile Justice Is Delinquent." Reprinted by permission of the author from the *Wall Street Journal*, May 27, 1992.

Charles Krauthammer, "School Birth Control Clinics; Necessary Evil." From the *Washington Post*, December 3, 1986. Copyright © 1986, The Washington Post Writers Group. Reprinted with permission.

Charles R. Lawrence III, "On Racist Speech." From *The Chronicle of Higher Education*, October 25, 1989. Reprinted by permission of the author.

John Leo, "Cozy Little Homicides." Copyright November 11, 1991, *U.S. News & World Report*. "Hillary's Children's Crusade" copyright © August 31/September 7, 1992, *U.S. News & World Report*.

Michael Levin, "The Case for Torture." Reprinted by permission of the author.

C. S. Lewis, "Vivisection." From *Undeceptions* edited by Walter Hooper. Copyright © 1971 by William Collins Sons & Company, Ltd. Reprinted by permission of William Collins Publishers, an imprint of HarperCollins Publishers Limited.

Rush H. Limbaugh III, "Animals Have No Rights — Go Ahead and Lick That Frog." From *The Way Things Ought to Be* by Rush Limbaugh. Copyright © 1992 by Rush Limbaugh. Reprinted by permission of Pocket Books, a division of Simon & Schuster, Inc.

Daniel C. Maguire, "Death by Choice." From *Death by Choice* by Daniel Maguire. Copyright © 1973, 1974 by Daniel C. Maguire. Used by permission of Doubleday, a division of Bantam Doubleday Dell Publishing Group, Inc.

Paulette Mason, "I'm Thirty-eight and Running Out of Time." From the *New York Times*, October 3, 1992. Copyright © 1992 by The New York Times Company. Reprinted by permission.

Michael Medved, "Hollywood's Poison Factory." Reprinted by permission from the November 1992 issue of *Imprimis*.

Metropolitan Energy Council advertisement, "Gas heat makes me nervous." Reprinted by permission of the Metropolitan Energy Council.

Richard Miniter, "Saving the Species." Copyright © 1992 by National Review, Inc., 150 East 35th Street, New York, NY 10016. Reprinted by permission.

Donna Minkowitz, "Why Heterosexuals Need to Support Gay Rights." Copyright © 1989 by Donna Minkowitz. Originally published in *The Village Voice*; subsequently adapted in *The Utne Reader*. Reprinted by permission of Jed Mattes, Inc., New York.

Mutual of America advertisement, "The Strength. The Stability. The Spirit of America." Reprinted by permission of Mutual of America.

Jacob Neusner, "The Speech the Graduates Didn't Hear." Copyright © 1983 by Jacob Neusner. Reprinted from the *Daily Herald*, June 12, 1983. Used by permission of the author.

New York State Social Studies Syllabus Review and Development Committee, "Report on Minority Cultures in the Classroom." From "One Nation, Many Peoples: A Declaration of Cultural Interdependence," a report submitted to the New York State Board of Regents by the Social Studies Syllabus Review and Development Committee (June 1991). As the report of an external advisory body, this report does not state or constitute the policy of the New York State Board of Regents, nor does any portion quoted herein represent New York State policy. From the *New York Times*, June 21, 1991. Copyright © 1991 by The New York Times Company. Reprinted by permission.

Florence A. Nolan, "Making Painful Choices on Deformed Fetuses." From the *New York Times*, January 28, 1992. Reprinted by permission of the author.

Dale O'Leary, "Condom Issues: Should Children Have Sex?" From the *New York Times*, October 10, 1991. Reprinted by permission of the author.

"An Open Forum on Ethnic Studies." From *Thatch* by Jeff Shesol. Copyright © 1991 by Jeff Shesol. Reprinted by permission of Vintage Books, a division of Random House, Inc.

George Orwell, "Politics and the English Language." Copyright 1946 by Sonia Brownell Orwell, renewed 1974 by Sonia Orwell. Reprinted from his volume *Shooting an*

Elephant and Other Essays by permission of Harcourt Brace & Company and the estate of the late Sonia Brownell Orwell and Martin Secker & Warburg Ltd.

David M. Oshinsky and Michael Curtis, "Freedom of Speech and Holocaust Revisionism." From the *New York Times*, December 11, 1991. Copyright © 1991 by The New York Times Company. Reprinted by permission.

Mortimer Ostow, "That Right Belongs Only to the State." Reprinted by permission of the author.

J. A. Parker, "Capital Punishment — An Idea Whose Time Has Come Again." From *Lincoln Review*, Summer 1986. Reprinted by permission.

Tony Parker and Robert Allerton, "A Criminal Justifies Himself." From *The Courage of His Convictions* by Tony Parker and Robert Allerton. Reprinted by permission of Random Century Group.

E. L. Pattullo, "Public Shouldn't Pay." From the *New York Times*, November 27, 1989. Copyright © 1989 by The New York Times Company. Reprinted by permission.

Stanton Peele, "Addiction Is Not a Disease." Reprinted with the permission of Lexington Books, an imprint of Macmillan, Inc., from *Diseasing of America: Addiction Treatment Out of Control* by Stanton Peele. Copyright © 1989 by Stanton Peele.

"Philip has questioned my stewardship." Drawing by Weber; © 1992 The New Yorker Magazine, Inc.

Planned Parenthood advertisement, "Nine Reasons Why Abortions Are Legal." Copyright revised version Planned Parenthood Federation of America, Inc., April 1990. Copyright PPFA 1985. All rights reserved. Reprinted by permission of Planned Parenthood® Federation of America, Inc.

Anna Quindlen, "Death Penalty's False Promise." From the *New York Times*, September 17, 1986. Copyright © 1986 by The New York Times Company. Reprinted by permission.

James Rachels, M.D., "Active and Passive Euthanasia." From *The New England Journal of Medicine*, Vol. 292, pp. 78–80, 1975. Reprinted by permission.

William Rathje and Cullen Murphy, "The Landfill Excavations." *From Rubbish! The Archeology of Garbage* by William Rathje and Cullen Murphy. Copyright © 1992 by William Rathje and Cullen Murphy. Reprinted by permission of HarperCollins Publisher, Inc.

Diane Ravitch, "Multiculturalism: E Pluribus Plures." Reprinted from *The American Scholar*, Volume 59, No. 3, Summer 1990. Copyright © 1990 by the author.

Carol Roye, "Protect Our Children." From the *New York Times*, September 12, 1992. Reprinted by permission of the author.

Saturn advertisement, "Cheryl Silas had a highway collision, was hit twice from behind, and then sold three cars for us." Reprinted by permission of the Saturn Corporation.

Arthur Schlesinger, Jr., "Toward a Divisive Diversity." From the *Wall Street Journal*, June 25, 1991. Reprinted by permission of the author.

Lawrence J. Schneiderman, "Euthanasia: Can We Keep It a Special Case?" First appeared in the May/June 1990 edition of *The Humanist* and is reprinted with permission.

Albert Shanker, "Value Free?" From the *New York Times*, January 6, 1991. Copyright © 1991 by The New York Times Company. Reprinted by permission.

Fred Siegel, "Ugh! Oops." Reprinted by permission of *The New Republic*, © 1991, The New Republic, Inc.

John Silber, "Don't Roll Back *Roe*." From the *New York Times*, January 3, 1990. Copyright © 1990 by The New York Times Company. Reprinted by permission.

Peter Singer, "Animal Liberation." Reprinted from the April 15, 1973 issue of *The New York Review of Books* by permission of the author. Copyright © 1973 by Peter Singer.

Roger Sipher, "So That Nobody Has to Go to School If They Don't Want To." From the *New York Times*, December 22, 1977. Copyright © 1977 by The New York Times Company. Reprinted by permission.

Joseph Sobran, "Bogus Sex: Reflections on Homosexual Claims." Reprinted from *Single Issues* by Joseph Sobran. Copyright © 1983 The Human Life Press. Reprinted by permission.

Glossary and Index of Terms

Abstract language: language expressing a quality apart from a specific object or event; opposite of *concrete language*   *184–188*

Ad hominem: "against the man"; attacking the arguer rather than the *argument* or issue   *225–226*

Ad populum: "to the people"; playing on the prejudices of the *audience*   *229–230*

Analogy: a *comparison* in which a thing is inferred to be similar to another thing in a certain way because it is similar to the thing in other ways   *156–157*

Appeal to tradition: a proposal that something should continue because it has traditionally existed or been done that way   *230*

Argument: a process of reasoning and advancing proof about issues on which conflicting views may be held; also, a statement or statements providing *support* for a *claim*   *3–22*

Audience: those who will hear an *argument;* more generally, those to whom a communication is addressed   *12–13*

Authoritative warrant: a *warrant* based on the credibility or trustworthiness of the source   *151*

Authority: a respectable, reliable source of evidence   *151–152*

Backing: the assurances upon which a *warrant* or assumption is based   *145*

Begging the question: making a statement that assumes that the issue being argued has already been decided   *227–228*

Cause and effect: reasoning that assumes one event or condition can bring about another   *153–155*

Claim: the conclusion of an argument; what the arguer is trying to prove   *10–11*

Claim of fact: a *claim* that asserts something exists, has existed, or

Index of Authors
and Titles

WARRANTS

TYPE OF WARRANT	SUBTYPE	EXAMPLE
Authoritative Warrants are based on the credibility of a source		CLAIM: Cigarette smoking is harmful.
Substantive Warrants are based on beliefs about the reliability of factual evidence.	A **Generalization Warrant** is a substantive warrant based on the belief that it is possible to derive a general principle from a series of examples.	CLAIM: Marijuana is a potent medicine for relief of pain in seriously ill patients.
	A **Sign Warrant** is a substantive warrant based on the belief that an observable datum is an indicator of a particular condition.	CLAIM: Press reports and TV news programs deal in lies and deception.
	A **Cause and Effect Warrant** is a substantive warrant that assumes that one event or condition can bring about another.	CLAIM: Giving free food to poor countries can be counterproductive.
	A **Comparison Warrant** is a substantive warrant that assumes that what is true in one case ought to be true in another.	CLAIM: The United States should set an annual budget for physician spending, then let doctors do their work.
	An **Analogy Warrant** is a substantive warrant that assumes a resemblance in some characteristics between dissimilar things.	CLAIM: Sports have become the secular religion of America. (Harry Edwards)
Motivational Warrants are based on the values of the arguer and the audience.		CLAIM: People in this country work too hard to enjoy God and family.